*These functions return a value
**These are macros

D1295554

VOLUME I

AMIGA P R O G R A M M E R ' S **HANDBOOK**

AMIGA™
Programmer's Handbook
VOLUME I / SECOND EDITION

EUGENE P. MORTIMORE

San Francisco ■ Paris ■ Düsseldorf ■ London

Book design by Amparo Del Rio, Graphic Design

Illustrations by Van Genderen Studios
Cover art by Thomas Scott Nelson
Cover produced using the Aegis Images™ program by
  Aegis Development Inc.
  2210 Wilshire Blvd., Ste. #277
  Santa Monica, CA 90403
Cover image ©1985 The Robert Jacob Agency DIV The
Next Frontier Corporation.

Library of Congress Card Number: 86-62805
ISBN 0-89588-367-8
Manufactured in the United States of America
10 9 8 7

I dedicate this book to my mother, to the memory of my father, to my son Scott, and to my daughter Lori, who, each in their own way, helped me write this book.

ACKNOWLEDGMENTS

I would like to thank Robert Peck, Director of Descriptive Graphics Arts at Commodore-Amiga, for his help in resolving technical questions. Mr. Peck has been with the Amiga project almost from the beginning, and his insight into the details of some of the function calls was very helpful.

At Commodore Business Machines, Inc. Amiga Technical Support, I would like to thank Lisa A. Siracusa for her help in obtaining up-to-date information.

I would also like to thank William Volk of Aegis Development Corporation for his help in resolving technical questions and his perspective on future directions for the Amiga.

Rudolph Langer, Carole Alden, Barbara Gordon, and Karl Ray deserve thanks for their helpful suggestions and guidance in the organization of the project.

I want to especially thank Valerie Robbins, editor, for her extensive help in preparing the second edition. Her planning and attention to detail ensured a balanced, precise final result. Thank you Valerie!

Special thanks also to Olivia Shinomoto for her help with the second edition. In addition to her expert word processing, Olivia prepared the index of functions for the inside cover.

Finally, thanks to Dawn Amsberry and Cheryl Vega, typesetting; Suzy Anger, proofreading; and Jannie Dresser, indexing.

TABLE OF CONTENTS

1 The Exec Functions

2 The Graphics Display and Drawing Functions

3 The Graphics Animation Functions

4 The Graphics Text Functions

5 The Layer Functions

6 The Intuition Functions

7 The Workbench Functions

A Glossary   588

B Amiga Display Modes

Index   627

Introduction

The purpose of this book is to present detailed explanations and discussions of the graphics-related functions in the Amiga ROM kernel. These functions were designed to be accessed from any language that follows the standard interface conventions of the Amiga software system. These conventions define the proper naming of symbols, the correct usage of 68000 CPU registers, and the format of RAM data structures.

This book is Volume I of a two-volume series. Volume I covers the graphics-related functions and structures in the Amiga software libraries. Volume II (to be released) covers Exec support functions, hardware Device functions and commands, Math Library functions, Resource Library functions, Debug Library functions, Dos Library functions, and Expansion Library functions. Many of the structures used and referenced by these functions are also discussed in these two volumes. Together these two books define and describe all the functions (and most of the structures) in the Amiga software system.

The audience for this book falls into two broad categories. First, there are those people with extensive backgrounds in C or assembly language programming who want to investigate the programming capabilities of the Amiga. These people know what other computers offer and want to decide whether the Amiga represents a worthwhile investment in line with their programming goals.

Second, there are those people who own and use an Amiga and now want to learn how to program it to extract the most from its many features. These people will most likely read this book in conjunction with books on programming in C or assembly language. However, you can use these functions with any programming language (BASIC, Pascal, Modula 2, etc.) for which there is an Amiga compiler if you follow the interfacing requirements of the ROM kernel software system.

In order to to use the ROM kernel functions in a C language program, you must have the Lattice C language compiler or the equivalent (Manx C), together with a set of C language INCLUDE files to interface the Amiga function libraries with the compiler. These INCLUDE files usually appear on the same disk as the compiler.

To use these functions in assembly language, you must have the assembly language macro assembler, together with a set of assembly language INCLUDE files to interface the Amiga function libraries with the assembler. These INCLUDE files appear on the same disk as the macro assembler.

The Amiga System

The Amiga represents the state of the art in personal and business computers. This is true not only of the hardware but also of the software. The hardware provides for capabilities never before offered in a business or home computer, including 880K-byte, double-sided 3½-inch floppy disks, a multitasking operating system, multiple scrollable display screens, complex animation capabilities, and the capability to display up to 4,096 colors.

In addition, the system offers both high-resolution and low-resolution mode displays, both interlaced and noninterlaced mode displays, and a set of special-purpose chips to allow a programmer detailed control of the display. Another set of special-purpose components allows you to create very speedy graphics and area-fill operations. All of these hardware features lead to very sophisticated graphic displays.

The software system is designed to allow you to access these hardware features at different levels. It provides for function groupings into libraries—both system libraries and libraries created by you. Both types of libraries have the same structure and usage conventions.

Because of the library approach to system function definition, there is only one fixed hardware address in the system (address 004, called AbsSysBase). All other addresses in the system are related to this one address. This means that your program routines do not have to be loaded into specific memory locations; they can be placed anywhere in the eight-megabyte memory space of the Amiga.

Also, in contrast to other computers, the bitmaps you define for graphics are not required to be in one memory location. Bitmaps can be placed anywhere in the first 512K of RAM. The advantages of multitasking and unconstrained memory allocation allow you to design sophisticated programs that make full use of the Amiga's hardware.

The functions in the Amiga kernel are built in a hierarchy. At the top of the hierarchy is the Workbench, which allows you to develop applications programs that use icons and the AmigaDOS file system in a uniform manner. Next in the hierarchy is Intuition. The Workbench uses Intuition to produce its displays and to interact with the filing system. Intuition, in turn, uses the Graphics Library and Layers Library functions to produce its output on the display screen. The Intuition and Workbench functions provide a higher-level interface to develop programs that incorporate a uniform user interface.

Summaries of the Chapters

This book is written in a reference format. The syntax, usage, results, and interactions of the functions are presented and examined.

Chapter 1 discusses the Exec Library functions, which provide the mechanism for managing tasks, devices, libraries, system lists, and other aspects of the Amiga system. In particular, the Exec functions direct task switching using task priorities and interrupts in the system. All of the other library functions rely on the Exec functions and macros, especially for task and memory management.

Chapter 2 discusses the Graphics Library display and drawing functions. These functions provide the mechanism for creating bitmaps, drawing into those bitmaps, and controlling bitmaps to display information on the Amiga screen. The emphasis is on defining the stationary playfields of the Amiga display. These functions and macros allow you to access the five major graphic display modes of the Amiga to build complex graphic displays; they form the first of three groups of Graphics Library functions.

Chapter 3 discusses the Graphics Library animation functions, which allow you to define and use hardware sprites, virtual sprites, and bobs (Blitter objects) to create movable objects on the Amiga display screen. Bobs can be grouped into more complex animation components and animation objects to produce very sophisticated animation effects. These movable objects can be combined with the stationary playfield graphic displays produced by the functions in Chapter 2. These animation functions and macros form the second of three groups of Graphics Library functions.

Chapter 4 discusses the Graphics Library text functions, which allow you to create and manipulate fonts and text in your displays. You can use these functions to create new fonts, save those fonts on disk, and later call those fonts into memory for drawing your text onto the Amiga display. These functions and macros form the third of three groups of Graphics Library functions.

Chapter 5 discusses the Layers Library functions, which allow you to design the multilayered display screens that give the Amiga its windowing capability. They also allow you to define and use a common bitmap between graphics tasks, thus allowing more than one task to draw into a bitmap. These functions and macros define the entire Layers Library.

Chapter 6 discusses the Intuition Library functions, which allow you to create applications programs that have a uniform user interface. Intuition allows you to define screens and windows with very simple functions. These high-level Intuition functions allow you to avoid using the more difficult Graphics Library functions. However, you can also combine Intuition functions with any of the Graphics Library functions to produce sophisticated applications programs. These functions and macros comprise the entire Intuition Library.

Chapter 7 discusses the Icon Library functions, also referred to as the Workbench functions. These functions allow you to work with applications program icons on the standard Workbench screen of Intuition. In this way, you can associate icons with each of your applications programs and the data files that those programs create. Program users can then select icons to perform specific actions related to your applications program. These 14 functions define the entire Icon Library.

In addition to these seven chapters, this book includes two appendices. Appendix A is a glossary of the terms used in this book. Appendix B contains a summary of the four additional display modes unique to the Amiga and includes a program template for each mode.

Finally, the index provides pointers to the information presented in the function discussions. To find individual function discussions, see the Table of Contents.

The 1.2 Amiga Software Release

Release 1.2 provides a number of improvements, additions, and changes over the earlier 1.0 and 1.1 releases. These improvements include the addition of 40 new library functions, the addition of a number of new CLI commands, many improvements in Amiga-DOS, and a number of other miscellaneous improvements and changes.

The 40 functions new to version 1.2 are identified in this book by this symbol in the left margin. They can be summarized as follows:

■ There are 18 new Exec Library functions. These include three memory management functions (AddMemList, CopyMem, and CopyMemQuick); 11 semaphore management functions (AddSemaphore, AttemptSemaphore, FindSemaphore, Init-Semaphore, ObtainSemaphore, ObtainSemaphoreList, ReleaseSemaphore, Release-SemaphoreList, RemSemaphore, Procure, and Vacate); three resident code module management functions (FindResident, InitCode, and InitResident); and one data-stream formatting function (RawDoFormat). These new functions are all discussed in Chapter 1.

■ There are 13 new Graphics Library functions. These include four region management functions (AndRegionRegion, ClearRectRegion, OrRegionRegion, and Xor-RegionRegion); two ellipse drawing functions (AreaEllipse and DrawEllipse); two circle drawing functions (AreaCircle and DrawCircle); two layer management functions (AttemptLockLayerRom and InstallClipRegion); two Blitter management functions (BltBitMapRastPort and BltMaskBitMapRastPort); and one color register management function (SetRGB4CM). These are all discussed in Chapters 2 and 5.

■ There are nine new Intuition functions. These include four gadget management functions (ActivateGadget, AddGList, RefreshGList, and RemoveGList); two window management functions (ActivateWindow and RefreshWindowFrame); two IntuitionBase structure management functions (LockIBase and UnlockIBase); and one Screen structure management function (GetScreenData). These are all discussed in Chapter 6.

The 1.2 release includes five new Intuition macros whose purpose is briefly defined as follows:

■ SRBNUM(N) sets the number of read bits per character for the serial device to N.

■ SWBNUM(N) sets the number of write bits per character for the serial device to N.

■ SSBNUM(N) sets the number of stop bits per character for the serial device to N.

■ SPARNUM(N) controls the parity setting of the serial device.

■ SHAKNUM(N) controls the handshake setting of the serial device.

These macros allow you to directly change the serial-device settings in the Intuition Preferences structure inside your program. This is useful if you are designing a program that requires an interface to a device hooked onto the serial port on the back of the Amiga.

AmigaDOS has been modified and enhanced as follows:

■ The most significant improvement is the addition of a new command (Addbuffers) to the C (Command) directory commands. Addbuffers:NN will add NN buffers to the list of sector caches for drive NN. Use of the Addbuffers command speeds up disk access significantly. This can have a strong impact on the time required for compiling and linking your programs.

- The C directory DiskCopy command now lets you copy disks with bad sector blocks. Also, DiskCopy doesn't get confused by two disks on the Workbench screen with identical volume names. DiskCopy now works with disk partitions and won't change the disk's volume name when run under the CLI (Command Line Interface).

- The Initialize (equivalent to Format) C directory command now marks a disk as invalid if it doesn't complete the formatting stage of the initialization.

- You can now use named pipes to pass files between programs as in the Unix system. A PipeHandler utility (in the l:directory) is provided to handle pipes.

- You can arrange for the RAM disk to come up automatically after every machine boot. This is done by putting an appropriate line in your startup sequence file. Add the line

dir ram:

Conveniently, this allows you to do all your C language programming on a RAM disk if you have enough extended memory. Also, when the RAM disk is defined, it now has its own icon on the Workbench screen.

- The Exec functions now contain support for the fast 68881 math coprocessor in a multitasking environment.

- There is a new mode for opening files: MODE_READWRITE. This mode opens a file with an exclusive lock.

- The C directory contains the DiskDoctor command. DiskDoctor can be used to fix a corrupted disk.

- The C directory contains the Path command. The Path command allows you to inspect, add, or change the search path directories that AmigaDOS automatically searches when looking for a program to execute.

- The C directory SetTaskPri command allows you to change task priorities from the CLI.

- The Assign and CD (change directory) commands now display directory names.

- You can now halt output from the Dir command permanently by typing Control-C (versus Control-S which stops output only temporarily). This saves you a lot of time and trouble if you start looking at a long directory and don't want to see all of it.

- The Execute and Edit commands now create a T (temporary file) directory if it doesn't already exist.

The NotePad program can now be run from the CLI, which is useful for keeping notes as you write or program. It is in the Utilities directory on the Workbench disk. The NotePad program has a number of new features. The most important of these are as follows:

- A word wrap option has been added.

- A new menu has been added: the Edit menu. Among other things, the new Edit menu contains search and replace options.

- You can now change fonts within a note.

- Scroll gadgets have been added to the NotePad window.

The Apple ImageWriter printer is now supported with its own driver program. Therefore, if you own an Apple or a Macintosh, you can use the ImageWriter printer directly with the Amiga. Other additional printers are also now supported.

For the most part, release 1.1 and 1.2 INCLUDE-file structures are identical. This is necessary to allow your 1.1 programs to run under the 1.2 release. However, there are several important differences between 1.1 and 1.2 structures. You should be aware of these differences especially if you are trying to adapt 1.1 programs to the 1.2 release.

Note in particular that the Layer and LayerInfo structures of the Layer Library have been modified and extended significantly in the 1.2 release. Most notably, signal-semaphore locking mechanisms have been added to the Layer and LayerInfo structures to allow accurate and fast updating of layers in a multilayered–multitasking situation where several tasks may want to draw into the same layer bitmap; these signal semaphores allow each task to get its proper turn at accessing and changing these structures.

Also note that parameters have been added to these two structures. When all is said and done, it appears that the 1.1 and 1.2 Layer and LayerInfo structures will be substantially different. These differences are more than just extensions; they are changes to the existing parameter definitions in these structures.

The final definitions of the 1.2 Layer and LayerInfo structures were not completely resolved at the time of this writing. For this reason, Chapter 5 presents the 1.1 version of these structures. You should consult your 1.2 release Clip.h and Layers.h INCLUDE files to see the final definition of the Layer and LayerInfo structures. Also note that the precise name of the LayerInfo structure is Layer_Info (not LayerInfo) in both the 1.1 and 1.2 releases.

Several other structures have been changed in small ways that are unlikely to affect your 1.1 programs running under the 1.2 release. In particular, some of the formerly reserved (and structure padding) parameters in some 1.1 structures now have parameter values defined in the 1.2 release. Your 1.1 programs could not have referred to these parameters because they didn't exist; therefore, these types of structure changes should not concern you except where you want to refer to them in your new 1.2 programs.

Libraries

Libraries are so important in the Amiga system that it is worthwhile to make some general statements about them. First, it is important to understand that the five libraries discussed in this book are nothing more than specific instances of the general definition of Amiga libraries as discussed in Chapter 1. Libraries are either resident (already in memory—eventually perhaps in ROM) or transient (on disk and brought into and out of RAM as required by the task that is currently executing). To use a library, you must first call the MakeLibrary function (see Chapter 1). Once a library is made, it should be saved on disk. Then other programs can load that library with a call to the OpenLibrary function.

This form of the OpenLibrary function call is used when you want to allocate the GfxBase structure statically:

```
LONG GfxBase;
GfxBase = OpenLibrary ("graphics.library", 0);
if (GfxBase = = 0);
exit (NO_GRAPHICS_LIBRARY_FOUND);
```

In this sequence, the LONG statement defines a memory location where the GfxBase Graphics Library pointer variable will be stored when the Graphics Library is opened. GfxBase is the base address of the library; specifically, it is a pointer to the GfxBase structure, which contains a Library structure as a substructure. Each of the ROM kernel libraries in the Amiga system has a name for its base structure: ExecBase for the Exec Library, GfxBase for the Graphics Library, LayersBase for the Layers Library, DiskfontBase for the DiskFont Library, Intuition-Base for the Intuition Library, and IconBase for the Icon Library. Each of these structures includes a Library structure as its first substructure.

This form of the OpenLibrary call is used when you want to allocate the GfxBase structure dynamically:

```
struct GfxBase *GfxBase;

GfxBase = (struct GfxBase *) OpenLibrary (" graphics.library ",0);

if (GfxBase = = 0);
exit (NO_GRAPHICS_LIBRARY_FOUND);
```

In both forms of call, the constant NO_GRAPHICS_LIBRARY_FOUND must is defined in your program in a C language define statement. If the library cannot be opened due to some type of error (for example, no library present on disk or inadequate memory), the error-checking shown in these two examples will cause your program to exit at this point.

Another kind of a library is a device library. You can bring a device library into the system with a call to the OpenDevice function:

```
error = OpenDevice (DEVICENAME, unitnumber, ioRequest, flags)
```

Notice that the return value is an error condition rather than the base address of the library associated with the device. You do not have to declare a memory location for the base address; instead, the base address of the library is returned in the I/O Request Block structure. After the device is opened, this address is used to interface the device library routines to the system library routines.

Structures

Besides functions and macros, structures are the main mechanism for programming the Amiga. You can work with these structures in assembly language, C language, or any other language that interfaces with the Amiga software system. Each Amiga library system uses a number of structures that interface with the functions and macros in that library.

The precise definitions of these structures and their parameters are contained in the INCLUDE files associated with each library.

Most structures contain pointers to other structures, allowing a group of related structures to be linked together. This concept is used heavily throughout the Amiga software system. Some structures also contain substructures. An example is the Gadget structure inside the WBObject structure. In this case, an actual instance of the Gadget structure (rather than a pointer) appears inside the WBObject structure.

In general, structures fall into three types: structures that are not linked at all to structures of the same type or structures of another type (stand-alone structures), structures that are linked only in the forward direction (singly linked structures), and structures that are linked in both directions, both forward and backward (doubly linked structures).

Figure I.1 shows a set of doubly linked structures with the names Structure 1, Structure 2, and so forth until Structure N. Structure 1 is the first structure in a linked list of structures; Structure 2 is the second structure; and Structure N is the last structure. All of these structures are of the same type. For example, they could all be Bob structures.

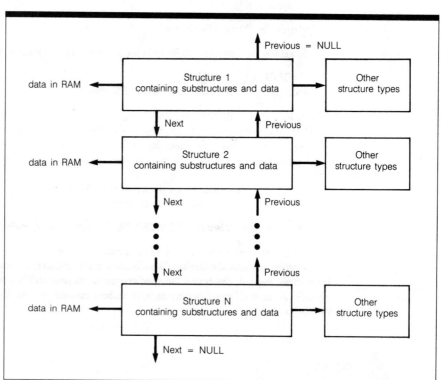

Figure I.1:
*Amiga
Doubly Linked
Structures*

The arrows in the figure represent pointer parameters, which are actually part of the structure definition and are stored in the memory allocated to the structure. Those arrows labeled Next and Previous point to specific instances of this same structure type. The C language compiler watches for these pointer parameters and constructs the linkages in the compiled program. It is important to understand that, because these structures are linked with pointer parameters, all the structures in a linked list are not required to be adjacent to each other in RAM. The compiler will reach their RAM location using the pointer parameters you specify in your program.

There are three general categories of parameters in structures: system, common, and user-defined. System parameters can be changed only by the system routines. An example is the NextVSprite pointer parameter in the VSprite structure. Common parameters can be changed by both the system and program tasks. An example is the Flags parameter in the VSprite structure. User-defined parameters can be changed only by your tasks. An example is the Height parameter in the VSprite structure.

Each parameter in these structures is of a specific parameter type. The type defines how much memory is required for that parameter and how the bytes and bits of that parameter are interpreted by the system and user routines. Consult the Types.h and Types.i Exec INCLUDE files to see the specific parameter types (BYTE, WORD, etc.) used by the programming structures.

There are three ways in which structure parameters are initialized: by Amiga system routines, by structure parameter assignment statements, or by specific library functions. For example, the NextVSprite parameter in the VSprite structure is initialized by system routines, the RxOffset and RyOffset parameters in the RasInfo structure are initialized by simple structure parameter assignment statements, and some of the RastPort structure parameters are initialized by the Graphics Library InitRastPort function.

The INCLUDE Files

The INCLUDE files associated with each function library are rich in information needed by the system to interface your programming tasks with the library function calls. In particular, the INCLUDE files fully define the library-related structures. When structure definitions are included in this book, they are the C language versions.

Each INCLUDE file contains two types of conditional compilation sequences. The first type allows the system to incorporate a specific INCLUDE file as necessary for the C language compiler. The second type allows the compiler to know about specific parameters necessary for the C language compiler.

Some of the INCLUDE files also contain a set of function return type declarations. From these you can determine the precise type of variable (BYTE, WORD, APTR, etc.) returned by each of the function calls. The best example of this is in the Icon Library INCLUDE file.

The complete set of structure definitions provided for each specific library includes the detailed layout of each structure in that library. Most often, you will also find a good set of structure parameter comments. These comments are helpful in understanding what a structure does and how it does it. Each parameter in the structure definition has its parameter type (BYTE, WORD, etc.) as part of the structure definition. You can use this information to determine how many bytes each instance of the structure occupies— structure storage requirement estimates are useful for allocating memory.

The INCLUDE files also contain definitions of any hardware constants and flag parameters used by that library. Flag parameters are sometimes used as one of the arguments in a function call. The INCLUDE files allow you to determine the exact numerical value corresponding to each flag parameter, flag parameter bit, or other use of a flag parameter.

A complete set of definitions for all macros used by each function library can also be found in the INCLUDE files. For example, the exact definitions of the Graphics Library CINIT, CEND, CMOVE, and CWAIT macros are presented in the Gfxmacros.h INCLUDE file. Often, these macros have arguments and are called in the same way functions are called.

INCLUDE file definitions of parameter equivalencies for software updates ensure compatibility. Each time the software is updated, some of the structure parameter definitions can change; a parameter might also change names between releases. This information enables you to compile your older programs under a new release. For example, if you have a program written under version 1.0, you can interface it with the version 1.1 parameter definitions (if they are different) because of these parameter equivalencies defined in the INCLUDE files.

Some of the INCLUDE files associated with the Exec Library are of special interest. The Alerts.h file contains the definition of all deadend alerts used throughout the entire system. Deadend alerts are discussed in Chapter 6; they inform the user of problems that will bring about a system crash. The Alerts.h file includes the names and numerical values attached to all the deadend alerts used by all the libraries in the system. You can use this information to debug your programs and to interpret error messages on the display screen.

The Errors.h file contains a list of I/O errors and the error numbers associated with them. Right now there are only four I/O errors listed in this INCLUDE file: IOERR_PENFAIL, IOERR_ABORTED, IOERR_NOCMD, and IOERR_BADLENGTH. These parameters have values of -1, -2, -3, and -4, respectively.

The ExecBase.h file contains the definition of the ExecBase structure, which contains all of the information needed by the system to start a task's execution, keep track of the time already used by a task, point to various routines needed by the task, keep track of the nesting of interrupts assigned to the currently executing task, and so forth.

The first part of the ExecBase structure is a library substructure, whose parameters are filled in when the Exec Library is loaded from disk by the OpenLibrary function call. The Library structure is followed by a set of parameters that allow the Exec system routines to keep track of everything in the system.

In particular, the ExecBase structure includes a definition of the time-slice period for equal-priority task execution; the amount of time actually consumed by the currently executing task; and pointers to task trap code, task exception code, and task exit code. The ExecBase structure also contains a set of ten List substructures that allow the Exec system to keep track of memory blocks and other things placed on lists. Read the introductions to the various chapters to see how Exec system lists are used throughout the system.

Conventions Used in the System

The following sections describe various conventions used in the system. You have to follow these conventions for the functions to interface correctly with the INCLUDE files and the system's internal routines.

Register Usage

The arguments used in function calls and the results returned by function calls are placed in 68000 registers according to certain rules. Knowing these rules will be useful if you want to program in assembly language or just use certain small assembly language routines in a C language program.

The arguments used in function calls fall into two categories: pointer arguments and data arguments. Pointer arguments can be subdivided into structure pointer arguments and memory block pointer arguments.

Address registers A0 through A7 are always used for structure and memory block pointer arguments. All memory address or structure pointer arguments are placed in these registers, starting from the leftmost pointer argument and moving toward the right side of the function call syntax. The first pointer argument in the function call is usually placed in register A0. Each successive pointer argument is usually placed in the next highest address register (A1, A2, etc.). This rule is adhered to exactly by the Intuition functions, but other libraries deviate slightly. You should examine the individual function calls to determine which address registers are used by each function.

Data registers are treated in a similar way to pointer registers. Each data parameter is placed into one of the 68000 CPU data registers (D0 through D7), starting from the left side of the function call syntax and moving toward the right. This rule is adhered to exactly by the Intuition functions, but other libraries deviate slightly. Once again, exceptions do occur, so it is best to check the definition of each function's syntax to verify correctness.

There are some additional rules about register usage. Register A6 has a special use in the system; it is always used to hold the base address of a library. In particular, when a library is opened, the Library structure address is always placed in the A6 register. The system looks at this address as a reference address from which it will find all the routines in that library.

Registers D0, D1, A0, and A1 are always scratch registers, meaning that you can modify them at any time. In particular, they can be used by any function without saving their previous contents. All other data and address registers must have their values preserved. If any of these registers are used by a function, their contents must be saved and restored appropriately.

The primary result returned by a function is always returned in register D0. However, if the function modifies other memory locations, you can see those effects by examining the individual structure parameters modified by the function call. In order to do this, you must determine which function modifies which structure parameter. You can usually do this by studying the function call and the structures with which the function deals.

Values Returned by Functions

Some Amiga library functions return no values; others return one of three types of values: structure pointer variables, memory block address variables, and data values of various sizes. You can place each instance of these values in temporary program variables and use any of them later in your program.

Table I.1 lists the kinds of values returned, along with their size, and an example of a function that returns such a value. Remember that all values returned by functions are returned in register D0. This is true even if one of the function's arguments is placed into register D0 before the function call is made.

Table I.1:
Values Returned by Function Calls

Value Returned	Size	Example
Structure pointer variable	4 bytes	InitRastPort
Memory block address variable	4 bytes	Allocate
Data value	32 bits	AllocSignal
Data value	16 bits	AllocTrap
Data value	1 byte	SetTaskPri
Data value	4 bits	SetIntVector

Four-byte data values are of type ULONG, or type LONGBITS when every bit is significant. Two-byte data values are of type WORD, or type WORDBITS when every bit is significant. One-byte data values are of type BYTE, or BYTEBITS when every bit is significant. Four-bit values are of type BYTEBITS with each bit in the nibble significant.

In addition to returning values, many functions also change the values of structure parameters indirectly. This is especially true for the functions that initialize structure definitions. The InitArea, InitBitMap, InitRastPort, InitTmpRas, InitView, and InitViewPort Graphics Library functions are examples of this type of function behavior, as are the SetAPen and SetBPen Graphics Library functions, which affect the RastPort structure parameters.

Flag Parameters

Flag parameters play a big part in Amiga C language programming. You can find a flag parameter in almost every structure. A good example is the Flag parameter in the Task Control Block structure. This parameter is a UBYTE (unsigned byte)—only the total value of this flag parameter is significant; the individual bits are not significant. This parameter takes on one of five values: TB_PROCTIME = 0, TB_STACKCHK = 4, TB_EXCEPT = 5, TB_SWITCH = 6, or TB_LAUNCH = 7.

Note that as a general rule, flag parameter names appear in all uppercase characters. As you can see from their names, each of the above Flag parameter values has something to do with maintaining the current task in the system. For example, if the Flag parameter is set to TB_PROCTIME, the system will keep track of the processor time used by this task.

On the other hand, the flag parameters in the Intuition structures are usually ULONG (32-bit) values, and their individual bits are usually significant. Study the individual INCLUDE files to determine the meaning attached to the values of each flag parameter in each structure.

There are two ways you can define flag parameters in the system. You can supply structure parameter assignment statements to define the flag parameter directly, or you can use a function that defines the value of a flag parameter as one of its arguments. The first method is by far the most common.

An example of the second method is the Layers Library CreateBehindLayer function, which contains the Layer structure Flags parameter as its seventh argument. When this function returns, the value of the flags argument used in the call will be placed into the Layer structure created by the call. This Flags parameter requires that you choose between three layer types: LAYERSIMPLE, LAYERSMART, or LAYERSUPER. Each of these types is mutually exclusive.

Notation Conventions Used in the Book

The notation used in this book is complex because of the complex nature of the subject material. You should be aware of the different ways in which general terms, structures, functions, and function arguments are referenced in this book. However, you should be able to tell which type of term is being used from the context. Following are some guidelines that will help you.

First, general terms appear in all lowercase notation. Examples of this are the terms task, message port, bitmap, and region.

Second, structure names begin with a capital letter and are otherwise lowercased, except when they are compound words. In this case, there is a capitalization variation in the middle of the name. Examples of this are the MsgPort structure, the List structure, and the BitMap structure. Structures that are referenced in a function call by pointer variables have pointer variable names that usually match the structure name. Examples of this are the msgPort pointer variable, which points to the MsgPort structure, and the interrupt pointer variable, which points to the Interrupt structure. Notice that the pointer name begins with a lowercase letter.

Occasionally, the structure pointer variable name will not match the name of the structure exactly. An example of this is the taskCB variable, which points to the Task structure of a task. In this case, the variable name was chosen to be more descriptive of the structure (a structure that controls a task) rather than to match the structure name. In any case, you will recognize the association between the pointer variable and the structure to which it points.

Structure parameters that are system constants are often written in all uppercase notation. This is how they appear in the structure definitions and function arguments.

Examples of this are the MEMF_CHIP and MEMF_CLEAR parameters, which refer to different types of RAM blocks in the Exec Library AllocMem functions.

Third, all ROM kernel function names begin with a capital letter and are otherwise lowercased, except for one or more case changes to indicate that they are compound words. Examples of this are the AddDevice, AddTask, Cause, and Insert functions in Chapter 1 and the AreaDraw, AreaMove, Draw, and Move functions in Chapter 2.

Fourth, most functions have one or more arguments. (Some functions have no arguments—for example, ColdReset, SuperState, OwnBlitter, and DisownBlitter.) Most function arguments, like structure pointer variables, start with a lowercase letter and have a case change in the middle of their spelling if they are compound words. If you flip through this book, you will find numerous examples of this in the syntax to the function calls.

Generally speaking, all uppercase characters are used in the following circumstances:

- Uppercase characters are used for the names of node types in a list of nodes of this type. Examples are the NT_INTERRUPT and NT_DEVICE, which represent categories of node types supported by the Exec Library list functions (AddHead, AddTail, etc.).

- Uppercase characters are used for the names of library or device code vectors. Examples are the OPEN and CLOSE library code vectors discussed in Chapter 1, which provide the names of required routine-entry points into each of the system and user software library structures.

- Uppercase characters are used for the names of function flag parameter arguments. Examples are the PF_ACTION and PA_IGNORE flag parameter names used in the message port functions. Typically, each value of a flag parameter has its own name and meaning. The exact meaning for each flag parameter value is defined in the appropriate INCLUDE file. These flag parameter values are sensed and used by the Amiga library functions to control specific individual actions in the system. Other examples are the HIRES and LACE parameters in the ViewPort and View structures in the Graphics Library.

- Uppercase characters are used for the names of assembly language macros. Examples are the ADDHEAD and ADDTAIL list-management macros in the Exec Library, which are used by the list functions (AddHead, AddTail, etc.) and the ON_DISPLAY and OFF_DISPLAY macros associated with the Graphics Library functions. These macros are used generally by the system to turn graphics displays on and off.

- In some cases, uppercase characters are used for the names of macros in the system libraries. The Graphics Library has four examples of these: CINIT, CEND, CMOVE, and CWAIT. These four macros are capitalized because they are closely related to low-level Copper instructions.

■ Uppercase characters are used for assembly language or C language variable type declarations. Examples are UBYTE and UWORD. In standard fashion, these are used in C language or assembly language programs to indicate the type of data (for example, byte or word) in a structure.

The meaning of each of these uppercased words should always be clear from the context.

You will become familiar with the exact spelling and capitalization rules if you study the function and macro definitions. You will find the INCLUDE files on the Lattice compiler C language disk under the INCLUDE directory. If you have this disk, you should print the entire contents of the INCLUDE files associated with each of the libraries. These files will help you understand all of the system lists, structures, structure parameters, structure linkages, macros, variable types, and so forth used by the Amiga library functions and macros. In fact, a thorough study of the INCLUDE files is one of the best ways to learn about the Amiga Exec and Graphics systems.

The Exec Functions

Introduction

This chapter defines and discusses the Amiga Exec functions. The Exec functions provide a way for you to manage tasks, devices, libraries, lists, and other aspects of the Amiga system. The Amiga Exec functions fall into fourteen categories:

- The library management functions: AddLibrary, CloseLibrary, MakeLibrary, RemLibrary, SumLibrary, and SetFunction, to use in creating and managing system and user software libraries

- The task management functions: AddTask, FindTask, RemTask, and SetTaskPri, for adding, managing, and removing tasks from the Amiga multitasking system

- The memory management functions: Allocate, AllocEntry, AllocMem, AvailMem, Deallocate, FreeEntry, and FreeMem, for allocating, deallocating, and otherwise managing RAM blocks for your tasks

- The device management functions: AddDevice, CloseDevice, OpenDevice, and RemDevice, for adding, managing, and removing I/O devices

- The device-I/O-control management functions: CheckIO, DoIO, SendIO, and WaitIO, for controlling input and output going to or coming from various I/O devices tied into your tasks

- The message-port management functions: AddPort, FindPort, RemPort, and Wait-Port, for adding, managing, and removing message ports

- The message-port-message management functions: GetMsg, PutMsg, and Reply-Msg, for placing and retrieving intertask messages in the message and reply ports assigned to your tasks

- The task-signal management functions: AllocSignal, SetExcept, FreeSignal, Set-Signal, and Wait, for allocating, managing, and freeing intertask signals

- The list-node management functions: AddHead, AddTail, Enqueue, Insert, Remove, RemHead, and Rem/Tail, for creating and managing lists of data and data structures needed by your programs

- The task-interrupt-vector management functions: AddIntServer, Cause, RemIntServer, and SetIntVector, for adding and controlling the 68000 interrupt vectors associated with each of your tasks

- The task-trap-vector management functions: AddTrap and FreeTrap, for specifying the 68000 trap-handling routines to be used with each of your tasks

- The resource management functions: AddResource, OpenResource, and RemResource, for adding, managing, and removing resources

- The 68000 microprocessor direct management functions: ColdReset, GetCC, SetSR, SuperState, and UserState, for resetting the Amiga hardware system, setting the 68000 status register to a specific bit pattern, and placing the 68000 into supervisor or user mode

- The data structure explicit initialization function, InitStruct, which allows you to initialize explicitly the contents of a data structure in RAM, supplementing some of the other functions (AddTask, OpenDevice, MakeLibrary, and so forth) that also initialize specific RAM memory structures

Results of Exec Functions

The Exec functions return their results in several ways. In the first method, all results are returned internally through system-specified RAM locations. An example of this type of behavior is the AddDevice function, which causes a new device to be added to the system device list in RAM. The system device list is updated to reflect the addition of the new device. When you use this type of function in your programs, you do not place anything on the left side of the function statement. The function name with included arguments becomes the entire program statement.

In contrast, the second method of function usage requires you to place a variable name on the left side of the program statement. For example:

memBlock = Allocate (memHeader, byteSize)

The Allocate, AllocEntry, and AllocMem functions work in this way. They return a structure or memory-block pointer variable as one of their results. The AllocTrap and AllocSignal functions also operate in this way; they return trap numbers and signal numbers, respectively. For each function call, this type of function returns one value as the value of a single variable. For example, Allocate and AllocMem return a value for the memory block pointer variable memBlock, AllocEntry returns a pointer to a MemList structure, and AllocTrap returns a value for the trap number variable trapNum.

In many cases, the single value returned by these functions is a pointer to a C language type structure in RAM. In these cases, the function has also initialized or changed the C language structure in RAM. When you try to understand how a function works and what it does, keep these ideas in mind. Always ask what information is input to a function and what information the function changes. Often the function changes more than is directly apparent. A close study of the system structures (for example, the Task Control Block structure and the I/O Request Block structure) will tell you precisely what each function changes.

In some cases, Exec functions return a single value for a specific variable. That specific variable is an error variable (not an error number). It has one of two specific values. For example, the DoIO function returns a nonzero error value if it is unsuccessful; it returns a zero error value if it is successful. The OpenDevice, RemDevice, RemLibrary, and WaitIO functions all work in this way. You can have your program test this error value and act accordingly.

Finally, it is important to understand one other aspect of Exec function usage: some functions return structure pointer variable values. You can use these specific pointer variable values later in your task programming. For example, the AllocEntry function returns the value of the MemList structure pointer variable; it also initializes a block of RAM where the MemList structure is stored. Later in your task, you may want to free these specific blocks of RAM for other uses in your task. If you saved the value of the memList variable in a temporary variable, you can use it to point to that same RAM block with the FreeEntry function, whose second argument is a MemList structure pointer variable. This type of sequence also works with some other pairs of Exec functions—AllocTrap and FreeTrap, and AllocSignal and FreeSignal, for example.

Exec System Structures

The Exec functions work with a number of important structures. The two most important ones are the Task structure and the IORequest structure. In this book, these are referred to as the Task Control Block structure and the I/O Request Block structure. Both of these structures are dynamic; their contents are initialized in some way and then keep changing as the tasks and devices assigned to tasks relate and move through a series of steps determined by your task's definition and the system routines.

The Task Control Block Structure

The form of the Task Control Block structure appears in the Exec INCLUDE files named Tasks.h (for C language programmers) and Tasks.i (for assembly language programmers). If you want to learn the details of the Task Control Block structure, print these files and study the structure layouts and parameters. See the discussion of the AddTask function for more about the Task Control Block structure.

The I/O Request Block Structure

The I/O Request Block structure is used by the device functions (AddDevice, OpenDevice, CloseDevice, and RemDevice). This structure is initialized by a call to the OpenDevice function. One of the arguments in the OpenDevice function call is a pointer to the I/O Request Block structure in memory. When OpenDevice returns, some of the I/O Request Block structure parameters are initialized to standard values. Then, as you use your devices to process data, various parameters of the I/O Request Block structure change during your task's execution.

The definition of the I/O Request Block structure appears in the Exec INCLUDE files named Io.h (for C language programmers) and Io.i (for assembly language programmers). If you want to learn the details of the I/O Request Block structure, print these files and study the structure layout and the meaning of the various structure parameters. See the discussion of the OpenDevice function for more about the I/O Request Block structure.

System List Structures and the Node Substructure

The Node structure is the basic structure used to link together a series of related structures in the Exec software system. All system structures that belong on a system list start with a Node structure, which is a substructure in these structure definitions.

For example, if you examine the Task Control Block structure in the Exec INCLUDE files (Tasks.h and Tasks.i), you will see that it contains a Node substructure as the first statement in its structure definition. The same is true of the List structure, the Interrupt structure, the Library structure, the MemHeader structure, the MemList structure, the MsgPort structure, and the Message structure. You can convince yourself of these structure-substructure relationships by printing the Exec INCLUDE files and studying the individual structure parameters. The names of these files are listed in Table 1.1.

Table 1.1:
System List Structures and their INCLUDE File Names

	Exec INCLUDE File Name	
Structure	**C Language**	**Assembly Language**
Node	Nodes.h	Nodes.i
Task Control Block	Tasks.h	Tasks.i
List	Lists.h	Lists.i
Interrupt	Interrupts.h	Interrupts.i
Library	Libraries.h	Libraries.i
MemHeader	Memory.h	Memory.i
MemList	Memory.h	Memory.i
MsgPort	Ports.h	Ports.i
Message	Ports.h	Ports.i

In general, any structure that the system maintains on a list will begin with a Node substructure to allow each instance of that structure to be named, to have a priority assigned to it, and to be placed in a list of structures in that structure category. For example, for tasks, the priority parameter (ln_Pri) of the Node substructure in the Task Control Block structure is actually the task priority. This is a number between -127 and $+128$ that works in combination with other factors to control the task-switching operations in the Amiga multitasking system. See the discussion of the AddHead function for a listing of the Node structure.

The List structure is used to define and arrange all structures in a system structure list. It defines the beginning of a list and links the initial Node substructure into the list. See the discussion of the AddTail function for a listing of the List structure.

Anytime you read the words node and list in this chapter, think of the Node and List structures and how these two general structures are used to tie specific instances of other structures together into a list.

The Interrupt structure is used to link a list of interrupt-server routines together. The first part of the Interrupt structure is the interrupt server Node substructure. This substructure allows every one of a group of related interrupt-server routines to be linked together in an interrupt-server routine priority chain.

The Library structure is used to define the parameters of a software library definition. The first item in the Library structure is the Library Node substructure, which allows named libraries to be linked together into a list of libraries maintained by the system. Each time you add a new library to the system with the AddLibrary function, this list is extended. A Device structure and a Resource structure are formally identical to a Library structure. These two structures allow you to build related device and resource routines into libraries.

The MemHeader structure is used to tie together memory-block allocations in your tasks. It is used when you want to set up a list of free memory that will be managed by the program rather than by the system. The MemList structure is also used to tie together memory-block allocations in your tasks.

The MsgPort structure is used to define the message ports assigned to each of your tasks. The Message structure is used to contain message information passed back and forth between communicating tasks and devices in the Exec system.

Other Structures

There are several other Exec system structures whose INCLUDE files are worth printing and studying. These structures and their Exec INCLUDE file names are listed in Table 1.2.

Table 1.2:
Other Exec System Structures and their INCLUDE File Names

	Exec INCLUDE File Name	
Structure	**C Language**	**Assembly Language**
ExecBase	ExecBase.h	ExecBase.i
IntVector	Interrupts.h	Interrupts.i
SoftIntList	Interrupts.h	Interrupts.i
MemChunk	Memory.h	Memory.i
MemEntry	Memory.h	Memory.i
Unit	Devices.h	Devices.i
I/O Request Block	Io.h	Io.i
IOStdReq	Io.h	Io.i
Resident	Resident.h	Resident.i

You will find the Exec INCLUDE files on the Lattice C compiler disk under the INCLUDE directory. You should print the entire contents of these files. They will help you understand all of the structures used by the Exec system routines and functions. In fact, a thorough study of these structures is one of the best ways to learn about the Exec functions.

Tasks, Message Ports, Messages, and Signals

Getting tasks to talk to each other can be confusing and complex. However, if you break down the process into simple parts you can see how message ports, messages, and signals are used to pass information from one task to another and to get one task to direct the actions of another task.

First of all, it is important to understand that message ports and messages are nothing more than structures in the Amiga system. In addition, signals are nothing more than bits in a longword (32-bit word). To bring these ideas into focus, it is worthwhile to first look at the MsgPort and Message structures, which play a big part in intertask communication. The definition of these structures is as follows:

```
struct MsgPort {
    struct Node mp_Node;
    UBYTE mp_Flags;
    UBYTE mp_SigBit;
    struct Task *mp_SigTask;
    struct List mp_MsgList;
};

struct Message {
    struct Node mn_Node;
    struct MsgPort *mn_ReplyPort;
    UWORD mn_Length;
};
```

The meaning of the parameters in the MsgPort structure is as follows:

- The mp_Node parameter is the name of a Node substructure that is used to add this message port to a message-port list for this task.

- The mp_Flags parameter contains the flag bits of the MsgPort structure. You can initialize this parameter to one of three values: PA_SIGNAL, PA_SOFTINT, or PA_IGNORE. If set to PA_SIGNAL, the task will be signaled when a message arrives in this message port. The task can decide what to do once it recognizes the signal. If set to PA_SOFTINT, the task will be signaled and a software interrupt will begin execution; the task will temporarily lose the CPU. If set to PA_IGNORE, the task will be signaled when a message arrives in this message port, but the signal will cause no action to occur. It is important to understand that these actions (or no action) take place irrespective of the origin of the message (this task, another task, whatever).

■ The mp_SigBit parameter contains the signal bit number that is sent to the task when a message arrives in the message port. It is important to understand that each MsgPort structure is associated with one and only one signal bit. The meaning (action) attached to this signal bit is defined in the mp_Flags parameter.

■ The mp_SigTask parameter is a pointer to the Task structure of the task to notify (signal) when a message arrives in the message port. This task can be any task in the system including the current task.

■ The mp_MsgList parameter is the name of a List substructure that is used by the system to place all messages arriving at this message port on a message list. This is a FIFO list that defines the queue of all messages currently in this message port.

The meaning of the parameters in the Message structure is as follows:

■ The mn_Node parameter is the name of a Node substructure that is used to add this specific message to the message list as defined by the mp_MsgList parameter in the MsgPort structure.

■ The mn_ReplyPort parameter is a pointer to a MsgPort structure, which acts as the reply port for the message defined by this Message structure. It is important to recognize that the pointer to the reply port occurs in the Message structure. Once the receiving task has processed the message, the message will be sent back to this reply port. This reply port will usually be attached to the task that originally sent the message; however, it can be any currently defined message port that receives messages, some of which may be reply messages.

■ The mn_Length parameter contains the length of the message defined by this Message structure and its data. This parameter is the number of bytes of data in the message that actually define the information content of the message. These data bytes are appended to the Message structure. This is usually done by creating another structure containing the Message structure as a substructure. The Message structure is placed at the top of the new structure. The next part of this new structure contains the data definition.

If you study the definition of the parameters in these structures, you can begin to see how messages are passed between tasks in the system. These are some of the most important points to remember:

■ The system can contain any number of tasks. Each task is defined by a Task structure. (See the AddTask function.)

■ Each task can deal with up to 32 signals assigned to it. Each signal is represented by a signal bit number. The signals that are allocated to a task are contained in the bits of the 32-bit tc_SigAlloc parameter of the Task structure; if a bit is set, that signal number is allocated. You can use 16 of these signals (bit numbers 16 to 31) to get your tasks to talk to each other. The other 16 (bit numbers 0 to 15) are reserved for use by the system.

- Each task can have any number of message ports assigned to it. Every time a MsgPort structure is declared, a new message port is created for that task. The system automatically keeps track of the message ports assigned to each task using the mp_Node parameter of the MsgPort structure to place all message ports for a task on a message-port list for that task.

- Each message port signals only one task with one signal bit number. It is important to understand that this could be the task that owns the message port or it could be any other task currently defined in the system. The task that is signaled is defined by the mp_SigTask parameter in the MsgPort structure.

- All messages placed in a specific message port produce the same signal (the same signal bit number) whenever any message is placed in that message-port queue by PutMsg (or ReplyMsg). The signaled task always sees the same signal regardless of where the message originated. Message structures themselves do not contain any information to define signals; it is the arrival of messages in message-port queues that induces signals. This is an important concept to understand.

- Messages are placed in message-port queues by the PutMsg (or ReplyMsg) function. PutMsg directs the message to a message-port queue in another (or the same) task. ReplyMsg is used to reply (send back to the sending task) a message once the receiving task has accessed and/or changed the data in the message.

- Message passing is handled purely by placing messages on message-port lists. The Message structure is never copied or moved in RAM. Instead, it is first placed on a message-port message list (by PutMsg), then removed from a message-port message list (by GetMsg or Remove), then placed on a reply-port list (by ReplyMsg), then removed from the reply-port list (by GetMsg or Remove). The contents of the data portion of the extended message (Message structure plus data) may change during these steps, but the message is never moved or copied in RAM.

- Messages are retrieved from message-port queues with GetMsg. GetMsg gets the current top (first) message in a message-port queue. You can also use the Remove function to get a message; this is useful for getting messages before they reach the top of the message-port queue.

- When any message arrives in a message port, it causes the signal associated with that message port (if any) to be sent to the task designated in the mp_SigTask parameter. That is, the designated task is always signaled on arrival of any message in that message-port queue. The important word here is arrival; a task is not signaled when the message is removed from the message-port queue (when it is processed by GetMsg or Remove). If a message never reaches the top of its message-port queue, it can always still signal a task (if mp_SigTask is specified).

The simplest possible case that illustrates these concepts is that of one task with one message port, one reply port, and two signals. Figure 1.1 illustrates this situation. Although this is a somewhat artificial situation—a task passing messages to itself—it portrays how message ports, reply ports, messages, and signals behave.

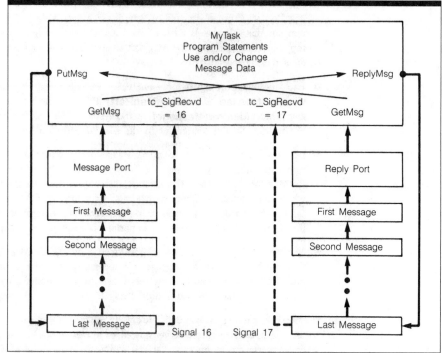

Figure 1.1:
One Task, One
Message Port,
One Reply Port,
Two Signals

The task statements to represent the connections of Figure 1.1 are as follows:

```
struct Task MyTask
struct MsgPort MsgPort
struct MsgPort ReplyPort

struct Message MsgPortMessage
struct Message ReplyPortMessage

MsgPort.mp_Node.In_Name = "MyTaskMsgPort"
MsgPort.mp_Node.In_Type = NT_MSGPORT
MsgPort.mp_SigTask = MyTask
MsgPort.mp_SigAlloc = 16
MsgPort.mp_SigWait = 16
MsgPort.mp_Flags = PA_SIGNAL

ReplyPort.mp_Node.In_Name = "MyTaskReplyPort"
ReplyPort.mp_Node.In_Type = NT_MSGPORT
ReplyPort.mp_SigTask = MyTask
ReplyPort.mp_SigAlloc = 17
ReplyPort.mp_SigWait = 17
```

ReplyPort.mp_Flags = PA_SIGNAL

MsgPortMessage.mn_ReplyPort = ReplyPort
ReplyPortMessage.mn_ReplyPort = MsgPort

PutMsg(MsgPort,MsgPortMessage)

MsgPortMessage = GetMsg(MsgPort)
ReplyMsg(MsgPortMessage)

ReplyPortMessage = GetMsg(ReplyPort)

The task operates in the following way:

1. PutMsg is used to place a message in the message-port queue of the task. As the arrow indicates, this message is placed at the end of the message-port queue, where it becomes the last message.

2. As soon as the message arrives (as soon as PutMsg returns), the task is signaled with signal bit number 16. The task can then recognize this signal (examine the tc_SigRecvd parameter of the Task structure) and go off immediately and do some processing in another routine.

3. The task gets the top (first) message in the message-port queue using GetMsg. Notice that, in general, this is not the same message placed in the message-port queue by the most recent PutMsg call. Rather, it is the message that has worked its way to the top of the queue (now the first message in the list). Other messages in that queue are moved up in the message list.

4. GetMsg tells the task that a message is now available. A pointer to the Message structure for that message is returned by GetMsg.

5. The task can now access, use, and possibly change the data in the message. Task statements to accomplish this are placed between the GetMsg and ReplyMsg (or GetMsg and PutMsg) statements. These task statements—represented by the long lines with arrows inside the MyTask rectangle—make use of the data information in the message.

6. Once the task uses (and perhaps changes) the data information in the message, it is ready to send a reply message back to the reply port specified in the Message structure. The mn_ReplyPort parameter in the Message structure tells the task where to send the reply message. This is done with ReplyMsg inside the task. When ReplyMsg returns, the message will be placed as the last message on the message-port message list of the reply port.

7. When the message arrives at the reply port, the task is immediately signaled of its arrival. The message is queued in the reply port, the reply-port message list is updated and the task is signaled. Signal bit number 17 is used for this purpose.

8. The task can now reference the reply message. It can access, use, and change the data in it. Once it does these things, the task is ready to send the message again using the same extended Message structure with new data defined.

If you study this simple example, you will understand how a task sends messages and signals to itself and how these are implemented using Amiga C language programming statements. In essence, this process specifies a number of memory structures (MsgPort, Message, and List structures) that are defined, changed, queued, and requeued in a specific sequence.

The PutMsg, GetMsg, and ReplyMsg functions direct the bookkeeping operations required to do the following:

- Get appropriate pointers to the Message structures at various times in the sequence

(GetMsg returns a pointer to a Message structure, but GetMsg doesn't know where the message originated.)

- Update the message-port message lists when PutMsg or ReplyMsg adds a message to a list or GetMsg (or Remove) removes a message from a list

- Provide a license to a task to allow that task to change Message structures at the correct times

Only after GetMsg (or Remove) gets a message from a message-port (or reply-port) queue can a task change the data information in that message. Anytime a message is still queued in a message-port message list, the task cannot access, process, or change the data information in that message.

Two Tasks, Two Message Ports, Two Reply Ports, and Four Signals

Figure 1.2 shows a two-task message-passing situation. Each task has one message port, one reply port, one message type (the type of data in the message), one reply message type, and two signals. These tasks and ports could represent any two tasks in the system. For example, when programming in Intuition, user-defined task (window) message ports are named UserPort. These are the message ports on the user task (window) side of the task–Intuition intertask communication. Intuition task message ports are named Window-Port (see Chapter 6). These are the message ports on the Intuition side of the task–Intuition intertask communication.

In Figure 1.2, each task has one message port and one reply port giving a total of four message ports. The PutMsg, ReplyMsg, and GetMsg functions are used to move messages onto and from the lists maintained for each of these four message-port message queues.

In addition, each task has two signals. Signal bit numbers 16 and 17 are used for both tasks. This demonstrates that signal bit numbers do not have to be unique to each task. The mp_SigTask parameter in each MsgPort structure is set to indicate the appropriate task to signal for that message port. In each case, this is the task that "owns" (declared as part of its task statements) the message port.

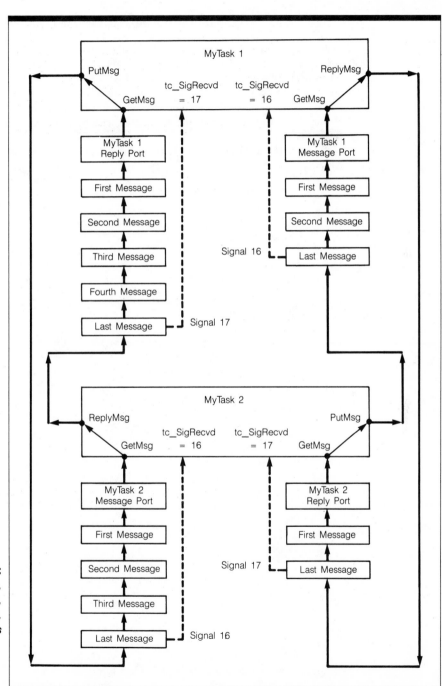

Figure 1.2:
Tasks,
Message Ports,
Messages,
and Signals

Multiple Tasks, Message Ports, Messages, and Signals

Figure 1.3 illustrates all the possible connections in a four-task situation. Each task has one message port and one reply port. Each task can send messages to each of the other three task's message ports. In addition, each task can reply messages back to the reply ports of the other three tasks. As you can see, this leads to a lot of connections.

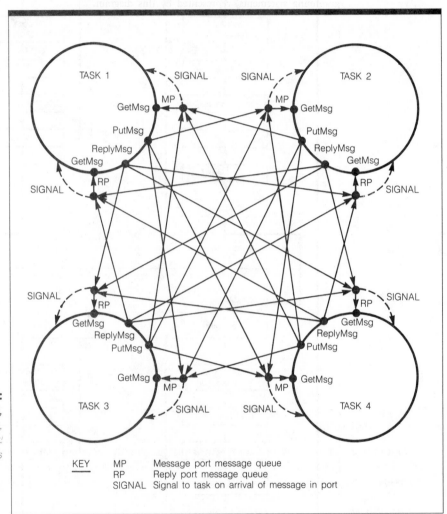

Figure 1.3:
Multiple Tasks,
Message Ports,
Messages, and
Signals

Each message port signals its task when a message arrives in either its message-port queue (one signal bit number) or its reply-port queue (usually another signal bit number).

Each of the four tasks can share the same signal bit numbers. The messages in each message port (a message port or a reply port) form a FIFO queue and move progressively to the top of the message-port message list.

To learn to program the Amiga multitasking system, you could attempt to specify all the C language statements required to fully define the situation in Figure 1.3. However, this figure depicts the most general situation involving four tasks. You can safely assume that in most situations your program will not need all the connections (and associated programming statements) represented by this diagram.

AddDevice

Syntax of Function Call

AddDevice (device)
A1

Purpose of Function

This function adds a new device to the system device list automatically maintained by the system and makes the device available to every task in the system. Note that this function merely places a node for this device on the system device list. The device should be ready to be called before this function is used.

Inputs to Function

device   A pointer to a properly initialized Device structure

Discussion

There are eight Exec functions that are directly concerned with device input/output: AddDevice, CheckIO, CloseDevice, DoIO, OpenDevice, RemDevice, SendIO, and WaitIO. Each of these functions performs a device service. There is more information on device I/O in the discussions of each of these calls.

The System Device List

The system maintains a list of all devices added to the system. Every time you make a call to the AddDevice function, this list is automatically updated to reflect the addition of that device to the system device list. Each device added uses certain resources of the system, memory in particular. A certain amount of memory is assigned to the device when you call the OpenDevice function. Therefore, unless a device is essential to the continuation of a particular task, you may want to close it with a CloseDevice function call. The CloseDevice function returns the memory used by this device to the system free-memory pool. If you also know that no task will need that device again, you should remove it with the RemDevice function as soon as you are sure you will not need to open it again.

Sequence of Device Handling

The general sequence of device handling proceeds along these lines:

1. First, the device is added to the system device list using the AddDevice function. This function operates similarly to the AddLibrary function, the AddResource function, and other Exec functions that add the named software resources to a system list. To this point, only the memory required to add the device to the system device list has been used. Once the device is added, it can be accessed by every task in the Amiga multitasking system—your specific programming tasks as well as other tasks (overhead and system tasks).

2. Each task that wants to use this device must open the device with a call to the OpenDevice function. The purpose of the OpenDevice function is similar to the OpenLibrary function, the OpenResource function, and other "open" functions in the Amiga Exec system. They allow a task in the system (the task that has the OpenDevice statement) to gain access to the device. Since this is a multitasking system, many tasks can use the same device. Each issues an OpenDevice call when it becomes the active task.

At any given time, then, there can be many tasks in the system that have issued OpenDevice calls to a single device. This is true even though only one task can be active at a time. Each call to the OpenDevice function assigns this device to a new task. This device then becomes a shared resource in the system: data comes and goes from it to only one task (the current task), even though many other tasks may subsequently use the same device to send and receive data.

The Device Library

The structure of a device library related to a device driver routine is very similar to a software library of any other type in the Exec system. The device driver routines are stored in a library format similar to the format of the standard library. As with other libraries, the device library has a number of code vectors that are a part of the library structure. These include the eight standard code vectors that are always required in a library: the vectors that point to the OPEN, CLOSE, EXPUNGE, and EXTFUNC routines, plus four others that are reserved for future use. A device library also contains fifteen additional required code vectors that point to the GoIO, DoIO, SendIO, AbortIO, Read, Write, Reset, Update, Clear, Flush, Stop, and Start routines, plus three additional reserved entries. Finally, each device can have a number of device-specific code vectors that point to routines specifically appropriate to that device.

Using Devices

Consider the flow of your program as you use devices in the system. If you think about the flow of code in this multitasking system, you will begin to appreciate how Exec handles devices. Assume you have three tasks in the system. Each task wants to use a specific device, whose characteristics are known to your program and which can help satisfy some of the data needs of that program. You have developed device-specific routines to handle the input/output of this device, coding and debugging them separately, and now you want to include them in the system.

To do this, you have to build a device library for this device, using the MakeLibrary function. This is done after you have constructed the library data and vectors according to the required rules.

Using standard programming tools, you put your device-specific routines in RAM at specific locations. These RAM offsets are then built into the device library as various RAM vectors from the Library structure of that library. That is, once you know what those offsets will be, you specify the code vectors to reach those routines. Of course, you must also specify the code vectors to reach the eight standard library routines and the fifteen standard device routines in the library. You must also define the data area for this device library.

Once all of this is done, you are ready to add the device library to the system with the MakeLibrary function. If all goes well, your library definition will be accepted. Now you are in a position to add that device to the system device list with the AddDevice function. Once you do this, any number of tasks can open that device for their own use.

As each task finishes (for the last time) with that device, you should close that device with a call to the CloseDevice function. Once all tasks have closed on that device and if you know that no task will need to open it again, you can remove the device from the system device list with a call to the RemDevice function. This will free all resources (memory and other overhead) allocated to and associated with that device. Now you can do the same for other devices in the system. If you have a large memory system, you won't have to remove devices as frequently.

Device handling on the Amiga is done by passing messages through device I/O Request Block structures. I/O Request Block structures allow devices to send and receive data and other information (for example, status) from the various devices currently in the system. The requesting information needed by the device driver is passed through the I/O Request Block structure to the device. Each device is referred to by its name in the Open-Device function call.

As the requesting task waits (or in some cases, does not wait) for the information to come back from the device, the device can send a message back to the task to tell it that the I/O request has been properly processed. This reply message is sent through the reply message area of the I/O Request Block structure of that device.

Device Memory Variables

A number of variables in the I/O Request Block structure are worthy of discussion. The io_Actual variable specifies the actual length of the data transferred from the device to the calling task. If an error occurs during the transfer, the request length (the value of the io_Length variable) in the original I/O Request Block structure and the actual length (the value of the io_Actual variable) may differ.

Sometimes differences are really due to errors in data transfer; for instance, information could not be found where expected (in memory buffers, on disk, and so forth). Some differences in two variables may not be critical; for instance, perhaps a disk read detected an EOF (end of file) condition that was no problem for the calling task (all the needed information was transferred). Therefore, a difference in the value of these two variables is not necessarily an indication of an error. Your program should examine each situation and determine the appropriate action for that case.

The io_Flags variable usually specifies some flags used only by the system. One of these is the IOF_QUICK flag bit, which indicates that QUICKIO is to be used for an I/O operation. However, under certain circumstances, this variable can contain information useful to the calling task.

The io_Error variable specifies a potential error condition. The expected device action did not occur as designed. Perhaps a disk wasn't in a disk drive, the information in a memory buffer did not make sense, or the wrong area of memory was referenced in the call. Every error must be treated differently. You can build error routines and call them individually, based on the error number, to tell the user what happened and how to correct it (insert a disk, for example). Note that what appears to be an error condition might, in some cases, not be a problem at all. Your program will have to make these types of decisions.

Standard Exec Devices

The standard device drivers installed in the Exec system are mostly ROM-based; that is, they are immediately available at power-up time. Exceptions are the serial device, the parallel device, and the printer device. These can be loaded from disk when needed.

There are two timer devices in the system. The first one uses the video vertical-blanking interval as a timing interrupt. This produces an interrupt every 1/60 of a second. The second uses the 8250 CIA chip to produce interrupts on a tighter time scale.

The Track-Disk device provides direct access to the disks to read and write information, as well as a number of functions, including Read, Write, and Format. The Amiga-DOS operating system uses the Track-Disk device for I/O operations. You can access it directly with the Track-Disk driver. The Track-Disk driver is part of a device library stored in the Disk.Resource file.

The Keyboard device handles input from the keyboard and converts it into input events that your program can retrieve and interpret. Keyboard input events are queued, so that the user can continue to type without losing keystrokes.

The Gameport device handles information from the mouse, joystick, or any potentio-meter device. Like keyboard input, gameport events are queued. You can tell the system what type of device is connected and how often to check and report the current status of the device.

The Console device is both an input and an output device. When treated as an input device, it combines the Keyboard and Gameport devices: the Console device-driver routines process input events from both of these sources and merge them into a single input event stream. Events are queued on a FIFO basis. When treated as an output device, the Console device handles the I/O for a window using the upper-level software in the Intuition system.

The audio device controls how the audio channels are used.

The serial device controls serial communications with external devices through the serial port of the Amiga. It controls I/O buffering, the baud rate, data-transfer error conditions, and more. In contrast to the other Exec devices, the serial device driver is loaded from disk when needed. Once in memory, it is initialized to some fixed parameter settings; your program can modify these settings as desired. The serial device has a baud range of 110 to 38400 baud.

The parallel device controls parallel communications with external devices through the parallel port of the Amiga. It controls the buffering of I/O data, data-transfer error conditions, and more. Like the serial device driver, the parallel device driver is loaded from disk when needed. Once in memory it is initialized to some fixed parameter settings; your program can modify these settings as desired. The parallel device is most often used with the parallel printer driver.

The printer device supports various printers attached to the Amiga. You can add more device drivers for different printers as you need them. Just like the serial and parallel device drivers, the printer device driver is loaded from disk when needed—whenever a user issues a print command.

You can add any number of devices, including any devices that you want to hook into either the serial port, the parallel port, the printer port, or the expansion connector port. Develop and debug a device routine and use the MakeLibrary, AddDevice, and OpenDevice functions to place it into the system. Then you can access it just like any other device.

AddHead

Syntax of Function Call

```
AddHead (list, node)
         A0   A1
```

Purpose of Function

This function adds a new Node structure to the head of a doubly-linked list.

Inputs to Function

list	A pointer to the List structure that will contain this node
node	A pointer to the Node structure to insert at the head of the list

Discussion

Exec has a number of macros and functions designed to operate on nodes (Node structures) and doubly-linked lists (List structures) built from nodes. These functions fall into several categories:

- Functions for adding and removing nodes in lists (Insert and Remove)

- Functions for adding and removing head and tail nodes in lists (AddHead, RemHead, AddTail, and RemTail)

- A function for inserting nodes sorted by priority (Enqueue)

- A function for searching for a node by name throughout a list (FindName)

Note that the Insert, Remove, AddHead, and AddTail functions do not use the priority field in the Node structure.

The basic element of a List structure is a doubly-linked list node represented by a Node structure. Here is the C language structure of a Node structure:

```
struct Node {
    struct Node *ln_Succ;
    struct Node *ln_Pred;
    UBYTE ln_Type;
    BYTE ln_Pri;
    char *ln_Name;
};
```

where the variables are defined as follows:

- ln_Succ (successor) is a pointer to the next Node structure in the list.

- ln_Pred (predecessor) is a pointer to the previous Node structure in the list.

- ln_Type is a decimal number from 0 to 255, used by other Exec functions to verify that all nodes in a particular list are of the same type.

- ln_Pri (priority) is a decimal number from +127 to −128 that associates a priority with a Node structure in a list. Nodes of higher priority are placed at the head of the list.

- ln_Name is a pointer to a null-terminated string of characters used to give a name to a particular Node structure

The relationship between a list, the list Head node, the list Tail node, and the list Tail Predecessor node are illustrated in Figure 1.4, which shows a complete list having N data nodes.

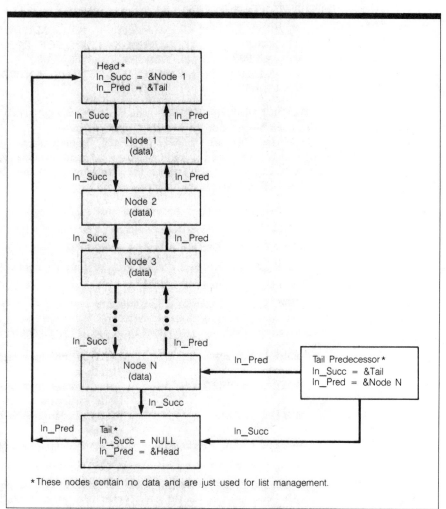

Figure 1.4:
List Linkages

In this figure, Node structures with the label data contain some ln_Name, ln_Pri, and/or ln_Type parameters. Note that the Head node, the Tail node, and the Tail Predecessor Node structures do not contain these data items; these three nodes are used only to manage the list. Initially, when the List structure is first defined, the list is empty. You can always test for an empty list; a list is empty if the ln_Pred parameter in the Tail

Predecessor node is equal to &Head or if the ln_Succ parameter in the Head node is equal to null.

It is important to note that *all* standard system structures begin with the Node substructure information. Exec now supports the following Node structure types, whose names imply their use:

NT_DEVICE	NT_MEMORY	NT_SEMAPHORE
NT_FONT	NT_MESSAGE	NT_SOFTINT
NT_FREEMSG	NT_PROCESS	NT_TASK
NT_INTERRUPT	NT_REPLYMSG	NT_UNKNOWN
NT_LIBRARY	NT_RESOURCE	

The INCLUDE files for these node types are called Nodes.h (for the C language interface) and Nodes.i (for the assembly language interface).

In addition, there are a number of assembly language macros you can use to embed list operations within your assembly language code and thereby optimize that code. The assembly language file List.i contains the current set of macros for assembly language code. These macros include the following:

ADDHEAD	Adds a Node structure at the head of a list
ADDTAIL	Adds a Node structure at the tail of a list
REMOVE	Removes a Node structure from a list
REMHEAD	Removes a Node structure from the head of a list
REMTAIL	Removes a Node structure from the tail of a list
NEWLIST	Initializes a List structure

For example, the following instructions are a part of the REMOVE macro:

```
MOVE.L (A1),A0          ; get a pointer to a successor Node
                          structure
MOVE.L LN_PRED(A1), A1  ; get a pointer to a predecessor
                          Node structure
MOVE.L A0,(A1)          ; fix up predecessor's successor
                          pointer
MOVE.L A1,LN_PRED(A0)   ; fix up successor's predecessor
                          pointer
```

You can also determine whether a list is empty. To do this, check whether the tail predecessor Node structure has the same pointer value as the Node structure of the head node, using the following instructions:

```
CMP.L LH_TAILPRED(A0), A0
BEQ emptylist
```

To scan a list, you must scan until the tail node is reached. Just compare the next node pointer with the tail pointer. Or, even better, you can maintain an element-pointer look-ahead register for the list by using the following instructions:

```
        MOVE.L (A1), D1       ; first node
scanLoop:
        MOVE.L D1, A1         ; make look-ahead to next
        MOVE.L (A1), D1       ; look-ahead to next
        BEQ.S scanExit        ; end of list
        <body>                ; use A1 for node
        BRA.S scanLoop
scanExit:
```

These assembly language instructions store the address (a pointer variable) of the next node in a list in the A1 register. This allows your program to look at this Node structure before it is used. You can perform a list scan in C language by using a For loop as follows:

```
for (node = list-> lh_Head; node-> ln_Succ; node = node-> ln_Succ)
{
<body of list-scan routine>
};
```

AddIntServer

Syntax of Function Call

```
        AddIntServer (intNumber, interrupt)
                      D0: 0–4    A1
```

Purpose of Function

This function adds a new interrupt-server routine to a specified server chain. This server routine is located in the server chain in a priority-dependent position; the interrupts corresponding to higher priority routines will be serviced first. If this server routine is the first one in this chain, interrupts will be enabled on this chain. This means that any server routine in the server chain list can be interrupted if a higher priority interrupt comes along while it is executing.

Inputs to Function

intNumber	The Paula (peripherals-sound custom chip) interrupt bit (0–14)
interrupt	A pointer to the Interrupt structure that contains an entry point for an interrupt-server routine belonging to this interrupt bit

Discussion

There are four functions that manage the interrupt servers: AddIntServer, Cause, RemInt-Server, and SetIntVector. See the discussions of each of these functions for more information on interrupt servers.

Servers are called with the following register conventions:

D0	Scratch
D1	Scratch
A0	Scratch
A1	On entry, server data segment pointer; scratch once inside routine
A5	On entry, jump vector register; scratch once inside routine
A6	On entry, system base pointer; scratch once inside routine

All other registers must be preserved. The term *scratch* means that the register can be used to manipulate data once you are inside the interrupt-server routine.

There are two types of routines used to service interrupts in the Amiga system:

1. Interrupt-handler routines directly handle the specific processing requirements of an interrupt associated with a specific Paula (the peripherals-sound custom chip) bit.

2. Interrupt-server routines are reserved for several interrupt routines that need to be linked together because they are related. Some or all of these routines will be called when such an interrupt occurs. These routines form an interrupt-server chain. Each interrupt-server routine in the chain has a priority. Each is called in the sequence determined by the priority field of the interrupt server Node structure, which is a substructure of the Interrupt structure.

There are two types of interrupts on the Amiga: software and hardware. Usually, all hardware interrupts are preprocessed by the Exec routines prior to calling the interrupt routines. This is where the Amiga-specific interrupts are identified: seven levels of 68000 CPU interrupts are decoded into the 15 individual Amiga interrupt vectors.

Because of the way things are arranged, multiple pieces of server code can share the same interrupt number. For example, several routines will execute when the vertical-blanking interrupt (Amiga interrupt 5) occurs; this happens every 1/60 of a second. For this reason, priority-sorted interrupt chains are provided. Then, when that specific interrupt occurs, the code from each interrupt vector in that interrupt-server chain is executed in turn, each with its own priority.

As you might imagine, higher priority routines are executed first. This ensures quick turnaround of certain interrupt routines that must be promptly executed when an interrupt occurs.

In addition, the hardware supports a means of generating software interrupts for invoking low-priority interrupt routines. This type of interrupt routine is not related to any particular hardware device. The 68000 TRAP instruction is one of the ways used to implement software interrupts.

Interrupts are also related to task switching. Most of the time, a task switch occurs as a result of an interrupt—either a hardware or software interrupt. Therefore, the interrupt system is at the heart of the task-switching mechanism for the Amiga.

Refer to the discussion of the Cause function for a list of the possible interrupt sources. Each interrupt, when it occurs, sets a bit in Paula's (the peripherals-sound custom chip's) interrupt request register. There are 15 interrupt bits, but there are only six interrupt levels (out of the seven supported by the 68000) that are actually used.

Within each level of interrupt service routine, there is a software priority established by the order in which the various interrupt bits are examined. See the discussion of the Cause function for the current prioritization within the various levels. There are six levels of interrupt prioritization, level 6 is highest priority; level 1 is lowest priority.

Interrupt Priority Levels

The Copper display control coprocessor has the highest priority interrupt, level 6. The Copper's operation is synchronized with the movement of the video beam as it scans across and down the display screen of the Amiga. If the Copper generates a special interrupt, it may be signaling that something should be done right away. Usually, this means that something should be done just as the video beam passes a certain pixel location on the display-screen scanning line. On the other hand, the external expansion-box interrupt, which is also at level 6, will usually be less important and can wait until the Copper is serviced.

The disk and UART (Universal Asynchronous Receiver Transmitter) are placed at level 5. Critical response time is very short for the disk (approximately 16 microseconds). The response of the UART is less demanding (approximately 250 microseconds).

All four audio channels are placed at level 4. Audio channels 0 and 2 on the Amiga are used to modulate the outputs of audio channels 1 and 3. Usually, audio channels 1 and 3 are used to produce and output audio-modulation waveforms. In this case, the interrupt overhead for audio channels 1 and 3 is minimized by placing them at the head of the software chain.

The Blitter, Copper (sometimes), and vertical-blanking interrupts are placed at level 3. The graphics routines keep the Blitter as busy as possible, which is why the graphics and animation in the system are so fast. For this reason, the Blitter DMA channel is serviced first at this level. On the other hand, if the Copper coprocessor should have a higher priority, it can write into bit 15 instead of bit 5 of Paula. This will cause a level 6 interrupt instead of a level 3 interrupt. Vertical blanking is usually a relatively slow sequence. Therefore, the vertical-blanking interrupt is at the bottom of the interrupt list.

The level 2 interrupts consist of the I/O ports, keyboard, clock, and printer. These are medium-speed devices whose interrupt routines are only required to execute at medium speed.

The UART TBE (transfer-buffer-empty), software, and disk-block interrupts are placed at level 1. The transmit-buffer-empty interrupt is at the head of the chain to speed serial communications. Next is the disk-block transfer interrupt. The last interrupt is for the software interrupts, which are the least demanding (time critical) type of interrupt.

System-Defined Server Chains

Note that the Exec system routines automatically build a server chain for six types of interrupts:

- The level 3 vertical-blanking interrupt

- The level 2 external interrupt coming from devices connected to the external expansion box

- The level 6 external interrupt coming from devices connected to the external expansion box

- The level 3 Copper coprocessor interrupt

- The levels 2 and 6 I/O port interrupts

- The level 3 Blitter interrupt

Currently, there is no system code entry point for creating an interrupt-server chain as a handler on any of the other interrupt bits. However, you can create your own interrupt handler by using the same type of sequencing as used for these four server chains.

AddLibrary

Syntax of Function Call

AddLibrary (library)
A1

Purpose of Function

This function adds a new library to the system and makes it available to every task in the system. The name of this library is added to the system library list. The library should be ready to be called before this function is used. This function also calculates the checksum on the library entries.

Inputs to Function

library   A pointer to a properly initialized Library structure

Discussion

There are seven Exec functions that deal with libraries in the Amiga system: AddLibrary, CloseLibrary, MakeLibrary, OpenLibrary, RemLibrary, SetFunction, and SumLibrary. Libraries are identified by their names and version numbers, and they can contain all of your most often used routines. By changing the version number of a library, you can have many closely related libraries.

You can keep a collection of different libraries on disk. These libraries are classified as system libraries and user libraries. If a library is in ROM, it is said to be *resident;* if it is on disk, it is said to be *transient.*

Tasks use libraries to satisfy their extra coding and data needs. Many tasks can reside in the system at one time. This means that several—perhaps many—tasks may be using the same library as these tasks switch in and out of execution according to their task priorities.

Figure 1.5 illustrates the general block structure of a library. If you design a library with MakeLibrary, you must force your library into this format. Formally speaking, the large rectangle represents the library. The small rectangles at the top of the figure represent the library routines; these are not formally a part of the library definition—only the jump vectors to these routines are said to be "in the library." The figure shows the three pieces of the library: the Library structure itself, the library data segment, and the library jump vector instructions.

Notice that the Library structure is sandwiched between the jump vectors and the library data. The first element of the Library structure is the Libnode Node substructure. For this reason, the Library structure is often referred to as a Library Node structure.

By convention, a code jump vector occupies six bytes. Six-byte jump vectors are used to allow the vector to reference code segments at some distance from the Library structure. The Library structure is the fulcrum point in memory for the other parts of the library. The jump vectors are located at negative offsets from the Library structure; the library data areas are located at positive offsets from the Library structure.

If your code routines are within 32K bytes of the Library substructure, you can use four-byte jump vectors in the definition of your library. If, by your library design, your library code routines are even closer in memory to the Library substructure, you can use two-byte jump vectors.

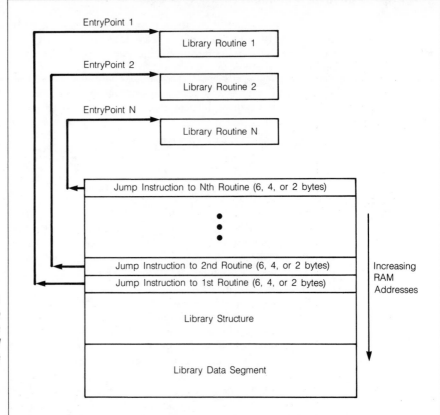

Figure 1.5:
Relationship
between a
Library and
Library Routines

The data segment is of variable size. Its contents and size depend on the intended use and needs of the library. Data segment locations are accessed as positive displacements from the Library structure. Library data is usually accessed from the library code routines themselves rather than from code outside of the library code routine sections. Different programming languages have different interface requirements. When you design your own libraries, you can decide how the associated data segments should be arranged and used.

The purpose of the AddLibrary function is to add a new library to the system library list. It only adds the library to the list—it does not open the library. You must have the library properly initialized before you call the AddLibrary function. You can initialize a library with the MakeLibrary function.

To access an already initialized library, you must perform two steps:

1. First, you must open the library with the OpenLibrary function. If the library is on disk, it will be brought into RAM at this time.

2. Second, you must access the jump-vector instructions or data by specifying an offset, either negative (for the jump vectors) or positive (for the data), from the Library structure pointer returned by the OpenLibrary function.

From this form of indirection you can see that your code is not necessarily dependent on the absolute locations of the system routines. For this reason, accessing the system routines through properly constructed libraries and subsequent library calls is the most efficient way of ensuring that your programs will work on different Amiga machines where the hardware may have different characteristics that impact program routine calls.

The Library Structure

The purpose of a library is to provide an organized grouping of related routines that can each be called in a convenient fashion. A Library structure contains all the information the system needs to manage a library. In C language notation, the Library structure is defined as follows:

```
struct Library {
    struct Node lib_Node;
    UBYTE lib_Flags;
    UBYTE lib_pad;
    UWORD lib_NegSize;
    UWORD lib_PosSize;
    UWORD lib_Version;
    UWORD lib_Revision;
    APTR lib_IDString;
    ULONG lib_Sum;
    UWORD lib_OpenCnt;
};
```

These are the parameters in the Library structure:

- The lib_Node parameter contains the name of a Node substructure that allows this particular library to be linked into the system library list. The ln_Name parameter in the Node structure will become the name of the library, thus allowing you to refer to the library by name. The ln_Pri parameter in the Node structure will determine where the library sits in the list of libraries. You should predefine these two parameters before you enter the library into the system. You should also set the ln_Type parameter in the Node structure to NT_LIBRARY to indicate that this Node structure represents a library.

- The lib_Flags parameter contains a set of flag parameters for this library. The flag bits are detailed below.

- The lib_pad parameter is a 1-byte padding parameter for the Library structure required to maintain proper word alignment in the Library structure.

- The lib_NegSize parameter contains the number of bytes in the library before the Library structure itself. This area of the library contains the library code vectors.

■ The lib_PosSize parameter contains the number of bytes in the library after the Library structure itself. This area of the library contains the library data.

■ The lib_Version parameter contains the version number of the library.

■ The lib_Revision parameter contains the revision number of the library.

■ The lib_IDString parameter contains a null-terminated text string, which identifies this library.

■ The lib_Sum parameter contains the current value of the checksum for the library. Each time the contents of the library are changed, this parameter should be updated. See the SetFunction discussion.

■ The lib_OpenCnt parameter maintains a count of the number of tasks that currently have this library open. Each time a task calls the OpenLibrary function to open the library associated with this Library structure, this parameter is incremented. Each time a task calls the CloseLibrary function for the library associated with this Library structure, this parameter is decremented.

AddMemList

Syntax of Function Call

```
error = AddMemList (size, attributes, priority, basePointer, name)
D0                  D0    D1          D2        A0           A1
```

Purpose of Function

This function adds a new memory block to a named free-memory pool. This block will consist of one or more subblocks. The first few bytes of this block will hold the MemHeader structure defining the memory block and each of its subblocks. The subblocks do not have to be in contiguous memory; the MemHeader and MemChunk structures provide the pointers and links for each subblock. The remainder of the block (other subblocks) will be available to the system and any other tasks that want to use it.

Inputs to Function

size   The number of bytes in the total memory block that are to be added

attributes	This is the set of attributes that the total memory block will have. See the AllocMem function for a discussion of these attributes.
priority	This is the priority for this memory block. Chip memory (memory in the first 512K) has a priority of -10 and extended—fast—memory (memory beyond 512K bytes) has a priority of 0. The priority of a memory block is contained in the ln_Pri parameter of the Node substructure inside the MemHeader structure.
basePointer	The base RAM location of the new memory block
name	This is the name of the free-memory pool. This name will be used in the MemHeader structure; use null if no name is to be assigned to this free-memory pool. The name is not copied; therefore, it must remain valid for as long as that MemHeader structure is present in the system.

Discussion

There are three functions in the 1.2 software release that deal with memory management: AddMemList, CopyMem, and CopyMemQuick. Read the discussions of each of these functions to understand the new memory management features offered by the 1.2 release.

Before the 1.2 release, there was no efficient way to add a set of memory blocks to a named free-memory pool. AddMemList provides a convenient way to do this. In previous releases, the Deallocate function was available to add one block of memory to a named free-memory pool and FreeEntry was available to add more than one block to the system free-memory pool, which consists of unnamed blocks.

The MemHeader structure provides a convenient way for the system to define an explicitly named free-memory pool; it is discussed under the Allocate function. You should note the following with respect to the AddMemList function:

- Each MemHeader structure contains a Node substructure, which contains the name (ln_Name) and priority (ln_Pri) parameters for that MemHeader structure. The AddMemList call uses its arguments to define these parameters in the MemHeader structure.

- Each MemHeader structure contains an attributes parameter (mh_Attributes). This is the attributes parameter in the AddMemList function call.

- Each MemHeader structure contains an upper and a lower bound parameter, which define the RAM limits of the memory block controlled by this MemHeader structure. In addition, each MemHeader structure contains the total number of free bytes (the total size of the free-memory pool) in the total memory block controlled by the MemHeader structure.

■ Each MemHeader structure contains a pointer to the first of one or more Mem-Chunk structures, which define a linked list of memory blocks—the total free-memory pool. Each MemChunk structure contains a link to the next memory block in the linked list.

You should study the MemHeader and MemChunk structures in the Memory.h INCLUDE file to further understand these relationships.

AddPort

Syntax of Function Call

        AddPort (msgPort)
               A1

Purpose of Function

This function adds a new message port to the system message-port list and makes it available to every task in the system. The message port is then said to be public. The name and priority fields of the Node substructure of the MsgPort structure should be initialized prior to calling this function. If the user does not require the name and priority fields, they should be initialized to zero. As with the name field in other system lists, the name is useful when more than one task needs to rendezvous at this message port to exchange data and other information.

Inputs to Function

        msgPort   A pointer to a MsgPort structure

Discussion

There are four Exec routines that are explicitly concerned with message ports in the Amiga system: AddPort, FindPort, RemPort, and WaitPort. AddPort, FindPort, and RemPort all deal exclusively with public ports that are added to the system message-port list with the AddPort function. WaitPort deals with both public and private ports. These routines manage the ports where messages are passed between tasks in the Amiga system. Messages passed through message ports are the mechanism by which tasks cooperate in the Amiga multitasking system.

Closely related to the message-port routines are the message-management routines: PutMsg, GetMsg, and ReplyMsg. To understand the operation of the message-port routines, you should also study the operation of the message-management routines. They work hand in hand to allow the multitasking operating system to exchange information between tasks and devices in an efficient manner.

Message Ports and Reply Ports

In general, ports fall into two classifications: message ports and reply ports. Each time a task is assigned a message port (using the AddPort function), an associated reply port is also automatically assigned to that task if the Message structure for messages coming to that port contains a pointer to a reply port. This is the mn_ReplyPort pointer parameter in the Message structure. Once a task gains control of the 68000 through a switch in priorities (or any other mechanism that switches tasks) it can send messages to all other tasks in the system if the appropriate message ports have been set up.

By definition, only one task is currently active; all other tasks are said to be "sleeping." The messages sent by the sender task are piling up in their message-port queues. Then, when a task switch occurs again, a previously inactive receiver task may gain control of the system. The messages in each message port of that task can then be examined to determine the action they require. Any signals assigned to the message ports where these messages are queued can also be examined to determine subsequent task actions based on these signals.

The original sender task needs to know when a message is processed by the receiver. This is the purpose of the reply port. Once the receiver task processes a message-port message, a reply-port message is automatically sent back to the reply port of the original sender task, which is now sleeping (it's no longer the active task). Then, when the original sender task reawakens, it will know that its original message has been received and processed by the intended receiver task. The sequence of its continued actions will be dependent on this knowledge.

Message-Port Characteristics

While there can be many tasks in the system at one time, only one task can be active at any given time. Which task is active is determined in part by the relative priority of all tasks placed into the system by the AddTask function. All tasks, both active and inactive, can have a group of message ports assigned to them. These ports are assigned to each task by the AddPort function, which can assign any number of ports to each task in the system.

When a message port is added to a task, it is placed on the message-port list for that task. The system automatically maintains a message-port list for each task currently in the system. Each message port can have a name and a priority. The names and priorities are useful if more than one pair of tasks need to be exchanging messages through this message port. The priority is used to tell the task which message port to look at first when it becomes active. The messages contained in a message port can be of any length.

Message ports can be public or private. A *public port* is one that is known to all code in the system; therefore, all tasks can use it. You must use the AddPort function to make a message port public. A public port must be given a name. A *private port* is used only by closely cooperating pieces of code. The system itself maintains and uses a number of private ports for its own needs. These system message-port linkages are achieved without using a name for the port.

AddResource

Syntax of Function Call

AddResource (resource)
A1

Purpose of Function

This function adds a new resource to the system resource list and makes it available to all tasks in the system. Note that the resource is merely placed on one of the system's lists by this function. The resource should be ready to be called before this function is used.

Inputs to Function

resource   A pointer to a properly initialized Resource structure

Discussion

Although resources have not been fully defined by Commodore-Amiga at this time, there are three Exec functions that are directly concerned with resource handling in the Amiga system: AddResource, OpenResource, and RemResource. Each of these functions performs a resource service; their names suggest the particular service they perform. Note that there is no CloseResource function.

The System Resource List

The system maintains a list in RAM of all resources added to the system. Every time you make a call to the AddResource function, the system resource list is updated automatically to reflect the addition of that resource. Each resource added uses certain system resources—memory in particular. This memory is assigned when you call the Open-Resource function.

Sequence of Resource Handling

The general sequence of resource handling proceeds along these lines:

1. The resource is added to the system resource list using the AddResource function. This function operates similarly to the AddLibrary function, the AddDevice function, and other Exec functions that add software resources to the system. Once the resource is added, it can be accessed by every task in the system—your specific programming tasks as well as other tasks (overhead and system) in the system. To this point, only the memory required to add the resource to the system resource list has been used.

2. Each task that wants to use this resource must open the resource with a call to the OpenResource function. The purpose of the OpenResource function is similar to the OpenLibrary function, the OpenDevice function, and other "open" functions in the Amiga Exec system. They allow a task (the task that has the OpenResource statement) to gain access to the resource. Because this is a multitasking system, many tasks can use the same resource. Each can issue an OpenResource function call when it is active.

At any given time, then, there may be many tasks in the system that have issued OpenResource calls to a single resource. This is true even though only one task can be active at a time. Each call to the OpenResource function assigns this resource to a new task. This resource then becomes a shared resource in the system. This ensures that data will be coming from and going to any one resource to and from only one task (the current task), even though many other tasks can subsequently use the same resource to send and receive data.

The Resource Library

A resource is represented in the system by a library pointing to a set of resource routines. These routines are stored in a library format similar to the format of the standard library. You can use the MakeLibrary function to create the resource library. As with other libraries, the resource library has a number of code vectors that are a part of the Library structure. These vectors have not yet been fully defined. In the case of a resource library, they usually point to dummy routines.

Using Resources

Consider the flow of your program as you use resources in the system. If you think about the flow of code in this multitasking system, you will begin to appreciate how Exec handles resources. Assume you will have three tasks in the system. Each task wants to use a specific resource, whose characteristics are known to your program and which can help satisfy some of the data needs of that program. You develop resource-specific routines to handle the data interchange mechanisms of this resource, coding and debugging them separately, and now you want to include them in the system.

To do this, you have to build a resource library for this resource. You put your resource-specific routines in the library at various offsets from the Library Node structure of that library. Once you know what those offsets are, you specify the code vectors to reach those routines. You must also specify the code vectors to reach the mandatory resource library routines and define the data area for this resource library.

Once you have done all of this, you are ready to construct the resource library by calling the MakeLibrary function. If all goes well, your library definition will be accepted. Now you can use the AddResource function to add that resource to the system resource list, where any number of tasks can open it.

As each task finishes (for the last time) with a resource, you can remove it with RemResource. This frees up all memory and other overhead resources allocated for and associated with that resource. If you have a large memory system, you won't need to continually remove resources.

The Amiga system currently has five resources. See the OpenResource function for information about these resources.

AddSemaphore

Syntax of Function Call

> **AddSemaphore (signalSemaphore)**
> **A1**

Purpose of Function

This function attaches a SignalSemaphore structure to the system signal-semaphore list. The name (ln_Name) and priority (ln_Pri) parameters of the SignalSemaphore Node substructure should be initialized before AddSemaphore is called. If you do not want other tasks to rendezvous (gain access to a named SignalSemaphore structure) with this semaphore, you should use the InitSemaphore function instead, which does not require you to initialize the name parameter of the SignalSemaphore Node substructure.

Inputs to Function

signalSemaphore   A pointer to a properly initialized SignalSemaphore structure. Both the name and priority parameters must be initialized by simple structure parameter assignment statements before the AddSemaphore function call.

Discussion

There are seven functions in the 1.2 release that deal with signal semaphores: Add-Semaphore, AttemptSemaphore, FindSemaphore, InitSemaphore, ObtainSemaphore, ReleaseSemaphore, and RemSemaphore. Each of these deals with an individual Signal-Semaphore structure. In addition, the 1.2 release provides two functions that deal with the signal-semaphore list (ObtainSemaphoreList and ReleaseSemaphoreList) and two functions that deal with message-based semaphores (Procure and Vacate). Read the discussion of each of these functions to understand how and why semaphores are used in the Amiga software system.

The first nine functions work with the SignalSemaphore structure directly or with parameters in the SignalSemaphore structure.

The SignalSemaphore Structure

The SignalSemaphore structure has the following definition in the Semaphores.h INCLUDE file:

```
struct SignalSemaphore {
    struct Node ss_Link;
    SHORT ss_NestCount;
    struct MinList ss_WaitQueue;
    struct SemaphoreRequest ss_MultipleLink;
    struct Task *ss_Owner;
    SHORT ss_QueueCount;
};
```

These are the parameters in the SignalSemaphore structure:

- The ss_Link parameter is the name of the Node substructure within the Signal-Semaphore structure. This Node structure contains the name (ln_Name) and priority (ln_Pri) parameters and other node parameters that allow this SignalSemaphore structure to be placed on a named signal-semaphore list.

- The ss_NestCount parameter is a counter that keeps track of the number of times this particular semaphore was obtained (by a call to ObtainSemaphore) and released (by a call to ReleaseSemaphore) within the current task. Only when this parameter is zero can another task gain access to this SignalSemaphore structure.

- The ss_WaitQueue parameter is the name of a MinList substructure, which defines the list of tasks waiting to gain access to this SignalSemaphore structure. The MinList structure is a shortened form of a List structure; it is defined in the Exec Nodes.h INCLUDE file. When the ss_NestCount parameter is zero, the system will consult this list to determine which tasks are queued to use this Signal-Semaphore structure.

- The ss_MultipleLink parameter is the name of a SemaphoreRequest substructure within the SignalSemaphore structure. The SemaphoreRequest structure is allocated by the ObtainSemaphore function when another task tries to obtain (gain access to) this SignalSemaphore structure. In this case there is a multiple link across tasks where each task is trying to use the signal semaphore represented by this Signal-Semaphore structure.

- The ss_Owner parameter is a pointer to the Task structure of the task that currently owns (has access to) this SignalSemaphore structure. The system will change this parameter only when a new task gains access to this SignalSemaphore structure.

- The ss_QueueCount parameter is the current count of the number of tasks that are queued waiting to use this SignalSemaphore structure. It tells the system the length of the ss_WaitQueue list. Each time another task tries to access this Signal-Semaphore structure, this parameter is incremented.

AddTail

Syntax of Function Call

```
AddTail  (list,node)
          A0   A1
```

Purpose of Function

This function adds a new Node structure to the tail of a doubly-linked list.

Inputs to Function

list
: A pointer to the List structure whose list will contain this node

node
: A pointer to the Node structure to insert at the tail of the list

Discussion

The Amiga Exec system has a number of macros and functions designed to operate on nodes and doubly-linked lists built from nodes. See the discussion under the AddHead function for a complete list.

Because an Exec list is a doubly-linked list, insertions and deletions can occur anywhere in the list without the need to scan the entire list. Each list has a List structure, which is built like this in the C language:

```
struct List {
    struct Node *lh_Head;
    struct Node *lh_Tail;
    struct Node *lh_TailPred;
    UBYTE lh_Type;
    UBYTE l_pad;
};
```

The lh_Head and lh_Tail fields together make up the first node in the list. The lh_Tail and lh_TailPred fields make up the last node in the list. The lh_Type field is used to verify individual nodes in the list; it should not be used in every case. There are 14 node types; they are defined under the Addhead function. The l_pad field is a single byte of padding to word-align data in the List structure; this item is currently not used.

The List structure is linked to the rest of the list in these ways:

1. The List structure lh_Head field points to the first Node structure in the list.

2. The List structure lh_TailPred field points to the last Node structure in the list.

3. The first Node structure points back to the List structure lh_Head field.

4. The last Node structure points back to the List structure lh_Tail field; it does *not* point back to the List structure lh_TailPred field.

These linkages are illustrated in Figure 1.4.

You should initialize the List structure prior to using it. It is not adequate to initialize the entire List structure to zero; the lh_Head and lh_Tail entries must point to each other. To initialize the List structure, follow these steps:

1. Assign the lh_Head Node structure to point to the lh_Tail Node structure.

2. Assign the lh_TailPred Node structure to point to the lh_Head Node structure.

3. Assign the proper data type to the lh_Type parameter of the List structure.

Here is an example of List structure initialization in assembly language:

```
MOVE.L A0, (A0)
ADDQ.L #LH_TAIL, (A0)
CLR.L LH_TAIL(A0)
MOVE.L A0, LH_TAILPRED(A0)
```

To give you some idea of how these list management functions are used, consider the types of lists that the Exec routines deal with to manage the system tasks and your tasks. An explanation of each of the principal types of lists follows.

The Task-Ready-Queue List

This is a list of all tasks that have been added to the system using the AddTask function. One task may be currently executing; other tasks are not currently executing but are said to be in the task-ready queue. Three things can happen to take a task out of the task-ready-queue list: a wakeup message can arrive at one of the task's message ports, an interrupt can reawaken the task, or a higher priority can be assigned to the task by the SetTaskPri function.

The task-ready-queue list grows as tasks are added to the system with the AddTask function; it shrinks as tasks are removed from the system with the RemTask function.

It is important to note that there is a fundamental difference between making a task active or inactive versus adding or removing the task from the system. Adding or removing affects the resources in the system as well as the task list.

The System Library List

This list grows as libraries are added to the system with the AddLibrary function; it shrinks as libraries are removed from the system with the RemLibrary function.

The System Device List

This list grows as devices are added to the system with the AddDevice function; it shrinks as devices are removed from the system with the RemDevice function.

The System Free-Memory List

This list grows as memory blocks are freed for other system uses with the FreeEntry and FreeMem functions. Notice that the system does not keep a list of memory areas actually in use—only a list of available (free) memory blocks is maintained.

The System Message-Port List

This list grows as message ports are added to the system with the AddPort function. The list shrinks as ports are removed with the RemPort function.

The System Reply-Port List

This list grows as message ports are added to the system with the AddPort function. The list shrinks as ports are removed with the RemPort function.

The Interrupt-Server List

This list grows as more interrupt-routine libraries are added to the system with the AddIntServer function. This list shrinks as interrupt-routine libraries are removed with the RemIntServer function.

The System Resource List

This list grows as resources are added to the system with the AddResource function. It shrinks as resources are removed with the RemResource function.

AddTask

Syntax of Function Call

AddTask (taskCB, initialPC, finalPC)
         A1   A2   A3

Purpose of Function

This function adds a new task to the system. Certain fields of the Task Control Block structure must be initialized and a minimal task stack should be allocated prior to calling this function.

AddTask temporarily uses space in the new task's stack area for the task's initial set of registers. This space is allocated starting at the SPReg parameter location specified in the Task Control Block structure (not from SPUpper). This means that the task stack area may contain static data put there before this task's execution. This is useful for providing initialized global variables that can then be used by the task to satisfy some of its data needs. In addition, some tasks may want to use this space for passing the task its initial arguments. A task's initial registers are set to zero, with the exception of the 68000 PC (program counter).

Inputs to Function

taskCB	A pointer to the Task Control Block structure for this task
initialPC	A pointer to the initial RAM entry point for this task
finalPC	A pointer to the finalization code RAM entry point for this task. If this value is zero, the system will automatically use a general finalizer routine. This pointer is placed on the task stack as if it were the outermost return address.

Discussion

There are four Exec functions that specifically relate to task handling in the Amiga system: AddTask, FindTask, RemTask, and SetTaskPri. See the discussions of each of these functions for more information on task handling.

The ROM executive of the Amiga is a real-time, message-based, multitasking operating environment. However, it is important to understand that the Exec functions are not an operating system in the usual sense of the term. AmigaDOS comes closer to a definition of an operating system.

As real-time functions, the Exec functions can respond to events as they happen. This is because they are cleverly written to run at maximum speed. Also, the special Amiga custom chips assist and speed task-related operations. In particular, the Blitter DMA (direct memory access) channel can transfer data at very high data rates. Up to 24 other channels of DMA also speed system operations.

As multitasking functions, the Exec functions make it possible for many programs to execute concurrently without each being aware of the others. For example, a task can signal another task that it needs information from the disk. When this disk subtask starts executing, there will be a disk-related task in the system. While the disk task moves the read/write head of the disk drive, another task can perform part of its work. This avoids the waste of time that occurs while the read/write head is moving, thus keeping the system busy at all times.

When tasks are entered into the system, they are assigned a priority. This is a number between +127 and −128. Each task's priority is contained in the ln_Pri parameter of the Node substructure (tc_Node) inside the Task Control Block structure. Internal task switching is automatically handled by the Exec task-management system routines, using messages passed between tasks through their message and reply ports.

The Exec functions are message based; individual tasks communicate with each other through messages. Each task can have one or more message ports where messages are placed. These messages are then queued: they are processed in FIFO order. When a message is received, a task can continue with its normal operations, it can get and perhaps respond to the message, or it can enter a special exception routine to respond to the message.

Messages are received by the message ports assigned to a task. These message ports allow you to pass hardware interrupt signals (or possibly software interrupts) to the task. That task, in turn, decides how these messages, when received, will affect the execution of that task.

When a message is received by the message port of a task, the message is appended to the end of the list of messages in that task's message queue. The PutMsg function is used to place messages in the message queue of a message port. The receiver task can then call the GetMsg routine to process messages in one of its message ports. PutMsg can perform one of two actions:

■ It can activate the task by processing a signal bit associated with that message port, thus starting execution of the task.

■ It can activate the task and cause a software interrupt. This will force the task to enter its exception code. However, this will happen only if the signal bit associated with this message port can cause exceptions. When the interrupt is finished, the task will continue at the same position as before the interrupt occurred.

To define and add a task, first initialize a Task Control Block structure that gives the system information about your task. Here you specify the variables to define the task's stack, the exception-routine definition variables, the trap-routine definition variables, the memory-allocation variables, and finally any other variables you need to define the task.

Now add your task to the system with the AddTask function. It shares the system with all other tasks already present. You need to answer the following questions about this task:

1. Where is the Task Control Block structure for this task? The AddTask function requires a pointer to the Task Control Block structure for this task. You must initialize the Task Control Block structure before you call the AddTask function.

2. Where is the starting address of this task's code instructions? The AddTask function requires this value in the initialPC pointer variable. You can place your program code anywhere (including above 512K) in RAM.

3. What is the starting address of the cleanup routine this task should use when finished? The AddTask function requires this value in the finalPC pointer variable.

Finally, if your task will need to communicate with other tasks in the system, create a message port that this task can use to send and receive messages. You can use the Add-Port function for this purpose.

The data structure that defines a task's Task Control Block structure appears in the Exec INCLUDE files; these files are called Tasks.h (for the C language interface) and Tasks.i (for the assembly language interface).

When you add a task to the system, you must initialize some variables in the task's Task Control Block structure, as follows:

1. The stack definition variables:

tc_SPUpper	The address of the upper byte of the RAM stack for this task
tc_SPLower	The address of the lower byte of the RAM stack for this task
tc_SPReg	The beginning user stack-pointer register value for this task

2. The exception-routine definition variables:

tc_ExceptCode	A pointer to this task's exception-handler code
tc_ExceptData	A pointer to this task's exception-handler data area
tc_SigExcept	A mask that tells the system which received signal bits will cause an exception
tc_SigRecvd	The actual signals that have occurred in intertask communication up to this time—this keeps changing as the task executes

tc_SigAlloc   The signal bits that have already been allocated—initialize this to zero when you enter the task into the system with the AddTask function

3. The trap-routine definition variables:

tc_TrapCode   A pointer to the trap-handling code for this task

tc_TrapData   A pointer to the trap-handling data area for this task

tc_TrapAlloc   A variable to tell the system which traps have already been allocated

tc_TrapAble   Reserved for future use

4. The memory-allocation variable:

tc_memEntry   This is a pointer to a List structure that tells the system which memory locations should be allocated for your new task. These memory areas can also be deallocated (freed) later during the execution of that task. There are a number of Exec memory management routines to manage the memory used by your task while it is in the system.

5. Other variables: In general, initialize all other variables in the Task Control Block structure to zero before you add the task to the system with the AddTask function.

After these variables are initialized, you should dynamically allocate memory for the Task Control Block structure with this statement:

```
struct Task *MyTask;
MyTask = (struct Task *) AllocMem (sizeof (structure Task),
    MEMF_PUBLIC);
```

Here, MyTask is a name for the Task Control Block structure of this task. Now this task can create other tasks (referred to as child tasks). Note that this task has been placed into public memory and is therefore accessible to all tasks in the system.

The Task Structure

The Task structure is defined as follows:

```
struct Task {
    struct Node tc_Node;
    UBYTE tc_Flags;
    UBYTE tc_State;
    BYTE tc_IDNestCnt;
    BYTE tc_TDNestCnt;
    ULONG tc_SigAlloc;
    ULONG tc_SigWait;
    ULONG tc_SigRecvd;
```

```
        ULONG tc_SigExcept;
        UWORD tc_TrapAlloc;
        UWORD tc_TrapAble;
        APTR tc_ExceptData;
        APTR tc_ExceptCode;
        APTR tc_TrapData;
        APTR tc_TrapCode;
        APTR tc_SPReg;
        APTR tc_SPLower;
        APTR tc_SPUpper;
        VOID (*tc_Switch)();
        VOID (*tc_Launch)();
        struct List tc_MemEntry;
        APTR tc_UserData;
};
```

The parameters in the Task structure are as follows:

■ The tc_Node parameter contains the name of a Node substructure, which is used to place this task on a list of tasks that the system maintains automatically. The ln_Name parameter in the Node structure will become the name of the task, thus allowing you to refer to the task by name. The ln_Pri parameter in the Node structure will be the execution priority of the task. You should define these two parameters before you enter the task into the system. You should also set the ln_Type parameter in the Node structure to NT_TASK to indicate that this Node structure represents a task.

■ The tc_Flags parameter contains a set of flag bits for the task. Each task can have up to five task flag bits. You should set some or all of these flag bits before you enter the task into the system.

■ The tc_State parameter contains the current state of the task in the system. Each task can be in one of six states. Task states are detailed below. The system automatically maintains this parameter.

■ The tc_IDNestCnt parameter contains the nesting count of the number of times interrupts have been disabled for the task represented by this Task structure. Every time a task enters a routine that disables interrupts, this parameter is incremented; interrupts are enabled just before the routine returns, thereby incrementing this parameter. This parameter is also changed directly by the system routines Enable and Disable.

■ The tc_TDNestCnt parameter contains the nesting count of the number of task-switching Forbid and Permit system calls. This parameter is automatically updated by the system each time these system routines are called.

■ The tc_SigAlloc parameter represents the set of signals actually allocated to the task represented by this Task structure. There are a total of 32 available signals, the lowest 16 (bits 0 to 15) of which are reserved for system use. You can allocate the other 16 (bits 16 to 31) to your task. You should set this optional parameter before you enter the task into the system.

■ The tc_SigWait parameter represents the set of signals for which this task is waiting. This set should always be a subset (or the entire set) of the 16 allocated signals (bits 16 to 31). You should set this optional parameter before you enter the task into the system.

■ The tc_SigRecvd parameter represents the set of signals that this task has actually received up to this time during its execution. The system automatically maintains and updates this parameter.

■ The tc_SigExcept parameter represents the set of signals that will cause task exceptions for this task when that signal is received by the task. This set is represented as a mask. There are 32 possible signal bits and 32 corresponding exception bits. Once again, 16 bits are used by the system and 16 bits can be used by the task. You should set this optional parameter before you enter the task into the system.

■ The tc_TrapAlloc parameter represents the set of trap numbers actually allocated to the task represented by this Task structure. Each trap number you set should have a corresponding trap routine to handle the trap as it occurs during the execution of this task. You should set this optional parameter before you enter the task into the system.

■ The tc_TrapAble parameter represents the set of trap numbers that are currently enabled for the task represented by this Task structure. You set this optional parameter before you enter the task into the system.

■ The tc_ExceptData parameter is a pointer to a set of exception data to be used with the exception routine associated with the task represented by this Task structure. Your exception routine will use this data when it gains control after an exception occurs. If you want your task to process exceptions needing data, set this optional parameter before you enter the task into the system.

■ The tc_ExceptCode parameter is a pointer to 68000 CPU exception code for this task represented by this Task structure. If you want your task to process exceptions when they occur, you should set this optional parameter before you enter the task into the system.

■ The tc_TrapData parameter is a pointer to a set of trap data for the task represented by this Task structure. If you want your task to process traps needing data, you should set this optional parameter before you enter the task into the system.

■ The tc_TrapCode parameter is a pointer to trap code for the task represented by this Task structure. If you want your task to process traps, you should set this optional parameter before you enter the task into the system.

■ The tc_SPReg parameter contains the value of the current stack pointer for the task represented by this Task structure. The system routines maintain (increase and decrease) this value as new data is added to the task's stack. You are required to set this parameter before you enter the task into the system.

■ The tc_SPLower parameter contains the value of the lower bound and the tc_SPUpper parameter contains the value of the upper bound of the stack pointer for the task represented by this Task structure. These values stay constant during task execution. You are required to set these parameters before you enter the task into the system.

■ The tc_Switch parameter is a pointer to a user-defined routine that will take control of the machine when the task represented by this Task structure loses the CPU. You should set this optional parameter before you enter the task into the system.

■ The tc_Launch parameter is a pointer to a user-defined routine that will take control of the machine when the task represented by this Task structure gains access to the CPU. This is the launch point code for this task. You should set this optional parameter before you enter the task into the system.

■ The tc_MemEntry parameter contains the name of a List structure, which tells the system about the memory to be allocated to the task on task entry and deallocated on task exit.

■ The tc_UserData parameter is a pointer to a set of user data that can be used exclusively by this task.

The Flag parameter in the Task structure includes the following flag bits:

■ TB_PROCTIME. Set this bit if you want the system to keep track of the 68000 processor time used by this task. If this bit is set, the system will automatically accumulate (as task switching occurs) the total CPU time used by the task in the variable TC_PROCTIME.

■ TB_STACKCHK. Set this bit if you want to maintain a current check on the condition of your task's stack.

■ TB_EXCEPT. The system sets this bit when the task is currently processing a task exception.

■ TB_SWITCH. Set this bit if you want to tell the system that there is a legitimate code vector in the tc_Switch( ) parameter in the Task structure; in this case you must also define the tc_Switch( ) parameter.

■ TB_LAUNCH. Set this bit if you want to tell the system that there is a legitimate code vector in the tc_Launch( ) parameter in the Task structure; in this case you must also define the tc_Launch( ) parameter.

Task States

A task in the RUN state is active and running. Only one task can be running at a time. Equal-priority tasks will time-slice the 68000 microprocessor memory cycles.

A task in the READY state is ready to run but is not currently running. It is not waiting for a message or signal but is currently not running because of its lower priority or because of some other condition in the system (for example, a currently active interrupt) that is causing some other task to run.

A task in the WAIT state is waiting for a signal to occur. This signal can come from any number of sources. The sources depend on the message ports connected to the task. These signals are defined in the Task Control Block structure when the task is entered into the system. One of the Task Control Block variables is tc_SigWait, a 32-bit variable that specifies which of 32 possible signal bits (one or more) a task is waiting for. At least one of the bits in the tc_SigWait variable must be active (set to 1) in the corresponding bit position in the tc_SigRecvd variable (this keeps track of which signals have actually arrived) before the task will again be ready to run.

A task in the ADDED state has just been added to the system with the AddTask function call. The Task Control Block structure and the task stack have been properly defined and all other parameters for this task have been initialized.

A task in the EXCEPT state is executing one of its exception routines. Something has happened that has caused task execution to be temporarily suspended in favor of an exception routine. This state continues until this task exception routine is finished. The exception routines associated with a task are assigned when the Task Control Block structure for that task is initialized.

A task in the REMOVED state is not on any task list at this time. It could have been removed from all task lists by the RemTask function. It is neither ready nor waiting. All system resources formerly used by that task have been freed for use by other tasks.

Figure 1.6 shows the behavior of the task stack at different times in the life of a task. Note that the task stack grows downward in memory toward lower addresses (toward tc_SPLower). The current (and initial) stack pointer is tc_SPReg; the system maintains the current stack pointer internally. If you want no parameters in the data area of the stack, then set tc_SPReg equal to tc_SPUpper.

The first rectangle in the figure shows the task stack as specified when you define the parameters in the Task structure. Note that you can set tc_SPReg to ensure that part of your task stack is protected during task execution. You can initialize this protected section of the stack with a set of parameter values. The task can then look at these locations (between tc_SPReg and tc_SPUpper) to get some initial parameter values before it starts execution. For example, another task might place values in these locations. The values in these parameter locations can also be changed during task execution by program statements inside the task.

The second rectangle in Figure 1.6 represents the state of the task just after the Add-Task function executes. This rectangle shows that the value of the finalPC parameter specified in the AddTask function has been pushed onto the stack. The current value of the stack pointer is then lowered by four bytes.

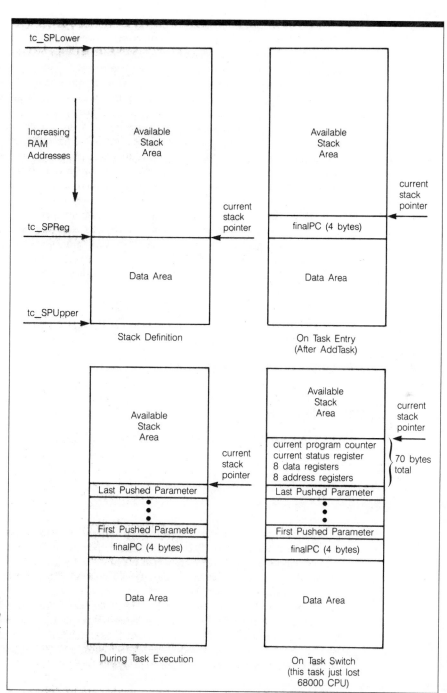

Figure 1.6:
Behavior of the Task Stack

The third rectangle represents the task stack after the task has taken control of the CPU and pushed some parameters onto (and possibly popped some parameters from) the stack. The first pushed parameter is just below the finalPC value (lower in memory). The last pushed parameter is located at the current stack pointer. Note that the data area could have changed if the task specified changes for the parameters in the data area.

The last rectangle in Figure 1.6 represents the task stack immediately after the task has lost the CPU. The task is now inactive; it has been put to sleep. In order to save the task context, the system has automatically pushed 70 bytes of information onto the task stack. The first items pushed are the current values of the 68000 address registers (eight 4-byte values). The next items pushed are the current values of the 68000 data registers (another eight 4-byte values). The next item pushed is the current value of the 68000 status register—two bytes. Finally, the 68000 program counter—four bytes—is pushed onto the stack. It is important to understand that the current value of the SP (stack pointer = tc_SPReg) is saved in the Task structure, not on the task stack.

This defines the behavior of the task stack for this task. Keep in mind that each task in the system must also have a task stack that behaves in the same way. Your definition of the Task structure guarantees part of this behavior while the Exec system routines guarantee the balance of that behavior, especially when tasks are switched in and out of execution.

Allocate

Syntax of Function Call

```
memBlock = Allocate (memheader, byteSize)
D0                    A0         D0
```

Purpose of Function

This function is used to allocate blocks of memory from a task-private free-memory pool. It will return the first free block that is greater than or equal to the requested size.

All blocks, whether free or allocated, will be block aligned. This means that all allocation sizes are rounded up to the next eight-byte value. This implies that the minimum allocation block size is eight bytes.

When used in conjunction with a private free-memory list, this function can manage an application's internal data memory. Allocate returns a pointer to the just-allocated free block in the variable memBlock. This block is now taken out of the system free-memory pool. If there are no free regions large enough to satisfy the request, or the amount of requested memory is invalid, this function returns zero.

Inputs to Function

memHeader A pointer to a MemHeader structure

byteSize The size of the desired block in bytes

Discussion

There are seven Exec functions that deal with memory management: Allocate, AllocEntry, AllocMem, AvailMem, Deallocate, FreeEntry, and FreeMem.

There are a few things you should know about memory management on the Amiga. First, the system maintains a free-memory list that tells it which regions of memory are now free for allocation. This list changes constantly as tasks, both your tasks and system tasks, allocate and deallocate memory in the system. The AllocMem and FreeMem functions are system-wide allocation and deallocation functions that use a free-memory list managed by the system outside of your control.

The AllocEntry and FreeEntry functions can be used to allocate and deallocate different sizes and types of memory areas. Several memory block allocations can be handled with just one call. No memory requirements other than size need be specified. In contrast, the Allocate and Deallocate functions manage one simple memory block at a time. Finally, the AllocMem function allows you to specify explicitly not only the size but also other requirements of your memory use.

The Allocate and Deallocate functions are specifically designed for use within your tasks. You use these functions with your own task-private free-memory lists. One of the arguments to these functions is a pointer to a task-private free-memory list structure—specifically, a pointer to a MemHeader structure.

In addition to the system free-memory list, each of your tasks can have a private free-memory list. Your task can set up and maintain its own list that tells it which regions of memory are now free for allocation. This list changes as you add more child tasks to your original parent task (using AddTask) and as other memory demands of your task change.

Whenever you ask that memory be allocated, it is always allocated in even multiples of eight bytes. Memory deallocation is also done in multiples of eight bytes. If you don't ask for an exact multiple of eight bytes, the system will round your request size up as required to arrive at an eight-byte multiple.

There are four types of memory in the Amiga system: MEMF_CHIP, MEMF_FAST, MEMF_PUBLIC, and MEMF_CLEAR. MEMF_CHIP memory is always in the lowest 512K of the memory space. MEMF_FAST means memory above the 512K point; this memory is fast because the special-purpose Amiga chips cannot use it. These chips do not, therefore, cause any bus contention with the 68000 for this memory, thus avoiding the inevitable slowdown that results from bus contention. MEMF_PUBLIC memory is to be used for shared memory resources. You can place your Task Control Block structures, MsgPort structures, and so forth, in public memory. MEMF_CLEAR memory is memory whose locations are zeroed (cleared) before it is used.

Each of your memory allocations can combine these attributes as needed to define the specific type of memory you need for your task.

The MemHeader Structure

The Allocate function uses a pointer to a MemHeader structure as part of the calling sequence. The MemHeader structure takes the following form:

```
struct MemHeader {
    struct Node mh_Node;
    UWORD mh_Attributes;
    struct MemChunk *mh_First;
    APTR mh_Lower;
    APTR mh_Upper;
    ULONG mh_Free;
};
```

These are the parameters to the MemHeader structure:

- The mh_Node parameter contains the name of a Node substructure inside the MemHeader structure. The ln_Name parameter of this Node structure contains the name of the complete memory block represented by this MemHeader structure. The ln_Pri parameter in the Node structure determines the location of this memory block on the system free-memory list. You should set the ln_Type parameter to NT_MEMORY.

- The mh_Attributes parameter contains the attributes for this memory block. See the AllocMem function for a discussion of memory block attributes.

- The mh_First parameter is a pointer to a MemChunk structure, which represents the first subblock in this memory block.

- The mh_Lower parameter is a pointer to a memory location where the first byte of the total memory block is located.

- The mh_Upper parameter is a pointer to a memory location where the last byte of the total memory block is located.

- The mh_Free parameter contains the total number of free bytes in the total memory block.

AllocEntry

Syntax of Function Call

```
memList = AllocEntry (memList)
D0                    A0
```

Purpose of Function

This function creates a MemList structure and allocates enough memory to hold the memory defined in the MemList structure as well as the MemList structure itself. These MemList structures can be linked together in a Task Control Block structure to keep track of the total memory usage of the task.

The MemList structure created by this function is filled with the actual memory allocated, together with the sizes of these pieces of memory. If enough memory cannot be obtained, the requirements of the failed allocation are returned and bit 31 of the returned memList variable is set to 1.

Inputs to Function

memList   A pointer to a MemList structure, which points to a series of MemEntry structures

Discussion

There are seven Exec functions that deal with memory management: Allocate, AllocEntry, AllocMem, AvailMem, Deallocate, FreeEntry, and FreeMem. There are a few things you should know about memory management on the Amiga in addition to the points discussed under the Allocate function.

First, each task in the machine has its own set of up to six memory areas assigned to it. The location of each of these memory areas is set at the time the task is created. This is done in the definition of a task's Task Control Block structure. The Task Control Block structure has a set of variables to assign appropriate areas of memory to different task needs:

tc_SPUpper   A pointer to the upper byte of the stack area for this task

tc_SPLower   A pointer to the lower byte of the stack area for this task

tc_ExceptCode   A pointer to the exception-handling code for this task

tc_ExceptData   A pointer to the exception-handling data for this task

tc_TrapCode   A pointer to the trap-handling code associated with this task

tc_TrapData   A pointer to the trap-handling data to be used with the trap-handling code

tc_MemEntry   A pointer to a List structure that tells the system about dynamic memory allocation while your task is in the system

The system automatically maintains a system free-memory list. Each time a task is added to the system, this list is updated. The system does not maintain a "used-memory" list. Once a block of RAM is allocated, the system does not know which task is using that block of RAM.

Often, a task will create one or more child tasks during its execution. This is done using the AddTask function to spawn a child-task within a task. When this happens, memory areas must be allocated for child tasks. This is a dynamic process. You can use the MemList structure to help you manage the memory allocations of the child-task creation process. The MemList structure allows you to build a list of all the memory areas your task has allocated dynamically.

When your task has finished, a call to the RemTask routine will automatically deallocate all memory associated with that task. All child task memory will also be deallocated at this time. These areas of memory will then both be added to the system free-memory list. In addition, if your task should abort prematurely, the MemList structure will once again allow the system to deallocate all the memory associated with your aborted task and any related child tasks automatically.

The AllocEntry and FreeEntry functions allow you to allocate and deallocate more than one block of memory at a time in a single call to each of these routines. AllocEntry uses a MemList structure that contains information about the size of the memory blocks you want to allocate. It also contains information about the attributes you want to assign to those memory blocks.

The MemList Structure

The MemList structure has the following form:

```
struct MemList {
    struct Node ml_Node;
    UWORD ml_NumEntries;
    struct MemEntry ml_ME;
};
```

There are three parameters to the MemList structure. The ml_Node parameter contains the name of a Node substructure inside the MemList structure. The ln_Name parameter of this Node structure contains the name of the complete memory block represented by this MemList structure. The ln_Pri parameter in the Node structure determines the location of this memory block on the system free-memory list. You should set the ln_Type parameter to NT_MEMORY. The ml_NumEntries parameter contains the number of memory blocks in the complete memory list represented by this MemList structure. Each memory block will have its own MemEntry structure. The ml_ME parameter is a pointer to a MemEntry structure that represents the first memory block in the memory list represented by this MemList structure.

AllocEntry allocates enough memory for all of the RAM blocks represented by the MemList structure you pass to it. Sometimes AllocEntry will have problems allocating all of the memory areas implied by your MemList structures. In this case, instead of returning the address of the new MemList structure, the AllocEntry function will return the memory requirement value with which it had a problem. Your task can then decide what to do next.

Example

Following is an assembly language example of how to use the AllocEntry function. Suppose you want five regions of 8, 16, 24, 32, and 40 bytes in size. You want the requirements for these pieces of memory to be as follows: MEMF_CLEAR, MEMF_PUBLIC, MEMF_CHIP or MEMF_CLEAR, MEMF_FAST or MEMF_CLEAR, and MEMF_PUBLIC or MEMF_CLEAR, respectively. The following code fragment would do this:

```
MyMemList:
DS.B LN_SIZE                          ; reserve space for list node
DC.W 5                                ; number of entries
DC.L MEMF_CLEAR                       ; entry number 0
DC.L 8
DC.L MEMF_PUBLIC                      ; entry number 1
DC.L 16
DC.L MEMF_CHIP.OR.MEMF_CLEAR          ; entry number 2
DC.L 24
DC.L MEMF_FAST.OR.MEMF_CLEAR          ; entry number 3
DC.L 32
DC.L MEMF_PUBLIC.OR.MEMF_CLEAR        ; entry number 4
DC.L 40
start:
LEA MyMemList,A0
CALLLIB _LVOAllocEntry,A5
BTST.L #31,D0
```

The first part of this example (down to the "start" label) defines a MemList structure in RAM. The second part of the example first places the address of the MemList structure in register A0, then calls the AllocEntry function. Register A5 contains the entry address into the Exec Library routines. This address is placed in the SysBase variable when you open the Exec library with an OpenLibrary call. The LVOAllocEntry variable is the assembly language notation for the load-vector offset to the entry point for the AllocEntry function in the Exec Library. The next line tests bit 31 of register D0. If this bit is set to 1, the memory allocation was unsuccessful.

You can follow the pattern of this example to do the same thing in C.

AllocMem

Syntax of Function Call

```
memBlock = AllocMem (byteSize, requirements)
D0                    D0         D1: 0–31
```

Purpose of Function

This function is the memory allocator to be used by system code and applications programs. Memory must be allocated properly for system code to be compatible with memory-mapped systems. Memory mapping allows programs to be dynamically relocated. AllocMem provides a means of specifying whether the allocation should be made in a memory area accessible to the chips (the first 512K of RAM) or to shared system RAM (512K up to the maximum Amiga memory size of eight megabytes).

Memory is allocated based on the requirements listed. The rule is that the requirements plus the attributes equal the total requirements for any particular memory block.

AllocMem will try all free memory spaces until one is found with the requested attributes and room (contiguous block of free memory) for the memory request.

The result of the AllocMem function is a memBlock pointer to the allocated freememory block. If there are no free regions large enough to satisfy the request—or if the amount of requested memory is invalid—this function returns zero. Remember that the minimum block size is eight bytes. In all cases, memory request sizes are rounded up to the nearest eight bytes.

Inputs to Function

byteSize	The size of the desired block in bytes. This number is rounded up to the next larger block size (a multiple of eight bytes) for the actual allocation.
requirements	Still not precisely set. Here are some typical memory attributes:
MEMF_PUBLIC	Memory must not be mapped, swapped, or otherwise made nonaddressable. This refers to the type of situation where you have a memory board that is swapped in and out of logical memory under software control. All memory that is referenced via interrupts and/or by other tasks must be public. This includes both code and data.
MEMF_CHIP	This attribute refers to certain parts of memory that are reachable by the special chip set's DMA circuitry. This is all memory in the first 512K of RAM. The special chips include the three VSLI chips of the Amiga: Agnus (the animation custom chip), Denise (the graphics custom chip), and Paula (the peripherals-sound custom chip). Anything that will use on-chip DMA must be in memory with this attribute. DMA includes screen memory, things that are moved with the Blitter DMA channel, audio blocks, raw disk buffers, and so on.

MEMF_FAST	This attribute refers to nonchip memory. It is possible for the 68000 CPU to get locked out of chip memory (the first 512K) under certain circumstances. This occurs most often when the custom chips demand all the memory cycles for a DMA data-transfer operation. If you cannot accept these delays, you should use fast memory (by default the system will allocate from fast memory first).
MEMF_CLEAR	This attribute causes the allocated RAM blocks to be initialized to all zeros. Use this attribute if you want to zero all involved memory locations before you do anything else with those locations.

Discussion

There are seven Exec functions that deal with memory management in the Amiga system: Allocate, AllocEntry, AllocMem, AvailMem, Deallocate, FreeEntry, and FreeMem. Read the discussions of each of these functions for more information on memory management.

The System Free-Memory List

The system tags and maintains only a list of free memory. This is done using a free-memory list for all available free memory in the system. This list keeps changing as your current task (and perhaps others) allocates and deallocates memory. Memory currently in use by the system and tasks is not tagged or arranged in a list. Once a memory block is allocated, the system has no way of knowing which task has control of that block of memory.

Multitasking Programming Styles

You can use two styles of programming in the Amiga multitasking system. You can use each separately or mix them up as desired.

The first method uses only the AllocMem and FreeMem functions. Here you use AllocMem and FreeMem to allocate and deallocate memory blocks globally. When you do this, the system will automatically maintain a MemList structure that belongs to that task. See the AllocEntry function for a description of the MemList structure. Your task's MemList structure will be updated automatically each time you make a call to either of these two functions.

The second method uses the AllocEntry function together with the Allocate and Deallocate functions. Here, just as your task begins executing, you allocate one or more large memory blocks from the system free-memory pool using AllocEntry. Try to anticipate how much total memory your task will need before you make this call, then manage subblocks of this large block internally using the Allocate and Deallocate functions.

Note that this second method requires you to anticipate the memory needs of your task throughout its execution. If you cannot do this, or if you are squeezed for memory, you should use the first method of step-wise, explicit allocation for your task.

AllocSignal

Syntax of Function Call

signalNum = AllocSignal (signalNum)
DO   DO

Purpose of Function

This function is used to allocate signal bits from the current task's pool of available signal bits. It allocates either a particular bit or the next free bit and returns the signal bit number actually allocated. It also initializes (clears) the signal associated with the newly allocated bit. If the signal is already in use (or no free signals are available), the function returns a −1. This function changes the tc_AllocSignal parameter in the Task Control Block structure.

Inputs to Function

signalNum   The desired signal bit number (one of 0–31) or −1 for no preference

Discussion

There are four Exec functions that deal with task signals in the Amiga system: AllocSignal, FreeSignal, SetSignal, and Signal. In addition, the GetMsg, PutMsg, and ReplyMsg functions fall in the category of signal-handling functions (messages cause signals). Read the discussions of these calls for more information on task signals.

Tasks communicate with each other by passing messages through their message ports. Tasks also send and receive messages from devices in this way.

The Message Port

To pass messages between tasks, you must set up a message port for each task that is to communicate with other tasks in the system. You can set up more than one message port for each task you create. Just initialize a MsgPort structure for each message port assigned to a task. Then add that message port to the task with the AddPort function. In fact, you can set up as many MsgPort structures as you need to handle the message-passing needs of the task you are defining. The only limit you might face in this situation is insufficient available memory to hold the Message and MsgPort structures. The message ports you assign to a task can be used for any type of communication with other tasks, system devices, custom chips, external devices, and so on.

The Message-Port Queue

All messages arriving at a message port of a task are either acted on immediately or queued into the message queue of that port. Each message that arrives at a particular port produces a signal according to the mp_SigBit parameter in the MsgPort structure. The message-port queue is a FIFO queue—the first message to arrive is the first message to be processed.

The tc_SigAlloc Variable

You can dynamically allocate signal bits to a task using the Task Control Block structure's tc_SigAlloc variable. You should initialize this variable to zero before you add a task to the system. tc_SigAlloc is a 32-bit variable that contains one bit for every signal bit allocated. Note that the lower 16 bits are reserved for system use (bits 0–15); you can use the upper 16 bits (bits 16–31) to pass signals between your tasks.

Keeping Track of Your Signals

As you add more and more message ports and signals to your program tasks, things can become complicated. If you try to keep track directly of which signals are in use and which are available, you will probably get very confused. Keeping track of signals is the purpose of the AllocSignal and FreeSignal routines. In fact, you *must* use AllocSignal to add signals to a task, because some system library routines require signals and use Alloc-Signal to get them.

Warning: Signals cannot be allocated or freed from exception-handling code. There is no message-passing capability between different pieces of exception code and/or other tasks in the system.

AllocTrap

Syntax of Function Call

trapNum = AllocTrap (trapNum)
D0   D0

Purpose of Function

This function allocates a trap number from the current task's pool of available trap numbers and returns the trap bit number actually allocated. These trap numbers are associated with the 68000 TRAP instructions. The AllocTrap function allocates either a particular trap number or the next free trap number. If the trap is already in use (or no free traps are available), the function returns a -1.

Inputs to Function

trapNum   The desired trap number (one of 0–15) or -1 for no preference

Discussion

There are two functions that deal explicitly with traps in the Amiga Exec routines: AllocTrap and FreeTrap. AllocTrap allocates a trap and FreeTrap returns a specific trap to the task's available-trap pool. The system automatically maintains a list of available trap numbers to assign to tasks.

The Amiga multitasking machine allows each task to gain full control of the system hardware, making each task a virtual terminal in the machine. This capability extends to the 68000 traps as well as all other types of exception conditions. Note, however, that traps are distinct from exceptions in the terminology of the Exec functions, which is not consistent with the terminology for the 68000 itself as detailed in the Motorola literature. For instance, traps in the 68000 are separated into hardware and software traps. The hardware traps are assigned vector numbers from 2 to 15. These cover such things as address error, zero-divide illegal instruction, and eleven other conditions. The trap numbers on the 68000 are numbered from 0 to 255.

All Amiga trap vectors result in a 68000 software trap and cause an entry into the Exec kernel routines. The kernel determines which task is running and adds the trap number to the task's stack before jumping to the task's trap-handling routine. Note that this procedure does no other preparation before giving the trap to you to process. In particular, no working registers are saved when you enter a trap routine. On entry to the trap routine, the user stack contains the state of the machine when the trap occurred.

It is also important to note that the system handles all trap processing in supervisor mode. Therefore, the task-switching features are disabled when a trap occurs.

Allocating traps is a bookkeeping process within your task. Exec does nothing to ensure that your task is prepared to handle this trap; it merely calls your trap subroutine. To make trap handling work correctly, you must compare the trap number that Exec gives you with the allocated trap numbers belonging to the task in which the trap occurred. Each distinct task in the system has its own set of assigned trap numbers tied to distinct trap-handling routines. You can look at the task's tc_TrapAlloc variable in its Task Control Block structure to see which trap numbers are allocated to each task.

When a trap occurs, a task should first suspend what it is doing; then it should enter a subroutine to process the trap. Usually, the task will first execute some instructions, which might include posting an error message. Then the task should clean up and exit.

You can use four Task Control Block structure variables to specify your trap-handling routines:

tc_TrapCode   This is the address of the trap routine that will process the trap. Each task has only one trap routine. However, you can design that routine to respond to different trap numbers in different ways. See the FreeTrap function.

tc_TrapData   This is the address of the data area for data needed by the trap routine.

tc_TrapAlloc   This is a trap assignment mask. You initialize this before you call the trap. This variable is optional; Exec initializes this variable to zero when the task starts.

tc_TrapAble   This parameter describes the set of traps currently enabled for this task.

Once you design a trap-handling routine, you must initialize the tc_TrapCode and tc_TrapData variables to point to your trap code and data areas, respectively. This can be done as follows:

```
VOID MyTrapRoutine( );
MyTask.tc_TrapCode = &MyTrapRoutine;
/* this will initialize a pointer to the address of the trap routine that will
    handle traps */
MyTask.tc_TrapData = &MyTrapData;
/* Here it is assumed that you have allocated and initialized a memory
    block labeled MyTrapData. This memory block will be used as the
    data area for this subroutine. */
```

To allocate a trap number you make the following type of call:

```
mytrap = AllocTrap ( - 1);
if(mytrap == - 1){
    printf(" This task has no more traps to allocate. ");
    cleanup( );
};
```

Or you can select a specific trap like this:

```
mytrap = AllocTrap (3);
if(mytrap == - 1){
    printf (" Trap 3 is already allocated. ");
};
```

The 68000 exception instructions include the trap instructions, TRAP and TRAPV. Here, TRAP is the explicit software trap instruction, and TRAPV is the trap-on-overflow instruction. Note that both of these instructions can execute in the user mode of the 68000. However, the trap routine itself executes in supervisor mode. The TRAP instruction allows a program to cause an exception directly through the software instructions of a program. On the other hand, other types of exceptions are usually caused by hardware conditions.

When the 68000 starts exception processing, a vector number is generated to reference the TRAP instruction exception vector specified by the four low-order bits of the TRAP instruction code format. Sixteen TRAP instruction vectors are thus available on the 68000. You can use these trap vectors to jump to short trap-processing routines. These routines can be designed for specific purposes tied to your program's processing needs.

Warning: Traps cannot be allocated or freed once inside exception-handling code. There is no message-passing capability between different pieces of trap exception code and/or other tasks in the system.

AttemptSemaphore

Syntax of Function Call

```
success = AttemptSemaphore (signalSemaphore)
D0                                        A0
```

Purpose of Function

This function attempts to obtain (gain access to) a SignalSemaphore structure. Attempt-Semaphore is very similar to ObtainSemaphore except that it will not put the calling task to sleep if the SignalSemaphore structure cannot be obtained. AttemptSemaphore will return TRUE if the SignalSemaphore structure can be obtained; it will return FALSE if some other task has already obtained the semaphore. In contrast, note that ObtainSemaphore, which also tries to obtain a SignalSemaphore structure, returns no value and will put the calling task to sleep if that SignalSemaphore structure is currently being used by another task.

Inputs to Function

signalSemaphore   A pointer to a properly initialized SignalSemaphore structure

Discussion

There are seven functions in the 1.2 release that deal with signal semaphores and two functions that deal with the signal-semaphore list. These functions are listed under the AddSemaphore discussion.

Tasks interact with semaphores by obtaining (AttemptSemaphore and Obtain-Semaphore) and releasing (ReleaseSemaphore) semaphores. Each time a semaphore is obtained by the current task, the ss_NestCount parameter in the SignalSemaphore structure is incremented; each time a semaphore is released by the current task, this parameter is decremented.

Whenever the ss_NestCount parameter is not zero, the SignalSemaphore structure is locked and a specific task has exclusive control of the semaphore. In this case, any task other than the specific task that calls ObtainSemaphore will not be able to obtain the semaphore and will be put to sleep. AttemptSemaphore will also be unable to obtain the semaphore. However, AttemptSemaphore will not put the calling task to sleep but will return a TRUE or FALSE value, thus allowing the calling task to continue execution. This is the difference between these two functions.

AvailMem

Syntax of Function Call

```
size = AvailMem (requirements)
D0                D1
```

Purpose of Function

This function returns the size of memory (the total free space remaining) given certain requirements.

Inputs to Function

requirements   A requirements mask of RAM attributes as specified in the AllocMem function

Discussion

There are seven Exec functions that deal with memory management: Allocate, AllocEntry, AllocMem, AvailMem, Deallocate, FreeEntry, and FreeMem. There is more information on memory management in the discussions of each of these functions.

As you allocate and deallocate memory blocks to your tasks, the amount of memory in the system free-memory pool keeps changing. To make matters more complicated, the amount of memory in each memory classification (MEMF_CHIP, MEMF_FAST, MEMF_PUBLIC, and MEMF_CLEAR) keeps changing. Therefore, at any given time, the amount of memory available to your task might not satisfy the requirements that you would like to specify for additional current-task memory needs. This is when the AvailMem function is useful.

You can call the AvailMem function, before you call the other memory allocation functions, to tell you if there is enough memory to satisfy your anticipated memory allocation. Note that the size returned by AvailMem is the total free memory remaining with the specified requirements. However, this free memory might be scattered over the entire system. If you need a large block of contiguous memory (for example, for one of the bitplanes in a multiplane bitmap), your call to the AvailMem function might not give you all the information you need to ensure success in your memory allocation.

If you allocate a large block of memory from the system free-memory pool, you should be sure that the task cleanup routine pointed to by the finalPC variable (as specified when you called AddTask to create your task's Task Control Block structure) deallocates this large block of memory as your task exits from the system at the completion of its execution. The advantage of allocating a large block to your task is that you can avoid a lot of bookkeeping details. You would have to attend to these if you used the AllocMem and FreeMem functions explicitly for each block.

With all this talk about memory, a question naturally comes up: just what is in Amiga RAM memory at different times and in the different situations that the Amiga finds itself? To answer this question, consider the various structures that are a part of each task in the system. This will also answer another question: what structures are in memory for each task in the system?

Structures in Memory for Each Task in the System

First, there is the Task Control Block structure for each task. The Task Control Block structure itself takes a certain amount of memory. Then you must add the memory implied by the different variables of the Task Control Block structure. Memory is assigned for each task as follows:

- For the task stack
- For the task exception code
- For the task exception-code data
- For the task trap code
- For the task trap-code data

- For the task–control signal information, memory–control information, and so on

- For the code (and possibly the data) of the task itself

Second, there are the libraries used by the task. The memory for the libraries is allocated by the OpenLibrary function and includes the following:

- The library jump-code instructions needed to reach the various routines in the library

- The Library structure for the library

- The data segment of the library

- The library routines themselves (to be precise, note that the routines are not formally a part of the library)

Third, there is the I/O Request Block structure for any devices in the system that are assigned to this task. This memory is initialized with the OpenDevice function and is usually smaller than the memory assigned to a library or a Task Control Block structure. Some of the memory is assigned as follows:

- For the device command you want to perform

- For the size of the message you are passing

- For the number of bytes in the I/O transfer

- For the address to which the data should be written

- For the byte offset into a block-structured device (for example, a disk device)

Fourth, there is the memory assigned to the MsgPort structure for each device and intertask communication channel attached to this task. For example, if a task works with ten devices, there could be ten or more message ports attached to it. The number and size of Message structures whose messages are queued in these message ports depends on the amount of data transferred, the way the device buffering is handled, and so on.

Fifth, there is the memory assigned to each reply-port MsgPort structure associated with each message assigned to a task. If the task has ten message ports, it could also have ten reply ports. As with message-port MsgPort structures, the size of the memory assigned to these reply-port MsgPort structures depends on the amount of data transferred, the way the buffering is handled, and so on.

Sixth, there is the memory assigned to the memory-management structures needed to manage all of these memory areas.

Seventh, there is the memory assigned to all the various miscellaneous Exec functions, the Graphics Library functions, and the Animation Library functions.

Last, there is the memory devoted to the graphics information to develop the display—the display raster memory. This could be the biggest part of the memory used for a task. Suppose you have a dual-playfield mode display with a total of six bitplanes required to define the display. Each bitplane takes 8,000 bytes of memory. Add any memory you might use for sprites in your display. You can see that graphics memory can become the biggest part of memory used by a task.

Cause

Syntax of Function Call

Cause (interrupt)
A1

Purpose of Function

This function causes a software interrupt to occur. If it is called from 68000 user mode, the software interrupt will preempt the current task.

Only five software interrupt priorities are currently implemented. These are -32, -16, 0, $+16$, and $+32$. Priorities in between these values are truncated. Priorities outside the -32 to $+32$ range are not allowed. (If all goes well, an interrupt will occur immediately.) The interrupt priority is contained in the ln_Pri parameter of the Node substructure of the Interrupt structure.

Inputs to Function

interrupt   A pointer to a properly initialized Interrupt structure

Discussion

Most of the time, a task switch occurs because of an interrupt—either hardware or software (for example, a software trap). During the interrupt, the system task rescheduler examines the priority of the task that was interrupted. Sometimes, just as the interrupt routine finishes execution, a new task will come into the system whose task priority exceeds that of the suspended task. (Perhaps this task was just added with the AddTask function or made active when a task message reached its message-port queue.) In this case, when the current interrupt routine has finished its job, the new task will commence execution. Thus, the previously executing task will be put to sleep. This is the principal mechanism whereby an interrupt induces task switching in the Amiga.

Each task has its own task stack space defined in the Task Control Block structure of the task before it is entered into the system. However, the task stack space doesn't have to allow for interrupts; when an interrupt occurs, the supervisor stack space handles all the data needs of the interrupt. This is especially important for nested interrupts, where the stack can grow as the data needs of the interrupt routines grow. If the task stack were used for nested interrupts, the allotted task stack capacity could easily be exceeded.

The only exception to this rule is the situation that occurs when you use the Super-State function in your program. The SuperState function tells the system to enter the supervisor mode of the 68000. Once there, nested interrupts will use the task stack rather than the supervisor stack. In this case, you must be sure that your task stack is big enough to handle nested interrupts. Either use a large stack space or stay out of supervisor mode.

Table 1.3 provides a list of the fifteen possible interrupts on the Amiga and shows how those interrupts are mapped into the six interrupt levels used and recognized by the 68000. Note that the Cause routine deals with the software interrupt positioned at CPU priority level 1, Amiga priority level 0. This is the lowest priority for all types of interrupts in the Amiga system.

Table 1.3:
Amiga Interrupts Mapped to 68000 Interrupt Levels

6800 Priority Level	Amiga Priority	Amiga Interrupt
6	14	High-priority Copper coprocessor
	13	I/O Ports (fast), external expansion box
5	12	Disk byte return on DMA (fast)
	11	UART RBF (receive buffer full) (fast)
4	10	Audio channel 1
	9	Audio channel 3
	8	Audio channel 0
	7	Audio channel 2
3	6	Blitter DMA done (start next Blitter operation) (medium speed)
	4	Copper coprocessor (fast)
	5	Vertical blanking (slow, lots of things to do)
2	3	I/O ports (medium speed), keyboard, clock, printer; external level 2 hardware interrupt
1	2	UART TBE (transmit buffer empty) (fast)
	1	Disk block transfer finished (medium speed)
	0	Software interrupt (fast)

CheckIO

Syntax of Function Call

```
result = CheckIO (ioRequest)
D0                 A1
```

Purpose of Function

This function determines the current state of a device I/O request of a task. It returns FALSE if the I/O transfer is not yet complete. This function effectively hides the internal workings of the I/O completion mechanism from the task.

If the I/O is complete, the CheckIO function will not remove the returned I/O request message from the reply port. You can use the Remove function for that purpose. Nor should the CheckIO function be used to create a busy loop waiting for an I/O operation to complete.

CheckIO returns a null if the I/O operation is still in progress; otherwise, the result variable points to the I/O Request Block structure. This pointer variable can then be used in other I/O functions.

Inputs to Function

ioRequest A pointer to a properly initialized I/O Request Block structure

Discussion

There are eight Exec functions that are directly concerned with device I/O: AddDevice, CloseDevice, OpenDevice, RemDevice, CheckIO, DoIO, SendIO, and WaitIO. Each of these functions performs a device service. Read the discussions of each of these functions for more information on device I/O.

When a task issues an I/O request, it has two choices: it can wait for the I/O to complete (synchronous I/O), or it can go on to other things while queuing the I/O request in the device's message port (asynchronous I/O). The choice depends on the specific point in the program where this choice has to be made. Ask yourself this question: Why is this task asking for I/O and what does it intend to do with it? If it is sending data to a device, it might be sufficient to place that data in a memory buffer and go on to other things; the device will find the data in good time.

If a task is trying to get data from a device, it might need that data to continue with its operations, calculations, and so on—the task might have to wait on the data before it can go on executing. If a task can issue an I/O request and not have to wait on the return of device information or data, it can perform asynchronously with respect to that device. If the device must wait on data to arrive at or return from a device, the task must operate synchronously with respect to that device. Within any given task, some devices might operate synchronously and some asynchronously (with respect to that task), depending on the flow of information in the system. These same devices may operate differently with respect to other tasks also in the system.

Picture a situation where you have a task that deals with several devices, perhaps as many as ten. A task might be dealing with the disk drive, the keyboard, the console, the mouse, the gameport, and several external devices attached to the expansion connector of the Amiga. Each call to one of these devices is accomplished by constructing an I/O Request Block structure and passing a message in it to the device.

Depending on the specific logic of the program, it might have to wait on certain devices but not others. This program can operate synchronously with some devices and asynchronously with others. As your program executes, all device I/O requests are sent to the devices. These devices respond in one of several ways:

1. If there are no queued I/O requests in its message port, the device will try to service an I/O request immediately. This will make the calling task happy regardless of whether it can wait on I/O to finish; it will soon find its data (and/or other information) in the reply message area associated with that I/O Request Block structure. That is, the I/O Request Block structure both sends information to a device and returns information to the calling task.

2. If there are queued I/O requests in the message port of the device, this new I/O request will be queued behind the others. If the task does not need to wait on I/O, it can go on to other things it needs to do (asynchronous I/O); if it must wait for the I/O request to complete, it must wait until that I/O request works its way to the top of the message queue in the device's message port (synchronous I/O). When the device finally processes the I/O request, a message is returned to the reply message area of that I/O Request Block structure. The task will then know that the I/O request has been completed.

The CheckIO routine only checks to see whether an I/O request has been satisfied. It looks for the presence of a reply message in the I/O Request Block structure. For this reason, it is only a status checker. Check I/O does not remove the I/O request from the message-port queue. If you want to remove the I/O request, use the Remove function with the node pointer set to point to the Node substructure in the Message substructure inside the I/O Request Block structure.

CloseDevice

Syntax of Function Call

CloseDevice (ioRequest)
A1

Purpose of Function

This function informs the system that access to a device previously opened has been concluded. The device routines can then perform certain house-cleaning operations. The
device will no longer be associated with this task. The memory previously allocated to its
I/O Request Block structure can then be used by another task.

Inputs to Function

ioRequest   A pointer to a properly initialized I/O Request Block structure

Discussion

There are eight Exec functions that are directly concerned with device I/O in the Amiga
system: AddDevice, CloseDevice, OpenDevice, RemDevice, CheckIO, DoIO, SendIO, and
WaitIO. Each of these functions performs a device service. Read the discussions of each
function for more information on device I/O.

Consider the general flow of code in a multitasking system that deals with devices
implemented using device routine libraries. Assume you want to place three concurrent
tasks into the system. These tasks all communicate with each other through messages
passed through their respective message and reply ports.

In addition, assume that each task uses one particular device. For the purpose of this
discussion, assume this device is a printer, but not a standard printer in the Amiga
resource files. You need to place a library of printer-driver routines for this printer into
the system before you can use it. Assume you have done this with the MakeLibrary function and that the printer library is available for use by your tasks.

The general programming sequence to share this device among three tasks is as
follows:

1. Add the first task to the system using the AddTask function and make it the active
   task. This can be done by assigning it a high priority with the SetTaskPri function.

A message sent to one of this task's assigned message ports can also cause this task to become active. Because only one task can be active at a time, all other tasks are now sleeping.

2. Add the printer to the system using the AddDevice function. Note that you have already placed the device library at the disposal of this task with a MakeLibrary function call. AddDevice adds the printer to the system device list. Now this device can be used by all tasks in the system. However, each has to open it individually (using the OpenDevice function) to gain access to the printer library routines.

3. Open the printer device for the first task using the OpenDevice function. This is a program statement within the code framework of the first task. Have this task print its information using the printer-driver routines in the printer device library.

4. Add the second task to the system using the AddTask routine and make it the active task. Note that this puts the first task to sleep. This can be done by assigning the second task a high priority. A message arriving in one of this task's assigned message ports can also cause this task to become active.

5. Open the printer device for the second task using the OpenDevice function call within the code framework of the second task. Have this task print its information using the printer-driver routines in the printer device library.

6. Add the third task to the system using the AddTask function and make it the active task. Note that this puts the second task to sleep. This can be done by assigning the third task a high priority.

7. Open the printer device for the third task using the OpenDevice function call within the code framework of the third task. Have this task print its information using the same printer-driver library routines.

8. Make the first task active (by either giving it a high priority or sending a message to one of its message ports). This puts the third task to sleep. Issue a CloseDevice call to close the printer device inside the first task. Repeat this procedure for the second and third tasks.

9. Make any one of the three tasks active again. Remove the printer device from the system using the RemDevice function as a code statement within the code framework of any of the three tasks. This frees the system resources assigned to the printer device—specifically the memory requirements of its device library and library driver routines.

Note that the printer device library has to be created with the MakeLibrary call only once. It could have been created in any one of the three tasks. Of course, it must first be created before it is added and subsequently opened by any task.

When a new task becomes active, it is not necessary to close the printer device in the prior active task—it can remain open for that task. However, before you remove the printer device from the system with a RemDevice call, you must first close the printer device in all three tasks using three separate calls to the CloseDevice function.

If you close the printer device library in one task, it still remains open in other tasks that have already opened it. In addition, you can come and go from tasks leaving devices open. If you have left a device open within a task and you decide to use that device again when that task becomes active again, you do not need to reopen it.

CloseLibrary

Syntax of Function Call

CloseLibrary (library)
A1

Purpose of Function

This function informs the system that access to a given library has been concluded. The task that issues the CloseLibrary call should not reference that library or any of its library routines until an OpenLibrary call is executed again inside that task.

Inputs to Function

library   A pointer to a Library structure

Discussion

There are seven Exec functions that deal with libraries in the Amiga system: AddLibrary, CloseLibrary, MakeLibrary, OpenLibrary, RemLibrary, SetFunction, and SumLibrary. Read the discussions of each of these functions for more information on libraries.

Libraries can contain all of your most often used routines. Libraries are identified by their names and (optionally) version numbers. If you use version numbers, you can have many closely related libraries to serve your programming needs. You can keep a collection of different libraries on disk. A call to the OpenLibrary function will then pull each of these libraries into RAM.

Once you initialize a library with the MakeLibrary function, you can bring your library into effect for a particular task by first adding that library by a call to the AddLibrary function, then calling OpenLibrary inside that task. That task can then use the code and data in the library both now and later as this task switches in and out of execution.

The system automatically maintains a system library list. Each time you add a library to the system with the AddLibrary function, this list is updated to reflect that addition. Then, when you use the OpenLibrary function to open a library for access to its routines, the system library list is searched for the name of that library. If it finds a library of that name, OpenLibrary returns a pointer to the Library structure for that library. In this case, the library's OPEN routine is called. If the OpenLibrary function cannot find a library with the name you have given, it will return a zero.

ColdReset

Syntax of Function Call

ColdReset ( )

Purpose of Function

This function causes a cold-start hardware reset sequence identical to that which occurs at power-on. All current system activities will be stopped: the entire software system will be reinitialized and nothing will be preserved. This function will also cause a 68000 processor hardware reset to reset all hardware devices.

Inputs to Function

This function has no arguments.

Discussion

ColdReset operates only in the 68000 supervisor mode. Any attempt to perform this function from 68000 user mode will result in a privilege-violation exception.

The reset operation provides the highest exception level for the 68000 microprocessor. There are two ways to generate the reset signal: you can either press the Ctrl key and both Amiga keys simultaneously or use the 68000 RESET instruction in a program. Two reset vectors are located at the very top of the 68000 exception-vector assignment table. This table contains a total of 255 exception-vector assignments. The first reset vector requires four words, unlike the other exception vectors (which require only two words), and is located in the supervisor-mode program space.

The reset signal is designed for system hardware initialization and recovery from cata-strophic failure conditions. For example, if a bus error occurs during the exception pro-cessing resulting from another bus error, an address error, or a memory-read error, the 68000 processor is halted and all processing ceases. When this happens, the 68000 removes itself from the system, thereby saving all memory contents. Under these circum-stances, only a RESET can restart the halted processor.

Any processing in progress at that time is aborted and cannot be recovered. The 68000 is forced into supervisor mode and instruction execution tracing is turned off. The 68000 interrupt mask is set at level 7—the highest level possible. This means that no other interrupt can gain control of the machine after a reset signal is asserted.

The reset vector number is then generated internally to reference the reset exception vector at location 0 in the supervisor-mode program space. No assumptions can be made about the validity of any of the register contents at this time. In particular, the exact bit-by-bit contents of the supervisor stack pointer is not known. For this reason, neither the program counter nor the status register is saved after a reset occurs.

Next, the address in the first two words of the reset exception vector is fetched as the initial value of the supervisor stack pointer. The address in the last two words of the reset exception vector is also fetched as the initial program counter.

Instruction execution is then started at the now current address in the program counter. The power-up/restart code (boot-up code) should be pointed to by this initial program-counter value.

Note that the RESET instruction (available only in supervisor mode), unlike the hardware reset, does not cause loading of the reset vector, but instead asserts the reset line low to reset all external hardware devices to their initial condition. This allows the soft-ware instructions in a task to reset the system hardware to a known state and then con-tinue processing with the next instruction in a program. However, if you try to execute the RESET instruction when the system is in user mode, a trap exception, due to an instruction privilege violation, will result. Note that as far as the 68000 is concerned, the RESET instruction affects only the program counter; it does not affect any other registers in the processor.

CopyMem

Syntax of Function Call

CopyMem (srcPointer, destPointer, size)
          A0   **A1**   **D0**

Purpose of Function

This function copies a memory block in a very fast, efficient manner from one location in RAM to another location in RAM. It can deal with any size memory block with its pointers pointing to any RAM locations. CopyMem attempts to optimize larger copies using more efficient copies of subblocks of the larger memory block. It uses byte copies for small copies or when memory block pointers are misaligned (not on longword boundaries).

Inputs to Function

srcPointer	A pointer to the source data region that marks the beginning of a memory block to be copied
destPointer	A pointer to the destination data region that defines where the memory block is to be copied
size	The size of the memory block

Discussion

There are three functions in the 1.2 software release that deal with memory management: AddMemList, CopyMem, and CopyMemQuick. You should read the discussion of each of these functions to understand the new memory management features offered by the 1.2 release.

Whenever you want to copy a section of memory from one location to another, you should consider using the CopyMem or CopyMemQuick function. For example, if you wanted to copy a bitmap definition from one RAM location in extended memory (above 512K) to another in chip memory (below 512K) where the Amiga special-purpose chips can work with that bitmap, you can use either of these two functions. Keep in mind that CopyMem and CopyMemQuick are copy functions, not move functions. When these functions return, you will have two copies of your memory data in two different RAM locations.

You should use CopyMem when you cannot guarantee that the source and destination blocks are longword aligned. Use CopyMemQuick when this alignment is always guaranteed.

CopyMemQuick

Syntax of Function Call

```
CopyMemQuick (srcPointer, destPointer, size)
                 A0          A1         D0
```

Purpose of Function

This function is a highly optimized memory block copy routine. It imposes restrictions on the source and destination RAM locations as well as on the size of the memory block.

Inputs to Function

srcPointer This is a pointer to the source data region that defines the memory block to be copied. The memory block can be anywhere in RAM but must be longword aligned; that is, it must start at a memory location that is an even multiple of four bytes.

destPointer This is a pointer to the destination data region that defines where the memory block is to be copied. The memory block can be anywhere in RAM but must be longword aligned.

size This is the size (in bytes) of the data region memory block. This parameter can represent a memory block of any size, but it must be an even multiple of longwords (it must be divisible by four).

Discussion

There are three functions in the 1.2 software release that deal with memory management: AddMemList, CopyMem, and CopyMemQuick.

Whenever you want to copy a section of memory from one location to another, you should consider using the CopyMem or CopyMemQuick function. For example, if you wanted to copy a bitmap definition from one RAM location to another, you can use either of these two functions. Keep in mind that CopyMem and CopyMemQuick are copy functions, not move functions. When these functions return, you will have two copies of your memory data in two different RAM locations.

You should use CopyMemQuick when you can guarantee that the source and destination blocks are longword aligned and when you need or want the extra speed offered by the CopyMemQuick function. Otherwise use the CopyMem function.

Deallocate

Syntax of Function Call

Deallocate (memHeader, memBlock, byteSize)
                 A0   A1   D0

Purpose of Function

This function deallocates memory by returning it to a task-private free-memory pool. You can use this function to free an entire block allocated with the Allocate function. It can also be used to free a subblock of a previously allocated block.

If the memBlock address is not on a block boundary (MEM_BLOCKSIZE, normally set at eight bytes), it will be rounded down. This will work correctly with all the memory allocation routines. However, this may cause some problems if you are freeing only part of a memory block. If byteSize is null, nothing happens; otherwise, the size of the block will be rounded up to the nearest eight-byte block. If this happens, the freed block will span an integer number of eight-byte memory blocks.

Inputs to Function

memHeader	A pointer to a MemHeader structure
memoryBlock	A pointer to the memory block to return
byteSize	The size of the desired block in bytes

Discussion

There are seven Exec functions that deal with memory management: Allocate, AllocEntry, AllocMem, AvailMem, Deallocate, FreeEntry, and FreeMem. Read the discussions of each of these functions for more information on memory management on the Amiga.

You can tell the system to maintain a number of free-memory lists. Some of these can be private and some can be public. If a list is private, it can be used and consulted by only a few cooperating tasks. If a list is public, any task in the system can refer to it to determine how much memory is free in every memory category. The system itself automatically maintains a number of private free-memory lists for its own use.

The system also maintains a number of free-memory pools. You can point to the MemHeader structure that controls these using the memHeader pointer variable in your Allocate function call. The memBlock variable returned by the Allocate function points to the area of memory (the memory block) you just allocated.

You should return memory to the system when your task completes. Keep in mind that the system keeps track only of free memory; the location of allocated memory is not stored in any list comparable to the free-memory list. Therefore, if you don't explicitly return the memory used by your task when the task finishes for the last time, the system will not automatically free it, and that memory will not be available to other tasks in the system that might need it. Obviously, this can be a problem if you don't have a large physical memory space on your Amiga (for example, if you have the 256K machine).

In addition, even with the 512K machine, if you need a large contiguous memory block for a bitplane in a multiplane bitmap, you should always make it a habit to free that memory as soon as possible before any of your tasks exit the system using a RemTask function call. You can use the Graphics Library memory-management functions for this purpose. Then, when you later need a large memory block in another task, it has a greater chance of being available.

The Deallocate function uses a memHeader pointer to point to a specific MemHeader structure as part of the calling sequence. This structure coordinates a task-private free-memory list defined by one MemHeader structure and a series of MemChunk structures. The layout of these structures is shown in the Allocate function discussion.

DoIO

Syntax of Function Call

```
error = DoIO (ioRequest)
D0            A1
```

Purpose of Function

This function requests that a device driver perform the I/O command specified in the I/O Request Block structure. This function will always prevent any other task from executing until the I/O request is completed (synchronous I/O). If the I/O request is successful, error contains a zero; otherwise, an error number is returned.

Inputs to Function

ioRequest   A pointer to a properly initialized I/O Request Block structure

Discussion

There are eight Exec functions that are directly concerned with device I/O: AddDevice, CloseDevice, OpenDevice, RemDevice, CheckIO, DoIO, SendIO, and WaitIO. Each of these functions performs a device service; read the discussions of each of these functions for more information about device I/O.

The Exec device I/O functions allow tasks in the Amiga multitasking system to send and receive data and/or other information, including messages from devices. The DoIO function sends an I/O request to a task and waits for completion. You should use this function when you know that the continued execution of your task depends on information going to or coming from a device; that is, when your task must wait on the I/O to complete. If the device has a number of queued requests in its message port, your task might have a considerable wait. If the device has no queued requests, your task will get immediate service by the device. The task must synchronize with the device; for this reason, DoIO function requests are classified as synchronous I/O requests.

DoIO puts your task to sleep waiting for the I/O request to complete. While your task is sleeping, another task (or sequence of tasks) can become active. When the reply message returns to your task, that task can be reawakened to access the information in the reply message area of the I/O Request Block structure. Now it can continue execution, no longer waiting on the device-supplied information that previously held it up. When the reply message arrives, DoIO automatically notifies your suspended task.

Enqueue

Syntax of Function Call

Enqueue (list, node)
A0 A1

Purpose of Function

This function inserts or appends a node into one of the system queues. The insertion is performed based on the Node structure priority parameter (ln_Pri); Enqueue keeps the list properly sorted. New nodes are inserted in front of the first node with a lower priority. Hence, this type of list forms a FIFO (first-in first-out) queue for nodes of equal priority.

Inputs to Function

list	A pointer to the List structure whose list will contain this node
node	A pointer to the particular Node structure to enqueue

Discussion

Exec has a number of functions designed to operate on nodes and doubly-linked lists built from nodes: Insert and Remove; AddHead, RemHead, AddTail, and RemTail; Enqueue; and FindName. Note that the Insert, Remove, AddHead, and AddTail functions, in contrast to the Enqueue function, do not use the priority field in the Node structure. For this reason, Enqueue is the equivalent of Insert for a sorted list. It always inserts on a priority basis, keeping the higher priority nodes toward the head of the list.

Because of this arrangement, all nodes passed to the Enqueue function must have a priority assigned prior to the call. Recall that the node priority is assigned when the Node structure is defined for this particular node. (See the definition of the Node structure under the AddHead function.) Highest priority is at the head of the list; lowest priority is at the tail of the list. RemHead removes the node with the current highest priority, while RemTail removes the node with the current lowest priority. If you insert a node that is equal in priority to a node already on the list, Enqueue gives FIFO ordering; the new node is inserted following the last node of equal priority.

FindName

Syntax of Function Call

```
node = FindName (start, name)
D0                A0    A1
```

Purpose of Function

This function traverses a system node list until a Node structure with the given name is found. To find multiple occurrences of a name-node string, this function can be called with a Node structure starting point. The result of FindName is a pointer to the Node structure with the same name; otherwise, a zero is returned to indicate that a Node structure with that name was not found.

Inputs to Function

start	A pointer to a List structure or a Node structure with which to start the search; if a Node structure, this Node structure is skipped and the search starts with the next Node structure in the list

name   A pointer to the Node structure name, a null-terminated text string; this is the ln_Name parameter in the Node structure

Discussion

Exec has a number of functions designed to operate on nodes and doubly-linked lists built from nodes: Insert and Remove; AddHead, RemHead, AddTail, and RemTail; Enqueue; and FindName.

Recall that each Node structure in a list has a node name. This is the ln_Name variable in the Node structure. FindName lets you find the first node with a given name within a specified list. To find multiple occurrences of a Node structure with the same name on a particular list, you can call FindName that number of times. If you want to start the search at the head of the list, specify a start variable that points to a List structure rather than a specific Node structure. If you want to start the search with a specific Node structure, specify a start variable that points to that Node structure. Note that this pointer will point to the predecessor Node structure, so the search starts with the Node structure following the Node structure you point to. Once you get the pointer to the named Node structure, you can use the other list functions to work with that node in your program as desired.

FindPort

Syntax of Function Call

```
msgPort = FindPort (name)
D0                  A1
```

Purpose of Function

This function searches the system message-port list for a public port with the given name. A pointer to the MsgPort stucture matching this name is returned; if the message port is not found, a zero is returned.

Inputs to Function

name   The name of the message port to find, a null-terminated text string

Discussion

There are four Exec functions that are explicitly concerned with task message ports in the Amiga system: AddPort, FindPort, RemPort, and WaitPort. AddPort, FindPort, and RemPort all deal exclusively with public ports. These are ports that are added to the system message-port list with the AddPort function. WaitPort deals with both public and private ports. Closely related to the port routines are the message-management routines: PutMsg, GetMsg, and ReplyMsg.

The system automatically maintains a system message-port list for each message port attached to each task in the system. Therefore, if you have several tasks, each with a number of message ports, there are quite a few of these lists in the system at one time. Each list is automatically updated each time you add a message port to a task.

Message ports can be added to the system with or without names attached to them. If the message port is public, it must have a name. This is the ln_Name parameter in the Node substructure of the MsgPort structure. If the message port is private, meaning that only a few closely cooperating routines use it, it can remain nameless. Communication can still take place between these closely knit routines even if their message ports don't have names.

If a port (whether public or private) is named, many separate, unrelated pieces of code can use this message port, referring to it by its name. Each piece of code (actually every task) can send and receive messages connected to that port. This provides a network of task-to-task communication that can lead to very complex interactions under a variety of circumstances.

The FindPort function returns a pointer to the MsgPort structure associated with the name argument. Once you get this structure pointer, you can examine and change the contents of the associated MsgPort structure. You can also use the msgPort pointer variable as the argument in the RemPort and WaitPort functions.

FindResident

Syntax of Function Call

```
resident  =  FindResident (name)
DO                         A1
```

Purpose of Function

This function attempts to find the Resident structure that represents a resident module of the specified name. Once your program has a pointer to the Resident structure, it can determine all the characteristics (initialization, priority, pointer to initialization code, etc.) associated with that resident module. If FindResident is successful, it returns a pointer to the Resident structure; otherwise it returns a zero value.

Inputs to Function

name   A pointer to a null-terminated string representing the name of the resident module; this is the string pointed to by the rt_Name parameter in the Resident structure

Discussion

There are three functions in the 1.2 release that deal with resident modules: FindResident, InitCode, and InitResident. You should read the discussion of each of these functions to understand how resident modules are used and managed in the Amiga software system.

The Resident Structure

The Resident structure is used to manage a resident module. Each resident module has its own Resident structure. The Resident structure is defined in the Resident.h INCLUDE file as follows:

```
struct Resident {
    UWORD rt_MatchWord;
    struct Resident *rt_MatchTag;
    APTR rt_EndSkip;
    UWORD rt_Flags;
    UWORD rt_Version;
    UWORD rt_Type;
    BYTE rt_Pri;
    char *rt_Name;
    char *rt_IDString;
    APTR rt_Init;
};
```

At the time of writing, the resident module functions and structures were still under development. For this reason, their use and meaning were not fully defined. However, a brief indication of the meaning of the various parameters in the Resident structure follows:

■ The rt_MatchWord parameter is the word to match on when searching for a resident module associated with a specific Resident structure.

■ The rt_MatchTag parameter is a pointer to another Resident structure. This parameter is used to continue the search for a matching Resident structure if this Resident structure does not match the resident module.

■ The rt_EndSkip parameter is a pointer to the RAM location to continue the scan for the resident module.

■ The rt_Flags parameter is the flags parameter in the Resident structure. Flags can have the following values: RTF_AUTOINIT if this Resident structure represents a resident module that will be auto-initialized; RTF_COLDSTART if this Resident structure represents a resident module that will be initialized upon a cold start.

■ The rt_Version parameter is the version number of the resident module. The rt_Version parameter is used by the InitCode function to initialize all resident modules with a specific version number.

■ The rt_Type parameter is the type of resident module. Resident module types have not been fully defined at the time of this writing.

■ The rt_Pri parameter is the initialization priority of the resident module. The InitCode function initializes resident modules in a specific order determined by the rt_Pri parameter in their Resident structure.

■ The rt_Name parameter is a pointer to a null-terminated string containing the name of the resident module. This parameter is used by the FindResident function to locate a Resident structure of a specific name.

■ The rt_IDString parameter is a pointer to the identification string of the resident module. The identification string is a null-terminated text string. The precise use of this parameter has not been defined at the time of this writing.

■ The rt_Init parameter is a pointer to the RAM location where the initialization code of the resident module begins. The system uses this parameter to locate and initialize the resident module code.

Each resident module has a name. The name is used together with the version number and the identification string to identify the resident module. Once a resident module is loaded into RAM, you can use the FindResident function to locate the Resident structure assigned to it. Once you have a pointer to the Resident structure, your program can deal with the resident module code in any way you please.

FindSemaphore

Syntax of Function Call

```
signalSemaphore = FindSemaphore (name)
D0                               A1
```

Purpose of Function

This function attempts to find a SignalSemaphore structure with a particular name. Find-Semaphore will search the system signal-semaphore list for a SignalSemaphore structure with the given name. If FindSemaphore is successful, a pointer to the first Signal-Semaphore structure with that name will be returned; otherwise FindSemaphore returns a zero value.

Inputs to Function

name   The name of the semaphore you want to find. This is the ln_Name parameter in the Node substructure inside the SignalSemaphore structure

Discussion

There are seven functions in the 1.2 release that deal with signal semaphores and two functions that deal with the signal-semaphore list. These functions are listed in the Add-Semaphore discussion.

At some point in a task you may need to locate a specific SignalSemaphore structure. FindSemaphore provides the means to do this. Once you know the name of the semaphore, you can use FindSemaphore to get a pointer to that SignalSemaphore structure. You can then use any of the C language structure parameter assignment statements to examine and alter selected parameters in that SignalSemaphore structure.

FindTask

Syntax of Function Call

```
taskCB = FindTask (name)
D0                  A1
```

Purpose of Function

This function checks all task queues for a task with the given name: if it finds such a task, it will return a pointer to its Task Control Block structure. If a null name pointer is given as input, a pointer to the current task's Task Control Block structure will be returned.

Inputs to Function

name   A pointer to the name of the task, a null-terminated text string; this is the node name used in the definition of the Task Control Block structure, the ln_Name parameter in the Node substructure inside the Task Control Block structure

Discussion

There are four Exec functions that specifically deal with task handling: AddTask, Find-Task, RemTask, and SetTaskPri. Read the discussions of each of these functions for more information on task handling. The data structure that defines a Task Control Block structure appears in the Exec INCLUDE files; these files are called Tasks.h (for the C language interface) and Tasks.i (for the assembly language interface).

Sometimes it is necessary to know where the Task Control Block structure for a task is placed in RAM. This is useful if you want to modify some of the parameters inside a particular Task Control Block structure. This is the purpose of the FindTask function. FindTask looks through a list of task-ready queues (different from message and library queues) and finds where the Task Control Block structure of this task is stored. It then returns a pointer to this memory location. Other task-handling functions can now look at and modify this Task Control Block structure.

FreeEntry

Syntax of Function Call

FreeEntry (memList)
A0

Purpose of Function

This function looks inside a MemList structure and frees all the entries. A pointer to the MemList structure was previously returned by a call to the AllocEntry function. When FreeEntry returns, all the memory blocks represented by the MemList structure will be deallocated.

Inputs to Function

memList   A pointer to a MemList structure, which defines a number of MemEntry structures

Discussion

There are seven Exec functions that deal with memory management: Allocate, AllocEntry, AllocMem, AvailMem, Deallocate, FreeEntry, and FreeMem. There is additional information on memory management in the discussions of each of these functions.

Three Ways to Free Memory

Just as you can allocate memory in several ways (one large block or several explicit smaller blocks), you can deallocate (free) memory in several ways. Whatever method you choose, you always return this memory to the system free-memory pool. You can use the Deallocate function, the FreeMem function, or the FreeEntry function. Each function operates in a different way:

1. The Deallocate function frees an explicit block of memory previously allocated with the Allocate function. It returns this block to an explicitly named free-memory list. The system can maintain a number of separate free-memory lists. You can reach each using the appropriate MemHeader structure pointer variable. If you use the Deallocate function, you know which free-memory list this freed block is assigned to. This information can be useful later if you want to allocate that specific block of memory again.

2. The FreeMem function frees a block of memory allocated by the Allocate or AllocMem functions. Here, however, the memory is not returned to any particular free-memory list in the system. In other words, you give up some control; you do not know to which free-memory list this block now belongs.

3. The FreeEntry function returns all the entries in a MemList structure previously allocated by the AllocEntry function. Here, again, the freed block of memory is not returned to any particular free-memory list in the system.

These functions all free memory, but only the Deallocate function returns this memory to a specific free-memory list.

Structures and Pointers

The memory-management functions deal with a number of structures and pointers:

1. The MemList structure consists of lists of free-memory areas that can be allocated in function calls to the memory allocation routines. In other words, this is just a another list—a list of memory areas that are free to be allocated. The MemList structure is used by the AllocEntry and FreeEntry functions.

2. The MemEntry structure is a substructure within the MemList structure. It consists of these parameters: meu_Reqs, the AllocMem requirements for this memory; meu_Addr, the address of this memory region; and me_Length, the size of this memory request.

3. The memBlock parameter points to a single specific allocated or deallocated block of memory. The Allocate and AllocMem functions, which deal with a specific block of memory, both return this pointer. The AllocEntry function, which deals with many blocks of memory at once, does not return this pointer.

4. The memList parameter is a pointer to a MemList structure where the parameters of a list of memory blocks are stored. Note that this is both an argument to and a return variable from the AllocEntry function. It is also an argument to the Free-Entry function.

5. The memHeader parameter is a pointer to a MemHeader structure that contains a list of free-memory blocks now available in the system. Of the three allocation functions, only the Allocate function uses this pointer. The Deallocate function also uses this memHeader pointer. The AllocMem and AllocEntry functions do not work with the memHeader pointer. Instead, they search through the system free-memory list to find blocks of memory that satisfy the explicit memory requests of the AllocMem and AllocEntry functions.

FreeMem

Syntax of Function Call

FreeMem (memBlock, byteSize)
A1   D0

Purpose of Function

This function frees a block of memory, returning it to the system free-memory list. If the memBlock pointer is properly specified and the size is less than or equal to the original size of that particular memory block, it will be added once again to the system free-memory list.

Inputs to Function

memBlock   A pointer to the specific memory block to free; this pointer was previously allocated by either the Allocate or Alloc-Mem functions

byteSize   The size of the block in bytes

Discussion

There are seven Exec functions that deal with memory management: Allocate, AllocEntry, AllocMem, AvailMem, Deallocate, FreeEntry, and FreeMem. There is more information about memory management in the discussions of each of these functions.

The FreeMem function needs the memBlock variable as an argument. Of the three memory allocation functions, only the Allocate and AllocMem functions return this pointer variable. Therefore, you cannot use the FreeMem function to free memory allocated with the AllocEntry function. Use the FreeEntry function for this purpose.

An example of freeing memory with the FreeMem function is

FreeMem (memptr,100)

This frees up 104 bytes of memory at the location pointed to by the memptr variable. Note that the original 100 bytes is rounded up to the next even multiple of eight bytes, which is the minimum memory block size with which the system can deal. This is acceptable because the original allocation function allocated memory in the same way, at this same RAM location.

The FreeMem function does not return any status to indicate whether your selection of a memory location to free a block is valid. If you try to free a memory block in the middle of a block that the system believes is already free, you will cause a system crash. If this happens, the only solution is to reboot the system.

FreeSignal

Syntax of Function Call

FreeSignal (signalNum)
D0

Purpose of Function

This function frees a previously allocated signal bit for reuse. This call must be performed while executing the same task in which the signal was originally allocated. After the FreeSignal call, the signal bit with signalNum (0–31) will be available for allocation once again. This function changes the tc_AllocSignal parameter in the Task Control Block structure.

Inputs to Function

signalNum   The signal bit number to free bit (one of 0–31)

Discussion

There are four Exec functions that deal with task signals in the Amiga system: AllocSignal, FreeSignal, SetSignal, and Signal. In addition, the GetMsg, PutMsg, and ReplyMsg functions can be included in the category of signal-handling functions; signals are induced by the messages these functions communicate from task to task. There is more information on task signals in the discussions of each of these functions.

Tasks communicate with each other by passing messages back and forth through message ports using the MsgPort structures set up for each task. Tasks also send and receive messages from devices by passing information through the I/O Request Block structures.

Task signals can be allocated using the AllocSignal function. Each signal comes from one of the message ports of the task as a result of a message sent to that port. Each message is queued or processed immediately if no other messages are presently queued. Task signals were defined in the Task Control Block structure for your task before it was added to the system with the AddTask function. Each message port is assigned a specific signal bit to allow that message port to respond to some expected activity in the system. If you want to change the assignment of some of these signal bits, you must first free that bit; this is the purpose of the FreeSignal function.

Signal bit allocation and deallocation is done on a per-task basis. If you free a signal bit from one task, you in no way affect any signal bits used by other tasks currently in the system. If you have ten tasks in the system, each using the full allotment of signals (32), you will have 320 signal bits being processed between tasks.

To reuse a signal bit of a task later, you simply deallocate it now. This returns it to the task signal-bit pool for later reassignment to that same task. Your task's Task Control Block structure also contains the tc_SigRecvd variable. This is a longword (32 bits) containing the signal bits that have already been received by this task as it executes.

If you set up exception-handling routines, you must initialize a mask to indicate which signals, when received, will cause an exception to occur. This is done using the tc_SigExcept mask variable in the Task Control Block structure of your task. This variable contains bits that define whether a signal bit, when received, should cause an exception.

The tc_SigExcept mask variable should be initialized to zero if you do not want to have any exception processing for that task. Just as there are 32 potential signal bits, there are 32 potential exception bits you can use. Any bit set to 1 in the tc_SigExcept variable will cause your task to enter the exception coding routine belonging to that exception bit if a message port with the signal bit set receives a message.

Warning: Signals cannot be allocated or freed from exception-handling code. There is no message-passing capability between different pieces of exception code and other tasks in the system.

FreeTrap

Syntax of Function Call

FreeTrap (trapNum)
D0

Purpose of Function

This function frees a previously allocated trap number for reuse in a task. This call must be performed while running the same task in which the trap was originally allocated by the AllocTrap function. After FreeTrap executes, the trap number whose value is trap-Num is free to be assigned to a different trap for this task.

Inputs to Function

trapNum   The trap number to free (one of 0–15)

Discussion

There are two functions that deal explicitly with traps in the Amiga Exec system: AddTrap and FindTrap. The AddTrap function allocates a trap number to a task. The FindTrap function returns a specific trap number to the available-trap-number list for this task. This list is automatically maintained by the system.

As you add and delete traps from your own tasks and programs, you should keep in mind that when the 68000 senses a trap, your program loses control; the Exec system routines gain control of the system. The Exec system routines determine which task is currently executing and whether this trap should go to that task and its trap code. If it should, the task-specific trap-handling routine belonging to that trap will be executed.

Recall that this routine is pointed to by the tc_TrapCode pointer variable in the Task Control Block structure of that task.

When a trap occurs, the 68000 supervisor stack contains the following information:

■ The trap frame. This is the 68000 exception frame as documented in the Motorola 68000 manual.

■ The trap number. A number from 0 to 255 as detailed in the 68000 manual.

When the system senses a trap it executes the assembly language code instruction

Trap *#n*

where *n* is a number from 0 to 15. This is a 68000 software trap instruction. However, when the system enters trap processing, the number that is placed on the stack is *n* + 32. This means that, by convention, Amiga software trap instructions generate trap numbers from 32 to 47.

You might not be able to handle all traps that occur. This will depend on the traps that you explicitly allocate with the AddTrap function. Therefore, in your trap code, you must first determine whether you can process this trap. Look at the item on the top of the stack and use this information to create a mask that you can compare to the allocate trap variable (tc_Trap-Alloc) you specified in the Task Control Block structure and later modified with the Alloc _Trap function. You can use an assembly language routine to do this:

1. Save the registers you will be using in the assembly language routine.

2. Get the trap number.

3. Compare the actual trap number to all of your assigned trap numbers for that task. This tells you whether you have assigned a trap routine to handle this particular trap in that task. If you find a match, you can process the trap. If you do not find a match, pass the trap to the system to handle as it will. Of course, this will cause the system to dump your current task.

4. Clean up and exit from this trap routine.

Always remember that trap processing takes place in supervisor mode. At this time, all the multitasking features of the system are disabled; no task switching can occur. You do not want this to go on for too long. For this reason, you should keep your trap-processing routines as short as possible; they should be optimized to execute as fast as possible.

GetCC

Syntax of Function Call

```
conditions = GetCC( )
D0:0–4
```

Purpose of Function

This function gets the condition codes of the Motorola 68000 in a way that is compatible with the 68010 and 68020. It provides a means of obtaining the condition codes in a way that will make the 68010 and 68020 upgrades transparent; programs written for the 68000 can be run on the 68010 and 68020 if the GetCC function is always used to get the condition codes. Note that the five condition code bits are returned in the D0 register in bit positions 0 to 4; these bits correspond to the first five of the 16 bits in the status register in all three microprocessors.

Inputs to Function

This function has no inputs.

Discussion

The Motorola 68000, 68010, and 68020 CPUs each generate five condition codes during the execution of their arithmetic, logical, and other classes of instructions. The condition codes are always contained in the first five bits of the 68000, 68010, or 68020 status register. The condition code bits are identified as follows:

N (negative)	This bit (bit 3) is set if the most significant bit of a result of a CPU operation is set; otherwise it is cleared.
Z (zero)	This bit (bit 2) is set if the result of a CPU operation equals zero; otherwise it is cleared.
V (overflow)	This bit (bit 1) is set if there was an arithmetic overflow in an arithmetic operation. This implies that the result of the arithmetic operation could not be represented in the operand size (one byte, two bytes, or four bytes) assigned to that operation. This bit is cleared otherwise.
C (carry)	This bit (bit 0) is set if a carry is generated out of the most significant bit of the operand of an addition operation. This bit is also set if a borrow is generated in a subtraction. Otherwise, it is cleared.
X (extend)	This bit (bit 4) is transparent to data movement. When it is effected, it is set the same as the carry bit.

Note that the first four bits are true condition codes; they reflect the result of a CPU operation. The X bit is made available for multiprecision (extended) operations. The C carry bit and the X multiprecision bit are separate in the Motorola 68000 and 68010 to simplify the programming model.

If you want your programs to be upwardly compatible with the 68010 and 68020 CPUs, you must avoid certain assembly language instructions. Also you must not make any assumptions about the processor supervisor stack frame. In particular, the MOVE SR,<ea> instruction is a privilege instruction on the 68010 and 68020 CPUs. If you want your programs to work correctly on all three CPUs, always use the GetCC function to get the condition codes.

GetMsg

Syntax of Function Call

```
message = GetMsg (msgPort)
D0                 A0
```

Purpose of Function

This function gets the next message from a specified message port. It provides a fast, non-copying, message-receiving mechanism. The received message is removed from the message-port queue.

This function will not wait. If a message is not present in the message-port queue, the function will return zero. If a program must wait for a message, it can wait on the signal attached to that message port, or it can use the WaitPort function. There can be only one task waiting for any given message port.

GetMsg returns a pointer to the first message available. This will be the oldest message (the first put there by the PutMsg function) in the message-port queue.

Getting the message does not imply that the message is free to be reused. When the receiver is finished with the message, it may send it back to the sending task through the reply port assigned to that message. You can use the ReplyMsg function for that purpose.

Inputs to Function

msgPort   A pointer to the receiver MsgPort structure

Discussion

There are three Exec functions that are explicitly concerned with intertask message processing in the Amiga system: PutMsg, GetMsg, and ReplyMsg. These functions manage the messages coming and going from the message ports assigned to each task in the

Amiga multitasking system. Because messages use message ports, it is also important to keep in mind the role of the message-port management functions: AddPort, FindPort, RemPort, and WaitPort. See the discussions of these functions for more information on their purpose and role in message processing.

There are some things you should know about messages in the Amiga system. When the system first powers up, there are several tasks already resident and operating in the system. These resident tasks are waiting for messages from user-defined tasks. They manage the I/O devices installed in the system: the keyboard, the floppy-disk drive, the hard-disk drive, the mouse, the Gameport device, and any other hardware attached to the system.

Each device is managed by a set of device-driver routines. The job of these routines is to wait for you to send data (input events) through the device into each of these routines. You can classify these tasks as device-management tasks. Their job is to sit and wait for input events.

All tasks communicate with each other through messages placed in the message ports assigned to each task. Messages are queued in FIFO fashion in these message ports. The system automatically keeps a message-port message list for each message port assigned to all tasks in the system. Messages can pile up in the queue of each message port; they must wait their turn to be processed.

When a message is sent to one of the message ports of a task, the PutMsg function appends that message to the end of the message-port queue of that task. The message-port message list of that message port is updated to reflect its addition.

Once it arrives, a message can be processed in a number of ways. If the message port contains the address of a Task Control Block structure, the PutMsg function can perform one of two actions:

1. It can activate a task by activating a signal bit associated with that message port.

2. It can activate a task and at the same time cause a software interrupt. This forces the task to enter one of its exception-handling routines. After this exception code is executed, the task continues at the same position it was executing when it lost control. Of course, this is all true only if the signal bit associated with that message port can cause exceptions.

These messages allow tasks (the one active task and all other presently inactive tasks) to communicate between themselves to do the following:

1. Put a task to sleep explicitly so that some other task of lower priority can take over use of the machine.

2. Wake up a sleeping task when an appropriate message arrives at one of its message ports.

3. Any number of other things, depending on the arrival and processing of messages in a message port and the status of the signal mask bits for that message port.

InitCode

Syntax of Function Call

InitCode (startClass, version)
          D0   D1

Purpose of Function

This function initializes all resident modules with a specific startClass value and version number. The startClass argument can assume three values: COLDSTART, COOLSTART, and WARMSTART. Resident modules are initialized in a prioritized order determined by the priority parameter (rt_Pri) in the Resident structure associated with each resident module.

Inputs to Function

startClass	The startup class of the resident module; either COOL-START, COLDSTART, or WARMSTART
version	The release version number of the resident module; this parameter appears as the rt_Version parameter in the Resident structure

Discussion

There are three functions in the 1.2 release that deal with resident modules: FindResident, InitCode, and InitResident. You should read the discussion of each of these functions to understand how resident modules are used and managed in the Amiga software system.

The InitCode function provides a way to initialize the code of a resident module represented by a particular Resident structure. Recall that each resident module has a specified startup class which indicates under what conditions the code in that resident module should by initialized and executed. In addition, as each resident module is updated, the version number of that module will change. The version argument provides a way to restrict initialization to modules of a specified and higher than specified version number.

InitResident

Syntax of Function Call

InitResident (resident, segList)
              A1   D1

Purpose of Function

This function initializes a resident module associated with a specific Resident structure using the segment list identified by the segList pointer argument.

Inputs to Function

resident	A pointer to a Resident structure representing a particular resident module
segList	A pointer to a segment list for the specified resident module

Discussion

There are three functions in the 1.2 release release that deal with resident modules: FindResident, InitCode, and InitResident.

The code of each resident module is made up of code segments. Each segment contains some executable code and a pointer to the next segment. A segment list is a list that ties together all code segments belonging to a specific unit of executable code; in this case, the code of a resident module.

The InitResident function uses the Resident structure and segment list associated with a specific resident module to initialize that resident module. Once initialized, the resident module remains in RAM ready to be executed at any time without further loading from disk.

InitSemaphore

Syntax of Function Call

InitSemaphore (signalSemaphore)
               A0

Purpose of Function

This function initializes a SignalSemaphore structure and prepares it for use in the system. InitSemaphore does not allocate memory; it only initializes list pointers and semaphore counters.

Inputs to Function

signalSemaphore   A pointer to a not yet initialized SignalSemaphore structure

Discussion

There are seven functions in the 1.2 release that deal with signal semaphores and two functions that deal with the signal-semaphore list. These functions are listed in the AddSemaphore discussion, where you will also find a discussion of the SignalSemaphore structure.

The SignalSemaphore structure has two counter parameters and two linkage parameters. The counter parameters are ss_NestCount and ss_QueueCount. The linkage parameters are ss_Link and ss_WaitQueue. These are the four parameters that the InitSemaphore function initializes.

There are two ways to initialize a SignalSemaphore structure. Either you can use a set of C language program structure parameter assignment statements or you can use the InitSemaphore function. If you decide to use the InitSemaphore function, you should normally call the InitSemaphore function before you use a SignalSemaphore structure with any other signal semaphore function. Note that InitSemaphore does not initialize the ln_Pri parameter of the Node substructure inside the SignalSemaphore structure. You must initialize this with a simple structure parameter assignment statement to establish the position of this semaphore on the semaphore list.

Semaphores in the Amiga System

One of the most significant additions to the Exec function library is the ability to define and use semaphores. Semaphores provide a way for a group of tasks to prevent and permit access to a number of shared data structures in the system. This need arises because the Amiga multitasking system otherwise allows a number of tasks to access the same structures and data areas in memory without restriction. Signal semaphores are used internally in the Graphics, Layers, and Intuition Libraries to allow and restrict mutually competing tasks from simultaneously drawing into shared bitmaps during system graphic updates.

If there is no way to lock a shared data structure when a specific task begins to access that structure, then each task cannot guarantee the data or rely on the data in that structure to remain the same as that task proceeds to access that data; another task may take over the machine and proceed to change the data in some way when the present task temporarily loses control of the CPU through a task switch. For example, Exec memory block lists (lists that tie together memory subblock allocations in a longer block) should only be accessed by one task at a time. If one task alters a memory list after another task starts looking at the list, the altering task will confuse the task that is inspecting the list, thus leading to memory corruption.

There are several ways to protect a RAM block while a particular task is modifying or accessing it. The first method is to use the Forbid and Permit system routines to surround the program statements that define these task actions. This scheme looks like this:

Forbid ( )
A set of program task statements to access (read) or alter (write) struc-
ture or data block data.
Permit ( )

Here the Forbid and Permit functions prevent another task from taking over the machine while the current task statements between Forbid and Permit are executing. This ensures that no other task will interrupt the execution of these statements before they have completed execution.

The disadvantage of this method is that *all* task switching is prevented between the Forbid and Permit statements. This creates the problem that no other task gets the CPU even though it may not want to modify the protected RAM block; that is, all task switching is prevented. Therefore, entry into tasks that would not cause a problem is also prevented, thus placing an undue burden on the task-switching capabilities of the machine.

This disadvantage can be overcome using semaphores. With this method of data structure locking, all appropriately involved tasks agree on a set of locking conventions before any task tries to access or modify shared data structures. In this way, tasks that do not attempt to modify a set of data structures currently shared by a second set of tasks are not prevented from running when one of the tasks in the second set gains control of the machine; that is, task switching is not unduly prevented. Mutual exclusion of data structure access takes place only between tasks that may try to alter the shared data structures.

There are two types of semaphores available in the Exec system: signal semaphores and message-based semaphores. There are nine new functions in the 1.2 release that deal with signal semaphores and two new functions that deal with message-based semaphores. Both types of semaphores are discussed in the 11 new functions definitions in this chapter.

Signal semaphores use the RequestSemaphore and SignalSemaphore structures and do not use the message-passing features of the Exec system; that is, they do not deal with MsgPort or Message structures in any way. Signal semaphores allow a number of tasks to lock and unlock shared data structures at appropriate times during the intertwined execution of those tasks.

On the other hand, message-based semaphores use the Semaphore structure and the message-passing features of the Exec system. The Semaphore structure contains a MsgPort substructure to pass semaphore-related messages back and forth between a set of tasks that share a set of shared data structures.

The in-program use of signal semaphores closely parallels the use of the Forbid( ) and Permit( ) system routines; just surround the set of protected statements with calls to ObtainSemaphore and ReleaseSemaphore as follows:

ObtainSemaphore ( )
A set of program task statements to access (read) or alter (write) structure or data block data.
ReleaseSemaphore ( )

Then use the function discussions to see how semaphores are managed.

InitStruct

Syntax of Function Call

InitStruct (initTable, memBlock, size)
         A1   A2   D0: 0–15

Purpose of Function

This function clears a memory area except for those words whose data and offset values are provided in the initialization table pointed to by the initTable pointer variable. This function allows you to build a data structure in RAM from a set of unstructured data somewhere else in RAM. You can then refer to the structured data in the usual C language style, as a related set of information in which each RAM location has a variable name associated with it.

Inputs to Function

initTable
A pointer to the beginning of the commands and data to use to initialize memory. This is a pointer to the raw (unstructured) data area. Both data and commands must be on even-byte boundaries if the size parameter is specified.

memBlock
A pointer to the beginning of the memory block to initialize. This must be on an even-byte boundary if the size parameter is specified.

size   The size of the memory block to initialize. This number is used to clear the to-be-structured memory area before initializing it via the initTable data. If the size variable is zero, the memory is not cleared before it is initialized. Before it is used, the size variable value is rounded down to the nearest even-byte number.

Discussion

InitStruct is the only Exec function that allows you to initialize memory areas directly. Contrast this to the MakeLibrary, OpenLibrary, OpenDevice, and OpenResource functions, which merely assign data to specific memory structures indirectly through the various structures that these functions manipulate. For instance, the MakeLibrary function specifically initializes a library routine vector and data area in memory. It sometimes initializes the library data area by calling the InitStruct function indirectly through its struc-Init pointer variable. The OpenDevice function specifically initializes at least part of an I/O Request Block structure in memory. The OpenResource function specifically initializes a Resource structure in memory.

You can also contrast InitStruct to the AddTask and AddPort functions. The Add-Task function specifically defines and initializes the Task Control Block structure of a task. The AddPort function specifically defines and initializes the MsgPort structure assigned to a message port that you assigned to a task.

You can also contrast InitStruct with the Allocate, AllocMem, AllocEntry, Deallocate, FreeMem, and FreeEntry memory-management functions. These functions merely modify the list of memory blocks that are assigned to a task. They allocate or free blocks of memory accordingly. They do not, however, explicitly initialize (except for clearing a memory block) the referenced memory areas with data values; this is the job of the InitStruct function.

Don't be intimidated by the complexity of the InitStruct function definition. Although it has many combinations, once you break it down, you can see what it can accomplish. The key idea is that InitStruct takes unstructured data in memory and turns it into structured data—data that is organized into a C language type structure. This structure data can then be referred to by its structure name, manipulated, and used as a unit in subsequent function calls in your program that need to access a data structure.

To use the InitStruct function properly, it's helpful to know the number of bytes of memory you will require for the data you want to place into the data structure. If you know what this value should be, you can use it as the third argument (size) in the Init-Struct function call. You also need to know how much memory you will need to hold the raw information in the initialization table. Try to estimate these two numbers; because of data memory-byte alignment requirements they are not necessarily the same value.

Make sure that the currently free memory blocks can accommodate both of these memory requirements at the same time, at least while you are developing the InitStruct data structure. You can call the AvailMem function to determine the memory available to the system before you start to place your initialization table in memory. (AllocMem returns the total free space remaining for memory of certain specified requirements.) After you create the InitStruct structure, you can free and reuse the initialization table's raw-data memory area pointed to by the initTable variable.

If you don't know how many bytes will be required for the InitStruct data structure information, you can use zero for the size argument. In this case, you will have to assume that a large enough block of memory is available for both the initialization table and the resulting InitStruct data structure. When you use zero for the size argument, the Init-Struct structure memory area will *not* be cleared to zero before your data is placed into it. Just be sure that any values in the final InitStruct structure data are not interpreted incorrectly in subsequent function calls that use this memory area.

For example, if you want to place your InitStruct structure data into the first 512K of RAM (MEMF_CHIP), you can call AllocMem with this memory requirement. If there is a block of memory satisfying both the initialization table and the final structure memory-block-size requirements simultaneously, you can use part of it for your initialization table raw data and part of it for the InitStruct data structure itself. If you want to clear the block first, call AllocMem with the MEMF_CHIP and MEMF_CLEAR compound requirement arguments.

If you can estimate an upper limit to the number of bytes required in the InitStruct structure, you can use the Allocate function to determine the location of a block of memory where you can place your resultant InitStruct structure. Once you get this pointer from the Allocate routine, use this memBlock value as the memory argument to the Init-Struct function call. If you already know of an area of memory large enough to hold your InitStruct structure data, use a pointer to that location as the memory argument.

The InitStruct function works with the initTable variable. This variable points to the memory location of the initialization table commands, which consist of commands and pointers to raw data areas (sources and destinations). These commands tell the InitStruct function where to take the data from and where and how to place that data in a structured form, thereby creating an InitStruct C-language type data structure.

These byte commands consist of several intertwined parts or categories of information that implement all the combinations of the InitStruct function. These commands can do the following:

- They can load data into memory. The data is either one value (a) or a range of values (count). The data is either a byte, a word (two bytes), or a longword (four bytes).

- They can load this data into a known (specified) memory location or into the next memory location in a sequence of known memory locations.

- They can load data at a specified byte location or at a location relative to a specified location.

- They can load the data at a memory offset relative to the memBlock pointer argument of the InitStruct function call.

- They can load the data once or repeatedly.

Not all combinations of these five operations are supported. You will have to experiment to discover which combinations work. A little common sense is helpful here. The offset, when specified, is relative to the memBlock pointer variable provided and is initially zero.

The eight bits of the initialization table's data byte commands are interpreted as follows:

ddssnnnn

The destination (dd) bits contain the information that tells the InitStruct function where to put the data in the resulting InitStruct structure.

The source (ss) bits contain commands that tell the InitStruct function where to find the raw data. These bits also tell the InitStruct function what type of data—byte, word, longword, or rptr (relative pointer)—is at these memory locations. Following are the possible combinations of information these bits can contain:

00   Means the source is a longword (four bytes) located in the next two aligned words

01   Means the source is a word (two bytes) located in the next aligned word

10   Means the source is the next byte (one byte)

Do not set both source bits to 1. If you do, you will cause an error condition that will cause an alert in the system.

The count or repeat (nnnn) bits contain the information that tells the InitStruct function how to count bytes as it moves the source and destination pointers. Count and repeat tell the InitStruct function the number of source items to copy (count) or the number of times the source is to be copied (repeat).

The count bits work with the destination bits in these combinations:

00   Means put data into the next destination location; nnnn (the last four bits of the command word) is the number of source items to copy (count)

01   Means put data into the next destination location; nnnn (the last four bits of the command word) is the number of times the source is to be copied (repeat)

10   Means destination offset is next byte; nnnn (the last four bits of the command word) is the count (how many bytes to copy)

11   Means destination offset is next relative pointer; nnnn (the last four bits of the command word) is the count (how many bytes to copy)

The initialization table commands are always read from the next even byte. The destination data offsets are always relative to the memBlock argument pointer variable value (the memory pointer variable placed in the A2 register), specified in the InitStruct function call. The 00000000 command ends the initTable stream: use 00010001 (dd = 00, ss = 01, nnnn = 0001) if you want to copy one longword.

You are free to pick a memory location anywhere in memory for the initialization table pointer (initTable), but this memory block must begin on an even byte address unless byte-by-byte initialization is used.

The assembly language implementation of the InitStruct function call is as follows:

- The D0 register holds the size, command, count, and repeat data values as they change from command to command in the command table.

- The D1 register holds the destination offset command type (for dd equal to 10 or 11) as it changes from command to command in the command table.

- The A0 register holds the current C language type structure memory-pointer variable as it changes inside the target structure as the commands in the command table are processed.

- The A1 register holds the current command-byte pointer variable as it changes from command to command in the command table.

The contents of the D0, D1, A0, and A1 registers are destroyed at the end of the InitStruct function execution.

Insert

Syntax of Function Call

Insert (list, node, listNode)
    A0 A1   A2

Purpose of Function

This function inserts a Node structure into a doubly-linked list *after* a given node position. You can insert a Node structure at the head of a list by using zero as the listNode argument.

Inputs to Function

list	A pointer to the List structure whose list will contain this node
node	A pointer to the Node structure whose node you want to insert
listNode	A pointer to the Node structure after which you want to insert this node

Discussion

Exec has a number of functions designed to operate on nodes and doubly-linked lists built from nodes. See the discussion of the AddHead function for a complete list of these functions.

Because an Exec list is a doubly-linked list, insertions and deletions can occur anywhere in the list without the need to scan the entire list. The new list is artomatically in correct order because of the double-linkage feature. Each list has a List structure that organizes the nodes in the list.

The Insert function is used for inserting a new Node structure into any position in a list. The function always inserts the Node structure following a specified predecessor Node structure.

Note that if the listNode argument points to the Node structure corresponding to the lh_Head parameter in the List structure, the new node will be inserted at the head of the list. In the same way, if the listNode argument points to the Node structure corresponding to the lh_Tail parameter in the List structure, the new node will be inserted at the tail of the list.

The Insert function does not use the priority parameter of the Node structure. For this reason, you cannot easily build a FIFO or LIFO list with the Insert function; use the Enqueue function for that purpose.

MakeLibrary

Syntax of Function Call

        library = MakeLibrary (funcInit, structInit, libInit, dataSize, segList)
        D0   A0   A1   A2   D0   D1

Purpose of Function

This function constructs a library vector and data area. Space for the library is allocated from the system free-memory pool. The size fields of the Library structure are filled with appropriate size data. The data portion of the library is initialized. A library-specific entry-point routine (INIT) is called if present.

The MakeLibrary function returns a pointer to the Library structure for this library. This is the pointer used in any further references to the library in the AddLibrary, Open-Library, CloseLibrary, and RemLibrary functions.

Inputs to Function

funcInit   This is a pointer to a table of library routine addresses. If the first word of the table is − 1, the array contains relative word displacements (based off of vectors); otherwise, the array contains absolute function pointers. If vectors are used, a six-byte vector is usually specified. However, if the library routines are close to the Library structure in RAM, four-byte and even two-byte vector displacements can be used.

structInit   This is a pointer to the InitStruct function data region. If this argument is null, the InitStruct function will not be called. The InitStruct function provides a way to initialize data in the library from a table of data stored elsewhere in memory. Read the InitStruct function description to see how this is done.

libInit   This is a pointer to the INIT routine that is called before adding the library to the system. If this argument is null, the INIT routine will not be called. When it is called, it will be called with the library pointer variable in D0. On return from INIT, D0 will still contain the library pointer variable.

dataSize   This is the size in bytes of the library data area. This includes the library's Library structure data as well as data for the library routines. See the discussion of the AddLibrary function for the Library structure definition.

segList   This is a pointer to an AmigaDOS memory segment list. It is used only for libraries loaded by AmigaDOS.

Discussion

There are seven Exec functions that deal with libraries in the Amiga system: AddLibrary, CloseLibrary, MakeLibrary, OpenLibrary, RemLibrary, SetFunction, and SumLibrary. There is more information on libraries in the discussions of each of these functions.

Libraries are identified by their names and version numbers. Libraries that are part of ROM or RAM are said to be *resident;* libraries that are on disk are said to be *transient.*

The MakeLibrary function call requires five arguments; four are pointer arguments.

The funcInit argument is a pointer to a table of six-, four- or two-byte library routine addresses. This argument must specify a valid table address. The vectors that begin at this location are used to jump to the various routines in the library. If these routines are close in memory to the Library structure itself, you can use the smaller four- and two-byte jump vectors, depending on the design of your library. As long as you are consistent between your library vectors and the actual location of your library routines, you can use the smaller vectors.

The strucInit variable points to the base of the InitStruct data region. This is the initTable pointer variable when the InitStruct function is called directly. The InitStruct function initializes various memory areas (actually creating structures in the process) from tables in other regions of memory. The strucInit variable points to the first item within a table that the InitStruct function can use to perform its initialization. Most often, the Init-Struct function will be used to initialize the data segments of the library. If strucInit is zero, the InitStruct function is not called; the library either has no data area or the data area is specified in some other way.

It is important to understand that the Task Control Block structures of the various tasks in the system (not part of a library definition), and the I/O Request Block structures (also not part of a library definition), are *not* initialized by the MakeLibrary function.

The libInit variable points to a routine (the library INIT routine) to be executed after the Library structure, together with the code and data areas, has been allocated and initialized. When this routine is called, the address of this library is placed into data register D0. If libInit is zero, the INIT routine is not executed; the library will not be initialized in the usual way.

The dataSize argument is used to fix the actual memory area used for the library routine data in the library. If you include any null entries in a funcInit vector table, MakeLibrary will generate a null (six bytes of zeroes) jump entry for this function. The jump vectors used in the library can be short jumps, long jumps, branches, and so on. The MakeLibrary function generates a consistent form of jump code to match the library routine jump vectors in the library; that is, the placement of the actual code for the library routines will be consistent with the assembly language instructions that represent the library routine vectors.

The dataSize variable specifies the size of the data area to be reserved for this library. The size includes the standard Library structure data and the library data area. Enough memory must be set aside for the system to make a library successfully. The total memory requirement in bytes of RAM is

$$(codeSize \times 1.5) + dataSize$$

To be precise, the library routines themselves are not a part of the library (only jump vectors to these routines) and therefore do not contribute to the library memory requirement calculation.

If enough memory is available, the MakeLibrary call will return a pointer to the Library structure. You can use this value as a pointer in future references to this library in the other library functions.

Memory for each part of the library (the Library structure, the library routine vectors, and library data itself) is automatically allocated from the system free-memory pool. If the library vector table requires more system memory than is available, the Make-Library function will cause a system crash. The only solution is to reboot the system.

The lib_Flags Variable

Part of the Library structure is the lib_Flags variable. There are several lib_Flags flag bits that you should know about.

If the LIBF_SUMMING flag is set, it indicates that a task is currently running a checksum on this library. A library checksum is initiated by calling the SumLibrary function. Tasks will do this from time to time to ensure that the libraries they access are properly initialized and the most up-to-date version. A checksum comparison indicates whether the library data has become corrupt or inconsistent for some reason.

If the LIBF_CHANGED flag is set, it indicates that one or more entries have been changed in the library code vectors. This flag is used by the SumLibrary function. Each time a library is changed, the SumLibrary function should be called to calculate a new checksum and store that value in the library for future consistency checks.

If the LIBF_SUMUSED flag is set, it tells the system that the designer of this library wants a checksum fault to cause a system panic—usually a crash. A checksum fault is any difference between the checksum value returned by a SumLibrary function call and the checksum value stored in the library itself. If you set the sum_Used bit and change your library without recalculating and restoring the checksum for your library, the Exec routines will detect this inconsistency and cause the system to crash. You can avoid this by always calling the SumLibrary function for any library that is updated in any way. See the discussion of the SumLibrary function for more on checksum calculations and updating.

ObtainSemaphore

Syntax of Function Call

> **ObtainSemaphore (signalSemaphore)**
> **A0**

Purpose of Function

This function allows the executing task to gain exclusive access to a SignalSemaphore structure. If another task currently has that SignalSemaphore structure locked, the Obtain-Semaphore call will cause the current task to go to sleep until the SignalSemaphore structure is available. ObtainSemaphore does not return a value.

Inputs to Function

signalSemaphore A pointer to a properly initialized SignalSemaphore structure

Discussion

There are seven functions in the 1.2 release that deal with signal semaphores and two functions that deal with the signal-semaphore list. These functions are listed in the Add-Semaphore discussion.

Signal semaphores can be obtained and released by calls to the ObtainSemaphore and ReleaseSemaphore functions. The current state (number of obtains and releases) of each SignalSemaphore structure is maintained in the ss_NestCount parameter in each Signal-Semaphore structure. ObtainSemaphore increases this parameter and ReleaseSemaphore decreases this parameter. When the counter returns to zero, the semaphore is finally released and the next waiting task can access that semaphore.

At any given time a number of tasks can be competing for access to each Signal-Semaphore structure. The system maintains a list of these tasks using the ss_WaitQueue parameter in the SignalSemaphore structure. Note that ss_WaitQueue is the name of a MinList substructure inside the SignalSemaphore structure. Each time the ss_NestCount parameter is reduced to zero for a specific task that currently has exclusive access to the SignalSemaphore structure, the system will use this list of waiting tasks to determine which task will gain access to the SignalSemaphore structure.

Note that signal semaphores are different from message-based semaphores. Signal semaphores require less CPU time, especially if the SignalSemaphore structure is not currently locked. Signal semaphores also require less setup—just a call to the InitSemaphore function—and programmer thought. On the other hand, the Procure and Vacate message-based semaphores are completely general and make no assumption on how they are used. However, they are not as efficient as signal semaphores and require the locking task to do some setup before making the function call.

The SemaphoreRequest Structure

The ObtainSemaphore function automatically allocates memory for a SemaphoreRequest structure. The definition of a SemaphoreRequest structure is as follows:

```
struct SemaphoreRequest {
    struct MinNode sr_Link;
    struct Task *sr_Waiter;
};
```

The sr_Link parameter is the name of a MinNode substructure within the Semaphore-Request structure. The MinNode structure is a shortened form of the Node structure; it is defined in the Exec Nodes.h INCLUDE file and is used to link each instance of the SemaphoreRequest structure into a linked list of SemaphoreRequest structures. The sr_Waiter parameter points to a Task structure. This is the Task structure that represents the task that has just requested and is now waiting for a particular signal semaphore.

ObtainSemaphoreList

Syntax of Function Call

ObtainSemaphoreList (list)
A0

Purpose of Function

This function attempts to simultaneously obtain (gain access to) all signal semaphores represented by a list of signal semaphores. Calling ObtainSemaphoreList is preferable to calling ObtainSemaphore for each semaphore on the list because ObtainSemaphoreList prevents deadlocks if another task attempts to obtain these SignalSemaphore structures in some other order.

Inputs to Function

list   This is a pointer to a List structure representing a list of signal semaphores. Signal semaphores in this list are linked together by the ss_Link Node substructure in the Signal-Semaphore structure.

Discussion

There are seven functions in the 1.2 release that deal with signal semaphores and two functions that deal with the signal-semaphore list. These functions are listed in the discussion of AddSemaphore.

ObtainSemaphoreList assumes that only one task will attempt to obtain the entire list of semaphores at any given time. Because you cannot always guarantee this condition, you should specify a higher level lock (perhaps another signal semaphore) to lock the signal-semaphore List structure before you call ObtainSemaphoreList. This higher-level semaphore can prevent another task from changing the signal-semaphore list before the ObtainSemaphoreList function finishes execution.

Note that deadlocks (two tasks mutually preventing each other's execution) may occur when you call ObtainSemaphoreList and another task attempts to use ObtainSemaphore to lock one of the semaphores on the list. If you wish to lock more than one semaphore (but not all of them), then you should also first obtain the higher level lock to lock the List structure that defines all the signal semaphores in the list.

OpenDevice

Syntax of Function Call

error = OpenDevice (devName, unitNumber, ioRequest, flags)
D0   A0   D0   A1   D1

Purpose of Function

This function opens the named device and initializes the specified I/O Request Block structure. OpenDevice returns a zero if it is successful; otherwise, an error number is returned.

Inputs to Function

devName	The name of the requested device
unitNumber	The unit number to open on that device. The format of the unit number is device specific. For instance, the floppy-disk drive controller can handle up to four disk drives, so the disk device has four units, numbered 0 to 3.
ioRequest	A pointer to the I/O Request Block stucture to be returned with appropriate fields initialized. The I/O Request Block structure is used for task-device communications to pass commands to a device and return messages, data, and other information from the device back to the task.
flags	A 32-bit flag variable containing additional device-specific information. This variable is sometimes used to request opening a device with exclusive access. The flags variable provides a way to control the detailed behavior of the task-device interaction.

Discussion

There are eight Exec functions that are directly concerned with device I/O: AddDevice, CloseDevice, OpenDevice, RemDevice, CheckIO, DoIO, SendIO, and WaitIO. Each of these functions performs a device service; read the discussions of each of these functions for more information on device I/O.

In the Amiga Exec system, devices are commanded (issued a command) to perform their operations. There is a standard set of commands that all devices in the system recognize, including the following:

- The Read command tells the device to perform a read operation. For example, the TrackDisk device can read information from one of the floppy-disk drives in the system.

- The Write command tells the device to perform a write operation. For example, the TrackDisk device can write information from an internal memory buffer to one of the floppy-disk drives in the system.

- The AbortIO command tells the device to terminate an ongoing I/O request. For example, it can tell a printer to stop printing a file.

- The Reset command tells the system to reinitialize a device. Usually, this occurs when the system is restarted, after either a power-up or crash condition. See the ColdReset function for more information about the reset operation. Any device registers and internal buffers are reset to their initial values.

- The Update command tells the system to write all known device-related buffers to the device. It is important to note that this command does not affect the status of the buffers associated with that device, empty the information from the buffers, nor clear the buffers. It merely copies the contents of each "dirty buffer" to the device. The term "dirty buffer" means a buffer that has not yet been written to the device. For instance, this command is useful in a program that deals with disk files. In the event of a power failure, all track buffers in RAM can be written to disk to avoid losing data.

- The Clear command tells the system to clear the buffers assigned to a device. Clearing means setting all bytes in the buffer to zero. Note that, in contrast to the Update command, these buffers are not first written to the device. When you close your files you should certainly use Update. If you want to clear the buffers assigned to a device, you can also issue a Clear command.

- The Start command tells the system to restart I/O following a Stop command. If I/O was suspended by the Stop command, the message queue for this device can still contain a number of pending I/O requests. Processing of requests will be restarted on a FIFO basis. If the I/O was terminated by the Flush command, it will be restarted with an empty device I/O message queue. In this case, if the affected tasks want to send or receive their formerly specified I/O information from this device, they will have to reissue their I/O requests and once again place them in the I/O queue of this device.

All of these commands are placed in the I/O Request Block structure of the device, specifically in the io_Command variable of that structure.

Device Names

Devices are identified by a name that is a null-terminated text string. When you specify a devName argument in your call to the OpenDevice function, Exec finds the corresponding device library for this name in the system. In this way, the system can manage your devices without affecting your device drive code.

If you want to change the specification of a device (by issuing a new MakeLibrary call for that device), you should use the same name in the new MakeLibrary call. Then, any program that uses that device name will still find a set of device driver routines in the device library under that device name; the name is still the same, only the driver code has changed. Some examples of device names are TD_NAME (for floppy-disk-drive—Track-Disk—driver routines) and AUDIONAME (for audio driver routines).

Here is a complete list of device names:

- Audio.device

- Clipboard.device

- Console.device

- Gameport.device

- Input.device

- Keyboard.device

- Narrator.device

- Parallel.device

- Printer.device

- Serial.device

- Timer.device

- TrackDisk.device

The I/O Request Block

The standard I/O Request Block structure for a device contains several variables. The io_Command variable specifies the specific command for this device. The commands are Read, Write, and so forth, as detailed above. In addition, the I/O Request Block structure contains a Message substructure named io_Message. This Message structure contains a number of useful parameters, as follows:

- The mn_ReplyPort variable is a pointer to the MsgPort structure for the reply port associated with the device and its I/O Request Block structure. The reply port is used to tell the calling task that the specific I/O request for that task has completed. This information reaches the I/O-dependent task as a message added to the reply port at this address. If the calling task was waiting for the data, it can now access that data (probably placed in some other memory buffer area by the device, but pointed to by the I/O Request Block structure) and proceed with its operations.

- The mn_Length variable specifies the size of the message you are passing. Note that this is the size of the message (not the expected returned length of data) passed to the device. As of this writing, it is acceptable to pass a message length of zero. Future system software upgrades might use this variable differently.

- The io_Length variable specifies how many bytes you want to transfer from the device to the task. For instance, if a task wants to read one sector of a disk track, io_Length will be 512 bytes. If the task wants to read a whole track, it will be 5632 bytes (11 tracks times 512 bytes per track).

- The io_Data variable is used for Read and Write commands. For a Read command, it specifies the buffer address to which the device data should be written. For a Write command, it specifies the buffer address from which this data should be read.

- The io_Offset variable specifies the byte offset into a block-structured device. This value must be an integer multiple of the block size. The block size for each device is specified in the INCLUDE file for that device. For example, the block size for the floppy-disk-drive device is 512 bytes; the offset is then an integer multiple of 512 (512, 1024, and so on).

Using OpenDevice

Device libraries fall into two classes: system and user. To use a device library in a program, you have to get its base address in memory. Once you have the address of the Device structure (identical to a Library structure) for the library that contains jump vectors to routines to service that device, you can reach these vectors indirectly. The OpenDevice call does this for you by placing the base address (the address of the Library structure) inside the I/O Request Block structure for that device. So, after the device is opened, the I/O Request Block structure contains the base address for that device. This base address is used along with the jump vectors in the library to access the device routines. If your user device library is on disk, the OpenDevice call will load it into RAM.

OpenLibrary

Syntax of Function Call

```
library = OpenLibrary (libName, version)
D0                      A1       D0
```

Purpose of Function

This function returns a pointer to a library that was previously installed using the Make-Library function. The specified library version must be greater than or equal to the requested version. If this is not true, the OpenLibrary function will fail, and a zero will be returned.

Inputs to Function

libName	The name of the library to open; this is the lib_IdString parameter in the Library structure
version	The version of the library required (zero in early releases of the Amiga Exec software); this is the lib_Version parameter in the Library structure

Discussion

There are seven Exec functions that deal with libraries in the Amiga system: AddLibrary, CloseLibrary, MakeLibrary, OpenLibrary, RemLibrary, SetFunction, and SumLibrary. There is additional information on libraries in the discussions of each of these functions.

You can keep a collection of different libraries on disk. When you execute the OpenLibrary function and specify a library by name in the libName variable, that library is loaded into memory. Libraries can contain all of your most often used routines. The version number is set in the version variable so that libraries of the same name will be compatible with previous versions of those same libraries having the same name but lower version numbers. If a library is not upwardly compatible with an earlier version of a closely related library, it should be assigned a different name to avoid a potential library-inconsistency problem that confuses the system and can cause a system crash. By changing the version number, you can have many closely related libraries to serve your programming needs.

There are several steps to constructing a library in the Amiga system:

1. You must create the library using the MakeLibrary function. MakeLibrary allocates memory space for the code vectors, the Library structure, and data areas in the library and initializes the Library structure and data areas. Note that the actual library routines are not a part of the library. These routines are located in RAM at locations determined by the code-vector offsets specified in the library.

2. You must add the library to the system library list with the AddLibrary function. Note that this function merely adds the library to the system library list; it does not actually open the library. If the library is on disk, it remains on disk.

3. You must open the library with the OpenLibrary function; OpenLibrary returns the address of the library in the library pointer variable. In some ways, this is equivalent to opening a file in a disk-based file system. This step prepares the library for access to its code vectors and data areas. If the library is on disk, it is now loaded into RAM.

4. You must access the library code vectors and data areas. To do this, you use offsets from the library value returned by the call to the OpenLibrary function. These offsets are positive (in higher memory locations) for the data areas and negative (in lower memory locations) for the library routine vectors. You know what these offsets are because they were set when you designed and initialized the library with the MakeLibrary function call.

One of the advantages of Exec libraries is the freedom they give you to define the placement of code and data areas in memory. With this type of library interface, you can call any of the system library routines without knowing in advance what absolute location it occupies in the memory system of the machine. Because of this arrangement, there are no hard-coded addresses in the Amiga system. You need to know only one fixed address to get going. All other addresses can be related to this address by the library definitions, library linkages, and Library structures.

There are a number of libraries that are a part of the system library group. In early releases, these were brought into memory from the Kickstart and Workbench disks. Eventually, some of them will become part of the Amiga ROM code. These are the system libraries:

Library Name	Library Base Address Variable	Description
exec.library	SysBase	The system Exec function library
graphics.library	GfxBase	The Graphics function library
intuition.library	IntuitionBase	The Intuition function library
dos.library	DosBase	The DOS function library
layers.library	LayersBase	The Layers (graphic layers) function library
clist.library	CListBase	The Character list function library
math.library	MathBase	The Math function library
potgo.library	PotgoBase	The Potgo function library
diskfont.library	DiskfontBase	The DiskFont function library
mathtrans.library	MathtransBase	The Math Transcendental function library
translator.library	TranslatorBase	The Translator function library

To utilize these system libraries, you must declare a variable having the name of the library-base address. Here are examples of program statements that accomplish this for some of the system libraries:

```
LONG SysBase
LONG GfxBase
```

LONG IntuitionBase
LONG DosBase
LONG LayersBase
LONG CListBase
LONG MathBase
LONG PotgoBase

In your program, you open a library to get its base address as follows, using the graphics library as an example:

GfxBase = OpenLibrary ("graphics.library", 0)
if (GfxBase == 0)
exit (NO_GRAPHICS_LIBRARY_FOUND)

The base address returned by the OpenLibrary call is used together with the library vectors to reach routines in the library. A set of assembly language interface routines is used to link your routines with the rest of the system software automatically.

There are several things you can do to make your library calls more efficient. Use the 68000 LEA (load effective address) instruction to cache (bring into and keep in a 68000 register at all times) various pointers connected with the library. First of all, you can cache the library variable itself. Remember that library points to the Library structure. The Library structure, the fulcrum point of the library, cannot move while the library is open. Therefore, it is OK to bring it into register memory for all references as long as that library remains open.

You can also cache the address of each jump vector in the library. These values will also remain constant as long as the library remains open. You cannot, however, cache the values of the jump vectors themselves. They do not necessarily remain constant while the library is open; the SetFunction function can change these values at any time.

OpenResource

Syntax of Function Call

resource = OpenResource (resName)
D0   A1

Purpose of Function

This function opens a previously installed resource and returns a pointer to the Resource structure associated with that resource. If the function is unsuccessful, it returns a zero.

Inputs to Function

resName   The name of the requested resource; there are usually two equivalent names for each resource

Discussion

There are four Exec functions that are directly concerned with resources in the Amiga system: AddResource, CloseResource, OpenResource, and RemResource. Each of these functions performs a resource service. Note that there is no CloseResource function. There is more information on resources in the discussions of each of these calls.

The OpenResource function opens resources in the same way that the OpenDevice function opens devices. Resource names follow the same rules as device names.

At the present time (version 1.2 software), there are five resources in the Amiga system. They have the following names:

DISKNAME	or	disk.resource
MISCNAME	or	misc.resource
CIAANAME	or	ciaa.resource
CIABNAME	or	ciab.resource
POTGONAME	or	potgo.resource

The structures related to these resources are contained in the Disc.h, Misc.h, Cia.h, and Potgo.h INCLUDE files.

Procure

Syntax of Function Call

```
result  =  Procure (semaphore, message)
DO                     A0         A1
```

Purpose of Function

This function is used to obtain a message-based semaphore. If the semaphore is immediately available, Procure returns a TRUE value and the message pointer argument is not used. If the semaphore is already being used, Procure returns a FALSE value. In this case, the current calling task must wait for the message freeing that semaphore to arrive at its reply port.

Inputs to Function

semaphore   A pointer to a Semaphore structure

message   A pointer to a Message structure defining a request to use (bid for) this semaphore

Discussion

The 1.2 release provides two new functions to deal with message-based semaphores: Procure and Vacate. You can use two types of semaphores in the Amiga multitasking system. The first type is the signal semaphores. These are defined and managed by the SignalSemaphore and SemaphoreRequest structures. They are discussed under the nine functions that deal with signal semaphores.

The second type is the message-based semaphores that use the Semaphore structure. The Exec system provides the Procure and Vacate functions to define and manage this type of semaphore.

A Semaphore structure contains a MsgPort substructure and one other parameter as follows:

```
struct Semaphore {
    struct MsgPort sm_MsgPort;
    WORD sm_Bids;
};
```

The sm_MsgPort parameter is the name of the MsgPort substructure that will receive semaphore-related reply messages belonging to the message-based semaphore defined by this Semaphore structure. The sm_Bids parameter is a count of the number of messages currently queued in this message port.

Just as you can protect RAM data with Forbid–Permit and ObtainSemaphore–ReleaseSemaphore, you can also use the Procure–Vacate combinaton to accomplish the same thing. As with signal semaphores, message-based semaphores do not unduly restrict task-switching. In addition, message-based semaphores provide one other advantage over signal semaphores: message-based semaphores can be queued. Therefore, any given task can wait on more than one message-based semaphore at a time by examining the task reply port where the messsages related to message-based semaphores are queued.

It is important to note that the MsgPort substructure in the Semaphore structure should be initialized with the mp_Flags parameter set to PA_IGNORE. Also note that the system interprets the mp_SigTask parameter as a pointer to the current locking Message structure (not a pointer to a Task structure, as is usually the case).

Finally, note that new Semaphore structures must have the sm_Bids parameter initialized to −1. If you want to make the Semaphore structure public, also initialize the ln_Name and ln_Pri parameters of the Node substructure of the MsgPort substructure and add the message port to the system message-port list with the AddPort function.

PutMsg

Syntax of Function Call

PutMsg (msgPort, message)
       A0   A1

Purpose of Function

This function adds a message to a given message-port queue. It provides a fast, noncopy-ing, message-sending mechanism. The message body can be of any size or form. Because messages are not copied, cooperating tasks share the same message memory. The sender task should not recycle the message (use that Message structure again) until the receiver has replied to it. Of course, this depends on the message-handling conventions set up by the involved tasks. If the mn_ReplyPort parameter in the Message structure is nonzero when the reciever replies to the message, the message is sent back to the original message port for possible reuse by other tasks.

If all goes well, the message will be added to the bottom of the message-port message queue and processed when it gets to the top. The GetMsg function will dequeue it when it reaches the top of the message-port queue.

Inputs to Function

msgPort	A pointer to a MsgPort stucture
message	A pointer to a Message structure in that message-port message queue

Discussion

There are three Exec functions that are explicitly concerned with messages in the Amiga system: PutMsg, GetMsg, and ReplyMsg. These functions manage the messages coming to and going from the message ports assigned to each task in the Amiga multitasking sys-tem. Because messages use message ports, it is also important to keep in mind the role of the message-port management functions: AddPort, FindPort, RemPort, and WaitPort. See the discussions of these functions for more information on their purpose and role.

Any one of the following actions can be set to occur when a message is placed into a message-port queue by the PutMsg function and later removed by the GetMsg function:

■ The message can indicate that no special action should be taken. Set the MsgPort mp_Flags parameter to PA_IGNORE.

■ The message can signal a given task. Set the MsgPort mp_Flags parameter to PA_SIGNAL.

■ It can cause a software interrupt. Usually this is used to change the currently active task. Set the MsgPort mp_Flags parameter to PA_SOFTINT.

Message Signals

Processing of messages arriving at one of the message ports of a task can induce task signals. When the receiving task processes this message, it can look at these signals to define certain actions that this task should take when the information in that message is processed and understood. The Task Control Block structure contains a mask variable (tc_SigExcept) that defines which signal bits of a message will cause exception routine execution when that message is processed and that signal is recognized as present in the message.

The Task Control Block structure also contains the tc_SigRecvd variable. This variable keeps track of the signals that each task has received.

The Message Port

PutMsg places messages in a FIFO queue in the message port of a given task. Any given task can have more than one message port assigned to it. The number of public message ports belonging to a task is controlled by the AddPort function; each AddPort function call adds another public message port to a task. In addition, a task can have a number of private message ports. When a message arrives at a message port of a task, that task is eventually notified of its arrival. Therefore, each task can be dealing with a lot of information coming into its message ports. This information is waiting to be processed by that task.

Two things have to happen before a task can get to a message: first, the task must become the active task, and second, that message must come to the top of that particular message-port queue. No task can process messages until it has become active and gains control of the machine. Task switching occurs according to the current priorities of all tasks in the system.

If all tasks have equal priority, the memory cycles of the 68000 CPU will be time-sliced (currently each receives 64 milliseconds of time), giving equal time to all tasks. Each task will then have this amount of time to process the messages in each of its message-port queues. If the queue is deep, a given message may not reach the top of the queue in this time span; it will have to wait for the next time-slice to try to reach that message.

Managing the Message-Port Queue

The order of messages in the message-port queue is kept in a message list for that message port. This is maintained by the mp_MsgList List substructure in the MsgPort structure. Depending on the complexity of the programming situation, a number of messages can pile up in these message ports. The Exec system routines manage the bookkeeping operations required for task-message queuing and processing, which can be a considerable job when there are a number of tasks in the system.

Sometimes you will want a task to wait for a particular signal to arrive. This signal will be coming as part of a message from another task or perhaps a device in the system. Any message that arrives at a message port whose MsgPort structure has its mp_SigBit parameter set to this signal bit number will eventually transmit this signal to the task. The WaitPort function is used to set up this situation. The WaitPort function instructs the system to keep looking for any message (and its associated signal) to arrive at this message port. The message port of the task must be initially empty for this function to operate. The WaitPort function returns immediately after any message arrives.

RawDoFormat

Syntax of Function Call

RawDoFormat (formatString, dataStream, putCharFunction, putCharData)
             A0   A1   A2   A3

Purpose of Function

This function performs a C language style formatting of a data stream. The result is output one character at a time to a programmer defined buffer.

Inputs to Function

formatString	A pointer to a C language format string, which is represented as a null-terminated character string
dataStream	A pointer to a buffer containing an unformatted stream of data, which will be processed (reformatted) according to the above format string
putCharFunction	A pointer to a data stream formatting function designated as PutCharFunction
putCharData	A pointer to a RAM location that will contain the data stream after it is formatted

Discussion

Often times you may have a data stream consisting of unformatted data. Your program may need to work with this data stream in formatted form. This is the purpose of the

RawDoFormat function. It takes an unformatted data stream and turns it into a formatted data stream.

The RawDoFormat function requires four pointers. The first pointer, formatString, defines the formatting you want to impose on the data stream; you are free to define this format string according to your needs and purposes using the usual rules for C language format strings.

The second pointer, dataStream, points to a buffer containing the data stream itself. The characters in the data stream can originate from any source; in fact, they can originate from any of the Amiga devices.

The third pointer, putCharFunction, points to a user-defined PutCharFunction function that will process the data stream according to the format string you specified. PutCharFunction is called for every character output by the RawDoFormat function; that is, for every character in the original data stream. You are free to design this function to suit your needs and purposes.

The fourth pointer, putCharData, points to a destination buffer; this argument is passed to the user-defined PutCharFunction function.

The RawDoFormat function can be illustrated by an example. Suppose you have a data stream you want to format according to the following format string:

"%dth character: %c/hex: %2x"

You can place this format string definition in RAM at a labeled location. This label then provides a pointer to the format string; this location defines the first argument in the function call.

A pointer to the data stream buffer is known by the design of your program. For example, you may have read in a series of bytes from the serial device and now you want to format that data stream. The dataStream pointer would then point to the task-defined data buffer assigned to the serial device.

You would design a PutCharFunction function to process the data stream according to the format string. The entry point for this function would be set by your function definition. You would use this entry point as the third argument in the RawDoFormat function call.

You are free to pick the pointer to the destination buffer. This pointer argument will then be passed through the RawDoFormat function to the PutCharFunction function. When both the PutCharFunction and RawDoFormat functions return, you can look at this location for the formatted version of the data stream.

The PutCharFunction function is called as follows:

PutCharFunction (character, putCharData)
D0: 0–8 A3

Here, character is a pointer to the current character being processed by the PutCharFunction function and putCharData is the pointer value (fourth argument) passed by the Raw-DoFormat function.

ReleaseSemaphore

Syntax of Function Call

ReleaseSemaphore (signalSemaphore)
A0

Purpose of Function

This function is the inverse of the ObtainSemaphore function. It makes the semaphore obtainable by other tasks in the system. These tasks can then gain access to this particular SignalSemaphore structure. If any tasks are waiting for the semaphore (in the ss_Wait-Queue list) and this task is finished with the semaphore (ss_NestCount = 0), then the next waiting task is signaled. The next waiting task is the first task in the wait queue maintained by the ss_WaitQueue MinList structure.

Inputs to Function

signalSemaphore A pointer to a properly initialized SignalSemaphore structure

Discussion

There are seven functions in the 1.2 release that deal with signal semaphores and two functions that deal with the signal-semaphore list. These functions are listed in the discussion of AddSemaphore.

Each ObtainSemaphore call must be eventually balanced by a corresponding call to the ReleaseSemaphore function. This is true of all tasks that use each signal semaphore. The nesting counter (ss_NestCount) parameter in the SignalSemaphore structure maintains a running total of the number of obtains and releases made by the current task.

The SignalSemaphore structure is not released to other tasks until the ss_NestCount parameter is reduced to zero for the current task. Needless to say, the system will probably crash if the number of releases exceeds the number of obtains for any Signal-Semaphore structure.

It is important to note the difference between the purpose of the AddSemaphore and RemSemaphore function pair and the ObtainSemaphore and ReleaseSemaphore function pair. AddSemaphore and RemSemaphore affect the signal-semaphore list whereas Obtain-Semaphore and ReleaseSemaphore affect the ss_NestCount parameter in the Signal-Semaphore structure. What we see here is the difference between adding versus obtaining (locking a structure) and removing versus releasing (unlocking a structure). This is an important difference to keep in mind.

ReleaseSemaphoreList

Syntax of Function Call

ReleaseSemaphoreList (list)
A0

Purpose of Function

This function is the inverse of the ObtainSemaphoreList function. ReleaseSemaphoreList releases each SignalSemaphore structure in the signal-semaphore list. The system will crash if any task (or all tasks taken together) tries to release more semaphores than it has obtained.

Inputs to Function

list   A pointer to a List structure representing a list of signal semaphores; this list is updated by the ss_Link parameter in the SignalSemaphore structure every time a signal semaphore is added to the list

Discussion

There are seven functions in the 1.2 release that deal with signal semaphores and two functions that deal with the signal-semaphore list. These functions are listed in the Add-Semaphore discussion.

Just like ObtainSemaphoreList, ReleaseSemaphoreList is a convenience to the programmer. If you have obtained a number of signal semaphores that have been placed on a list, ReleaseSemaphoreList will release all of them for you. Note that you did not have to use ObtainSemaphoreList to create the list; some of them could have been created using AttemptSemaphore or ObtainSemaphore directly.

RemDevice

Syntax of Function Call

error = RemDevice (device)
D0   **A1**

Purpose of Function

This function removes an existing device from the system device list. Once the device is removed, it cannot be opened unless it is once again added to the system with the Add-Device function. The function returns a zero if it is successful; otherwise, it returns an error number.

Inputs to Function

device   A pointer to a Device structure.

Discussion

There are eight Exec functions that are directly concerned with device I/O: AddDevice, CloseDevice, OpenDevice, RemDevice, CheckIO, DoIO, SendIO, and WaitIO. Each of these functions performs a device service. Read the discussions of each of these calls for more information on device I/O. A Device structure is identical to a Library structure. See the AddLibrary function.

RemHead

Syntax of Function Call

```
node = RemHead (list)
D0              A0
```

Purpose of Function

This function gets a pointer to a head Node structure and removes it from a list. The RemHead function returns a pointer to the removed Node structure. If the list is an empty list, RemHead returns a zero value.

Inputs to Function

list   A pointer to the target List structure

Discussion

Exec has a number of functions designed to operate on nodes and doubly-linked lists built from nodes. There is a complete list in the discussion of the AddHead function.

The RemHead and RemTail functions are used in combination with AddHead and AddTail to create special list ordering. When you combine AddTail and RemHead, you produce a FIFO list; AddTail adds a node to the bottom of a list and RemHead removes the first node from the list (FIFO). When you combine AddHead and RemHead, you produce a LIFO list which is equivalent to a memory stack structure; AddHead adds a node to the top of a list and RemHead removes the first node in a list (LIFO). You can also use these functions in other combinations to manage your lists. For example, combining AddTail and RemTail also produces a LIFO list, but in this case you are working with the bottom of the list.

RemIntServer

Syntax of Function Call

RemIntServer (intNumber, interrupt)
D0: 0–4   A1

Purpose of Function

This function removes an interrupt server node from the given server chain. Only the resources tied to the maintenance of the interrupt server list will be freed. The interrupt server will still be in memory as part of a set of library routines.

Inputs to Function

intNumber   The Paula (peripherals-sound 4703 custom chip) interrupt bit (0–14)

interrupt   A pointer to an Interrupt structure that contains an entry point for an interrupt server routine belonging to this interrupt bit

Discussion

The interrupt system uses the 68000 registers in the following way:

1. On entry to an interrupt server, the Exec routines automatically save the A0, A1, A4, A5, A6, D0, and D1 registers.

2. Inside your interrupt code, you can treat A0, A1, A5, D0, and D1 as scratch registers.

3. The A4 and A6 registers can be considered special system registers. Following Exec system routine conventions, use register A4 to point to functions you want to call. Then use register A6 to point to the Library structure of any system library you want to use during the execution of your interrupt routine. This library has the interrupt routine stored as one of its library routines.

4. Any of the other registers *must* be restored to their original contents before you execute your interrupt server or handler. If not, system operation is unpredictable.

5. After you leave the interrupt handler or server you can copy to the system stack any registers that you need.

RemLibrary

Syntax of Function Call

error = RemLibrary (library)
D0   A1

Purpose of Function

This function removes an existing library from the system. It deletes it from the system library list, so the library cannot be used again until it is again added with the AddLibrary function call. If the function is successful a zero is returned; otherwise, an error number is returned.

Inputs to Function

library   A pointer to a Library structure, previously returned by an OpenLibrary function call

Discussion

There are seven Exec functions that deal with libraries in the Amiga system: AddLibrary, CloseLibrary, MakeLibrary, OpenLibrary, RemLibrary, SetFunction, and SumLibrary. Libraries are identified by their names and version numbers. There is more information on libraries in the discussions of each of these functions.

The Exec system automatically maintains a system library list. Each time you add a library with the AddLibrary function, this list is updated to reflect the addition of this new library. In the same way, each time you remove a library from the system with the RemLibrary function, this list is updated to reflect one less library in the system. The system library list acts as a directory of libraries.

The only argument to the RemLibrary function is the library argument, a pointer to the Library structure of this library. Note that the AddLibrary function also has only one argument and that argument is also the Library structure pointer variable. This pointer is the same one returned from the original call to the OpenLibrary function.

If you remove a library from the system library list, you can later restore it to that list with another call to the AddLibrary function. You can optimize your library memory usage by adding and removing libraries from the system library list as the needs of your programs dictate.

Remember, however, that it is the CloseLibrary call that removes a library from the system memory; the RemLibrary call merely removes the library from the system library list. You will gain some, but not much, memory from a call to the RemLibrary function.

Remove

Syntax of Function Call

Remove (node)
A1

Purpose of Function

This function removes a Node structure from a doubly-linked list. A Node structure is a data structure that holds all linkage information about a node in a list. All system structures begin with a Node structure. If the Node structure cannot be found in any list in the system, an error condition will result.

Inputs to Function

node	A pointer to the Node structure whose node you want to remove

Discussion

Exec has a number of functions designed to operate on nodes and doubly-linked lists built from nodes. See the discussion of the AddHead call for a complete list of these functions.

Note that there is no List structure pointer argument for the Remove function. Whatever list the node belongs to will have that node removed. Recall that each list is of a specific type according to the lh_Type parameter of the List structure. Therefore, to find a node in a specific list, that node must also be of the type; that is, have the same ln_Type parameter in the Node structure. Node types are defined under the AddHead function. Exec will find the appropriate list and remove your specified node from it. You should always make sure that the node you are specifying is part of a list currently in the system.

RemPort

Syntax of Function Call

RemPort (msgPort)
A1

Purpose of Function

This function removes a public message port from the system message-port list. Subsequent attempts to rendezvous by name with this message port will fail. If the message port cannot be found in the system message-port list, an error condition will result. The message port must have been previously added to the system message-port list with the AddPort function.

Inputs to Function

msgPort	A pointer to a MsgPort structure

Discussion

There are four Exec routines that are explicitly concerned with ports in the Amiga system: AddPort, FindPort, RemPort, and WaitPort. AddPort, FindPort, and RemPort all deal exclusively with public ports. These are ports that are added to the system message-port list with the AddPort function. WaitPort deals with both public and private ports. These routines manage the message ports where messages are passed between cooperating tasks in the Amiga multitasking system. Three message management routines (PutMsg, GetMsg, and ReplyMsg) manage the messages that are queued in these message ports.

All tasks in the system are allowed to have their own set of message ports. These are task-private ports. In addition, all tasks in the system can use the public message ports. These are ports assigned to each task by the AddPort function. A task can have any number of public ports. Each public port is added to achieve a specific objective; some ports reach out to other tasks or devices in the system to pass information and signals that are vital to the operation of that task or device.

As the system message-port list gets longer and longer, the number of message ports can become too large for the system to manage and too demanding on your own programming bookkeeping procedures. This is the time to consider removing some of these ports. If nothing else, this may help you keep track of what is going on in the system. In addition, it can free up other system resources, such as memory, for more pressing uses. You can use the RemPort function to remove public message ports; you cannot use this function to remove private message ports.

To use the RemPort function, you need the pointer to the MsgPort structure. You can use the FindPort function to get this pointer if you know the name of the port. The name of the port is the one argument you need for the FindPort function; it is the ln_Name parameter in the Node substructure for the MsgPort structure for that message port. You initialized the name parameter before you called the AddPort function. You will always know the name if the port is public.

When you use the RemPort function, you are removing the message port from only one task—the task with the RemPort call. When RemPort executes, the system message-port list is updated to reflect one less message port assigned to that task. The associated resources (memory in particular) will be deallocated (freed) for other uses.

RemResource

Syntax of Function Call

RemResource (resource)
A1

Purpose of Function

This function removes an existing resource from the system resource list. No new opens for this resource can occur until it is once again added to the system with the Add-Resource function.

Inputs to Function

resource   A pointer to a properly initialized Resource structure, previously returned by the OpenResource function

Discussion

There are three Exec functions that are directly concerned with resources: AddResource, OpenResource, and RemResource. Each of these functions performs a resource service. Note that there is no CloseResource function. There is more information on resources in the discussions of each of these functions. A Resource structure is formally identical to a Library structure. See the AddLibrary function.

RemSemaphore

Syntax of Function Call

RemSemaphore (signalSemaphore)
A1

Purpose of Function

This function removes a signal semaphore from the system signal-semaphore list. Subsequent attempts to rendezvous (gain access to a named SignalSemaphore structure) with this semaphore by name will fail.

Inputs to Function

signalSemaphore A pointer to a properly initialized SignalSemaphore structure

Discussion

There are seven functions in the 1.2 release that deal with signal semaphores and two functions that deal with the signal-semaphore list. These functions are listed in the discussion of AddSemaphore.

Signal semaphores are maintained on a signal-semaphore list by the system. Each time the AddSemaphore function executes, this list is updated to reflect the addition of another named signal semaphore to the list. Each time RemSemaphore executes, the signal-semaphore list is updated to reflect one less named semaphore.

The signal-semaphore list is maintained using the ss_Link Node substructure in the SignalSemaphore structure. This Node substructure provides the mechanism to place and link new SignalSemaphore structures on the signal-semaphore list.

RemTail

Syntax of Function Call

```
node = RemTail (list)
D0              A0
```

Purpose of Function

This function returns a pointer to the Node structure corresponding to the tail node of a list and removes the tail node from the node list. If the list is empty, a zero is returned.

Inputs to Function

list   A pointer to the List structure whose tail node you want removed

Discussion

Exec has a number of functions designed to operate on nodes and doubly-linked lists built from nodes. See the discussion of the AddHead entry for a complete list of these functions.

The RemHead and RemTail functions are used in combination with AddHead and AddTail to create special list ordering. When you combine AddTail and RemHead, you produce a FIFO list; AddTail adds a node to the bottom of a list and RemHead removes the first node from the list. When you combine AddHead and RemHead, you produce a LIFO list (which is equivalent to a memory stack structure); AddHead adds a node to the top of a list and RemHead removes the first node in a list. You can also use these functions in other combinations to manage your lists as necessary. For example, combining AddTail and RemTail also produces a LIFO list, but in this case you are working with the bottom of the list.

RemTask

Syntax of Function Call

> RemTask (taskCB)
> A1

Purpose of Function

This function removes a task from the system task-ready queue list. Memory resources should be deallocated before this function is called. This function frees other resources, which can then be assigned to other tasks in the system. If a pointer to the Task Control Block structure of the task cannot be found in any task list in the system, an error condition will result.

Inputs to Function

taskCB   A pointer to the Task Control Block structure representing the task to be removed. A zero value indicates task self-removal: this task takes itself out of the system, causing the next ready task to begin execution.

Discussion

There are four Exec routines that specifically relate to task handling: AddTask, FindTask, RemTask, and SetTaskPri. There is more information on task handling in the discussions of each of these functions.

The data structure that defines a Task Control Block structure appears in the Exec INCLUDE files; these are called Tasks.h (for the C language interface) and Tasks.i (for the assembly language interface).

Preventing a Task from Running

There are two methods of preventing a task from running at any particular time. First, you can assign the task a low enough priority so that higher priority tasks will always have use of the CPU. You do this by calling the SetTaskPri function or directly changing the ln_Pri parameter of the Node substructure inside the Task Control Block structure. At any given time, only the highest priority task will run. If your task has a low priority, it must wait until higher priority tasks go to sleep to gain access to the CPU. These other tasks can go to sleep for a variety of reasons. For example, if a task requires a system resource that is not presently available, it will go to sleep. If your task has the next highest priority, it can now take over the system.

Second, you can use the Forbid and Permit private system routines. These routines are usually used only in the system software itself. If you surround critical code sections in your task routines with these two statements, you can forbid and later permit task-switching into and out of your code segment. You should also use these two commands when a task is modifying data structures that are also accessible to other tasks. You do not want any task to try to access memory data while the data is changing.

As a task is running, you can specify that certain conditions will cause exception routines to begin execution. However, sometimes your routines will not need to process exceptions; in that case, you will not need any exception routines and you should set the tc_ExceptCode and tc_ExceptData variables to zero.

Each task has 32 task signal bits and 32 task exception bits assigned to it. If any bit in the tc_SigExcept variable is set to 1, the associated exception code will begin executing. Usually, you initialize the exception code and data variables before you add a task to the system. This is done in your definition of the Task Control Block structure for that task. Alternatively, you can initialize the signal and exception bits of your code after it begins executing.

ReplyMsg

Syntax of Function Call

ReplyMsg (message)
A1

Purpose of Function

This function sends a message to a task's reply port. ReplyMsg is usually called when the receiver task has finished with a message and wants to return it to the sender task, so that the message can be reused, deallocated, or whatever. If the message pointer is incorrectly specified and the Message structure cannot be found at that memory location, an error condition will result.

Inputs to Function

message   A pointer to a Message structure, originally placed by the PutMsg function and later retrieved from the message-port queue with the GetMsg function

Discussion

There are three Exec routines explicitly concerned with messages in the Amiga system: PutMsg, GetMsg, and ReplyMsg. These routines manage the messages coming and going from the message ports assigned to each task in the Amiga multitasking system. Because messages use message ports, it is also important to keep in mind the role of the message-port management routines. These routines are AddPort, FindPort, ReplyPort, and Wait-Port. See the discussion of these routines for more information on their purpose and role.

Messages can be passed between message ports in one task or between message ports belonging to different tasks. In the first case, the sender and receiver tasks are identical. In the second case, the sender and receiver tasks are distinct.

Each task has a reply port in addition to its message port. The purpose of the reply port is to tell the sender task that the message has been received and processed by the receiver task. It is important that the sender task know this. Then, once the sender task regains control (remember, only one task is active at a time), it will have received notification from at least one receiver task that a message has been processed.

The reply port message itself can contain information vital to the continued execution of the sender task. In fact, the sender task may have to wait for the receiver task to send back information through one of its reply ports. If you consider all the tasks in the system, all the message ports assigned to these tasks, and all the reply ports associated with these message ports, you can begin to see how complex task interaction can become.

The Exec routines enable you to manage the various steps in these complex procedures. Note that the sender task cannot reuse (send and assign to another task) a message until the receiver task has replied to it. Therefore, individual messages are truly connected between two intertwined tasks. Once the reply port receives a message, the sender can send this same message to other tasks. The same process of waiting for a reply is required before this message can be sent a third time, and so on.

The need for a reply port to reply before the same message can be sent a second time is not a limitation, because a sender task can send duplicates of the same message to a number of receiver tasks. These messages use different Message structures. Therefore, they appear as distinct messages in the system.

Each message in the system has a sender and a receiver task associated with it. The sender uses the PutMsg function to send a message to a receiving task. Note that the PutMsg function is called from within a task when that task is active. This task is then the sender task. As it executes, it can send a lot of messages to various other tasks in the system. These messages are queued into the respective destination message-port queues of the receiver tasks.

At some point, the active task will change. This can occur because of a reassignment of priorities, the appearance of a new task with higher priority in the system, or the current task finishing its work. When that happens, control passes to another task in the system. This task may be one of the receiver tasks of the first task. If it is, it will have messages queued in one or more of its message ports. Now it will process these messages on a FIFO basis.

Once a message is processed by the receiver task, it is dequeued (taken out of the queue of its message port). The message list for that message port is then updated to reflect this change.

Each message can induce a task signal when it is processed. The receiver task looks for and processes these signal bits. The important bits depend on the receiver task's signal-mask arrangements previously set up in its Task Control Block structure. The receiver task can sense and act on only the actual signals associated with the message port where the message is queued and processed. As the receiver task processes these queued messages, it will examine the message signal bits and act accordingly.

SendIO

Syntax of Function Call

SendIO (ioRequest)
A1

Purpose of Function

This function requests the device driver to initiate the command specified in the given I/O Request Block structure. If the I/O Request Block structure is properly designed, the device will process the I/O request and then return to the calling task. The device will return control to the requesting task regardless of whether the I/O has completed.

Inputs to Function

ioRequest   A pointer to a properly initialized I/O Request Block structure

Discussion

There are eight Exec functions that are directly concerned with device I/O: AddDevice, CloseDevice, OpenDevice, RemDevice, CheckIO, DoIO, SendIO, and WaitIO. Each of these functions performs a device service. There is additional information on device I/O in the discussions of each of these functions.

In general, the device calls in your programs fall into two classes. The first class includes calls to devices to or from which you must have immediate information to continue with the execution of your program (or subtask of the program). You know what those device calls are by the design, data flow, and data needs of your program. All calls in this class should use the DoIO function. DoIO makes the device call and waits for completion of the device-task data exchange; it is called a synchronous device call.

The second class includes calls to devices where your program is not dependent (at least for a while) on the information going to or coming from that device. All calls in this class should use the SendIO function. SendIO makes the call and does not wait for completion of the device-task data exchange; it is termed an asynchronous device call.

DoIO and SendIO are the two functions usually used to transmit an I/O request to a device. In addition to these two functions, there are two system routines that are direct entries into the device driver routines stored in your device library. These are the BeginIO and AbortIO routines. These routines provide the quickest method to begin and abort an I/O transfer. The BeginIO routine is especially useful when you want to do Quick I/O.

Quick I/O gives an I/O request a higher priority and effectively jumps it to the front of the task queue (if other circumstances permit this to happen). You specify Quick I/O by setting the IOF_QUICK flag in the io_Flags parameter of the I/O Request block structure. The advantage of Quick I/O is that your task's I/O request will be replied to immediately and can then continue its execution, no matter how many I/O requests are in the device I/O request queue. It is up to the system to decide whether Quick I/O is possible; if not, your I/O request will be queued and the equivalent of a SendIO call will be performed, returning immediately to the task without completing the requested I/O.

Using Quick I/O presents some problems in the I/O request completion-detection mechanism. If the Quick I/O works, the reply message is returned to the reply message area of the I/O Request Block structure before the task itself returns from the BeginIO call—Quick I/O can be very quick indeed.

If the Quick I/O didn't take place as intended, the I/O request may still be pending in the queue of the device. In this case, when your program reaches a certain convenient logical location, you can call CheckIO to determine whether that I/O request has completed. CheckIO merely looks for a message in the reply message area of that I/O Request Block structure in the message's reply port. If it finds a message, it will know that the I/O request was satisfied, even though it may not have been a Quick I/O as originally intended.

SetExcept

Syntax of Function Call

oldSignals = SetExcept (newSignals, signalMask)
D0   D0   D1

Purpose of Function

This function defines which of the task's 32 signal bits will cause exceptions. This changes the value of the tc_SigExcept parameter in the Task Control Block structure. When any of these signals occur, the task exception handler associated with that signal is dispatched. If the signal occurred prior to calling the SetExcept function, it is stored in the tc_SigRecvd variable of the Task Control Block structure. In this case, the exception routine begins execution as soon as that task becomes active. The function returns the prior exception signals in oldSignals.

Inputs to Function

newSignals	A 32-bit variable whose individual bits specify new values for the signals in the signalMask variable
signalMask	A 32-bit mask for the set of signals to be affected

Discussion

Exceptions fall into two categories: 68000 exceptions, which execute in supervisor mode, and task-private exceptions, which execute in user mode. 68000 exceptions are grouped into three categories:

1. Reset, address error, bus error

2. Trace, interrupt, illegal instruction, processor privilege violation

3. TRAP, TRAPV, and CHK instructions, together with the zero divide condition

A privilege violation is an attempt to execute a supervisor mode instruction while in user mode. A trap is a user mode instruction that allows you to jump to 16 memory addresses (it has 16 jump vectors) where trap routines are stored. The routines stored at these addresses should be short to allow quick processing and return from the exception routine to a task.

This discussion covers the 68000 microprocessor exceptions. Exception processing on the 68000 occurs in supervisor mode in four steps:

1. The 68000 makes an internal copy of the status register. After the copy is made, the supervisor mode bit (S) of the status register is set to 1 to place the 68000 into supervisor mode processing. Also, the trace mode bit (T) of the new status register is set to 1 to prevent trace mode operation.

2. The 68000 determines the vector number of the particular exception. This number is then used to generate the address of the routine that processes the exception. The 68000 provides 16 exception vectors.

3. The 68000 saves the current processor status. The current program counter and the saved value of the status register are then placed on the supervisor stack.

4. The 68000 fetches a new program counter value from the exception vector. The 68000 then resumes instruction execution at this new address location in the usual way—fetching, decoding, and so forth—until an RTE (return from exception) instruction is encountered.

Amiga Task-Private Exceptions

The Amiga handles its task-private exceptions in user mode. An Amiga task-private exception can be thought of as a task executing within a task. The system mechanisms used for processing exceptions preserve the entire 68000 register set of the first task to use once the task regains control (after the exception routine finishes execution). If an exception occurs while your program is executing, the 68000 goes into user mode if it is not already there. Remember that your task stack must be large enough to handle the stack needs of the exception code. Some exception routines require a lot of stack space during their execution.

Once your exception code begins executing, the system sets the A1 register as a pointer to your exception routine data memory area. The system sets the D0 register to the exception signal mask. This allows you to determine why your program called this exception routine. The system also establishes your user-mode task stack to look like this (from lowest to highest address):

User Task Stack

PC (program counter)
SR (status register (16 bits))
D0 through D7
A0 through A7
(the rest of the stack)

Once you are through with exception processing, you must first set register D0 to the exception event mask of your task. This sets the bits that will allow exceptions once you return to your current task's execution.

Then you must execute a 68000 RTS (return from subroutine) instruction to complete the task exception-handling process. The RTS instruction restores the contents of all the task's registers and restarts the task at the point where it was interrupted by the exception signal.

SetFunction

Syntax of Function Call

```
oldFunc = SetFunction (library,funcOffset,funcEntry)
D0                     A1    A0.W      D0
```

Purpose of Function

This function provides a method of changing those parts of the library for which a check-sum is calculated. They are changed in such a way that the summing process will never declare a library to be invalid. If all goes well, the new library routine vector (referred to as a function vector with the pointer variable funcEntry) will be inserted into the library at the appropriate vector offset from the Library structure of that library.

Inputs to Function

library	A pointer to the Library structure of the library to be changed, previously returned from a call to the Open-Library function
funcOffset	The library word offset where the new funcEntry vector should go
funcEntry	A pointer to the RAM location of the beginning of a new function to be added to this library

Discussion

There are seven Exec functions that deal with libraries in the Amiga system: AddLibrary, CloseLibrary, MakeLibrary, OpenLibrary, RemLibrary, SetFunction, and SumLibrary. Libraries are identified by their names and version numbers. There is more information on libraries in the discussions of each of these functions.

Library Code Vectors

Each library you create must have a minimum number of library code vectors. At this time this number is eight; four vectors are assigned, and four are reserved for future use. The four assigned vectors point to the OPEN, CLOSE, EXPUNGE, and EXTFUNC required library routines.

The OPEN routine is automatically called when you use the OpenLibrary function to open a library. Each task in the system that needs this library will execute an OpenLibrary function call. As a result, this library can be simultaneously open under more than one task; these tasks each become active in turn and use this library.

All these tasks have access to the contents of this library, both the code vector and data areas. Each time a task opens this library, the OpenCnt variable, which is stored in the library, is incremented. This tells the system how many tasks have already opened this library. However, remember that only one task will actually be using any library at any given time; the system can have only one active task at a time.

The CLOSE routine is automatically called when you use the CloseLibrary function to close a library. The routine at this vector decrements the OpenCnt variable when a CloseLibrary function call is made. Each time a task no longer needs this library, it should call the CloseLibrary function to free some system resources. If that task is indeed the only task using that library, a CloseLibrary function call followed by a RemLibrary function call can be very productive to free system resources, especially memory.

The EXPUNGE routine prepares the library for removal from the system. In other words, the EXPUNGE routine explicitly reverses the effect of a MakeLibrary function call. This includes deallocating the memory resources reserved by MakeLibrary. EXPUNGE is called by the RemLibrary function; its effect is to remove this library from the system library list. EXPUNGE frees the memory allocated for library routines and data, as well as the data areas reserved for the Library structure itself.

The EXTFUNC routine tells the system how to exit from one of the library routines. After these eight mandatory routine vectors come your own library routine vectors. These vectors can point to any routines of your own design that you want to include in this library.

Using SetFunction to Change Library Vectors

From time to time as your libraries evolve, you may want to change some of your routines in those libraries. You may want to update a particular routine, add a new routine, or delete a routine that's no longer useful. You can do all of these things by adding or replacing one of the library routine vectors. These types of library operations are accomplished with the SetFunction function. A discussion of each of the SetFunction function arguments follows.

The library argument is a pointer to the Library structure of the library for which a routine vector entry will be changing. Recall that the library variable was returned when you opened the library with the OpenLibrary function; library points to the memory address of the Library structure. This is the fulcrum point of this library.

The funcOffset argument is the negative number offset (with respect to the library pointer) at which the routine vector to be changed is located. The funcOffset variable must be a multiple of six. It must also be within the range specified by the negSize Library structure variable, which you set when you initialized the Library structure.

The funcEntry variable is a longword (four bytes) value that indicates the absolute address of the library routine to be inserted. This routine will be inserted at the func-Entry memory location.

When you use SetFunction to modify a function entry in a library, it automatically recalculates the checksum for that library. You do not have to make a separate call to the SumLibrary function.

SetIntVector

Syntax of Function Call

oldInterrupt = SetIntVector (intNumber, interrupt)
D0   D0: 0–4   A1

Purpose of Function

This function provides a mechanism for setting the system interrupt vectors. Both the code (is_Code) and data (is_Data) pointers for this interrupt vector are set to the new values. A pointer to the old Interrupt structure is returned. When the system calls the specified interrupt code, the registers are set up as follows:

D0   Scratch

D1   Scratch (on entry: active Paula—peripherals-sound custom chip—interrupts)

A0   Scratch (on entry: pointer to chip-base register)

A1   Scratch (on entry: interrupt's data segment)

A5   Jump vector register (scratch on entry)

A6   Exec Library base pointer—SysBase (scratch on entry)

All other registers must be preserved.

Inputs to Function

intNumber   The Paula (peripherals-sound custom chip) bit number (0–14)

interrupt	A pointer to the Interrupt structure containing the interrupt routine's entry point and data segment pointer. It is a good idea to give the Interrupt Node structure a name so that other tasks in the system can identify which task currently has control of the interrupt.

Discussion

The following steps are usually performed by an interrupt-handler routine:

1. The routine disables the particular interrupt tied to its particular interrupt bit. It does this by writing into the interrupt enable register. Then, if another interrupt belonging to this particular interrupt bit comes along, it cannot interrupt its own interrupt routine.

2. Optionally, it clears the interrupt bit in the interrupt request register. (However, you may want to clear it later when you execute this interrupt routine.)

3. It executes its own handler code.

4. It clears the interrupt request bit. (This should be done at this time if it wasn't done in Step 2 above.)

5. It reenables the input enable bit for this routine. This allows future instances of this particular interrupt to regain control if they occur.

Note that Steps 4 and 5 are performed to ensure that your code doesn't get caught in an endless loop, processing repeats of the same interrupt occurring close together in time. This prevents the overflow of the supervisor stack.

The contents of the registers on entry to the interrupt routines are as follows:

A0	This is a pointer to the base address of the special-purpose chip registers of the Amiga. These are the registers for the Agnus, Denise, and Paula (plus other) custom chips. At the present time, this value is 0xDFFE00. If you need to address the special-purpose registers more specifically, you should specify word address offsets from this base address.
A1	This is a pointer to the data segment of the interrupt routine that you assigned when the particular interrupt vector was created. This register contains the is_Data parameter of the new Interrupt structure.
A5	This is the address of the interrupt routine that is currently being executed. This register contains the is_Code parameter of the new Interrupt structure.
A6	This is the SysBase pointer to the system base library. You can get this value with a call to the system base library:

```
LONG SysBase
SysBase = OpenLibrary ("system.library", 0)
```

Now the system assembly language routines will automatically interface the routines in SysBase (the system Exec routines). Each time you issue an Exec function call, the call will find the appropriate system assembly language routines it needs. If the SysBase library is disk resident, as it is in earlier versions of the Amiga system, it will be retrieved from disk at this point.

D1   This register contains the active bits of the Paula (peripherals-sound custom chip) interrupt register, including the current interrupt being processed. See the discussion of the AddIntServer function for a list of the Paula interrupt bits and their meaning.

SetSignal

Syntax of Function Call

oldSignals = SetSignal (newSignals, signalMask)
D0   D0   D1

Purpose of Function

This function defines the state of the task's received signals. It returns the prior values of all signals in oldSignals. This function changes the tc_SigRcvd parameter in the Task Control Block structure.

Inputs to Function

newSignals   A 32-bit variable whose individual bits represent new signal values received by a task

signalMask   A 32-bit mask variable whose individual bits represent individual signal bits to be affected

Discussion

There are four Exec functions that deal with task signals in the Amiga system: AllocSignal, FreeSignal, SetSignal, and Signal. Because messages induce signals, the GetMsg,

PutMsg, and ReplyMsg functions can also be included in the category of signal-handling functions.

Tasks communicate with each other through message ports by passing messages back and forth between tasks currently residing in the system. Tasks communicate with devices in much the same way.

Each task has two kinds of signals: task-communication signals and exception-handler signals. There are a total of 32 signal bits available to each task in the system. The lower 16 bits (0–15) are reserved for system use; the upper 16 bits (16–32) can be used by the task. Some subset of these 32 signals can cause exceptions. The signals that can cause exceptions are determined by the tc_SigExcept variable specified in the task's Task Control Block structure.

Messages arrive at a task's message port through the message-passing mechanism of the Exec routines. Each message port will then send a specific signal bit to a task when that message is processed. However, to put a task into a known state, you can use the SetSignal and SetExcept routines to specify directly the signals a task will see. This is done in the following way:

```
oldSignals = SetExcept ($00000000, $FFFFFFFF)
/* set entire exception mask to zero */
oldSignals = SetSignal ($00000000, $FFFFFFFF)
/* set entire signal set to zero */
```

The first statement sets the tc_SigExcept parameter in the task's Task Control Block structure to all zeros to mask out any exception calls; any signals received by the task will not now cause an exception. The second statement sets the tc_SigRcvd parameter in the Task Control Block structure to all zeros. Now all task received signal bits have been set temporarily to zero values. You can restore things to their former condition by issuing appropriate SetSignal and SetExcept calls later in the task. Alternatively, any incoming messages can set the signal bits back to ones.

Recall that there is a variable called tc_SigRecvd in the Task Control Block structure of every task. This variable contains the signal bits of all signals that have been received by the task up to this time. Every time a message with a signal bit arrives at the message port of this task and is dequeued and processed, the tc_SigRecvd variable is updated.

The SetSignal function provides a way of dynamically controlling how a task responds to its outside environment; it can either recognize or ignore outside events according to the arguments of the SetSignal function.

Using SetSignal you can make a task behave in a number of ways, actually performing many different tasks from the basic code of one task. For example, you can use Set-Signal to simulate a device signal such as might come from the keyboard. Just set the task to respond to keyboard events transmitted from the keyboard device to the task in a message port, using a signal assigned to that message port. Associate that signal with the keyboard device. Now, as you debug your program, you may want to isolate the effect of the keyboard interaction with this task. You want to simulate the keyboard's action without having the keyboard actually talking to your task. You can do this by using the SetSignal function to simulate the signal usually sent to the task by the keyboard. This can be a convenient debugging technique.

The SetSignal function can be dangerous, because it alters the normal behavior of a task. Signals are usually assigned to a task for a good reason: to modify its behavior as events happen in the system. The SetSignal function allows you to modify this behavior arbitrarily. In most cases, this is not a good idea.

The code to get the current state of all signals is

oldSignals = SetSignal ($00000000, $00000000)

OldSignals is then the current value of the tc_SigRcvd parameter in the Task Control Block structure.

The code to clear all signals is

oldSignals = SetSignal ($00000000, $FFFFFFFF)

This says that all signals will be affected and all signal bits will be set to zero. It sets the tc_SigRcvd parameter to all zeros in the Task Control Block structure.

SetSR

Syntax of Function Call

```
oldSR = SetSR (newSR, mask)
D0              D0     D1
```

Purpose of Function

This function provides a means of modifying the 68000 CPU status register in a controlled way from inside a task. This function will affect only the CPU status register bits specified in the mask parameter. It returns the prior content of the entire status register.

Inputs to Function

newSR	The new values for 68000 CPU status register (SR) bits
mask	A mask of the bits that can be changed

Discussion

These are the bits in the Motorola 68000 microprocessor status register (SR):

0	Carry
1	Overflow

2	Zero
3	Negative
4	Extend
5	Not used
6	Not used
7	Not used
8	First interrupt mask bit
9	Second interrupt mask bit
10	Third interrupt mask bit
11	Not used
12	Not used
13	Supervisor state
14	Not used
15	Trace mode

The 16-bit 68000 status register is divided into two halves: the user byte (bits 0 through 7) and the system byte (bits 8 through 15).

Notice that there are three status register bits devoted to the interrupt mask. This mask handles the priority of the seven interrupt levels used by the 68000 CPU. If an interrupt occurs and the interrupt has a higher priority than the value currently stored in this three-bit mask, the interrupt routine associated with that interrupt will take over the machine.

If an interrupt occurs with a lower priority than the value of the interrupt mask, the new interrupt must wait until the current processing sequence is completed. See the discussion of the AddIntServer, Cause, and RemIntServer functions to relate the mapping of these seven 68000 interrupt levels to the 15 specific interrupts actually used in the Amiga.

To get the current status register, use this call:

currentSR = SetSR ($0000, $0000)

To change the processor interrupt level to level 3, use this call:

oldSR = SetSR ($0300, $0700)

This allows changes in bits 8, 9, and 10 (due to $0700) and sets bits 8 and 9 to 1 and bit 10 to 0. The oldSR variable now contains the previous 16-bit SR values. To set the processor interrupts back to their prior level, use this call:

oldSR = SetSR (oldSR, $0700)

This allows changes in bits 8, 9, and 10 (due to $0700) and sets bits 8, 9, and 10 back to their old values. When the SetSR function returns, the variable oldSR contains the previous 16-bit SR value.

SetTaskPri

Syntax of Function Call

oldPriority = SetTaskPri (taskCB, newpriority)
DO: 0–8   A1   DO: 0–8

Purpose of Function

This function changes the priority of a task regardless of its state. The old priority of the task is returned. Reschedule, a private system routine, is called to reschedule this task based on its new priority. A task context switch may also occur because of the change in task priorities.

Inputs to Function

taskCB   A pointer to the Task Control Block structure for a task
newpriority The new priority for that task

Discussion

There are four Exec routines that specifically relate to task handling in the Amiga system: AddTask, FindTask, RemTask, and SetTaskPri. See the discussion of each of these functions for more information on task handling. The data structure that defines a Task Control Block structure is in the Exec INCLUDE files; these are called Tasks.h (for the C language interface) and Tasks.i (for the assembly language interface).

Each task in the system has exclusive use of the 68000, the custom chips, and other hardware while it is running. In addition, each task has complete control over the full set of registers, the 68000 status register, its own task stack area, its own trap-handling routines, and its own exception-handling routines.

When a task is active, all other tasks are sleeping. One of them can wake up automatically when the current task has finished executing, or one may reawaken if it receives an appropriate signal to restart its execution. In addition, an appropriate interrupt can often wake up a sleeping task.

You can control the priority of each user task in the system. However, you cannot control the priority of system tasks. System tasks execute in the background to accomplish their work. Their priorities are set by the internal workings of the private Schedule and Reschedule Exec routines.

Usually, all tasks in the system run using a priority of zero; the variable ln_Pri is set to 0 in the Node substructure of the Task Control Block structure of that task. However, you can set the priority to a number from +127 to −128. The task with the current highest priority is the task that will get current complete control of the 68000.

Equal priority tasks will time-slice the time and instruction execution cycles of the 68000 CPU. Currently the time-slice is set at 64 milliseconds. To give you an idea of this time duration, note that this is roughly equivalent to the time needed to scan (paint) four video display frames ($^1/_{25}$ second). If you have many equal priority tasks in the system, these tasks continually switch in and out of processor execution at this time-slice rate.

For fully memory-resident tasks, task switching merely involves jumping to a different location in memory to gain access to the instructions for the task. At the same time, the 68000 user mode stack pointer is changed to the stack pointer for the new stack.

When a task is preempted, the Exec system automatically saves all the task's registers in the task's stack area. The only exception is that the task's stack pointer is saved in the task's Task Control Block structure memory area.

Most of the time, task switching occurs as a result of actions performed during an interrupt. For example, the disk drive can signal the task that it has data ready for that task. The task may have been waiting on this data to arrive through one of the I/O Request Block structures assigned to the disk-drive device. When the disk data interrupt finishes execution, the task system rescheduler automatically looks at the priority of the task that was interrupted. One of the equal or higher priority tasks in the system task-ready queue, if present, now gains control of the machine.

A task can relinquish control of the system by going to sleep while waiting for a signal to arrive. In addition, a task can lose control if a system event originating from a system Exec routine's internal operation puts a higher priority task into a ready condition and starts its execution.

Signal

Syntax of Function Call

> Signal (taskCB, signals)
> A1 D0

Purpose of Function

This function signals a task with the signals specified in the function call. This bypasses the normal task signaling that occurs when messages in message ports are processed with the PutMsg function. If the task is currently waiting for one or more of these signals, it will be made ready to execute. The system will use the private system Reschedule routine to activate that task if other conditions are satisfied.

If the task is not waiting for any signals, signals will be posted to the task for possible later use. Both of these situations change the tc_SigRcvd parameter in the Task Control Block structure. A signal can be sent to a task regardless of whether the task is running, ready, or waiting.

Inputs to Function

taskCB   A pointer to the Task Control Block structure of the task to be signaled

signals   A 32-bit variable containing one bit for each signal to be sent

Discussion

There are four Exec functions that deal with task signals in the Amiga system: AllocSignal, FreeSignal, SetSignal, and Signal. The GetMsg, PutMsg, and ReplyMsg functions can also be included in the category of signal-handling functions.

The Signal function is considered low level. Its main purpose is to support higher level functions, like PutMsg. Generally, a task need not directly specify its signals. Instead, the task, devices, and system software together establish and control the generation and processing of signals. This is accomplished by the message-port message mechanism. However, the Signal function together with the SetSignal function can provide a useful mechanism for debugging tasks and programs.

Posting Signals to a Task

Signal posting (delivery of and reply to message signals) is usually automatic. It is usually controlled by the Exec kernel routines acting together with the Task Control Block structure and I/O Request Block structures associated with a task and the devices used by that task. Therefore, you will not usually use the Signal function to post signals to a task.

If the Signal routine is used to send signals to a task, nonmessage signals will be treated like message signals coming from other sources. In particular, if a task cannot act immediately on the signals that it receives, these signals merely change the tc_SigRecd parameter in the Task Control Block structure. As a result, the Signal function does not lend any special priority or quality to the signals it sends.

SumLibrary

Syntax of Function Call

SumLibrary (library)
A1

Purpose of Function

This function computes a new checksum on a library. It can also be used to check an old checksum. If an old checksum does not match the currently calculated checksum and the library has not been marked as changed, the system will alert the task to a possible inconsistency between the expected library contents and the actual library contents.

Inputs to Function

library　　　　A pointer to the Library structure for which a checksum is to be calculated, previously returned by a call to the OpenLibrary function

Discussion

There are seven Exec functions that deal with libraries in the Amiga system: AddLibrary, CloseLibrary, MakeLibrary, OpenLibrary, RemLibrary, SetFunction, and SumLibrary. There is more information on libraries in the discussions of each of these calls.

Because the Exec system relies heavily on libraries, it tries to maintain internal consistency between the actual information and the expected information in a library. It does this by using the checksum feature.

If you use the MakeLibrary routine or the SetFunction routine, you will change the contents of a library. Each time you change a library, you should calculate and store a new checksum value in that library. The current checksum is stored in the lib_Sum parameter of the Library structure. Use the SumLibrary function for this explicit purpose; call it whenever you change a library. Your call to SumLibrary will ensure that the currently stored checksum is consistent with the information actually in the library. (Every time you execute an AddLibrary routine, the system automatically calculates and stores a new checksum for that library.)

You can also use the SumLibrary routine merely to check (versus compute and update) the checksum on a library. The information currently in the library is used to calculate a new checksum. This value is then compared to the value of the checksum presently stored in the library. If these two values do not match, there is an inconsistency between the assumed and actual library contents. In this case, the system panics and perhaps crashes. You may have to reset or restart the system to recover from this.

The LIBF_SUMUSED and LIBF_CHANGED flag bits in the Library structure Flags parameter control the operation of the checksum feature. So long as the LIBF_SUMUSED flag is not set, the checksum feature will not be used; the checksum will be neither calculated nor checked. If you want to restore the checksum feature, set this flag.

If the LIBF_SUMUSED and LIBF_CHANGED flags are set, indicating that the library has been changed, a new checksum will be calculated. If the LIBF_SUMUSED flag is set and the LIBF_CHANGED flag is not set, a newly calculated checksum is tested against the currently stored checksum for that library. If they do not match, the system will probably crash. This means that you should be careful when you change libraries. Always make sure the checksum is up to date by using the SumLibrary function.

SuperState

Syntax of Function Call

```
oldSysStack = SuperState ( )
D0
```

Purpose of Function

This function causes the system to enter the supervisor mode of the 68000 CPU microprocessor chip, allowing your task to execute the privileged instructions available only in supervisor mode. Supervisor mode is entered while running on the current task stack. For this reason, the calling task still has access to current task stack variables. Be careful, though—the task stack must be large enough to accommodate space for all the interrupt data, including all possible nesting of interrupts. The system stack pointer returned in oldSysStack should be saved; you will need it when you return to user mode. This function does nothing when called from supervisor mode. If the system is already in supervisor mode, oldSysStack is zero.

Inputs to Function

This function uses no arguments.

Discussion

There are two Exec functions that allow you to switch the operating mode of the 68000 microprocessor chip: SuperState and UserState. There are some things you should keep in mind if you decide to use either of these functions.

The Motorola 68000 microprocessor operates in two modes: user mode and supervisor mode. The S bit of the 68000 status register (SR) determines the operating mode of the 68000 chip; if the S bit is set to 1, the 68000 is in supervisor mode. Supervisor mode is a state of higher privilege for the 68000 microprocessor. All of the 68000 user-mode instructions can be executed in supervisor mode. In addition, some instructions are available only in supervisor mode:

ANDI TO SR	*And* immediate to the status register
EORI TO SR	Exclusive *Or* immediate to the status register
ORI TO SR	*Or* immediate to the status register
MOVE TO SR	Move to the status register
MOVE FROM SR	Move from the status register
MOVE USP	Move user stack pointer
MOVEC	Move to/from control register
MOVES	Move to/from alternate address space
RESET	Reset external devices
RTE	Return from exception
STOP	Load status register and stop

Note that six of these instructions directly manipulate the status register. One manipulates the user stack pointer (USP), one manipulates the control register, one manipulates memory addresses, one resets the machine, one returns from exception processing, and one stops the machine in its tracks.

While the 68000 is in supervisor mode, all instructions that use either the system stack pointer (implicitly) or the address register (explicitly) access the supervisor mode stack pointer. All exception processing is done in supervisor mode regardless of the status of the S bit when the exception occurs.

Most of the time, the system operates in user mode. When a task signal causes a task exception, on entry to the exception code the system establishes the following register contents:

A0   This register contains a pointer to the exception routine data frame. This is the data area in memory used by the exception routine.

D0   This register contains a signal mask so that the currently executing task can determine why this task exception occurred.

Also on entry to your exception code, the system establishes your stack frame as follows (from lowest to highest address):

Task Stack Frame

Program counter
Status register (16 bits)
D0 through D7
A0 through A7
(the rest of the stack)

On exit from task exception processing, you have to set D0 to the new value of the exception enable mask; set whichever bits you want to allow further exceptions once you return from exception processing. Note that this new mask can be the same as the mask used before the exception occurred. Finally, you must execute an RTS (return from subroutine) instruction to complete the exception processing.

The Amiga system handles traps in supervisor mode. This means that all task switching is disabled when a trap occurs. When the 68000 senses and subsequently performs a trap, the Exec routines gain control of the system. These routines determine which task is presently executing and whether this trap should go to that task. If Exec decides that the trap belongs to the current task, the trap-handling routine assigned to that task is executed. Recall that the address of this trap routine was stored in the tc_TrapCode parameter in the Task Control Block structure setup for this task.

Once the 68000 enters supervisor mode, the supervisor stack contains the trap frame information and the trap number. (See the Motorola 68000 microprocessor *Reference Manual* for details about the trap frame and trap numbers.) To return from a trap, remove the exception number from the supervisor stack. Then perform an RTE (return from exception) instruction.

It is important to note that your trap routines should be made very short. While they are executing, all task switching is disabled. You do not want this condition to continue for too long.

UserState

Syntax of Function Call

> **UserState (sysStack)**
> **D0**

Purpose of Function

This function returns the 68000 CPU to the user mode. Now your task can no longer execute the privileged instructions available only in supervisor mode. This function is usually used in conjunction with the SuperState function; it must be called from the 68000 CPU supervisor mode state.

Inputs to Function

sysStack   The value of the supervisor stack pointer (SSP)

Discussion

There are two Exec functions that allow you to switch the operating mode of the 68000 microprocessor chip: SuperState and UserState. Read this discussion in conjunction with the discussion of the SuperState function to learn the things you should keep in mind if you decide to use either of these functions.

The user mode of the 68000 is a state of lower privilege than the supervisor mode. If the S bit of the status register is 0, the 68000 is running in user mode. Most instructions execute in identical fashion in both modes. However, some instructions that have important system effects are declared to be privileged; these can be used only in supervisor mode. In particular, programs are not allowed to use the STOP or RESET instructions while in user mode.

The 68000 is designed to ensure that a user's program cannot enter supervisor mode accidentally. This is accomplished by making all instructions that can modify the 68000 status register privileged instructions. The MOVE to USP (move to user stack pointer) and MOVE from USP (move from user stack pointer) are also privileged instructions. Once the 68000 is in user mode processing program instructions, only exception processing can change the privilege state.

During exception processing the following occurs:

1. The current state of the S bit of the status register is saved.

2. The S bit in the status register is set to 1. This puts the 68000 into supervisor mode.

3. When processing continues with the instructions of the exception-handling routine, the system is in supervisor mode.

The transition from supervisor mode back to user mode can be accomplished using any one of four different instructions:

■ RTE (return from exception)

■ MOVE word to SR (move a new value into the status register)

■ ANDI to SR (*And* an immediate value to the status register)

■ EORI to SR (exclusive *Or* an immediate value to status register)

If you need to know more about these instructions, consult the Motorola 68000 microprocessor *Reference Manual.*

Vacate

Syntax of Function Call

Vacate (semaphore)
A0

Purpose of Function

This function releases a previously locked message-based Semaphore structure. If a second task is waiting for this message-based semaphore, the Message structure presently belonging to this message-based semaphore will be queued in the reply port of that second task.

Inputs to Function

semaphore   A pointer to a Semaphore structure containing the MsgPort substructure that will process the message

Discussion

The 1.2 release release provides two functions to deal with message-based semaphores: Procure and Vacate. Each Procure function call should be followed eventually by a Vacate function call. Vacate releases a Semaphore structure so that another task can use the semaphore associated with that structure. In this sense, Procure and Vacate are very similar to the ObtainSemaphore and ReleaseSemaphore functions, which deal with signal semaphores.

Wait

Syntax of Function Call

signals = Wait (signalSet)
D0   D0

Purpose of Function

This function causes the current task to suspend execution while it waits for one or more signals induced by a message arriving at one of its message ports. When any of the specified signals is detected and processed, the task returns to the ready state. If a signal arrives and is sensed prior to calling Wait, the wait condition is satisfied and the task continues to run. This function cannot be called while in the 68000 CPU supervisor mode, because the signal may call for a task switch. All task switching is prevented while the system is in supervisor mode.

Inputs to Function

signalSet   This is the tc_SigWait parameter in the Task Control Block structure—a 32-bit variable representing the set of signals for which to wait; each bit represents a particular signal

Discussion

There are four Exec routines that deal with task signals in the Amiga system: AllocSignal, FreeSignal, SetSignal, and Signal. In addition, GetMsg, PutMsg, and ReplyMsg fall in the category of signal-handling routines. Tasks communicate with each other through message ports by passing messages (which induce signals) back and forth between tasks currently residing in the system. Tasks communicate with devices in much the same way.

There are some things you should remember about posting signals to a task. A task can have up to 32 signal bits assigned to it. Of these, 16 (0 to 15) are used by the system routines. The other 16 (16 to 31) can be used directly by the task to control its behavior and interaction with other tasks. In particular, you can stop a task's execution until a signal (or signals) is induced by a message arriving at one of the message ports assigned to that task. That signal may be vital to some decision (for example, branching to a different subroutine) to be made in the task at that point, and no decision can be made until that signal arrives from another task or device.

The Wait function, together with the SetSignal and Signal functions, is useful for debugging programs. You can simulate the operation of devices usually attached to tasks with these three functions. Use Signal to simulate a signal coming to a task; use SetSignal to set signal bits to represent signals normally coming from the devices this task will use when fully debugged; use Wait to control the execution of the task once a signal is supplied by the other two functions. Once the task (its main program and subroutines) is fully debugged, remove the Signal and SetSignal statements from the task statements. Then attach task statements that bring the other tasks and devices and their associated messages and signals into this task definition.

WaitIO

Syntax of Function Call

        error = WaitIO (ioRequest)
        D0   A1

Purpose of Function

This function waits for the specified I/O request to complete. If the I/O has already completed, this function will return immediately. Use WaitIO with care, because it does not return until the I/O request completes; if the I/O never completes, WaitIO will never return and your task will hang. In this case, you may have to reboot the Amiga. If this situation is a possibility, it is safer to use the Wait function; it returns when a specific signal or signals is received. This is how to handle I/O time-out situations properly. A zero is returned if the I/O request is successful; otherwise an error number is returned.

Inputs to Function

ioRequest   A pointer to a properly initialized I/O Request Block structure

Discussion

There are eight Exec functions that are directly concerned with device I/O in the Amiga system: AddDevice, CloseDevice, OpenDevice, RemDevice, CheckIO, DoIO, SendIO, and WaitIO. There is more information on device I/O in the discussions of each of these functions.

Tasks send their I/O requests to devices in several ways. You can use the DoIO function, the SendIO function, or the BeginIO routine if you want synchronous, asynchronous, or Quick I/O, respectively. Note that even though BeginIO is not one of the Exec functions, it can be called in the same way.

Sometimes, the logic of your program will dictate that you absolutely must wait on an I/O operation to complete. If you use the DoIO function to send an I/O request, the task will wait on the I/O request to complete. In this case, you don't need the WaitIO function.

However, if you send the original I/O request with the SendIO function, it can be parked in the I/O request queue of that I/O device. Because you want your program to take some action when that specific I/O request is satisfied, you must use the WaitIO function: WaitIO looks for a specific I/O request to complete. As you can see, the one argument that WaitIO takes is the ioRequest pointer variable—a pointer to a specific I/O Request Block structure in memory.

Your intention in this case is to proceed further in program execution once you find the data and/or other information in the reply message area of that I/O Request Block structure. Because of this arrangement, it is possible for this function to hang up your program. This occurs when you execute the WaitIO function to wait on a specific I/O request to complete, and for one reason or another (for example, a very long device I/O request queue), the I/O request is delayed for a long time. In this case, your program must wait a long time to continue its execution.

WaitPort

Syntax of Function Call

```
message = WaitPort (msgPort)
D0                   A0
```

Purpose of Function

This function waits for the given message port queue to become nonempty. If necessary, the Wait function will be called (indirectly by the system) to wait for a message signal. If a message is already present at the message port, the function will return immediately. The return value is always a pointer to the Message structure for the first message queued; its presence in the message-port queue is sensed and the waiting task is notified of its presence. However, this message is not removed from the queue.

Inputs to Function

msgPort   A pointer to a MsgPort structure

Discussion

There are four Exec routines that are explicitly concerned with ports in the Amiga system: AddPort, FindPort, RemPort, and WaitPort. AddPort, FindPort, and RemPort all deal exclusively with public ports added to the system message-port list with the AddPort function. WaitPort deals with both public and private ports. These routines manage the ports where messages are passed between cooperating tasks in the Amiga multitasking system. Closely related to the port routines are the PutMsg, GetMsg, and ReplyMsg routines. These routines manage the messages that are queued in these message ports.

When you add a message port to a task for communication with other tasks, that message port can sometimes later become empty. It is empty at power-on time just after the system boots up; there are no messages in any message ports at that time.

Some of the system task-related ports will soon start receiving messages, as devices and events in the system move information from one place to another. Even so, some of the tasks in the system may sit with empty message ports in the beginning before any other task is talking to them. This may also be true later in an Amiga session when some of the message ports of some of the tasks have been completely dequeued because all of their messages have been removed. This is another time when a task message port is empty.

Note that the WaitPort function returns a pointer to the first Message structure that arrives at the specified message port, regardless of that message's characteristics. You cannot tell this function to wait on a particular message having this and that characteristic. Note also that the function returns with a pointer to the first Message structure queued, even though more than one message may arrive in quick succession. Any other messages that arrive later, even immediately after the first message, are not attended by the current WaitPort function call.

If you want to use the WaitPort function to wait on a specific message, you must arrange your coding in such a way that the message-port queue is empty while you wait for the message, and ensure that no other message can get into that message-port queue. Then you can use the Wait function to examine the incoming message for specific signals needed to reawaken a sleeping task or perform any other task operation that you desire.

Additional System Functions

Beyond the functions already discussed in this chapter, there are 14 additional functions that are normally used by the system but can also be useful to a programmer under some circumstances. Here, for completeness, is a brief description of each of these functions. Note that, in contrast to most of the other functions already discussed, only two of these functions have any arguments.

Debug( )

This function is used by the system to enter the Wack debug library in preparation for debugging a program. The Debug library itself has six functions that can aid the debugging process.

Delay (systemticks)

The system uses this function to delay the current task for a specified period of time. The argument is the number of microseconds that the task should be held. Note that this type of delay is different from the type of delay that occurs when a task is waiting on a message or signal. In that case another task will usually take over the 68000 CPU. With Delay( ) however, the entire system merely goes to sleep for a specified period of time.

Disable( )

This function is used by the system to disable task interrupts. It ensures that a task can go on executing without being interrupted by outside sources.

Dispatch( )

This function is used by the system to initiate execution of a task. It provides a way to start task execution without waiting on task messages, signals, or interrupts.

Enable( )

This function is used by the system to reenable interrupts once disabled. Now the task will, once again, be sensitive to interrupts when they occur.

Exception( )

This function is used by the system to start execution of a task exception routine. It provides a mechanism to directly initiate task exception routines without using task signals and task exception parameters in the Task structure.

Exit(return_code)

This function is used by the system to force immediate exit from a executing task.

ExitIntr( )

This function is used by the system to force an exit from a executing interrupt routine.

Forbid( )

This function is used by the system to disable task switching. It provides one way to protect structures from changes by other tasks while the current task is accessing that structure. However, note that semaphores provide a better way to do this.

Permit( )

This function is used by the system to reenable task switching if it was disabled by the Forbid function.

Reschedule( )

This function is used by the system to reestablish the schedule (priority of execution) for a task. This provides a mechanism for a task to directly relinquish the 68000 CPU without waiting for a signal to arrive at one of its message ports.

Schedule( )

This function is used by the system to establish the schedule (priority of execution) for a task. Its use is very similar to the SetTaskPri function.

Supervisor( )

This function is used by the system to put the 68000 CPU in supervisor mode. Its use is similar to the SuperState function.

Switch( )

This function is used by the system to switch to execution of another task from the currently executing task. It provides a way to start task execution without waiting for task messages, signals, or interrupts.

The Graphic Display and Drawing Functions

Introduction

This chapter discusses the nonanimation and nontext graphics functions in the Amiga ROM kernel Graphics Library. The functions in this chapter can be divided into two major groups: the display functions and the drawing functions. Generally speaking, the display functions initialize the bitplanes, bitmaps, and various structures that support bitmaps. The drawing functions set and/or reset the bits in the bitmaps to fill the bitmaps with drawing information.

A *bitplane* is a memory block consisting of an even number of memory bytes. A *bitmap* or *raster* is a set of bitplanes; a bitmap in the Amiga system can consist of from one to six bitplanes. The number of bitplanes that define a bitmap depends on the specific display mode used with the bitmap. Each position of each bit in a bitplane can be related to a pixel location in an eventual screen display.

As Figure 2.1 shows, the bits in a bitmap, each coming from a different bitplane in that bitmap, are combined to produce a binary value at a specific pixel location. That binary value is used to determine the color register number used at that pixel location. The color assigned to each color register is controlled by your program.

The Display Functions

The display functions cause memory to be allocated for all the bitplanes and bitmaps; many of these RAM areas are also initialized to values predetermined by the system routines. However, no real drawing information is present in the bitmaps at this point; they are essentially cleared areas of RAM. The display functions also place the structures that support the display in RAM at various locations. These RAM locations are automatically assigned by the system memory-allocation routines, which are called indirectly when you call the initialization functions. Once memory is allocated and the structures are initialized, everything is in place to define how the drawing information should be placed into the bitmaps.

In the course of designing your display, you need to establish the exact composition of all the video frames you will need for your program. (The system is capable of displaying a completely new video frame every 1/60 of a second.) To do this, you build each video frame into a view. Each view is composed in turn of a number of viewports. A *viewport* is a rectangular area on the display screen similar to an Intuition window, but with certain limitations that Intuition windows do not have.

The result of this procedure is one view (one video-frame definition) consisting of one or more rectangular viewports. If you want to present an unchanging screen display, it is only necessary to load the definition of this view (its Copper instructions) into the video display hardware once. The system will automatically repeat that frame 60 times a second. If you want to change the display screen, you must define several views and load their Copper instructions when appropriate. Your display design strategy consists of identifying and defining all viewports in all views. You then link these viewports together to form views. Finally, you load appropriate view definitions when you want to change the screen display.

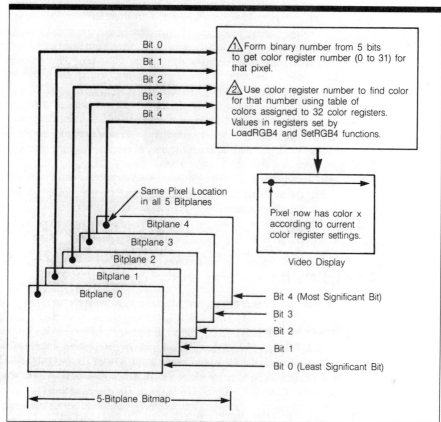

Figure 2.1:
Bitplanes, Bit-maps, Color Registers, and Pixel Colors

The display functions fall into eight categories: the bitmap functions, the superbit-map functions, the RastPort structure initialization function, the view functions, the view-port functions, the region-definition functions, the layer functions, and the hardware-control functions. The hardware-control functions fall into a number of sub-groups: the Copper control functions, the Blitter control functions, and the video-beam position-sensing and control functions. Read the section in this introduction on graphic structures for more information on these function groupings.

The Drawing Functions

Actual drawing information is added to bitmaps by the drawing functions; these comprise the second major category of ROM kernel graphics functions discussed in this chapter. They allow you to place drawing information into each bitmap you have already allocated. Drawing information ultimately results in appropriate settings of specific bits in the bit-planes of each raster's bitmap.

The drawing functions allow you to draw in fairly high-level pieces. You can deal with whole rasters, regions in a raster, rectangles in regions, areas, lines, polygons, and so forth. In addition, you can directly set and reset specific bits in raster bitmaps by specifically addressing those points in C language For loops. This second approach represents a very detailed, low-level approach to drawing, which the higher-level drawing functions allow you to avoid most of the time.

Generally, you use the drawing functions to set drawing modes, drawing pens, raster section boundaries, and so on, and then you use a specific drawing function to place the drawing information into some portion of a raster bitmap. You do this for an entire raster bitmap until you have defined all parts of that raster. Then you can move on to the next raster bitmap and do the same thing.

The drawing functions fall into seven categories: the pixel-color read and write functions, the drawing-pen color-control functions, the RGB color-control functions, the drawing-mode functions, the area-fill functions, the colormap functions, and the region-drawing functions.

Graphics Macros

In addition to the display and drawing functions, the graphics system includes sixteen macros: CINIT, CMOVE, CWAIT, CEND, SetOPen, SetDrPt, SetWrMsk, SetAfPt, ON-DISPLAY, OFF-DISPLAY, ON-SPRITE, OFF-SPRITE, RASSIZE, BNDRYOFF, ON-VBLANK, and OFF-VBLANK. The precise definition for each of these macros (in terms of lower-level system routines) is contained in the Gfxmacros.h INCLUDE file. Their definition appears as a set of sixteen C language #DEFINE statements.

The CINIT, CMOVE, CWAIT, and CEND macros allow a programmer to define a set of Copper instructions. You can use these to control the display hardware in a very detailed fashion. The SetOPen, SetDrPt, SetWrMsk, and SetAfPt macros provide direct control over various parameters in the RastPort structure.

You should note that the calling syntax for these macros follows the same pattern and rules as that of the other Graphics Library functions. These macros appear to be "patches" that were made as new system needs were discovered. It is possible that they will become functions in later revisions of the Amiga software libraries.

Structure Linkages in the Graphics System

The key to defining a graphics program (in single-playfield, dual-playfield, double-buffer, hold-and-modify, or any other video mode) lies in defining the proper linkages between the five major structures in the graphics system. These are the RastPort, View, ViewPort, RasInfo, and BitMap structures. Once these linkages are defined, other parameters in these five structures can also be declared and initialized. The same is true of the other graphics-related structures (Layer, AreaInfo, etc.)—a linkage definition is sometimes necessary—but the linkage is not as complicated or as universal as for these five major structures.

The required linkage of the five major structures is shown in Figure 2.2. Note that the particular order (top to bottom) of structures in this diagram is arbitrary. The small rectangles on the right side of the figure represent other structures that these five major structures point to. The arrows on the diagram represent pointer parameters whose names are written along each arrow.

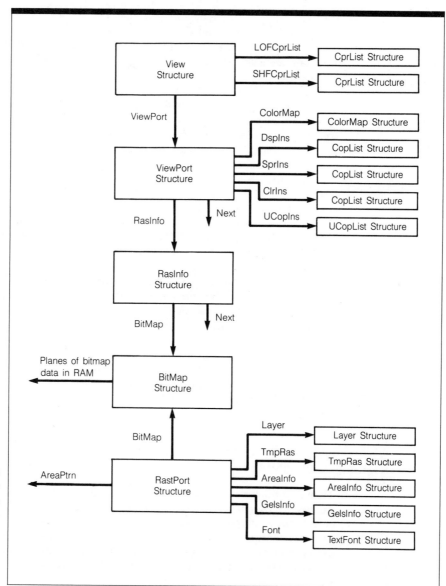

Figure 2.2:
Structure Linkages in the Graphics System

Note that the RastPort structure is linked only to the BitMap structure. In addition, the RastPort structure points to the Layer, TmpRas, AreaInfo, GelsInfo, and TextFont structures. The RastPort structure also points to the RAM data area labeled AreaPtrn.

The View structure defines the display screen view, which may consist of one or more viewports separated vertically on the display screen. The View structure points to the first ViewPort structure for a linked list of ViewPort structures that define the complete view. In addition, the View structure points to two CprList structures; these define the Copper lists for the complete view. Note that the RastPort structure and the View structure are not directly linked.

The View structure is linked to the ViewPort structure. To be more precise, the View structure is linked to the first ViewPort structure representing the first viewport in a list of one or more viewports in that view. Subsequent ViewPort structures are linked to each other with the Next parameter in the ViewPort structure. In addition, each Viewport structure points to a maximum of five other structures. These are the ColorMap, DspIns, SprIns, ClrIns, and UCopIns structures. The ColorMap structure defines the colortable array for the viewport. Each viewport can have its own colortable array and therefore, its own color palette. The other four structures define the complete set of Copper instructions for that viewport.

The ViewPort structure is linked to the RasInfo structure. To be more precise, the first ViewPort structure is linked to the first RasInfo structure. A second RasInfo structure is linked to the first with the Next parameter in the RasInfo structure; only the dual-playfield mode display uses a second RasInfo structure (see Appendix B). The RasInfo structure is also linked to the BitMap structure, which points to each of the bitplanes in RAM. These are the RAM data areas where the blocks of bitplane pixel data are stored. Together these bitplanes define the total bitmap for one viewport.

Each video display mode uses these linkages in various combinations to define that display mode. For example, the single-playfield mode, hold-and-modify mode, and extra-half-brite mode displays link one RastPort structure, one RasInfo structure, one BitMap structure, one View structure, and as many ViewPort structures as necessary to define the view.

The dual-playfield mode display links one RastPort structure, two RasInfo structures, two BitMap structures, one View structure, and as many ViewPort structures as necessary. Finally, the double-buffer mode display links one RastPort structure, one RasInfo structure, two BitMap structures, one View structure, and as many ViewPort structures as necessary.

Graphics Structures

There are a number of important structures with which the graphics functions work. Generally speaking, for each structure there is a corresponding structure-initialization function (for example, the InitBitMap and InitRastPort functions). These structure-initialization functions set up default values in the structure definition in memory. You then place explicit values into the parameters of these structures using individual program statements. Once the current values of a structure are fully defined, you can use that structure to help carry out a specific step in your graphics program. For example, the RastPort structure controls all aspects of the drawing definition for a raster bitmap. This is a very important concept in the operation of the graphics functions. In other words, defining the structure in itself determines how the drawing will appear in the bitmap associated with that structure.

The RastPort structure is such an important structure in the graphics system that it is useful to list its contents here and briefly explain the meaning of each of its parameters:

```
struct RastPort {
    struct Layer *Layer;
    struct BitMap *BitMap;
    USHORT *AreaPtrn;
    struct TmpRas *TmpRas;
    struct AreaInfo *AreaInfo;
    struct GelsInfo *GelsInfo;
    UBYTE Mask;
    BYTE FgPen;
    BYTE BgPen;
    BYTE AOlPen;
    BYTE DrawMode;
    BYTE AreaPtSz;
    BYTE linpatcnt;
    BYTE dummy;
    USHORT Flags;
    USHORT LinePtrn;
    SHORT cp_x, cp_y;
    UBYTE minterms[8];
    SHORT PenWidth;
    SHORT PenHeight;
    struct TextFont *Font;
    UBYTE AlgoStyle;
    UBYTE TxFlags;
    UWORD TxHeight;
    UWORD TxWidth;
    UWORD TxBaseline;
    WORD TxSpacing;
    APTR *RP_User;
    UWORD wordreserved[7];
    ULONG longreserved[2];
    UBYTE reserved[8];
};
```

The Layer parameter points to a Layer structure, which allows the RastPort structure to control the drawing settings for layer bitmaps. The Layer structure is used directly by the LockLayerRom, UnlockLayerRom, CopySBitMap, and SyncSBitMap functions. It is also used by the functions in the Layers Library.

The BitMap parameter points to a BitMap structure, which allows the RastPort structure to control the drawing settings for a bitmap. The BitMap structure points to a bitmap in RAM and defines its size. The BitMap structure is initialized by the InitBit-Map function; other functions use the BitMap structure indirectly.

The AreaPtrn parameter points to an area-fill pattern data region in RAM. This data region defines the specific pixels of the area-fill pattern used by the AreaEnd and Flood functions. The block of memory that defines the area-fill pattern is filled by the SetAfPt macro, which is defined in the Gfxmacros.h INCLUDE file.

The TmpRas parameter points to a TmpRas structure, which is used to control an auxiliary buffer. This buffer holds small, temporary areas of a larger bitmap during an area-fill sequence involving the AreaDraw, AreaMove, and AreaEnd functions. The TmpRas structure is initialized with the InitTmpRas function.

The AreaInfo parameter points to an AreaInfo structure, which controls an auxiliary buffer that stores end-point vertices defining a set of areas to be filled with the AreaEnd function. The AreaInfo structure is initialized by the InitArea function.

The GelsInfo parameter points to a GelsInfo structure, which is used to link the virtual sprite and Bob (Blitter object) animation details into the current bitmap display definition. The GelsInfo structure is used directly by the animation functions in the Graphics Library.

The Mask parameter is a write mask that controls the specific bitplanes in a bitmap that will be affected by a drawing operation. The Mask parameter is not controlled directly by any Graphics Library function. You can set the mask parameter by using either a simple structure parameter assignment statement or the SetWrMsk macro, which is defined in the Gfxmacros.h INCLUDE file.

The FgPen parameter holds the current value of the foreground pen number, which determines the color for drawing the foreground pixels in a bitmap. This parameter is set by the SetAPen function.

The BgPen parameter holds the current value of the background pen, which determines the color for drawing the background pixels in a bitmap. This parameter is set by the SetBPen function.

The AOlPen parameter is the current value of the area-outline pen, which determines the color for drawing line pixels in a bitmap. This pen is used for outlining areas produced by the AreaEnd function. It is also used in Flood fill operations. This parameter is set by the SetOPen macro, which is defined in the Gfxmacros.h INCLUDE file.

The DrawMode parameter is the value of the drawing mode, which determines how the drawing pens are used in drawing pixels in a bitmap. This parameter is set by the SetDrMd function.

The AreaPtSz parameter is the number of words in the area pattern definition. This defines the size of the area pattern used in area-fill functions such as AreaEnd and Flood. This parameter is set by the SetAfPt macro, which is defined in the Gfxmacros.h INCLUDE file.

The linpatcnt parameter is the current value of the line pattern count, which helps to define the line pattern drawing produced by the Draw and PolyDraw functions. This parameter is not affected directly by any Graphics Library function; it is controlled by the system.

The dummy parameter is a dummy byte inserted to keep the RastPort structure properly aligned through the various software updates.

The Flags parameter is a set of bits used by the system software to control various internal details of the drawing process. This parameter is not directly affected by any Graphics Library function. You can set it with a simple assignment statement. The flag bits are defined in the RastPort.h INCLUDE file.

The LinePtrn parameter is the current value of a two-byte line pattern whose individual bits are used to define the on-and-off pixels in a line. This line pattern is used by the Draw and PolyDraw functions. It is defined by the SetDrPt macro, which is listed in the Gfxmacros.h INCLUDE file.

The cp_x and cp_y parameters are the current pen x,y coordinates as measured in the current bitmap coordinate system. These define the location where the next drawing operation will occur in a bitmap. Each time a function (AreaDraw, AreaMove, AreaEnd, Draw, Flood, Move, or PolyDraw) moves the drawing pen, these values may change. Other drawing functions affect these values indirectly. The Graphics Library text functions can also affect these values as they add text to a raster bitmap.

The minterms[8] parameter is a set of eight bytes used to control the logic operations of the Blitter. These parameters are set and controlled by the BltBitMap, ClipBit, and other Blitter functions.

The PenWidth and PenHeight parameters hold the current width and height of the drawing pen in pixels. There are no Graphics Library functions that control these parameters directly.

The Font parameter points to a TextFont structure used by the Graphics Library text functions. The AlgoStyle, TxFlags, TxHeight, TxWidth, TxBaseline, and TxSpacing parameters are the current values of the text drawing parameters. The AlgoStyle parameter is a one-byte value used to keep track of style changes (bold, italic, and so forth) in a text font definition. TxFlags contains the current value of the Flags parameter; it is related to the Flags parameter in a TextFont structure. TxHeight, TxWidth, TxBaseline, and TxSpacing hold the current values of the text height, width, baseline, and spacing parameters; these are also related to values in a TextFont structure. Read Chapter 4 to see how these parameters are defined and modified.

The RP_User parameter points to an Exec reply port (a message port) of the task that is currently using this RastPort structure for drawing. This parameter is not controlled directly by any Graphics Library function.

The wordreserved[7], longreserved[2], and reserved[8] parameters are reserved for future enhancements and expansion to the RastPort structure.

To understand the importance of the RastPort structure, you should focus on the key word *control;* the RastPort structure is the main structure used to control the drawing into a raster bitmap. (In this book, *raster, bitmap,* and *raster bitmap* will all be used synonymously.) Once parameters in the RastPort structure are set by the other drawing functions (for example, SetAPen and SetBPen), they are placed into the updated RastPort structure. Then, when you call one of the actual drawing functions (for example, AreaEnd or Rect-Fill), the parameters in the current definition of the RastPort structure control how that part of the bitmap is actually *drawn,* meaning how bits in the bitmap are set and reset and how these bits are interpreted by the display hardware. The RastPort structure changes dynamically throughout the drawing process.

In addition to the RastPort structure, the graphics display and drawing functions deal with the following structures:

- The RasInfo structure contains two parameters that define the upper-left corner of a viewport bitmap within the larger raster bitmap. It also contains a pointer to a BitMap structure. You initialize this structure with three simple program statements.

- The BitMap structure tells the system where to find the display area RAM blocks (the raster bitmap) and how those areas of RAM are organized into bitplanes. The BitMap structure is initialized by the InitBitMap function.

- The ViewPort structure contains parameters to control the display of one of the viewports in a specific screen view. The ViewPort structure is initialized by the InitVPort function.

- The View structure has parameters that control the display of one of the video frames in your program. Each unique video frame you define has a separate View structure to control its display. Any given view can have a number of viewports with their associated ViewPort structures. The View structure is initialized by the InitView function.

- The Region structure has parameters that control the definition of a region. A *region* is the subsection of the total bitmap to which a drawing operation is limited. The Region structure is initialized by the NewRegion function. Once a region is initialized, you can use the AndRectRegion, OrRectRegion, and XorRectRegion functions to extend the definition of that region.

- The Rectangle structure has parameters that control the definition of clipping-rectangles in regions. Clipping-rectangles allow you to build a region definition which limits the area of a bitmap that drawing operations will affect. The Rectangle structure is initialized by individual assignment statements that define the boundary points of clipping rectangles.

- The Layer structure has parameters that control layer bitmaps. *Layers* are used to build a multiwindow screen, where different parts of the screen display come from different layer bitmaps. Layer structures maintain video priorities (which layer is displayed on top, which is next displayed, and so forth) in a complex video-display definition. The Layer structure is initialized by the CreateUpfrontLayer and Create-BehindLayer Layers Library functions.

- The ColorMap structure allows you to control the color mapping between the hardware system color registers and the actual colors used to define various parts of each viewport display. The ColorMap structure is initialized by the GetColorMap function.

- The CopList structure has parameters that control the use and definition of a set of intermediate (not yet final) explicit low-level Copper instructions required to define the display of a single viewport. It is defined and initialized by the MakeVPort function. Each ViewPort structure has a set of three pointers to CopList structures that define the intermediate Copper instruction list for the playfield and sprite parts of a display frame.

- The CprList structure has parameters that control the use and definition of the final, full set of explicit low-level Copper hardware instructions. It is initialized by the system routines.

- The AreaInfo structure has parameters that control the definition of area-fill operations produced by the AreaDraw, AreaMove, and AreaEnd functions. It is initialized by the InitArea function.

- The TmpRas structure has parameters that aid the area-fill operations of the AreaDraw, AreaMove, and AreaEnd functions. It is initialized by the InitTmpRas function.

- The ClipRect structure provides the linkages between a set of clipping-rectangles used to define clipping-rectangle regions and to update layer bitmaps. It is used indirectly by the region functions, but it is used most extensively by the Layers Library functions.

- The UCopList structure is used to maintain the linkages between the various user-defined Copper lists. These lists are created by the CINIT, CMOVE, CWAIT, and CEND Copper control instructions, and the UCopList structure is referenced directly by these functions.

- The LayerInfo structure is used to control a layer bitmap when more than one task can draw into that bitmap. It is used indirectly by the LockLayerRom and UnlockLayerRom functions, but it is used most extensively by the Layers Library functions.

Coordinate Systems

There are three coordinate systems you must be aware of and able to use when you are programming with the Graphics Library functions: the raster bitmap coordinate system, the display frame or view co-ordinate system, and the viewport coordinate system. You should examine each function to make sure you understand the coordinate system used by that function.

The raster coordinate system is the largest. The x,y values in this system can range up to 1024,1024, that is, 1,024 pixels in each raster direction. Most of the drawing functions, among them the area-fill functions (AreaDraw, AreaMove, and AreaEnd) and the line drawing functions (Draw, Move, and PolyDraw), use this coordinate system to fill the raster with drawing information.

The display frame or view coordinate system is the next largest. The maximum co-ordinates for this system depend on the drawing mode you set with the SetDrMd function. For example, if you choose a low-resolution, noninterlaced mode display, the maximum x,y values will be 320,200. If you choose a high-resolution, interlaced mode display, the maximum x,y values will be 640,400. (The Amiga display hardware is actually capable of maximum x,y values of 352,232 in low-resolution, noninterlaced mode and 704,464 in high-resolution, interlaced mode. However, because of the display overscan of most monitors you will probably want to limit the maximum x,y values to 320,200 and 640,400, respectively.)

The viewport coordinate system is the smallest of the coordinate systems. The maximum coordinates for this system depend once again on the drawing mode you set with the SetDrMd function. In addition, the maximum coordinates depend on the size of your biggest viewport. If you define a viewport that takes up the entire display screen, your viewport will be as large as your view. In this case, the maximum x,y values in the viewport coordinate system could be as large as 640,400.

Creating an Amiga Video Display Frame

There are seven main steps involved in creating an Amiga video display. First, you must use the AllocRaster function to allocate enough memory to hold all of the bitplanes in a bitmap. You must also ensure that you have enough memory in the system for the following structures:

- Each ViewPort structure in a view

- Each View structure with which your task deals

- Each RastPort structure

- Each BitMap structure

- Each ColorMap structure

- Each Layer structure

- Each LayerInfo structure

- Each RasInfo structure

- Each Region structure

- Each Rectangle structure

- Each CopList structure

- Each CprList structure

- Each UCopList structure

- Each TmpRas structure

- Each BlitNode structure

This list contains most of the graphics-related structures. You can determine the number of bytes required by each structure by studying the function definitions and the INCLUDE file listing for each structure. The memory requirements for your structures will, of course, vary from task to task; in fact, most of the above structures will not be used in most of your graphics tasks. Also, you can allocate and deallocate memory for these structures as you proceed through a task. Use the Exec Allocate and Deallocate function calls when there is no explicit function to allocate memory for one of these structures.

Second, you must define all the ViewPort structures that will be combined into the final View structure. Each of the ViewPort structures is a node in a linked set of ViewPort structures. Each node in this list has a pointer variable to point to the next ViewPort structure in the list. When taken together, these linked ViewPort structures define the total View structure that will be used to define one final display screen image.

Third, you must initialize the RasInfo structure, which tells the system the RAM location of a bitmap to be used with a viewport definition. It also tells the system how the viewport display area should be positioned with respect to the complete drawing area (the raster) definition in memory.

Fourth, you must initialize the View structure using the InitView function. Link the first ViewPort structure into the View structure. Note that because ViewPort structures are linked, this step will also link the other ViewPort structures into the View structure.

Fifth, you must use the MakeVPort function to create most of the actual display instructions that will be used by the Copper to define each complete frame of the display. Other Copper display instructions may come from other sources.

Sixth, you must merge all of the Copper instructions to form a complete Copper instruction list. The Copper will use this instruction list to control the scanning of the video beam to define each part of the video display. These Copper instructions come from three sources: those provided by the MakeVPort function, those provided by the animation routines, and those provided in a UCopList structure by a programmer. The MrgCop function merges all of these together to define the total display for a single video frame.

It is important to note that these Copper instructions can change from frame to frame. In fact, it is possible that the full set (or part of a set) of instructions will change during the vertical-blanking interval as the scanning beam retraces vertically every 1/60 of a second. This allows you to change the details of the display every 1/60 of a second.

The last step is to use the LoadView function to load the display view represented by the detailed Copper instructions into the display hardware. This is the step that actually produces the display. Up to this step, all video information existed in memory purely in the form of bitmaps and Copper instructions. The LoadView function takes the merged Copper list instructions and sends these instructions to the system display hardware.

AllocRaster

Syntax of Function Call

```
bitplane_Pointer = AllocRaster  (width, height)
D0                               D0    D1
```

Purpose of Function

This function calls the system memory-allocation routines to allocate memory space for a single bitplane in a raster bitmap. It returns a pointer to a memory block in RAM, if successful, or 0, if unsuccessful.

Inputs to Function

width   The number of bits in the x direction of the raster coordinate system

height   The number of bits in the y direction of the raster coordinate system

Discussion

There are four Graphics Library display functions that work specifically with the raster: AllocRaster, FreeRaster, InitTmpRas, and ScrollRaster. There is more information on working with the raster in the discussions of each of these functions.

A *raster* is essentially areas of memory consisting of bitplanes that, taken together, define one of the bitmaps of the Amiga display. In this book, *raster, bitmap,* and *raster bitmap* will all be used synonymously. AllocRaster allocates the memory area devoted to the bitplanes and the bitmaps that are formed from these bitplanes. The AllocRaster function uses no pointer arguments and therefore does not work directly with any structure; it merely returns a pointer to a single memory block in RAM. You must call the AllocRaster function for each bitplane in a bitmap.

AllocRaster works with two arguments: width and height. For example, if you want a noninterlaced, low-resolution mode display, you will have 320 pixels on each horizontal line and 200 pixels on each vertical line. In this case, the width variable will be 320 and the height variable will be 200.

You can used a C language For loop to allocate the memory space required for more than one bitplane. Just call the AllocRaster function each time in the For loop. In this way, you can allocate memory for all the bitplanes you need to define a single bitmap (up to six in hold-and-modify mode). The For loop looks like this:

```
for (i = 0; i<depth, i+ +) {
   MyBitMap.Planes[i] = (PLANEPTR) AllocRaster (width, height);
};
```

Table 2.1 shows the number of RAM bytes required for different video-display mode combinations. You can use this information to estimate your display memory requirements.

Picture Size	Display Mode	Number of Bytes per Bitplane
320 by 200	Low-resolution, noninterlaced	8,000
320 by 400	Low-resolution, interlaced	16,000
640 by 200	High-resolution, noninterlaced	16,000
640 by 400	High-resolution, interlaced	32,000

Table 2.1:
Display Memory Requirements

The Amiga hardware system has 32 registers that control colors on the display screen. Each of these registers contains 12 bits. Four bits control the shade of red; four bits control the shade of green, and four bits control the shade of blue produced by that color register. Therefore, each color register can represent up to 4,096 colors. A colormap table is an assignment of each of these specific color registers to color numbers used in the drawing routines. Color 1 is associated with color register 1, color 2 is associated with color register 2, and so on.

Color 0 is reserved for the background color. The background consists of any area on the display screen where there is no other object present. The background color is also displayed outside the defined display window, in the border area. Color 1 is often the alternate color selection for a two-color playfield. (See Appendix A for a definition of a playfield.) These are the bitplanes required for colors in a single-playfield display:

Number of Colors	Number of Bitplanes Required
1 or 2	1
3 or 4	2
5 to 8	3
9 to 16	4
17 to 32	5

AndRectRegion

Syntax of Function Call

```
AndRectRegion   (region,  rectangle)
                 A0       A1
```

Purpose of Function

This function performs a two-dimensional And operation of a clipping-rectangle with a region. The result is left in the region. AndRectRegion clips away any. portion of the region that exists outside of the clipping-rectangle.

Inputs to Function

region	A pointer to a Region structure
rectangle	A pointer to a Rectangle structure

Discussion

There are six Graphics Library drawing functions that deal specifically with regions and the clipping-rectangles that define these regions: AndRectRegion, ClearRegion, Dispose-Region, NewRegion, OrRectRegion, and XorRectRegion. A *clipping-rectangle* is an area of the display where drawing will take place when the display definition changes. These functions allow you to build a customized drawing region as part of the total definition of a layer. There is more information on drawing regions and clipping-rectangles in the discussions of each of these functions.

The AndRectRegion function performs an And operation on the current contents of a region with a clipping-rectangle that may or may not be already a part of that region. The new clipping-rectangle is then made a part of that region. Note that this is not the same as performing an And operation on the bits of a rectangle bit-by-bit with the bits in a region of a bitmap.

To understand the clipping-rectangle concept better, suppose that you want to draw a solid square into a layer. There are at least two ways you can do this. The first way is the more obvious: you decide where you want that square to appear in that layer, then you use the AreaDraw, AreaMove, and AreaEnd functions (or the RectFill function) to define and draw that square. You use the drawing functions (SetAPen, SetBPen, etc.) to prepare the RastPort structure so it properly controls the drawing colors for your square's borders. Then, when you finally execute the AreaEnd or RectFill function, the square will be drawn into your bitmap.

Alternatively, you can use the AndRectRegion and OrRectRegion functions together with one region defined by two clipping-rectangles to limit the drawing into this portion of your bitmap. To do this, first define a ClipRect structure using four simple statements to define the vertices of a clipping-rectangle. Make this a very large clipping-rectangle. In fact, you can make it as big as the entire layer bitmap itself.

Then call the NewRegion function to allocate and initialize a new region of size zero. Next, use the OrRectRegion function to include this large clipping-rectangle in the new region. This step is necessary because the AndRectRegion function will not add anything to an empty region.

Next, define a second clipping-rectangle using the same procedure. In this case, define a clipping-rectangle that is actually a small square. Then place a call to the AndRectRegion function. This adds the small square to the region's definition and restricts any additional drawing in that region to the small square defined in the clipping-rectangle.

Follow this immediately with a call to the BeginUpdate function to begin the update of that layer bitmap (see Chapter 5 for a discussion of the BeginUpdate function). Here, however, you are updating only that part of the layer bitmap that is contained in the region definition; you are changing only those parts of the layer bitmap that are inside the clipping-rectangle added by the AndRectRegion function. The drawing process will be clipped to the area inside this clipping-rectangle square.

Next, just as in normal drawing procedure, use the drawing functions (SetAPen, SetBPen, etc.) to prepare the RastPort structure so it can control the drawing colors, borders, and so forth for the added square. Then use the RectFill function to fill the square with the color you want. Usually, the entire raster receives this color. But now the small, square clipping-rectangle ensures that only the small square is filled with your chosen color.

You can extend this indirect drawing process using other instances of the AndRectRegion function. For example, before you call the BeginUpdate function, you could define another clipping-rectangle. Then you could execute the AndRectRegion function to include that clipping-rectangle into your region definition.

The way you proceed from here depends on the position of the two rectangles in relation to one another. First, assume that the second clipping-rectangle is at the identical bitmap position as the first clipping-rectangle. In this case, when you call the BeginUpdate function the result will be the same as the first case; the region definition is not changing because the And operation has not extended the region definition.

Next, assume that the second clipping-rectangle does not overlap the first clipping-rectangle; it is a different size and located in an entirely different position in the raster bitmap. In this case, when you call the BeginUpdate function the layer will have no rectangles added to it; the region definition has changed because the And operation has reduced it to a region of zero size.

The third case, shown in Figure 2.3, is the most interesting, because it shows how the AndRectRegion function really works. Here, assume that the second clipping-rectangle

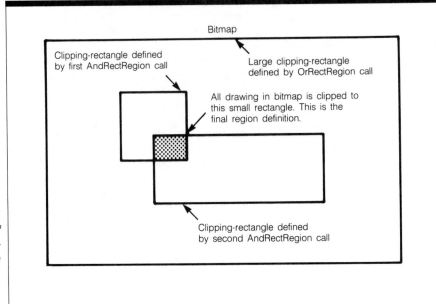

Bitmap

Clipping-rectangle defined
by first AndRectRegion call

Large clipping-rectangle
defined by OrRectRegion call

All drawing in bitmap is clipped to
this small rectangle. This is the
final region definition.

Clipping-rectangle defined
by second AndRectRegion call

Figure 2.3:
*Illustration of
the AndRect-
Region Function*

partially overlaps the first clipping-rectangle (the square). All drawing will be clipped outside of all parts of the region that do not belong to the intersections of these two rectangles; once again, the region definition is changing because the And process has reduced
the size of the final clipping-rectangle in the region definition.

In this case, the intersection is a rectangle no bigger than the smaller of the two
clipping-rectangles. The precise size of this final clipping-rectangle depends on the relative
size, shape, and position of the two clipping-rectangles.

Finally, note that the order of the clipping-rectangles added to the definition of a
region by the AndRectRegion function does not matter: for any given set of clipping-
rectangles, the final region they define does not depend on the order in which they are
added to produce the final region. You can convince yourself of this with a piece of paper
and some simple examples.

AndRegionRegion

Syntax of Function Call

```
success = AndRegionRegion  (region1, region2)
D0                          A0       A1
```

Purpose of Function

This function performs a two-dimensional And operation of one region with another region. AndRegionRegion clips away any portion of the total region not common to the two regions; only the area of overlap remains. The result is left in the second region. The first region is not changed.

Inputs to Function

region1   A pointer to the first of two Region structures whose regions are to be combined

region2   A pointer to the second of two Region structures whose regions are to be combined

Discussion

There are four functions in the 1.2 Amiga software release that deal with regions exclusively: AndRegionRegion, ClearRectRegion, OrRegionRegion, and XorRegionRegion. You should read the discussions of each of these functions to understand how regions are combined to aid the drawing process.

The intention and use of the AndRegionRegion function is very similar to that of the AndRectRegion function. Recall that regions are merely collections of clipping-rectangles and that regions are defined using the AndRectRegion, OrRectRegion, and XorRectRegion functions.

The only difference between the AndRegionRegion and AndRectRegion functions is that AndRegionRegion combines two regions whereas AndRectRegion combines one region and one clipping-rectangle. Two regions form a more versatile combination because a region does not have to be a simple rectangle; it can be any shape with straight-edge boundaries.

Read the discussion of the AndRectRegion function to see how and why regions and clipping-rectangles are combined; the ideas and concepts discussed there apply equally well to a combination of two regions into a third region.

AreaCircle

Syntax of Macro Call

error = AreaCircle (rastPort, centerX, centerY, radius)
D0   A1   D0   D1   D2

Purpose of Macro

This macro adds a circle to the area information used for area-fill in a raster bitmap. When drawn, the circle will be filled with a solid color or a pattern according to the current drawing control settings in the RastPort structure. AreaCircle does its job by calling the AreaEllipse function. It returns a 0 value if the macro call was successful and 1 if no room was left in the vector table list defined by the AreaInfo structure.

Inputs to Macro

rastPort	A pointer to a controlling RastPort structure
centerX	The x-coordinate of the center of the circle measured in the raster bitmap coordinate system
centerY	The y-coordinate of the center of the circle
radius	The radius of the circle (in number of pixels) measured in the horizontal resolution of the raster bitmap coordinate system

Discussion

There are two macros in the 1.2 release that deal with circles: AreaCircle and DrawCircle. AreaCircle is a macro that calls the AreaEllipse function and DrawCircle is a macro that calls the DrawEllipse function.

There are two ways you can add a circle to a raster bitmap. First, you can call the DrawCircle macro to draw the circle immediately into your raster bitmap. Or second, you can call the AreaCircle macro to place information about your circle into the vector table associated with an AreaInfo structure to suspend the actual drawing of your circle.

If you proceed the second way, drawing information for the circle (the arguments of the macro call) will provide the data required by the AreaInfo structure vector table. The circle will be added to the bitmap only when the AreaEnd function is finally called. Other circles, ellipses, and rectangles currently represented by that vector table will also be drawn at that time.

AreaCircle appends the centerpoint coordinates and size of the circle to the vector table list maintained by the AreaInfo structure. The circle will be drawn when the AreaEnd function is finally called.

The action of the AreaCircle and AreaEnd macro-function pair is very similar to the action of the AreaDraw, AreaMove, and AreaEnd function triplet. You should read the discussions of these three functions to better understand how the AreaCircle macro works.

AreaDraw

Syntax of Function Call

```
error = AreaDraw  (rastPort, x,  y)
D0                 A1        D0 D1
```

Purpose of Function

This function adds a point to a vector buffer that consists of sets of x,y values used to define areas to be filled by the AreaEnd function. AreaDraw returns a 0 if there is no error; it returns a −1 if there is no space left in the vector buffer allocated by the Init-Area function.

Inputs to Function

rastPort	A pointer to a controlling RastPort structure
x	The horizontal coordinate of a pixel in the raster coordinate system
y	The vertical coordinate of a pixel in the raster coordinate system

Discussion

There are six Graphics Library drawing functions that deal specifically with area development in the Amiga system: AreaDraw, AreaEnd, AreaMove, InitArea, RectFill, and

Flood. These functions allow you to define bitmap areas (initially part of a ViewPort structure) that can be used to build a complex display from a group of areas defined with these functions. There is more information on area development in the discussions of each of these functions.

AreaDraw allows you to define the vertices of an enclosed screen area. This area will later be filled with specific pattern and color combinations. You can use the AreaDraw function to define all the rectangular areas of your raster bitmap. You do this by defining all the sets of vertices required to fix the corners of all of those areas.

Once you allocate space in RAM for a raster, you must define the drawing information that will eventually be used to define all the views associated with that raster. This is where the drawing routines come into play. They draw information into the raster using the RastPort structure to control the drawing process. Effectively, this amounts to setting the raster bitmap bits to zeros and ones in an indirect manner.

A specific raster consists of a bitmap, which in turn consists of one or more bitplanes. After you have called the AllocRaster function to allocate enough RAM for each of the bitplanes required to define a given bitmap or raster, you must fill in the raster drawing information. There are at least two ways you can approach this job. The first procedure controls the bitplane bits directly. The second procedure uses the drawing functions to set and reset bitplane bits.

First Drawing Procedure

You can specifically address each bit in a bitplane and set or reset that bit to a specific value. First choose a set of bitplane bit values that together define a specific color at that point in the raster bitmap. Then set up your FgPen, BgPen, and AOlPen numbers by calls to SetAPen, SetBPen, and SetOPen to choose the color register you want. Next, set the proper bitplane bits.

You can vary FgPen, BgPen, and AOlPen as you define different parts of a raster. For instance, if you have a one-bitplane raster, you can only assign two colors to each point in that raster; one color is associated with a 0 bit and the other with a 1 bit. If your drawing mode is JAM2 (see the SetDrMd function discussion), the 1 bits in the raster will receive the FgPen color and the 0 bits will receive the BgPen color.

You can use the LoadRGB4 or SetRGB4 functions to set up the colormap table values (which color goes with which register), and the SetAPen and SetBPen functions to assign a primary pen number and a secondary pen number to the RastPort structure to which this raster is connected. In this way, you will be drawing directly into each bit of this single-bitplane bitmap. You can extend this procedure for drawing to a raster bitmap that consists of more than one bitplane. Here, however, things get fairly complicated.

Second Drawing Procedure

You can use the drawing routines to make things much easier. They provide the higher level drawing control you need to define the most common features of your video displays. In particular, you can use these routines to draw solid lines, patterned lines, solid rectangles, pattern-filled rectangles, solid polygons, and pattern-filled polygons. Because of their ability to deal with large sections of the raster at one time, these routines considerably speed complex video-display view definition.

The AreaDraw routine works with a specific RastPort structure that is controlling the drawing of a specific raster in memory. You can have a number of simultaneous rasters and coexisting RastPort structures in RAM to control the drawing in these rasters. You should arrange the programming logic of your task to work on one raster at a time, define all the polygon areas to be filled for that raster, and then move on to the next raster. In this way, you can optimize your use of scarce RAM by deallocating temporary buffer areas as you proceed from one raster to another.

A raster uses a number of bitplanes to define its total bitmap. The bits in each individual bitplane must all be in a single, contiguous section of RAM; however, the full bitmap of a raster doesn't have to be in one contiguous section of RAM—each bitplane can start at its own RAM location, as fixed by the AllocRaster function. Remember that the x,y values in a raster can range from 0,0 to 1024,1024; you are drawing into the raster, not into the display screen where x,y values are limited to 640,400.

It is important to note that the AreaDraw function does not actually draw an area on the display screen; it merely adds a new point to a growing list of vectors (x,y points) in a vector buffer that will eventually be used to define a set of filled areas with the AreaEnd function. Keep in mind that previously you must have set aside enough RAM with the InitArea function to hold all of the required vectors.

You do not have to call the AreaEnd function immediately after you define a single polygon area with a sequence of AreaDraw function calls. Instead, you can build up a growing set of area-definition vectors in the buffer area set aside by the InitArea function. Once you have defined all the polygon areas you need for one raster, you can execute the AreaEnd function to produce the actual fill. Then you can release the buffer area (by using the Exec Deallocate function).

In this way, you can define all the polygon areas to be filled for one raster. Once you are convinced that you will not need the InitArea vector buffer again for this raster, you can deallocate the memory set aside for it. Then you can move on to the next raster, set aside a buffer for it, and proceed to use the AreaDraw, AreaMove, and AreaEnd functions to define its vectors and area-fill polygon areas.

Don't be confused by the difference between the AreaDraw function and the Draw function. AreaDraw builds up a set of lines (vectors) to define an eventual area to be filled with a pattern; Draw produces a series of lines (often connected) between x,y values without any intention of filling the area enclosed by these lines. Use the Draw function if you want to draw lines and the AreaDraw function if you want to fill areas.

Also keep in mind the distinction between the AreaDraw and PolyDraw functions: again, PolyDraw deals with lines, while AreaDraw deals with areas. PolyDraw allows you to specify a series of x,y values that will define a closed polygon; however, this polygon will not be filled with the AreaEnd function.

AreaEllipse

Syntax of Function Call

```
error = AreaEllipse (rastPort, centerX, centerY, horiz_radius, vert_radius)
D0                   A1        D0:16    D1:16    D2:16         D3:16
```

Purpose of Function

This function adds an ellipse to the area information used for area-fill in a raster bitmap. When drawn, the ellipse will be filled with a solid color or a pattern according to the current drawing control settings in the RastPort structure. AreaEllipse returns a 0 value if the function call was successful or 1 if no room was left in the vector table list represented by the AreaInfo structure.

Inputs to Function

rastPort	A pointer to a controlling RastPort structure
centerX	The x-coordinate of the left-focal point of the ellipse measured in the raster bitmap coordinate system
centerY	The y-coordinate of the left-focal point of the ellipse
horiz_radius	The horizontal radius of the ellipse (in number of pixels) measured in the horizontal resolution of the raster bitmap coordinate system
vert_radius	The vertical radius of the ellipse (in number of pixels) measured in the vertical resolution of the raster bitmap coordinate system

Discussion

There are two functions in the 1.2 release that deal with ellipses: AreaEllipse and Draw-Ellipse.

There are two ways you can add an ellipse to a raster bitmap: first, you can call the DrawEllipse function to draw the ellipse immediately into your raster bitmap. Or second, you can call the AreaEllipse function to place information about the ellipse into the vector table associated with an AreaInfo structure to suspend the actual drawing of your ellipse.

If you proceed the second way, drawing information for the ellipse (the arguments of the function call) will provide the data required by the AreaInfo structure vector table. The ellipse will be added to the bitmap only when the AreaEnd function is finally called. Other circles, ellipses, and rectangles represented by that vector table will also be drawn at that time.

AreaEllipse appends the coordinates and size of the ellipse to the vector table coordinate list maintained by the AreaInfo structure. The ellipse will be drawn when the AreaEnd function is finally called.

The action of the AreaEllipse–AreaEnd function pair is very similar to the action of the AreaDraw, AreaMove, and AreaEnd function triplet. You should read the discussions of these three functions to better understand how the AreaEllipse function works.

AreaEnd

Syntax of Function Call

```
AreaEnd  (rastPort)
         A1
```

Purpose of Function

This function processes a table of x,y vectors and produces an area-fill by triggering the area-fill sequence. It processes the vector buffer built by the AreaDraw and AreaMove functions. It generates the required area-fill in the raster bitplanes. After the fill is complete, this function reinitializes the end-point vector table for the next AreaMove function. The AreaEnd function uses the temporary work-area buffer set up by InitTmpRas when generating an area-fill mask.

Inputs to Function

rastPort   A pointer to a controlling RastPort structure

Discussion

There are six Graphics Library drawing functions that deal specifically with area development in the Amiga system: AreaDraw, AreaEnd, AreaMove, InitArea, RectFill, and

Flood. These functions allow you to display screen areas that can be used to build a complex display from a group of areas defined with these functions. There is more information on area development in the discussions of each of these functions.

The Area-Filling Procedure

Suppose you are in the process of adding drawing information to fill in the bitplanes of a bitmap to define explicit polygon areas that will be filled with area-fill information.

As you continue to add different areas to the growing list of areas to be filled, you can keep changing the values of the various pens and patterns to define the next area to fill with your eventual AreaEnd function call. Your task will consist of a series of calls to the SetAPen, SetBPen, and SetDrMd functions and the SetAfPt macro, followed immediately by a call or calls to the AreaDraw or AreaMove functions.

In this way, you can change the drawing mode, drawing pen, line pattern, and area pattern as you progress through a series of polygon areas to be filled. All of the current drawing control information is stored in the RastPort structure; all of the vector x,y values are stored in the AreaInfo structure. The information in the AreaInfo structure changes as you add more and more vectors and polygons to your list of areas to be filled with the AreaEnd function.

You should postpone your call to the AreaEnd function until all the line vectors for each of your areas have been fully set up with the AreaDraw and AreaMove functions. Your task typically will have quite a few AreaDraw and AreaMove calls, but fewer AreaEnd calls for any given raster. Each AreaEnd call will take all the accumulated line definitions stored in the AreaInfo structure along with the drawing-control information stored in the RastPort structure and produce the actual area-fill.

You can also use the InitTmpRas function to set aside a specific work area in memory to hold temporary drawing information needed by the AreaEnd function. If your area-fill drawing information is extensive, you may need this temporary buffer; just call the InitTmpRas function with the appropriate buffer size argument. If you use the Init-TmpRas function, you will also have to provide a tmpRas pointer argument as its first argument. Once you set up this temporary buffer, your RastPort structure can use it to develop intermediate values to be used in your drawing definition.

Finally, note that the AreaEnd function also draws boundary lines on the area it fills. The line-pattern setting in the current definition of the RastPort structure is used to add patterned boundary lines around the area. If you do not want to add these lines, you must fool the AreaEnd function by arranging the line pattern defined in the current RastPort structure definition to match the background color and pattern where these lines are usually drawn. Then, even though these boundary lines are indeed drawn, they will match the background. Thus, the area will not appear to have any boundary lines.

AreaMove

Syntax of Function Call

```
error = AreaMove (rastPort, x,  y)
D0                      A1       D0 D1
```

Purpose of Function

This function defines a new starting point for a unique new shape in the area-fill vector buffer. It automatically closes the last area created by the AreaDraw function call and starts another area at the x,y location in the AreaMove function call. AreaMove returns a 0 if there is no error; it returns a −1 if no space is left in the vector buffer allocated by the InitArea function.

Inputs to Function

rastPort	A pointer to a controlling RastPort structure
x	The horizontal pixel position in the raster coordinate system
y	The vertical pixel position in the raster coordinate system

Discussion

There are six Graphics Library drawing functions that deal specifically with area development in the Amiga system: AreaDraw, AreaEnd, AreaMove, InitArea, RectFill, and Flood. These functions allow you to define screen areas that can be used to build a complex display from a group of areas defined with these functions. There is more information on area development in the discussions of each of these functions.

AreaMove defines a new starting point and a new unique area shape. You define the first point of this new area with the AreaMove function; subsequent points for this area are defined with the AreaDraw function.

The AreaDraw, AreaMove, and AreaEnd functions together provide a way to define filled areas in specific rasters stored in RAM. These functions provide a high-level approach to filling the raster bitmap information with color, line-pattern, and area-pattern information. If you had to do this on a bit-by-bit basis, your job would take much longer.

The AreaMove function provides a way to start a new area definition for a later area-fill. Specifically, AreaMove allows you to define a starting point (an x,y value) for a new enclosed area to be filled with a specific pattern. This pattern must be set in the RastPort structure associated with the raster bitmap to which you are now supplying drawing information. The effective area pattern will be the one set by your last call to the SetAfPt macro.

The RastPort structure has a line-pattern setting in addition to the area-pattern setting. The current line pattern is set by your last call to the SetDrPt macro. Finally, the governing RastPort structure has a set of FgPen, BgPen, and AOlPen settings. These are the primary pen number, secondary pen number, and outline pen number set by your last call to the SetAPen, SetBPen, and SetOPen functions, respectively.

Two other parameters in the RastPort structure are the cp_x and cp_y parameters. These are the current x,y locations of the drawing pen as it moves around the raster. Each time you make a call to the AreaMove or AreaDraw functions, you affect the value of these location parameters. Remember that the x,y values in a maximum-sized raster can range from 0,0 to 1024,1024; you are drawing into the raster, not into the display screen where x,y values are limited to 640,400.

If your current raster is small, you must be careful that the x,y values you specify in the AreaMove function don't exceed the boundaries you set previously by an AllocRaster or InitBitMap function call. If you specify a set of x,y values outside the range assigned by these functions, you probably will cause the system to crash when you try to call AreaDraw or AreaMove.

You should also be aware of the write-mask parameter in the RastPort structure. This parameter determines which of the current bitplanes are write-enabled. Usually, all planes in a bitmap can be written into; they are all write-enabled. In this case, the value for the write-enable parameter is a set of all ones.

If you want to prevent the AreaEnd function from affecting certain bitplanes in a bitmap, you can use the RastPort structure write-mask parameter; just set this parameter to a binary value to block writing into the bitplanes in which you don't want to write information.

Don't be confused by the difference between the AreaMove and Move functions. AreaMove moves the drawing pen to a new location in a raster to define a starting point as the beginning of a new area for a later area-fill; Move moves the drawing pen to a new location to begin drawing a new line in the raster or to start adding text characters at that new point.

AttemptLockLayerRom

Syntax of Function Call

```
success  =  AttemptLockLayerRom  (layer)
D0                               A5
```

Purpose of Function

This function attempts (tries, then continues with the current task) to lock the Layer structure pointed to by the layer argument. If the AttemptLockLayerRom call is successful, all other tasks will be prevented from changing the Layer structure until one of the unlocking functions (UnLockLayerRom, UnLockLayer, or UnLockLayers) is used to unlock that layer. AttemptLockLayerRom will not put the calling task to sleep if the layer cannot be locked. It returns a TRUE value if successful; otherwise a FALSE value is returned.

Inputs to Function

layer   A pointer to a Layer structure

Discussion

AttemptLockLayerRom is the only function in the 1.2 release that deals with layer locking. It is very similar to the LockLayerRom function; both are ROM based. However, it differs in one important respect: AttemptLockLayerRom returns a success value that your program can test to determine if the specified layer can be locked. If TRUE is returned, the specified layer was appropriately locked by the AttemptLockLayerRom call. If FALSE is returned, the specified layer was already locked and AttemptLockLayerRom could not lock it. In this case, however, the current task can recognize the FALSE return value and continue execution without going to sleep. This sequence is not possible with the LockLayerRom function, which does not return a value.

BltBitMap

Syntax of Function Call

```
planes = BltBitMap  (srcBitMap, srcX, srcY, destBitMap, destX,
D0                   A0         D0    D1    A1          D2
                     destY, sizeX, sizeY, minTerm, mask, tempA)
                     D3     D4     D5     D6       D7    A2
```

Purpose of Function

This function performs a Blitter copy operation that moves a rectangle from a source area in a raster bitmap to a destination area. The destination area can be in another raster bitmap. The BltBitMap function returns the number of bitplanes actually involved in the Blitter operation. BltBitMap does not test for or report any error conditions (for example, rectangle specifications outside of a raster bitmap). The number of planes returned by the BltBitMap function will be less than expected if tempA chip memory is not allocated properly.

Inputs to Function

srcBitMap	A pointer to the source BitMap structure, which contains a pointer to source bitmap information
srcX, srcY	The x and y pixel coordinates of the upper-left corner of the source rectangle in the source bitmap coordinate system
destBitMap	A pointer to the destination BitMap structure, which contains a pointer to the destination bitmap information
destX, destY	The x and y pixel coordinates of the upper-left corner of the destination rectangle in the destination bitmap coordinate system
sizeX, sizeY	The size in pixels of the rectangle to be moved
minTerm	An unsigned byte whose leftmost four bits indicate the logic function to apply to the source and destination rectangles to produce the new destination rectangle
mask	The write mask to apply to the Blitter operation
tempA	A pointer to a temporary buffer area of chip memory where a line of source data (data for up to 1,024 pixels) can be stored; this buffer is used only if the source and destination rectangles overlap

Discussion

There are ten Graphics Library display functions that work specifically with Blitter operations in the Amiga system: BltClear, BltPattern, BltBitMap, BltTemplate, ClipBlit, DisownBlitter, OwnBlitter, QBlit, QBSBlit, and WaitBlit.

The BltBitMap function uses the Blitter to move a rectangular portion of a bitmap to another area of the same size in the same bitmap or in another bitmap. The BltBitMap function can also be used to change data as you are moving it. The Blitter is ideally suited for this purpose, because it can transfer up to one million bits per second. This is the number of bits required to paint four one-color screens.

The BltBitMap function works with a source bitmap and a destination bitmap. You specify a rectangle position in both bitmaps. If you transfer bitmap data in the time between video frames, you can produce an effect similar to the Bobs in Amiga animation.

Only those bitplanes with identical plane numbers and a nonzero write mask (see the RastPort structure definition in the introduction to this chapter) will be copied from the source to the destination. Also, only those bitplanes whose plane numbers are less than the maximum plane count will be copied.

The srcX, srcY, destX, and destY variables are restricted to values between 0 and 976. However, you must make sure that these two sets of values are chosen so that the copy operation does not exceed the boundaries of the destination raster bitmap.

The valid range of the sizeX argument is from 1 to 976; the valid range of the sizeY argument is from 1 to 1023. Both arguments must also be chosen to ensure that the copy operation does not exceed the boundaries of the destination raster bitmap.

The minTerm byte controls the specific way the logic of the data transfer is handled during the Blitter operation. You can write a logic equation to define each type of logic transfer operation between a source bitmap (bits denoted by B), an original destination bitmap (bits denoted by C), and a final bitmap (bits denoted by A).

You can then reorganize that logic equation to an equivalent equation that involves a set of minimum terms using the rules of Boolean algebra. Each of these terms will have two factors in it (for example, $A = B\overline{C} + B\overline{C}$). Each term in this equation can be used to help specify one bit of the minTerm argument for that particular data transfer.

The bits set in the mask variable indicate which bitplanes are to participate in the operation. Typically, the mask variable is set to 0xFF (11111111), indicating all bitplanes will be involved.

The tempA argument is used to allow copies where the source and destination overlap. If the copy overlaps exactly to the left or right on an address boundary (that is, the source and destination addresses both occur on a word boundary) and the tempA is argument nonzero, tempA points to enough chip memory to hold a line of the source for the Blitter operation. You must have allocated this memory previously. You can use an Exec allocation function for this purpose.

BltBitMapRastPort

Syntax of Function Call

```
BltBitMapRastPort  (sourceBitMap, sourceX, sourceY, destRastPort,
                    A0            D0       D1       A1
                    destX, destY, sizeX, sizeY, minterm)
                    D2     D3     D4     D5     D6
```

Purpose of Function

This function performs a Blitter operation from a source bitmap to a destination bitmap. The destination bitmap is defined indirectly through the BitMap structure pointer in the RastPort structure. The details of the Blitter operation are completely controlled by the minterm logic value, which specifies how the source and destination pixel values are to be combined.

Inputs to Function

sourceBitMap	A pointer to the BitMap structure that represents the source bitmap
sourceX	The x-coordinate in the source bitmap coordinate system of the initial point (the upper-left point) in the source bitmap
sourceY	The y-coordinate of the initial point in the source bitmap
destRastPort	A pointer to the RastPort structure that contains the appropriate pointer to the destination BitMap structure
destX	The x-coordinate in the destination bitmap coordinate system of the initial point (the upper-left point) in the destination bitmap
destY	The y-coordinate of the initial point in the destination bitmap
sizeX	The number of x-direction pixels to blitter from the source to the destination bitmap measured in the source bitmap coordinate system
sizeY	The number of y-direction pixels to blitter from the source to the destination bitmap
minterm	The precise minterm (set of logic terms) to use for the Blitter operation

Discussion

There are two new functions in the 1.2 release that deal with Blitter operations: BltBitMapRastPort and BltMaskBitMapRastPort. Both functions carry out a Blitter operation from a source bitmap to a destination bitmap using a logic combination (a set of minterms) to control the Blitter operation. In addition, BltMaskBitMapRastPort uses a mask to control the Blitter operation. You should read the discussions of the other Blitter functions (BltBitMap, BltClear, BltPattern, and BltTemplate) to better understand how and why Blitter operations are specified and carried out.

BltClear

Syntax of Function Call

BltClear   (memBlock,   bytecount,   flags)
                    A1   D0   D1

Purpose of Function

This function uses the Blitter to clear a block of memory. The memory block must be in the first 512K of RAM. BltClear accepts the starting memory location and count and clears that block to zeros.

In the row/bytes-per-row mode, the rows variable must be less than or equal to 1024 and the bytes-per-row variable must be less than or equal to 128. In standard bytecount mode, multiple runs of the Blitter can be used to clear all the memory.

Inputs to Function

memBlock   A pointer to the memory block to be cleared; the memBlock variable must be an even number so that the clearing operation starts on a word boundary

bytecount   If the second bit (bit 1) of the flag variable is not set to 1, there is an even number of bytes to clear (standard byte-count mode); otherwise, the lower 16 bits of this variable are the number of bytes per row and the upper 16 bits are the number of rows (bytes-per-row mode)

flags   This is a one-byte variable; set bit 0 to 1 to force the Blt-Clear function to wait until the Blitter operation is finished

Discussion

There are ten Graphics Library display functions that deal specifically with Blitter operations in the Amiga system: BltClear, BltPattern, BltBitMap, BltTemplate, ClipBlit, OwnBlitter, DisownBlitter, QBlit, QBSBlit, and WaitBlit. These functions allow you to control the very fast DMA operations of the Blitter to accomplish the following:

■ Clear memory to zero (BltClear)

■ Perform area-fill operations (BltPattern)

- Transfer blocks of memory from a source to a destination (BltBitMap, BltTemplate, and ClipBit)

- Grab the Blitter for your current task (OwnBlitter)

- Give the Blitter back to other tasks for their use (DisownBlitter)

- Queue a request for Blitter usage (QBlit)

- Synchronize a task's Blitter request with the position of the video-scanning beam on the display screen (QBSBlit)

- Wait for the Blitter to finish before proceeding with operations in your current task (WaitBlit)

BltClear provides a mechanism to clear blocks of RAM at very fast rates. Keep in mind that BltClear is limited to the Amiga chip-memory area. This is the first 512K of RAM and is used by the Amiga special-purpose custom chips: Agnus (the animation custom chip), Denise (the graphics custom chip), and Paula (the peripherals-sound custom chip). These chips, together with some other Amiga special-purpose chips, can read and write only into the first 512K of memory. In addition, all of your bitmaps are confined to this area of memory.

The BltClear function requires three arguments. The first is the memBlock pointer variable, which points to the start of the memory block where the clearing operation is to take place. Under most circumstances, this variable must be an even number; BltClear generally clears an even number of bytes.

The second argument is the bytecount variable. This is the number of bytes of memory you want to clear. It can be an even or odd number, depending on other BltClear argument values.

The third argument is the flags variable, which can have several values that determine the mode of function execution. If the 0 bit of the flags variable (in register D1) is 0, the BltClear function will not return until the BltClear Blitter operation has completed. This means that the current task (the task that called the BltClear function) must wait until the Blitter operation is complete before it can execute additional task statements. Note that this is similar to the WaitBlit function, which will hold back further task execution until a series of queued Blitter requests have all completed.

If bit 1 of the flags variable is 0, the BltClear function assumes there is an even number of bytes to clear. The BltClear function then operates in even-number-of-bytes-to-clear mode.

If bit 1 of the flags variable is 1, the BltClear function operates in bytes-per-row mode; the lower 16 bits of the bytecount variable is taken as the number of bytes per row and the upper 16 bits is taken as the number of rows to clear. Most often, you will use this mode to clear an area of a bitmap, specifically a block of memory assigned to a bitplane in that bitmap. You can use the memory pointer returned by the AllocRaster function (when you allocated that bitplane) to get a pointer to that block of memory. Then call the BltClear function with that pointer. Use a memory location offset to point to another position in the bitplane.

Note that if you use bytes-per-row mode, you are limited to 1,024 rows or 128 bytes. If the total block you want to clear is larger than that, you can call the BltClear function a number of times to clear it.

BltMaskBitMapRastPort

Syntax of Function Call

BltMaskBitMapRastPort (sourceBitMap, sourceX, sourceY, destRastPort,
                     A0   D0   D1   A1
                  destX, destY, sizeX, sizeY, minterm, bltMask)
                  D2   D3   D4   D5   D6   A2

Purpose of Function

This function performs a Blitter operation from a source bitmap to a destination bitmap. The destination bitmap is defined indirectly through the BitMap structure pointer in the RastPort structure. The details of the Blitter operation are controlled partly by the minterm logic value, which specifies how the source and destination pixel values are to be combined, and partly by a single bitplane mask, which defines the pixels that are combined under the logic rules of the minterm. That is, the Blitter mask determines which pixels pass through the Blitter operation from source to destination.

Inputs to Function

sourceBitMap	A pointer to the BitMap structure that represents the source bitmap
sourceX	The x-coordinate in the source bitmap coordinate system of the initial point (the upper-left point) in the source bitmap
sourceY	The y-coordinate of the initial point in the source bitmap
destRastPort	A pointer to the RastPort structure that contains the appropriate pointer to the destination BitMap structure
destX	The x-coordinate in the destination bitmap coordinate system of the initial point in the destination bitmap

destY	The y-coordinate of the initial point in the destination bit-map
sizeX	The number of x-direction pixels to blitter from the source to the destination bitmap measured in the source bitmap coordinate system
sizeY	The number of y-direction pixels to blitter from the source to the destination bitmap
minterm	The precise minterm to use for the Blitter operation; either (ABC|ABNC|ANBC) if you intend to copy the source and blitter it through the mask or (ANBC) if you want to first invert the source and then blitter it through the mask
bitMask	A pointer to a one-bitplane mask in RAM; the mask bit-plane must be the same size and dimensions as the bitplanes of the source bitmap

Discussion

There are two functions in the 1.2 release that deal with Blitter operations: BltBitMap-RastPort and BitMaskBitMapRastPort. Both functions carry out a Blitter operation from a source bitmap to a destination bitmap using a logic combination (a set of minterms) to control the Blitter operation.

In addition, BltMaskBitMapRastPort goes one step further and uses a mask to control the Blitter operation. You should read the discussion of these two functions together with the discussion of the other Blitter functions (BltBitMap, BltClear, BltPattern, and BltTemplate) to better understand how and why Blitter operations are specified and carried out.

BltPattern

Syntax of Function Call

BltPattern (rastPort, maskBitMap, x1, y1, maxx, maxy, bytecount)
          A1   A0   D0 D1 D2   D3   D4

Purpose of Function

This function performs a Blitter operation using the drawing mode, area-fill pattern, outline, and raster write-mask of the current RastPort structure. The rectangular area is defined by the x1,y1 and maxx,maxy coordinates. The image bitmap must begin on a word boundary.

Inputs to Function

rastPort   A pointer to a controlling RastPort structure

maskBitMap   A pointer to a two-dimensional mask bitmap

x1, y1   Raster coordinates of the upper-left corner of a rectangular region in the raster

maxx, maxy   Raster coordinates of the lower-right corner of a rectangular region in the raster

bytecount   The number of bytes per row using bytes-per-row mode

Discussion

There are ten Graphics Library display functions that specifically manage Blitter operations in the Amiga system: BltClear, BltPattern, BltBitMap, BltTemplate, ClipBlit, DisownBlitter, OwnBlitter, QBlit, QBSBlit, and WaitBlit. These functions allow you to control the very fast DMA operations of the Blitter. There is more information on Blitter operations in the discussions of each of these functions.

BltPattern is the only Graphics Library function that deals specifically with drawing using the Blitter to set things up. Specifically, BltPattern handles drawing through a stencil (called a *mask*). Use BltPattern when you have a block of memory bits that you want to change in a specific way, and you want only certain of these memory bits to remain 1 bits after the BltPattern function has executed. In effect, you want to put a stencil or mask over a block of memory and change selected bits to 0 if your stencil mask has 0 bits at those locations.

For example, suppose you have a four-word (eight-byte) section of memory that you want to place a mask (stencil) over. Your mask has 1 bits only in certain bit locations, as shown here:

```
0000000000000000
0000001111000000
0000001111000000
0000000000000000
```

You can see that most of the bits in this mask bitmap are 0. Only eight bits in the center of the mask are 1 bits.

Assume your area of memory has all 1 bits:

```
1111111111111111
1111111111111111
1111111111111111
1111111111111111
```

You want to use the mask bitmap as a stencil over the second bitmap. This job is accomplished with the BltPattern function. This is the result:

```
0000000000000000
0000001111000000
0000001111000000
0000000000000000
```

When you use the BltPattern function, you must first establish how big your memory block should be—how much memory you want to stencil over. Generally, you will be dealing with one bitplane. Use the x1, y1, maxx, and maxy variables to set these size limits. The coordinates will be in the raster coordinate system. Keep in mind that large rasters can have x,y pairs as large as 1024,1024. You can use either maxx,maxy values or bytes-per-row mode to specify the limits of your bitplane once you specify the initial x1,y1 values.

Next, establish a memory block for the mask bitmap of the same size as the area of memory you want to mask. Use the second argument (maskBltMap) to point to this mask. Set the bits in the mask bitmap words according to the specific mask you want to design. You can use either hex values or bit values to define the mask in your program.

Then supply the rastPort pointer variable. This will be a pointer to the RastPort structure that is controlling the drawing into this particular raster. Note that the BltPattern function also draws into a piece of raster using the drawing rules already set up by the current RastPort structure definition.

Before you call the BltPattern function, make sure that the drawing settings in the associated RastPort are what you want for your drawing. Set the drawing mode, area pattern, FgPen, and BgPen to the settings you want for the resulting bitmap. JAM1 mode will use FgPen at the 1 bits in the result; JAM2 mode will use FgPen at the 1 bits and BgPen at the 0 bits. Read the discussion of the SetDrMd function for more information on these combinations.

BltTemplate

Syntax of Function Call

```
BltTemplate (source, srcX, srcModulo, destRastPort,
             A0      D0     D1          A1
             destX, destY, sizeX, sizeY)
             D2     D3     D4     D5
```

Purpose of Function

This function uses the Blitter to extract a rectangular area from a source array and place it into a destination area in a bitmap. The current FgPen, BgPen, and drawing mode settings are used for the drawing transfer operation.

Inputs to Function

source	A pointer to the source array of data bits; a subsection of this array contains a rectangular bitmap area to be transferred
srcX	The x coordinate of the upper-left corner of the source rectangle in the source array coordinate system
srcModulo	The source modulo; this value is used to find the next row of source rectangle data bits within the source array
destRastPort	A pointer to the destination RastPort structure, which contains an indirect pointer to the destination bitmap information
destX, destY	The x and y coordinates of the upper-left corner of the destination rectangle in the destination bitmap coordinate system
sizeX, sizeY	The x and y size of the rectangle to be moved; these values are measured in the source bitmap coordinate system

Discussion

There are ten Graphics Library display functions that work specifically with Blitter operations in the Amiga system: BltClear, BltPattern, BltBitMap, BltTemplate, ClipBlit, DisownBlitter, OwnBlitter, QBlit, QBSBlit, and WaitBlit.

You can use the BltTemplate function to transfer any rectangular area of a bitmap array to a specific bitmap in the system. BltTemplate differs from BltBitMap in part because the copy is a straight copy without any logic operations on the transferred data.

BltTemplate also differs from BltBitMap in the way it specifies the source and destination data. The source rectangle used in the BltTemplate function is pointed to directly. It is part of a bit data array in RAM.

The other difference between the BltBitMap and BltTemplate functions is that the BltTemplate function points to a RastPort structure to specify the destination bitmap. Thus, the destination bitmap is determined indirectly through the pointer to the BitMap structure in the RastPort structure. The BitMap structure referenced in the RastPort structure contains a pointer to a specific bitmap. The BitMap structure also defines the size of that bitmap.

The srcModulo variable tells the BltTemplate function where to find every row of the source data in the source data array. The value of the srcModulo argument is the number of bytes of data to add to the start of one row of source rectangle data to point to the next row of source rectangle data. This tells the BltTemplate function how the larger data array is organized and allows the function to extract each line of source rectangle data correctly. The value of srcModulo must be an even number of bytes.

The source data array is assumed not to overlap the destination, even though they may both be part of the same bitmap. In fact, if part of the data transfer falls outside the destination raster bitmap boundary, it is clipped to the destination bitmap boundary.

The srcX variable is measured in the source data array. The upper-left corner of the source data array is location 0,0. You can vary the srcX, sizeX, and sizeY arguments to make repeated copies of different subsections of the source data array for the destination raster bitmap.

The destX and destY coordinates are measured in the destination bitmap coordinate system with the upper-left corner of that bitmap at the 0,0 location.

You can use the BltTemplate function to transfer character templates (for example, text) from one memory area, where you separately prepare them, to their final drawing location in a large raster bitmap definition, which may later become part of a display screen view.

BNDRYOFF

Syntax of Macro Call

> **BNDRYOFF (rastPort)**
> **A1**

Purpose of Macro

This macro turns off boundary line drawing when the AreaEnd or RectFill function executes. It resets the AREAOUTLINE flag parameter in the RastPort structure.

Inputs to Macro

rastPort   A pointer to a controlling RastPort structure

Discussion

Any function that uses the AOlPen pen will normally draw a boundary line around the drawn object. This includes the AreaEnd function and the RectFill function. Note that the AOlPen pen setting is normally determined by calling the SetOPen function. If you want to avoid drawing a boundary when these functions execute, call the BNDRYOFF macro before you call these drawing functions. BNDRYOFF will then set the AREAOUTLINE parameter in the RastPort structure to indicate that boundaries should not be drawn.

After the current drawing operation is complete, you may want to restore boundary drawing once again. Note that there is no function or macro to do this. Instead, you will have to set the AREAOUTLINE flag in the RastPort structure with a statement such as the following:

```
MyRastPort.Flags = AREAOUTLINE;
```

CEND

Syntax of Macro Call

```
CEND (uCopList)
      A1
```

Purpose of Macro

This macro terminates a growing list of user-defined Copper instructions. It calls the low-level Copper routine CWait. When CEND returns, a specific user-defined Copper instruction list will have been fully defined.

Inputs to Macro

uCopList   A pointer to a UCopList structure

Discussion

There are four macros that deal specifically with user-defined Copper instructions: CINIT, CMOVE, CWAIT, and CEND. All four of these macros use the uCopList variable pointer argument and therefore work with the UCopList structure. Read the discussions of the CINIT, CMOVE, and CWAIT macros to learn more about user-defined Copper instructions.

The CEND macro terminates a list of user-defined Copper instructions being placed into a buffer set aside by the CINIT macro. Each time you want to end the definition of one complete set of user-defined Copper instructions, you should call the CEND macro.

CINIT

Syntax of Macro Call

```
CINIT (uCopList, numInst)
       A1        D0
```

Purpose of Macro

This macro initializes the UCopList structure to accept a set of user-defined Copper instructions. It calls the low-level Copper routine UCopperListInit. When CINIT returns, you can start defining Copper instructions with the CMOVE and CWAIT macros, then terminate the Copper instruction list with a call to the CEND macro.

Inputs to Macro

uCopList   A pointer to a UCopList structure

numInst   The maximum number of Copper instructions you expect to place into the Copper instruction buffer

Discussion

There are four macros that deal specifically with user-defined Copper instructions: CINIT, CMOVE, CWAIT, and CEND. All four of these macros use the uCopList variable pointer argument and therefore work with the UCopList structure. Read the discussions of the CMOVE, CWAIT, and CEND macros to learn more about user-defined Copper instructions.

The CINIT macro sets aside a buffer to contain a growing set of user-defined Copper instructions. This is done indirectly through the UCopList structure. The UCopList structure contains a pointer to the buffer area that will be used to contain these instructions. Before you call the CINIT macro, you should estimate how many instructions you will place into this buffer. Once the buffer is assigned, the CMOVE, CWAIT, and CEND macros will automatically place their Copper instructions into that buffer.

If the uCopList pointer variable is zero, this macro will allocate memory for the UCopList structure and a buffer to hold the number of Copper instructions in the numInst variable. If the uCopList pointer variable is not zero, the CINIT macro reinitializes an existing Copper instruction list to accept new Copper instructions; in this case the numInst argument is ignored.

ClearRectRegion

Syntax of Function Call

```
success  =  ClearRectRegion  (region,  rectangle)
D0                            A0       A1
```

Purpose of Function

This function performs a two-dimensional clearing operation of a clipping-rectangle with a region, leaving the result in the region. All areas in the region that are also inside the clipping-rectangle are cleared, thereby eliminating part of the region. ClearRectRegion returns a TRUE value if the operation was successful; it returns a FALSE value if not.

Inputs to Function

region   A pointer to the Region structure that represents the region to be combined with the rectangle

rectangle   A pointer to the Rectangle structure that defines the clipping-rectangle inside of which the region is to be cleared

Discussion

ClearRectRegion is one of the four functions in the 1.2 Amiga software release that deal with regions.

ClearRectRegion provides some additional region-definition control not provided by the AndRegionRegion, OrRegionRegion, and XorRegionRegion functions; it allows you to clear parts of a region. This has the effect of placing a hole in the region. Any subsequent drawing will not draw anything in the part of the bitmap that is inside this hole.

Note that clearing is different from Anding, Oring, or Xoring. However, you can also arrive at the same final region definition using some or all of the region-region and rectangle-region functions if you define the rectangles and regions appropriately and use the functions in the correct order. ClearRectRegion just provides you with an easier way to do this.

You should read the discussion of the AndRectRegion, OrRectRegion, and XorRect-Region functions to see how and why regions and clipping-rectangles are combined. These ideas carry over directly to the clearing of part of a region using a clipping-rectangle.

ClearRegion

Syntax of Function Call

ClearRegion (region)
A0

Purpose of Function

This function clears all the clipping-rectangles in a region. ClearRegion will set this Region structure and the associated Rectangle structures to size zero.

Inputs to Function

region   A pointer to a Region structure

Discussion

There are six Graphics Library drawing functions that deal specifically with regions and the clipping-rectangles that define these regions: AndRectRegion, ClearRegion, Dispose-Region, NewRegion, OrRectRegion, and XorRectRegion. These functions allow you to build a customized drawing region as part of the total definition of a layer.

The ClearRegion function clears a region to size 0,0, thereby eliminating all the clipping-rectangles associated with that region's current definition. The ClearRegion function uses the region pointer variable; its value was previously returned by a call to the NewRegion function.

Whenever you use the clipping-rectangle region-manipulation facilities to draw into your layer, you must follow this procedure:

1. Initialize all the structures you will need for your layer drawing: the View structure, the ViewPort structure, the ColorMap structure, the RasInfo structure, the BitMap structure, the RastPort structure, the LayerInfo structure, the Rectangle structure, and the Region structure. Use a series of structure declaration statements to initialize these structures and allocate the necessary memory for later definitions of their parameters.

2. Open the Graphics and Layers Libraries using the OpenLibrary function. OpenLibrary returns a pointer to each of these Library structures.

3. Use a series of simple program statements to fill in the specific parameters of the structures you initialized and allocated in step 1.

4. Use the AllocRaster function to allocate memory for all the bitplanes you will need for the layer bitmap you are about to define.

5. Use the MakeVPort function to assign a ViewPort structure to this layer.

6. Use the CreateUpfrontLayer or CreateBehindLayer Layers Library functions to allocate and initialize a Layer structure to define the layer you are about to draw into.

7. Use a series of simple program statements to define the vertices of all clipping-rectangles you intend to place into your region definition.

8. Use the NewRegion function to get a zero-sized region to use.

9. Use the AndRectRegion, OrRectRegion, and XorRectRegion functions to bring your clipping-rectangles into your region definition. Plan this step carefully so that you correctly define the drawing area you are trying to achieve.

10. Save a pointer to the current DamageList structure for this layer as a temporary variable. Then assign the layer's damageList pointer variable to point to the region's clipping-rectangle definition list. This is actually a pointer to the ClipRect structure that belongs to the region's definition.

11. Call the BeginUpdate function. Use the SetAPen, SetBPen, and SetDrMd drawing setup functions to define the RastPort structure to control the drawing. Use the AreaDraw, AreaMove, and AreaEnd functions (or any other drawing functions) to generate a drawing into the layer bitmap using the region clipping-rectangles as a type of mask through which to draw.

12. Call the EndUpdate function to terminate the region-controlled drawing process for that layer. Switch the damageList pointer variable back to the value previously stored in the temporary variable so that it points to the ClipRect structure once again.

13. Use the MrgCop function to define the total set of Copper instructions needed to define this layer. Use the LoadView function to load the view into the display hardware of the Amiga.

14. Use the ClearRegion function to clear the existing region definition. Now you can redefine the same region and proceed as before. Or, you can use the DisposeRegion function to free the memory assigned to this region.

15. Free all memory you don't need for further steps in your drawing progression for this layer.

ClipBlit

Syntax of Function Call

ClipBlit (srcRastPort, srcX, srcY, destRastPort, destX, destY, sizeX, sizeY, minTerm)
      A0   D0   D1 A1   D2   D3   D4   D5   D6

Purpose of Function

This function performs a Blitter operation between a source and a destination bitmap where the data transfer is clipped in the destination bitmap.

Inputs to Function

srcRastPort   A pointer to a controlling RastPort structure that points to the source bitmap for the Blitter operation

srcX, srcY   The x and y pixel coordinates of the upper-left corner of the source rectangle in the source bitmap coordinate system

destRastPort   A pointer to a controlling RastPort structure that points to the destination bitmap for the Blitter operation

destX, destY	The x and y pixel coordinates of the upper-left corner of the destination rectangle in the destination bitmap coordinate system
sizeX, sizeY	The size in pixels of the rectangle to be moved
minTerm	An unsigned byte whose leftmost four bits indicate the logic function to apply to the source and destination rectangles to produce the new destination rectangle

Discussion

There are ten Graphics Library display functions that work specifically with Blitter operations in the Amiga system: BltClear, BltPattern, BltBitMap, BltTemplate, ClipBlit, DisownBlitter, OwnBlitter, QBlit, QBSBlit, and WaitBlit.

The ClipBlit function is very similar to the BltBitMap function in that it copies bitmap information from one place to another. However, the ClipBlit function differs from BltBitMap because it works with RastPort structures. Each of these two RastPort structures (source and destination) contains a pointer to a Layer structure. Each RastPort structure also contains a pointer to a BitMap structure. Each BitMap structure contains pointers to each of the bitplanes that make up a bitmap. Therefore, the ClipBlit function provides an indirect way to reach the bits in a bitmap.

Because it works with RastPort structures, the ClipBlit function knows about the layer (or layers) controlled by the source and destination RastPort structures. It looks at those layers to see if there are any overlapping areas between them. If there are overlapping areas, ClipBlit splits the overall operation into a set of suboperations. Each of these suboperations transfers data from the appropriate source bitmap to one of the areas in the destination bitmap. Read the discussion of the BltBitMap function to learn how the Blitter operations are controlled by the ClipBlit function arguments.

CMOVE

Syntax of Macro Call

```
CMOVE  (uCopList, regnum, regvalue)
        A1        D0      D1
```

Purpose of Macro

This macro adds a Copper instruction to move value regvalue to hardware register regnum. It calls the low-level Copper routine CMove and then calls the low-level Copper routine CBump to bump the local Copper instruction pointer to the next instruction.

Inputs to Macro

uCopList	A pointer to a UCopList structure
regnum	A hardware register number
regvalue	A 16-bit value to be written into that register

Discussion

There are four macros that work specifically with user-defined Copper instructions: CINIT, CMOVE, CWAIT, and CEND. All four of these macros use the uCopList variable pointer argument and therefore work with the UCopList structure. Read the discussions of the CINIT, CWAIT, and CEND macros to learn more about user-defined Copper instructions.

CMOVE and CWAIT are the direct counterparts of the MOVE and WAIT assembly language Copper routine calls. You can access MOVE and WAIT directly through assembly language if you want to control the hardware at that level. In fact, your call to CMOVE or CWAIT does nothing more than call the MOVE and WAIT instructions indirectly. With CMOVE and CWAIT, you can alter the characteristics of the video display hardware directly at any point in the development and specification of a specific view.

When you specify Copper instructions with CMOVE and CWAIT, you build a UCopList structure in memory. This structure contains only the CMOVE and CWAIT calls you make for a particular view frame. When you call the MrgCop function, these instructions are merged with the Copper instructions generated by the MakeVPort and MakeView functions to form the complete list of Copper instructions that define the next frame. In addition, if you have animation effects in the upcoming frame, the animation Copper instructions are also merged into the complete Copper instruction stream when you execute the MrgCop function.

If the next frame is the same as the currently displayed frame, this total set of Copper instructions will be the same as used for the previous frame. On the other hand, if you have redefined your sprites, viewports, or UCopList structure for this new view, the merged set of Copper instructions will be changed from those of the last frame.

If there was no change, the system special-purpose hardware registers will not need to be changed during the vertical-blanking interval prior to the start of the next frame. On the other hand, if the merged set of Copper instructions has been changed from its definition in the last video frame, some system registers may have to be reset; this will be done during the vertical-blanking interval when the Copper takes over control of the system hardware from the 68000.

The first argument to the CMOVE macro is the uCopList pointer variable. This variable points to the UCopList structure, which points to all the user-defined Copper instructions in the definition of the next video frame. This structure will reference a list of MOVE and WAIT instructions to specify detailed changes in the next video frame definition.

These CMOVE-generated Copper instructions take the simple form of a MOVE instruction to move a value into a register. This is similar to the 68000 MOVE instruction.

You specify the value to move as the third argument in the CMOVE call. You specify the register number to receive the value as the second argument in the CMOVE call. It is important to note that the CMOVE macro does not actually move a value into a register; it merely adds an instruction to make a change to the UCopList structure instruction pool. The data value is not moved until first the MrgCop and then the LoadView functions have executed.

There are a number of important system hardware registers that you can control with CMOVE, including the color registers used to set up the color palette for the next video frame. Another set of registers that you can control with CMOVE includes those registers that define the display mode (high- or low-resolution mode, single- or dual-playfield mode, hold-and-modify mode, and so forth) to be used for the next part of the display.

The Copper can control the following register groups:

1. Any register whose address is hex 20 and above. This includes all the registers up to register number decimal 255 (hex FF), a total of 224 system hardware registers.

2. Any register whose address is between hex 10 and hex 20 and whose Copper Danger bit is set to 1. These are the second 16 registers in the system.

Note that any register whose address is lower than hex 10 cannot be controlled by the Copper. These are the first 16 registers in the system.

If you want to write your own Copper instruction lists, you will need detailed Amiga hardware information. This information will tell you the specific register name and purpose for each register associated with each of these register numbers.

CopySBitMap

Syntax of Function Call

CopySBitMap (layer)
A0

Purpose of Function

This function is the inverse of the SyncSBitMap function. CopySBitMap copies the current contents of part of the superbitmap assigned to a layer into the layer bitmap. The CopySBitMap function works only with layers that are specifically set up as superbitmap layers.

Inputs to Function

layer   A pointer to a Layer structure that in turn contains a pointer to a BitMap structure for a superbitmap; the Layer structure should already be locked by the calling task

Discussion

There are two Graphics Library display functions that deal specifically with superbitmaps and the layers associated with superbitmaps: CopySBitMap and SyncSBitMap. These functions work with the BitMap structure that defines a raster superbitmap and a Layer structure that defines a layer bitmap.

The CopySBitMap and SyncSBitMap functions allow you to synchronize the contents of a superbitmap with a layer bitmap. *Synchronize* here means to combine for the purpose of refreshing the screen. A *layer bitmap* is the on-screen portion of a layer.

A superbitmap is a single, often large, raster bitmap where obscured as well as off-screen portions of a layer bitmap are permanently stored to aid on-screen refreshing; it is a backup bitmap area for a layer bitmap. It is called a superbitmap for two reasons: first, it is often larger than the on-screen bitmap for a layer, and second, it alone can satisfy the entire refreshing needs of the superbitmap layer without help from other bitmaps in other sections of RAM.

When you use the Graphics Library drawing functions (for example, AreaDraw, AreaMove, and AreaEnd) to draw into a superbitmap layer, only part of the drawing is rendered into the current on-screen layer bitmap. In addition, any part of the layer that is presently obscured (not visible on the display screen) will also be affected by the drawing functions. The bitmap information for those portions of that layer are stored in the superbitmap. Therefore, it is superbitmap bitplane bits that the drawing functions alter to create the off-screen portion for that layer.

Once the drawing functions have finished their work, both the on-screen and off-screen portions of the bitmap have been defined. When your task (or the user) brings that layer to the front (or exposes additional portions of it), those portions previously obscured will be correctly rendered with the latest drawing information.

Also, when the layer is scrolled or resized, the superbitmap is used together with the layer bitmap to accomplish the changes. As scrolling proceeds, portions of the superbitmap are copied into the layer bitmap and portions of the layer bitmap are copied simultaneously into the superbitmap.

A similar type of bitmap copy operation takes place when the layer is resized. If the layer is made bigger, portions of the superbitmap are copied into the on-screen bitmap. If the layer is made smaller, portions of the off-screen bitmap are copied into the superbitmap.

The CopySBitMap function is used to copy appropriate bits from the bitplanes of a current superbitmap into the layer bitmap. The idea here is that you have used the drawing functions to redefine obscured portions of a layer. As you have seen, this drawing was done in the off-screen portion of the superbitmap.

To display these currently obscured areas on the visible screen, you must copy the appropriate section of the superbitmap into the layer bitmap. This is precisely what the CopySBitMap function does. Note that this operation is the opposite of the operation produced by the SyncSBitMap function, which copies a layer bitmap into a superbitmap. See the discussion of SyncSBitMap for more on superbitmaps and their interactions with layers.

CWAIT

Syntax of Macro Call

            CWAIT   (uCopList, vertbpos, horizbpos)
                    A1   D0   D1

Purpose of Macro

This macro adds an instruction to the list of user-defined Copper instructions already associated with this task. CWAIT waits for the vertical video-beam position v and horizontal video-beam position h. CWAIT calls the low-level CWait Copper routine and then the low-level CBump Copper routine to bump the local Copper instruction pointer to the next instruction.

Inputs to Macro

uCopList	A pointer to the UCopList structure
vertbpos	The vertical video-beam position relative to the top of the viewport measured in vertical-resolution pixels
horizbpos	The horizontal video-beam position relative to the left side of the viewport measured in horizontal-resolution pixels

Discussion

There are four macros that deal specifically with user-defined Copper instructions: CINIT, CMOVE, CWAIT, and CEND. All four of these macros use the uCopList variable pointer argument and therefore work with the UCopList structure.

You can use the CWAIT macro together with the CMOVE macro to achieve detailed control over the display screen. Use the CWAIT macro to wait for a specific horizontal and vertical video-beam position in a given view frame. For example, you can write an instruction to wait until the video beam reaches horizontal position 640 in line 100 in a high-resolution, noninterlaced mode display frame. When you write this call to the CWAIT macro, a specific Copper WAIT instruction will be appended to the information controlled by the UCopList structure in RAM.

Follow that CWAIT instruction immediately with the CMOVE instruction to move a specific value into a specific special-purpose hardware register in the Amiga system. For example, you can move a value into the register that controls the horizontal resolution of the display screen to change to a low-resolution display mode after the position 640,100 is reached. You might do this to specify a new low-resolution mode viewport as part of the new view frame you are defining.

Continue in this way, specifying pairs of CWAIT and CMOVE instructions to regulate the details of the new display screen view frame. However, it is important to understand that you want to exhaust all the higher level Graphics Library functions before you use CMOVE and CWAIT. It is much easier to program the higher level functions to do most of your screen definition. After all, they are designed to do more work with less programming effort. Use CMOVE and CWAIT only when higher level functions do not provide the kind of detailed, local screen attributes and mode definition that you need to define your viewports and their views.

Remember that the specific order of the Copper instructions is very important: the Copper instruction list must have a sequence that corresponds to the progression of the video beam as it creates a view frame. This is a top-to-bottom, left-to-right progression on the display screen. The video beam traverses the screen from the 0,0 position in the upper-left corner to the 320,200 position in the lower-right corner at the end of the display screen. Therefore, a CMOVE or CWAIT instruction that does something at 100,200 should come after an instruction that does something at 100,100; both the increasing x-coordinate and increasing y-coordinate ordering must be observed.

The MrgCop function expects the Copper instructions coming from each of its three sources to be properly sorted in this order, as does the UCopList structure. By contrast, the MakeVPort function sorts its contribution to the merged three-source Copper instruction list automatically. So do the animation routines that generate sprite-control Copper instructions for the upcoming video frame.

Like the CMOVE macro, the CWAIT macro contains the uCopList variable pointer argument. This tells the system to which UCopList structure to add this Copper WAIT instruction. The CWAIT macro deals specifically with both the vertical and horizontal video beam positions. The horizontal beam position is measured in terms of the last setting of the HIRES display mode parameter—either 320 or 640.

However, it is important to remember that the vertical beam position is always measured in terms of the noninterlaced mode setting of the LACE display mode parameter, and is therefore always a maximum of 262 lines. Note that because the Copper can operate in the overscan region of the display, you can write CMOVE and CWAIT calls to detect and change system registers while the video beam is in the overscan portion of the video display. This includes the first 31 lines (lines 0 to 30) and the last 31 lines (lines 232 to 262). These off-screen sections are sometimes useful when you need to make detailed changes before the start of the next video frame display.

DisownBlitter

Syntax of Function Call

DisownBlitter ( )

Purpose of Function

This function frees the Blitter so that other tasks can use it.

Inputs to Function

This function has no arguments.

Discussion

There are ten Graphics Library display functions that deal specifically with Blitter operations in the Amiga system: BltClear, BltPattern, BltBitMap, BltTemplate, ClipBlit, DisownBlitter, OwnBlitter, QBlit, QBSBlit, and WaitBlit. These functions allow you to control the very fast DMA operations of the Blitter.

Task control and ownership of the hardware in the system is an aspect of programming you do not need to consider in nonmultitasking systems. While the multitasking feature gives you great power in the types of programs you can produce, it requires additional bookkeeping on your part. One aspect of this bookkeeping is control and ownership of the Blitter—the fastest data mover in the Amiga system. This is where the OwnBlitter and DisownBlitter functions come into play.

The OwnBlitter function allows you to gain exclusive control of the Blitter for your current task's data movement needs. In this way, you can queue Blitter requests and wait for them to finish. The DisownBlitter function does just the opposite. It frees ownership of the Blitter hardware so that other tasks can use it.

You can see that these two functions are especially peculiar to a multitasking system where tasks often need temporary ownership of certain critical hardware resources while they process vital information. Once that information is fully processed, those hardware resources can be freed. At that point, another task can gain ownership of that same piece of hardware.

This temporary, one-task ownership ensures an orderly flow of program execution; you know which of your tasks owns which parts of the system when it is the active task, easing your bookkeeping chores.

If you combine the OwnBlitter, DisownBlitter, and WaitBlit functions, you can control closely just how and when the Blitter is used among your tasks. Read the discussions of the OwnBlitter and WaitBlit functions for more on this topic.

Generally speaking, you execute the DisownBlitter function near the end of your current task definition. When you enter into a task, you know that you need the Blitter's attention. Therefore, you execute the WaitBlit function first. This suspends your task until the current Blitter request queue empties. Then you execute the OwnBlitter function. Now your task owns the Blitter for its exclusive use, and you can proceed to generate Blitter requests with the QBlit and QBSBlit functions.

These requests are automatically added to the Blitter queue. Then you execute the WaitBlit function. Once again, all activity in your current task is suspended until the Blitter finishes with the newly queued Blitter requests. Once WaitBlit returns, your task should execute the DisownBlitter function to return the Blitter hardware to the system for other tasks to use. Those tasks will proceed in the same way to wait, own, wait, and finally disown the Blitter. This is the general logic of Blitter use in the multitasking Amiga system.

It is interesting to note that in contrast to the Blitter, the Copper is not owned and disowned by tasks. The Copper is tied mostly to the generation of the video display and is needed by the system and other tasks at all times.

DisposeRegion

Syntax of Function Call

DisposeRegion (region)
A0

Purpose of Function

This function first frees the memory allocated to all associated Rectangle structures for this region. Then it frees the memory allocated to the Region structure itself. DisposeRegion returns all memory for this region to the system free-memory pool.

Inputs to Function

region   A pointer to a Region structure

Discussion

There are six Graphics Library drawing functions that deal specifically with regions and the clipping-rectangles that define those regions: AndRectRegion, ClearRegion, Dispose-Region, NewRegion, OrRectRegion, and XorRectRegion. They allow you to build a customized drawing region as part of the total definition of a layer. There is more information on drawing regions and rectangles in the discussions of each of these functions.

A region is defined as a set of clipping-rectangles. Once all the clipping-rectangles are appropriately defined, you can draw into this region under control of the clipping-rectangles. The clipping-rectangles define and limit (clip) drawing operations inside that region.

In this way, you can create customized portions of your drawing using very quick drawing procedures. You can alter part of a layer bitmap in a very selective fashion. This method of drawing exists in addition to the other techniques for drawing discussed in this chapter. The main advantage to region drawing techniques is the ability to customize parts of a layer bitmap and thus speed the drawing operations.

However, you still have to allocate bitplanes, associate raster bitmaps with these bitplanes, and define a Layer structure. All of these steps lead up to the definition of regions. Don't confuse these types of regions with the explicit drawing regions created by such drawing functions as AreaDraw, AreaMove, AreaEnd, and RectFill. Also, be careful that you don't confuse clipping-rectangles with the rectangles filled by the RectFill function.

Six key structures play a big part in the use and definition of regions: the Layer structure, the LayerInfo structure, the Region structure, the Rectangle structure, the Clip-Rect structure, and the DamageList structure. Read Chapter 5 to learn more about the Layer, LayerInfo, ClipRect, and DamageList structures. When you allocate a new region with the NewRegion function, you are automatically allocating memory for the Region and Rectangle structures that are combined into the ClipRect structure. The ClipRect structure defines all the clipping-rectangles associated with that region.

The DisposeRegion function frees the memory previously allocated to a Region, a Rectangle, and a ClipRect structure by the NewRegion function. This frees memory for other uses in the system. The DisposeRegion function uses the region pointer variable argument. The value for this pointer variable was previously returned by a call to the NewRegion function.

Draw

Syntax of Function Call

```
Draw  (rastPort, x,  y)
        A1       D0 D1
```

Purpose of Function

This function draws a line from the current drawing pen position to the point with raster coordinates x,y.

Inputs to Function

rastPort	A pointer to a controlling RastPort structure
x	The horizontal coordinate of a pixel in the raster coordinate system
y	The vertical coordinate of a pixel in the raster coordinate system

Discussion

There are two Graphics Library drawing functions that deal specifically with drawing lines in the Amiga system: Draw and PolyDraw. These functions allow you to add lines to your RastPort structure definitions. The Draw function draws a line between the current pen position and a specified x,y point. PolyDraw uses an array of x,y points to draw a set of lines that potentially define a polygon in a RastPort structure definition.

The Draw and PolyDraw functions both use the rastPort pointer argument to point to a specific RastPort structure where these lines are to be added. In addition, PolyDraw uses an array pointer argument to point to the first of a set of x,y pairs that can be used to define a polygon.

The Draw function works with a specific RastPort structure; this RastPort structure is controlling the drawing of a specific raster in memory. You can have a number of simultaneous rasters and coexisting RastPort structures in RAM to control the drawing in these rasters. You should arrange the programming logic of your task to work on one raster at a time. Define some or all of the lines for that raster with Draw and PolyDraw function calls, then move on to the next raster.

As you continue adding different lines to your current raster drawing definition, you can keep changing the values of various drawing settings: you might change the drawing mode and drawing pen to define the line pattern for the next line to be drawn with your next Draw function call. In this way, you can change the drawing mode, drawing pen, and line pattern as you progress through a series of lines to be added to the raster you are defining.

Your task will then consist of a series of calls to the SetDrMd, SetAPen, and SetB-Pen functions and to the SetOPen macro, followed by a call to the Draw and/or Move functions to actually draw a line. Any line drawn will affect the contents of the bitmap that the RastPort structure is controlling. All of this drawing control information is stored in the current RastPort structure definition. The RastPort structure is a dynamic structure; it changes each time you change one of its parameters. For this reason, you must use its settings to draw your line before you move on to the next line if those settings change for the next line. Alternatively, you can have a number of different RastPort structures for the same bitmap. Each of these would have different drawing settings; just change the structure pointer when you want to point to another one.

Don't be confused by the difference between the Draw function and the AreaDraw function. AreaDraw builds a set of lines (vectors) to define an eventual area to be filled with a pattern; Draw produces a series of lines (often connected) between x,y values with no intention of actually filling any area enclosed by these lines. However, you can use the Flood function to fill the areas enclosed by these lines.

Also remember that the AreaDraw function requires a memory buffer to provide a temporary work area to build a set of area definition vectors (x,y values); the Draw function doesn't require such a buffer.

In addition, keep in mind the distinction between the Draw and PolyDraw functions. PolyDraw requires you to define all x,y values at once in a table. Draw requires you to define a single x,y point at a time; a single line is then drawn between the current drawing pen position and this point.

Neither the Draw nor PolyDraw functions provides directly for the area-fill mechanism. If you want to fill the areas defined using Draw and PolyDraw, you must use the Flood function; you cannot use the AreaEnd function for this purpose.

DrawCircle

Syntax of Macro Call

DrawCircle (rastPort, centerX, centerY, radius)
            A1   D0   D1   D2

Purpose of Macro

This macro draws a circle with the specified center and radius in the raster bitmap currently controlled by the specified RastPort structure. Only an outline of the circle is produced; the circle is not filled with a solid color. DrawCircle does its job by calling the DrawEllipse function. This macro returns no value.

Inputs to Macro

rastPort   A pointer to a controlling RastPort structure

centerX   The x-coordinate of the center of the circle measured in the raster bitmap coordinate system

centerY	The y-coordinate of the center of the circle
radius	The radius of the circle (in number of pixels) measured in the horizontal resolution of the raster bitmap coordinate system

Discussion

There are two macros in the 1.2 release that deal with circles: AreaCircle and DrawCircle. AreaCircle is a macro that calls the AreaEllipse function and DrawCircle is a macro that calls the DrawEllipse function.

There are two ways you can add a circle to a raster bitmap. First, you can call the AreaCircle macro to defer the drawing of your circle by placing the parameters for that circle in the information controlled by the AreaInfo structure vector table.

Or second, you can draw the circle immediately using the DrawCircle macro. Note that the DrawCircle macro produces only an outline of the circle. The circle is drawn in the current AOlPen color set by the most recent SetOPen function call. If you want to fill the circle, you can then call the Flood function to fill it with a solid color or pattern.

DrawEllipse

Syntax of Function Call

```
DrawEllipse  (rastPort, centerX, centerY, horiz_radius, vert_radius)
             A1        D0:16    D1:16    D2:16         D3:16
```

Purpose of Function

This function draws an ellipse with the specified center and radii in the raster bitmap controlled by the specified RastPort structure. Only an outline of the ellipse is produced; the ellipse is not filled. This function returns no value.

Inputs to Function

rastPort	A pointer to a controlling RastPort structure
centerX	The x-coordinate of the left focal point of the ellipse measured in the raster bitmap coordinate system

centerY   The y-coordinate of the left focal point of the ellipse

horiz_radius   The horizontal radius of the ellipse (in number of pixels) measured in the horizontal resolution of the raster bitmap coordinate system

vert_radius   The vertical radius of the ellipse measured in the vertical resolution of the raster bitmap coordinate system

Discussion

There are two functions in the 1.2 release that deal with ellipses: AreaEllipse and Draw-Ellipse. There are two ways you can add an ellipse to a raster bitmap. First, you can call the AreaEllipse function to defer the drawing of your ellipse by placing the parameters for that ellipse in the information controlled by the AreaInfo structure vector table. Or second, you can draw the ellipse immediately using the DrawEllipse function. Note that the DrawEllipse function produces only an outline of the ellipse. This outline is drawn in the current AOlPen color set by the most recent SetOPen function call. If you want to fill the ellipse, you can then call the Flood function to fill it with a solid color or pattern.

Flood

Syntax of Function Call

```
Flood   (rastPort,  floodmode,  x,   y)
         A1          D2          D0  D1
```

Purpose of Function

This function fills the raster much like an area-fill operation. Flood searches the bitmap starting at raster location x,y. It then fills all adjacent pixels according to the floodmode setting. Flood uses the drawing options (drawing modes and patterns) that apply to standard area-fill operations.

Inputs to Function

rastPort	A pointer to a controlling RastPort structure
floodmode	A variable to control the mode used to flood the area; when set to 0, the Flood function fills pixels if they are not the same as the current AOlPen color setting; when set to 1, the Flood function fills pixels if they have the same color as the pixel at x,y
x	The horizontal pixel coordinate in the raster coordinate system
y	The vertical pixel coordinate in the raster coordinate system

Discussion

There are six Graphics Library drawing functions that deal specifically with area development in the Amiga system: AreaDraw, AreaEnd, AreaMove, InitArea, RectFill, and Flood. These functions allow you to define screen areas that can be used to build a complex display from a group of areas. There is more information on area development in the discussions of each of these functions.

There are several ways to fill an area of the raster with drawing information. The first is to use the SetRast function to set an entire raster to one color; this provides no area-pattern or line-pattern capability. Second, you can use the AreaEnd function to fill a set of areas defined by the AreaDraw and AreaMove functions. You set the drawing mode, FgPen, BgPen, AOlPen, area-fill pattern, and line-fill pattern with prior calls to the appropriate drawing functions. A third procedure uses the RectFill function to fill rectangular areas with specific area-fill patterns; again, you can control the drawing characteristics. The Flood function is the fourth way to fill an area.

The Flood function stands apart from the other area-fill functions in that it has two operating modes. The first, called outline mode or mode 0, uses two pieces of information to carry out its operations. In mode 0, the Flood function first looks at the current setting for the AOlPen. Then it looks at the colors of all x,y points branching out in all directions from the x,y point to the borders of the area. If the colors of these points do *not* match the current AOlPen color, they will be filled using information in the current RastPort structure definition.

Any time a point is reached where the pixel color already matches the current AOlPen color, no further filling takes place beyond that point in that direction. For example, if the x,y point is 100,100 and the color at 105,100 matches the AOlPen color, points with x-values of 105 or more will not be filled.

The second mode, called color mode or mode 1, operates differently. It fills pixels based on a different criterion for choosing the pixel to be filled. Specifically, pixels whose present color matches the color of the pixel at the Flood function x,y point will be filled using information in the current RastPort structure definition. If they don't match the color at the x,y point, they will not be affected by the Flood function. The search for points that satisfy this criterion continues until the first pixel on the borders of the chosen area is reached.

Mode 1 continues to the border, whereas mode 0 will often stop searching and filling before a border is encountered. In mode 1, any filling operation that does occur will affect every pixel that satisfies the appropriate mode criterion until the first pixel of the border of the enclosed area is hit; that is, the area is flooded from a given x,y point outward in all directions until every border is encountered. You can see that the Flood function incorporates an algorithm to sense the borders of shapes, even very complex shapes. The Flood function operation is generally slower than comparable area-fill functions.

FreeColorMap

Syntax of Function Call

FreeColorMap (colorMap)
                A0

Purpose of Function

This function frees the memory previously allocated to a ColorMap structure and returns its memory to the system free-memory pool.

Inputs to Function

colorMap   A pointer to the ColorMap structure originally allocated with the GetColorMap function

Discussion

There are two Graphics Library drawing functions that deal specifically with the colormap in the Amiga system: FreeColorMap and GetColorMap. GetColorMap allocates memory for a ColorMap structure that is to be attached to a specific ViewPort structure. FreeColorMap frees the memory assigned to the ColorMap structure. The memory is returned to the system free-memory pool. This memory can then be allocated by this task or other tasks as required.

The GetColorMap function takes no structure pointer arguments; the FreeColorMap function uses the colorMap variable pointer argument to point to the ColorMap structure originally assigned by GetColorMap. The most important parameter in the ColorMap structure is the ColorTable pointer. The colormap table is a memory table that contains a set of color-number color-register definition pairs. This table allows you to vary the colors used in a viewport.

FreeCopList

Syntax of Function Call

FreeCopList (copList)
A0

Purpose of Function

This function deallocates all memory associated with the intermediate Copper list CopList structure. This includes all the memory for the intermediate Copper instructions required to define one frame of the video display. This block of memory is returned to the system free-memory pool.

Inputs to Function

copList   A pointer to a CopList structure

Discussion

There are three functions that free the memory assigned to hold Copper instructions to define the upcoming display frame: FreeCopList, FreeCprList, and FreeVPortCopLists. Each of these functions deals with a different category of Copper instructions.

There are four categories of Copper instructions: intermediate, hardware, viewport, and user-defined. The FreeCopList function frees the memory assigned to the intermediate instructions. The FreeCprList function frees the memory assigned to the hardware instructions. The FreeVPortCopLists function frees the memory assigned to the viewport instructions. The memory assigned to user-defined instructions must be allocated and freed with the Exec memory-management functions.

The CopList structure deals with the intermediate Copper instructions; it contains a pointer to the next block of intermediate Copper instructions. All the intermediate instructions in the complete intermediate Copper instruction set are contained in a linked list. The CopList structure contains a count of the number of intermediate Copper instructions in each linked instruction block.

To understand the distinction between the intermediate Copper instructions and the hardware Copper instructions, you need to understand how the graphics system arrives at the final set of Copper hardware instructions. It is done in two stages. The first stage takes all the viewport and view definitions (including any user-defined Copper instructions) and arrives at an intermediate set of Copper instructions. This set represents the display, color, sprite, and user-defined Copper instructions. (Although the user-defined instructions are a separate category, they are eventually merged into the intermediate instructions.)

This set of Copper instructions is called *intermediate* because they are not yet in the final form (specifically, the order is not in final form) necessary to drive the Copper co-processor hardware to define a display frame; they represent an intermediate step in the progression toward the final, full, per-frame set of hardware Copper instructions. The MrgCop function sorts these instructions to put all four components of the intermediate Copper instruction list into proper order.

The system automatically allocates a block (or blocks) of memory for these intermediate Copper instructions. The FreeCopList function deallocates this memory. See the discussions of the FreeCprList and FreeVPortCopLists functions for more on freeing memory used for Copper instructions.

FreeCprList

Syntax of Function Call

FreeCprList (cprList)
A0

Purpose of Function

This function deallocates all memory associated with a hardware Copper list structure. This block of memory is returned to the system free-memory pool.

Inputs to Function

cprList   A pointer to a CprList structure

Discussion

There are three functions that handle memory deallocation for the memory assigned to hold Copper instructions that define the upcoming display frame: FreeCopList, Free-CprList, and FreeVPortCopLists. Each of these functions deals with a different category of Copper instructions.

All three of these functions deallocate the memory assigned to the particular category of Copper instructions with which they work. There are four categories of Copper instructions: intermediate, hardware, viewport, and user-defined.

The Copper instructions contained in the CprList structure represent the final (as opposed to intermediate) *hardware* Copper instructions. These instructions originate directly from the results of the MrgCop function call. They contain all of the WAIT, MOVE, and SKIP instructions required to define one video frame. These instructions are sorted in y,x order. The CprList structure deals with the Copper hardware control instructions; it contains a pointer to a linked set of Copper hardware instructions. All of the Copper hardware instructions needed to define one display frame are contained in this linked list. The CprList structure's start variable points to the first Copper hardware instruction block in this series of linked instruction blocks.

These hardware Copper instructions change the color register assignments at the beginning and at intermediate points in a display frame and change the sprite color definitions in midframe. If you are an ambitious assembly language programmer, you could have written these instructions yourself as a large assembly language program containing the WAIT, MOVE, and SKIP Copper instructions.

This set of hardware Copper instructions is used to define one frame of the video display; of course, you can reuse it for any number of display frames. When you are finished with this set of explicit Copper hardware instructions, you should deallocate its memory with the FreeCprList function.

FreeRaster

Syntax of Function Call

FreeRaster (memBlock, width, height)
         A0   D0   D1

Purpose of Function

This function frees the memory assigned to this part of a raster bitmap and returns it to the system free-memory pool. This memory block was originally allocated with an

AllocRaster function call. Use the same values of width and height as you used when you originally called AllocRaster.

Inputs to Function

memBlock	A pointer to a memory block returned as a result of a call to AllocRaster
width	The width in bits of the bitplane
height	The height in bits of the bitplane

Discussion

There are four Graphics Library display functions that deal specifically with the raster: AllocRaster, FreeRaster, InitTmpRas, and ScrollRaster. A *raster* is an area of memory consisting of bitplanes that, taken together, form one of the bitmaps of the Amiga display.

The memory requirements of extensive graphic displays can be quite demanding. In addition to the display bitmaps, you have to define and store a number of graphics-related structures in memory. (These structures are listed in the introduction to this chapter.) Because of these memory requirements, you will want to free display memory as quickly as possible. Of course, this is more important if you have a small-memory Amiga (256K or 512K RAM) and less important if you have more memory.

Take a look at the bitmap memory requirements of various types of displays. To do this, consider Table 2.2, which defines the possible display mode combinations for the Amiga.

Table 2.2:
Number of Colors and Bitplanes for the Various Display Modes

Number of Colors	Number of Bitplanes	Modes Allowed
2	1	All modes except hold-and-modify
4	2	All modes except hold-and-modify
8	3	All modes except hold-and-modify
16	4	All modes except dual-playfield and hold-and-modify
32	5	All modes except high-resolution, dual-playfield, and hold-and-modify
4,096	6	All modes except high-resolution and dual-playfield

There are three things to note from Table 2.2:

- You are restricted to eight colors at most if you want to use the dual-playfield mode display. If you want more than eight colors, you will not be able to have two playfields.

- You are restricted to 16 colors at most if you want to use the high-resolution mode display.

- If you want more than 32 colors in a display, you *must* use hold-and-modify mode.

Consider a 320-by-200-pixel display. This is a low-resolution, noninterlaced mode display. This is the least memory-demanding type of display. Suppose you want only one color in this display. For one color, you will need only one bitplane to define a bitmap for each ViewPort structure in the display. Each line in the display has 320 pixels. With one color (one bitplane per bitmap), each pixel takes only one bit. Therefore, each line takes only 20 words (40 bytes) of bitmap information. You can see that this display would take 8,000 bytes of memory, just for one color. If you want to have four colors (two bitplanes per bitmap), you will need an additional 8,000 bytes. A 32-color display (five bitplanes per bitmap) requires 40,000 bytes of display memory information for one frame of the display.

This defines the memory requirements for the most basic type of display. You can figure out the memory requirements of more involved displays by relating it to this basic display. If you want a dual-playfield mode display with eight colors per playfield, you will need 24,000 bytes for each playfield, giving a total of 48,000 bytes to define both playfields of an eight-color, dual-playfield mode display.

Now consider a 640-by-200-pixel display. This is a high-resolution, noninterlaced mode display. This display has twice as many pixels on each horizontal line as the low-resolution mode display. Therefore, each horizontal line of the display requires 80 bytes of information for just one color. This gives 16,000 bytes for just one frame of bitmap information to define just one color. In this case, a 16-color display with four bitplanes per bitmap (the maximum allowed in high-resolution mode) would require 64,000 bytes of bitmap display information. If you want an eight color display, you will need 24,000 bytes per playfield, for a total of 48,000 bytes to define a dual-playfield mode display.

Now consider a 640-by-400-pixel display. This is a high-resolution, interlaced mode display. Each frame requires 32,000 bytes of information for just one bitplane to define one color. If you want a 16-color display, you need four bitplanes per bit-map. Therefore, you must have 128,000 bytes of bitmap display information per frame.

Now consider a single-playfield hold-and-modify mode display that is 320 by 200 pixels. This is a low-resolution, noninterlaced mode display. The advantage of the hold-and-modify mode display is that you can display up to 4,096 colors in a single frame. To do this, you must specify six bitplanes to define the two bitmaps that make up the separate parts of this type of display. From this you can see that a single-playfield hold-and-modify mode display requires 8,000 bytes per bitplane times six bitplanes, to give a total of 48,000 bytes of display information required to define just one frame of the display.

The technique of double-buffering, used to smooth the changes as you develop a fast-changing screen display, requires yet more memory. You have to set aside two memory areas to hold two sets of bitmap display information. One is used to drive the display hardware to produce the current frame. At the same time, the second bitmap is being updated to produce the display information required to define the next video frame. It is obvious that this double-buffering technique doubles the memory requirements of any display.

From all of this, you can see how important the FreeRaster function can be in your programs. As soon as you see that you are finished with bitplane and/or bitmap information, return that memory to the system free-memory pool with the FreeRaster function.

FreeVPortCopLists

Syntax of Function Call

FreeVPortCopLists (viewPort)
A0

Purpose of Function

This function deallocates the memory assigned to all intermediate Copper lists and their headers connected to a given viewport. FreeVPortCopLists searches the display, color, sprite, and user Copper lists recursively and calls the FreeMem function to deallocate the memory assigned to these lists. The function sets the DspIns, ClrIns, SprIns, and UCopIns pointers in the ViewPort structure to nulls.

Inputs to Function

viewPort   A pointer to a ViewPort structure

Discussion

There are three functions that free the memory assigned to hold Copper instructions to define the upcoming display frame: FreeCopList, FreeCprList, and FreeVPortCopLists.

The FreeVPortCopLists function works with the ViewPort structure and the full collection of intermediate CopList structures needed to define the display of a particular viewport.

The FreeVPortCopLists function deals with all the memory assigned to all Copper lists connected to a given viewport of the display. Specifically, you can use this function to free the RAM dedicated to these display Copper instruction lists: the color-register change lists, the animation routine lists, and the user-defined lists stored in the UCopList structure.

FreeVPortCopLists works with only one viewport at a time. If you want to free the memory assigned to all viewports in a view, you must execute the FreeVPortCopLists function for each of these viewports; each will have its own viewPort pointer variable, which you will know from your call to the InitVPort function.

The ViewPort structure contains four pointers:

DspIns   A pointer to a CopList structure for the display Copper instructions

SprIns   A pointer to a CopList structure for the sprite Copper instructions

ClrIns   A pointer to a CopList structure for the sprite color register Copper instructions

UCopIns   A pointer to the UCopList structure for the user-defined Copper instructions

Each of these is set to null (0) by the FreeVPortCopLists function. When the function returns, there are no display, sprite, or color-register Copper instructions, and there is no UCopList structure tied to this ViewPort structure.

GetColorMap

Syntax of Function Call

colorMap = GetColorMap (entries)
DO   DO

Purpose of Function

This function allocates memory for a ColorMap structure, initializes that structure, and returns a pointer to it. The resulting ColorMap structure is attached to the ViewPort structure to save color values. A value of 0 (null) will be returned if this routine cannot allocate the required memory for the structure.

Inputs to Function

entries   The number of color register entries in the colortable pointed to by a ColorMap structure

Discussion

There are two Graphics Library drawing functions that deal specifically with the colormap table and ColorMap structure in the Amiga system, FreeColorMap and GetColorMap. GetColorMap allocates memory for a ColorMap structure associated with a specific View-Port structure. The ColorMap structure allows you to specify the colors used for a specific viewport.

FreeColorMap frees the memory assigned to the ColorMap structure. The memory is returned to the system free-memory pool and can then be allocated by this task or other tasks as required.

The GetColorMap function takes no structure pointer arguments, but it returns a pointer to the ColorMap structure it has initialized. The FreeColorMap function uses the colorMap variable pointer argument returned by GetColorMap to point to the ColorMap structure. Read the discussion of the LoadRGB4 function to see how the entries in the colortable are defined.

GetRGB4

Syntax of Function Call

```
colorvalue = GetRGB4 (colorMap,entry)
D0                    A0        D0
```

Purpose of Function

This function determines and returns the value of an entry in a ColorMap structure's colortable array. GetRGB4 returns -1 if the entry argument is not a valid entry in the table associated with this ColorMap structure; otherwise, it returns a UWORD (two-byte) RGB value, four bits per gun (red, green, or blue), right-justified. Bits 0 to 3 are assigned to blue; bits 4 to 7 are assigned to green; bits 8 to 11 are assigned to red. This bit assignment allows any entry to represent any one of 4,096 colors.

Inputs to Function

colorMap   A pointer to a ColorMap structure that contains a pointer to a colortable array of RGB color-register values assigned to a viewport

entry   An index into the colortable array

Discussion

There are three Graphics Library drawing functions that deal specifically with the colors assigned and used in viewports in the Amiga system: GetRGB4, LoadRGB4, and SetRGB4.

LoadRGB4 loads a set of RGB color values into the colortable array associated with a ColorMap structure, allowing you to change the colors assigned to a given viewport. GetRGB4 allows you to find the value of a specific color assigned by a ColorMap structure through its associated colortable. Once you know what this color is, you can use or change it, according to your needs, to define the detailed appearance of a specific viewport on the display screen. SetRGB4 allows you to set one specific color in the colortable associated with a given ColorMap structure.

The GetRGB4 function uses the colorMap variable pointer argument to point to a ColorMap structure. This is the same pointer variable returned by the GetColorMap function.

InitArea

Syntax of Function Call

```
InitArea (arealnfo, buffer, maxvectors)
           A0        A1      D0
```

Purpose of Function

This function allocates memory for and initializes the vector collection matrix—a collection of end-point (vertex) specifications that define an area. The initialized area has a size of maxvectors x,y pairs. The size of the region pointed to by the buffer pointer variable should be five times as large as the maxvectors variable. This size is given in bytes.

Area-fills produced with the AreaMove, AreaDraw, and AreaEnd functions must have enough memory space allocated in the vector collection matrix to store all the points for the area with the greatest number of vertices. If there is not enough memory space, this routine will return a -1. When InitArea returns, pointers are set up to begin storing vectors produced by AreaMove and AreaDraw. The underlying low-level graphics routines actually split the vector collection matrix into two parts to save coordinates and flags.

Inputs to Function

arealnfo   A pointer to an AreaInfo structure

buffer   A pointer to a memory block where vertex x,y pairs will be
                  stored; the buffer must start on a word boundary

maxvectors   The maximum number of x,y pairs (vectors) this buffer will
                  be designed to hold

Discussion

There are six Graphics Library drawing functions that deal specifically with area development in the Amiga system: AreaDraw, AreaEnd, AreaMove, Flood, InitArea, and Rect-Fill. These functions allow you to define bitmap areas (initially part of a viewport bitmap) that can be used to build up a complex display screen from a group of areas. There is more information on area development in the discussions of each of these functions.

The AreaDraw, AreaMove, and AreaEnd functions deal with area-fill drawing vectors. Vectors are sets of x,y values required to define lines that go between these x,y points. If you are building a fairly complicated set of areas to be filled, you might need a great number of x,y points to fully define that area. This is where the InitArea function comes into play.

The InitArea function has two basic purposes. First, it sets aside a buffer area in RAM to hold all the x,y values you need to define a specific area to be filled. Second, it provides a bookkeeping mechanism through the AreaInfo structure. The current controlling RastPort structure stores a pointer to the AreaInfo structure.

The AreaInfo structure acts as a bookkeeping structure. It consists in part of two pointer variables, a Count variable and a Maxcount variable. The Count variable is the number of vertices (x,y values) actually stored in the current vector buffer table. The first pointer variable points to the vector buffer table where the x,y values are stored. The second pointer variable points to the current vector (or vertex) being processed by the AreaInfo structure.

Note that the buffer specified in the InitArea function call must be large enough to hold the largest area-fill that you are designing through the current AreaInfo structure. Recall that you have to begin your area-fill sequence by defining the appropriate drawing mode, area-fill pattern, line-fill pattern, FgPen, BgPen, and AOlPen. These requirements limit how large a buffer you will need at any one time in your drawing progression; each call to the AreaEnd function will use very specific drawing settings. Therefore, you can draw and fill only those areas that have the same characteristics.

You can collect all your areas with common drawing characteristics into subgroups. This is true even though your drawing areas can be scattered widely throughout the raster you are defining. The buffer size set aside by the InitArea function should be based on the maximum number of x,y values required to define all areas in the largest subgroup. Once you know this number, call InitArea and follow this with calls to AreaDraw, AreaMove, and, finally, AreaEnd.

When your AreaEnd call has completed, you can proceed in the same way for the next subgroup in that raster. Do this for all subgroups in the first raster. When that raster is complete, go through the same procedure for the next raster. Continue in this way until you define all the areas to be filled.

Because of this procedure, the required buffer may not have to be very large; it depends mostly on the sequence of your drawing operations, which is entirely up to you to define. If you are squeezed for RAM space, you can limit the size of the InitArea buffer by treating only a selected section of your drawing even if other sections have the same drawing characteristics.

InitBitMap

Syntax of Function Call

InitBitMap (bitMap, depth, width, height)
A0   D0   D1   D2

Purpose of Function

This function initializes a BitMap structure with input values. It places values in the Bit-Map structure to reflect correctly the depth, width, and height of a specific bitmap. Init-BitMap must be called before you can use this bitmap in other graphics calls. The bitmap bitplanes are not allocated; the calling task must do this with the AllocRaster function.

Inputs to Function

bitMap	A pointer to a BitMap structure
depth	The number of bitplanes this bitmap will have
width	The number of bits wide (columns) this bitmap will be
height	The number of bits tall (rows) this bitmap will be

Discussion

There are three Graphics Library display functions that work specifically with bitmaps: CopySBitMap, InitBitMap, and SyncSBitMap. There is more information on bitmaps in the discussions of the CopySBitMap and SyncSBitMap functions.

The procedure for developing a view on the Amiga display screen consists in part of specifying the bitmaps used to define that view. You must do three things to finalize the information in a bitmap: initialize the BitMap structure, set aside an area of memory to hold the bitmap, and supply pixel information to each bitplane of the bitmap.

Initializing the BitMap structure is the job of the InitBitMap function. When you make your call to InitBitMap, one of the arguments you must specify is the depth of the bitmap; you will know this value by the design of that bitmap. You will also know how many colors you want to display and which display mode (low-resolution, high-resolution, dual-playfield, or hold-and-modify) you plan for this part of the final view display. When you call InitBitMap, you must also supply the width and height arguments. These variables define the size of the bitmap in memory. Both width and height can be as large as 1,024 pixels.

Generally speaking, you will use these same variables when you call the AllocRaster function to allocate memory for each of the bitplanes of this bitmap. Note that the BitMap structure is a part of the INCLUDE file for the Graphics Library; it is called Gfx.h (for the C language interface) and Gfx.i (for the assembly language interface).

Use the AllocRaster function to set aside an area of memory to hold the bitmap. AllocRaster tells the memory allocation system how much memory to allocate to a single bitplane. Once you decide on the depth (number of bitplanes per bitmap) of your bitmap, you can decide how many calls to AllocRaster you will need to set aside the memory space for each bitplane in that bitmap; make one call to AllocRaster for each bitplane in the bitmap you are defining.

Keep in mind that the bitmap stored in RAM can be as large as 1,024 by 1,024 pixels. At any one time, you can show only a part of this large display. You do this by specifying the raster offset parameters (RxOffset and RyOffset) to select a portion of the bitmap to define the specific viewport you want to appear. The RxOffset and RyOffset parameters are part of the RasInfo structure. The purpose of the RasInfo structure is to select a subsection of a large bitmap to define a viewport bitmap.

Recall that the RasInfo structure provides information to the system about the location of the BitMap structure as well as the positioning of the display area. These positioning variables are measured with respect to the upper-left corner of the bitmap in memory, which has pixel coordinates 0,0; the lower-right corner can have pixel coordinates as large as 1024,1024.

You can supply pixel information to each bitplane of the BitMap structure in two ways. First, you can use a C language running For loop index to specify every pixel in each bitplane directly, one by one. Second, you can use any and all of the drawing functions to draw information into each bitplane. If you add information to your bitplane in this way, you will usually be working with high-level geometric structures such as lines, areas, and vectors.

InitRastPort

Syntax of Function Call

InitRastPort (rastPort)
A1

Purpose of Function

This function initializes a RastPort structure to standard values. The RastPort structure is the main drawing control structure for a bitmap. The RastPort structure describes how the bits of a complete, single-playfield bitmap will be written. This structure is referenced by any drawing functions that perform operations on a section of a bitmap in RAM.

When InitRastPort returns, all entries in the RastPort structure are zeroed except for the Drawing Write Mask, FgPen, AOlPen, and LinePtn parameters, which each get a value of − 1.

In addition, the InitRastPort function sets the drawing mode to JAM2. The font choice for text characters is set to the standard system font—Topaz-60 or Topaz-80, depending on the specific display mode currently being used.

Inputs to Function

rastPort   A pointer to a controlling RastPort structure

Discussion

InitRastPort is the only Graphics Library display function that deals directly with the RastPort structure. It allows you to initialize the contents of the RastPort structure in memory. You should call the InitRastPort function whenever you need to restore a Rast-Port structure to its initial default parameter settings. For more information about the RastPort structure, see the introduction to this chapter.

You can create a variety of RastPort structures that can then be used to define various ViewPort structures. These ViewPort structures can be linked together to define various View structures. View structures can be combined to define a wide range of distinct views leading to a wide range of display screens.

The section of memory that is being written may or may not be part of the current on-screen display memory. For example, if you are using the double-buffering display mode, this memory could be the memory devoted to the off-screen display buffer. The actual memory area defined by the RastPort structure is referred to as either a *raster* or a *bitmap*.

Calling the InitRastPort function establishes various defaults in the RastPort structure. It does not establish where the rasters are located in memory. To do graphics with this RastPort, the task must set up a pointer to the BitMap structure in the RastPort. This is done by first creating a BitMap structure with assignment statements and then using a pointer to the BitMap structure in the RastPort structure.

Remember also that the bitmap that defines the characteristics of the raster in memory can be as large as 1,024-by-1,024 pixels. It can also be as small as 1-by-1 pixel. Most often, the raster will be one of four sizes: 320-by-200 pixels, 640-by-200 pixels, 320-by-400 pixels, or 640-by-400 pixels.

These size combinations define rasters that are precisely the size of the display screen in the various display modes that the Amiga can present. If you are using one of these sizes, the view size will match the raster size exactly. In this case, you will not be able to scroll the view inside the raster; they are one and the same. However, depending on other relationships, you may still be able to scroll your viewports inside the view to which they belong.

Also remember that each viewport bitmap can be equal to or less than the raster in size but limited to the maximum viewable area of the current display mode. For example, if your raster size is 320-by-200 pixels (a low-resolution, noninterlaced mode raster), your viewport bitmap can be as large as 320-by-200 pixels. However, if your raster is 1,024-by-1,024 and you want a low-resolution, noninterlaced mode display viewport, the size of your viewport is still limited to 320-by-200 pixels.

These size limitations depend on the combination of the number of colors and the specific display mode you want in your final view. See the discussion of the FreeRaster function for a table of available display modes and the number of colors you can have in those display modes.

With these size considerations in mind, you can define some key variables used in the various structures to fix the relationship between the raster information in memory and the viewport and view information that is actually shown on the display screen. These variables are RHeight, RWidth, RxOffset, and RyOffset; DWidth, DHeight, DxOffset, and DyOffset.

The RHeight variable is the vertical size of the raster measured in number of pixels in the y direction of the display screen. This number can be as large as 1024 and as small as 1. This variable is used in the calls to the AllocRaster and InitBitMap functions. It appears in the BitMap structure as the rows parameter. If RHeight is greater than 400, it is obvious that only a part of the raster information can be put on the display screen at any given time. However, you should keep in mind that you can still draw into other parts of the raster while a smaller section is being shown. Once that drawing operation is completed, you can redefine which part of the raster is to become a new viewport to be used as part of a new view. In this way, you can define a very large raster in memory and present different parts of it for each video frame presented to the display hardware.

The RWidth variable is the horizontal size of the raster measured in number of pixels in the x direction of the display screen. Just like RHeight, this number can be as large as 1024 and as small as 1. This variable is used in calls to the AllocRaster and InitBitMap functions. It is directly related to the BytesPerRow parameter in the BitMap structure. If RWidth is greater than 640, only a part of the raster information can be on the display screen at any one time. However, just as with the RHeight variable, you can still draw into other parts of the raster while a smaller section is being shown.

RxOffset is the raster offset x-direction variable. RxOffset specifies the starting x-coordinate for the definition of a viewport bitmap that is pulled from a larger bitmap in memory. RxOffset is measured from the upper-left corner of the raster bitmap as stored in memory. The coordinates of the upper-left raster corner are 0,0. If, for example, you have a 1024-by-1024 pixel raster, you can set RxOffset equal to 200. If your viewport bitmap is defined as a low-resolution mode display, the pixel information to define that viewport bitmap will come from the pixel locations of the raster bitmap in RAM where x is a value between 200 and 520.

RyOffset is the raster offset y-direction variable. RyOffset specifies the starting y-coordinate for the definition of a viewport bitmap that is pulled from a larger raster bitmap in memory. Like RxOffset, RyOffset is measured from the upper-left corner of the raster bitmap as stored in memory. For example, if you have a 1024-by-1024 pixel raster, you can set RyOffset equal to 300. If your viewport bitmap is defined as an interlaced mode display, the pixel information to define that viewport will come from the pixel locations of the raster bitmap in RAM where y is a value between 300 and 700.

DWidth, DHeight, DxOffset, and DyOffset are all variables in the ViewPort structure definition. The DWidth variable is the width (in pixels) of the viewport bitmap that you pull from the larger raster bitmap in memory. For example, if you want a low-resolution mode viewport, you can set DWidth equal to 320. Remember that the starting location for pixel information taken from the raster bitmap will have been set by the RxOffset variable in the RasInfo structure.

The DHeight variable is the height of the viewport bitmap that you pull from the larger raster bitmap in memory. For example, if you want an interlaced mode viewport, you can set DHeight equal to 400. Note that the starting location for pixel information taken from the raster bitmap will have been set by the RyOffset variable in the RasInfo structure.

The DxOffset variable sets the on-screen x-coordinate starting position of the viewport bitmap that you pulled from the larger raster bitmap. Here, distances are referenced to the Amiga physical display screen, not the raster bitmap in RAM. This places the 0,0 point in the upper-left corner of the Amiga display screen. For example, if you want this viewport to appear centered on the Amiga display, use a value of 0 for this variable. If you want this viewport to appear shifted left or right on the display screen, use a nonzero value for this variable. Negative values shift the viewport to the left; positive values shift the viewport to the right.

The DyOffset variable sets the on-screen position of the viewport bitmap that you pulled from the larger raster bitmap. Just as with the DxOffset variable, distances are referenced to the Amiga physical display screen, not the raster bitmap in RAM. A value of 0 for this variable will center the viewport on the Amiga display. Negative values shift the viewport down; positive values shift the viewport up. These relationships are illustrated in Figure 2.4.

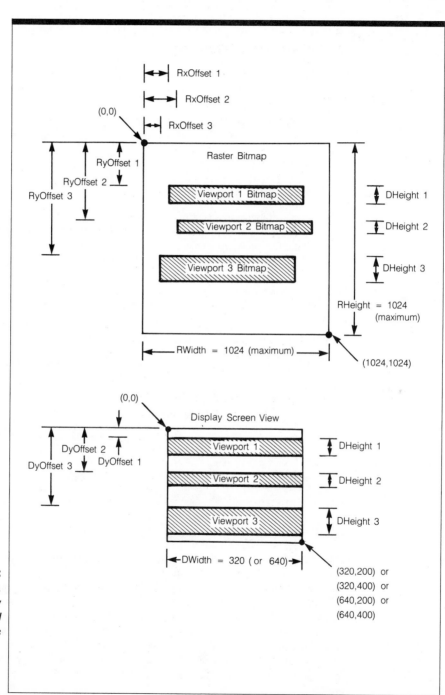

Figure 2.4:
Raster Bitmap, Viewports, View Offsets, and Dimensions

InitTmpRas

Syntax of Function Call

> InitTmpRas (tmpRas, buffer, size)
>   A0   A1   D0

Purpose of Function

This function initializes an area of memory in the first 512K of RAM for use by the area-fill, flood-fill, and text functions. The buffer variable points to an area of RAM set up for the area-fill functions (AreaDraw, AreaMove, and AreaEnd). These functions use this memory for intermediate bitmap sections in preparation for putting these sections into the full raster bitmap. InitTmpRas makes the buffer available to all tasks that use the current controlling RastPort structure. The tmpRas variable is a pointer to a TmpRas structure. The TmpRas structure is very simple; it merely contains a pointer to a temporary raster bitmap in RAM and the size of that bitmap.

Inputs to Function

tmpRas   A pointer to a TmpRas structure to be linked into a RastPort structure

buffer   A pointer to a contiguous piece of memory in the first 512K of RAM

size   The size of the buffer in bytes

Discussion

There are four Graphics Library display functions that deal specifically with the raster bitmap: AllocRaster, FreeRaster, InitTmpRas, and ScrollRaster. There is more information on defining and manipulating rasters in the discussions of each of these functions.

It is important to understand that the InitBitMap function does nothing more than initialize your raster bitmap. It is up to you to place drawing information into it. Once all drawing information is appropriately placed into each raster bitmap, you can use the viewport functions to extract specific sections of that raster to define your viewports. You can then combine selected viewports to define your views. In this way, you build a sequence of display frames that can be used by your tasks.

It would be nice if you could do this all in one step by calling some magic Graphics Library function. You cannot, however, so you are forced to use sometimes complex sequences of drawing steps to define the graphic information content of your rasters. In particular, when you use the AreaDraw, AreaMove, and AreaEnd functions, you will be defining (drawing into) specific areas of a specific raster that were previously initialized with the InitBitMap function.

One result of this procedure is that the AreaEnd function places some additional memory requirements into your task. Specifically, you must set aside a buffer to hold all the vectors (x,y points) needed to define all the vertices of areas that will be filled when the AreaEnd function is executed. This is also true of the Flood function; it too requires a temporary buffer to handle its intermediate data-handling requirements. For more on this extra buffer requirement, see the discussion of the InitArea function.

In addition to the InitArea buffer for vectors, the Amiga drawing system is set up to provide temporary buffers for temporary subsections of the current raster bitmap. This is where raster bitmap information is designed by the AreaEnd and Flood functions. Each time you call either of these functions, they develop that section of final raster information in a temporary buffer. This temporary area is pointed to by the buffer variable in your most recent call to the InitTmpRas function.

The AreaEnd function draws into this temporary buffer. Then, when the buffer is fully defined, it takes that piece of raster bitmap information and places it into the targeted raster that you are filling with the AreaEnd function.

You can see that this is an indirect approach to filling your raster bitmap with drawing information. Once the AreaEnd function has executed, the buffer is automatically released for the next series of AreaDraw, AreaMove, and subsequent AreaEnd function calls. Because of this internal system procedure, you must allow RAM space for the maximum buffer you will need in this series of buffers in the design of your graphics tasks.

Note that these buffers and the corresponding bitmap areas for all of your raster bitmaps all have to coexist in the first 512K of RAM. For a complicated graphics design involving several rasters, viewports, and views, this means that you will have to plan a graphics development strategy.

There are two ways you can allocate memory for a temporary raster buffer. First, you can estimate the maximum buffer size and give this size argument directly to the InitTmpRas function. The InitTmpRas function will then allocate and deallocate the memory for this buffer automatically.

Second, you can use the AllocRaster function to allocate a buffer of known size. For example, if you know that you need three 100-by-100-bit areas to hold your TmpRas structure for a specific area-fill, just call the AllocRaster function with a width variable of 300 and a height variable of 100.

Use the pointer returned by the AllocRaster function as the second argument (the buffer pointer argument) in your call to the InitTmpRas function. If you proceed in this way, you must remember to free this temporary buffer explicitly with the FreeRaster function. The FreeRaster function also uses the same buffer pointer as that returned by your call to the AllocRaster function.

You want to design a programming strategy to avoid a "memory squeeze" due to all the current requirements imposed by your graphics design. If you produce your drawing in a specific sequence, drawing only limited-size parts at any given time, the InitTmpRas and InitArea functions will automatically allocate and deallocate these auxiliary memory buffers, thus avoiding a conflict of memory requirements at each stage of your graphics design task.

Like the AreaInfo structure, the TmpRas structure is pointed to inside the RastPort structure. The RastPort structure contains a pointer to the TmpRas structure; when you call the InitTmpRas function, the first argument contains this pointer. The current controlling RastPort structure then knows where to place the final bitmap information needed to handle this step in the ongoing drawing sequence.

Finally, note that you will often have a series of rasters and associated RastPort structures to control the drawing in those rasters. If you set aside a buffer for one TmpRas structure with a call to the InitTmpRas function, that buffer is available again and again to that RastPort structure as a work area for any drawing steps in a sequence of AreaEnd functions for that raster. Therefore, if you can afford it, estimate the largest buffer you will need for all AreaEnd calls for the current raster you are drawing. Then use that buffer again and again throughout that raster's definition.

On the other hand, it is important to note that a buffer allocated by the InitTmpRas function for one raster bitmap is not necessarily available to other RastPort structures and their associated rasters to use; one buffer cannot be shared between RastPort structures.

This is the drawing system as it is set up now. It may change in the near future to allow multiple RastPort structures to share a common buffer. If this feature is added, it will not necessarily reduce memory requirements. Rather, it will be a convenience that will save a call to the InitTmpRas function for each new raster and controlling RastPort structure that you work with in your total drawing.

InitView

Syntax of Function Call

InitView (view)
A1

Purpose of Function

This function initializes the View structure to a set of default values. First, the View structure parameters are set to all zeros. Then values are placed into DxOffset and DyOffset to position the default display about half an inch in each direction from the upper-left corner of the Amiga monitor.

Inputs to Function

view   A pointer to a View structure

Discussion

There are five Graphics Library display functions that deal specifically with display screen viewports and views in the Amiga system: InitView, InitVPort, LoadView, MakeVPort, and ScrollVPort. These functions work with two types of structures: the ViewPort structure and the View structure. InitView and LoadView use the view argument and therefore work with the View structure. InitVPort and ScrollVPort use the viewPort argument and therefore work with the ViewPort structure. MakeVPort uses both the view and viewPort arguments and therefore works with both the ViewPort and View structures. For more information about these structures, see the introduction to this chapter.

This function positions the display about half an inch in each direction from the upper-left corner of the Amiga monitor to ensure that the view is contained on the visible portion of the monitor display (avoiding problems with video-beam overscan).

Viewport Display Modes

Every viewport can use one of five different modes. These modes are controlled by five bits (DUALPF, PFBA, HIRES, LACE, and HAM) in the ViewPort structure Modes parameter. A brief description of each of these five bits follows.

The DUALPF bit controls the number of playfields in the display. You can specify either single-playfield or dual-playfield display. If you choose the dual-playfield display mode (DUALPF set to 1), the raster specified by the viewport is the first of two separately controllable playfields. This choice modifies the manner in which raster bitplanes are grouped and the way colors are determined based on the bits in the bitplanes.

The PFBA bit is the priority bit in a dual-playfield display mode. You use this together with the DUALPF bit to describe a dual-playfield mode display. When this bit is a 1, it tells the system that the second playfield will have video priority over the first playfield. This means that it will appear in front of the first playfield on the video display.

The HIRES bit tells the system that the viewport specified by this ViewPort structure is to be displayed in high-resolution mode with 640 horizontal pixels. If HIRES is set to 0, a low-resolution mode display with 320 pixels on each horizontal line will be used.

The LACE bit tells the system that the viewport specified by this ViewPort structure will be displayed in interlaced mode. It will have 400 scanning lines per display frame. It is important to note that you cannot vary the LACE parameter from viewport to viewport within a given view; the LACE parameter is ignored in the definition of the ViewPort structure. Instead, the View structure has its own LACE parameter. When the View structure combines one or more viewports into a single display, it uses its own LACE parameter to define the vertical resolution of the display screen. On the other hand, the other display mode parameters (DUALPF, PFBA, HIRES, and HAM) are taken from each ViewPort structure.

The HAM bit, when set to 1, tells the system to use the hold-and-modify mode of screen display. The main advantage of hold-and-modify mode is that you can display up to 4,096 colors at once on the display screen. See Appendix B for definitions of each of the Amiga display modes.

InitVPort

Syntax of Function Call

InitVPort (viewPort)
A0

Purpose of Function

This function initializes the ViewPort structure to default values. All parameters in the ViewPort structure are set to zero values.

Inputs to Function

viewPort   A pointer to a ViewPort structure

Discussion

There are five Graphics Library display functions that work specifically with display screen viewports and views in the Amiga system: InitView, InitVPort, LoadView, MakeV-Port, and ScrollVPort. There is more information on viewports and views in the discussions of each of these functions.

All View structures are composed of one or more ViewPort structures. Before these ViewPort structures are added to the system, they must be initialized. This is the purpose of the InitVPort function. After this function executes, memory is set aside to hold a ViewPort structure with specific characteristics. Initially, most of the memory locations are set to zero. In particular, the Modes variable in that ViewPort structure is set to zero; this means that this viewport will generate a low-resolution mode display. Of course, these default settings can be overridden later when you define ViewPort structure parameters explicitly.

Restrictions on Viewports

There are several restrictions on viewports and their associated ViewPort structures that you should be aware of. First, viewports can only be stacked vertically on the display screen of the Amiga; you cannot define two viewports that appear next to each other horizontally on the display screen. If you want to define and work with overlapping windows, use just one viewport in a view and create windows inside this viewport. This is basically how the Intuition functions create and manage windows; in fact, if you want to use windows, you should use the Intuition functions.

Second, viewports cannot overlap in any way on the display screen. This includes both horizontal and vertical overlap. This restriction is implied by the other restrictions.

Third, viewports cannot be precisely adjacent to each other vertically on the display screen; they must be separated by at least one video display line. This is required to allow the hardware of the system to change viewport settings (modes, colors, etc.) between successive viewports in a view. In some cases, more than one vertical separation line is required. This is especially true if you are changing colors between vertically arranged viewports in the same view.

Viewport Definition

To define a viewport fully, you must define the height, width, depth, and display mode in the associated ViewPort structure. The height of the viewport is the number of pixels (vertical scanning lines) that this viewport will occupy when it is displayed. This is the DHeight variable in the definition of the ViewPort structure for this viewport. Most often this number will be either 200 or 400; this defines a single-viewport view in noninterlaced and interlaced mode, respectively. However, this parameter cannot be greater than 400 or the overscan of your monitor will prevent display of part of this viewport.

The width of the viewport is the number of horizontal pixels that this viewport will occupy when it is displayed. This is the DWidth variable in the definition of the ViewPort structure. Most often, this number will be either 320 or 640, but it can be between these two numbers. However, it cannot be greater than 640.

The depth of the viewport defines how many bitplanes are used to define the raster bitmap of this viewport. This is the Depth variable in the definition of the BitMap structure used to define the raster bitmap for this viewport. This number can vary between 1 and 6, depending on the number of colors you want in the viewport. For example, for 32 colors in a viewport, you must specify a depth of 5 when you call the InitBitMap function; you need five bitplanes per bitmap.

The display mode used for this viewport is controlled by five bits in the specification of the ViewPort structure. These mode bits are named DUALPF, PFBA, HIRES, LACE, and HAM. They tell the hardware system how to display this viewport when it is added to a view definition. The viewport display modes are summarized in the discussion of the InitView function.

Note that the LACE bit is ignored for each viewport; only the LACE bit of the associated View structure governs the display of all viewports in a given view made up of those viewports. For this reason, all viewports will appear in either interlaced or noninterlaced mode. There can be no change in the interlacing characteristics from viewport to viewport in a display view.

LoadRGB4

Syntax of Function Call

LoadRGB4 (viewPort, colorTable, count)
                   A0   A1   D0

Purpose of Function

This function assigns a set of RGB color-register values to the specified ViewPort structure. These colors (red, green, and blue) are held in the colortable array pointed to by the colortable array pointer.

Inputs to Function

viewPort	A pointer to the ViewPort structure where you want to change color register definitions
colorTable	A pointer to a colortable array of color-register definitions
count	The number of two-byte words to load from the colortable, starting at color 0 (the background color) and proceeding to the highest color number specified in the colortable array

Discussion

There are three Graphics Library drawing functions that work specifically with the colors assigned and used in viewports in the Amiga system: GetRGB4, LoadRGB4, and SetRGB4. LoadRGB4 loads a set of RGB color-register values from a colortable array into a viewport definition.

GetColorMap allocates the memory for and initializes a ColorMap structure; it requires as an argument the number of entries in the colortable. This is a number between 1 and 32, depending on how many color registers will be defined or redefined by a subsequent call to the LoadRGB4 function.

LoadRGB4 defines the specific entries for the colortable array and associates that colortable array with a given viewport. LoadRGB4 loads specific values into each of the colortable slots counted in the entry argument (1 to 32) to the GetColorMap function. See the discussion of the SetRGB4 function for examples of colors that can be placed into the 32 registers. The LoadRGB4 function directly affects the contents of the color registers eventually used to produce colors in the viewport associated with this ViewPort structure.

Recall that the Amiga has 32 system hardware color-control registers. It is interesting to note that each of these 32 registers has the capability to define up to 4,096 colors. This is possible because these color registers include four bits (bits 11 to 8) of red, four bits (bits 7 to 4) of green, and four bits (bits 3 to 0) of blue. This provides for 16 red variations, 16 green variations, and 16 blue variations for a total of 4,096 colors if you combine all the various shades of each color.

If you use hold-and-modify mode for a video display, you can produce 4,096 colors by assigning values to the 32 color registers and interpreting these register values in the hold-and-modify mode conventions.

In order to use the LoadRGB4 function, you must first define a colortable array in RAM. This table will have the number of entries indicated in the third argument of the LoadRGB4 function call. Each entry will be two bytes (16 bits). The meaning of these 16 bits is as follows:

    0000 rrrr gggg bbbb

where 0000 represents the four most significant bits of a color register; these bits are unused and are always set to zero. rrrr represents the four bits assigned to the red intensity variations; these four bits can vary from 0000 (no red) to 1111 (maximum red). gggg represents the four bits assigned to the green intensity variations; these bits can vary from 0000 (no green) to 1111 (maximum green). bbbb represents the four bits assigned to the blue intensity variations; they can vary from 0000 (no blue) to 1111 (maximum blue).

It is important to understand that you can have quite a few of these colortable arrays in memory at the same time. For any given viewport, you can create as many colortable arrays as you need. Each one is created with a call to the GetColorMap function to allocate memory, followed by a call to LoadRGB4 to fill in the values for that colortable. When you want to change the colors used in any viewport, call LoadRGB4 again using a different pointer argument to point to another (already defined) colortable array.

For example, you can have a display view that is composed of the same viewport drawn twice on the same display frame. There will be at least one horizontal scanning line between these two viewports. The first viewport uses a pointer to one colortable array. The second viewport is the same as the first, except that it uses a pointer to a second colortable array. In this way, you can present the same information in different colors on the same display view.

LoadView

Syntax of Function Call

LoadView (view)
A1

Purpose of Function

This function uses a Copper instruction list to create the current display screen view. This list was previously created by the InitVPort, MakeVPort, and MrgCop functions. When LoadView returns, the new view is displayed according to the view's bitmap definitions represented by the bit values stored in its raster bitmaps and the merged set of Copper instructions created by the MrgCop function.

Inputs to Function

view   A pointer to a View structure that contains a pointer to a hardware Copper instruction list

Discussion

There are five Graphics Library display functions that work specifically with display screen viewports and views in the Amiga system: InitView, InitVPort, LoadView, MakeVPort, and ScrollVPort. There is more information on viewports and views in the discussions of each of these functions.

The LoadView function works directly with the Copper coprocessor hardware instruction list. It generates the set of Copper instructions required to define one frame of the video display, based solely on the information in the View structure. The View structure has been developed by other view-building calls prior to this point in the task. The full set of Copper instructions can include additional instructions from two other sources: the Graphics Library animation functions and the user-defined Copper instructions defined in the UCopList structure.

The Copper instructions from these three sources are merged before the LoadView function is called. This merging operation is the job of the MrgCop function. Essentially, the LoadView function says, "using the complete set of Copper instructions provided by the MrgCop function, including those for the view I have created, display the result on the video display."

There are two system macros that can control display events prior and subsequent to your call to the LoadView function, ON_DISPLAY and OFF_DISPLAY. They work together with the LoadView function to determine precisely what happens when the Load-View function executes.

You can call these macros just before and after your call to the LoadView function. If you call ON_DISPLAY just before LoadView, the video display will update immediately after the LoadView function executes. If you call OFF_DISPLAY just before LoadView, the video display will not update immediately after your call to LoadView and the new view frame will not be shown. In fact, this view will not be shown until the ON_DISPLAY macro is executed. ON_DISPLAY is the default in the system; the display will update automatically after a LoadView call unless you first call OFF_DISPLAY.

Using these macros allows you to suppress the view temporarily. The main advantage of this is the possible suppression of visual confusion ("garbage") on the display screen caused by ongoing intermediate steps in the drawing definition of a view. To avoid this "garbage," do the drawing with OFF_DISPLAY active; then, once the drawing functions (AreaDraw, AreaEnd, etc.) have fully executed, call the ON_DISPLAY macro. This will restore the video display to normal operation and display the view created by the most recent LoadView function call.

LockLayerRom

Syntax of Function Call

LockLayerRom (layer)
A5

Purpose of Function

This function locks a Layer structure using ROM code in the Graphics Library. When the LockLayerRom function returns, the layer is locked for exclusive use by the calling task. No other task can modify this layer until this task calls the UnlockLayerRom function. The LockLayerRom function call does not destroy any registers.

Inputs to Function

layer   A pointer to a Layer structure

Discussion

There are two Graphics Library display functions that deal specifically with the Layer structure, LockLayerRom and UnlockLayerRom. The purpose of these functions is to lock and unlock the display layers to prevent and allow different tasks to draw into these layers. With these functions, you can prevent unwanted alteration of any layer bitmap graphics information by other tasks in the system.

Both the LockLayerRom and UnlockLayerRom functions take only one argument, the layer pointer variable. The value of this variable is known from a previous call to the CreateUpfrontLayer or CreateBehindLayer functions. (These two functions are described in Chapter 5.)

The Amiga system can deal with four types of layers: the simple-refresh layer, the smart-refresh layer, the superbitmap layer, and the backdrop layer. Read the discussions of the CopySBitMap and SyncSBitMap functions for information on superbitmap layers, and the introduction to Chapter 5 to learn about the Layer structure.

Suppose that you have your own graphics task in which you are creating layer bitmaps and drawing into those layer bitmaps. Suppose that graphics task is not the only task you have in the system but part of a much larger graphics program you are designing. This program will create and define several layers and will consist of several intertwined tasks. Unless something is done, each of these tasks can modify (draw into) the bitmap content of any layer in one way or another when it gains control of the system.

Suppose that a task is about to draw information into a specific layer. You want to prevent all other tasks in your program from affecting the layer that your current task is defining; you want to ensure that only this task can alter that layer's bitmap (until you tell the system otherwise). This is necessary because you don't know the exact sequence of steps another task will take. If these steps lead to a drawing sequence in that task, you can prevent any drawing from occurring if you execute the LockLayerRom function in the first task. Only when the first task again becomes the active task and executes the Unlock-LayerRom function can other tasks modify the bitmap definition of this layer.

LockLayerRom function calls can be nested. Suppose you have three graphics tasks in a graphics program. The first task creates a layer by placing a call to the Layers Library CreateUpfrontLayer function. This allocates a raster bitmap for this layer. This call also associates a RastPort structure to control the drawing into this layer. You can use some of the drawing functions (for example, the AreaDraw, AreaMove, and AreaEnd functions) to place drawing information into this layer's bitmap.

Once this drawing is done, you decide you want to switch tasks to the second of your three graphics tasks in that program. However, before you switch, you decide that your other tasks should not be allowed to draw into this first layer. Before you leave this task, you execute the LockLayerRom function to lock this layer.

When the second drawing task in your program becomes active and takes over the machine, it creates a second layer and draws into that second layer. Then, before it transfers control to a third task, it executes a LockLayerRom call for this second layer. Now only the second task can modify this second layer.

You can continue throughout your graphics program with this arrangement. Alternatively, you can go back into each of the three tasks and execute an UnlockLayerRom function call. In this way, you can control the changes in your layer bitmap definitions in a very detailed fashion, locking and unlocking layers as necessary.

MakeVPort

Syntax of Function Call

MakeVPort (view, viewPort)
A0   A1

Purpose of Function

This function uses the information in the View and ViewPort structures to generate an intermediate Copper list for a viewport.

If the ColorMap structure pointer in the ViewPort structure is null, MakeVPort uses colors from a system default colortable array. If the DUALPF bit is set in the Modes parameter in the View structure, there must be a second RasInfo structure pointed to by the first RasInfo structure.

Inputs to Function

view	A pointer to a View structure
viewPort	A pointer to a ViewPort structure that contains a valid pointer to a RasInfo structure

Discussion

There are five Graphics Library display functions that work specifically with display screen viewports and views in the Amiga system: InitView, InitVPort, LoadView, MakeVPort, and ScrollVPort. There is more information on viewports and views in the discussions of each of these functions.

The display information required to define one frame of the Amiga display is built up in a series of steps. These include the steps to allocate memory for bitmaps and structures, to define ViewPort structures, and to define View structures and views consisting of combinations of viewports. All of these steps lead up to the complete definition of a View structure and its associated display screen view—one frame of an ongoing display sequence.

It is important to remember that the display functions finally have to talk directly to the display-related hardware chips on the Amiga motherboard. The system needs a set of instructions to drive the display hardware—specifically, a set of instructions to drive the Copper coprocessor. The Copper tells the other display-related hardware chips how to fix the colors and other information needed to define the current frame of the video screen display. This is where the MakeVPort function comes into play.

The MakeVPort function looks at the View structure in memory and generates a set of Copper instructions to generate that view on the Amiga display screen. It provides one set of Copper instructions that will define one frame of the display. These Copper instructions are then merged with the animation sprite Copper instructions (if any) and the user-defined Copper instructions (those in the UCopList structure, if any) to arrive at the full set of Copper instructions required to define this frame of the display. If your display does not change from frame to frame, this merged set of Copper instructions can be used again and again (every 1/60 of a second) to drive the display hardware.

If, on the other hand, your current task wants to change the appearance of the display screen from frame to frame, it is necessary to change the Copper instructions with which the MakeVPort function deals. While the video beam is retracing from top to bottom of the display screen (the vertical-blanking interval), the Copper instructions are updated to define a new display screen frame. In this way, you can modify the appearance of the display screen on a very fine time scale.

Always remember that it is the LoadView function that actually loads the total view into the hardware. If you have more than one source of Copper instructions, these will be merged with the View structure Copper instructions just prior to calling the LoadView function. Use the MrgCop function to merge all three possible sources of Copper instructions.

These are the main principles that relate your current task to the changing appearance of the screen display. See the discussions of CINIT, CMOVE, CWAIT, and CEND for more information about the Copper coprocessor and its importance in the Amiga display system.

Move

Syntax of Function Call

Move (rastPort, x, y)
         A1   D0 D1

Purpose of Function

This function moves the graphics pen position relative to the upper-left corner of the raster coordinate system (the 0,0 point).

Inputs to Function

rastPort	A pointer to a controlling RastPort structure
x	A horizontal coordinate in the raster bitmap coordinate system
y	A vertical coordinate in the raster bitmap coordinate system

Discussion

There are five Graphics Library drawing functions that deal specifically with the use of drawing pens in the Amiga system: Move, SetAPen, SetBPen, SetOPen, and SetRast.

These functions allow you to move and otherwise manipulate drawing pens to define colors and other characteristics of each part of a raster bitmap.

The Move function moves the position of the graphics pen to a new location in a raster bitmap. The movement takes place and is measured inside the current raster coordinate system. This is the bitmap associated with the controlling RastPort structure. The Move function is often used together with the Draw function to define individual lines in a bitmap. In addition, the PolyDraw function provides an explicit way of adding sets of lines to a bitmap. These three functions, together with the AreaEnd and RectFill functions, which draw boundary lines on areas as they fill those areas, provide all the line-drawing capability you need to define your bitmaps.

The Move function differs from these other functions in one very important respect: Move does not add a line; it merely lifts the drawing pen off the bitmap drawing surface to be put down at another location in the bitmap you are currently defining. In this way, you can finish adding a line with the Draw function, pick up the drawing pen with the Move function, move to another x,y position, and start to draw again with the Draw, AreaDraw, AreaMove, PolyDraw, RectFill, or Text functions.

Just as with the other drawing functions, any moves you make must stay within the current raster bitmap bounds. If you specify an x,y position outside of the current raster bitmap, the system will probably crash. Just remember that the x,y values are in the raster bitmap coordinate system; you can use x,y pairs as large as 1024,1024 if you have designed a bitmap that large.

Although the Move function does not set and reset bits in the bitmap, a subsequent call to any of the other drawing functions will affect the bitmap bits.

MrgCop

Syntax of Function Call

MrgCop (view)
A1

Purpose of Function

This function merges together the display, color, sprite, and user-defined Copper instructions into a single Copper instruction stream. MrgCop creates a per-display-frame program for the Copper coprocessor. This function is used automatically by the graphics animation routines, which effectively add information into a static background display. This automatic procedure changes some of the user or sprite instructions, but not those that have formed the basic display. When all forms of the coprocessor instructions are merged, the task will have a complete per-frame instruction list for the Copper coprocessor.

Inputs to Function

view	A pointer to a View structure where Copper instructions are to be merged

Discussion

There are eight Graphics Library display functions and macros that deal specifically with the Copper coprocessor: CINIT, CMOVE, CWAIT, CEND, FreeCopList, FreeCprList, FreeVPortCopLists, and MrgCop. There is more information on the Copper in the discussions of each of these functions and macros.

All the effort of your graphics work is directed toward the final result: a series of views that you can present to the system hardware for display on the Amiga. To arrive at these views, you have to initialize a series of raster bitmaps, allocate memory for rasters, define viewports as parts of your bitmaps, combine viewports into views, and finally draw into your bitmaps. Then your program can load the hardware with this information and display a series of views. For example, in a menu-driven program, each new menu chosen can call forth a different Amiga display screen. In the background, unknown to the user, your program senses the menu selection and loads another view using the LoadView function.

When this happens, many (if not all) of the system hardware control registers must be reset to new values. In particular, if the color palette of the new view is different from the previous display screen color palette, the color registers must be reset. In addition, the Copper instruction list, which consists of all Copper display instructions, must be redefined to produce the display screen associated with that new menu selection.

Therefore, just prior to the LoadView function call, you must define where all the Copper instructions for that view will come from. There will generally be three sources: the internally generated Copper instructions associated with the specific view you just defined, the Copper instructions coming from the animation functions that define how the animation sprites are incorporated into each playfield and display view, and a set of custom Copper instructions you defined with the CMOVE and CWAIT macro calls.

The MrgCop function does the job of bringing all of these Copper instructions together, merging and sorting them to produce a full-frame Copper instruction list to define the display screen for that view. This internal sorting is necessary to produce a total set of instructions that are sorted in increasing y and x values measured in the coordinate system of the display screen. Once this sorting is completed, the total Copper instruction stream is arranged in top-to-bottom, left-to-right fashion to define the video frame as it is scanned by the video beam.

NewRegion

Syntax of Function Call

```
region = NewRegion ()
D0
```

Purpose of Function

This function creates a Region structure of size zero. It initializes the Region structure to empty; that is, there are no clipping-rectangles now assigned to this region. NewRegion returns a pointer to the new Region structure.

Inputs to Function

This function has no arguments.

Discussion

There are six Graphics Library drawing functions that deal specifically with regions and the clipping-rectangles that make up those regions: AndRectRegion, ClearRegion, Dispose-Region, NewRegion, OrRectRegion, and XorRectRegion. These functions allow you to build a region from a set of clipping-rectangles and then alter the region characteristics as desired. There is more information on regions and clipping-rectangles in the discussions of each of these functions.

To understand the purpose of regions, you first have to understand two key ideas used in the Graphics Library system: clipping-rectangles and damage-lists. These two concepts play a vital part in the definition and use of regions. They also play a big part in the definition and use of layers.

A *clipping-rectangle* is a rectangle that limits the area that the drawing functions (for example, AreaDraw, AreaMove, and AreaEnd) will draw into at any particular time. A set of these clipping-rectangles defines the total area of a layer bitmap that the drawing functions will affect. Clipping-rectangles get their names from the type of action that they cause; they clip any drawing that is outside of their boundaries.

For example, if a drawing function (Draw, Move, or PolyDraw, for instance) calls for the update of a layer, only those parts of the layer that are inside the currently defined set of clipping-rectangles will receive new bitmap bit definitions. Parts of the layer outside of the currently defined set of clipping-rectangle definitions will not receive new bitmap bit definitions. In other words, all drawing into the layer will be clipped to be purely inside the bitmap areas defined by the currently defined set of clipping-rectangles.

To make this idea more understandable, consider the multiwindow, multilayer Intuition screen. Suppose you have two windows open on the Intuition display screen. Call these windows 1 and 2. Suppose you opened window 2 after you opened window 1. At this point window 2 is the active window.

Further, suppose that these windows did not overlap when they were opened; instead, they were separated by the blue background screen along all of their borders. Now suppose you move (drag) window 2 so that it overlaps window 1. When you do this, window 1 becomes partially obscured; a certain rectangular portion of it is covered by window 2.

Now, move window 2 away from window 1 once again. Automatically, the Intuition routines restore the corner of window 1 that was previously obscured by the overlapping window 2. In this window-uncovering operation, window 1 is only partially refreshed—only the obscured corner is refreshed, not the whole window.

This restoration of the previously obscured corner is handled by using a clipping-rectangle and damage-list. These are implemented in ClipRect and DamageList structures, respectively.

In this case, there is only one clipping-rectangle involved. This clipping-rectangle represents only the small, obscured rectangle on the corner of window 1. Note that this small clipping-rectangle is not a visible rectangle. It exists only in concept; you do not see any borders around this rectangle, either now or at any time later in the progression of the display. Conceptually, it merely surrounds the obscured area of the display screen. This area is said to be *damaged;* it is repaired when the windows are separated again.

Any time the Intuition windows are moved or the depth-arrangement (windows brought to the front of other windows or sent behind other windows) of these windows is changed, the layer's damage-list and the set of associated clipping-rectangle boundary definitions change to represent the newly obscured portions of the display screen.

When windows are moved and depth-arranged again, the current set of clipping-rectangle boundary definitions and the associated damage-list are used to define the areas of the display screen that should be updated. In the case just described, only those areas that are damaged need be redrawn; no other areas need to be refreshed. This is one of the features that leads to the very quick screen updates of both Intuition screens and the screens your graphics programs create.

Damage-lists and clipping-rectangles can arise in at least two different ways. In the first case, they can arise as the user of a graphics program moves graphics elements around on a multilayered display screen. The speedy Intuition screen with multiple overlapping windows is the most common example of this type of dynamic damage-list clipping-rectangle behavior.

In the second case, clipping-rectangles and damage-lists can be purposely designed to define and control the drawing of a specific section (or the entire display) of a graphics layer bitmap. This is where regions and clipping-rectangles come into play. *Regions* are sets of clipping-rectangles that, when combined, become part of a customized damage-list to be used to control drawing in a layer bitmap. The Graphics Library region functions allow you to design and construct a customized DamageList structure, which contains pointers to a set of ClipRect structures that govern the definition of a region. With this list, you can selectively update a customized part of a specific layer bitmap without disturbing any of the other layer bitmaps that define the current display.

The idea here is that you use NewRegion to allocate memory for a new Region structure. This structure contains no information on how big the region will eventually be. At this point, the region contains no clipping-rectangles and is essentially empty. Only when you use the AndRectRegion, OrRectRegion, and XorRectRegion functions do you define the clipping-rectangles associated with this region. This is when you start to define the drawing-control characteristics of this region; it will grow (and shrink) as you use these three functions to combine clipping-rectangles to define its ultimate size.

Read Chapter 5 to learn more about layers, clipping-rectangles, damage-lists, and their associated structures.

OFF_DISPLAY

Syntax of Macro Call

OFF_DISPLAY

Purpose of Macro

This macro clears the display DMA (direct memory access) bit in the DMA control register. Any view subsequently loaded with the LoadView function will not be displayed until an ON_DISPLAY macro call.

Inputs to Macro

This macro has no inputs.

Discussion

There are two macros that deal with display DMA control: ON_DISPLAY and OFF_DISPLAY. Read the discussion of the ON_DISPLAY macro to learn more about the relationship between these two macros.

OFF_DISPLAY resets the BPLEN bit in the DMACON register. There are several times when you might want to use the OFF_DISPLAY macro. For example, when you are drawing into a display bitmap and you don't want the user to see intermediate steps in a drawing sequence, OFF_DISPLAY prevents the display of the changing view while it is being changed. Another example is when you want to provide additional memory cycles to the 68000 CPU or the Blitter. OFF_DISPLAY will shut down the display DMA and possibly speed up other DMA operations.

The Amiga DMA system provides for four hardware sound channels, a disk read/write channel, and a 16-color low-resolution mode display (or a 4-color high-resolution mode display) all operating at once with no slow down (7.1 megahertz) of the operation of the 68000 CPU. Therefore, you would not normally use OFF_DISPLAY to speed other DMA operations.

OFF_VBLANK

Syntax of Macro Call

OFF_VBLANK

Purpose of Macro

This macro clears the vertical blanking interrupt bit (bit 5) in the interrupt control register.

Inputs to Macro

This macro has no inputs.

Discussion

There are two macros that deal with interrupt control in the graphics system: ON_VBLANK and OFF_VBLANK. Read the discussion of the ON_VBLANK macro to learn the relationship between these two macros. This macro is the complement of the ON_VBLANK macro.

ON_DISPLAY

Syntax of Macro Call

ON_DISPLAY

Purpose of Macro

This macro sets the display DMA (direct memory access) bit in the DMA control register. Any view subsequently loaded with the LoadView function will then be displayed.

Inputs to Macro

This macro has inputs.

Discussion

There are two macros that deal with display DMA control: ON_DISPLAY and OFF_DISPLAY. Read the discussion of the OFF_DISPLAY macro to learn more about the relationship between these two macros.

ON_DISPLAY sets bit 8 (called the BPLEN bit) in the DMA control register (the register named DMACON). After you have loaded a new view with the LoadView function, you can use the ON_DISPLAY macro to allow the system DMA to display the new view.

ON_DISPLAY is the system default setting. That is, unless you specifically turn off display DMA with the OFF_DISPLAY macro, any view you load will be automatically displayed.

ON_VBLANK

Syntax of Macro Call

ON_VBLANK

Purpose of Macro

This macro sets the vertical-blanking interrupt bit (bit 5) in the interrupt control register. This enables the vertical-blanking interrupt.

Inputs to Macro

This macro has no inputs.

Discussion

There are two macros that deal with interrupt control in the graphics system: ON_VBLANK and OFF_VBLANK.

The Amiga system is often required to perform many tasks during the vertical-blanking interval; it must update various pointer registers and rewrite Copper lists as necessary to define the next video frame. The system has two interrupt control registers: INTENAR (interrupt enable register) and INTREQ (interrupt request). The settings in these two registers determine how events are handled during the vertical-blanking interval.

The ON_VBLANK macro sets bit 5 in the interrupt control register. When this bit is set, an interrupt will occur at the start of the vertical-blanking interval. ON_VBLANK is the system default. That is, unless you specifically turn off the vertical-blanking interrupt with the OFF_VBLANK macro, any view (old or new) you load will be displayed automatically.

The minimum vertical-blanking interval is 20 horizontal scan lines (beginning at line 0 and ending at line 20). If you find that you still require additional time during vertical blanking, you can use the Copper to create an interrupt.

OrRectRegion

Syntax of Function Call

OrRectRegion (region, rectangle)
A0   A1

Purpose of Function

This function performs a two-dimensional Or operation of a clipping-rectangle with a region, leaving the result in the region. If any portion of the clipping-rectangle is not already in the region, OrRectRegion adds that portion to the region definition.

Inputs to Function

region	A pointer to a Region structure
rectangle	A pointer to a Rectangle structure

Discussion

There are six Graphics Library drawing functions that deal specifically with regions and the clipping-rectangles that make up those regions: AndRectRegion, ClearRegion, DisposeRegion, NewRegion, OrRectRegion, and XorRectRegion. These functions allow you to build a customized drawing region as part of the total definition of a layer. There is more information on regions and clipping-rectangles in the discussions of each of these functions.

The OrRectRegion function performs an Or operation on the current clipping-rectangle contents of a region and a clipping-rectangle that may or may not be already a part of that region. That new clipping-rectangle is then made a part of that region. Note that this is not the same as performing an Or operation on the bits of a rectangle bitplane bit by bit with a region of a bitmap.

To understand this rectangle clipping concept better, consider this example. Suppose you want to draw a solid square into a layer. There are at least two ways you can do this. The first way is the more obvious: you simply decide where you want that square to appear in that layer. Then you use the AreaDraw, AreaMove, and AreaEnd functions (or the RectFill function) to define and draw that square. You use the drawing functions (SetAPen, SetBPen, etc.) to prepare the RastPort structure so that it properly controls the drawing colors, borders, and so forth for your square. Then, when you finally execute the AreaEnd function (or the RectFill function), the square will be drawn into your bitmap as required.

Alternatively, you can use the OrRectRegion function to limit the drawing into this portion of your bitmap. First, define a ClipRect structure using four simple program statements to define the vertices of the clipping-rectangle. In this case, suppose you define a clipping-rectangle that is actually a square. Call the NewRegion function to allocate and initialize a new region of size zero. Then call OrRectRegion to add the clipping-rectangle to the region.

Follow this immediately with a call to the BeginUpdate function to begin the update of that layer bitmap. (See Chapter 5 for a discussion of the BeginUpdate function.) Here, however, you are updating only that part of the layer bitmap that is contained in the region definition. To be specific, you are changing only those parts of the layer bitmap that are inside the clipping-rectangle added by the OrRectRegion function. The drawing process will be clipped to the area inside this clipping-rectangle square.

Next, just as in normal drawing procedures, use the drawing functions (SetAPen, SetBPen, etc.) to prepare the RastPort structure so that it can control the drawing colors, borders, etc. for your square. Then use the RectFill function to fill the square with the color you want. Normally, the entire raster would receive this color. But now the square clipping-rectangle ensures that only the small square is filled with your chosen color.

You can extend this indirect drawing process using other instances of the OrRect-Region function. For example, before you call the BeginUpdate function, you could define another clipping-rectangle. Then you could execute the OrRectRegion function to include that clipping-rectangle into your region definition. Following are several examples of this procedure.

First, assume that the second clipping-rectangle is at the identical bitmap position as the first clipping-rectangle. When you call the BeginUpdate function, the result will be the same as the first case; the region definition is not changed because the Or operation has not extended the region definition.

Next, assume that the second clipping-rectangle does not overlap the first clipping-rectangle; it is both a different size and located in an entirely different position in the raster bitmap. In this case, when you call the BeginUpdate function, the layer will have two rectangles (one a square) added to it; the region definition has changed because the Or operation has extended the region definition.

The third case, shown in Figure 2.5, is the most interesting, because it shows how the OrRectRegion function really works. Here, assume that the second clipping-rectangle partially overlaps the first clipping-rectangle (the square). All drawing will be clipped outside of all parts of the region that do not belong to the union of these two rectangles; once again, the region definition is changing because the Or operation has extended the region definition.

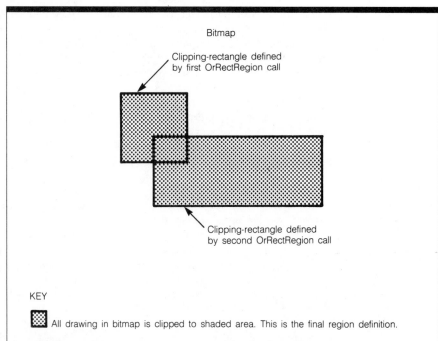

Bitmap

Clipping-rectangle defined by first OrRectRegion call

Clipping-rectangle defined by second OrRectRegion call

KEY

All drawing in bitmap is clipped to shaded area. This is the final region definition.

Figure 2.5:
Illustration of the OrRect-Region Function

In this case, the union is a squared-edged object that can vary from a cross to two side-by-side rectangles. The ultimate configuration depends on the relative size and shape of the two clipping-rectangles. If you study this example and extend the discussion yourself, you will see how the OrRectRegion function works.

Finally, note that the order of the clipping-rectangles added to the region definition by the OrRectRegion function does not matter; for any given set of clipping-rectangles, the final region defined by all of those clipping-rectangles does not depend on the order in which they are added to produce the final region. You can convince yourself of this with a piece of paper and some simple examples.

OrRegionRegion

Syntax of Function Call

```
success = OrRegionRegion (region1, region2)
D0                        A0       A1
```

Purpose of Function

This function performs a two-dimensional Or operation of one region with another. It combines the two regions into a third region; the result is placed into the second region. The first region is not changed. This usually results in a larger region. However, if the two regions are identical in size and shape, the resulting region will be identical to the incoming regions.

Inputs to Function

region1   A pointer to the first of two Region structures whose regions are to be combined

region2   A pointer to the second of two Region structures whose regions are to be combined

Discussion

OrRegionRegion is one of the four functions in the 1.2 Amiga software release that deal with regions.

Recall that regions are merely collections of clipping-rectangles. Regions are defined using the AndRectRegion, OrRectRegion, and XorRectRegion functions. The intention and use of the OrRegionRegion function is very similar to that of the OrRectRegion function. The only difference is that the OrRegionRegion function combines two regions whereas the OrRectRegion function combines one region and one clipping-rectangle.

You should read the discussion of the OrRectRegion function to see how and why regions and clipping-rectangles are combined. These ideas carry over directly to the combination of regions into additional regions.

At some point in the drawing process, you may have two odd-shaped regions. Each of these will have straight-edge boundaries but might have any shape and size under that restriction. Now if you combine these two regions with the OrRegionRegion function, you will produce a third (perhaps more oddly shaped) region that is bigger than either of the first two regions. This new region may be useful for your next drawing step. This is the purpose of the OrRegionRegion function.

OwnBlitter

Syntax of Function Call

OwnBlitter ( )

Purpose of Function

This function will return when the Blitter has been assigned to this task. The Blitter will then be locked from use by other tasks in the system. Before this task starts to use the Blitter, it should first call the WaitBlit function. WaitBlit waits for all queued Blitter operations to finish, thus emptying the Blitter request queue.

Inputs to Function

This function uses no arguments.

Discussion

There are ten Graphics Library display functions that deal specifically with Blitter operations in the Amiga system: BltClear, BltPattern, BltBitMap, BltTemplate, ClipBlit, DisownBlitter, OwnBlitter, QBlit, QBSBlit, and WaitBlit. These functions allow you to control the operation of the Blitter. There is more information on the Blitter in the discussions of each of these functions.

The Blitter DMA channel, which is part of the animation custom chip, is the fastest data mover in the Amiga system. When properly set up, it can move a million bits of information in one second. This amounts to moving the entire bitmap information required to develop the contents of over 15 one-color display screens. This gives you an indication of the power of the Blitter. It means that the Blitter is much faster than the 68000 for data movement and other types of data manipulation.

Once your task sets up the Blitter control registers, you could move data at these high rates to do a number of useful things. For example, the Blitter can be used to copy data and to do line drawing. In addition, the Blitter can simulate animation using what is called playfield animation. *Playfield animation* allows the Blitter to pick up a section of a display frame and move it to a new location by the time the next frame is displayed. The display screen observer then sees the object move as if animated.

Here is a list of some of the things the Blitter can do:

1. It can move bitplane image data anywhere. If it transfers bitplane data to another part of the same raster bitmap, playfield animation is produced.

2. It can get data from up to three RAM location source blocks, combine data bits from those sources in up to 256 different ways, and place the results in a RAM destination block.

3. It can work with ascending or descending addresses as it moves data between one RAM block and another.

4. It can bit-shift one or two of its data sources by up to 15 bits before applying its logic operations to the data. This allows movement of images in memory across word boundaries (even-byte addresses).

5. It can mask the leftmost and rightmost data word from each horizontal line of raster bitmap information. This is useful for performing logic operations on the data and allows movement of images in memory across word boundaries (even-byte addresses).

6. It can draw ordinary lines at any angle and can also apply a pattern to the lines it draws.

Because the Blitter can do so many things so fast, it is no surprise that graphics tasks, which deal with large amounts of bit data, find the Blitter so useful. However, with so many tasks (both graphic and nongraphic) in a multitasking system, each competing for exclusive use of the Blitter to get their jobs done as quickly as possible, there must be some way to assign the Blitter to a task for its exclusive use. This is especially true when a subtask is critical to the progression of a larger task. This is the job of the OwnBlitter function.

The OwnBlitter function gives exclusive use of the Blitter to the task that calls it. Note that the task that calls the OwnBlitter function does not necessarily get immediate use of the Blitter. Instead, any ongoing Blitter operation is allowed to complete, so that a data transfer operation is not left half-completed.

Once any ongoing Blitter operation is completed, the task that calls OwnBlitter will own the Blitter DMA channel, for at least one Blitter operation and perhaps more. This task becomes the only task that can place Blitter requests in the Blitter queue. If the Blitter queue is empty when a task calls the OwnBlitter function, its Blitter request will get immediate attention.

If the Blitter queue is not empty when the OwnBlitter function executes, all queued Blitter requests still have priority over any that the calling task places in the queue. Any requests added by this task will have to wait until they reach the top of the queue and are processed.

One way to ensure immediate access to the Blitter is to use the WaitBlit function in your task before you execute the OwnBlitter function. WaitBlit will return only when all prior queued Blitter requests have completed. Then, when the calling task starts queuing Blitter requests, it knows that all newly queued requests belong to it.

Once a task issues all its Blitter requests, it can once again call the WaitBlit function to ensure that no further task activity takes place until its queued Blitter requests are completed. When WaitBlit returns from this second call, a call to the DisownBlitter function will release the Blitter for other tasks to own temporarily. Once again, they will start with an empty Blitter queue.

PolyDraw

Syntax of Function Call

PolyDraw (rastPort, count, array)
A0   D0   A1

Purpose of Function

This function draws lines on the display screen. It starts with the first pair of x,y values in a polygon definition table and draws lines between that point and every succeeding point in the table.

Inputs to Function

rastPort	A pointer to a controlling RastPort structure
count	The number of points (x,y pairs) in the polygon definition table
array	A pointer to the first x,y pair in the polygon definition table

Discussion

There are two Graphics Library drawing functions that deal specifically with drawing lines in the Amiga system: Draw and PolyDraw. These functions allow you to add lines to your raster bitmap definitions. The Draw function draws a line between the current pen position and a specified x,y point. PolyDraw uses an array of x,y positions to draw a set of lines that potentially define a polygon in a raster bitmap definition.

There is one graphics function that deals with the simultaneous drawing of sets of lines into raster bitmaps: the PolyDraw function. Note that sets of lines can form closed polygons but are not required to. However, for the purposes of this discussion, we will assume that closed polygons are being drawn. You can adapt the discussion to enter lines only; most of the same ideas apply.

The PolyDraw function works with a specific RastPort structure; this RastPort structure is controlling the ongoing drawing definition of one specific raster bitmap in memory. You can have a number of simultaneous raster bitmaps and coexisting RastPort structures in RAM to control the drawing in these bitmaps. However, you should arrange the programming logic of your task to work on one raster bitmap at one time. Define some or all of the polygons for that bitmap with the PolyDraw function call, then move on to the next bitmap.

As with all bitmaps, this bitmap uses a number of bitplanes to define its total raster. These bitplanes must all be in contiguous sections of RAM. However, the full bitmap of a raster doesn't have to be in a contiguous section of RAM—each bitplane can start at its own RAM location as fixed by the AllocRaster function. Remember that the x,y values in a bitplane can range from 0,0 to 1024,1024; you are drawing into the bitmap, not into the display screen, where x,y values are limited to 640,400 under maximum conditions. You can use the write-mask parameter of the RastPort structure to control which bitplanes are affected by your PolyDraw function call.

As you continue to add different polygons to your current bitmap drawing definition, you can keep changing the values of various drawing settings in the RastPort structure. The current drawing mode, drawing pen, and pen pattern will then be used by your PolyDraw function call.

This part of your task will then consist of a series of calls to the SetDrMd, SetAPen, and SetBPen functions and to the SetOPen, SetDrPt, and SetWrMsk macros, followed by a call to the PolyDraw function to actually draw a polygon. Any polygon drawn will affect the contents of the bitmap that the RastPort structure is controlling. All of this drawing-control information is stored in the current RastPort structure definition. The RastPort structure is a dynamic structure; it keeps changing any time you change one of its parameters. For this reason, you must use its settings to draw your polygon before you move on to the next polygon, which may have different settings.

Don't be confused by the difference between the PolyDraw function and the Area-Draw function. AreaDraw builds a set of lines (vectors) to define an eventual area to be filled with a pattern; PolyDraw produces a polygon using a table of x,y values with no required intention of filling any area enclosed by these polygons. However, you can use the Flood function to fill the areas enclosed by the polygon boundary lines.

Also remember that the AreaDraw function requires a memory buffer to provide a temporary work area to build a set of area-definition vectors (x,y values). The PolyDraw function also requires such a buffer; however, the arrangements for its creation through the array and count arguments in the PolyDraw call are different from those used to define the buffer for an area-fill involving the AreaEnd function.

Register Name	Register Address*	Register Function
BLTDDAT	000	RAM destination address
BLTCON0	040	Control register 0
BLTCON1	042	Control register 1
BLTAFWM	044	First word mask for source A
BLTALWM	046	Last word mask for source A
BLTCPTH	048	Pointer to source C (high 3 bits)
BLTCPTL	04A	Pointer to source C (low 15 bits)
BLTBPTH	04C	Pointer to source B (high 3 bits)
BLTBPTL	04E	Pointer to source B (low 15 bits)
BLTAPTH	050	Pointer to source A (high 3 bits)
BLTAPTL	052	Pointer to source A (low 15 bits)
BLTDPTH	054	Pointer to destination D (high 3 bits)
BLTDPTL	056	Pointer to destination D (low 15 bits)
BLTSIZE	058	Start and size (bitmap width and height)
BLTCMOD	060	Modulo for source C
BLTBMOD	062	Modulo for source B
BLTAMOD	064	Modulo for source A
BLTDMOD	066	Modulo for destination D
BLTCDAT	070	Source C data register
BLTBDAT	072	Source B data register
BLTADAT	074	Source A data register

*register, address 000 corresponds to memory address $DFF000, i.e., 68000 address = (chip address) + $DFF000

Table 2.3:
Blitter Register Names, Addresses, and Functions

In addition, keep in mind the distinction between the PolyDraw and Draw functions. Like the Draw function, the PolyDraw function deals with a set of lines that are not necessarily absolutely closed polygons. The PolyDraw function allows you to specify a series of x,y values in a table that can define a closed polygon; this polygon cannot be filled with the AreaEnd function. The Draw function requires you to define a single x,y point at a time; a single line is then drawn between the current drawing-pen position and this x,y point. Both of these functions can lead to enclosed areas that can later be filled with the Flood function.

Neither of these two functions provides directly for the area-fill mechanism. If you want to fill the areas defined using the Draw and/or PolyDraw functions, you must use the Flood function; you cannot use the AreaEnd function for this purpose.

RASSIZE

Syntax of Macro Call

```
num_bytes = RASSIZE (width, height)
D0                    D0     D1
```

Purpose of Macro

This macro computes the memory required for a raster bitmap based on the width and height of that bitmap. Execution of RASSIZE results in the number of bytes required to contain the specified raster bitmap.

Inputs to Macro

width The width of the bitmap measured in pixels

height The height of the bitmap measured in pixels

Discussion

This macro is available as a convenience to save you some arithmetic. Many times you will know how many pixels you need in each direction in a raster bitmap. RASSIZE enables you to use this readily available information to compute the number of bitmap memory bytes required to contain that bitmap.

For example, you might want to use this macro to help you zero all bytes in a bitmap area before you draw into that area. A set of nested For loops to do that would look as follows:

```
#define WIDTH 320
#define HEIGHT 200
#define DEPTH 5

For(i = 0; i<DEPTH; i + +){
    displaybyte = (UBYTE)MyBitMap.Planes[i];
    For(j = 0; j< RASSIZE (WIDTH,HEIGHT); j + +);
        displaybyte + +  = 0;
};
```

QBlit

Syntax of Function Call

QBlit (blitNode)
A1

Purpose of Function

This function links a request for use of the Blitter to the end of the current Blitter queue. The blitNode pointer points to a BlitNode structure containing, among other things, the link information. The BlitNode structure also contains the address of a Blitter routine to be called when the Blitter gets to this newly queued Blitter request.

Inputs to Function

blitNode   A pointer to a BlitNode structure

Discussion

There are ten Graphics Library display functions that deal specifically with Blitter operations in the Amiga system: BltClear, BltPattern, BltBitMap, BltTemplate, ClipBlit, DisownBlitter, OwnBlitter, QBlit, QBSBlit, and WaitBlit. There is more information on the Blitter in the discussions of each of these functions.

There are two ways you can queue a request for the Blitter. The first is to use the QBSBlit function to place a Blitter request in the Blitter queue. In this case, the Blitter request will be synchronized with the position of the video beam as it scans a particular video frame. When the video beam reaches the x,y position specified in the BlitNode structure, the queued Blitter routine will begin executing. This procedure allows you to rewrite certain parts of the video display RAM for a specific frame after the video beam has passed a certain point in that frame. This prevents the screen flicker that often occurs when your task is rewriting the bitmap of a view it is also simultaneously displaying.

However, if the nature of your Blitter request does not involve simultaneous memory rewriting and display, you can use the QBlit function to queue a Blitter request. Use the QBlit function when you want to move data at a very fast rate between two RAM blocks that are not currently displayed.

The QBlit function works with a Blitter routine that you specify and link into the system. This routine is very similar to the routine used by the QBSBlit function; both are Blitter usage and controlling routines. Read the discussion of the QBSBlit function to better understand the elements of these routines.

When the task Blitter routine is called, the present task will now be in control of the Blitter; the Blitter is not busy with any other task's request. This means that you can directly specify the Blitter's register contents and start the Blitter's operation.

Any Blitter request queued by the QBSBlit function will take precedence over any request queued by the QBlit function when the video beam reaches the point specified in the BlitNode structure used with the QBSBlit function.

The Blitter registers are considered to be part of the system registers that have addresses starting at 000 and continuing up to address 1FE. The Blitter registers are scattered in this address range, as shown in Table 2.3.

In general, QBlit requests are put ahead (in front of) OwnBlitter and DisownBlitter requests. However, for short Blitter operations, there is more overhead in using the QBlit function than in using a combination of OwnBlitter and DisownBlitter functions.

QBSBlit

Syntax of Function Call

<pre>
QBSBlit (blitNode)
        A1
</pre>

Purpose of Function

This function synchronizes the Blitter request with the video-beam scanning position. QBSBlit calls a user routine for use of the Blitter. The request is queued separately from a request made by the QBlit function call. QBSBlit calls the user routine referenced in the BlitNode structure after the video beam has passed a specified on-screen position.

This is useful when you are trying to copy pixel data into the raster bitmap at a location that is part of a visible area of the display screen and want to move data after the video beam has passed that display area. This prevents showing part of an old display and part of a new display simultaneously. Blitter requests on the QBSBlit queue take precedence over those on the regular Blitter queue. The bitplane for Blitter data is specified in the BlitNode structure.

Inputs to Function

blitNode   A pointer to a BlitNode structure

Discussion

There are ten Graphics Library display functions that deal specifically with Blitter operations in the Amiga system: BltClear, BltPattern, BltBitMap, BltTemplate, ClipBlit, DisownBlitter, OwnBlitter, QBlit, QBSBlit, and WaitBlit. There is more information on the Blitter in the discussions of each of these functions.

The BlitNode structure is fairly short:

```
struct BlitNode {
   struct BlitNode *n;
   int (*function) ( );
   char stat;
   short beamsync;
   int (*cleanup)( );
};
```

The BlitNode structure contains the following:

- A pointer to another BlitNode structure in a linked list

- A pointer to the Blitter routine that your task should execute when it gets control of the Blitter

- A beam-sync value—a combination of the vertical and horizontal positions of the video beam; when the video beam reaches this position, your routine will start to execute

- A status flag that tells the system whether the Blitter should perform a clean-up routine when the last Blitter operation has completed

- The address of the clean-up routine that should be used if the status flag is set

The first line of the BlitNode structure definition

struct BlitNode *n;

is a pointer to the next BlitNode structure. In most cases, blitnodes will not be linked and this item will be zero. The second line

int (*function) ( );

is the address of the routine that the Blitter queuer will call when your Blitter request reaches the top of the Blitter queue. The third line

char stat;

is a value that when set to the CLEANUP value (0x40) will execute a clean-up routine after the Blitter routine has finished. If this value is zero, no clean-up routine will be executed. The fourth line

short beamsync;

is a value that should be in the hardware system's video-beam counter (called VBEAM). It is used to determine when a beam-synchronous Blitter operation, as specified by the QBSBlit function, should occur. The system uses this value to prevent execution of your Blitter routine until the video beam has passed the VBEAM value position. This feature is especially useful when you define single-buffered displays—it prevents the video screen flicker that occurs when a task displays video information while it is changing the definition of that video information in RAM. By waiting until the video beam reaches the VBEAM position, the video information above that point in the current video frame has already been displayed and can then be altered without causing screen flicker. The last line

int (*cleanup)( );

is the address of the clean-up routine. This routine will be called when the task finally returns from the QBSBlit function call; the return occurs when your Blitter routine finally returns a zero. At that time, the system routines will automatically call this clean-up routine. For instance, you can use the clean-up routine to deallocate any memory allocated for your Blitter routines. Do everything you need to make a clean exit. This routine is not optional and must be specified.

The routine the Blitter queuer will call must be formed as a subroutine ending with a 68000 RTS (return from subroutine) instruction. If you use a C language routine, the returned value will be in the D0 register. The system will automatically call your routine again and again until it returns a zero value. This is the way the system is set up to interact with your Blitter routine. It allows your routine to maintain control over the Blitter, for example, for all five bitplanes of a bitmap. This feature can also be used when you are using the Blitter to move multiple objects while saving and restoring the background display. Here, you want to make sure that all bitplanes of the object are positioned before another object is overlaid at that screen position. The zero return value requirement will hold back progress in the Blitter queue until all aspects of the current Blitter request are finished.

Usually, the routines written for use with the QBSBlit function are assembly language routines rather than C language routines. This allows the system-queue routines to pass your routine's parameters in the system registers. These are the register-passing conventions for these system routines:

■ The system places a pointer to the system hardware registers in A0; all other system hardware registers can be referenced as an offset from the address in A0.

■ The system places a pointer to the current BlitNode structure in A1. This allows you to deal with multiple queued Blitter requests that use the same Blitter routine. The data for each of these related Blitter requests can be obtained at various offsets from the address in A1. Your task should precalculate the hardware register values and place them into the appropriate registers during the routine's execution.

ReadPixel

Syntax of Function Call

```
pennum = ReadPixel ( rastPort, x,  y)
D0                   A1        D0 D1
```

Purpose of Function

This function combines the bits from each of the bitplanes at a specified pixel position. It then determines the color represented by the pen number corresponding to that bit combination.

If successful, ReadPixel returns a pen number (pennum). This is a value between 0 and 255. A value of −1 is returned if the ReadPixel function cannot determine the color at that pixel location.

Inputs to Function

rastPort	A pointer to a controlling RastPort structure
x	The x-coordinate in the raster coordinate system
y	The y-coordinate in the raster coordinate system

Discussion

There are two Graphics Library drawing functions that deal specifically with individual display screen pixels in the Amiga system, ReadPixel and WritePixel. These functions allow you to read and change the pen number (color-register number) of a specific pixel in a specific raster bitmap.

Occasionally, you will find it necessary to determine the color number assigned to a given pixel in a specific raster bitmap definition. This may be necessary to make some kind of program decision, or you may need to verify that your raster colors have been set appropriately. This is the purpose of the ReadPixel function.

Remember that the coordinates for the ReadPixel function are measured in the raster coordinate system, which can handle a raster as large as 1,024-by-1,024 pixels. The 0,0 location, or origin, is the upper-left corner of the raster bitmap. With this convention, positive x is to the right and positive y is down. Always keep this reference frame in mind. Don't get confused between the raster coordinate system and the display-screen coordinate system, which is limited to 640-by-400 pixels for a high-resolution, interlaced mode display and has its origin in the upper-left corner of the physical display screen.

The pen number can range from 0 to 255, giving a total of 256 pen-color numbers. Although the Amiga has 256 color registers, only the first 32 of these registers have meaning in the current system, which uses a maximum of five bitplanes to define a single-playfield display. A later version of the machine will allow eight bitplanes in a single-playfield display and then will use all 256 color registers.

RectFill

Syntax of Function Call

RectFill (rastPort, xmin, ymin, xmax, ymax)
      A1   D0   D1   D2   D3

Purpose of Function

This function fills the rectangular area specified by the parameters with the chosen pen colors and area-fill pattern using the current drawing mode.

nputs to Function

rastPort	A pointer to a controlling RastPort structure
xmin, ymin	The coordinates of the upper-left corner of the rectangle
xmax, ymax	The coordinates of the lower-right corner of the rectangle

Discussion

There are six Graphics Library drawing functions that work specifically with area development in the Amiga system: AreaDraw, AreaEnd, AreaMove, Flood, InitArea, and RectFill. There is more information on area development in the discussions of each of these functions.

There are several ways you can fill a rectangular area with a pattern. You can use the AreaDraw, AreaMove, and AreaEnd functions; you can use the Draw, Move, and Flood functions; or you can use the PolyDraw and Flood functions. However, the RectFill function provides the best and fastest way to fill a rectangular area with patterned information.

You perform rectangular area-fills on a specific raster bitmap. This is the raster bitmap associated with a specific controlling RastPort structure. Keep in mind that you can have several raster bitmaps in RAM at once. The memory for each of these was allocated with the AllocRaster function, and the total bitmap was initialized by the InitBitMap function. To make your programming job easier, you should draw into one raster bitmap at a time using the associated RastPort structure to control the drawing process. Finish with one raster, then move on to the next raster.

As you fill different areas, you can keep changing the values of the various pens and patterns. You set these to define the drawing characteristics of the next area to be filled with a RectFill function call. Your task will then consist of a series of calls to the SetDrMd, SetAPen, and SetBPen functions and the SetDrPt, SetWrMsk, and SetAfPt macros, followed immediately by a call (or calls) to the RectFill function.

In this way you can change the drawing mode, drawing pen, and area pattern as you progress through a series of rectangular areas to be filled. All of the current drawing control information is stored in the RastPort structure.

You can fill an entire raster bitmap with a RectFill call. The SetRast function, however, has been specifically designed for this purpose. There is one important difference between the RectFill and SetRast functions: the SetRast function allows you to change only a fill color, previously specified by the SetAPen function.

The RectFill function, on the other hand, allows you to change a fill pattern in addition to a drawing mode, FgPen, BgPen, AOlPen, line pattern, and area pattern. Therefore, the amount of information you can place into a raster with one function call is greatly enhanced by using the RectFill function over the SetRast function. A large raster consisting of 1,024 pixels in each direction can be filled very quickly with a specific pattern displaying several colors.

Note that the RectFill function does not use any explicitly named buffers to do its job. Whatever buffers are used are controlled entirely by the system. This is another difference between RectFill and the AreaDraw, AreaMove, and AreaEnd functions, which require an explicit buffer area and an additional structure (the TmpRas structure) to control the drawing operation. RectFill also contrasts with the PolyDraw function, which sets aside its own buffer to hold the x,y values that define the vertices of what may eventually be a closed polygon.

Finally, note that the RectFill function also draws boundary lines on the rectangle it fills. The line-pattern setting in the current definition of the RastPort structure is used to add patterned boundary lines on the rectangle. If you do not want to add these lines, you must fool the RectFill function. You can do this by arranging the line pattern defined in the RastPort structure to match the background color and pattern where these lines will be drawn. Then, even though these boundary lines are indeed drawn, they will match the background and the rectangle will not appear to have any boundary lines.

ScrollRaster

Syntax of Function Call

ScrollRaster (rastPort, dx, dy, xmin, ymin, xmax, ymax)
         A1   D0 D1   D2   D3   D4   D5

Purpose of Function

This function moves the bits in the raster by dx,dy toward the 0,0 raster coordinate system origin. The area vacated is filled (using RectFill) with the color of BgPen. This function limits the scrolling operation to the rectangle defined by xmin,ymin and xmax,ymax. Any bits outside this area will not be affected.

Inputs to Function

rastPort	A pointer to a controlling RastPort structure
dx, dy	The number of pixels to scroll; these are integers that can be positive, zero, or negative
xmin, ymin	Coordinates of the upper-left corner of the subrectangle
xmax, ymax	Coordinates of the lower-right corner of the subrectangle

Discussion

There are four Graphics Library display functions that deal specifically with the raster: AllocRaster, FreeRaster, SetRast, and ScrollRaster. The first three functions allocate, deallocate, and initialize the memory area devoted to bitplanes and the bitmaps that are formed from these bitplanes. ScrollRaster provides a means of scrolling the resulting raster information on the display screen.

The ScrollRaster function allows you to scroll a subrectangle inside a much larger rectangle, namely the raster bitmap itself. This function, together with the ScrollVPort function, implements some of the graphics magic that is peculiar to the Amiga—the ability to move graphics information on and off the screen. For example, in a graphics program, a completely different view can be scrolled onto the screen while another view already on the screen is scrolled off. If properly timed, this procedure can give the user the illusion of frames of a movie being brought slowly on and off the Amiga's display screen.

To use the ScrollRaster function, you must first specify which raster you are working with. Recall that you can have multiple raster bitmaps in the first 512K of RAM. When you call the ScrollRaster function, you must specify the RastPort structure that is controlling the drawing operations in this raster. Inside the RastPort structure is a pointer to the BitMap structure for that raster.

You must also specify six other arguments to the ScrollRaster function. These are the dx,dy, xmin,ymin, and xmax,ymax raster coordinate points required to define how big the subrectangle is and how far to scroll it. It is important to remember that all of these pieces of coordinate information are specified in the raster coordinate system, not in the display-screen coordinate system.

The dx,dy arguments define the distance the subrectangle should move inside the raster bitmap. This definition is a bit tricky; positive dx values mean that the subrectangle should be scrolled to the left; positive dy values mean that the subrectangle should be scrolled up. In other words, scrolling increments are defined as data values that move the subrectangle toward the (0,0) point of the larger bitmap.

The xmin, ymin, xmax, and ymax variables fix the size of the subrectangle. Keep in mind that for a very large raster, this can be a very large subrectangle. In fact, it could be the size of an entire view. For example, in low-resolution, noninterlaced mode display, the xmin,ymin xmax,ymax subrectangle could represent the entire 320-by-200-pixel view.

The portion of the subrectangle that is scrolled is actually filled with the current color in the BgPen setting in the controlling RastPort structure. An internal double-buffering procedure stores the old section of the subrectangle that now gets this new background color in another section of RAM. Then, when you want to scroll this old piece back onto the screen, the original raster bitmap drawing information is called back from this buffer. It is also important to understand that raster pixels outside the subrectangle will not be affected by the scrolling operation.

ScrollVPort

Syntax of Function Call

ScrollVPort (viewPort, dx, dy)
      A0   D0 D1

Purpose of Function

This function scrolls a viewport rectangle by dx,dy toward the raster bitmap coordinate system origin (0,0 point). ScrollVPort automatically changes the Copper instruction lists to reflect the viewport's scrolled position. This is done after the task has adjusted the viewport definition offset values in the RasInfo structure associated with this ViewPort structure.

ScrollVPort modifies the hardware and intermediate Copper instruction list to reflect new information in the RasInfo structure. Changing the BitMap structure pointer in the RasInfo structure without changing the offsets will have a double-buffering effect.

Inputs to Function

viewPort   A pointer to the ViewPort structure that is currently on display

dx, dy   The number of pixels to scroll; these are integers that can be positive, zero, or negative

Discussion

There are five Graphics Library display functions that deal specifically with display screen viewports and views in the Amiga system: InitView, InitVPort, LoadView, MakeVPort, and ScrollVPort. There is more information on viewports and views in the discussions of each of these functions.

One of the nicest features of the Amiga computer is the quick way that the video display responds to commands from a user. This shows up first and foremost in the speed at which windows can be moved on the display screen when you use the Intuition user interface. As soon as you move the mouse pointer, the entire window comes right along. This creates a very pleasing effect for the user, who does not have to wait on the machine. The Amiga's immediate response makes the user feel in control.

This same type of instant screen movement can also be accomplished under the control of your programs. This is where the ScrollVPort and ScrollRaster functions come into play.

Suppose you want to scroll a viewport rectangle inside a total screen view. The ScrollVPort function allows you to do this for a specified viewport that is a part of that view. If you want to move a viewport, just specify the ViewPort structure pointer and the number of dx and dy pixels that you want the viewport to move inside the current view.

Note that if dx is positive, the viewport moves to the left; if dx is negative, the viewport moves to the right. (Note that this is contrary to expected behavior in Euclidean geometry.)

In contrast to the behavior of the x-axis, if dy is positive, the viewport moves up. Of course, if dy is negative, the viewport moves down. Note that this y-axis movement is consistent with the conventions of an x,y coordinate system. In both cases, positive movement is toward the origin (0,0 point) of the raster.

A lot of things have to happen to scroll a viewport inside a view. A lot of information is being moved at a very quick rate. In particular, most (if not all) of the Copper instruction list for the involved view has to be rewritten every time the screen is changed in any way.

As usual, the Copper instruction list is redefined during the vertical-blanking interval (the time when the scanning beam is blanked and is retracing from the bottom to the top of the display screen). A complete rewrite of the Copper instruction list could take place during the vertical-blanking interval. This time resolution (a complete display definition rewrite in much less than 1/60 of a second) provides the kind of display update speed that sets the Amiga apart from other microcomputers.

Finally, note that the ScrollVPort function operates differently from the ScrollRaster function in the way that it treats the display area newly exposed by the scrolling operation. The ScrollRaster function fills this newly exposed area with the background pen color. The ScrollVPort function, on the other hand, fills the newly exposed area with the display information in the next lower layer of a multilayered display.

SetAfPt

Syntax of Macro Call

SetAfPt (rastPort, areaPtrn, powerOfTwo)
          A0   A1   D0

Purpose of Macro

This macro sets the area-fill pattern for areas filled with the area-fill drawing functions.

Inputs to Macro

rastPort	A pointer to a controlling RastPort structure
areaPtrn	A pointer to the first word of an area-fill pattern in RAM
powerOfTwo	The number of words in the area-fill pattern, expressed as a power of two

Discussion

There are four macros in the Graphics Library that deal specifically with the definition of drawing-control parameters in the RastPort structure: SetOPen, SetDrPt, SetAfPt, and SetWrMsk. These macros supplement the drawing functions.

When the SetAfPt macro returns, the value of the AreaPtrn parameter, the AreaPt-Size parameter or both is changed in the specified RastPort structure. Any area-fill operations using that RastPort structure will then use those definitions.

The area-fill pattern is a set of 16-bit words whose individual bits control how the areas are filled. The newAreaPtrn parameter points to the first word in that set. The number of words in the set is determined by the powerOfTwo parameter. If the powerOfTwo parameter is 1, there is only one word in the area-fill pattern definition; if the powerOfTwo parameter is 2, there are four words; if the powerOfTwo parameter is 3, there are eight words.

Before you call the SetAfPt macro, you must build these area-fill pattern words into a specific memory location. For example, if you want eight words in a named memory location set the powerOfTwo parameter to 3. You will then have control over 128 bits (8 times 16) that you can set or reset to produce the specific area-fill pattern you want.

When you next call the area-fill drawing functions (AreaEnd, Flood, etc.) this area-fill pattern will be used to define the pixels in your new area. Your settings for the drawing mode, FgPen, BgPen, etc. will determine what colors are placed into those areas. For example, if the drawing mode is JAM1, each bit with a 1 value will receive the FgPen color and each bit with a 0 value will not be changed. Any area-fill patterns defined in this way are always positioned with respect to the upper-left corner of the drawing defined by the RastPort structure and the drawing functions.

There is an option to the SetAfPt function that allows you to produce more colors in the area-fill pattern. This is achieved by using a powerOfTwo parameter with a −1 value. If you use this option, you must supply as many planes of area-fill pattern definitions as there are bitplanes in the bitmap into which you are drawing. For example, if you want to fill a rectangle that is part of a five-bitplane bitmap, you must define your area-fill with five sets of eight words. Each set of words can be different, allowing you to define the colors for your rectangle with as much detail as you want.

SetAPen

Syntax of Function Call

SetAPen (rastPort, pennum)
          A1   D0

Purpose of Function

This function sets the primary pen color for lines, area-fills, and text in the current Rast-Port structure.

Inputs to Function

rastPort	A pointer to a controlling RastPort structure
pennum	A pen number between 0 and 255

Discussion

There are two Graphics Library drawing functions that deal specifically with the definition of drawing pens in the Amiga system: SetAPen and SetBPen. In addition, the system provides the SetOPen macro. There is more information on using drawing pens in the discussions of each of these functions and macros.

Once you create a RastPort structure and its associated raster bitmap, you want to define colors to be assigned to each pixel in that raster bitmap definition. There are many ways to do this; all of the different methods use the three drawing pens (FgPen, BgPen, and AOlPen) and the four drawing modes (JAM1, JAM2, COMPLEMENT, and INVERSVID) in various combinations to produce the desired color. See the discussion of SetBPen, SetOPen, SetDrMd, SetDrPt, and SetAfPt for more information on drawing pens and drawing modes.

After you define all the pixel colors (and perhaps other characteristics, such as patterns and text attributes), you can make various parts of this raster into distinct viewports and later combine these viewports into a view. When this view is loaded (given to the display hardware for actual display) with the LoadView function, your program will produce the desired colors on the screen.

The SetAPen function uses the FgPen (also called the APen) to assign up to 256 colors to all pixels in a given raster. The FgPen is the foreground or primary drawing pen. The JAM1 drawing mode uses this pen exclusively. The JAM2 drawing mode uses this pen together with the BgPen. The COMPLEMENT and INVERSVID drawing modes also use this pen in various ways.

The FgPen parameter in the RastPort structure contains the current value of the A pen color. You can assign a particular FgPen color by calling the SetAPen function, pointing to a specific RastPort structure (using the rastPort variable pointer argument), and specifying a value for the foreground pen you want to use for the pixels in that raster. Pen numbers can vary from 0 to 255, for a total of 256 pen numbers you can assign. The assocation of colors with pen numbers is fixed by the SetRGB4 and LoadRGB4 functions.

Once you set this new pen number, you can call any of the drawing functions routines to draw lines, fill areas, or color text using that FgPen setting. For example, first call SetAPen specifying a RastPort structure and pen number. Then call AreaDraw and AreaMove repeatedly to define a set of end-points related to a set of areas you want to fill with the color set by SetAPen. Finally, call AreaEnd to fill those areas with the chosen color. (Remember that before you call AreaDraw, you must call InitArea to set aside a work area in RAM that will hold the end-point vectors defining the lines you want to draw.)

Continue in this way for other areas that need filling in that raster bitmap. Just execute the SetAPen, AreaDraw, AreaMove, and AreaEnd functions appropriately until you design all the filled areas you want for that RastPort structure.

You can follow a similar sequence for drawing lines. Just call SetAPen to set the pen number, call Move to move the pen and/or Draw to draw a line of that pen color between two points. You can also use the PolyDraw function to draw the outline of polygons in the current FgPen color.

You can continue in this way to define all the elements of your raster bitmap. Then you can change the RastPort structure pointer and do the same thing for a new raster bitmap. Do this on and on for all the raster bitmaps whose pixel colors you want to define. Always keep in mind that the raster exists only as a series of bitplanes tied into a bitmap. Actual on-screen colors are produced when this bitmap is loaded into the hardware with the LoadView function. The system color registers then look at the colormap table (see the GetColorMap function) to define how the bitmap bits are interpreted by the color registers.

Pen numbers correspond to color-register numbers of which the Amiga has 256. The first 32 of these are the ones you should use with the present version of the machine, which is limited to five bitplanes (2^5 = 32). A future version of the machine will probably have up to eight bitplanes per bitmap and will use all 256 color registers.

Read the discussion under the SetDrMd function to better understand more completely some of the drawing-pen/drawing-mode combinations.

SetBPen

Syntax of Function Call

SetBPen (rastPort, pennum)
          A1   D0

Purpose of Function

This function sets the secondary pen color for lines, area-fills, and text in the specified RastPort structure.

Inputs to Function

rastPort   A pointer to a controlling RastPort structure

pennum   A pen number between 0 and 255

Discussion

There are two Graphics Library drawing functions that deal specifically with the definition of drawing pens in the Amiga system: SetAPen and SetBPen. In addition, the system provides the SetOpen macro.

The SetBPen function uses the BgPen (also called the BPen) to assign up to 256 colors to all pixels in a given raster bitmap. The BgPen is the background or secondary drawing pen.

You can use the SetBPen function in much the same way that you use the SetAPen function, except that different pens are used in each of the drawing modes. The JAM1 drawing mode does not use the BgPen at all. The JAM2 drawing mode uses the FgPen pen where there are ones in the line or area-pattern definition and the BgPen where there are zeros. The COMPLEMENT and INVERSVID drawing modes also use this pen in various ways. To understand the drawing-pen/drawing-mode combinations more completely, read the discussion under the SetDrMd function.

SetDrMd

Syntax of Function Call

SetDrMd (rastPort, drawmode)
             A1   D0

Purpose of Function

This function sets the drawing mode for lines, area-fills, and text. The mode set is dependent on the mode variable bits selected.

Inputs to Function

rastPort   A pointer to a controlling RastPort structure
drawmode   A drawing mode specification

Discussion

SetDrMd is the only Graphics Library drawing function that deals specifically with the drawing modes used to define the elements of the Amiga display screen. SetDrMd allows you to set the drawing mode for lines, area-fills, and text in a given RastPort structure definition.

Whenever you specify a drawing mode, you always tie that specification to a particular RastPort structure. In other words, you draw into the raster bitmap associated with that RastPort structure. This is more fully explained in the introduction to this chapter and is an important idea to understand.

If you examine all the drawing function calls, you will see that they all have the rastPort pointer variable as one of their arguments. In fact, it is usually the first argument in these functions. All drawing functions are targeted to a specific RastPort structure. You can have a number of current RastPort structures; you can think of some as active and others as passive. You can then direct your drawing commands to each of these as the flow of your program and the current active task dictate.

Drawing Modes

There are four possible drawing modes you can use to define information in the RastPort structure. The first drawing mode is JAM1. If you specify this variable in the Rast-Port structure, you will be using the primary drawing pen to color pixels in the raster bitmap associated with that RastPort structure. You will be setting (or resetting) the bit-plane bits according to the current bit definition of the primary drawing pen. In JAM1 mode, you can jam only one color into the target raster bitmap; every addressed pixel in that raster will be drawn in the FgPen color. By varying the current FgPen color, you can vary the colors assigned to each pixel in a raster bitmap.

The second drawing mode is JAM2. This mode is only used with line pattern and area pattern drawing. If you specify this variable in the RastPort structure, you will be using both the primary and secondary drawing pens to set (and reset) bits in the raster bitmap associated with that RastPort structure. With this mode, you can jam only two colors into the target raster bitmap. Whenever there is a 1 bit in the pattern (area or line), the FgPen color replaces the color of the pixel at the drawing position. Whenever there is a 0 bit in the pattern, the BgPen color is used. By varying the current FgPen and BgPen colors, you can vary the colors assigned to each pixel in a raster where a line or area pattern is drawn.

The third drawing mode is COMPLEMENT. This mode first takes the bits in the established raster bitmap definition and complements them. For each bit in the FgPen parameter, the corresponding bit in the target drawing is complemented: 0 bits become 1 bits and 1 bits become 0 bits. From this it is obvious that specifying two COMPLE-MENT mode drawing steps back to back will reverse the effect of each other.

The drawmode parameter is written as JAM1 or JAM2 for simple cases. Drawing specifications involving COMPLEMENT or INVERSVID are usually written as com-pound statements; that is, a drawing specification is usually written

> **COMPLEMENT | JAM1**

or

> **COMPLEMENT | JAM2**

(The vertical bar in this argument is simply the logical And (bitwise OR) operator. This tells the SetDrMd function to use the combination of JAM1 and COMPLEMENT, for example.)

The fourth drawing mode is INVERSVID. This drawing mode must be used in combination with either JAM1 or JAM2 and is used primarily for text. If the compound drawing mode is

> **JAM1 | INVERSVID**

text characters appear as transparent letters surrounded by the current FgPen color. On the other hand, if the compound drawing mode is set as

> **JAM2 | INVERSVID**

the text characters appear in the background color surrounded by the current FgPen color. The only difference between this drawing mode and

> **JAM1 | INVERSVID**

is that the BgPen is used to draw the text character itself. From this discussion, you can see that the INVERSVID mode command essentially reverses the role and effect of the FgPen and BgPen colors.

SetDrPt

Syntax of Macro Call

SetDrPt (rastPort, linePtrn)
         A0   D0

Purpose of Macro

This macro sets the line-fill pattern for lines drawn with the Draw, Move, and PolyDraw functions. The line-fill pattern setting becomes part of the current RastPort structure.

Inputs to Macro

rastPort	A pointer to a controlling RastPort structure
linePtrn	A one-word line-fill pattern

Discussion

When you use the Draw, Move, AreaEnd, RectFill, or PolyDraw functions, you will often be drawing lines into your raster bitmap. To be more precise, you will fill the boundary lines of objects in your raster with a specific pattern of information. This pattern is known as the *line-fill pattern*. The current controlling RastPort structure definition contains the latest definition of the line-fill pattern in the LinePtrn parameter. You use the SetDrPt macro to define precisely what that line-fill pattern should look like when a line is drawn on the display screen. In fact, the SetDrPt macro provides a mechanism for you to define all the line-fill patterns you will need for your program and its graphics tasks.

Your line-fill patterns are limited to a width of 16 bits; therefore, they can be defined by a single memory word. When you make your call to the SetDrPt macro, specify that word as a hex number of the form 0xXXXX. For example, 0xFFFF defines a line-fill pattern in which all bits are set to 1 values; this gives a solid line. If you use 0x0000, you define a line-fill pattern in which all bits are 0; this gives a line drawn in the current BgPen color, thus possibly matching the background of the display at that location.

Your call to the SetDrPt macro will place your one-word line-fill pattern definition into the RastPort structure you are currently using to control your drawing operations. Then, when you call any of the drawing functions that produce lines using this RastPort structure as the controlling structure, the LinePtrn parameter in that RastPort structure will tell these drawing functions what specific line-fill pattern to use.

Note that you can design any number of line-fill patterns for your graphics program tasks. Each can define a unique pattern to satisfy all your line-fill needs. These can vary from solid lines to various types of dotted lines to lines that match the background pattern at various screen locations. You can vary the colors produced by these different line-fill patterns by calling the SetOPen macro at appropriate points in your drawing task. In this way, you can use a sequence of SetDrPt calls followed by Draw, Move, AreaEnd, and/or RectFill calls to draw all the lines in your raster.

SetOPen

Syntax of Macro Call

SetOPen (rastPort, pennum)
          A1   D0

Purpose of Macro

This macro sets the outline pen (AOlPen) color for text and area-outlines in the current RastPort structure.

Inputs to Macro

rastPort	A pointer to a controlling RastPort structure
pennum	A pen number between 0 and 255

Discussion

There are two Graphics Library drawing functions that deal specifically with the definition of drawing pens in the Amiga system: SetAPen and SetBPen. In addition, the system provides the SetOPen macro. These functions and macro allow you to define the characteristics of drawing pens that can then be used to define colors and other aspects of each part of the display screen.

The AOlPen, also called the OPen, is the outline-drawing pen. Neither the JAM1, JAM2, or COMPLEMENT drawing modes use this pen. However, the INVERSVID drawing mode uses this pen in various ways to draw text. Here, the AOlPen works together with the FgPen and the BgPen to produce on-screen text having various characteristics.

In addition, the AOlPen is used for two specific applications: area-fill and flood-fill. When used with an area-fill operation, the AOlPen will outline the filled area with the AOlPen color once that area has been filled with the FgPen color. When used with a flood-fill operation, you can fill the flooded area with the FgPen color until you reach the pixel having the color of the current AOlPen setting, when the flooding operation will be stopped.

Note that the current setting for the outline pen appears as the AOlPen parameter in the RastPort structure.

SetRast

Syntax of Function Call

       SetRast (rastPort, pennum)
               A1   D0

Purpose of Function

This function sets the entire contents of the specified raster to the specified pen color. When SetRast returns, the bits in the bitplanes of the entire bitmap have values consistent with the chosen pen color.

Inputs to Function

rastPort	A pointer to a controlling RastPort structure
pennum	The pen number that gives you the color you want

Discussion

SetRast is the only Graphics Library drawing function that allows you to set the color of an entire bitmap in one step.

Occasionally, you will find it necessary to preset the color assigned to an entire raster bitmap governed by a specific RastPort structure definition. This may be necessary to set the most pervasive color in a drawing. This is the purpose of the SetRast function. All SetRast drawing is done according to the current FgPen setting (determined by the last SetAPen function call) and the current drawing mode (determined by the last SetDrMd function call).

You can then use the pen functions together with the AreaDraw, AreaMove, AreaEnd, Draw, Move, Flood, and PolyDraw functions to color other parts of the raster bitmap. When you have used these line-drawing and area-drawing functions to their fullest extent, you can use the WritePixel function to fine-tune small areas in your raster bitmap. WritePixel sets a particular pixel in a raster bitmap to a given color; it allows you to vary the color explicitly from pixel to pixel.

The raster coordinate system can handle a raster as large as 1,024-by-1,024 pixels. The 0,0 location, or origin, is the upper-left corner of the raster. With this convention, positive x is to the right and positive y is down.

Always keep this reference frame in mind. Don't get confused between the raster coordinate system and the display-screen coordinate system, which is limited to 640-by-400 pixels for a high-resolution, interlaced mode display and has a 0,0 reference point in the upper-left corner of the physical display screen.

Because the raster can be so large, you can develop many viewports and views from it. Therefore, if you set it to a specific color with the SetRast function, each of these viewports and resulting views will also have that color until further modified by other color-setting functions.

Also remember that the pen number can range from 0 to 255, giving a total of 256 pen colors. See the ReadPixel function discussion for information on how the color registers are used.

SetRGB4

Syntax of Function Call

SetRGB4 (viewPort, n, red_intensity, green_intensity, blue_intensity)
         A0   D0 D1   D2   D3

Purpose of Function

This function stores the color definition value in the Colortable array for this viewport. Twelve bits in the selected color register will be changed to reflect this new RGB setting.

Inputs to Function

viewPort	A pointer to a ViewPort structure
n	A pen number for one of the system color registers; n ranges from 0 to 31

red_intensity   An integer from 0 to 15 to define the intensity of red in the color register setting

green_intensity   An integer from 0 to 15 to define the intensity of green

blue_intensity   An integer from 0 to 15 to define the intensity of blue

Discussion

There are three Graphics Library drawing functions that deal specifically with the drawing pen colors used in viewports: GetRGB4, LoadRGB4, and SetRGB4. LoadRGB4 loads a set of RGB (red, green, blue) color values from a colortable array, allowing you to change the colors in the colortable assigned to pens. GetRGB4 allows you to find the value of a specific color currently assigned by a colortable to a pen. Once you know what this color is, you can use or change it to define the detailed drawing steps of a specific viewport. SetRGB4 allows you to set one specific color register value in a given viewport bitmap.

The LoadRGB4 and SetRGB4 functions both work with a specific viewport. Remember that a viewport is one rectangular area of a view. All visual aspects of the viewport are controlled by the ViewPort structure; the view, which often consists of several viewports, is controlled by the View structure. The purpose of the SetRGB4 function is to set one of the color registers for this viewport. It directly affects the contents of one of the color registers on the Amiga motherboard.

It is important to place the SetRGB4 function in its proper context. Keep in mind that each call to SetRGB4 sets the color value of only one of the 32 color registers in the Amiga system. In addition, it deals with only one viewport, the one specified by the viewPort pointer argument.

Also note that the SetRGB4 function gives you control over each primary color (red, green, and blue) individually for that viewport and color register. You can vary the red (argument R), green (argument G), and blue (argument B) bits in the specified color register separately to control the intensity of each of the primary colors in 16 gradations. If, for example, you want a maximum red intensity, set the R argument to 15. If you want minimum red intensity, set the R argument to 0. The intensities of the other two colors work in the same way.

The Amiga color registers are 16-bit registers. However, only 12 of the 16 bits are used; bits 15 through 12 are not used. When you set the R, G, and B arguments in your SetRGB4 call, you set the corresponding bits in these registers. Bits 11 through 8 control red, bits 7 through 4 control green, and bits 3 through 0 control blue.

Contrast the SetRGB4 function to the LoadRGB4 and GetRGB4 functions. In particular, note that the LoadRGB4 function works with the entire colortable, allowing you to specify all 32 color registers at one time. The GetRGB4 function allows you to determine what color value is stored in one of the color registers, but does not provide a mechanism for changing color-register assignments.

The SetRGB4 function provides color-register fine-tuning in a specified viewport. This allows you to change color assignments in a viewport without redefining the entire colortable using the LoadRGB4 function. Make your initial viewport color assignments using LoadRGB4—once for each viewport. Later, if you need to change one or several color-register values for a specific viewport to get some new colors into that viewport, use SetRGB4 to make these additional changes.

Such a procedure, which avoids redefining the entire colortable over and over again, obviously saves task execution time, which is often critical in graphics work. In some cases, you may have to change viewport color-register assignments in the small time interval provided by the single scanning line between viewports. It is clear that the less code that has to execute in this small interval of time ensures success for your current task and the program with which it is associated.

If you use hold-and-modify mode for a video display, you can produce 4,096 colors by assigning values to the 32 color registers and interpreting these register values in the hold-and-modify mode conventions. See the discussion of hold-and-modify mode in Appendix B.

Table 2.4 lists a set of typical color-register values and the color produced by a color register when it has that setting. It is useful to keep the color extremes in mind. Notice from Table 2.4 that a color-register value of zero ($000) gives black. Black is the background color used on the Amiga. If all bits in the color register are set ($FFF), white is produced.

Table 2.4:
Typical Color Register Settings

Register Value	Color Produced	Register Value	Color Produced
$FFF	White	$6FE	Sky blue
$D00	Brick red	$6CE	Light blue
$F00	Red	$00F	Blue
$F80	Red-orange	$61F	Bright blue
$F90	Orange	$06D	Dark blue
$FB0	Golden orange	$91F	Purple
$FD0	Cadmium yellow	$C1F	Violet
$FF0	Lemon yellow	$F1F	Magenta
$BF0	Lime green	$FAC	Pink
$8E0	Light green	$DB9	Tan
$0F0	Green	$C80	Brown
$2C0	Dark green	$A87	Dark brown
$0B1	Forest green	$CCC	Light grey
$0BB	Blue-green	$999	Medium grey
$0DB	Aqua	$000	Black
$1FB	Light aqua		

SetRGB4CM

Syntax of Function Call

```
SetRGB4CM (colorMap, color_number, red_intensity
           A0         D0            D1:4
green_intensity, blue_intensity)
D2:4             D3:4
```

Purpose of Function

This function changes one of the color register definitions (entries) in the colortable array pointed to by a specific ColorMap structure. You can use SetRGB4CM to define a colormap table before assigning it to a viewport. SetRGB4CM returns no value.

Inputs to Function

colorMap   A pointer to a ColorMap structure whose colortable array you want to change

color_number   The color register number (0 to 31) whose color assignment you want to change

red_intensity   An integer value from 0 to 15 representing the red color intensity for the new red value

green_intensity An integer value from 0 to 15 representing the green color intensity for the new green value

blue_intensity   An integer value from 0 to 15 representing the blue color intensity for the new blue value

Discussion

SetRGB4CM is the only function in the 1.2 release that deals with color register changes.

There are several ways you can change the color register definitions in your programs to produce different colors on the Amiga display screen. First, you can use the LoadRGB4 function to associate a set of color register definitions with a viewport using the ColorMap structure to point to the colortable array.

Second, you can use the SetRGB4 function to define a specific color register (the red, green, and blue intensity) and assign that color register to a specific RastPort structure. All bitmaps controlled by that RastPort structure will then use that color register definition.

Or third, you can use the SetRGB4CM function to set one color in the colormap table associated with a specific ColorMap structure. You can then use that new colormap table with any RastPort structure you desire. This last method provides a more direct way to change colors in a colortable array.

SetWrMsk

Syntax of Macro Call

```
SetWrMsk (rastPort, newmask)
         A0        D0
```

Purpose of Function

This macro sets the bitplane write-mask parameter in a specific RastPort structure.

Inputs to Macro

rastPort	A pointer to a controlling RastPort structure
newmask	A 16-bit value whose lowest six bits determine which bitplanes in a bitmap can be written into

Discussion

There are four macros in the Graphics Library that deal specifically with the definition of drawing-control parameters in the RastPort structure: SetOPen, SetDrPt, SetAfPt, and SetWrMsk. These macros supplement the other drawing functions in the Graphics Library.

Usually, a drawing operation will write into all bitplanes of a bitmap without restriction. However, there are times when you may want to prevent a drawing operation from changing the bits in certain bitplanes in a bitmap. This is the purpose of the SetWrMsk macro. It assigns a specific value to the Mask parameter in a specific RastPort structure.

Then, when any drawing function that uses that RastPort structure executes, it will modify only those bitplanes in the raster bitmap where the Mask parameter has a 1 bit in that position.

For example, if the SetWrMsk macro is used to set the Mask parameter to 1111111111110111, all of the bitplanes can be changed by a drawing operation except for bitplane 3. Note that for a single-playfield mode display, only the lowest five bits of the Mask parameter have any meaning. However, for a dual-playfield mode display the lowest six bits can have meaning. Higher order bits can be used for future enhancements (more bitplanes in a bitmap) when more colors are added to the Amiga system. Also remember that you can use a simple structure parameter assignment statement to modify the Mask parameter in a RastPort structure. That method and the SetWrMsk macro method are equivalent.

SyncSBitMap

Syntax of Function Call

        SyncSBitMap (layer)
              A0

Purpose of Function

This function copies the current contents of a layer bitmap into the superbitmap associated with that layer.

Inputs to Function

layer   A pointer to a super bitmap Layer structure that is already locked by the calling task

Discussion

There are two Graphics Library display functions that deal specifically with superbitmaps and the layers associated with them: CopySBitMap and SyncSBitMap. These functions work with a BitMap structure that defines a raster superbitmap and a Layer structure that defines a layer bitmap.

Both the CopySBitMap and SyncSBitMap functions use the layer pointer argument, which points to the Layer structure with which this superbitmap is associated. Inside the

Layer structure is a pointer to a BitMap structure that defines the superbitmap associated with this layer.

The superbitmap screen-refreshing technique is one of three ways that obscured portions of the Amiga display screen can be refreshed. The other two are the simple-refresh method, which uses no backup bitmap, and the smart-refresh method, which uses a series of small, system-allocated backup bitmaps.

If you design a layer as a smart-refresh layer, the system automatically allocates a set of small RAM blocks to hold the currently obscured portions of that layer bitmap. The entire layer (both the visible and obscured portions) is not backed up as is done with a superbitmap layer. Only the obscured portions are placed in several small bitmaps scattered throughout RAM.

The superbitmap-refresh technique differs from the smart-refresh technique in several ways. First, only one backup bitmap is used for a superbitmap layer. Second, you must explicitly allocate the RAM memory for the backup superbitmap in the graphics task; use the AllocRaster function for this purpose. Third, the backup superbitmap can be larger than its associated layer bitmap. To see a larger portion of a superbitmap in the on-screen layer bitmap, you can use the SizeLayer function. To see a different portion of the superbitmap in the on-screen layer bitmap, you can use the ScrollLayer function. Both of these functions are in the Layers Library, which is discussed in Chapter 5.

The SyncSBitMap function is used when you need to back up an entire layer bitmap. To do that, you must copy the entire bitmap into the appropriate subsection of its associated superbitmap. Because of its internal bookkeeping procedures, the system knows where to place the current layer bitmap inside of the current superbitmap. This is precisely what the SyncSBitMap function does. Note that this operation is the opposite of the operation produced by the CopySBitMap function, which copies a part of a superbitmap into its associated layer bitmap. See the discussion of CopySBitMap for more on superbitmaps and their interaction with layers.

UnlockLayerRom

Syntax of Function Call

UnlockLayerRom (layer)
A5

Purpose of Function

This function unlocks the Layer structure using ROM code in the Graphics Library. There should be an UnlockLayerRom function call for every LockLayerRom function call. UnlockLayerRom decrements the task lock count in the Layer structure. Once all tasks that have locked this layer have also unlocked it, the lock count is reduced to zero. When this Layer structure is fully unlocked, any task can modify it and its associated layer bitmap.

Inputs to Function

layer   A pointer to a Layer structure

Discussion

There are two Graphics Library display functions that deal specifically with multitasking and Layer structures: LockLayerRom and UnlockLayerRom. The purpose of these functions is to lock and unlock the Layer structures used to define a multilayered display. Once a task locks a Layer structure, other tasks cannot modify that Layer structure. This is useful in a multitasking system where more than one task tries to define the graphics information in the same layer bitmap. When a Layer structure is locked, no task other than the locking task can modify its bitmap contents until it is unlocked.

In addition, no other task can change any of the parameters of the Layer structure itself. Both the LockLayerRom and UnlockLayerRom functions take only one argument, the Layer structure pointer variable; its value is known from a previous call to the CreateUpfrontLayer or CreateBehindLayer functions (described in Chapter 5).

The Intuition graphics interface provides the best visible use of layers in the Amiga graphics system. Once you are inside Intuition, you can use the mouse to open a number of windows on the Amiga display screen. You can then use the various gadgets that Intuition provides to manipulate these windows. In particular, you can use the gadgets in the upper-right corner of every window to bring a window to the front of the display screen, making it the active window, or to place a window behind all other windows on the display screen. Then this window is no longer the active window; instead, the previous active window becomes active.

When you use these types of Intuition operations to open and manipulate windows, you will be dealing with a multilayered display. Behind all of these windows will be the background screen. The formal definition of a background screen is a backdrop layer, usually all blue. This backdrop layer does not move as you open and close windows. Every window that opens is placed on top of this backdrop layer.

In addition, as you open more windows, each new window comes from a different layer bitmap. As a result of this layer-building process, some new windows may overlap other windows already visible on the screen. When this happens, some portion of an already visible window is obscured from view on the display screen. Windows also get obscured when you move a window around on the display screen. All of these effects are handled internally by calls to the Layers Library functions called indirectly by the Intuition software system.

Getting back to UnlockLayerRom, each task can create and draw into any number of layers. The only limitation is the amount of bitmap RAM required. Keep in mind that the bitmap information is confined to the first 512K of Amiga RAM. In a low-resolution, noninterlaced mode display, a 32-color layer requires 8,000 bytes per bitplane if that layer is the full size of the Amiga display screen. This gives 40,000 bytes for the entire layer, just for its bitmap. In addition, of course, you must allow RAM space for various structures such as the RastPort structure, the Task Control Block structure (see Chapter 1), the LayerInfo structure (see Chapter 5), and many others. Therefore, you want to develop a layer strategy that ensures that you are economizing on RAM space specifically assigned to layers in a graphics program.

Each LockLayerRom call should be paired with a comparable UnlockLayerRom call within the same task. Then, when that task finishes execution for the last time, that layer will be unlocked. If a task executes a LockLayerRom call on a specific layer, another task can execute a LockLayerRom or UnlockLayerRom call on that same layer. This situation can arise because each task cannot anticipate the exact sequence another task will follow once it gains control of the machine. However, the LockLayerRom or UnlockLayerRom call of the second task will have no effect on the state of that layer; it will still be locked to all but the task that executed the first LockLayerRom call. Only that task can unlock a layer it has locked.

Finally, note that the UnlockLayerRom function uses ROM code to accomplish its job, making it very fast. In contrast, the UnlockLayer function in the Layers Library does the same job, only slower, using RAM-based code.

VBeamPos

Syntax of Function Call

```
vertbpos = VBeamPos ()
D0
```

Purpose of Function

This function interrogates the hardware for the current vertical video-beam position and returns the value in the vertbpos variable. The vertbpos value is the scan-line number in a noninterlaced mode display. Because of hardware constraints, if the current vertical video-beam position is between 256 and 262, this function will return a value of 0 through 6. Because of multitasking, the actual value returned may be of no use to the current task.

Inputs to Function

This function uses no arguments.

Discussion

There are three Graphics Library display functions that deal specifically with the vertical video-beam position on the display screen of the Amiga: VBeamPos, WaitBOVP, and Wait-TOF. The purpose of these three functions is to sense the position of the video beam on the display screen and to take specific actions depending on the detected position.

Knowledge of the vertical video-beam position is vital to the operation of the Amiga graphics system. The system needs to know this position to develop and display video information on the screen properly. The VBeamPos function works together with the WaitTOF and WaitBOVP functions to use the vertical video-beam position as a variable in the control of the display system hardware.

There are several key times in the development of a video frame when the system needs to know the vertical position of the video beam. The first and most important time is when the beam reaches the bottom of the display frame and is about to retrace to the top of the next frame.

In this short time, the system hardware often needs to update the Copper instruction lists that specify the video contents of the next video frame. New Copper instructions come from three sources: those supplied by the MakeVPort function, those supplied by the animation routines, and any Copper instructions that a user has written to control the special-purpose registers directly outside the control of the Graphics Library function calls.

If the contents of the next video frame are in any way different from the contents of the previous frame displayed, the system's special-purpose video-control chip registers have to be rewritten. These register changes allow the system to change the characteristics (for example, the display mode and the color palette) of the next view, to reposition sprites on the next display frame (animation), and to set up the Blitter for its next set of actions.

You can use the vertical video-beam position returned by the VBeamPos function to make decisions in your current program task. For instance, you can use the LoadRGB4 or SetRGB4 functions to change the colors assigned to the system color registers while the vertical video-beam position is between two vertically stacked viewports on the screen. This is why viewports must have at least one vertical scanning line between them: this line allows the hardware control registers enough time to be changed so that the next viewport will have the new colors you want.

You can also use the current vertical video-beam position value to decide when to change a sprite with the ChangeSprite function, or when to free a sprite with the FreeSprite function (see Chapter 3). In general, you can use the current vertical video-beam position to decide when to change hardware settings in the system. You can also use CWAIT, CMOVE, DisownBlitter, OwnBlitter, and MoveSprite to change the next frame of the video display to accomplish things that you need to do in your graphics programs.

WaitBlit

Syntax of Function Call

WaitBlit ( )

Purpose of Function

This function is used to halt the current task's activity until all of the Blitter data moves already queued have been completed. Recall that the Blitter, under control of the QBlit and QBSBlit functions, is used to queue various requests for action.

Inputs to Function

This function uses no arguments.

Discussion

There are ten Graphics Library display functions that deal specifically with Blitter operations in the Amiga system: BltClear, BltPattern, BltBitMap, BltTemplate, ClipBlit, DisownBlitter, OwnBlitter, QBlit, QBSBlit, and WaitBlit. There is more information on programming the Blitter in the discussions of each of these functions.

The current task waits until the Blitter is finished. Because of multitasking, other tasks may saturate the Blitter with back-to-back requests. The current task cannot resume until there is a break in the action.

Generally speaking, all queued requests are processed in the order they are queued on a first-in first-out basis. The only exception to this is when a later QBSBlit request takes precedence over an earlier QBlit request. This situation can occur if the video beam reaches the position specified in the BlitNode structure associated with the QBSBlit function call before the queued QBlit request comes to the top of the Blitter request queue.

The Blitter request queue continues to build as long as the QBlit and QBSBlit functions are adding their requests to the queue. The system routines automatically keep the Blitter queue up to date as these requests are added. Sometimes the queue can get fairly long, especially if a number of tasks are currently competing for the Blitter's attention.

Some of these may be display tasks; others may not display anything; they may be just moving data in and between off-screen bitmaps. Most tasks will find various uses for the Blitter. As task switching occurs, each task can put its requests into the Blitter request queue. These will be queued back to back for all tasks in the system. Under these circumstances, you can quickly saturate the Blitter queue with a tremendous number of pending Blitter requests.

If nothing is done to prevent it, the queue will continue to fill. In this way, you can lose control of the system; you can have many tasks waiting for Blitter requests to finish, and those requests may still be near the bottom of the Blitter request queue. This is where the WaitBlit function comes into play.

The purpose of the WaitBlit function is to suspend other task activities until the Blitter queue has been emptied of all pending requests. This is most useful as it relates to task switching. For example, when you switch to a new task you can execute the WaitBlit function immediately. This tells the system to process all queued Blitter requests no matter where they originated. When the WaitBlit function returns, you will know that the Blitter request queue is indeed empty.

Then the current task can proceed to execute its other statements. Among these can be additional Blitter requests. These will be placed in an initially empty Blitter request queue. When you finish adding requests to the queue, you can once again execute the WaitBlit function. This will suspend all other system activity until all the requests queued by your current task have been processed by the Blitter. Therefore, the WaitBlit function allows you to maintain order in what could be a chaotic situation. See the discussion of the OwnBlitter function for more on the use of the WaitBlit function.

WaitBOVP

Syntax of Function Call

WaitBOVP (viewPort)
A0

Purpose of Function

This function tells the current task to wait until the vertical video-beam position value corresponds to the value at the bottom of a specified viewport.

Inputs to Function

viewPort   A pointer to a ViewPort structure

Discussion

There are three Graphics Library display functions that deal specifically with the vertical video-beam position on the display screen of the Amiga: VBeamPos, WaitBOVP, and Wait-TOF. The purpose of these three functions is to sense the position of the video beam on the display screen and to take specific actions depending on the detected position. Read the discussions of VBeamPos and WaitTOF for more information on this subject.

One of the key times you will want to change graphics settings is in the time interval between the end of one viewport display and the beginning of the next viewport display. Recall that the Amiga requires at least one vertical scanning line between two vertically stacked viewports.

While the video beam scans that line, the system updates the hardware control registers that define the characteristics of the next viewport displayed in that frame. This is when you can change the resolution, color palette, active sprites, and other characteristics of the next viewport in that frame.

The purpose of the WaitBOVP function is to wait for the video beam to reach the bottom of the specified viewport. Once the video beam reaches this point, you can go on to a set of task instructions to fix the hardware settings for the next viewport.

Using the WaitBOVP viewPort pointer argument, you can specify the viewport for which you want to wait. The WaitBOVP function will then suspend current task execution until the video beam reaches the known last line of that viewport. Then the task instructions that change the video display characteristics for the next viewport will execute. Keep in mind that you can change most of the viewport characteristics in this way. However, you cannot change the vertical resolution from one viewport to another within the same view frame; the LACE mode parameter of the View structure governs the vertical resolution of all viewports in a view.

WaitTOF

Syntax of Function Call

WaitTOF ( )

Purpose of Function

This function waits for the video beam to reach the top of the next video frame. This occurs just after the latest vertical-blanking sequence is completed. WaitTOF also waits for completion of execution of all vertical-blanking routines that occur during the vertical-blanking interval.

Inputs to Function

This function uses no arguments.

Discussion

There are three Graphics Library display functions that deal specifically with the vertical video-beam position on the display screen of the Amiga: VBeamPos, WaitBOVP, and Wait-TOF. The purpose of these three functions is to sense the position of the video beam on the display screen and to take specific actions depending on the detected position.

The VBeamPos and WaitBOVP functions allow you to alter the display screen characteristics at specific vertical positions in a display view frame. The purpose of the Wait-TOF function is to take this capability one step further: to allow a task to wait until the video beam reaches the top of the next video frame.

This procedure ensures that a complex set of Copper instructions leads to a complex set of control-register changes before the display of the next video frame actually begins. Recall that the system may have to make many changes in control registers and other hardware settings during the vertical-blanking interval. The WaitTOF function suspends further task execution until all of the system hardware settings have been properly changed.

If you want to change the next frame's definition in a major way, the system will need a little extra time to make the hardware setting changes. For this reason, you want to delay the further task execution until all these changes are known to have been made. For instance, a menu choice in a program may open up a completely new set of program windows. In this case, the system needs some time to specify the system control registers and other hardware settings that define those windows. An Intuition program will momentarily suspend execution until the system hardware is properly set up to display the new windows.

There are a few more things you should know about the Copper coprocessor and how it relates to the Amiga system as a whole. The Copper is a custom display coprocessor. This means that it has its own set of instructions. Just like the 68000 CPU instructions, Copper instructions are written and stored in RAM. There are only three Copper instructions: WAIT, SKIP, and MOVE. Just like all the other special-purpose Amiga hardware, Copper instructions are restricted to chip memory, the first 512K of RAM.

These Copper instructions allow a task to change the color palette in midscreen, splitting the screen into multiple horizontal slices (for example, Intuition windows or viewports in a view), each having its own horizontal resolution; change the bitmap depth; produce beam-synchronized interrupts for the 68000; and so on.

One of the key functions of the Copper is to wait (the Copper WAIT instruction) for a specific vertical video-beam position and then to move (the Copper MOVE instruction) information into one or more of the system's special-purpose registers.

During the waiting period, the Copper examines the contents of the system video-beam counter directly. This is important to system efficiency because it means that while the Copper is waiting for a specific video-beam position, it does not use the memory bus at all; it is effectively off the memory bus. During wait times, the bus is freed for use by the other DMA channels or by the 68000. Once the wait condition has been satisfied, the Copper steals memory cycles from the Blitter or the 68000 (whichever is then active) to move the specified data to the special-purpose registers addressed by the Copper instructions.

The Copper instructions work with the 68000 instructions. Most of the time, they do not compete for the memory cycles in the system. The 68000 runs at 7.16 megahertz and needs to use only alternate RAM memory cycles, the even-numbered cycles. This means that the Copper can use the odd-numbered RAM memory cycles to do its job. Under most circumstances the 68000 runs at its full speed. Only under rare circumstances does the Copper (or, for that matter, the Blitter) steal memory cycles from the 68000. In fact, these chips steal memory cycles only when they can do a particular job (for instance, data movement) faster than the 68000.

WritePixel

Syntax of Function Call

        WritePixel (rastPort, x, y)
                    A1   D0 D1

Purpose of Function

This function changes the color and other attributes of a selected pixel in the specified raster bitmap to that currently specified by the SetAPen function together with other current parameters in the controlling RastPort structure.

Inputs to Function

rastPort	A pointer to a controlling RastPort structure
x	The raster bitmap x-coordinate of the selected pixel
y	The raster bitmap y-coordinate of the selected pixel

Discussion

There are two Graphics Library drawing functions that deal specifically with individual display-screen pixels in the Amiga system, ReadPixel and WritePixel. These functions allow you to read and change the color of a specific pixel in a specific raster bitmap.

Occasionally, you will find it necessary to set the color assigned to a specific pixel in a raster bitmap, perhaps to control the drawing in a small part of a display. This is the purpose of the WritePixel function. All WritePixel drawing is done according to the current FgPen setting of the last SetAPen function call and the current drawing mode set by the SetDrMd function.

You can use the SetRast function to set the most common color in a RastPort structure definition. If the raster has a common, pervasive background color, SetRast allows you to set it. You can then use the SetAPen and SetBPen functions and the SetOPen, SetDrPt, and SetAfPt macros, together with the area-drawing functions (AreaDraw, AreaMove, and AreaEnd), to draw outlines and fill these outlines with specific color information, patterns included. You can also use the pen functions together with the Draw, Move, Flood, and PolyDraw functions to color other parts of that raster. Then, when you have used these line-drawing and area-drawing functions to their fullest extent, you can use the WritePixel function to take care of the fine-tuning in your raster display.

XorRectRegion

Syntax of Function Call

```
XorRectRegion (region, rectangle)
               A0      A1
```

Purpose of Function

This function performs a two-dimensional XOR operation of a clipping-rectangle with a region, leaving the result in the region definition. XorRectRegion clips away any portion of the region that exists both in the new clipping-rectangle and in the current region definition up to this point.

Inputs to Function

region	A pointer to a Region structure
rectangle	A pointer to a Rectangle structure

Discussion

There are six Graphics Library drawing functions that deal specifically with regions and the clipping-rectangles that define those regions: AndRectRegion, ClearRegion, Dispose-Region, NewRegion, OrRectRegion, and XorRectRegion. There is more information on regions and clipping-rectangles in the discussions of each of these functions.

The XorRectRegion function performs an XOR operation on the current clipping-rectangle contents of a region and a clipping-rectangle that may or may not already be a part of that region. That clipping-rectangle is then made a part of that region. Note that this is not the same as performing an XOR operation on the bits of a rectangle bitplane by bitplane with bits in a region of a bitmap.

Suppose that you want to draw two solid one-color squares that overlap on one corner. This corner where the two squares overlap should show the background color. The other parts of the two squares should show any other color. There are at least two ways you can draw this figure.

The first way is the more obvious. You merely decide where you want the new figure to appear in that layer. Then you use the AreaDraw, AreaMove, and AreaEnd functions (or the RectFill function) to define and draw that new figure. You use the drawing functions (SetAPen, SetBPen, etc.) to prepare the RastPort structure so that it properly controls the drawing colors, borders, and so forth, for your new figure. Then, when you finally execute the AreaEnd function (or the RectFill function), the new figure will be drawn into your layer bitmap.

Alternatively, you can use the XorRectRegion function together with one region defined by two clipping-rectangles to set and draw into this portion of your layer bitmap. To do this, first define a ClipRect structure using four simple program statements to define the vertices of a square clipping-rectangle. Then call the NewRegion function to allocate and initialize a new region of size zero. Next, use the XorRectRegion function to include this clipping-rectangle into the new region. Then define a second clipping-rectangle using another four program statements to define the vertices of a second square clipping-rectangle. In this case, you would define a clipping-rectangle that is the same size as the first one but located to overlap the first clipping-rectangle at a common corner. Now call the XorRectRegion function a second time to add this second square to the region's definition.

Follow this immediately with a call to the BeginUpdate function to begin the update of that layer bitmap (see Chapter 5 for a discussion of the BeginUpdate function). Here, however, you will be updating only that part of the layer bitmap that is contained in the region definition. To be specific, you will be changing only those parts of the layer bitmap that are inside the area that is *not* common to the two square clipping-rectangles added by the XorRectRegion function calls. This means that the drawing process will be clipped to the nonoverlapping area of the two squares.

Next, use the drawing functions (SetAPen, SetBPen, etc.) to prepare the RastPort structure so it can control the drawing colors, borders, and so forth, for the new figure. Then use the RectFill function to fill the figure with the color you want. In this case, your call to the RectFill function can specify a very large rectangle, in fact, a rectangle as large as the entire raster bitmap can be used. Notice that normally the entire raster would receive this color, but this clipping process ensures that only the current region definition is filled with your chosen color; the corner where the two squares overlap is left with the background color.

As Figure 2.6 shows, you can extend this indirect drawing process using other instances of the XorRectRegion function. For example, before you call the BeginUpdate function, you could once again define another clipping-rectangle. Then you could execute the XorRectRegion function to include that clipping-rectangle in your region definition. You can also mix XorRectRegion calls with AndRectRegion and OrRectRegion calls to produce a very complex region-boundary drawing definition.

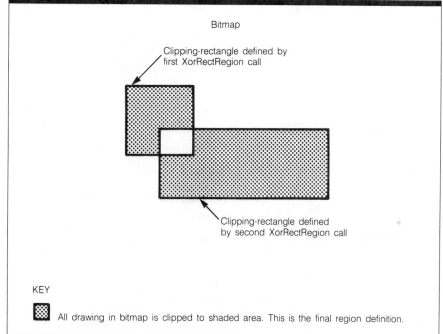

Figure 2.6:
Illustration of the XorRect-Region Function

Finally, note that the order of the clipping-rectangles added to the definition of a region by the XorRectRegion function does not matter; for any given set of clipping-rectangles, the final region they define does not depend on the order in which they are added to produce the final region. You can convince yourself of this with a piece of paper and some simple examples.

XorRegionRegion

Syntax of Function Call

```
success = XorRegionRegion (region1, region2)
D0                         A0        A1
```

Purpose of Function

This function performs a two-dimensional Xor operation of one region with another region. XorRegionRegion clips away any portion of the two regions that overlap. This has the possible effect of creating a hole in the new region. The result is left in the second region. The first region is not changed.

Inputs to Function

region1	A pointer to the first of two Region structures whose regions are to be combined
region2	A pointer to the second of two Region structures whose regions are to be combined

Discussion

XorRegionRegion is one of the four functions in the 1.2 Amiga software release that deal with regions. The intention and use of the XorRegionRegion function is very similar to that of the XorRectRegion function.

Recall that regions are merely collections of clipping-rectangles. Regions are defined using the AndRectRegion, OrRectRegion, and XorRectRegion functions. The only difference between XorRegionRegion and XorRectRegion is that the XorRegionRegion function combines two regions whereas the XorRectRegion function combines one region and one clipping-rectangle.

You should read the discussion of the XorRectRegion function to see how and why regions and clipping-rectangles are combined. These ideas carry over directly to the combination of regions into additional regions.

At some point in the drawing process, you may have two odd-shaped regions. Each of these will have straight-edge boundaries but might have any shape under that restriction. Now if you combine these two regions with the XorRegionRegion function you will produce a third (perhaps more oddly shaped region) that is smaller than either of the two incoming regions. This new region may be useful for your next drawing step. The new region will contain a hole where the two original regions overlapped. Any subsequent bitmap drawing will be clipped inside this hole. This is the purpose of the XorRegion-Region function.

The Graphics Animation Functions

Introduction

This chapter defines and discusses the Amiga animation functions found in the Graphics Library. These functions form a comprehensive system for managing movable objects—hardware sprites, virtual sprites, bobs (Blitter objects), animation components, and animation objects—on the Amiga display screen.

The animation functions fall into eight categories:

■ The hardware sprite functions: ChangeSprite, FreeSprite, GetSprite, and Move-Sprite, used for adding, moving, changing, and removing hardware sprites from the system

■ The virtual sprite functions: AddVSprite, InitMasks, and RemVSprite, used for adding, managing, and removing virtual sprites from graphics-element lists

■ The bob management functions and macro: the AddBob and RemIBob functions and the RemBob macro, used for adding and removing bobs from graphics-element lists

■ The animation-object functions and macro: the InitGMasks and AddAnimOb functions and the InitAnimate macro, used for initializing and adding animation objects to the system animation-object list

■ The Animate function, which causes the actual animation effects to take place on the display screen

■ The gel-to-gel collision management functions: DoCollision and SetCollision, used for detecting collisions between graphics elements and initiating the execution of user-defined collision-handling routines

■ The graphics-element list management functions: InitGels, SortGList, and DrawGList, used for initializing, sorting, and drawing the graphics elements in the current graphics-element list

■ The animation-object memory management functions: FreeGBuffers and GetG-Buffers, used for allocating and deallocating the memory buffers required by animation objects

Animation Entities

The Amiga animation system deals with five types of animation entities: hardware sprites, virtual sprites, bobs, animation components, and animation objects. Following is a short description of each type.

Hardware Sprites

These are the actual hardware sprites controlled by Amiga hardware sprite DMA channels. You can define up to eight hardware sprites. Each hardware sprite can be only 16 pixels wide, but it can be as high as the entire display screen.

Hardware sprites are paired as far as color choices are concerned; each sprite in a pair must have the same color as the other sprite in that pair. Each pair of hardware sprites can have four of 16 colors assigned to it. One of these colors will always be transparent, allowing the underlying playfield pixels to show through. The hardware sprites are useful for simple animation effects involving a few simple movable objects. For this reason, they are also known as simple sprites. If you need more than four movable objects, you should use virtual sprites and bobs.

Each hardware sprite is defined by a SimpleSprite and SpriteImage structure. You use the ChangeSprite, GetSprite, FreeSprite, and MoveSprite functions to manage hardware sprites.

It is important to understand that you cannot group hardware sprites into higher-level animation entities such as animation components or animation objects. Neither can you tell the system to check and report collisions between hardware sprites and other objects in the system.

Virtual Sprites

Virtual sprites are defined by associating a software definition of a sprite to an actual hardware sprite. This software-sprite to hardware-sprite mapping mechanism allows you to define a large number of virtual sprites and to create many different colored sprites on the display screen. However, you are still limited to eight virtual sprites at any given screen y-position. Like hardware sprites, virtual sprites are 16 pixels wide and can be as high as the entire display screen. The principal advantage of virtual sprites over hardware sprites is the large variety of shapes and colors you can display in one video frame.

Each virtual sprite is assigned to a different hardware sprite channel. At any given point in a display frame, virtual sprites are assigned to unused hardware sprites as the video beam traces from top to bottom and left to right on the Amiga display screen. This assignment is controlled by the system. Like hardware sprites, virtual sprites are each limited to four colors chosen from a set of 16 colors; one of the four colors is always transparent. Each virtual sprite is defined by a VSprite structure. You use the AddVSprite, RemVSprite, and other functions to manage your virtual sprites.

Sprites, whether they are hardware or virtual, cannot be grouped into higher-level animation entities such as animation components or animation objects. However, in contrast to hardware sprites, you can tell the system to check and report collisions between virtual sprites and other objects in the system.

Bobs

Bobs (Blitter objects) are similar to virtual sprites except that the system uses the Blitter rather than hardware sprite DMA channels to draw them. A bob is a rectangular section of a playfield bitmap that can be moved from one point in the bitmap to another point in that or another bitmap. Read the discussions of the Blitter functions in Chapter 2 to get an idea of how the Blitter works. Although the Blitter is very fast, a virtual sprite with the same image definition as a bob will produce quicker animation on the display screen. This is because the hardware sprite DMA channels are faster than the Blitter.

However, bobs do have two advantages over virtual sprites. The first advantage is the number of colors you can assign to bobs. A bob can display up to 32 colors, whereas each virtual sprite is limited to four colors. The second advantage is that a bob can be any width; it is not limited to 16 pixels. The third advantage is that Bobs can be grouped to create animation components, which can be grouped in turn to create animation objects.

Animation Components

Animation components are groups of bobs linked together. An example is the arms, legs, body, and head of a person. Each of these six pieces can be defined as a distinct bob and then linked together to form an animation component.

It is important to understand that animation components use only bobs, not hardware sprites or virtual sprites. Each animation component is defined by an AnimComp structure, which has a set of timing parameters that control the lifetime of the animation component when it is used as part of an animation object. There are no functions specific to animation components; they are defined by the structure linkages you define in your Bob structures.

Animation Objects

An animation object is the highest animation entity in the system. Animation objects are groups of animation components linked together. The system can cause an animation object to move, which makes all of its animation components move. You can perform two types of drawing with animation objects: sequenced-drawing animation and motion-control animation.

Animation System Lists

The animation system maintains a number of lists: graphics-element lists, bob lists, animation-object lists, and animation-component lists. A brief discussion of each type of list follows.

Graphics-Element Lists

Each graphics-element list is a doubly-linked list consisting of all graphics elements (virtual sprites and bobs) placed on that list. The graphics-element list is required so that graphics elements can be sorted in increasing y,x order by the SortGList function before the DrawGList function is called. This ordering is required because the Copper instructions generated by the DrawGList function define the display frame from top to bottom and from left to right.

Each graphics-element list is initialized with a call to the InitGels function. This adds a new active graphics-element list to the system. Each time the AddBob or AddVSprite functions are called, a new graphics element is added to one of the active graphics-element lists in the system. The NextVSprite and PrevVSprite parameters in the VSprite structure define the linkages in the graphics-element list for both virtual sprites and bobs.

Bob Lists

Each bob list consists of all the individual bobs that make up one animation object. The bob list determines the drawing priority (which bobs are drawn first, which last) of bobs in that animation object. The drawing order determines which bobs appear on top of other bobs in the screen display. The Before and After pointers in the Bob structure define the linkages in the bob list. The system DrawPath and ClearPath pointer parameters in the VSprite structure are also related to the drawing order for bobs.

Animation-Object Lists

Each animation-object list is initialized with a set of simple task statements or a call to the InitAnimate function. Both of these procedures specify the first animation object on the animation-object list and create a new active animation-object list. Each time the AddAnimOb function is called, a new animation object is added to one of the active animation-object lists. Once the initial animation object is defined, the NextOb and PrevOb pointers in the AnimOb structure define the linkages in each specific animation-object list.

Animation-Component Lists

The system maintains two types of animation-component lists. The first type defines all animation components that are part of an animation object. The second type of list defines the drawing order of the animation components that make up an animation object. Each animation-component list of the first type is initialized when the animation components in a specific animation object are defined. This list defines which animation components are a part of a specific animation object. Each list of this type is initialized by specifying the HeadComp pointer parameter in the AnimOb structure. Additional entries in an animation-component list are defined by the NextComp and PrevComp pointers in the AnimComp structure. These parameters define the linkages in that animation-component list.

Each animation-component list of the second type helps define the drawing order in sequenced-drawing animation. The NextSeq and PrevSeq pointers in the AnimComp structure initialize and define the linkages in this type of animation-component list.

Virtual Sprite Operations

This is a capsule summary of the procedure to use for virtual sprite operations:

1. Define a View structure whose Copper display instructions will later be merged with the virtual sprite Copper instructions.

2. Initialize the GelsInfo structure using the InitGels function; this needs to be done only once.

3. Define the virtual sprite parameters in the VSprite structure. (These are defined and discussed under the AddVSprite function.)

4. Add the virtual sprite to a graphics-element list using the AddVSprite function.

5. Display the virtual sprite by calls to the ON_DISPLAY and ON_SPRITE macros and the SortGList, DrawGList, MergeCop, and LoadView functions.

6. Change the appearance of the virtual sprite by changing the pointer to the Image-Data structure, the height of the virtual sprite, or the pointer to the sprite color data structure.

7. Move the virtual sprite with two structure-element definition statements that define a new set of virtual sprite coordinates in the VSprite structure.

8. Repeat step 5 to display the moved and changed virtual sprite once again.

Bob Operations

This is a capsule summary of the procedure to use for bob operations:

1. Define a View structure whose Copper instructions will contain information to display the bob.

2. Initialize the GelsInfo structure using the InitGels function; this needs to be done only once.

3. Create and link a Bob and a VSprite structure with a simple structure linkage statement.

4. Define the parameters in the Bob structure. (These are discussed under the Add-Bob function.)

5. Allocate memory space for the ImageShadow data.

6. Point to a DBufPacket data if you want to use double-buffering for this particular bob. If you don't want to use double-buffering, make this a null value.

7. Call the InitMasks function to create the bob ImageShadow data.

8. Add the bob to the graphics-element list using the AddBob function.

9. Display the bob by calls to the ON_DISPLAY and ON_SPRITE macros and the SortGList, DrawGList, MergeCop, and LoadView functions.

10. Change the appearance of the bob by changing either the pointer to the ImageData structure or the height, width, or depth of the bob.

11. Change the bob colors by changing either the definition of the playfield color set or the PlanePick and PlaneOnOff parameters in the Bob structure.

12. Move the bob with two structure-element definition statements that define a new set of bob coordinates in the Bob structure.

13. Repeat step 9 to display the moved and changed bob once again.

Types of Animation

The Amiga system can perform two types of animation: sprite animation and playfield animation. Sprite animation uses the hardware sprites or the virtual sprites. Playfield animation divides into three subcategories: single bob animation, multiple bob motion-control animation, and multiple bob sequenced-drawing animation.

Sprites cannot be linked together to define more complex geometric shapes. The sprite objects are moved against the stationary background called the playfield; that is, the sprites are superimposed on the stationary playfield background. Both hardware and virtual sprites use the hardware sprite DMA channels to create and move the sprite objects. This type of animation has its limitations. In particular, you are limited to one-entity geometric shapes that move as a unit. You cannot define more complex entities with relative motion between individual parts of those entities. You can use sprite animation in both the single- and dual-playfield modes of Amiga operation.

Playfield animation is much more powerful than sprite animation. Playfield animation uses the Blitter DMA channels to move certain areas of the playfield called bobs. The bobs created for playfield animation each have a video priority assigned to them. Their video priority is controlled by the Before and After pointers in the Bob structures that define each bob. A bob is physically a part of the playfield. As bobs are moved around in the playfield bitmaps, the system stores and restores the background bitmap information buffers assigned by the Bob structure.

The most interesting thing about bobs is that you can combine them into animation components, which you can combine in turn into animation objects. Once you have defined an animation object, you can use it in motion-control animation or sequenced-drawing animation.

Sequenced-drawing animation requires you to define a sequence of animation-object positions. These animation objects are then brought onto the screen in the order defined by the AnimOb structure. You must also supply a set of timing variables to control how long each animation object in the sequence remains on the screen.

Motion-control animation requires you to define the position, velocity, and acceleration of animation objects. The system uses this information to move each animation object at a certain speed and acceleration across the display screen.

If you study the function discussions and the Bob, AnimComp, and AnimOb structure definitions, you will see how to perform both sequenced-drawing and motion-control animation. Finally, you can combine sequenced-drawing animation and motion-control animation together with user-defined motion sensing and control routines to produce a hybrid type of animation.

User-Defined Animation Routines

The Amiga animation system can be highly customized by implementing user-defined motion control and collision-handling routines. Each AnimComp structure has a parameter that points to the address of a user-defined animation-component routine, AnimCRoutine. In the same way, each AnimOb structure has a parameter that points to the address of the user-defined animation-object routine, AnimORoutine. Both of these routines are called automatically when the Animate function executes.

You can design these routines to do almost anything you want. In particular, they can modify the Bob, AnimComp, and AnimOb structures during animation. Just design a routine that looks at the current values (position, velocity, acceleration, etc.) in each of these structures and uses an algorithm of your choosing to change those values.

Specifically, you can arrange your customized routines to sense and change the current positions of your animation objects, animation components, or bobs.

You can also use these routines to change the colors of the bobs in your animation objects or produce sound effects under certain circumstances. The well-known bouncing ball demo with its sound effects provides a good illustration of what can be done with these routines. Any position changes you make with these routines will be in addition to the changes produced by sequenced-drawing or motion-control animation as defined in the position parameters in the VSprite, AnimComp, and AnimOb structures.

The AnimCRoutine and AnimORoutine routines have only one parameter passed to them automatically when they are called by the Animate function. This parameter is a pointer to the controlling AnimComp or AnimOb structure. However, you can use the user-defined extensions to the AnimComp and AnimOb structures to write and read parameters that these routines can use.

Extending the Bob and VSprite Structures

The Bob and VSprite structures each have a set of parameters at the end that can be used to extend the definition of those structures. These parameters are called BUserStuff and BUserExt in the Bob structure; they are called VUserStuff and VUserExt in the VSprite structure.

User-defined extensions to the Bob and VSprite structures can be used to interface system activity to the AnimCRoutine and AnimORoutine routines. They can also be used to interface system activity to the user-defined collision-handling routines discussed in the SetCollision function.

A simple example can illustrate the mechanics of this procedure. Suppose that you have a structure called MyVariables that you want to add to the Bob structure. This is the definition of MyVariables:

```
struct MyVariables {
    SHORT xvelocity;
    SHORT yvelocity;
    SHORT xacceleration;
```

SHORT yacceleration;
    };

This structure allows you to add the current values of a bob's velocity and acceleration to the end of the Bob structure. Then, when that bob is moved as part of an animation object, you can update these values after each move by writing the new values into these locations. You can then use these values to make decisions in either your collision-handling routines or your AnimCRoutine or AnimORoutine routines. To achieve this you must add a statement to your program that reads as follows:

#DEFINE BUserStuff struct MyVariables

Once this is done, the Bob structure will be extended for customized velocity and acceleration sensing and changes in your animation program. You can take this idea further by defining your own extensions to the VSprite and Bob structures.

Animation System Structures

The animation system works with a number of structures that allow you to define, change, and otherwise manage all elements of the animation system. These structures are identified in the following paragraphs.

The SpriteImage structure contains the bit data required to define the image of a hardware sprite. See the ChangeSprite function for a full definition of the SpriteImage structure.

The SimpleSprite structure contains the height and position control data required to manage the image of a hardware sprite. See the GetSprite function for a definition of the SimpleSprite structure.

The VSprite structure contains all the parameters you need to define a virtual sprite. These parameters include pointers to the next and previous VSprite structure in the graphics-element list, as well as the current virtual sprite position. The VSprite structure is fully defined in the AddVSprite function discussion.

The Bob structure contains all the parameters you need to define a bob. These parameters include pointers to define the drawing order of bobs and a pointer to a VSprite structure associated with this Bob structure. The Bob structure is fully defined in the AddBob function discussion.

The AnimComp structure contains all the parameters you need to define an animation component. These parameters include pointers to the next and previous animation components in a linked list of animation components, pointers to the next and previous AnimComp structures in an animation component sequence, timing parameters for the animation component, and spatial translation values for the animation component. The AnimComp structure is fully defined in the Animate function discussion.

The CollTable structure contains a set of up to 16 pointers to user-defined collision-handling routines. These routines are called when the automatic collision-detection system senses a gel-to-gel collision. The CollTable structure is fully defined in the SetCollision function discussion.

The GelsInfo structure helps manage the graphics-element list. It contains a byte to indicate which hardware sprites can be currently assigned to virtual sprites. It also contains pointers to the first and last VSprite structures in the graphics-element list, as well as a pointer to the CollTable structure. The GelsInfo structure is fully defined in the InitGels function discussion.

The DBufPacket structure contains all the information you need to handle double-buffering for bobs in the system. The DBufPacket structure is fully defined in the GetGBuffers function discussion.

Linking AnimOb, AnimComp, Bob, and VSprite Structures for Motion-Control Animation

Designing a program to do motion-control animation is largely a matter of learning how to link the AnimOb, AnimComp, Bob, and VSprite structures, which define the animation objects, animation components, bobs, and virtual sprites of that animation.

Figure 3.1 shows all the linkages in the animation system between these four types of structures, represented by the four large rectangles.

This figure shows the following:

- The only structure pointer in the AnimOb structure that is user-defined is the HeadComp pointer, which points to the first AnimComp structure for an animation object. The PrevOb and NextOb pointers are defined and controlled by the system.

- There are four pointers in each AnimComp structure that you must define for motion-control animation: PrevComp, NextComp, HeadOb, and AnimBob. (For sequenced-drawing animation, you must also define the PrevSeq and NextSeq pointers.)

- There are two pointers in each Bob structure that you must define for both motion-control and sequenced-drawing animation: BobComp and BobVSprite. The Before and After pointers are optional; if you don't specify these pointers, the system will draw the bobs in the order it determines.

- There is only one pointer parameter in the VSprite structure that you must define for each virtual sprite. This is the VSBob parameter. The other four pointer parameters (PrevVSprite, NextVSprite, DrawPath, and ClearPath) in every VSprite structure are defined and controlled by the system. Note that each of these system-controlled parameters points to a specific VSprite structure.

In addition to these pointer parameters, there are a number of position-control parameters in the AnimOb, AnimComp, and VSprite structures that are required for a motion-control animation definition. However, there are no position-control parameters in the Bob structure. You should read the appropriate function discussion to learn more about the meaning of these parameters. Following is a brief summary:

- In each AnimOb structure, you must define the AnY,AnX, YVel,XVel, and YAccel,XAccel parameters. These pairs are the reference position, current velocity,

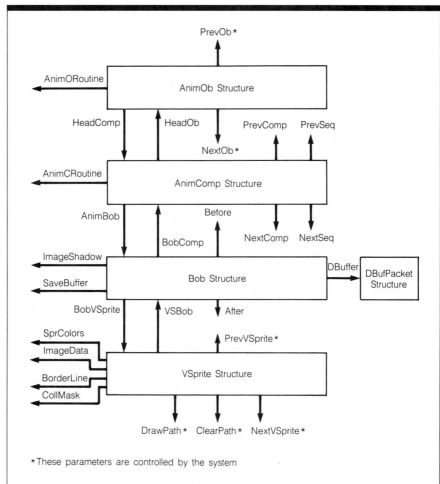

Figure 3.1:
Structure Linkages in the Animation System

and current acceleration of the animation object. (Note that two additional parameters are used for sequenced-drawing animation: RingYTrans and RingXTrans.) The other position-control parameters in the AnimOb structure are defined and controlled by the system.

■ In each AnimComp structure, you must define the YTrans and XTrans parameters. This pair is the desired initial Y and X translation of the animation component. (Two more parameters are used for sequenced-drawing animation: Timer and Time-Set.)

■ In each VSprite structure, you must define the Y,X position-control parameters. This pair is the current desired position of the virtual sprite. The other position-control parameters are defined and controlled by the system.

In addition to the structure-pointer parameters and the position-control parameters, these four animation structures also point to a number of other memory areas as shown on the far left side of the structure rectangles. The AnimORoutine and AnimCRoutine pointers fall into this category of parameters. You should read the appropriate function discussions to determine the meaning of each of these parameters.

An Example of Motion-Control Animation

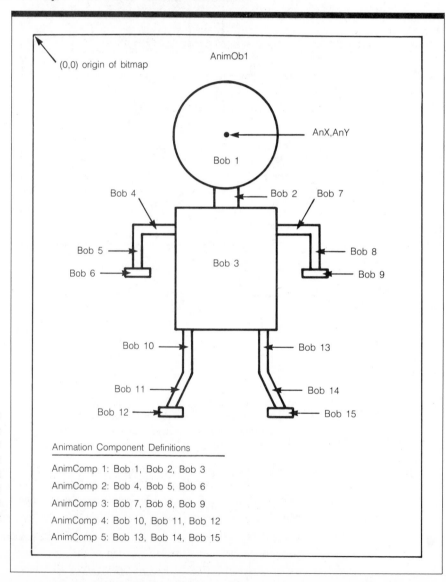

Figure 3.2:
Grouping Bobs into Animation Components and Animation Components into an Animation Object

AnimOb1

(0,0) origin of bitmap

AnX,AnY

Bob 1

Bob 4   Bob 2   Bob 7

Bob 5   Bob 8

Bob 6   Bob 3   Bob 9

Bob 10   Bob 13

Bob 11   Bob 14

Bob 12   Bob 15

Animation Component Definitions

AnimComp 1: Bob 1, Bob 2, Bob 3

AnimComp 2: Bob 4, Bob 5, Bob 6

AnimComp 3: Bob 7, Bob 8, Bob 9

AnimComp 4: Bob 10, Bob 11, Bob 12

AnimComp 5: Bob 13, Bob 14, Bob 15

Figure 3.2 shows a stick figure of a robot-like character. The idea is to get the figure to walk and move. This is an example of motion-control animation using one animation object, five animation components, 15 bobs, and therefore, 15 virtual sprites. The animation component definitions are given on the figure.

AddAnimOb

Syntax of Function Call

        AddAnimOb (animOb, animKey, rastPort)
                   A0   A1   A2

Purpose of Function

This function adds an AnimOb structure to the linked list of animation objects.

Inputs to Function

animOb	A pointer to the AnimOb structure to be added to the animation-object list
animKey	A pointer to the first AnimOb structure in the animation-object list
rastPort	A pointer to a controlling RastPort structure

Discussion

There are two functions and one macro that work with animation objects in the Graphics library: AddAnimOb, InitGMasks, and InitAnimate, respectively. Read the discussions of InitGMasks and InitAnimate to understand more completely how animation objects are managed in the graphics system.

There are two Graphics Library animation systems that are concerned with virtual sprites and bobs. These are the graphics-element system, which deals with both virtual sprites and bobs, and the animation-object system, which deals with bobs. Each of these systems maintains its own lists.

The AddAnimOb function adds a new animation object to the linked list of animation objects maintained by the system. The animKey argument always points to the first AnimOb structure in a specific animation-object list. AddAnimOb calls the AddBob function to initialize each component's Bob structure. In addition, AddAnimOb initializes all the timer parameters in each AnimComp structure in the newly added animation object to zero. This is done only for the animation components belonging to the newly added animation object; it is not done for every component in every animation object in the current animation-object list.

Note that the RastPort structure must be initialized before you call the AddAnim Ob function. The discussion of the InitRastPort function in Chapter 2 contains information on how this should be done. In particular, the GelsInfo structure inside the RastPort structure must be initialized properly. This is done with the InitGels function as described later in this chapter.

The AnimOb Structure

This is the definition of the AnimOb structure:

```
struct AnimOb {
    struct AnimOb *NextOb, *PrevOb;
    LONG Clock;
    WORD AnOldY, AnOldX;
    WORD AnY, AnX;
    WORD YVel, XVel;
    WORD YAccel, XAccel;
    WORD RingYTrans, RingXTrans;
    WORD (*AnimORoutine) ();
    struct AnimComp *HeadComp;
    AUserStuff AUserExt;
};
```

The system automatically sets and uses the following parameters in the AnimOb structure:

■ The NextOb and PrevOb parameters point to the next and previous animation objects in an animation-object list. Keep in mind that the animation-object list is distinct from the graphics-element list. These parameters are null for the last (NextOb is null) and first (PrevOb is null) animation objects added to the animation-object list.

■ The Clock parameter contains the number of calls to the Animate function that this animation object has experienced. This parameter starts at zero and is incremented each time the Animate function processes this animation object.

■ The AnOldY and AnOldX parameters contain the previous values of the y- and x-coordinates of the animation object. These are the values before the last call to the Animate function. These parameters are measured in the vertical and horizontal resolution of the bitmap that will receive this animation object.

Both the system and your graphics tasks can set and use the following parameters in the AnimOb structure:

■ The AnY and AnX parameters contain the current y- and x-coordinates of the animation object. These parameters are measured in the vertical and horizontal resolution of the bitmap that will receive this animation object.

Your graphics tasks can set and use the following parameters in the AnimOb structure:

■ The YVel and XVel parameters contain the current y- and x-velocities of the animation object. All velocities are positive or negative numbers or zero. The system treats the 16-bit velocity value as if it were a fixed point number. The decimal point is assumed to be between bits 5 and 6 (with bits numbered 0 to 15). Each call to the Animate function adds the values of YAccel and XAccel to the current values of YVel and XVel, respectively. You can use sequenced-drawing and motion-control animation simultaneously. Usually, these values will be zero for pure sequenced-drawing animation.

■ The YAccel and XAccel parameters contain the current y- and x-accelerations of the animation object. These values can be positive or negative, but they are usually zero for pure sequenced-drawing animation.

■ The RingYTrans and RingXTrans parameters contain the increments in the reference position for the animation object. They are the y- and x-translation values for this animation object. These parameters are measured in the vertical and horizontal resolution of the bitmap that will receive this animation object. These values are added to the current AnY and AnX values to produce the new value of AnY and AnX for the next video frame. This parameter allows a sequence of drawings to be described as a "ring"; the last position in the ring is the same as the first. This parameter works only when the RINGTRIGGER bit in the Bob structure Flags parameter is set. You should use these parameters only for sequenced-drawing animation.

■ The AnimORoutine parameter contains the address of a special animation-object routine that will be called each time the Animate function executes. If this value is zero, no routine will be called.

■ The HeadComp parameter points to the first AnimComp structure in the animation object defined by this AnimOb structure.

■ The AUserStuff and AUserExt parameters contain the name of the first and second user-defined memory areas, respectively, used to modify the AnimComp structure.

See the introduction to this chapter for the proper procedure to use to take advantage of these extensions to the AnimOb structure.

AddBob

Syntax of Function Call

                    AddBob (bob, rastPort)
                       A0   A1

Purpose of Function

This function adds a Bob structure to the current graphics-element list. AddBob first sets the appropriate flags in the Bob structure and then links this Bob structure into the graphics-element list using the AddVSprite function.

Inputs to Function

bob   A pointer to a Bob structure

rastPort   A pointer to a controlling RastPort structure

Discussion

There are two functions and one macro in the Graphics Library that work with bobs (Blitter objects) directly: AddBob, RemIBob, and RemBob, respectively. Read the discussions of RemBob and RemIBob to understand more completely how bobs are used in the graphics system.

The system maintains both virtual sprites and bobs on the graphics-element list. This list is separate from the animation-object and animation-component lists, which the system also maintains. The AddBob function adds another Bob structure to the graphics-element list.

The Bob Structure

This is the definition of the Bob structure:

```
struct Bob {
    WORD Flags;
    WORD *SaveBuffer;
    WORD *ImageShadow;
    struct Bob *Before;
    struct Bob *After;
```

```
    struct VSprite *BobVSprite;
    struct AnimComp *BobComp;
    struct DBufPacket *DBuffer;
    BUserStuff BUserExt;
};
```

Your graphics tasks can set and use all of the parameters in the Bob structure. Both the system and your graphics tasks can set and use the Flags parameter. Following is a description of each of the parameters in the Bob structure.

- The Flags parameter contains a group of bits that can be set and reset to control various aspects of a bob's behavior. The individual flag bits are listed later in this discussion.

- The SaveBuffer parameter points to a RAM buffer that is used when the portion of the display bitmap where this bob is drawn (the background) should be saved. When the bob is moved, the image data in this background buffer can be swapped back into the display bitmap to restore the screen area where the bob was drawn previously. The memory for this buffer is allocated and deallocated by the GetGBuffers and FreeGBuffers functions.

- The ImageShadow parameter points to a RAM buffer that holds the shadow mask bit array of the bob. The shadow mask defines the shadow of a bob. A shadow mask is a logical Or combination of all the bits of the various bitplanes of a bob image definition. The memory for this buffer is allocated and deallocated by the GetGBuffers and FreeGBuffers functions. The system uses the shadow mask data along with the PlanePick and PlaneOnOff parameters in the VSprite structure to determine bob colors. The ImageShadow parameter in the Bob structure and the CollMask parameter in the VSprite structure usually point to the same data.

- The Before and After parameters point to Bob structures whose bobs will be drawn before and after the bob defined by this Bob structure. These parameters are used to assign drawing priority to a group of bobs in an animation object.

- The BobVSprite parameter points to this bob's VSprite structure definition, which defines some of the bob's parameters. In particular, the VSprite structure contains the current position coordinates of the bob.

- The BobComp parameter points to this bob's AnimComp structure. This bob will become a part of the animation component represented by this AnimComp structure.

- The DBuffer parameter points to this bob's DBuffer buffer. This pointer should be null if you do not want to use double-buffering for this particular bob. The memory for this buffer is allocated and deallocated by the GetGBuffers and FreeGBuffers functions.

- The BUserStuff parameter contains the name of a user-defined memory area that can be used to modify the Bob structure.

■ The BUserExt parameter contains the name of a second user-defined memory area that can be used to modify the Bob structure.

See the introduction to this chapter for more on this topic.

These are the individual flag values for the Flags parameter of the Bob structure. Note that some of these flag bits are defined for the Bob structure and some are defined for the VSprite structure associated with the Bob structure.

■ VSPRITE. This flag parameter belongs to the VSprite structure. Set this flag value if you are using this VSprite structure to define a virtual sprite; do not set this flag value if you are using this VSprite structure to define a bob.

■ SAVEBACK. This flag parameter belongs to the VSprite structure. Set this flag value if you want to save the background bitmap information where a bob is newly drawn. If you choose to save the background, you must allocate the SaveBuffer buffer with the GetGBuffers function. This will also cause the background to be restored automatically when the bob is moved again.

■ OVERLAY. This flag parameter belongs to the VSprite structure. Set this flag value if you want the bob to be drawn using the ImageShadow data. In this case, you must first allocate and initialize the ImageShadow data array with the GetGBuffers function. If you do not set this flag value, the system uses the entire rectangle of bob definition words to draw the bob image on top of the background bitmap image. This means that the playfield colors (the background colors) show through in any section where there are 0 bits in the bob shadow mask.

■ GELGONE. This flag parameter belongs to the VSprite structure. The system sets this flag value when a bob has been moved to a drawing region entirely outside the current clipping region. The clipping region for this bob is defined in the GelsInfo structure. See the discussion of the InitGels function for a definition of the GelsInfo structure and the clipping region.

■ SAVEBOB. This flag parameter belongs to the Bob structure. If this flag value is set, the previous bob image will not be erased when the bob is moved, and the bitmap will contain a sequence of bob images. If these are spaced properly, a paint-brush effect can be simulated.

■ BOBISCOMP. This flag parameter belongs to the Bob structure. Set this flag value if this bob is part of an animation component. In this case, you must also define the value of the BobComp pointer parameter in the VSprite structure. See the discussion of the AddVSprite function for the definition of the BobComp structure pointer.

■ BWAITING. This flag parameter belongs to the Bob structure. The system sets and resets this parameter. If it is set, this bob is waiting to be drawn. This occurs only when the system has found a Before pointer in the Bob structure definition for this bob. If it is not set, the bob has already been drawn. The system clears this bit on return from each call to the DrawGList function.

■ BDRAWN. This flag parameter belongs to the Bob structure. The system sets and resets this parameter. If this bit is set, the bob has already been drawn. The system can then examine the Before and After pointers in each Bob structure to verify the correctness of the drawing sequence for bobs. The system clears this parameter on return from each call to the DrawGList function.

■ BOBSAWAY. This flag parameter belongs to the Bob structure. This parameter can be set and reset by either your tasks or the system. Set this parameter if you want the bob to be removed from the graphics-element list when the next DrawGList function executes. In that case, the system restores the background bitmap information where it has last drawn the bob. In addition, the system unlinks the Bob structure from the graphics-element list the next time the DrawGList function is called (unless you are using double-buffering). If you are using double-buffering, the bob will not be removed from the graphics-element list until the second call to the DrawGList function. At that point the bob image will have been removed from both bob image buffers.

■ BOBNIX. This flag parameter belongs to the Bob structure. The system sets and resets this flag. When the bob has been removed completely, the system sets this parameter on return from the DrawGList function. This occurs only after the bob has been removed from the graphics-element list and the background bitmap image has been restored. This parameter is especially important when you are using double-buffering for a bob. In that case, the system must be sure that the bob image has been removed from both the currently active drawing buffer and the current display buffer.

■ SAVEPRESERVE. This flag is set and reset by the system; it belongs to the Bob structure. This is a double-buffer version of the SAVEBACK flag. SAVEPRESERVE is used by the system to indicate whether the bob in the second buffer has been restored.

AddVSprite

Syntax of Function Call

```
AddVSprite (vSprite, rastPort)
           A0       A1
```

Purpose of Function

This function adds a VSprite structure to the current graphics-element list. The new VSprite structure is positioned in the list by the values of its y,x coordinates. AddVSprite also sets up the system VSprite structure flags.

Inputs to Function

vSprite	A pointer to a VSprite structure
rastPort	A pointer to a controlling RastPort structure

Discussion

There are three functions in the Graphics Library that work with virtual sprites directly: AddVSprite, InitMasks, and RemVSprite. Read the discussion of InitMasks and RemVSprite for more information on virtual sprites.

The system maintains both virtual sprites and bobs on the graphics-element list. The AddVSprite function adds another VSprite structure to the graphics-element list. Note that the AddBob function calls the AddVSprite function indirectly to add Bob structures to the graphics-element list.

The VSprite Structure

This is the definition of the VSprite structure:

```
struct VSprite {
    struct VSprite *NextVSprite;
    struct VSprite *PrevVSprite;
    struct VSprite *DrawPath;
    struct VSprite *ClearPath;
    WORD OldY, OldX;
    WORD Flags;
    WORD Y, X;
    WORD Height;
    WORD Width;
    WORD Depth;
    WORD MeMask;
    WORD HitMask;
    WORD *ImageData;
    WORD *BorderLine;
    WORD *CollMask;
    WORD *SprColors;
    struct Bob *VBob;
    BYTE PlanePick;
    BYTE PlaneOnOff;
    VUserStuff VUserExt;
};
```

The system automatically sets and uses the following parameters in the VSprite structure:

- The NextVSprite and PrevVSprite parameters point to the next and previous VSprite structures in the graphics-element list, respectively. All virtual sprites are sorted in increasing y,x order.

- The DrawPath and ClearPath parameters point to two VSprite structures. These parameters are used by the system to control the drawing process.

- The OldY and OldX parameters contain the previous y- and x-positions of the virtual sprite—the values used the last time the Animate function was called. For bobs, these parameters are measured in the vertical and horizontal resolution of the bitmap that will receive the bob. For virtual sprites, the OldY parameter is measured in the context of a noninterlaced mode display; the OldX parameter is always measured in terms of a low-resolution mode display.

Your graphics tasks can set and use these parameters:

- The Y and X parameters contain the current y- and x-positions of the virtual sprite. These are the positions that will be used when the Animate function is next called. For bobs, these parameters are measured in the vertical and horizontal resolution of the bitmap that will receive the bob. For virtual sprites, these parameters are measured in the context of a low-resolution, noninterlaced mode display.

- The Height and Width parameters contain the height and width of the virtual sprite image. The height parameter is measured in terms of a noninterlaced mode display and can range from 0 to 200 pixels. The width parameter is ignored if this VSprite structure defines a virtual sprite, because the width of virtual sprites is always 16 pixels. For bobs, the width is the number of 16-bit words required to define the pixel width of the bob image.

- The Depth parameter contains the number of bitplanes used to define the image data for this virtual sprite. If this VSprite structure defines a bob, up to five bitplanes can be used. If this VSprite structure defines a virtual sprite, two 16-bit words are always used to define each line of the sprite image and this parameter is ignored.

- The MeMask and Hitmask parameters contain masks that determine which collision-handling routine to call when two or more graphics elements collide. The system Ands the current HitMask parameter of the upper-leftmost object with the MeMask parameter of the lower-rightmost object. The 1 bits remaining after the Anding operation determine which of 16 possible collision-handling routines are called. (See the discussion of the SetCollision and DoCollision functions.)

- The ImageData parameter points to a set of image data for this virtual sprite. The image data is a set of 16-bit words, with a minimum of two words for each line of the virtual-sprite image. Bits in each of these two words are combined to determine the color assigned to a particular virtual-sprite pixel. The virtual-sprite image data is very similar to the data in the SpriteImage structure that is used to define hardware sprites.

■ The BorderLine parameter points to a memory location containing the logical Or combination of all the bits in the image data for a virtual sprite. The borderline data is used by the system to speed the collision detection process. The memory for this buffer is allocated and deallocated by the GetGBuffers and FreeGBuffers functions.

■ The CollMask parameter points to a RAM location containing the collision mask for the virtual sprite. The data that define a collision mask are usually the same as the data that define a shadow mask for the same virtual sprite. (See the definition of the Bob structure's ImageShadow parameter in the AddBob discussion.) Both are formed as the logical Or combination of all 1 bits in all planes of the image data. The collision mask is similar to the borderline mask, but the collision mask is a matrix rather than a word (for a virtual sprite) or a set of one or more words (for a bob). The memory for the collision mask buffer is allocated and deallocated by the GetGBuffers and FreeGBuffers functions.

■ The SprColors parameter points to the first of three sequentially stored 16-bit values. These values form a short colormap table in the same manner as the 32-entry colormap tables discussed in Chapter 2. Each of these three 16-bit values represents the contents of one color register; bits 0 to 3 represent the blue intensity, bits 4 to 7 represent the green intensity, and bits 8 to 11 represent the red intensity. (Bits 12 to 15 are not used.) The system uses these values to determine the set of three colors assigned to this virtual sprite. This parameter is not used if this VSprite structure defines a bob.

■ The VSpriteBob parameter points to a Bob structure; it is used only when this VSprite structure defines a bob.

■ The PlanePick parameter contains an eight-bit mask that selects the planes of a bob used to determine the color for that bob. This parameter is not used with virtual sprites. (See the discussion of the PlanePick parameter under the AddVSprite function.)

■ The PlaneOnOff parameter contains an eight-bit mask that determines what to do with the planes not selected by the PlanePick parameter. This parameter is not used with virtual sprites. (See the discussion of the PlaneOnOff parameter under the AddVSprite function.)

■ The VUserStuff and VUserExt parameters contain the names of the first and second user-defined memory areas, respectively, used to modify the VSprite structure. (See the introduction to this chapter for more on this topic.)

Both the system and your graphics tasks can set and use the VSprite structure Flags parameter, which contains the following flag values:

■ VSPRITE. Set this flag value if this VSprite structure defines a virtual sprite; do not set this flag value if you are defining a bob.

- MUSTDRAW. If this flag is set, it tells the system that the virtual sprite represented by this VSprite structure must be drawn on-screen when the current DrawGList call is made. If the system runs out of hardware sprites that it can assign to this virtual sprite, it can convert this virtual sprite to a bob for this one call to the DrawGList function. If the system decides that it must convert a virtual sprite to a bob, the colors assigned in the VSprite structure SprColors parameter will not be used for the bob. Instead, the PlanePick and PlaneOnOff parameters will be used to determine the bob colors for that DrawGList function call.

- VSOVERFLOW. This flag is set by the system. If the system determines that the number of virtual sprites defined for one horizontal line of the display exceeds the number of currently available hardware sprites (usually eight unless the SprRsrvd parameter in the GelsInfo structure says otherwise), it sets the VSOVERFLOW flag. This means that unless you set the MUSTDRAW bit for a particular virtual sprite, it will not be drawn when the next call to the DrawGList function is made.

- GELGONE. The system sets this bit when a bob or virtual sprite has been moved to a location entirely outside the current clipping region. The clipping region is defined by four parameters in the GelsInfo structure. (See the discussion of the InitGels function for a definition of the clipping region.) Because the system does not draw any bob or virtual sprite that is entirely outside the clipping region, you can remove that particular virtual sprite or bob from the graphics-element list for the current DrawGList call. This speeds the processing of the graphics-element list. It is important to understand that virtual sprites or bobs that are removed from the system are no longer managed or checked by the system.

The VSprite structure contains the ImageData parameter, which points to the image data for the bob or virtual sprite. The data arrangement for the structure containing both bobs and virtual sprites is very similar. However, there is enough difference to warrant a separate discussion of each.

The image data for a virtual sprite is very similar to the image data for a hardware sprite, as contained in the SpriteImage structure. The data for a virtual sprite image is

```
struct ImageData {
    UWORD sprdata[2][height];
};
```

where sprdata[2][height] is the actual data that define the virtual sprite image. These data consist of two words (indicated by the [2]) for each line (indicated by the height parameter) of the virtual sprite image. Note that the height parameter is set in the VSprite structure for this virtual sprite. For example, if you want to define a one-line virtual sprite image, you supply two words of data. If you want to define a virtual sprite that is as tall as the display screen (with height equal to 200 lines), you supply 400 words of data here.

Each word you supply has 16 bits; each line of the virtual sprite is defined by two of these words. The colors for each pixel in the virtual sprite are determined by the combination of bits from each of these two words. A simple example will illustrate this idea.

Assume you want to define a two-line virtual sprite image. You define the image data in the ImageData structure as follows:

    line 1 word 1: 1111111111111111
    line 1 word 2: 1111000000001111
    line 2 word 1: 1111000000001111
    line 2 word 2: 1111111111111111

This virtual sprite is 16 pixels wide (this is the maximum for both virtual sprites and hardware sprites). The color for the rightmost pixel (pixel 0) is determined by taking the combination of the 0 position bits in words 1 and 2 of line 1. For this particular image, this is binary 11, which translates to decimal 3. Therefore, this pixel will be assigned color 3. This is true of pixels 1 through 3 and 12 through 15 in both sprite lines; they all receive color 3.

However, pixels 4 through 11 of line 1 have a 10 binary value, which translates to a decimal 2. These pixels will receive color 2. In the same way, pixels 4 through 11 of line 2 have a 01 binary value, which translates to a decimal 1. These pixels will receive color 1.

The actual assignments of color registers to colors 1 through 3 is determined by the SprColors parameter in the VSprite structure. Color 0 always corresponds to transparent. Any sprite pixel with this color will let the background playfield pixel color show through at that location.

The ImageData structure for bobs is similar to the ImageData structure for virtual sprites. However, the data are laid out differently. This can be illustrated best with an example. Suppose you want to define a three-line, 16-pixel-wide bob image that is three bitplanes deep (with the Depth parameter in the VSprite structure equal to 3). The image data to define this bob could be as follows:

    line 1 word 1 bitplane 1: 1111111111111111
    line 1 word 2 bitplane 1: 1111000000001111
    line 1 word 3 bitplane 1: 1111000000001111
    line 2 word 4 bitplane 2: 1111000000001111
    line 2 word 5 bitplane 2: 1111000000001111
    line 2 word 6 bitplane 2: 1111000000001111
    line 3 word 7 bitplane 3: 1111000000001111
    line 3 word 8 bitplane 3: 1111000000001111
    line 3 word 9 bitplane 3: 1111111111111111

This shows that the bob image data is laid out in consecutive memory locations with data for bitplane 1, then data for bitplane 2, and so on. Note that this is the same data arrangement used for the ImageData structure in the Image structure in Intuition. See the discussion of the DrawImage function in Chapter 6.

The colors assigned to each pixel of this bob are determined by the PlanePick and PlaneOnOff parameters in the VSprite structure. Both of these parameters are one-byte values whose six least-significant bits (bits 0 through 5) are used by the system to control the drawing of bobs into raster bitmaps at the bob location. The PlanePick parameter picks the bitplanes of the receiving bitmap that will receive the bob image pointed to by the ImageData pointer in the VSprite structure.

This concept of bitplane selection can be illustrated with a simple example. Suppose you have a two-bitplane bob image (defined by an ImageData structure) that you want to draw into a specific five-bitplane raster bitmap. It is easy to see that you could place the bob bitplanes bits into any two of the five bitplanes in that bitmap. This leads to a large number of combinations. For example, you could place the bob image into the first two bitplanes (bitplanes 0 and 1) of the raster bitmap. In this case, you would use a 00000011 value for the PlanePick parameter. Or you could place the bob image into the last two bitplanes (bitplanes 3 and 4) of the raster bitmap. In this case, you would use a 00011000 PlanePick parameter value. The PlanePick parameter merely controls which bitplanes of the raster bitmap receive the bob image bit data.

This idea can be extended to other combinations. For example, if the bob requires three bitplanes for its definition, some of the PlanePick parameter values could be 00000111, 00001110, or 00011100. Other combinations involving nonconsecutive 1 values are also possible.

This scheme is useful because it allows you to use the bob image data in the Image-Data structure to define one or more bobs all having the same shape but different colors when displayed. Once the bob data is placed into the raster bitmap at the bob location, the color assigned to that pixel location is determined in the usual way using the binary value of the bits in all bitplanes at that pixel location. It is easy to see that the bits in those locations and their binary values can be varied simply with appropriate choices for the PlanePick parameter.

The PlaneOnOff parameter works together with the PlanePick parameter to determine the bit values that will be placed into the raster bitmap bitplanes not selected by the PlanePick parameter. If you have a two-bitplane bob and a five-bitplane raster bitmap and you specify the PlanePick parameter to be 00000011, the bob image will be placed into bitplanes 0 and 1 of the raster bitmap. Then, if you specify a PlaneOnOff value of 00011100, each bit of the raster bitmap in bitplanes 2 to 4 will receive a 1 value at each bob pixel location. On the other hand, if you specify a PlaneOnOff value of 00000000, each bit of the raster bitmap in bitplanes 2 to 4 will receive a 0 value at each bob pixel location.

Moreover, the system goes one step further with this scheme. It consults the bob shadow data to determine the precise pixel location to place the bit values specified by the PlaneOnOff parameter. Everywhere there is a 1 bit in the bob shadow mask at a specific pixel location, the receiving raster bitmap will get the bit value in the PlaneOnOff parameter at that location. For example, assume the shadow mask for a two-line bob image looks like this:

```
0000000000000000
0000001111000000
0000001111000000
0000000000000000
```

This is the shadow mask of a four-line bob image. If the PlanePick parameter is 00000011, the bob image will be drawn into the first two bitplanes of the receiving raster bitmap. Now assume that the PlaneOnOff parameter is set to 00011100. The raster bitmap will receive 1 bits in bitplanes 2 through 4. However, only the eight central pixel locations of the image will receive these 1 bit values. All other pixel locations in bitplanes

2 through 4 will maintain their present bit values. Whatever bits were present in those locations before the bob image was added to the raster bitmap will be present after the bob writing operation has completed; the bob writing operation will not affect these bits.

Note that the PlanePick and PlaneOnOff parameters do not affect the drawing of virtual sprite images. In fact, virtual sprites are not drawn into a bitmap definition. Instead, the system assigns each virtual sprite to a hardware sprite and generates a Copper instruction list for it. This is an important distinction to keep in mind. In addition, it is important to remember that the colors for virtual sprites are always determined by the SprColors pointer parameter in the VSprite structure; virtual sprite colors are not determined by the binary combination of bitplane bit values at each virtual sprite pixel location.

The PlanePick and PlaneOnOff parameters provide a very simple way to draw a one-color rectangle into a bitmap. You do this as follows:

1. Set all bits in all bitplanes in the receiving bitmap location of the rectangle to zero.

2. Define a VSprite structure for a dummy bob. Set the Height and Width parameters for the size of rectangle you want. Place a zero value into the Depth and Image-Data parameters in the VSprite structure. This will tell the system that there is no image data for the bob. Because the bob has no image data, all bits in the shadow mask, as computed by the system, will be zero. Therefore, define a dummy shadow mask with all 1 bits for this bob.

3. Set the PlanePick parameter to 00000000. This will tell the system that there are no bitplanes to place bob image data into.

4. Set the PlaneOnOff parameter to the color you want for the rectangle. For example, if the current color table assigns red to color register 5, set PlaneOnOff to 00000101 to place 1 bits into bitplanes 0 and 2 of the raster bitmap.

This procedure is also useful in Intuition to create one-color images with the Intuition Image structure. However, when you use the PlanePick and PlaneOnOff parameters in Intuition, you will not need to worry about the shadow mask, which plays a part only in the animation system. See the discussion of the Image structure under the DrawImage function in Chapter 6.

Animate

Syntax of Function Call

Animate (animKey, rastPort)
       A0   **A1**

Purpose of Function

This function moves the animation objects you have created. It processes every AnimOb structure in the current graphics-element list to produce animation.

Inputs to Function

animKey A pointer to the first AnimOb structure in the animation object list

rastPort A pointer to a controlling RastPort structure

Discussion

The Animate function is the only function of its kind. It processes the entire current animation-object list to produce animation in the system. The Animate function updates the position and velocity of every animation object in the graphics-element list and calls any special animation routine associated with that object. Read the discussions of the AddAnimOb and InitGMasks functions to understand more completely how animation objects are used in the graphics system.

The Animate function updates all of the animation-object positions associated with a specific bitmap pointed to by a specific RastPort structure. It also calls any special routines you may have specified in the AnimComp and AnimOb structures. See the introduction to this chapter for an explanation of the definition and use of these routines.

The Animate function does the following for each AnimOb structure:

■ It updates the list and velocity of the animation object according to current definitions in the Bob, VSprite, and AnimComp structure definitions.

■ It calls the animation object's special routine if one is pointed to by the AnimORoutine parameter in the AnimOb structure. This routine can also affect the positions of various parts of the animation object.

■ For each animation component in each animation object, Animate automatically switches to a new timing sequence if any animation component's sequence times out. (Timing of animation components is determined by the Timer and TimeSet parameters in the AnimComp structure.) It also calls the animation component's special routine if one is pointed to by the AnimCRoutine parameter in the Anim-Comp structure. Animate then sets the animation component y,x coordinates based on these actions.

These AnimORoutine and AnimCRoutine routines are called automatically by the Animate function each time it executes. Each of these routines can be designed to affect the position of graphics elements. This may make the order of graphics elements in the current graphics-element list incorrect.

When the Animate function returns, the bitmap positions of the various animation objects will have changed. Under most circumstances, their new positions will not be in increasing y,x order. Therefore, before telling the system to redraw the animation objects, you must tell it to reorder the animation objects in increasing y,x order; that is, you must once again call the SortGList function before you call the DrawGList function.

The AnimComp Structure

This is the definition of the AnimComp structure:

```
struct AnimComp {
    WORD Flags;
    WORD Timer;
    WORD TimeSet;
    struct AnimComp *NextComp;
    struct AnimComp *PrevComp;
    struct AnimComp *NextSeq;
    struct AnimComp *PrevSeq;
    WORD (*AnimCRoutine) ();
    WORD YTrans;
    WORD XTrans;
    struct AnimOb *HeadOb;
    struct Bob *AnimBob;
};
```

Following is a description of each of the parameters in the AnimComp structure:

■ The Flags parameter contains a set of bits that determine the behavior of this animation component. You should study the graphics Collide.h file to determine what these are.

■ The Timer and TimeSet parameters fix how long this animation component is kept alive in the system. These parameters are used in sequenced-drawing animation. The value of the TimeSet parameter is the initial value for Timer. If the TimeSet parameter is nonzero, the Timer parameter is initialized to TimeSet and decrements each time the Animate function is called. When the Timer parameter decrements to zero, the animation system switches to the next animation component in a sequence, defined by the NextSeq parameter.

■ The NextComp and PrevComp parameters point to the AnimComp structures for the next and previous animation components in the animation object.

■ The NextSeq and PrevSeq parameters point to the next and previous AnimComp structures in a sequence of AnimComp structures defined in a drawing sequence.

■ The AnimCRoutine parameter points to a special user-defined animation component routine that will be called when the Animate function executes. Set this parameter to zero if you have not created such a routine.

- The YTrans and XTrans parameters contain the values of the initial y- and x-translation of the animation component defined by this AnimComp structure. These parameters are measured in the vertical and horizontal resolutions of the bitmap that will receive the bob.

- The HeadOb parameter points to the AnimOb structure with which this animation component is associated.

- The AnimBob parameter points to the Bob structure that defines one of the bobs for this animation component. Other bobs in this animation component are linked into this animation component by the Before and After pointers in the Bob structure.

ChangeSprite

Syntax of Function Call

ChangeSprite (viewPort, simpleSprite, spriteImage)
           A0   A1   A2

Purpose of Function

This function changes the pixel content of a hardware sprite's image definition so that it uses data stored in a new SpriteImage structure. The SpriteImage structure must be in chip memory (the first 512K of RAM).

Inputs to Function

viewPort   A pointer to the ViewPort structure to which this sprite is attached

simpleSprite   A pointer to a SimpleSprite structure

spriteImage   A pointer to a SpriteImage structure

Discussion

There are four Graphics Library functions that work specifically with hardware sprites in the Amiga system: ChangeSprite, FreeSprite, GetSprite, and MoveSprite. There is more information on hardware sprites in the discussions of each of these functions and in the introduction to this chapter.

The ChangeSprite function changes the on-screen appearance of a particular hardware sprite. It allows you to give that sprite different colors and a completely different shape. It uses the viewPort argument to point to a specific ViewPort structure. The hardware sprite is said to be attached to that viewport. The ChangeSprite function links this hardware sprite's new data definition, contained in the SpriteImage structure, into an existing viewport definition.

The data supplied in the SpriteImage structure consists of two reserved words and the hardware-sprite pixel definition that you supply. The pixel definition consists of two words per line of sprite height. The first word contains bits to define the most significant bit of the color selection for that sprite; the second word contains bits to define the least significant bit of the color selection for that sprite.

It is important to understand that color selection for hardware sprites is restricted: you are limited to four colors per sprite. This is because each line of sprite data is defined with only two data words, giving at most four color combinations (corresponding to the 00, 01, 10, and 11 bit combinations) at each sprite pixel location. The 00 combination always makes this pixel transparent to allow the background playfield colors to show through at that pixel location. However, you can change the color assignments from one video frame to another and also between viewports in a given view. For more on the colors allowed for sprites, see the discussion of the MoveSprite function.

Don't confuse the SpriteImage data structure with the SimpleSprite structure used by the GetSprite function. The SimpleSprite structure contains a pointer to position-control data for the sprite, the sprite height, the current sprite position, and the number (a value from 0 to 7) assigned to that sprite. The SpriteImage structure contains two things: first, it contains two words of sprite position-control data. Each of the bits in these two words is managed by the system. Second, it contains the pixel (bitmap) definition of the sprite, two words per sprite line. This is the data that defines the ImageData structure for the hardware sprite.

The SpriteImage Structure

The SpriteImage structure is defined as follows:

```
struct SpriteImage {
   UWORD posctldata[2];
   UWORD sprdata[2][height];
   UWORD reserved[2];
};
```

The meaning of the parameters in the SpriteImage structure is as follows:

■ The posctldata[2] parameter contains two words of position-control data. These are the data that the SimpleSprite function refers to with its first parameter. (See the discussion of the GetSprite function.)

■ The sprdata[2][height] parameter contains the actual data that define the sprite image. This data consists of two words (indicated by the [2]) for each line (indicated by the height parameter) of the hardware sprite image. Note that the height parameter is set in the SimpleSprite structure for this hardware sprite. For example, if you want to define a one-line hardware sprite image, you supply two words of data. If you want to define a hardware sprite that is as tall as the display screen (with a height equal to 200 lines), you

The last two bytes in the SpriteImage structure are reserved for future enhancements.

The first word of this position-control data in the posctldata parameter has the following bit definitions:

- Bits 15 through 8 represent the starting vertical position for this hardware sprite.

- Bits 7 through 0 represent the starting horizontal position for this hardware sprite.

The second word of this position-control data has the following bit definitions:

- Bits 15 through 8 represent the stopping vertical position for this hardware sprite.

- Bit 7 is the attach bit. You can use this bit to get additional colors for a hardware sprite. In this way, you can get 15 colors instead of three (plus transparent). At this time, this feature has not been implemented.

- Bits 6 through 4 are unused.

- Bits 3 through 0 are related to sprite position control.

Generally speaking, the system controls the values of these two words; however, their values are also controlled indirectly by the ChangeSprite and MoveSprite functions. Each word you supply in the sprdata parameter has 16 bits. Each line of the hardware sprite is defined by two of these words. The colors for each pixel in the hardware sprite are determined by the combination of bits from each of these two words. A simple example will illustrate this idea. Assume you want to define a two-line hardware sprite image. You define the image data in the SpriteImage structure as

```
line 1 word 1: 1111111111111111
line 1 word 2: 1111000000001111
line 2 word 1: 1111000000001111
line 2 word 2: 1111111111111111
```

This hardware sprite is 16 pixels wide (the maximum for a hardware sprite). The color for the rightmost pixel (pixel 0) is determined by taking the combination of the 0 position bits in words 1 and 2 of line 1. For this particular image, this is a binary 11 bit combination, which translates into a decimal 3. Therefore, this pixel will be assigned color 3. This is true of pixels 1 through 3 and 12 through 15 in both sprite lines; they all receive color 3.

However, pixels 4 through 11 of line 1 have a 10 binary value, which translates to a decimal 2. These pixels will receive color 2. In the same way, pixels 4 through 11 of line 2 have a 01 binary value, which translates to a decimal 1. These pixels will receive color 1.

The actual assignments of color registers to colors 1 through 3 for hardware sprites is determined by the following table:

Hardware Sprite Number	Color Registers
0 and 1	16 to 19
2 and 3	20 to 23
4 and 5	24 to 27
6 and 7	28 to 31

This means that, for hardware sprites 0 and 1, a 01 bit combination will be assigned to color register 17, a 10 bit combination will be assigned to color register 18, and a 11 bit combination will be assigned to color register 19. The same type of assignment applies to the other sprite pairs. Color 0 always corresponds to transparent (registers 16, 20, 24, and 28). The system does not assign any color register when the 00 bit pair occurs at a sprite pixel location. Instead, it draws nothing at that location. For this reason, any sprite pixel with the 00 bit pair will let the background playfield pixel color show through at that location.

DoCollision

Syntax of Function Call

DoCollision (rastPort)
A1

Purpose of Function

This function tests every graphics element in the current graphics-element list for collisions. Both gel-to-boundary and gel-to-gel collisions are checked.

Inputs to Function

rastPort   A pointer to a controlling RastPort structure

Discussion

DoCollision and SetCollision are the two functions in the Graphics Library that deal with gel-to-gel and gel-to-boundary collisions directly. Gel-to-gel collisions occur when the images of two graphics elements overlap as these elements (virtual sprites or bobs) are moved by the Animate function. Gel-to-boundary collisions occur when the image of a graphics element overlaps with one of the boundaries of a playfield. This type of collision can also occur when the Animate function moves the graphics elements. Read the discussion of SetCollision to understand more completely how collision events are handled in the graphics system.

The DoCollision function tests every graphics element in the current graphics-element list for a gel-to-gel or gel-to-boundary collision. When a collision is detected, DoCollision calls the appropriate collision-handling routine.

There are several things you must do before you call the DoCollision function:

1. Use the SetCollision function to initialize the collision-handling table to point to each of your collision-handling routines.

2. Use the SortGList function to arrange the current graphics-element list in increasing y,x order.

3. Prepare the BorderLine, CollMask, HitMask, and MeMask pointer parameters in the VSprite structure. See the discussion of the InitGMasks function for more information about initializing the BorderLine and CollMask parameters. The Hit-Mask and MeMask parameters allow the system to determine which collision-handling routine to call when a collision is detected. See the discussion of the AddVSprite function for more information about these two parameters.

The DoCollision function uses the RastPort structure pointer variable as its only argument. This RastPort structure points to a BitMap stucture, which points to a specific bitmap. Each RastPort structure also has an associated GelsInfo structure that defines the order of the graphics-element list for this bitmap. Each GelsInfo structure also has a CollTable pointer parameter that points to the collision table associated with this particular graphics-element list.

Collisions in the system fall into two categories: gel-to-gel collisions and gel-to-boundary (bob or virtual-sprite to bitmap-boundary) collisions.

When DoCollision detects a collision, it causes the system to And the 16-bit HitMask parameter of the upper-leftmost object of the colliding pair bit by bit with the 16-bit MeMask parameter of the lower-rightmost object of the colliding pair. The 1 bits resulting from the And operation determine which of a possible 16 collision-handling routines the system will call. For example, if the Animate function causes two bobs to collide, the Hit-mask of bob 1 will be Anded with the MeMask of bob 2. If the HitMask Parameter in the VSprite structure for bob 1 (assumed to be above and to the left of bob 2) is 1111111111111111 and the MeMask Parameter in the VSprite structure for bob 2 is 0000000000000010, the Anded result will be 0000000000000010. In this case the second collision-handling routine will be called.

When bit 0 of the And result is a 1, the collision is a boundary collision. The system sets the BORDERHIT flag to indicate that a graphics element has landed on or moved beyond the boundary of the drawing area. The DoCollision function then calls the collision-handling routine corresponding to bit 0.

If one of the other bits (bits 1 to 15) is set in the And result, the system calls the collision-handling routine corresponding to the bit set. For example, if bit 1 is set to 1, the system calls the collision-handling routine corresponding to bit 1.

If more than one bit is set as a result of the And operation, the system calls the routine corresponding to the rightmost bit. For example, if the And result is 0000000000000110, the system calls the second (not the third) collision-handling routine.

The system does not pass any parameters to these collision-handling routines when it calls them. However, you can use the user-defined extensions (AUserStuff, BUserStuff, and VUserStuff) to the AnimOb structure, the Bob structure, or the VSprite structure to hold the variables you need for your collision-handling routines. This is discussed more fully in the introduction to this chapter.

In addition, if you check for gel-to-gel collisions after the Animate function moves your objects, the collision-handling routines themselves may affect the positions of your graphics elements. They will if they are designed to affect the positions of the animation objects that collide. Therefore, you should call the SortGList function after any collision-handling routines have executed. Use this sequence of function calls:

```
Animate (animKey, rastPort);
SortGList (rastPort);
DoCollision (rastPort);
SortGList (rastPort);
DrawGList (rastPort);
Animate (animKey, rastPort);
```

DrawGList

Syntax of Function Call

```
DrawGList (rastPort, viewPort)
           A1        A0
```

Purpose of Function

This function performs one drawing pass of the current graphics-element list. For all virtual sprites in the list, the associated virtual sprite definitions are built into the Copper list for that video frame. For all bobs in the list, the associated Bob structures are used to draw the bobs into the current raster bitmap definition.

▌nputs to Function

rastPort	A pointer to a controlling RastPort structure
viewPort	A pointer to the ViewPort structure with which to associate the virtual sprite Copper instructions

▌iscussion

There are three functions in the Graphics Library that work directly with the graphics-element list: DrawGList, InitGels, and SortGList. Read the discussions of InitGels and SortGList to learn more about how the graphics-element list is used in the graphics system.

The DrawGList function prepares the necessary Copper instructions and RAM areas to display all graphics elements currently defined in the graphics-element list. It is important to understand that the DrawGList function actually draws the bobs into the raster bitmap when it is called. For the virtual sprites, however, DrawGList merely defines a set of Copper instructions; the virtual sprites are not drawn into the raster bitmap. The system can use these Copper instructions to associate the virtual sprites with hardware sprites when they are displayed. The assignment of virtual sprites to hardware sprites is based on the positions you defined for the virtual sprites when you initialized the VSprite structure. These Copper instructions are later merged with the Copper instructions for the viewport by the MergeCop function. The whole picture is then brought onto the display screen with the LoadView function.

The DrawGList function uses the RastPort structure pointer to find the bobs in the graphics-element list. Recall that each Bob structure is linked to a specific RastPort structure and therefore to a specific bitmap drawing area. Each VSprite structure, on the other hand, is linked to a View structure.

The View structure points to a set of Copper instructions for constructing the screen display. (See the discussion of InitView function in Chapter 2.) Through a linked ViewPort structure, the View structure also includes a set of pointers to a set of virtual-sprite Copper instructions that have been defined by a call to the DrawGList function.

To install the currently defined virtual sprites into the display area, you must call the MergeCop function to merge the virtual sprite instructions with the other display definition instructions. (See the discussion of the MergeCop function in Chapter 2.) Follow the MergeCop call with a call to the LoadView function.

FreeGBuffers

Syntax of Function Call

FreeGBuffers (animOb, rastPort, doubleBuf)
                    A0   A1   D0

Purpose of Function

This function deallocates all buffers of an entire animation object previously allocated by the GetGBuffers function. It is new to the version 1.1 software release.

Inputs to Function

animOb	A pointer to an AnimOb structure
rastPort	A pointer to a controlling RastPort structure
doubleBuf	The double-buffer indicator; set this to TRUE if the original animation object was allocated with double-buffering

Discussion

There are two Graphics Library functions that work directly with animation-object memory management: FreeGBuffers and GetGBuffers.

For each animation-drawing sequence of each component of the AnimOb, the FreeGBuffers function deallocates memory for these buffers:

- The SaveBuffer buffer, which used to save the background bitmap when a bob is drawn

- The BorderLine and Collmask buffers, which contain data bits used in collision detection

- The ImageShadow buffer, which contains data bits used to draw bobs into bitmaps

Note that the CollMask and ImageShadow buffers usually share the same RAM space.

In addition, if the doubleBuf variable is set (TRUE), the graphics task uses double-buffering and the FreeGBuffers function will also deallocate memory for these buffers:

- The DBufPacket buffer, which contains the DBufPacket structure

■ The BufBuffer buffer, which contains the bob bitmap when double-buffering is used

Read the discussion of the GetGBuffers function to learn more about these buffers.

FreeSprite

Syntax of Function Call

FreeSprite (spritenum)
D0

Purpose of Function

This function frees a hardware sprite for use by other tasks in the system and for assignment to virtual sprites. FreeSprite makes the hardware sprite available to other tasks that issue GetSprite calls.

Inputs to Function

spritenum   An integer from 0 to 7 that denotes one of eight hardware sprites

Discussion

There are four Graphics Library functions that work specifically with hardware sprites in the Amiga system: ChangeSprite, FreeSprite, GetSprite, and MoveSprite. These functions enable sharing of sprite hardware and handle simple cases of sprite usage and movement. The system provides eight hardware sprites that can be used to create moving images on the display screen.

The FreeSprite function frees a previously assigned hardware sprite for other uses. You must free your hardware sprites if you want to use them again. If you do not free them and your task ends, the system has no way of allocating those sprites until it is rebooted.

When you use the GetSprite and FreeSprite functions together, remember that you are limited to eight hardware sprites. Because of this restriction, you should free the hardware assigned to hardware sprites as quickly as possible. This is especially true if you want to deal with only the hardware sprites and avoid using the more complex virtual-sprite functions.

Suppose that you have two viewports in a video frame view and you want to use four hardware sprites in the top viewport and *the same* four hardware sprites in the bottom viewport. You want to redefine the shape of these hardware sprites and assign a different set of colors to all four. Therefore, you have to free the hardware sprites between the first and second viewports.

To define the first viewport, use the GetSprite and ChangeSprite functions each four times to get and define four sprites. When you call the GetSprite function, define a SimpleSprite structure for each of the sprites; this structure gives the system position-control data for that sprite, the height of the sprite, the current x,y position of the sprite, and the number (0 to 7) assigned to that sprite. When you call the ChangeSprite function, you must also define eight SpriteImage structures for the pixel color and shape of each of the sprites.

Next, you must free the sprites with four calls to the FreeSprite function before you do the same thing for the second viewport. Assigning the same hardware sprites for the second viewport allows you to redefine the shapes and colors and reposition the sprites in the second viewport.

Therefore, once you build these structures (a total of eight SimpleSprite structures and eight SpriteImage structures) and make your calls to the GetSprite, ChangeSprite, and FreeSprite functions, each sprite will be associated with the proper viewport in that view. In addition, if you use the MoveSprite function, you can change the position of these eight sprite images between video frames, thus producing animation.

GetGBuffers

Syntax of Function Call

```
GetGBuffers (animOb, rastPort, doubleBuf)
              A0       A1        D0
```

Purpose of Function

This function allocates memory for all the buffers of an animation object. It returns TRUE if all buffer allocations were successful, or FALSE if any buffer allocations failed.

Inputs to Function

animOb   A pointer to an AnimOb structure

rastPort   A pointer to a controlling RastPort structure

doubleBuf   The double-buffering indicator; set this to TRUE if you want to use double-buffering

Discussion

There are two Graphics Library functions that work directly with animation-object memory management, FreeGBuffers and GetGBuffers. Each animation object can use a number of buffers to handle its drawing, double-buffering, and collision-detection requirements. These buffers are pointed to by various pointers in several structures in the animation system.

The GetGBuffers function allocates memory for these buffers: the BorderLine and CollMask buffers, pointed to in the VSprite structure; the SaveBuffer, DBuffer, and ImageShadow buffers, pointed to in the Bob structure; and the BufBuffer buffer, pointed to in the DBufPacket structure. The DBuffer and BufBuffer buffers are used only if double-buffering is specified for the animation object. Note that each Bob structure has a pointer to a distinct DBufPacket structure.

The DBufPacket Structure

The DBufPacket structure has this definition:

```
struct DBufPacket {
    WORD BufY, BufX;
    struct VSprite *BufPath;
    WORD *BufBuffer;
};
```

where BufX and BufY are system variables that represent the last on-screen x,y position of the bob. They are used to provide correct restoration of the playfield background bitmap using the double-buffering buffers assigned to this bob.

BufPath is a system parameter that helps control the drawing order the system uses to draw a specific bob into the playfield background bitmap. The RastPort structure contains a pointer to the BitMap structure that defines the bitmap for background playfields. The BufPath parameter ensures that the system restores the playfield background bitmaps in the correct sequence. The BufPath parameter is related to the DrawPath and ClearPath system parameters in the VSprite structure.

The BufBuffer parameter points to the block of memory set by your graphics task. The GetGBuffers function will attempt to allocate enough RAM buffer space for both of the playfield buffers used with a double-buffered bob. Each of these separate buffers must be at least as large as the bob image.

GetSprite

Syntax of Function Call

spritenum = GetSprite (simpleSprite, spritenum)
D0   **A0**   **D0**

Purpose of Function

This function allocates one of the eight hardware sprites to a specific animation task. If the spritenum value is 0–7, GetSprite attempts to allocate that hardware sprite. If the spritenum value is − 1, GetSprite allocates the next available hardware sprite. If no sprites are available or the hardware sprite is already allocated, GetSprite returns a − 1. If the hardware sprite is available for allocation, GetSprite marks it as allocated, fills in the Num entry of the SimpleSprite structure, and returns the sprite number.

Inputs to Function

simpleSprite   A pointer to a SimpleSprite structure

spritenum   An integer from 0 to 7, or − 1 for the next available sprite

Discussion

There are four Graphics Library functions that work specifically with hardware sprites in the Amiga system: ChangeSprite, FreeSprite, GetSprite, and MoveSprite. There is more information on hardware sprites in the discussions of each of these functions and in the introduction to this chapter.

The GetSprite function allows you to get a new hardware sprite from the sprite hardware system. This is sometimes called stealing a sprite. The term "stealing" is used because the GetSprite function assigns the sprite hardware for this sprite exclusively to this sprite. You are therefore limited to eight hardware sprites at a time. Although this is a restriction, you benefit from the easy-to-use hardware-sprite functions. If you use virtual sprites you can have an unlimited number of sprites, but you cannot use these hardware-sprite functions.

When you are defining hardware sprites, the GetSprite function is the first function you need to call. GetSprite does nothing more than assign a hardware sprite to a specific sprite image; that hardware sprite is then no longer available until you call the FreeSprite function to free it for other uses.

Note that if you assign one hardware sprite, you are effectively assigning two. This is because they occur in pairs (by convention in the system); sprites 0 and 1 form a pair, as do sprites 2 and 3, 4 and 5, and 6 and 7.

If you assign a hardware sprite, you assign its color registers as well. Color registers 16–19 are assigned to sprites 0 and 1; registers 20–23 are assigned to sprites 2 and 3; registers 24–27 are assigned to sprites 4 and 5; and registers 28–31 are assigned to sprites 6 and 7.

In addition, the color registers are shared with the viewports in a playfield. For example, if a viewport is five bitplanes deep, the upper 16 of the total 32 color registers will also be used by the playfield viewport display hardware. This means that 16 of the playfield colors will be identical to the hardware sprite colors. Of course, you can reload the color registers between viewports. This is one of the reasons you must have at least one scanning line between all viewports in a view.

Notice that one argument to the GetSprite function is a pointer to the SimpleSprite structure. Don't confuse the SimpleSprite structure with the SpriteImage structure used by the ChangeSprite function.

The SimpleSprite Structure

This is the definition of the SimpleSprite structure:

```
struct SimpleSprite {
    UWORD *posctldata;
    UWORD height;
    UWORD x,y;
    UWORD num;
};
```

The SimpleSprite structure contains the following data:

- A pointer to the SpriteImage stucture associated with this hardware sprite. The SpriteImage structure starts with a set of position-control data for this sprite. For this reason, the pointer parameter in the SimpleSprite structure is called posctldata. This is a set of values of the x,y coordinates for the hardware-sprite position. Usually, you can set these values to zero. The remainder of the SpriteImage structure consists of bit data to define the hardware sprite image. (See the discussion of the ChangeSprite function for a complete definition of the SpriteImage structure.)

- The height of the hardware sprite you are assigning. This is the number of noninterlaced-mode scanning lines you will use for this sprite. This number is limited to the number of noninterlaced-mode scanning lines in the viewport to which you will assign this sprite with the ChangeSprite function. If this viewport fills the entire display screen, you can make the sprite as tall as 200 scanning lines.

- The current x,y position for this hardware sprite in the viewport coordinate system. The MoveSprite function allows you to change these values.

- The sprite number assigned to this sprite. This number ties this instance of the SimpleSprite structure to the GetSprite function call.

InitAnimate

Syntax of Macro Call

        InitAnimate (animKey)
                     A0

Purpose of Macro

This macro initializes the animation system by pointing to the first AnimOb structure in the animation-object list.

Inputs to Macro

animKey   A pointer to the first AnimOb structure in a linked list of AnimOb structures

Discussion

There are two functions and one macro that work directly with animation objects in the Graphics Library. These are the AddAnimOb and InitGMasks functions and the InitAnimate macro. Read the discussions of AddAnimOb and InitGMasks to learn more about how animation objects are used in the graphics system.

Before you call the Animate function, you must initialize the animation system by defining a pointer to the first AnimOb structure in the animation-object list. Of course, you must also initialize the graphics-element list with a call to the InitGels function.

You can initialize the animation system by either calling the InitAnimate macro or using two simple task statements to specify a pointer to the first animation object in the animation-object list. Obviously, the InitAnimate macro provides the simpler approach.

InitGels

Syntax of Function Call

        InitGels (headVSprite,tailVSprite,gelsInfo)
                 A0   A1   A2

Purpose of Function

This function initializes a graphics-element list; it must be called before you can use any graphics element. InitGels assigns VSprite structures to the head and tail of the graphics-element list. It then links these two structures together to form the boundary nodes of the list.

Inputs to Function

headVSprite	A pointer to a dummy VSprite structure to be used as the head of the gel list
tailVSprite	A pointer to a dummy VSprite structure to be used as the tail of the gel list
gelsInfo	A pointer to the GelsInfo structure to be initialized

Discussion

There are three functions in the Graphics Library that work directly with the graphics-element list: DrawGList, InitGels, and SortGList. Read the discussions of DrawGList and SortGList to learn more about how the graphics-element list is used in the graphics system.

The InitGels function initializes a specific graphics-element list. Each graphics-element list is a linked list of all the bobs and virtual sprites currently defined as part of a specific group of graphics elements. You can have a number of graphics-element lists in the system simultaneously. Each of these lists is initialized with a call to the InitGels function.

The InitGels function requires a pointer to the first and last elements in the list. Each of these elements is a VSprite structure. Each of these VSprite structures can represent either a virtual sprite or a bob. The headVSprite and tailVSprite pointers should point to dummy VSprite structures. These structures contain no useful information but are required to set up the graphics-element list. Then, when the InitGels function executes, it automatically assigns the head VSprite structure a maximum negative x- and y-coordinate; it assigns the tail VSprite structure a maximum positive x- and y-coordinate. Here, maximum negative and maximum positive are numbers sufficiently negative and positive that the x,y position value of any graphics element would always fall between them. This ensures that these two dummy VSprite structures are always at the outermost limits of that graphics-element list.

Changing Graphics-Element Definitions

Before you add new elements to a specific graphics-element list, you may want to change the appearance of your bobs or virtual sprites. To do this, you need to change the Image-Data pointer in the VSprite structure. You can place a number of image data arrays in RAM. Then, when you want to point to new image data for a bob or virtual sprite, just change the ImageData pointer parameter in the VSprite structure. When you change the image data for a bob or virtual sprite, remember to call the InitMasks function to update the borderline and collision masks for that bob or virtual sprite.

To change the color choices for a virtual sprite, change the SprColor pointer parameter to a new value. You can place a number of SprColor words in RAM. Then, when you want to point to a new set of color definitions for a virtual sprite, just change the Spr-Colors pointer parameter in the VSprite structure.

To change the color choices for a bob, change the PlanePick and PlaneOnOff parameters in the VSprite structure associated with the bob. You can also change the Depth parameter in the VSprite structure if you want to add or delete bitplanes from the definition of the bob's image data. Note that you do not use the VSprite Structure SprColor parameter for bobs; this parameter is used only with virtual sprites.

To change a virtual sprite or bob location inside the drawing area, change the y,x coordinates in the VSprite structure.

To change the bob's drawing priority, change the drawing sequence by rearranging the Before and After pointers in the Bob structure.

To change the bob into a paintbrush, set the SAVEBOB flag in the Bob structure. This tells the system not to erase the old bob image when the bob is moved. A series of bob images will then appear simultaneously on the display screen, thereby simulating a paintbrush effect.

Note that none of these changes will occur until the SortGList and DrawGList functions have both returned.

The GelsInfo Structure

This is the definition of the GelsInfo structure:

```
struct GelsInfo {
    BYTE sprRsrvd;
    UBYTE Flags;
    struct VSprite *gelHead, *gelTail;
    WORD *nextLine;
    WORD **lastColor;
    struct collTable *collHandler;
    SHORT leftmost, rightmost, topmost, bottommost;
    APTR firstBlissObject, lastBlissObject;
};
```

These are the parameters in the GelsInfo structure:

■ The sprRsrvd parameter is a one-byte parameter whose individual bits determine which hardware sprites can be used by the virtual-sprite system. For example, if this parameter is 00000000, all hardware sprites can be used by the virtual-sprite system. If this parameter is 00000001, the first hardware sprite (sprite 0) cannot be used by the virtual-sprite system. If this parameter is 10000001, the first and last hardware sprites (sprites 0 and 7) cannot be used by the virtual-sprite system. You can set the bits in this parameter to restrict which hardware sprites are assigned to each virtual sprite.

- The Flags parameter is a one-byte parameter whose bits are set and used by the system.

- The gelHead parameter is a pointer to a VSprite structure to be placed at the head of the graphics-element list. This is a dummy VSprite structure to which the system assigns maximum negative y,x coordinates.

- The gelTail parameter is a pointer to a VSprite structure to be placed at the tail of the graphics-element list. This is a dummy VSprite structure to which the system assigns maximum positive y,x coordinates.

- The nextLine parameter is a pointer to an array of eight words that define the available sprite lines. These are video display lines between sprite images where the sprite definition registers (color, etc.) can be changed. This parameter is for system use only.

- The lastColor parameter is a pointer to an array of eight pointers (double indirection) for the color last assigned to virtual sprites. This parameter is for system use only.

- The collHandler parameter is a pointer to the collision-table array. The collision-table array contains a list of pointers to collision-handling routines that will be used when a gel-to-gel or gel-to-boundary collision is sensed by the system. Entries in the collision table are defined by the SetCollision function.

- The leftmost and rightmost parameters contain the x-coordinates and the topmost and bottommost parameters contain the y-coordinates of the clipping-rectangle used to limit the drawing of a bob in a specific raster bitmap. When a bob passes across these boundaries, the drawing routines automatically clip the drawing of that bob. These parameters are not used for virtual-sprite clipping. Note that you can also use these four parameters to detect gel-to-boundary collisions.

- The firstBlissObject and the lastBlissObject parameters are used by the system.

InitGMasks

Syntax of Function Call

InitGMasks (animOb)
A0

Purpose of Function

This function initializes all the masks of an AnimOb structure. It calls the InitMasks function for every drawing sequence of every AnimComp structure.

Inputs to Function

animOb   A pointer to an AnimOb structure

Discussion

There are two functions and one macro that work directly with animation objects in the Graphics Library: AddAnimOb, InitGMasks, and InitAnimate, respectively.

The InitGMasks function provides a quick way to initialize the borderline and collision masks of all animation components in an animation object with one function call. Any time you change the virtual sprite or bob image data that help define a specific animation component, you should call the InitMasks function. If you change several graphics-element definitions in an animation object, it may be more efficient to call the InitGMasks function to update the borderline and collision masks of each animation component in the object automatically.

The InitGMasks function calls the InitMasks function for each and every animation component in the specified animation object. Each of the animation component's virtual-sprite or bob masks will then be initialized. Read the discussion of the InitMasks function to see how the borderline and collision masks are defined and computed.

InitMasks

Syntax of Function

InitMasks (vSprite)
A0

Purpose of Function

This function initializes the borderline and collision masks of a virtual sprite. It takes the image data stored in the ImageData structure and computes these masks for the designated virtual sprite.

Inputs to Function

vSprite   A pointer to a VSprite structure

Discussion

There are three functions in the Graphics Library that work directly with virtual sprites: AddVSprite, InitMasks, and RemVSprite. Read the discussions of AddVSprite and RemVSprite to understand more completely how virtual sprites are used in the graphics system.

The InitMasks function initializes the borderline and collision masks associated with a VSprite structure. The BorderLine and CollMask pointer parameters are both in the VSprite structure.

The collision mask of a graphics element is usually the same as the shadow mask of that graphics element. For each pixel location in a graphics-element image bitmap (the ImageData data), bits in the first bitplane are Ored with each bit in all other bitplanes at the same pixel location. The result is stored in the collision mask data area. Therefore, the size (height and width) of the collision mask bitmap is the same size as the individual bitmaps of the planes of the graphics element.

For example, if a graphics element image has two planes and each plane is 16-by-32 bits, the collision mask bitmap is also 16-by-32 bits. At each location in the collision mask bitmap, a bit is set if any of the planes of the graphics element image has a bit set at that location. If none of these planes has a bit set at that location, the bit in the collision mask bitmap at that location is 0.

The collision mask is used to control the drawing of a graphics element and to define where a bit is set in the bitmap for that graphics element for collision detection. Each bit set in the collision mask indicates that some part of the graphics-element image exists at that location. When that image pixel overlaps the pixel of another screen object, a collision has occurred.

The borderline mask is also used to detect collisions. The borderline mask is creating by Oring all words that define the graphics-element image with each other. For example, the borderline mask would be 0011111111000000 if a graphics-element image is defined by these six words:

```
0011000011000000
0001100110000000
0000111100000000
0001100110000000
0011000011000000
0000000000000000
```

In other words, there is a 1 bit in any location where any of the words that define the graphics-element image has a 1 bit. This procedure is similar to taking the whole image and condensing it into a single line.

The borderline mask always has a 1 bit at graphics-element image borders. In the example, the borders of the image are at bit locations 6 and 13 (bit 0 is the rightmost bit). The system uses the borderline mask to determine quickly whether the bob or virtual

sprite is touching the left or right boundaries of a drawing area. This mechanism supplements collision detection using only the collision mask.

The size of the data area you allocate for the borderline mask must be at least as
large as the width of the graphics-element image expressed in words. For example, if it
takes three 16-bit words to hold each line of bob image data, the RAM assigned to the
borderline mask must have at least three words allocated to it.

Note that both bobs and virtual sprites participate in software collision detection.
Therefore, you should call the InitMasks function for each graphics element that you
want to check for collisions. Alternatively, you can call the InitGMasks function to initialize the mask for each graphics element in an animation object with one function call.

MoveSprite

Syntax of Function Call

MoveSprite (viewPort, simpleSprite, x, y)
            A0   A1   D0D1

Purpose of Function

This function moves a hardware sprite image to a new point in a viewport display. The
x,y coordinates are measured in the viewport coordinate system.

Inputs to Function

viewPort	A pointer to a ViewPort structure
simpleSprite	A pointer to a SimpleSprite structure
x	The new horizontal position for the sprite relative to the left edge of the viewport bitmap
y	The new vertical position for the sprite relative to the top edge of the viewport bitmap

Discussion

There are four Graphics Library functions that work specifically with hardware sprites in the Amiga system: ChangeSprite, FreeSprite, GetSprite, and MoveSprite.

The MoveSprite function allows you to move a hardware sprite inside a viewport. This movement can produce the animation effects you are trying to achieve in your programs. The MoveSprite function, like the ChangeSprite function, is tied to a specific viewport.

In contrast, the GetSprite and FreeSprite functions do not deal with a specific viewport; they make hardware sprites available to the system to be assigned to viewports with the ChangeSprite function.

You can use the MoveSprite function to define a series of different video-frame definitions to achieve your animation effects. Specify a new x,y hardware sprite position that is a small number of pixels different from frame to frame. The sprite will then appear to move on the display screen.

When the MoveSprite function returns, the sprite will be moved to a new x,y position in the viewport bitmap. Note that the coordinates specified in the MoveSprite function call are in the viewport coordinate system. The origin for this coordinate system is the 0,0 point of the viewport bitmap—the upper-left corner of the viewport as it would appear on the display screen.

The x,y arguments are the new pixel coordinates to which the sprite should be moved. Movement resolution is tied to a low-resolution, noninterlaced mode display. If the viewport is part of a high-resolution and/or interlaced mode display, the system can move the sprite only in increments of two high-resolution mode pixels or two interlaced mode pixels per MoveSprite call.

OFF_SPRITE

Syntax of Macro Call

OFF_SPRITE

Purpose of Macro

This macro clears the sprite DMA (direct memory access) bit in the DMA control register. Any sprites subsequently loaded with the LoadView function will not be displayed until an ON_SPRITE macro call.

Inputs to Macro

This macro has no inputs.

Discussion

There are two macros that deal with sprite DMA control: ON_SPRITE and OFF _SPRITE. Both macros reset the SPREN bit in the DMACON register.

The ON_SPRITE and OFF_SPRITE macros are very similar to the ON_DIS-PLAY and OFF_DISPLAY macros discussed in Chapter 2. You should read those discussions to learn about macros that control the Amiga DMA channels.

ON_SPRITE

Syntax of Macro Call

ON_SPRITE

Purpose of Macro

This macro sets the sprite DMA (direct memory access) bit in the DMA control register. Any sprites (hardware or virtual) subsequently loaded with the LoadView function will then be displayed.

Inputs to Macro

This macro has no inputs.

Discussion

There are two macros that deal with sprite DMA control: ON_SPRITE and OFF _SPRITE. ON_SPRITE sets bit 5 (called the SPREN bit) in the DMA control register (the register named DMACON). After you have loaded a new view with the LoadView function, you can use the ON_SPRITE macro to allow the system DMA to display your sprites.

ON_SPRITE is the system default setting. That is, unless you specifically turn off sprite DMA with the OFF_SPRITE macro, any sprites you define will be displayed.

RemBob

Syntax of Macro Call

RemBob (bob, rastPort)
      A0   A1

Purpose of Macro

This macro removes a Bob structure from a graphics-element list and raster bitmap definition. It unlinks the Bob structure from the graphics-element list and erases it from the raster bitmap definition.

Inputs to Macro

bob	A pointer to a Bob structure
rastPort	A pointer to a controlling RastPort structure

Discussion

There are two functions and one macro in the Graphics Library that work with bobs (Blitter objects) directly: the AddBob and RemIBob functions and the RemBob macro. The RemIBob function and RemBob macro both remove a bob from the current graphics-element list. Unlike the RemBob macro, the RemIBob function erases the bob from the current raster bitmap immediately. Read the discussions of AddBob and RemIBob to understand more completely how bobs are used in the graphics system.

The RemBob macro does three things:

1. It tells the system to erase the bob from the drawing area. If appropriate flags are set, the background information in the area where that bob was positioned will be restored from off-screen buffers.

2. It tells the system to erase any bob that has been drawn subsequent to this one at the same location.

3. It removes the bob from the graphics-element list.

In contrast to the RemIBob function, the bob is not removed immediately. Instead, the system removes the bob during the next execution of the DrawGList function. If the bob is double-buffered, the on-screen version is removed during the next DrawGList call and the off-screen version is removed during the DrawGList call following that.

In any case, the system unlinks the Bob structure from the system graphics-element list. To redraw any bobs that were drawn on top of the one just removed, you must make another call to the DrawGList function.

RemIBob

Syntax of Function Call

RemIBob (bob, rastPort, viewPort)
          A0   A1   A2

Purpose of Function

This function removes a Bob structure from a graphics-element list and the raster bitmap definition immediately. It unlinks the Bob structure from the graphics-element list and erases it from the raster bitmap definition.

Inputs to Function

bob	A pointer to a Bob structure
rastPort	A pointer to a controlling RastPort structure
viewPort	A pointer to a ViewPort structure

Discussion

There are two functions and one macro in the Graphics Library that work with bobs directly: the AddBob and RemIBob functions and the RemBob macro. Read the discussions of AddBob and RemBob to learn more about how bobs are used in the graphics system and to compare the different behavior of the RemIBob function and the RemBob macro.

The RemIBob function does three things:

1. It tells the system to erase the specified bob from the drawing area. If the appropriate double-buffering flags are set, the background information in the area where that bob was positioned will be restored.

2. It tells the system to erase any bob that has been drawn subsequent to this one at the same location.

3. It removes the bob from the graphics-element list immediately by unlinking the Bob structure from the graphics-element list. To redraw any bobs that were drawn on top of the one just removed, you must make another call to the DrawGList function.

RemVSprite

Syntax of Function Call

RemVSprite (vSprite)
A0

Purpose of Function

This function unlinks and removes a VSprite structure from the current graphics-element list.

Inputs to Function

vSprite   A pointer to a VSprite structure

Discussion

There are three functions in the Graphics Library that work with virtual sprites directly: AddVSprite, InitMasks, and RemVSprite. Read the discussions of AddVSprite and InitMasks to learn more about how virtual sprites are used in the graphics system.

The action of the RemVSprite function is very simple. It simply removes a virtual sprite from the current graphics-element list. Note that you can have several graphics-element lists all active at once; each was initialized with a call to the InitGels function. Each graphics-element list starts and finishes with VSprite dummy structures. These head and tail VSprite structures were specified in the call to the InitGels function.

Each virtual sprite added with an AddVSprite call places a new virtual sprite on a specific graphics-element list. The same virtual sprite can be placed on a number of different graphics-element lists by initializing a specific graphics-element list with a new InitGels call before you call the AddVSprite function. Each of these virtual sprites is associated with a different RastPort structure, a different raster bitmap, and a different GelsInfo structure.

Your call to the RemVSprite function removes the specific instance of a VSprite structure from the same graphics-element list on which it was placed originally by the AddVSprite function call.

SetCollision

Syntax of Function Call

SetCollision (numroutine, routine, gelsInfo)
           D0   A0   A1

Purpose of Function

This function sets a pointer to a user collision-handling routine. It sets entry h (h varies from 0 to 15) in the user's collision-handling routine pointers to the pointer p (the RAM address of the collision-handling routine).

Inputs to Function

numroutine   The number of the collision-handling routine (0 to 15)

routine   A pointer to a collision-handling routine

gelsInfo   A pointer to a GelsInfo structure

Discussion

There are two functions in the Graphics Library that work with gel-to-gel and gel-to-boundary collisions directly: DoCollision and SetCollision. The DoCollision function tests every graphics element in the current graphics-element list for collisions. If a collision is detected, an appropriate collision-handling routine is called automatically.

The SetCollision function sets a pointer to a collision-handling routine. It allows you to place various collision-handling routines in RAM at different locations. In this way, you define a collision table where pointers to your collision-handling routines are stored. The SetCollision function does nothing more than define the values in the collision-handling routine pointer table.

The SetCollision function works with the CollTable structure. The CollTable structure consists of a pointer to a set of collision-handling routine pointers (called collPtrs). Each of these 16 parameters points to a specific collision-handling routine in the system. You must define and debug these routines before you install them in the system. Once they are operational and you know their startng RAM location, you can use the SetCollision function to place them into the system.

When the DoCollision function detects a collision between any two graphics elements, it tells the system to call one or more of your collision-handling routines. The MeMask and HitMask parameters assigned to each graphics element determine which collision-handling routine it calls. Each of the collision-handling routines can take some action that is useful and specific to your graphics task. See the introduction to this chapter for more on collision-handling routines.

When the View structure is first initialized, the system sets all the collision-handling routine pointers in the CollTable structure to zero values. Therefore, in order to use the collision-handling routines, you must initialize those entries in the collision table that correspond to the HitMask and MeMask bits that you have set.

SortGList

Syntax of Function Call

SortGList (rastPort)
          A0

Purpose of Function

This function sorts the current graphics-element list according to the graphics elements' y,x coordinates. Graphics elements are then placed on the new list in increasing y,x order.

The list must be sorted in this order before you call the DrawGList and DoCollision functions.

Inputs to Function

rastPort	A pointer to a controlling RastPort structure that contains a pointer to the GelsInfo structure

Discussion

There are three functions in the Graphics Library that work directly with the graphics-element list: DrawGList, InitGels, and SortGList. Read the discussions of DrawGList and InitGels to understand more about how the graphics-element list is used in the graphics system.

Both virtual sprites and bobs are added to the specific graphics-element list you define with the InitGels function. Each of your graphics-element lists can get out of order for several reasons.

First, each time the position of a virtual sprite or bob changes due to an animate function call, you must re-sort all of the graphics elements into the correct drawing order. Second, a call to either the AnimORoutine or AnimORoutine routines may move virtual sprites or bobs, thereby getting them out of correct y,x order. Third, a call to any of 16 possible collision-handling routines may move virtual sprites or bobs. These last two types of events depend on your design of the special and collision-handling routines.

Remember that you can have a number of current graphics-element lists. If you do, you must put all of them in the correct y,x order. To do this, you merely change the RastPort pointer argument in the SortGList function and call the SortGList function for each of your RastPort structures that use a different GelsInfo structure.

You should call the SortGList function after the Animate function returns. The Animate function itself can change the on-screen position of your animation objects. In addition, the AnimORoutine and AnimCRoutine routines automatically called by the Animate function can change the y,x coordinates of graphics elements in the current graphics-element list.

You should also call the SortGList function after the DoCollision function returns. The DoCollision function, through its collision-handling routine calls (if any), can change the on-screen position of the graphics elements.

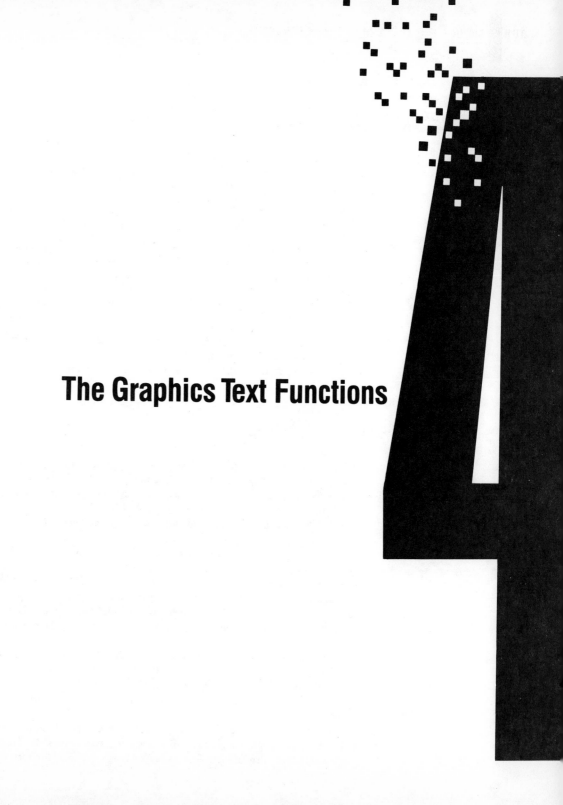

The Graphics Text Functions

Introduction

This chapter defines and discusses the Graphics Library text functions and the DiskFont Library functions. These functions enable you to manage text and fonts in the Amiga system. They fall into three categories:

■ The text-management functions: ClearEOL, ClearScreen, Text, and TextLength, for placing text into each of your raster bitmaps

■ The font-management functions for RAM-resident fonts: AddFont, AskFont, AskSoftStyle, CloseFont, OpenFont, RemFont, SetFont, and SetSoftStyle, for adding, managing, and removing fonts in the system

■ The font-management functions for disk-resident fonts: AvailFonts and OpenDisk-Font, for adding and using font information on disks in the system

The functions in the first two categories appear in the Graphics Library. The AvailFonts and OpenDiskFont functions appear in the DiskFont Library and are included in this chapter because of their relation to the RAM-resident font-management functions.

Lists in the Font System

The font functions work with two lists. One is maintained in RAM and the other is maintained on disk. The first list keeps track of the RAM-resident fonts; it is called the system font list. Each call to the AddFont function adds a new font to this list. In addition, each call to the AvailFonts function adds one or more fonts to this list. Each call to the RemFont function removes a font from this list.

The list that is maintained on disk is a list of all fonts stored in separate files on disk—the disk font list. This list is updated automatically by the structure definitions that define and add new fonts to that disk. The purpose of this list is to link together all font files on a specific disk. The complete set of all fonts on a given disk is usually composed of one or more family subcategories. Using the DiskFontHeader, FontContents, and Font-ContentsHeader structures, the disk font list links together all font definition files that belong to the same family. Then, when any particular font file in a font family is loaded, all other font files in that family are also loaded. This reduces the number of disk accesses the system must make.

A family most often consists of a set of fonts having the same name but different heights. For example, the system Topaz-60 and Topaz-80 fonts belong to the same family. These two fonts have the same name; they differ only in size. The sapphire fonts are another example of a font family. Of course, other criteria besides size can be used to define a font family.

The system is capable of separating font family members from the full set of fonts on a disk by their family names. The disk operating system uses the FontContentsHeader and FontContents structures to find its way through the font directory on that disk to a disk to a specific font family and from there to a specific font.

The FontContentsHeader and FontContents structures are each contained in what is called a font-descriptive file, which always has the characters .font appended to its file name. This file contains a description of a font family; it does not contain the actual font. (The FontContentsHeader and FontContents structures are discussed under the OpenDisk-Font function.)

In addition to the font-descriptive file, each font in a font family has a unique font-definition file on the same disk. This is the file that contains the DiskFontHeader structure and the actual definition of the font. The DiskFontHeader structure contains a TextFont substructure and other information needed to define a font. This is the file that contains the bitmap definitions for each character in the disk font definition. The Disk-FontHeader structure uses a Node substructure to link all fonts in a family. The DiskFontHeader structure is also discussed under the OpenDiskFont function.

Defining and Using Fonts

To define a specific font, you must build a TextFont structure that contains all the necessary parameters to define the characteristics of a specific font and provides pointers to the actual font data for each character in that font. But first you must allocate memory for the TextFont structure and the data areas to which it points. You can use the Exec memory-allocation functions to allocate memory for the TextFont structure and its associated data blocks. (The TextFont structure and its associated data blocks must be in public memory—memory type MEMF_PUBLIC.) These functions return memory-block pointers that you can use to specify where the TextFont structure and its associated font data blocks are located. These font data blocks contain the bitmap information for each character in the font. Each font character is defined by a one-bitplane bitmap.

Once the TextFont structure and its associated data blocks are set up in RAM, the AddFont function can use the pointer to the TextFont structure to add the font to the system font list. When AddFont returns, any task can access this font by calling the OpenFont function.

For each task in which you want to use a specific font, you must issue an OpenFont call. You can specify the TextAttr structure for the OpenFont call using structure parameter assignment statements to define each of its four parameters. Alternatively, you can use the AskFont function to create a TextAttr structure based on the current font settings of a specific RastPort structure.

If the TextFont structure was constructed previously and saved on disk, however, it is a disk-resident font. In this case, the AddFont and OpenFont calls are replaced by Avail-Fonts and OpenDiskFont calls. The AvailFonts function searches the disk for all fonts and builds a set of structures in memory to count and characterize the disk fonts. It builds one AvailFonts structure for each font on disk. Each AvailFonts structure contains a TextAttr structure, which contains the font attributes for a specific disk font. When you call the OpenDiskFont function to open a disk font having a specific set of attributes, it consults the set of AvailFonts structures to see whether a font with those attributes exists on disk. If the font exists on disk, OpenDiskFont loads the specified font file for use.

Once a font is opened in a particular task, you can use the AskSoftStyle and SetSoft-Style functions to create underlined, bold, or italic versions of the font (or combinations of these) for drawing into a raster bitmap at different times in your raster bitmap drawing sequence. If the font has these characteristics in its original definition, however, you cannot use AskSoftStyle and SetSoftStyle to take these characteristics away from the font. You can use the same font or a modified version of it in any task that issues an OpenFont call. Once a task has access to a font, that task can issue text function calls to place text characters into any bitmap with which that task is currently working.

Each task can issue OpenFont (or OpenDiskFont) calls for any font that has been added to the system with the AddFont or AvailFonts function. This means that there can be a number of fonts currently open in any given task. A task can switch the font currently used in its text operations by using the SetFont function.

In addition, each task can inquire about the style characteristics of any font it has opened by using the AskSoftStyle function. Once it knows what the style characteristics are for any particular font, it can change those characteristics by calling the SetSoftStyle function. This will change the style characteristics of that font only while it is being used by that task. Moreover, the task can always change the style characteristics back to their original values before it finishes accessing that font.

When each task is finished with a font for the last time, it can issue a CloseFont call to free the memory assigned to that TextFont structure and its associated font data structures in RAM. Each task should issue a CloseFont call for all fonts previously opened by that task before the task is removed from the system with the Exec RemTask function. This will ensure that the memory resources assigned to all fonts in that task will be available to other tasks in the system.

Text-Related Structures

The two most important structures in the font system are the TextFont structure and the TextAttr structure. The TextFont structure is the main structure in the text system. It contains all of the information you need to define a font for use by any and all tasks in the system. In particular, the TextFont structure contains the size characteristics of the font and pointers to a set of bit-packed data that define all characters in the font.

The parameters in the TextFont structure are fully discussed under the AddFont function. Note that the first item in the TextFont structure is a Node substructure. This Node structure allows various TextFont structures to be linked together into the system font list maintained automatically by the system.

The TextAttr structure contains only four parameters: a pointer to the name of the font, the pixel height of the font, a one-byte definition of the intrinsic style bits of the font, and a one-byte font flags parameter. The parameters in the TextAttr structure are fully discussed under the AskFont function.

The TextFont and TextAttr structures are listed in the Text.h INCLUDE file (for C language programmers) and in the Text.i INCLUDE file (for assembly language programmers).

In addition to these two structures, the font library functions deal with five structures specifically related to disk fonts. These are the AvailFontsHeader, AvailFonts, FontContentsHeader, FontContents, and DiskFontHeader structures.

The AvailFontsHeader and AvailFonts structures define all fonts currently in the system—RAM fonts as well as disk fonts. The AvailFontsHeader structure contains only one entry, the number of disk and RAM fonts in the system at any given time. This structure is constructed in RAM when the AvailFonts function is called; it is listed in the discussion of that function.

The AvailFonts structure, also constructed in RAM when the AvailFonts function is called, consists of two items. The first indicates where the font definition came from—disk or memory. The second item is a TextAttr substructure for that font. There is one AvailFonts structure for each font in the system. See the discussion of the AvailFonts function for more information on the AvailFonts structure.

The FontContentsHeader and FontContents structures are contained in font-descriptive files on disk. These structures provide a mechanism to count the number of files on disk and to direct the disk operating system to those files. The FontContentsHeader structure contains two entries. The first entry is the file type definition, which identifies this file as a font header file. The second entry is the number of font files in the font family. The FontContentsHeader structure is defined under the OpenDiskFont function.

The FontContents structure is very similar to the TextAttr structure. In fact, the last three parameters are the same as the those of the TextAttr structure. The first parameter defines the directory path the system must follow to reach the font described in that structure. The FontContents structure is discussed under the OpenDiskFont function.

The DiskFontHeader structure is found in the disk file that actually contains a font definition. There is a corresponding font-definition file for each FontContents structure. The DiskFontHeader structure contains a Node substructure to link this font definition file into the font family and a TextFont substructure to define the details of this specific font's characteristics. The DiskFontHeader structure is discussed under the OpenDiskFont function.

AddFont

Syntax of Function Call

AddFont (textFont)
A1

Purpose of Function

This function adds a font to the system font list. When AddFont returns, the font it has added will be available to any task that wants to use it. The font will remain on the system font list until it is removed by the RemFont function.

Inputs to Function

textFont   A pointer to a TextFont structure

Discussion

The Addfont function belongs to the category of font-management functions for the RAM-resident fonts. Of this group, the AddFont, CloseFont, OpenFont, RemFont, and SetFont functions all deal with a TextFont structure specifying a particular font.

The TextFont Structure

This is the definition of the TextFont structure:

```
struct TextFont {
    struct Node TextNode;
    struct Message tf_Message;
    UWORD tf_YSize;
    UBYTE tf_Style;
    UBYTE tf_Flags;
    UWORD tf_XSize;
    UWORD tf_Baseline;
    UWORD tf_BoldSmear;
    UWORD tf_Accessors;
    UBYTE tf_LoChar;
    UBYTE tf_HiChar;
    APTR tf_CharData;
    UWORD tf_Modulo;
    APTR tf_CharLoc;
    APTR tf_CharSpace;
    APTR tf_CharKern;
};
```

These are the parameters to the TextFont structure:

- TextNode. This is a Node substructure within the TextFont structure. It allows a set of TextFont structures to be linked together in the system font list maintained by the system. Each time you add a font (with AddFont) or remove a font (with RemFont), the system updates the system font list. It is important to understand that the name of the font is contained in the Node substructure.

- tf_Message. This is a Message substructure. It is the first parameter in the Text-Font structure that allows a number of different tasks to access the same font. This Message structure is used as the reply message to a task when a specific TextFont structure and its associated font have been removed from that task.

■ tf_YSize. This parameter contains the height of the font in pixels, measured in the vertical resolution of the current raster bitmap. For example, if this parameter is 8, each character will occupy eight lines in the vertical resolution of the receiving bitmap.

■ tf_Style. The bits of this one-byte parameter specify the intrinsic font style. At present, these bits identify five possible styles: normal, underlined, bold, italic, and extended. These bits are called intrinsic style bits because they comprise the first definition of the font style; this value is never changed in the TextFont structure. Corresponding style bits in the AlgoStyle parameter of the RastPort structure can be changed by the SetSoftStyle function only in those cases where the bits are originally 0 values in the TextFont structure tf_Style parameter. (See the discussions of the AskSoftStyle and SetSoftStyle functions.)

■ tf_Flags. This parameter is composed of the preference settings. Each preference setting is indicated by a specific value for the Flag parameter. Some examples of preference settings are ROMFONT, REVPATH, and PROPORTIONAL. The ROMFONT preference setting (value = 0) should not be used unless you are burning new system ROMs yourself. The REVPATH preference setting (value = 2) is used when a font is to be rendered from right to left, that is, along a reverse path. A Hebrew font is an example of a reverse font. The PROPORTIONAL preference setting (value = 32) is used when each character has its own width and positioning in the receiving bitmap. That is, the characters of the font are not always XSize pixels wide. You can read about other Preferences settings in the INCLUDE files.

■ tf_XSize. This parameter contains the nominal character width in pixels, measured in the horizontal resolution of the receiving raster bitmap.

■ tf_Baseline. This parameter contains the number of lines from the top of a font character to its baseline. It is based on the tallest character in this font. The baseline position is the same for all characters in this font. When a character is drawn into a bitmap, the current value of the cp_y parameter in the controlling RastPort structure represents the current baseline position.

■ tf_BoldSmear. This two-byte parameter is used to produce bold characters in a font. A smear is a set of bits added to the text character to make it appear bolder.

■ tf_Accessors. This parameter contains a count of the number of tasks that have accessed this particular font; it changes as different tasks open and close this font. This is the second parameter that helps more than one task access this font once it is added to system font list. Each time a new task calls the OpenFont or OpenDiskFont function, this variable is incremented. A call to CloseFont decrements this parameter; however, it is never reduced below zero. This parameter should be initialized to zero before you link a new font into the system, but it is managed by the system once the font has been linked.

■ tf_LoChar. This parameter contains the numerical value (1 to 255) of the first character described by this TextFont structure. These values provide a method of indexing the font character array; they are distinct from the font characters themselves. Each specific font can have no more than 255 characters. If you need more characters, you must use two or more fonts and TextFont structures. Note that you do not need to use a 1 value for the first character in a font; instead, you can choose any value from 1 to 255. In addition to the font character numbers for the actual characters in your font definition, you must assign a number to an extra dummy character. This extra dummy character is used for all program references to a font character whose numerical value does not actually exist in the font definition. For example, if you design a font that has the characters A, B, and C and your program refers to any character other than A, B, or C, this dummy character will be drawn into the raster bitmap.

■ tf_HiChar. This parameter is the numerical value (1 to 255) of the last character described by this TextFont structure. See the previous discussion of the tf_LoChar parameter.

The next five parameters are the font descriptors for this font; they define how the font character data is packed into an array. Note that for all proportional fonts there must be one set of font descriptors (charData, modulo, charLoc, charSpace, and charKern) for each character in the character set.

■ tf_CharData. This is a pointer to a memory area where the character bits that define this font are located. Each character in the font has a rectangular area of memory assigned to it. Zero and one bits are placed into each memory rectangle to represent the pixel definition of the character. This memory area contains a bit-packed representation of the font. The system handles the exact packing definition.

■ tf_Modulo. This parameter contains the number of bytes per font character line. The bit data for each font are organized with the bits of the top line of the first character adjacent to the bits of the top line of the second character, and so on. This parameter tells the system where to find the bit information for the next line of a character. For example, if the bit-packed character set needs 20 words of 16 bits each to hold the top line of all characters in a set, tf_Modulo is equal to 40 bytes. The system must add 40 to the character matrix pointer to go from one line of a character definition to the next line in the same character.

■ tf_CharLoc. This is a pointer to the memory location where an array of paired values exists for each character in the font. The font data is arranged in two-word sets; the first word is the bit-offset into the bit-packed array for this character, and the second word is the width of each specific character in bits. The system uses this array to determine the pixel width of each character in the font and to locate the start of a specific character's bit definition.

■ tf_CharSpace. This is a pointer to an array of words defining the proportional spacing of this font. Each word in the array contains the width of a character rectangle. This is the edge-to-edge pixel width of this character's bit definition. This includes the spacing defined in the character rectangle. For example, although an I might be defined to be only three bits wide, its character rectangle could be seven bits wide, to allow for two bits of space on either side of the character. If this pointer is zero, the system will use the nominal width for each character as specified in the XSize parameter.

- tf_CharKern. This is a pointer to an array of words used to define the kerning data for this font. Kerning data tells the system where the bits for each font character actually begin in the character rectangle. For example, if the edge-to-edge width of the character rectangle is ten pixels and a character starts in pixel position 2 in the rectangle, the kerning word for that letter would have the value 2. If this pointer is null, there is no kerning data.

AskFont

Syntax of Function Call

```
AskFont ( rastPort, textAttr)
          A1        A0
```

Purpose of Function

This function fills the TextAttr structure with the text attribute parameters in the RastPort structure for the current font. Some of these parameters are obtained indirectly from the TextFont structure, to which the RastPort structure points.

Inputs to Function

rastPort   A pointer to a controlling RastPort structure

textAttr   A pointer to a TextAttr structure

Discussion

The AskFont function is one of the Graphics Library font-management functions for RAM-resident fonts. It looks up the font attributes of the font currently assigned to a given RastPort structure in a given task and uses that information to fill the TextAttr structure.

Each task can use a number of fonts. In addition, each task can draw text into a number of raster bitmaps. Drawing into each raster bitmap is controlled by the RastPort structure associated with that particular bitmap. Remember that each RastPort structure contains a pointer to a particular BitMap structure. In addition, each RastPort structure contains seven parameters specifically related to text drawing control in the bitmap associated with that particular RastPort structure. These are the text-drawing parameters in the Rast-Port structure:

■ Font. This parameter points to the current TextFont structure associated with this particular RastPort structure. This parameter gives any function that points to this RastPort structure access to the parameters in the TextFont structure. In particular, the intrinsic style bits parameter in the TextFont structure (the tf_Style parameter) is made available to the AskSoftStyle and SetSoftStyle functions in this way. Note that the SetFont function can change the value of the Font parameter in the RastPort structure so that you can use several different fonts to draw text into a specific raster bitmap.

■ AlgoStyle. This one-byte parameter is used in a similar way to the tf_Style parameter in the TextFont structure. This is a single byte whose individual bits contain a definition of the algorithmically generated style bits of this particular font. This parameter is changed by calls to the SetSoftStyle function. The system initializes it to zero. (See the discussion of the TextFont structure in the AddFont function for a definition of the style bits.)

■ TxFlags. This is a one-byte parameter whose bits define the current font preference bits. It is comparable to the tf_Flags parameter in the TextFont structure. Read the description of the TextFont structure under the AddFont function to see what the various flag bits mean.

■ TxHeight. This is a one-word (two-byte) parameter that defines the current height (in number of pixels) of the text font used to draw text in the bitmap associated with this RastPort structure. This parameter is related to the tf_YSize parameter in the TextFont structure.

■ TxWidth. This is a one-word (two-byte) parameter that defines the current width (in number of pixels) of the text font used to draw text in the bitmap associated with this RastPort structure. This parameter is related to the tf_XSize parameter in the TextFont structure.

■ TxBaseline. This is a one-word (two-byte) parameter that defines the current baseline position of the text font used to draw text in the bitmap associated with this RastPort structure. This parameter is related to the tf_Baseline character in the TextFont structure.

■ TxSpacing. This is a one-word (two-byte) parameter that defines the current per-character spacing (in number of pixels) of the text font used to draw text in the bitmap associated with this RastPort structure. This parameter is related to the tf_CharSpace parameter in the TextFont structure.

The TextAttr Structure

The TextAttr structure is used by the AskFont, OpenFont, and OpenDiskFont functions. This is the definition of the TextAttr structure:

```
struct TextAttr {
    STRPTR ta_Name;
    UWORD ta_YSize;
    UBYTE ta_Style;
    UBYTE ta_Flags;
};
```

Each of the parameters in the TextAttr structure can be either assigned by simple structure parameter assignment statements or obtained from the font attribute parameters (AlgoStyle, TxFlags, etc.) in the RastPort structure. The TextAttr structure serves two purposes. First, it provides a four-parameter definition of a font that a task *wants* to use. This is its meaning when used in the OpenFont or OpenDiskFont function calls. Second, it provides a four-parameter definition of fonts that are actually in the system. This is its meaning in the AvailFonts structures constructed by the AvailFonts function. At each stage of a text-drawing task, the system can compare what is wanted with what is available and take appropriate action. These are the parameters in the TextAttr structure:

- ta_Name. This is a pointer to a null-terminated text string that represents the name of the font. For example, if you want to use the system default fonts, either Topaz-60 or Topaz-80 will be used for this parameter. On the other hand, if you have designed your own font (or want to use someone else's font), the AskFont function will supply the appropriate font name here. The name parameter specified here will be compared to the font name in the Node substructure inside a specific TextFont structure.

- ta_YSize. This parameter is the height in pixels of the font. The font you specify in the name parameter should have this height.

- ta_Style. This parameter contains either the desired or the intrinsic style bits for this font, depending on where the TextAttr structure is used.

- ta_Flags. This parameter contains either the desired or the actual preference settings for this font, again depending on where the TextAttr structure is used.

AskSoftStyle

Syntax of Function Call

```
enable = AskSoftStyle (rastPort)
D0                     A1
```

Purpose of Function

This function returns a modified version of the AlgoStyle parameter in the current Rast-Port structure. The AlgoStyle parameter contains the style bits that are algorithmically generated by the activities of various tasks that have accessed and manipulated the style bits of a font up to this point in the task. AskSoftStyle returns the modified version of the algorithmically generated style bits in the enable variable. The resulting enable variable can be used as a mask for further style changes using the SetSoftStyle function. In other words, the enable variable becomes an enable mask when used as an argument in the Set-SoftStyle function.

Inputs to Function

rastPort   A pointer to a controlling RastPort structure, which contains the AlgoStyle parameter representing the algorithmically generated style bits of the current font

Discussion

The AskSoftStyle function is one of the Graphics Library font-management functions for RAM-resident fonts.

Each font in the system has a set of style bits. The original style bits assigned to a font are contained in the one-byte tf_Style parameter in the TextFont structure. These are called the intrinsic style bits. The bits in this parameter define various styles as follows:

Style	Style Byte
Normal	00000000 (value = 0)
Underlined	00000001 (value = 1)
Bold	00000010 (value = 2)
Italic	00000100 (value = 4)
Extended	00001000 (value = 8)

Because each bit in this variable indicates a specific style, you can combine font styles. For example, if the style byte has a value of 3, it indicates a bold, underlined font. (As you can see, bits 5 through 8 in the style byte allow room for additional styles, as yet undefined.)

Each font in the system has a number of intrinsic style bits and possibly a set of algorithmically generated style bits. The intrinsic style bits are the bits you set in the TextFont structure when you originally defined and initialized it. Note that a font can have all 0 style bits; in this case, it is a normal font.

The algorithmically generated style bits are defined as those bits that were changed by the ongoing font manipulations of a program task. For example, a particular task could redefine the style bits of the original normal font (all style bits are 0) to have the least significant bit set (bit 0 = 1). In this case the algorithmically generated style bits would indicate an underlined font. This would be done by changing the AlgoStyle parameter in the RastPort structure to *ask* for an underlined font. A TextAttr structure defining this situation could be defined. Then a call to OpenFont would look at the AvailFonts structures to determine whether the named font exists with underlining. If the font was designed as normal, the system will modify it to underlined for the upcoming drawing operation.

When the style bits are modified by a program task, they are called algorithmic. The style bits are usually changed by the SetSoftStyle function inside a program algorithm. SetSoftStyle gets its name from the action of the software algorithm on the setting of the style parameter.

Because style bits can change under program control, they are dynamic within a task; the intrinsic style bits in the TextFont structure returned by the OpenFont or OpenDiskFont functions are not always the only styles you can use to draw into raster bitmaps.

For this reason, style bits are contained in three different parameters in three different structures: the AlgoStyle parameter in the RastPort structure, the ta_Style parameter in the TextAttr structure, and the tf_Style parameter in the TextFont structure.

The initial definition of the style bits is contained in the TextFont structure. The TextFont structure version of the style bits is the intrinsic version. No styles that are defined as intrinsic (that is, their bits are set) can be changed; those styles will always be used in that font's character definition. However, those styles that were not defined as intrinsic (their bits are 0) can be generated algorithmically by using the SetSoftStyle function. This means that you can add boldface, underlining, or italics to a normal font, but you cannot take these characteristics away from a font that has been designed to include them. You should know, however, that generally speaking, the system does not do a good job of adding boldfacing or italics to a font that has not been designed to include them— the resulting characters may be difficult to read or unattractive when drawn. Also note that the system cannot create an extended font if this is not an intrinsic style. To be safe, therefore, it is best to use the system to create only underlining for a nonunderlined font. All other font styles should be created as intrinsic styles in the font definition.

The current definition of the algorithmically generated style bits, used for text drawing, is contained in the RastPort structure's AlgoStyle parameter. These style bits define how text is actually drawn into a particular raster bitmap at a specific time; the algorithmically generated style bits in this RastPort structure could be changed again later with the SetSoftStyle function.

A third definition of the style bits is used to search the set of AvailFonts structures for a specific font with certain characteristics. This version of the style bits is kept in the ta_Style parameter of the TextAttr structure. Each time you want to open a new font to use as the starting font definition in a specific RastPort structure, you define and initialize a TextAttr structure. This is done either by defining the parameters in the TextAttr structure directly with structure parameter assignment statements or by using an AskFont function call. If you use the AskFont function, appropriate parameters in the RastPort structure (AlgoStyle, TxFlags, etc.) will be used to define the TextAttr structure. Then you call the OpenFont or OpenDiskFont functions to search the list of available fonts for a font having the characteristics defined in the ta_Style parameter of the TextAttr structure.

The AskSoftStyle function merely reports a modified version of the current value of the algorithmically generated style bits as contained in a specific RastPort structure. AskSoftStyle gets a copy of the AlgoStyle parameter from the current definition of the RastPort structure and modifies it before placing it into the enable variable returned by the function.

For example, suppose you want to use the current font (the font pointed to in the Text-Font structure) to draw italic characters into a bitmap. The intrinsic style bits in that TextFont structure indicate that the font was originally defined as a bold, extended, underlined font. The style parameter in the TextFont structure is 00001011. Because you want to change the font to include italics, you change the AlgoStyle parameter in the RastPort structure to 00000100. Under these conditions, AskSoftSytle will return a 00000100 value in the enable variable. This value is defined to have a bit set for every bit in the AlgoStyle parameter as well as a bit set for every bit not set in the style parameter of the TextFont structure. In this case, bit 2 was the only bit that was not set in the style parameter of the TextFont structure. It was also the only bit set in the AlgoStyle parameter. The enable variable returned by AskSoftStyle tells the system that is is okay to modify the font to generate italics characters. This variable can later be used in the SetSoftStyle function to alter the set of algorithmically generated style bits further. Read the discussion of the SetSoftStyle function for more about style-bit manipulation.

AvailFonts

Syntax of Function Call

> error = AvailFonts (buffer, number_bytes, types)
> D0   A0   D0   D1

Purpose of Function

This function builds an AvailFontsHeader structure containing the number of fonts in memory and on disk. It also builds an AvailFonts structure (which contains a TextAttr structure) for each of those fonts. The AvailFonts function also adds each font it finds to the system font list.

Inputs to Function

buffer   A pointer to a memory location to be filled with the data to define the AvailFontsHeader structure and a series of Avail-Fonts structures

number_bytes   The number of bytes allocated to the buffer area

types   One or both of two values indicating whether you want to search for fonts in memory (AFF_MEMORY) or on disk (AFF_DISK)

Discussion

There are two functions that work directly with disk fonts: AvailFonts and OpenDiskFont. The AvailFonts function allows you to build an array of all disk and memory fonts into an AvailFontsHeader structure and a series of AvailFonts structures in memory. The OpenDiskFont function loads a font from disk into memory and makes it available to the task. These two functions are contained in the DiskFont Library, but are included here because they relate directly to the Graphics Library functions that operate on RAM-resident fonts.

The AvailFonts function fills a specified buffer with information to define one AvailFontsHeader structure and a series of AvailFonts structures, which contain information about all fonts available in memory and on disk. This function also places each font it finds on the system font list. Once these structures are properly constructed, the fonts that reside on disk must be loaded with calls to the OpenDiskFont function. The fonts that already reside in memory can be opened with a call to the OpenFont function.

One of the results of the AvailFonts function call is the definition of a TextAttr structure for each font in the system. Read the discussion of the AskFont function for the definition of the TextAttr structure.

The AvailFonts function returns when the above structures are placed into the memory buffer. Note that there will be duplicate entries for fonts found both in memory and on disk; these will differ only by type (AFF_DISK or AFF_MEMORY). Set the types argument to AFF_MEMORY to search memory for fonts to fill these structures; set it to AFF_DISK to search a disk for fonts to fill these structures. Both AFF_MEMORY and AFF_DISK can be specified if you want to add all disk and memory fonts to the system. The existence of an AvailFonts structure in this buffer indicates only that the font exists as an entry in a font definition somewhere in the system; the AvailFonts function does not check the underlying font definition for validity. Thus, a subsequent OpenDisk-Font function call may fail if the TextFont structure that defines the font is constructed incorrectly.

If the error variable returned by the AvailFonts function is nonzero, it indicates the number of additional bytes needed in the memory buffer to hold the structure information generated by the AvailFonts function. In this case, all of the font information was not included in the buffer because the buffer was not large enough. Therefore, if you get a nonzero error value, you should increase the buffer size by the amount indicated and call the AvailFonts function again.

The AvailFonts function searches the fonts directory path to locate all available disk font files in that directory. You can issue an AmigaDOS ASSIGN command to change the fonts directory path for which the search is made. If you don't change the search directory, the system will search the sys:fonts directory.

The AvailFonts function builds the AvailFontsHeader structure in a RAM buffer followed by a set of AvailFonts structures. All of these structures are placed in the buffer you assign in the AvailFonts function call. This buffer contains only one occurrence of the AvailFontsHeader structure, followed by one or more instances of the AvailFonts structure.

The AvailFontsHeader Structure

The AvailFontsHeader structure is very simple:

```
struct {
    UWORD afh_NumEntries;
};
```

The afh_NumEntries variable contains the number of AvailFonts structure entries in the RAM buffer, starting at zero and incrementing for each font found in RAM or on disk. Each RAM or disk font is counted once even if there are duplicate entries.

The AvailFonts Structure

The AvailFonts structure is also very simple:

```
struct AvailFonts {
    UWORD af_Type;
    struct TextAttr af_Attr;
};
```

The af_Type variable contains the type of font; this is either a font already in RAM (AFF_MEMORY) or a font still on disk (AFF_DISK).

The af_Attr variable contains a specific TextAttr substructure that describes the attributes of a specific font. The TextAttr structure consists of the font name, height, style, and flags parameters. The TextAttr structure is discussed under the AskFont function.

ClearEOL

Syntax of Function Call

```
ClearEOL (rastPort)
         A1
```

Purpose of Function

This function clears a rectangular area (defined by the height of the current text font) from the current pixel position to the right edge of the raster bitmap. The current pixel position in the raster bitmap is defined by the cp_x parameter in the RastPort structure.

Inputs to Function

rastPort   A pointer to a controlling RastPort structure

Discussion

There are four Graphic Library functions that deal with the actual placement of text in a raster bitmap: ClearEOL, ClearScreen, Text, and TextLength.

The ClearEOL function clears a rectangular area from the current pixel position to the right edge of the raster bitmap. The height of the rectangular area is taken from the height of the current text font; this is the TxHeight parameter in the controlling RastPort structure. The vertical position of the rectangular area is fixed by the current pen vertical position (the cp_y parameter) in the controlling RastPort structure. This guarantees that any text output in this newly cleared rectangular area will not exceed the vertical boundaries of this area. Clearing consists of setting the color of the rectangular area to color 0 (the color currently defined to color register 0) or, if the DrawMode variable is JAM2, to the color of BgPen.

ClearScreen

Syntax of Function Call

ClearScreen (rastPort)
                     A1

Purpose of Function

This function clears a specific area in a raster bitmap in preparation for adding text characters to the drawing definition of that bitmap. Text can then be added to the bitmap from the current pixel location to the very last pixel location in that specific bitmap.

Inputs to Function

rastPort   A pointer to a controlling RastPort structure

Discussion

The ClearScreen function belongs to the group of text-management functions in the Graphics Library. ClearScreen clears a rectangular area from the current pen position to the right edge of the raster bitmap definition by calling the ClearEOL function. Then it clears the rest of the bitmap definition from just beneath that rectangular area to the bottom of the raster bitmap definition. The current pen position in the raster bitmap is defined by the cp_x and cp_y parameters in the RastPort structure. Clearing consists of setting the color of the cleared area to color 0 (the color currently defined for color register 0) or, if the DrawMode variable is JAM2, to the color of BgPen.

CloseFont

Syntax of Function Call

CloseFont (textFont)
A1

Purpose of Function

This function closes a specific font opened by the OpenFont or OpenDiskFont function. In this way, fonts that are no longer needed will not tie up system resources, specifically memory. CloseFont prevents the task that called it from using that particular font again until another OpenFont or OpenDiskFont call is issued for that particular font.

Inputs to Function

textFont   A pointer to a TextFont structure

Discussion

The CloseFont function belongs to the category of RAM-resident font-management functions in the Graphics Library. At any given time, the system can have a fair number of coresident tasks. Each of these tasks can have several open fonts. These fonts, together with all the other information required by a task, can impose a memory squeeze on the system. To alleviate this problem, you should close your fonts using the CloseFont function as soon as possible in any task. This will free memory in the system for the memory requirements of this task as well as others.

Note that there is no specific function for closing disk-resident fonts. This is because once a disk-resident font is opened, it is RAM-resident. Therefore, you close both types of fonts with the CloseFont function.

Also note that the font remains on the system font list when CloseFont returns. If you want to remove the font from the system list, call the RemFont function.

OpenDiskFont

Syntax of Function Call

```
textFont = OpenDiskFont (   textAttr)
D0                          A0
```

Purpose of Function

This function searches the disk for the font specified in the TextAttr structure. It then loads the TextFont structure and associated font data into memory and returns a pointer to the TextFont structure. This pointer can then be used in subsequent calls to the Set-Font and CloseFont functions. The OpenDiskFont function will return a zero value if the desired font cannot be found on disk.

Inputs to Function

textAttr   A pointer to a TextAttr structure

Discussion

There are two functions that work directly with disk fonts: AvailFonts and OpenDiskFont. These two functions are contained in the DiskFont library and are included here because they relate directly to the Graphics Library functions that manage RAM-resident fonts.

The process of accessing a font is called opening the font; the OpenDiskFont function opens disk-resident fonts by loading them into memory. It is important to match all OpenDiskFont function calls with corresponding calls to the CloseFont function. This sequence results in proper management of font memory. If the font is already in memory, OpenDiskFont uses the copy in memory; it does not reload the disk copy. If the font cannot be found, the OpenDiskFont function returns a zero value.

Note that the specific font opened by the OpenDiskFont function call is determined solely by the current contents of the TextAttr structure referenced in the function call. This structure consists of four parameters—the font name, the font height, the font style, and the font flags. Read the chapter introduction and the discussion of the AskFont function to see how the TextAttr structure is defined and used.

The OpenDiskFont function searches the disk for a TextFont structure having the characteristics specified in that TextAttr structure. OpenDiskFont then loads this TextFont structure and its associated font character definition arrays into memory.

If the OpenDiskFont function call is successful, it returns a pointer to the specific TextFont structure. This pointer can then be used in SetFont, CloseFont, and RemFont functions in the specific task that issued the OpenDiskFont function call. If the OpenDiskFont function call is unsuccessful, it returns a null value.

Each task that wants to use a specific font must issue an OpenDiskFont or OpenFont function call. In this way, a font can be assigned to a number of tasks simultaneously. When each of these tasks becomes active, it can access the font to draw text characters into any number of the raster bitmaps it controls.

Each disk font file is constructed as a loadable, executable file module. For this reason, AmigaDOS can load and allocate memory for the font just as if it were a program module. AmigaDOS can also deallocate the memory for the disk font when it is removed from the system. This means that you do not have to allocate and deallocate memory for disk fonts.

To gain access to a disk font file, follow these steps:

1. Open the DiskFont Library with an OpenLibrary function call as explained in the book introduction.

2. Place a call to the AvailFonts function to determine all fonts on the disk and in RAM. The AvailFonts function builds the AvailFontsHeader and AvailFonts structures in RAM. For every font in RAM and on disk, there is an AvailFonts structure (which contains a TextAttr structure). (See the discussion of the Avail-Fonts function.)

3. Open the disk font with the OpenDiskFont function, referencing a specific TextAttr structure as its argument. You can define the TextAttr structure by a set of program structure parameter assignment statements or by using the AskFont function. The TextAttr structure must define a specific font in a family of fonts. Of course,

you can always design font families with only one font. When you use the Avail-Fonts function to build the AvailFonts structures, the AskFont function will try to find the appropriate TextAttr structure in one of the AvailFonts structures.

Each font in the system belongs to a font family. For example, Topaz-60 and Topaz-80 both belong to the system default Topaz font family. Another example is the sapphire family of fonts; each font in this family has a different height. Font families allow related fonts on disk to be grouped.

A font directory usually contains two names for each font family. A typical pair of entries for a font family called sapphire is

sapphire.font
sapphire(dir)

The Sapphire.font file contains a description of the contents of a particular font family in a FontContentsHeader structure and a set of FontContents structures. Each FontContents Header structure defines how many FontContents structures are needed to define all disk fonts in a disk-font family.

The TextFont structures and other information required to define each font for all fonts in a particular family are contained in the files defined by the sapphire directory. The Font-Contents structures tell the system how to reach and load each of these font files.

The FontContentsHeader Structure

The definition of the FontContentsHeader structure is

```
struct FontContentsHeader {
    UWORD fch_FileID;
    UWORD fch_NumEntries;
};
```

The fch_FileID variable contains a numerical file identifier to indicate that the file that contains the FontContentsHeader structure is a font-related file. At this time, its value is always hexadecimal F00. This number tells the system to treat this file as a font file.

The fch_NumEntries variable contains the number of fonts in the font family. Each font will have its own FontContents structure, its own disk font file, and its own Text-Font structure.

The FontContents Structure

This is the definition of the FontContents structure:

```
struct FontContents {
    char fc_FileName[MAXFONTPATH];
    UWORD fc_YSize;
    UBYTE fc_Style;
    UBYTE fc_Flags;
};
```

The meaning of the parameters in the FontContents structure is as follows:

■ The fc_FileName[MAXFONTPATH] parameter contains the directory path name that AmigaDOS must follow to find the file that contains the DiskFontHeader and TextFont structures for this font. Once AmigaDOS reaches the path named in the fonts directory, it finds the specific font file name by the path name contained in this parameter. For example, this parameter could be FONTS:sapphire/14. This tells the system to look for a subdirectory named sapphire in the FONTS directory and to find the file named 14 in that subdirectory. The MAXFONTPATH argument allows the specific path name to be as large as 256 characters. In this way, you can specify a very long directory-subdirectory path name, involving a number of subdirectories, to reach the specific font file.

■ The fc_YSize variable contains the height of the font in pixels. This parameter also appears in the TextAttr structure.

■ The fc_Style variable contains the style of the font. This parameter also appears in the TextAttr structure.

■ The fc_Flags variable is the flags parameter of the font. This parameter also appears in the TextAttr structure.

The DiskFontHeader Structure

Each font file loaded from disk has an associated DiskFontHeader structure, which allows all members of the same disk font family to be linked together into the family definition. The definition of the DiskFontHeader structure is as follows:

```
struct DiskFontHeader {
    struct Node dfh_DF;
    UWORD dfh_FileID;
    UWORD dfh_Revision;
    LONG dfh_Segment;
    char dfh_Name[MAXFONTNAME];
    struct TextFont dfh_TF;
};
```

The meaning of the parameters in the DiskFontHeader structure is as follows:

■ The dfh_DF parameter contains the name of a Node structure used to link all disk fonts in a disk font family.

■ The dfh_FileID parameter contains the name of the file containing the TextFont structure for this particular font in the disk font family.

■ The dfh_Revision parameter identifies the font revision for this particular font.

■ The dfh_Segment parameter contains the segment address of the font when it is loaded. All font-definition files are loaded as executable files. This is just a system convention for loading; the system never tries to execute a font file.

- The dfh_Name[MAXFONTNAME] parameter contains a null-terminated text string that represents the font name. Every font name has the characters .font appended to it. For example, sapphire/14.font is a valid font name. The MAX-FONTNAME argument contains the number of characters in the font name. MAXFONTNAME can range from 1 to 32. Five of these characters are devoted to the .font characters.

- The dfh_TF parameter contains the name of the TextFont structure that defines this particular font.

OpenFont

Syntax of Function Call

```
textFont = OpenFont ( textAttr)
D0                    A0
```

Purpose of Function

This function searches the system font list for a TextFont structure that best matches the attributes specified in the TextAttr structure. It returns a pointer to the closest matching TextFont structure. If the named font is found but the requested size and style specified in the TextAttr structure are unavailable, a pointer to the TextFont structure with the nearest attributes is returned. The OpenFont function will return a zero value if the desired font (or a similar font) cannot be found.

Inputs to Function

textAttr   A pointer to a TextAttr structure

Discussion

The OpenFont function belongs to the group of functions that manage RAM-resident fonts in the Graphics Library.

The system can contain a number of fonts at one time. Some of these fonts could have come from disk; others could already be in RAM. The process of accessing a font is called opening the font. The system has two functions that open fonts: the OpenFont function, which opens RAM-resident fonts, and the OpenDiskFont function, which opens disk-resident fonts.

Note that the specific font opened by the OpenFont (or OpenDiskFont) function is determined solely by the current contents of a TextAttr structure. Read the introduction to this chapter and the discussion of the AskFont function to see how the TextAttr structure is defined and used.

The OpenFont and OpenDiskFont functions use the font characteristics specified in the TextAttr structure to search the system (RAM or disk) for a particular TextFont structure having those characteristics. If a font that matches the TextAttr structure parameters exactly cannot be found, OpenFont will look for a closely matching font. That is, if the named font is found but the size and style specified in the TextAttr structure are not available, a pointer to the TextFont structure with the most similar font attributes is returned. If the OpenFont call is successful, the font can be used by the specific task that issued the call.

Each task that wants to use a specific font must issue an OpenFont (or OpenDisk-Font) function call. In this way, a font can be assigned to a number of tasks simultaneously. When each of these tasks becomes active, it can access the font to draw text characters into any of the raster bitmaps it controls. A task can also have a number of fonts currently open to use in drawing text characters into any of several raster bitmaps at any particular time.

The TextFont structure pointer returned by the OpenFont function call can be used in subsequent SetFont and CloseFont calls. It is important to match each call to the OpenFont function with a corresponding call to the CloseFont function. This ensures that system resources are freed as soon as possible once a task finishes with a particular font.

RemFont

Syntax of Function Call

```
error = RemFont (textFont)
D0                A1
```

Purpose of Function

This function removes a font from the system font list.

Inputs to Function

textFont   A pointer to a TextFont structure

Discussion

RemFont belongs to the RAM-resident font-management functions in the Graphics Library.

When your task has finished with a particular font for the last time, you should call the CloseFont function to free the memory resources assigned to that font. This is as far as you should go if you will need that font for other tasks in the system.

On the other hand, if all tasks are finished with the font, you should call the RemFont function to remove it from the system font list. However, it is important to note that although the RemFont function prevents additional tasks from opening that specific font, any tasks that currently have the font open can continue to use it. These tasks will have a current pointer to the TextFont Structure, which will still be in RAM, together with other required font data. When these tasks issue their CloseFont calls, they too will be unable to open that specific font until it is once again added to the system font list with the AddFont or AvailFonts functions.

SetFont

Syntax of Function Call

error = SetFont (rastPort, textFont)
D0   A1   A0

Purpose of Function

This function resets the text font parameters currently defined in a RastPort structure to those in the specified TextFont structure. It also changes the TextFont structure pointer in the RastPort structure to the value specified as the second argument of the function call. If the textFont argument is 0, the RastPort structure will be left with zero values in the font-related parameters.

Inputs to Function

rastPort	A pointer to a controlling RastPort structure
textFont	A pointer to a TextFont structure

Discussion

The SetFont function is one of eight functions in the Graphics Library that work directly with RAM-resident fonts.

Your program can deal with a number of raster bitmaps at the same time. Each of these bitmaps has an associated RastPort structure that controls the drawing of graphics and text into that bitmap. By changing the pointer to the TextFont structure in the Rast-Port structure with the SetFont function, you can place characters from several text fonts into each raster bitmap—using as many fonts as memory restrictions allow.

SetFont takes a set of font attributes in a TextFont structure and places them into a specific RastPort structure. Read the discussion of the AskFont function to see which RastPort parameters are affected. From that point forward in the drawing process (or until another change is made), all text drawn into that raster bitmap will be added in the font defined by that TextFont structure.

Note that the font must have been opened previously with the OpenFont (or Open-DiskFont) function before you call the SetFont function.

SetSoftStyle

Syntax of Function Call

```
newStyle = SetSoftStyle (rastPort,style, enable)
D0                       A1        D0    D1
```

Purpose of Function

This function alters the style bits contained in the AlgoStyle parameter of the RastPort structure. The enable argument acts as a bit-change mask variable; only those style bits that are set in the enable argument can be affected. The SetSoftStyle function returns the new style in the newStyle variable.

Inputs to Function

rastPort	A pointer to a controlling RastPort structure
style	A one-byte variable whose bits represent the new font style bits that are desired
enable	A mask variable that indicates the particular style bits that can be changed; this is the variable returned by a previous call to the AskSoftStyle function.

Discussion

The SetSoftStyle function belongs to the group of functions in the Graphics Library that manage RAM-resident fonts. Read the discussion of the AskSoftStyle function for more information on changing a font style.

Note that requests for style changes will not be honored if the intrinsic style bits in the TextFont structure preclude changing them. For example, you cannot make a font normal if the UNDERLINED bit (bit 0) was set in the original TextFont structure. The newStyle variable is the amalgam of two things: the soft style selection as represented by the style argument and the intrinsic style bits in the TextFont structure. The system knows about the intrinsic style bits through the enable argument, which is generated previously by the AskSoftStyle function.

Each font in the system has a set of style bits. These are explained in the discussion of AskSoftStyle. The purpose of the SetSoftStyle function is to change the value of the algorithmically generated style bits in a specific RastPort structure associated with a specific task. Recall from the AskSoftStyle function discussion that the current algorithmically generated style bits for a specific font are contained in the RastPort structure AlgoStyle parameter. The AskSoftStyle function gets a current copy of this parameter and returns a modified version of it in the enable variable.

The SetSoftStyle function can change the AlgoStyle parameter in the RastPort structure. However, there are certain restrictions. Only the bits set in the enable variable as returned by the AskSoftStyle function can be changed. For example, suppose a TextFont structure contains a bold, underlined, italic, extended font. In this case, AskSoftStyle would always return 00000000 value in the enable variable, regardless of the value of the AlgoStyle parameter of the RastPort structure. Under these conditions, SetSoftStyle cannot change any of the AlgoStyle parameter bits.

On the other hand, suppose a TextFont structure contains a normal font. In this case, AskSoftStyle could return nonzero values in the enable variable. The particular value returned would depend on the current value of the AlgoStyle parameter in the RastPort structure when the AskSoftStyle call was made. In particular, if AskSoftStyle returns a value of 3 (00000011) indicating that it is okay to modify this normal font with underlining and boldface, SetSoftStyle can change the AlgoStyle parameter to 3 (00000011), 2 (00000010), or 1 (00000001), giving a bold underlined font, an underlined font, or a bold font, respectively.

Only the 0 bits in the tf_Style parameter of the original TextFont structure can be altered. For example, if the original font was normal (tf_Style = 00000000), SetSoftStyle could change any of the style bits. If the original font was underlined, extended, italic, and bold (tf_Style = 00001111), SetSoftStyle could not alter any of the bits in the Algo-Style parameter of the RastPort structure. Both of these restrictions are handled by the enable mask argument in the SetSoftStyle function call.

Text

Syntax of Function Call

```
error = Text (rastPort, stringPointer,count)
D0            A1        A0            D0: 0–15
```

Purpose of Function

This function writes text characters into the specified raster bitmap starting at the current pixel position.

Inputs to Function

rastPort	A pointer to a controlling RastPort structure
stringPointer	A pointer to a string of characters to draw into a raster bit-map
count	The number of characters in the string; if this is 0, there are no characters to be output

Discussion

There are four Graphics Library functions that deal with the actual placement of text in a raster bitmap: ClearEOL, ClearScreen, Text, and TextLength. Each of your tasks can add text characters to each of one or more raster bitmaps. Each of these bitmaps has an associated RastPort structure that is used to control the drawing of the text additions to that raster bitmap. The RastPort structure's drawing-control parameters are usually used to define and control the graphics added to a raster bitmap definition. However, some of these parameters are also used to control text drawing.

Text Drawing Modes

One of the RastPort structure parameters that controls text drawing is DrawMode. If the DrawMode parameter is set to JAM1, text will be drawn in the color of the foreground pen, indicated by the value of the FgPen parameter in the RastPort structure. Whenever there is a 1 bit in the text-character pixel pattern, the FgPen color will overwrite the raster bitmap data present at that pixel location.

If the DrawMode parameter is set to JAM2, the color of the FgPen will be used as the color of the text character pixels and the color of the BgPen will be used as the background color for the pixels surrounding the text character. Each text character has a surrounding rectangle of pixels. The pixels that define this rectangle completely overwrite the pixels in the same location in the destination raster bitmap.

If the DrawMode parameter is set to COMPLEMENT, text characters are drawn in one of the following ways:

1. If a text character pixel contains a 1 bit and the destination raster bitmap has a 0 bit in a bitplane at the same pixel location, the destination bit is changed to a 1 at that location.

2. If a text character pixel contains a 1 bit and the destination raster bitmap also has a 1 bit in a bitplane at the same pixel location, the destination bit is changed to 0 at that location.

3. If a text character pixel contains a 0 bit and the destination bitmap has either a 0 or a 1 bit in a bitplane at the same pixel location, the destination bit is not changed.

In addition, if the INVERSVID flag in the RastPort structure is set, all bits in the text-character pixel definition will be reversed (0 bits to 1 bits and vice versa) before the text character is drawn into the raster bitmap. If the drawing mode at that time is JAM2, the text character colors will be reversed.

Only text on the current line is output by the Text function. For this reason, you must plan your Text function calls carefully. If the characters in the specified string run past the raster bitmap boundary, the text pixels are clipped at that boundary. In this case, the current pen position parameters (cp_x and cp_y) in the RastPort structure are set at the bitmap boundary. If this happens, the pen position parameters in the RastPort structure do not represent the drawing pen position that would result if all text characters were added to the raster bitmap.

The Text Function and Algorithmically Generated Characters

The Text function must be able to deal with two types of characters: characters that come directly from the font definition without modification (the intrinsic font characters) and characters that are generated algorithmically. For example, if the original font is a normal font and you want underlined characters, you have to generate them using the SetSoftStyle function.

On the other hand, if you want underlined characters and the original font definition is for underlined characters, you can use the font definition characters directly without modification. In this case, the internal character size and spacing data in the TextFont structure is the same for all characters you output with the Text function. Therefore, the spacing of individual characters output by the Text function is always correct.

However, algorithmically generated text characters present a potential problem. This is because the Text function always calculates character positioning and width based on the nominal width and intercharacter spacing as defined by the tf_XSize and tf_Char-Space parameters, respectively, in the TextFont structure.

After it draws each character, the Text function automatically positions the drawing pen at the pixel location that it thinks is right for the next character using these two parameters. This procedure may cause adjacent algorithmically generated characters to overlap when drawn individually. For example, algorithmically generated italic characters could lean over into the next character rectangle. You can solve this problem by taking the following steps:

1. To increase the intercharacter spacing used for the text drawing operation, set the Tx_Spacing parameter in the RastPort structure to the number of pixels you want between text characters. You may have to do some experimentation to get things right.

2. Build your output characters into a text string before you call the Text function. You can do this using the C language string-handling functions.

3. Call the Text function to draw the correct style with correct intercharacter spacing.

TextLength

Syntax of Function Call

```
numPixels = TextLength (rastPort, stringPointer,  numchars)
D0                      A1        A0             D0: 0–15
```

Purpose of Function

This function determines the length in pixels of text data to be output to a specific raster bitmap. The length is based on the font attributes in the RastPort structure used to define the font text characters. TextLength returns the pixel length of the character string in the numPixels variable.

Inputs to Function

rastPort	A pointer to a controlling RastPort structure
stringPointer	A pointer to the text string whose pixel length is to be determined
numchars	The number of characters in the text string; a value of zero means that there are no characters in the string

Discussion

There are four Graphics Library functions that deal with the actual placement of text in a raster bitmap: ClearEOL, ClearScreen, Text, and TextLength. The value returned by the TextLength function is the number of x-direction pixels the specified text will occupy, including any negative kerning (see tf_CharKern under AddFont) that may take place at the beginning of the text string. To determine what the current pixel position will be after a Text function call using this string, add the numPixels variable to the current value of the cp_x parameter in the RastPort structure before you call the Text function. In this way, you can determine whether a particular text string can be drawn into a particular raster bitmap without being clipped at the right edge of the bitmap. Once you verify that this is true, you can call the Text function to draw the text string into the bitmap. (Note that the cp_y variable in the RastPort structure is unchanged by the addition of these text characters to the bitmap.)

Read the introduction to this chapter to see how the RastPort structure parameters affect the width and spacing of characters added to a raster bitmap.

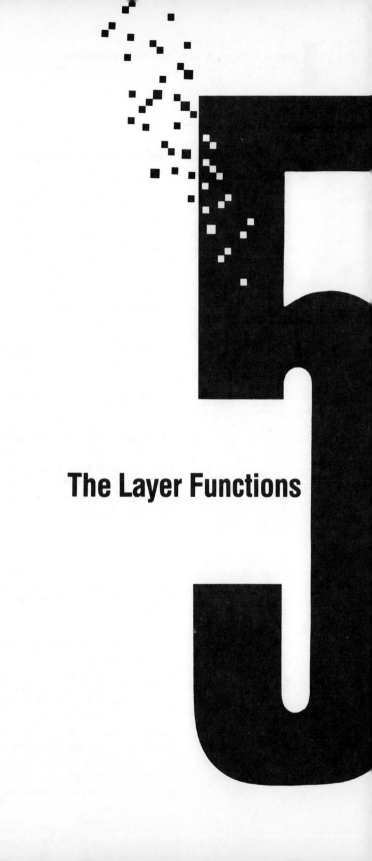

The Layer Functions

Introduction

This chapter defines and discusses the Layers Library functions. These functions are used to create and manipulate layers on the display screen of the Amiga, producing many interesting effects. In fact, the Amiga's layering capability makes its graphic behavior unique among microcomputers. The best example of this is the behavior of the windows and screens in the Intuition system. All Intuition windows and screens are managed with the Layers Library functions.

To understand the operation of layers and the associated Layers Library functions, you must first understand a number of concepts that characterize the operation of the Amiga display screen and its multilayering capability. The first of these is that the display screen itself is not multilayered. *Multiple layers do not actually exist on-screen;* instead, layers exist in memory.

This brings up the question of what does exist on the display screen. The simple answer is that the display screen is a quilt of pixel-information rectangles. Each of these rectangles can come from a different layer in memory. Each layer in memory can have a different bitmap associated with it, or different layers can use the same bitmap. If you look at the display screen at any given time, you will be seeing an amalgam of rectangles that can come from many different layer bitmaps in memory.

To make these ideas more understandable, consider how the Intuition screen/window system works. The Intuition example and the facts and conclusions you can draw from it are worth stating here, because you can achieve the same types of display effects in your own programs. Studying the Intuition example will help you understand the operating principles of the Layers Library functions as implemented in the Intuition software system. For purposes of simplification, the example is based on these assumptions: only Intuition custom screens are considered, and only one drawing task is controlling the Intuition display screen.

Each Intuition display consists of a number of screens. Each of these screens can be depth-arranged with respect to each other using Intuition screen functions, specifically the ScreenToFront and ScreenToBack functions. It is important to understand that when your program calls these two functions, the system actually calls the underlying Layers Library functions to move these screen layers around. Intuition screens are therefore very similar to layers.

Each Intuition screen can contain a number of windows. Intuition windows are also very similar to layers. Each of these windows can be depth-arranged with respect to each other within that screen, using Intuition window functions (specifically, the WindowTo-Front and WindowToBack functions). Once again, it is important to understand that when your program calls these two functions, the system actually calls the underlying Layers Library functions to move these windows around in their screen layers. Each window in each screen can be moved and resized, causing some windows to overlap other windows already on the screen. When two windows overlap, the window belonging to the lower layer will be partly obscured from view.

At any given time, then, the Intuition screen displays a complex set of graphics information coming from many different in-memory layers. Your program could zero in on any particular pixel and find out how that pixel got there and where it came from. Each display screen pixel is produced by using a specific layer bitmap to fix the color at that pixel location; that is, at any given time, each pixel is associated with one and only one layer bitmap.

If the screen display were static and unchanging, you could find the specific layer responsible for producing each display screen pixel. To get a better idea of how the layers work, it is useful to map each part of the display screen to its associated layer bitmap conceptually. The first step is to map out a current pixel-layer assignment. Then you could combine this map with the known memory position of each layer bitmap. Then you would be down to the raw bitplane information; you would know where every pixel on the screen came from in memory. You would find that the pixels on the screen came from a number of layer bitmaps in memory. You would then know everything about the current screen's definition. In fact, this mapping procedure can be accomplished with the WhichLayer function.

Assume that you change the screen by moving a window to a new location. When you do this, you expose new areas of other windows on the screen. If you now developed a pixel-layer map for the whole screen, you would find that the map changed for those parts of the screen where the visible screen changed. The moving window either covered up or exposed something. Because this window, like all windows, is rectangular, it is easy to see that each of the areas where a change occurred is also rectangular.

As you study the Layers Library functions, keep this overall picture in mind, because it will help you understand how the Layers Library functions work. Ask yourself where the pixel information for each screen location is coming from and what happens to that information when the screen is changed. The answers to these questions are contained in the remainder of the chapter introduction and the discussion of the individual functions.

Layers and Multitasking

There is another important aspect of layer behavior you should be aware of. This has to do with multiple tasks drawing into the same layer. The Layers Library provides a number of functions to deal with this feature of the Amiga multitasking system. When your program is designed so that more than one task can draw into a single layer bitmap, any given task may at any given time want to prevent other tasks from drawing into that layer. This is the purpose of the intertask management functions in the Layers Library. They allow a specific task to lock out other tasks from any drawing operations on a specific layer bitmap.

This layer locking is necessary because the exact execution path followed by a specific task is not always the same; sometimes a task will be lead into a drawing sequence when it gains control of the machine, and sometimes it will not. Therefore, the system needs a mechanism outside of that task to prevent it from drawing into a specific layer bitmap when it gains control of the machine.

Any time a task gains control of the machine from a task that has locked a specific layer bitmap and that second task tries to execute a set of drawing statements for that locked layer, the system puts the second task to sleep. Only when the locking task regains control and unlocks the locked layer can other tasks produce drawing changes in that layer bitmap.

This locked state of affairs, where only the locking task can make changes in the layer bitmap, continues until the locking task issues an unlock call using one of the Layers Library unlocking functions. These ideas will become clearer when you study the LockLayer, LockLayers, LockLayerInfo, UnlockLayer, UnlockLayers, and UnLockLayerInfo functions.

Layer Types

The Layers Library works with four types of layers: backdrop layers, simple-refresh layers, smart-refresh layers, and superbitmap layers. A backdrop layer can be combined with each of the other three layer types; that is, you can define a backdrop layer that is a simple-refresh layer, a smart-refresh layer, or a superbitmap layer. The simple-refresh, smart-refresh, and superbitmap layer types are, on the other hand, mutually exclusive; any specific layer can be only one of these three types.

If you study the definition and operation of each of these layer types, you will begin to understand how layer bitmaps are managed to produce the changing quilt of the Amiga display screen. Following is a discussion of the characteristics of each of these types of layers.

Simple-Refresh Layers

The simple-refresh layer is the only layer type that does not use an off-screen bitmap to aid in the screen refreshing process for that layer. Instead, when an obscured area of the display screen belonging to a simple-refresh layer is once again exposed, the task that is currently controlling this layer must redraw the obscured portions of the screen.

This means that the task must execute the Graphics Library drawing functions to reproduce the obscured areas. If the task drawing procedures draw into large sections of the layer bitmap, including areas outside the previously obscured areas, the Layers Library BeginUpdate function automatically clips the drawing to the rectangular boundaries of the obscured areas. This procedure avoids drawing into the already visible portions of the simple-refresh layer. The bookkeeping for the clipping process is handled by the system software once it is told that this is a simple-refresh layer.

Smart-Refresh Layers

The smart-refresh layer provides one or more off-screen backup bitmaps that hold the pixel information for the obscured areas of a layer. This usually involves a set of small bitmaps scattered throughout the available memory space. These backup bitmaps contain the pixel information for a number of obscured rectangular areas of the smart-refresh layer.

As the user or your program changes the display screen, different parts of different layers are obscured and exposed. For each newly exposed area, a small off-screen bitmap is swapped automatically into the layer display memory to produce that new part of the display. Then, as you or the user manipulates the display screen again, the bitmap information for any more newly obscured rectangles is placed into off-screen bitmap areas, one for each small rectangle that is obscured.

Note that whenever these off-screen bitmaps are not being used, you can arrange for your graphics tasks to use the Graphics Library drawing functions to draw into them. This changes their pixel information. When these redrawn bitmaps are swapped back into the layer display memory to refresh a newly exposed area, you have a different image on the screen. In essence, this process simulates a double-buffering mode of screen display, but it works only with the small rectangles representing the obscured areas of the display screen.

Superbitmap Layers

The superbitmap layer has a single, large, off-screen bitmap associated with it. In contrast, the smart-refresh layer uses one or more small off-screen bitmaps. One advantage of a superbitmap layer is that it can be scrolled; you cannot scroll either a simple-refresh layer or a smart-refresh layer.

This off-screen superbitmap can be as large as or larger than the on-screen layer bitmap for the same layer. At any given time, the off-screen superbitmap can contain some or all of the same bitmap information as the on-screen layer bitmap. In fact, the superbitmap usually will contain an exact duplicate of all of the layer bitmap bits plus additional bits. These additional bits define pixels not currently in the layer bitmap; that is, at all times, the pixels in the superbitmap are a superset of the pixels in the layer bitmap. The layer bitmap acts as a window inside the superbitmap.

Therefore, at any given time, the superbitmap contains two categories of pixel information. The first category is the pixel information corresponding to the on-screen layer bitmap. This subset of information will be an exact copy of the current layer bitmap information if no task has redrawn this part of the superbitmap since it was last copied from the layer bitmap.

The current x,y position of the layer bitmap origin inside the superbitmap is determined by which part of the superbitmap is currently displayed in the layer bitmap, which is determined by the ScrollLayer and SizeLayer functions.

The second category of superbitmap information is the bitmap data for pixels that are not currently in the on-screen layer bitmap definition. In some cases, these are the parts of the superbitmap that have been scrolled off the layer bitmap by the operation of the ScrollLayer function. The size of this second category of superbitmap pixels varies with the parameters of the SizeLayer function. At other times, these parts are just the extra parts of the superbitmap that have not as yet been displayed.

It is important to understand that the superbitmap exists completely independently of the layer bitmap itself. For this reason, you can arrange for your tasks to draw into all areas of the superbitmap bitplanes at any given time. In this sense, a superbitmap layer is a true double-buffering mode of screen display, where the second off-screen display buffer is larger than the first on-screen display buffer.

Backdrop Layers

A backdrop layer always appears behind all other layers that you create. Note that the current implementation of backdrop layers prevents them from being resized, moved, or depth-arranged in any way. Also, remember that you can combine the backdrop layer type with the other three types to create a simple-refresh backdrop layer, a smart-refresh backdrop layer, or a superbitmap backdrop layer. Finally, note that you can change the backdrop layer flag in the Layer structure to create and delete a backdrop layer. If you do this, you will be able to resize, move, and depth-arrange backdrop layers by manipulating the Flags parameter.

Layers Library Structures

The Layers Library works with three structure types in particular: the Layer structure, the LayerInfo structure, and the ClipRect structure. It also works with one or more controlling RastPort structures.

The Layer Structure

The Layer structure is used to define the characteristics of layers in the system. Fundamentally, it contains information to define the position of a layer in the current layer stacking order. It also contains information to allow the system to define and control the clipping-rectangles associated with that layer and to allow the system to lock and unlock that layer when multiple tasks draw into its bitmap. The Layer structure contains several key parameters that you should be aware of. The first of these is a set of two (front and back) Layer structure pointers, which allows each particular Layer structure to be placed into a linked list of related Layer structures.

Also note that the Layer structure contains a pointer to the controlling RastPort structure and an optional pointer to a SuperBitMap structure, which defines the characteristics of a superbitmap layer. The fourth parameter of interest is the Flags parameter, which takes one of four values that define the layer type.

The definition of the Layer structure is listed in the discussion of the CreateBehindLayer function and in the INCLUDE files, called Clip.h for C language programmers and Clip.i for assembly language programmers.

The LayerInfo Structure

The purpose of the LayerInfo structure is to provide a mechanism to control drawing operations on a related group of layers. Specifically, the LayerInfo structure provides the mechanism for individual tasks to lock and unlock a specific Layer structure from drawing changes by other tasks in the system. For this reason, the LayerInfo structure has both a LockPort and a ReplyPort pointer parameter. By using these and other parameters, the LayerInfo structure keeps track of the number of tasks that have locked a specific layer.

The definition of the LayerInfo structure is listed in the discussion of the NewLayerInfo function and in the INCLUDE files, called Layers.h for C language programmers and Layers.i for assembly language programmers. Note that in versions 1.1 and 1.2, the structure name has been changed from LayerInfo to Layer_Info.

The ClipRect Structure

The purpose of the ClipRect structure is to maintain a list of clipping-rectangles associated with layers. These clipping-rectangles define the portions of a layer that require drawing updates when additional portions of those layers are newly exposed on the display screen. The most important parameters in the ClipRect structure are the Layer structure pointer, the clipping-rectangle boundary points, and the two ClipRect structure pointers. These last two parameters point to the next and previous ClipRect structures linked into a clipping-rectangle list maintained by this ClipRect structure.

The definition of the ClipRect structure is listed in the discussion of the UpfrontLayer function and in the INCLUDE files, called Clip.h for C language programmers and Clip.i for assembly language programmers.

The RastPort Structure

Finally, it is important to remember that the layer-creation functions (CreateUpfrontLayer and CreateBehindLayer) always assign a controlling RastPort structure to a newly created layer. You can get a pointer to this RastPort structure using a simple program statement, then place that RastPort structure pointer into a temporary variable. You can then use a set of these temporary variables to point to a set of RastPort structures when you want to specify parameters in the RastPort structure in preparation for a drawing sequence in that layer. See Chapter 2 for more information about the RastPort structure.

Creating and Manipulating Layers

Figure 5.1 shows two bitmaps. The first bitmap has four layers; the second has three. Notice that the height and width of these two bitmaps are different, which illustrates that this can be the case.

In the first bitmap, the layers are placed in the bitmap in the following order:

1. Layer 1 is added using the CreateUpFrontLayer function.

2. Layer 2 is added using the CreateBehindLayer function.

3. Layer 3 is added using the CreateUpFrontLayer function.

4. Layer 4 is added using the CreateBehindLayer function.

This creates one bitmap with four layers depth-arranged as illustrated in Figure 5.1, where unseen boundaries of layers are shown by dashed lines.

Note that this order of layer creation also produces a number of clipping-rectangles: clipping-rectangle 1 is created when Layer 2 is placed behind Layer 1; clipping-rectangle 2 is created when Layer 3 is placed in front of Layer 1; clipping-rectangles 3 and 4 are created when Layer 4 is placed behind Layers 2 and 3.

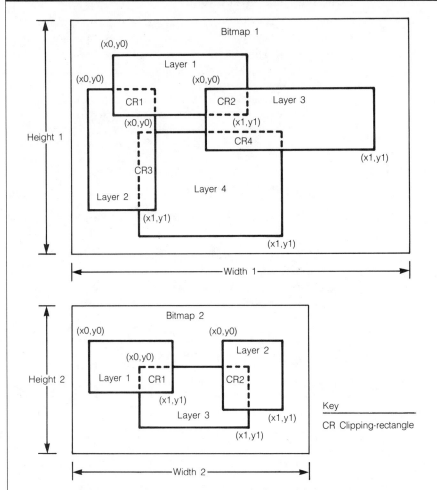

Figure 5.1:
Bitmaps,
Layers, and
Clipping-
Rectangles:
Layer Creation

In the second bitmap, the layers are placed in the bitmap in the following order:

1. Layer 1 is added using the CreateUpFrontLayer function.

2. Layer 2 is added using the CreateUpFrontLayer function.

3. Layer 3 is added using the CreateBehindLayer function.

Once again, the order of placing layers creates a specific set of clipping-rectangles. Both clipping-rectangles 1 and 2 are created when Layer 3 is placed behind Layers 1 and 2.

Once these layer definitions are complete, you can use the Graphics Library drawing functions to add drawing information to the layers; you can also use the Layers

Library functions to change their depth-arrangement and resize them. If the layers are declared as superbitmap layers, you can also scroll them.

It is important to understand that the number, location, size, and other characteristics of the clipping-rectangles will change as you manipulate these layers with the Layers Library functions. However, the Layers Library automatically keeps track of these changes. Then when you change these layers again, the Layers Library system routines will automatically restore the display correctly.

BeginUpdate

Syntax of Function Call

BeginUpdate (layer)
A0

Purpose of Function

This function readies the system to repair a damaged simple-refresh layer. It first exchanges the DamageList structure pointer with the ClipRect structure pointer in the Layer structure. Then it swaps the damage-list for the clipping-rectangle list so that the graphics task can redraw the damaged portions of a simple-refresh layer.

Inputs to Function

layer A pointer to a Layer structure that represents a simple-refresh layer

Discussion

The BeginUpdate and EndUpdate functions allow you to control the drawing update of simple-refresh layers. Read the EndUpdate function discussion to learn more about these two functions.

You use the BeginUpdate function when you want to make pixel definition changes in the obscured portions of a simple-refresh layer. These changes can consist of any type of drawing effect achieved using any of the Graphics Library drawing functions.

The BeginUpdate function is used only for simple-refresh layers, which are the only layers that do not have an off-screen bitmap that stores the obscured portions of their on-screen bitmaps. As a result, when one of these layers is obscured by moving, resizing, scrolling, or placing another layer partly or wholly in front of it, the drawing information in the obscured areas is lost. In contrast, obscured areas of a superbitmap or smart-refresh layer are saved in an off-screen buffer or buffers.

If one of your tasks wants to draw into a simple-refresh layer while it is partly or wholly obscured, the obscured part will receive no drawing information, because there is no off-screen buffer to receive new pixel definitions. This is when the BeginUpdate function is used.

Before you can redraw the obscured portions of a simple-refresh layer during a drawing update of that layer, you need to identify those portions. This is the job of the damage-list. A damage-list is simply a clipping-rectangle list that keeps track of the obscured (damaged) portions of a simple-refresh layer.

The general procedure for redrawing only the obscured portions of a damaged simple-refresh layer using the BeginUpdate function is as follows:

1. Call the BeginUpdate function. BeginUpdate automatically saves a pointer to the current ClipRect structure and replaces it with a pointer to the current DamageList structure for this layer. The system automatically updates the DamageList structure when a simple-refresh layer is manipulated, thereby keeping track of all the damaged (obscured) portions of that layer. Once the system has a pointer to the DamageList structure, the drawing functions will use the damage-list to define the set of clipping-rectangles that require drawing changes.

2. Execute the Graphics Library drawing functions. For example, you can used the AreaDraw, AreaMove, and AreaEnd functions to define new drawing contents for selected areas of your simple-refresh layer. You can specify drawing functions for the entire surface of the layer. However, due to the damage-list, the graphics functions will draw only into the damaged parts of the simple-refresh layer; that is, the drawing will be clipped. If these are a few small areas, the drawing process can occur very quickly. No time is wasted drawing into the undamaged portions of the simple-refresh layer.

3. Call the EndUpdate function to terminate the drawing process. EndUpdate will replace the DamageList and ClipRect structure pointers with their original values. Other parts of the layer can now be redrawn in the usual way.

See the discussion of the CreateBehindLayer function for a description of the Layer structure.

BehindLayer

Syntax of Function Call

```
success = BehindLayer (    layerInfo, layer)
D0                          A0        A1
```

Purpose of Function

This function places the specified layer behind all other layers. It does this by swapping bits with other layers in and out of the current display bitmap. If the other layers are simple-refresh layers, the BehindLayer function collects their damage-lists and sets bits in the flags of those layers with sections that were previously hidden by the specified layer but are now revealed. If the specified layer is a backdrop layer, the BehindLayer function places this layer behind all other backdrop layers. Otherwise, it places this layer in front of the top backdrop layer and behind all other layers. This function returns a Boolean value: TRUE if successful; FALSE if unsuccessful.

Inputs to Function

layerInfo	A pointer to a LayerInfo structure
layer	A pointer to a Layer structure

Discussion

The BehindLayer, UpfrontLayer, and MoveLayerInFrontOf functions deal with the relative positions of the layers in the layer stack, which sets the video priority for the display screen. These functions allow you to reorder your layers, which is especially useful in a windowing environment such as Intuition or in an applications program that wants to mimic Intuition-style windows and screens. Each time you want to change the stacking order of your layers, you should call one of these three functions.

It is important to note that the BehindLayer function takes into account all backdrop layers in the system. Also note that the system automatically calls the LockLayers function and the LockLayerInfo function during the restacking operation. This prevents all the other layers in the system from changing while you are moving this particular layer to the backmost position.

See the discussion of the CreateBehindLayer function for a description of the Layer structure. See the discussion of the NewLayerInfo function for a description of the Layer-Info structure.

CreateBehindLayer

Syntax of Function Call

```
layer = CreateBehindLayer (layerInfo, bitMap, x0, y0, x1, y1,
D0                         A0       A1      D0 D1 D2 D3
                           flags, [bitMap2])
                           D4     [A2]
```

Purpose of Function

This function creates a new layer of the type indicated in the flags argument. If the type is a superbitmap layer, this function uses the bitMap2 argument to point to a BitMap structure for a superbitmap associated with this layer and copies the superbitmap pixel contents into the layer bitmap. If this layer is a backdrop layer, it is placed behind all other layers, including other backdrop layers. If it is not a backdrop layer, it is placed behind all nonbackdrop layers. The CreateBehindLayer function returns a pointer to the Layer structure associated with the layer it creates.

Inputs to Function

layerInfo	A pointer to a LayerInfo structure
bitMap	A pointer to a BitMap structure whose bitmap is used by all layers in a group
x0, y0	The pixel coordinates of the upper-left corner of the layer bitmap
x1, y1	The pixel coordinates of the lower-right corner of the layer bitmap
flags	A set of bits indicating various types of layers
bitMap2	[optional] A pointer to a second BitMap structure if the flags variable indicates this is a superbitmap layer

Discussion

There are three functions that allow you to create and delete layers. The CreateBehindLayer and CreateUpfrontLayer functions provide the only mechanism you can use to create layers.

These two functions create a new layer and place it behind all other layers (CreateBehind-Layer) or in front of all other layers (CreateUpfrontLayer). The DeleteLayer function provides the only mechanism you can use to delete a layer from a layer list.

Usually, you create and add layers in sets. All of the layers in a given set can have a common bitmap. That is, all layers are created with the same bitMap argument in the CreateBehindLayer (or CreateUpfrontLayer) function. The only difference between these layers is the position of the upper-left corner (x0,y0) and the size of the layer (x1,y1). The resulting arrangement is that each layer in a set of layers shares the same bitmap. This is a very important idea in the use of the Layers Library functions.

As you create different layers, all sharing the same bitmap, you create the raster bitmap quilting effect mentioned in the introduction to this chapter. Each added layer partly overlaps or partly underlies each of the other layers already defined for a specific bitmap. The more layers you add that share a particular bitmap, the more small rectangles you create in the quilt. When this particular bitmap is displayed on screen, each visible sub-rectangle in the full display-screen quilt can belong to a different layer.

In addition, some or all of these layers can share the same LayerInfo structure if the same LayerInfo pointer argument is used in calls to CreateBehindLayer or CreateUp-frontLayer. Because of this, all layers associated with a specific LayerInfo structure can be treated as a unit by the other Layers Library functions. Note that the two groups—layers that share the same bitmap and layers that share the same LayerInfo structure—are not required to be the same group and do not have to have the same layers.

The Layer Structure

The definition of the Layer structure is as follows:

```
struct Layer {
    struct Layer *front, *back;
    struct ClipRect *ClipRect;
    struct RastPort *rp;
    struct Rectangle bounds;
    UBYTE Lock;
    UBYTE LockCount;
    UBYTE LayerLockCount;
    UBYTE reserved;
    UWORD reserved1;
    UWORD Flags;
    struct BitMap *SuperBitMap;
    struct ClipRect *SuperClipRect;
    APTR Window;
    SHORT Scroll_X, Scroll_Y;
    struct MsgPort LockPort;
    struct Message LockMessage;
    struct MsgPort ReplyPort;
    struct Message I_LockMessage;
    struct Region *DamageList;
    struct ClipRect *_cliprects;
```

```
    struct Layer_Info *LayerInfo;
    struct Task *LayerLocker;
    struct ClipRect *SuperSaveClipRects;
    struct ClipRect *cr, *cr2, *crnew;
    APTR _p1;
};
```

These are the parameters in the Layer structure:

■ The front and back parameters point to the Layer structures associated with the layers that are currently in front of and in back of the layer defined by this Layer structure.

■ The ClipRect parameter points to the ClipRect structure associated with this layer.

■ The rp parameter points to the controlling RastPort structure associated with this layer.

■ The bounds variable contains a set of clipping-rectangle bounds to use with the ClipRect structure associated with this layer.

■ The Lock variable contains the task lock indicator for this layer.

■ The LockCount and LayerLockCount parameters count the number of tasks that have locked this layer.

■ The Flags parameter contains 16 bits that determine the type of layer and indicate whether parts of this layer are currently obscured.

■ The SuperBitMap parameter points to a BitMap structure for a superbitmap if this is a superbitmap layer.

■ The SuperClipRect parameter points to a ClipRect structure associated with a superbitmap if this is a superbitmap layer.

■ The Window parameter points to an Intuition Window structure.

■ The Scroll_X and Scroll_Y variables contain the x- and y-direction scrolling distances (in pixels) to be used in superbitmap layer scrolling.

■ LockPort is the name of a MsgPort substructure. It is the first message port that deals with layer locking messages and is used to receive locking messages from tasks that want to lock this layer.

■ LockMessage is a layer locking Message substructure. Messages received from locking tasks are placed here.

■ ReplyPort is the name of a MsgPort substructure. It is used as the reply port in intertask layer locking.

■ l_LockMessage is a Message substructure for handling intertask layer locking. It is used to hold messages that will be sent to tasks.

- The DamageList parameter points to a Region structure; it is used only for simple-refresh layers.

- The _cliprects parameter points to a ClipRect structure. This is used only by the system.

- The LayerInfo parameter points to a LayerInfo structure, which represents a layer list for layers at the head of the list.

- The LayerLocker parameter points to a Task structure for the task that has locked this layer.

- The SuperSaveClipRects parameter points to a ClipRect structure, which represents a set of clipping-rectangles preallocated by the system for a superbitmap layer.

- The cr, cr2, and crnew parameters each point to a ClipRect Structure, which the system uses to manage the clipping-rectangles associated with this layer.

- The P1 parameter is a pointer used only by the system.

CreateUpfrontLayer

Syntax of Function Call

```
layer = CreateUpfrontLayer (layerInfo, bitMap, x0, y0, x1, y1,
D0                          A0       A1      D0  D1  D2  D3
                            flags, [bitMap2])
                            D4     [A2]
```

Purpose of Function

This function creates a new layer of the type indicated in the flags argument and places it in front of all other layers. If this is a superbitmap layer, this function uses the bitMap2 argument to point to a BitMap structure for a superbitmap associated with this layer, then copies the superbitmap pixel contents into the layer bitmap. You should not use this function for backdrop layers; use CreateBehindLayer for that purpose. The CreateUpfrontLayer function returns a pointer to the Layer structure associated with the layer it creates.

Inputs to Function

layerInfo	A pointer to a LayerInfo structure
bitMap	A pointer to a BitMap structure whose bitmap is used by all layers in a group
x0, y0	The pixel coordinates of the upper-left corner of the layer bitmap
x1, y1	The pixel coordinates of the lower-right corner of the layer bitmap
flags	A set of bits indicating various types of layers
bitMap2	[optional] A pointer to a second BitMap structure if the flags variable indicates this is a superbitmap layer

Discussion

There are three functions that allow you to create and delete layers. CreateBehindLayer and CreateUpfrontLayer provide the only mechanism you can use to create layers. You can use these two functions to create a new layer and place it behind all other layers (CreateBehindLayer) or in front of all other layers (CreateUpfrontLayer). The DeleteLayer function provides the only mechanism you can use to delete a layer from a layer list. See the discussion of the CreateBehindLayer function for a more complete discussion, including an explanation of the Layer structure.

DeleteLayer

Syntax of Function Call

DeleteLayer (layerInfo, layer)
           A0   A1

Purpose of Function

This function deletes the specified layer from a list of layers maintained by the system. In doing so, the DeleteLayer function releases the memory associated with this layer bitmap and Layer structure.

Inputs to Function

layerInfo	A pointer to a LayerInfo structure
layer	A pointer to a Layer structure

Discussion

The DeleteLayer function provides the only mechanism you can use to delete a layer from a layer list maintained by a specific LayerInfo structure. It also restores the display of other layers that may have been previously obscured by this layer, refreshing those newly exposed layers. If this is a superbitmap layer, you must make sure that the superbitmap definition is up to date. After the DeleteLayer function returns, the superbitmap for this superbitmap layer continues to be available in the system; it is not removed. Therefore, you can use CreateBehindLayer or CreateUpfront layer later in the task to restore the contents of this layer, using the up-to-date superbitmap definition.

DisposeLayerInfo

Syntax of Function Call

DisposeLayerInfo (layerInfo)
A0

Purpose of Function

This function deallocates the memory previously assigned to a LayerInfo structure by the NewLayerInfo function. It is new to the version 1.1 software release.

Inputs to Function

layerInfo	A pointer to a LayerInfo structure

Discussion

There are eight functions that deal with the LayerInfo structure: DeleteLayer, Dispose-LayerInfo, FattenLayerInfo, InitLayers, LockLayerInfo, NewLayerInfo, ThinLayerInfo, and UnlockLayerInfo. DisposeLayerInfo, FattenLayerInfo, NewLayerInfo, and ThinLayer-Info are new to the version 1.1 software release. Read the other function discussions to learn more about working with the LayerInfo structure.

The NewLayerInfo function allows you to create, allocate memory for, and initialize a new LayerInfo structure. The LayerInfo structure arranges related layers into an organized list so that various operations can be performed on that list. When you are finished with all the layers tied into a specific LayerInfo structure, you can remove the LayerInfo structure from the system. The DisposeLayerInfo function allows you to deallocate the memory previously assigned to a LayerInfo structure by NewLayerInfo.

EndUpdate

Syntax of Function Call

                    EndUpdate (layer, flag)
                              A0   D0

Purpose of Function

This function terminates the drawing update of the damaged portions of a simple-refresh layer. To do this, EndUpdate exchanges the DamageList structure pointer with the ClipRect structure pointer in the current definition of the Layer structure. This reverses the exchange that was made by the BeginUpdate function and effectively removes the DamageList structure from control of the drawing process for this layer. This allows the simple-refresh layer ClipRect structure to once again control the drawing process.

Inputs to Function

layer   A pointer to a Layer structure that represents a simple-refresh layer

flag   A set of flag bits as defined in the Layer structure

Discussion

The BeginUpdate and EndUpdate functions allow you to control the drawing update of simple-refresh layers. You use the BeginUpdate function when you want to change (or restore) drawing contents in the obscured portions of a simple-refresh layer using any of the Graphics Library drawing functions. You use the EndUpdate function when you want to end the pixel-update process in a simple-refresh layer.

The EndUpdate function is used only for simple-refresh layers. It exchanges the ClipRect and DamageList structure pointers that were used in the drawing update of the damaged portions of a simple-refresh layer bitmap. Read the discussion of the Begin-Update function to understand how the BeginUpdate, drawing, and EndUpdate functions work together with the ClipRect and DamageList structures to accomplish the drawing update of a simple-refresh layer.

The EndUpdate function should be called after all graphics tasks have redrawn the obscured portions of a simple-refresh layer bitmap. You should use a flag variable of 0 if you are making a partial update of the obscured areas. You can use the Graphics Library region functions to define a clipping region smaller than the total area defined by the DamageList structure. This will further reduce the effective drawing area, thus giving a partial update of the simple-refresh layer. Note that you would do this only if you wanted to speed the refreshing process and you did not care about how certain sections of the simple-refresh layer appeared on the screen.

FattenLayerInfo

Syntax of Function Call

> **FattenLayerInfo (layerInfo)**
> **A0**

Purpose of Function

This function allocates additional memory for the LayerInfo structure when the InitLayers function is used, allowing the InitLayers function to be used in version 1.1 programs. This function is new with the version 1.1 software release.

Inputs to Function

> **layerInfo**   A pointer to a LayerInfo structure

Discussion

There are eight functions that deal with the LayerInfo structure: DeleteLayer, Dispose-LayerInfo, FattenLayerInfo, LockLayerInfo, InitLayers, NewLayerInfo, ThinLayerInfo, and UnlockLayerInfo. DisposeLayerInfo, FattenLayerInfo, NewLayerInfo, and Thin-LayerInfo are new to the version 1.1 software release.

The FattenLayerInfo and ThinLayerInfo functions are provided for backwards compatibility with the version 1.0 software release. They allow you to adapt your 1.0 programs that use the InitLayers function to the 1.1 release. These two functions allocate and deallocate the extra memory needed for the additional information the LayerInfo structure contains in version 1.1.

If you are compiling with the 1.1 release and you still want to use the InitLayers function to initialize the LayerInfo structure, you must follow the InitLayers call with a call to the FattenLayerInfo function. This will allocate the additional memory needed for the 1.1 version LayerInfo structure. Alternatively, you can use the NewLayerInfo and DisposeLayerInfo functions and thus avoid using the AllocMem, InitLayers, FattenLayer-Info, ThinLayerInfo, and FreeMem functions.

InitLayers

Syntax of Function Call

InitLayers (layerInfo)
A0

Purpose of Function

This function initializes the version 1.0 LayerInfo structure. To allocate the memory for this structure, you must call the Exec AllocMem function.

Inputs to Function

layerInfo   A pointer to a LayerInfo structure

Discussion

There are eight functions that deal with the LayerInfo structure: DeleteLayer, Dispose-LayerInfo, FattenLayerInfo, LockLayerInfo, InitLayers, NewLayerInfo, ThinLayerInfo, and UnlockLayerInfo. InitLayers and NewLayerInfo both allow you to initialize a new LayerInfo structure. NewLayerInfo also allocates the necessary memory for this structure. NewLayerInfo is new to version 1.1, in which the LayerInfo structure has been extended with additional information.

If you use the InitLayers function to initialize the LayerInfo structure, you must first allocate the memory for this structure with a call to the Exec AllocMem function. To use InitLayers with version 1.1 of the Amiga software, you must follow the InitLayers call with a call to FattenLayerInfo. This will allocate the additional memory needed for the LayerInfo structure in version 1.1. When you want to free all the memory assigned to the LayerInfo structure, you should call the ThinLayerInfo function (to deallocate the extra memory allocated by FattenLayerInfo) and then the Exec FreeMem function.

InstallClipRegion

Syntax of Function Call

```
oldClipRegion = InstallClipRegion (layer, region)
D0                                  A0     A1
```

Purpose of Function

This function installs a region into a layer. All subsequent drawing additions in that layer will be clipped to the boundary of this region. If the call is successful, InstallClipRegion returns a pointer to the most recent (old) Region structure installed in the layer; a 0 value is returned if no previous region was installed in that layer.

Inputs to Function

layer   A pointer to the Layer structure that represents the layer where you want to add a region definition

region   A pointer to the Region structure that represents the region you want to add to the layer definition

Discussion

InstallClipRegion is the only 1.2 release function that deals jointly with layers and regions. It allows you to modify the area of a layer bitmap where subsequent drawing occurs by installing (combining) the current definition of the layer with a region definition.

If the system runs out of memory while computing the resulting clipping-rectangles required by the layer-region combination, the LAYERS_CLIPRECTS_LOST flag will be set in the Layer structure flags parameter. In this case the clipping-rectangle list representing the new region-layer combination may get lost. However, as soon as there is enough memory and the Graphics Library is called again, this clipping-rectangle list will be rebuilt.

It is important to note that you must make the following call before calling the Graphics Library DeleteLayer function or the Intuition Library CloseWindow function if you have previously installed a nonnull clipping-region in the layer:

InstallClipRegion (layer, NULL)

LockLayer

Syntax of Function Call

LockLayer (layerInfo, layer)
A0   A1

Purpose of Function

This function locks a layer so that only this task can change its bitmap or clipping-rectangle definition. If another task is drawing into this layer, this task will wait for that task to finish using the layer before locking it.

Inputs to Function

layerInfo	A pointer to a LayerInfo structure
layer	A pointer to a Layer structure

Discussion

There are seven functions that allow you to manipulate individual layers in the group of layers handled by a specific LayerInfo structure: DeleteLayer, LockLayer, MoveLayer, ScrollLayer, SizeLayer, UnlockLayer, and WhichLayer. There is more information on working with individual layers in the discussions of each of these functions.

If the current task is making some changes to a particular layer, such as moving or resizing that layer, it must inhibit other tasks from changing that layer. This is the purpose of the LockLayer function; LockLayer blocks other tasks from changing the drawing or clipping-rectangle definition of a layer bitmap. This locking condition continues until the current task issues an UnlockLayer function call. If you are locking just one layer with a single LockLayer call, you do not need to precede that call with a call to the LockLayerInfo function. Note that you can also use the quicker Graphics Library LockLayerRom function for this purpose.

Task switching is still allowed after a LockLayer function call. However, if a new task takes over the machine and tries to draw into the locked layer, that task will be put to sleep. It is important to understand that that task can do other things; it is only forbidden from drawing into the locked layer until the original locking task unlocks the layer.

If you want to lock more than one layer at the same time, there are two ways to go about it. First, you can issue a number of LockLayer calls. In this case, each call must be preceded by a call to the LockLayerInfo function and followed by a call to the UnlockLayerInfo function to protect the LayerInfo structure from inadvertent changes while LockLayer executes.

Second, you can simultaneously lock all the layers represented by a LayerInfo structure by calling the LockLayers function. Of course, you should then follow that call with a call to the UnlockLayers function. With this procedure, you do not need to call LockLayerInfo and UnLockLayerInfo.

LockLayerInfo

Syntax of Function Call

LockLayerInfo (layerInfo)
A0

Purpose of Function

This function locks the LayerInfo structure so that only the current task can modify it. This function is the inverse of the UnlockLayerInfo function.

Inputs to Function

layerInfo   A pointer to a LayerInfo structure

Discussion

There are seven functions that deal with the LayerInfo structure: DeleteLayer, Dispose-LayerInfo, FattenLayerInfo, LockLayerInfo, NewLayerInfo, ThinLayerInfo, and Unlock-LayerInfo. Read the other function discussions to learn more about these functions.

The LockLayerInfo function allows you to lock the data in a LayerInfo structure from change by any task other than the current task. The UnlockLayerInfo function allows you to unlock a previously locked LayerInfo structure so that other tasks can change the data in that LayerInfo structure.

If a previous task has issued a current LockLayerInfo function call with no corresponding UnlockLayerInfo call, the current task must wait for the previous task to regain control and execute an UnlockLayerInfo call for this specific LayerInfo structure. The current task will go to sleep if it tries to lock or modify that LayerInfo structure before the previous task unlocks it.

There are several occasions when the system calls the LockLayerInfo function automatically:

■ When you call the MoveLayer function

■ When you call the SizeLayer function

■ When you call the BehindLayer function

■ When you call the UpfrontLayer function

At other times, you will have to call the LockLayerInfo function whenever there is any chance that other tasks could change the LayerInfo structure at an inappropriate moment. For example, you should call LockLayerInfo before you call the WhichLayer function. This will ensure that no task changes the sequence of layers before your task processes the Layer structure pointer returned by WhichLayer. You also need to call the LockLayerInfo function before you call the CreateUpfrontLayer, CreateBehindLayer, or DeleteLayer functions. This will ensure that other tasks do not affect the LayerInfo structure until these functions have returned. You do not need to call the LockLayerInfo function when you scroll a superbitmap layer, because the ScrollLayer function changes only the portion of the superbitmap being shown, not the layer size or on-screen position of the superbitmap layer.

LockLayers

Syntax of Function Call

LockLayers (layerInfo)
A0

Purpose of Function

This function locks all layers associated with the specified LayerInfo structure so that only the current task can change their bitmap or clipping-rectangle definitions. Layers in other LayerInfo structures are not locked by this call.

Inputs to Function

layerInfo   A pointer to a LayerInfo structure

Discussion

There are two functions that allow you to manipulate simultaneously all the layers associated with a specific LayerInfo structure: LockLayers and UnlockLayers. You can use these two functions in your current task to lock a group of related layers from changes produced by tasks other than the current task. Then, when you want to allow other tasks to change some or all of these layers, you can use the UnlockLayers function to unlock all related layers.

Because the LayerInfo structure ties together a group of related Layer structures, the LockLayers function can reference it to lock a group of related layers all at once. The best example of this function in action is the orange rubber-band box that represents the outline of the window on the display screen when you are moving or resizing an Intuition window. The only way for Intuition (or, for that matter, any program) to draw such a box without interference from other tasks is to make sure that all drawing to all layers other than the layer in which the rubber-band box is placed is halted while the rubber-band box is being drawn. This is exactly what happens in Intuition; the LockLayers function is used to lock all Intuition screen layers while the user is manipulating the window.

MoveLayer

Syntax of Function Call

MoveLayer (layerInfo, layer, delta-x, delta-y)
          A0   A1   D0   D1

Purpose of Function

This function moves a nonbackdrop layer to a new position in a layer bitmap. If this operation reveals any parts of other simple-refresh layers, MoveLayer collects the damaged areas and sets a REFRESH bit in the Layer structure's Flags variable.

Inputs to Function

layerInfo	A pointer to a LayerInfo structure
layer	A pointer to a Layer structure that represents a nonbackdrop layer
delta-x	The number of pixels to move the layer bitmap in the x direction
delta-y	The number of pixels to move the layer bitmap in the y direction

Discussion

There are seven functions that allow you to manipulate individual layers in the group of layers handled by a specific LayerInfo structure: DeleteLayer, LockLayer, MoveLayer, ScrollLayer, SizeLayer, UnlockLayer, and WhichLayer. Read the other function discussions to learn more about working with individual layers.

MoveLayer is used any time you want to move a layer on the screen. For example, if you define a layer as an Intuition window and you want to move the layer when the user presses the mouse Menu button, you can call MoveLayer to do that.

The MoveLayer function affects the list of layers that is being managed by the LayerInfo structure. For this reason, the system automatically locks the LayerInfo structure while the MoveLayer function is executing.

MoveLayerInFrontOf

Syntax of Function Call

```
success = MoveLayerInFrontOf (layerToMove, targetLayer)
D0                            A0           A1
```

Purpose of Function

This function moves a nonbackdrop layer to a new position in the layer stacking order. If this is a simple-refresh layer and this operation reveals any parts of it, this function automatically collects the damaged areas into a damage-list and sets a REFRESH bit in the damaged layer's Flags variable. The MoveLayerInFrontOf function is new to the version 1.1 software release. MoveLayerInFrontOf returns a Boolean value. If the function is successful, this value will be TRUE; if unsuccessful, this value will be FALSE.

Inputs to Function

layerToMove   A pointer to a Layer structure representing the nonbackup layer to be moved

targetLayer   A pointer to a Layer structure representing the nonbackup layer in front of which this layer will be placed

Discussion

There are three functions that deal with the relative position of a layer in the layer stack on the display screen: BehindLayer, UpfrontLayer, and MoveLayerInFrontOf. These functions allow you to reorder your layers on the display screen of the Amiga. This capability is especially useful in a windowing environment such as Intuition and in an applications program that wants to mimic Intuition-style windows and screens.

The MoveLayerInFrontOf function allows you to move a specific layer in front of another specific layer. This operation permits detailed control of the stacking order of the layers in the system. Note that you can reorder a backdrop layer with this function if you first clear the BACKDROP bit in the Layer structure's Flags parameter.

See the discussion of the CreateBehindLayer function for a description of the Layer structure.

NewLayerInfo

Syntax of Function Call

layerInfo = NewLayerInfo (layerInfo)
DO   A0

Purpose of Function

This function allocates memory for and initializes a LayerInfo structure. All newly created layers are assigned to a specific LayerInfo structure. Once this is done, the other Layers Library functions can operate on the list of layers associated with this LayerInfo structure. NewLayerInfo also has the effect of unlocking the layers so that their bitmap definitions can be changed. The NewLayerInfo function is new to the version 1.1 software release.

Inputs to Function

layerInfo   A pointer to a LayerInfo structure

Discussion

There are eight functions that deal with the LayerInfo structure: DeleteLayer, DisposeLayerInfo, FattenLayerInfo, LockLayerInfo, InitLayers, NewLayerInfo, ThinLayerInfo, and UnlockLayerInfo. Read the other function discussions to learn more about working with the LayerInfo structure.

Both the InitLayers and NewLayerInfo functions allow you to initialize a new LayerInfo structure. NewLayerInfo also allocates the necessary memory for this structure, while InitLayers must be preceded by a call to AllocMem. InitLayers is in both version 1.0 and 1.1 Layers Libraries; it must be used with FattenLayerInfo and ThinLayerInfo. NewLayerInfo is in version 1.1 only and should not be used with the FattenLayerInfo and ThinLayerInfo functions.

The LayerInfo Structure

The version 1.1 LayerInfo structure is defined as follows:

```
struct Layer_Info {
    struct Layer *top_layer;
    struct Layer *check_lp;
    struct Layer *obs;
```

```
        struct MsgPort RP_ReplyPort;
        struct MsgPort LockPort;
        UBYTE Lock;
        UBYTE broadcast;
        UBYTE LockNest;
        UBYTE Flags;
        struct Task *Locker;
        BYTE fatten_count;
        UBYTE bytereserved;
        UWORD wordreserved;
        UWORD LayerInfo_extra_size;
        ULONG longreserved;
        struct LayerInfo_extra *LayerInfo_extra;
    };
```

Following is a brief discussion of some of the parameters contained in the LayerInfo structure:

■ The top_layer parameter points to the top layer in the layers represented by this LayerInfo structure.

■ The check_lp and obs parameters are for system use only.

■ The RP_ReplyPort is the name of a MsgPort substructure for the reply port used to handle intertask communications for this LayerInfo structure. It is used to prevent other tasks from making changes to this LayerInfo structure.

■ The LockPort is the name of a MsgPort substructure used to handle intertask communications for this LayerInfo structure. It is used to keep other tasks from making changes to this LayerInfo structure definition.

■ The Locker parameter points to the Task structure for the task that issued a call to lock all layers represented by this LayerInfo structure.

The rest of the information is either byte padding to ensure correct positioning of information bytes in the LayerInfo structure, information to extend the version 1.0 LayerInfo structure to version 1.1, or reserved bytes that will be used for future software upgrades.

ScrollLayer

Syntax of Function Call

```
ScrollLayer (layerInfo, layer, delta-x, delta-y)
             A0        A1     D0       D1
```

Purpose of Function

This function scrolls a superbitmap layer. It copies bits between the superbitmap and the on-screen layer bitmap (the visible portion of the layer) to change the portion of the layer that is shown on-screen.

Inputs to Function

layerInfo	A pointer to a LayerInfo structure
layer	A pointer to a Layer structure for a superbitmap layer
delta-x	The number of pixels to scroll the layer bitmap in the x direction
delta-y	The number of pixels to scroll the layer bitmap in the y direction

Discussion

There are seven functions that allow you to manipulate individual layers in the group of layers handled by a specific LayerInfo structure: DeleteLayer, LockLayer, MoveLayer, ScrollLayer, SizeLayer, UnlockLayer, and WhichLayer. If you want to control operations on individual layers, these are the functions to use. Read the other function discussions to learn more about working with individual layers.

The ScrollLayer function works only with superbitmap layers. Recall that a superbitmap layer is a layer that has a single backup bitmap area. This backup bitmap, referred to as the superbitmap of the layer, stores the pixel information that is not in the on-screen layer. In addition, it contains a recent copy of the on-screen layer bitmap. By design, the superbitmap can be (and usually is) bigger than the on-screen layer bitmap. However, it can also be equal in size to the on-screen bitmap. In this case, the ScrollLayer function could not produce any scrolling.

The ScrollLayer function changes the portion of the superbitmap that is shown in the on-screen bitmap. It works with the superbitmap layer to provide an easy mechanism to change the on-screen view associated with a layer. In general, there are two ways to change the on-screen view of a layer. The first way is to change the pixel definitions of the layer bitmap by using the Graphics Library drawing functions. The other method is to use a bitmap larger than the on-screen view and to present different parts of it on-screen at different times. In this method, the bitmap (a superbitmap) is drawn and different parts of it are scrolled onto the display screen by copying those parts into the on-screen bitmap.

The main advantage of the superbitmap layer is the easy way you can scroll layer information on the display screen. The main disadvantage is the extra area of memory you must set aside to contain the superbitmap bitplanes. For a full-screen layer, this memory requirement will often be large.

For example, a full-screen, 320-by-200 pixel, 32-color layer requires 8,000 bytes per bitplane, or 40,000 bytes for the on-screen bitmap alone. In addition, the off-screen super-bitmap requires at least this amount of memory. If you want to scroll the layer over greater distances, you will need even more off-screen superbitmap memory.

SizeLayer

Syntax of Function Call

```
SizeLayer (layerInfo, layer,  delta-x,  delta-y)
           A0         A1       D0        D1
```

Purpose of Function

This function increases or decreases the size of a layer bitmap.

Inputs to Function

layerInfo	A pointer to a LayerInfo structure
layer	A pointer to a Layer structure for a nonbackdrop layer
delta-x	The number of pixels to add to the current layer bitmap size in the x direction
delta-y	The number of pixels to add to the current layer bitmap size in the y direction

Discussion

There are seven functions that allow you to manipulate individual layers in the group of layers handled by a specific LayerInfo structure: DeleteLayer, LockLayer, MoveLayer, ScrollLayer, SizeLayer, UnlockLayer, and WhichLayer. Read the other function discussions to learn more about working with individual layers.

The SizeLayer function changes the size of a layer by modifying the coordinates of the lower-right corner of the layer bitmap. It leaves the coordinates of the upper-left corner of the layer bitmap unchanged. If the layer bitmap is made larger, the coordinates of the lower-right corner are increased. If the layer bitmap is made smaller, the coordinates of the lower-right corner are decreased.

If the layer is a superbitmap layer, the SizeLayer function copies pixels into and out of the superbitmap as required to make the size change in the layer bitmap. In addition, the SizeLayer function collects the damage-lists for those simple-refresh layers that may need to be refreshed if damage occurred during the sizing operation. These damage-lists can then be used to redraw the damaged portions of all simple-refresh layers as they become newly exposed during the resizing operation. Note that the system automatically locks the LayerInfo structure while it is resizing a layer.

SwapBitsRastPortClipRect

Syntax of Function Call

```
SwapBitsRastPortClipRect (rastPort, clipRect)
                          A0        A1
```

Purpose of Function

This function swaps bits between a layer bitmap (the bitmap referenced by the BitMap structure referenced in the RastPort structure) and an off-screen bitmap (the bitmap referenced by the BitMap structure in the ClipRect structure). This procedure avoids the need to create a new layer for the off-screen bitmap and results in a very fast update of the display screen.

Inputs to Function

rastPort	A pointer to a RastPort structure
clipRect	A pointer to a special ClipRect structure designed for use by this function

Discussion

The SwapBitsRastPortClipRect function allows you to swap pixel bits between a layer bitmap and a set of off-screen bitmaps. This mechanism provides a quick way to update the definition of the layer bitmap.

The SwapBitsRastPortClipRect function is used when you want to avoid creating a new layer when you need additional on-screen display information. It can also be used to speed up display operations. Among other things, the SwapBitsRastPortClipRect function produces the very fast menu operations you experience when you use Intuition. These menu operations would not be as speedy if the SwapBitsRastPortClipRect function was not available.

To understand how this function works, suppose you have several windows open on an Intuition display screen. Each of these windows is part of a layer. Now suppose you want to bring a menu onto the screen. You can do this in two different ways.

In the first method, you create a layer using the CreateUpfrontLayer function. Then you draw the menu into it using the Intuition and Graphics Library drawing functions for menu creation and manipulation. Of course, you first have to set aside enough memory for the new layer bitmap and associated Layer and LayerInfo structures. You also have to create all of the clipping-rectangles for the existing windows that will be obscured when the new menu is brought on-screen.

In the second method, you use the SwapBitsRastPortClipRect function to produce the menu directly on the display screen. To do this, you first draw the menu in an off-screen bitmap area. Then you lock all of your present layers using the LockLayers function. This prevents any task from modifying these layers and thereby drawing over your menu once it is displayed.

Next, you swap the on-screen bitmap bits (the bitmap referenced by the BitMap structure referenced in the RastPort structure) with the off-screen bitmap bits (the bitmap referenced by the BitMap structure referenced in a special ClipRect structure) using the SwapBitsRastPortClipRect function. This makes the menu appear immediately on the display screen. When you are finished with the menu display, use the SwapBitsRastPortClipRect function to swap the bitmaps again and restore the original appearance of the display screen.

Note that this second drawing procedure is faster than the first procedure. In addition, the second procedure leaves the normal ClipRect structures and most other window-display related structures unchanged. This obviously reduces the bookkeeping chores of your task.

Also note that all of the display layers must be locked while the menu is displayed. Therefore, any task that is drawing into any of the layers will be put to sleep temporarily while the menu is displayed. Obviously, this will slow down any background tasks that attempt to draw into these layers. In contrast, if you use the first procedure and produce the menu in a separate layer bitmap, no task will need to be halted while the menu is displayed. Instead, each task can continue to draw into the off-screen portions of the layer bitmaps associated with other layers in the system.

ThinLayerInfo

Syntax of Function Call

ThinLayerInfo (layerInfo)
A0

Purpose of Function

This function deallocates the extra memory allocated to the LayerInfo structure by the FattenLayerInfo function. It allows the InitLayers function to be used in version 1.1 programs. This function is new to the version 1.1 software release.

Inputs to Function

layerInfo   A pointer to a LayerInfo structure

Discussion

There are eight functions that deal with the LayerInfo structure: DeleteLayer, Dispose-LayerInfo, FattenLayerInfo, LockLayerInfo, InitLayers, NewLayerInfo, ThinLayerInfo, and UnlockLayerInfo. DisposeLayerInfo, FattenLayerInfo, NewLayerInfo, and ThinLayer-Info are new to version 1.1 of the Amiga software release. The LayerInfo structure is defined in the discussion of NewLayerInfo.

The FattenLayerInfo and ThinLayerInfo functions are provided for backwards compatibility with the version 1.0 software release. These two functions allow you to adapt your 1.0 programs that call the InitLayers function to the 1.1 release. They allocate and deallocate the extra memory needed for the LayerInfo structure when the InitLayers function is used in a version 1.1 program.

If you use the InitLayers function to allocate memory for the LayerInfo structure, you must follow the InitLayers call with a call to FattenLayerInfo to allocate the extra memory used by the version 1.1 LayerInfo structure. When you want to deallocate the extra memory allocated by FattenLayerInfo, call the ThinLayerInfo function. You should follow this with a call to the FreeMem function to deallocate the memory for the version 1.0 LayerInfo structure you originally allocated with the AllocMem function. The Alloc-Mem and FreeMem calls are necessary because the InitLayers function initializes, but does not allocate, the memory for the version 1.0 LayerInfo structure.

UnlockLayer

Syntax of Function Call

UnlockLayer (layer)
A0

Purpose of Function

This function unlocks the specified layer and allows other tasks to modify this layer bit-map definition. Call the UnlockLayer function when your locking task has finished draw-ing into or changing the clipping-rectangles associated with that layer bitmap.

Inputs to Function

layer   A pointer to a Layer structure

Discussion

There are seven functions that allow you to manipulate individual layers in the group of layers handled by a specific LayerInfo structure: DeleteLayer, LockLayer, MoveLayer, ScrollLayer, SizeLayer, UnlockLayer, and WhichLayer. Read the other function discus-sions to learn more about working with individual layers.

Recall that the LockLayer function locks a layer for exclusive modification by the current task. When you want to end the one-task ownership of this layer and allow other tasks to modify its bitmap or clipping-rectangle definition, call the UnlockLayer function.

Once the UnlockLayer function has been called to balance a call to the LockLayer function, any task that was previously put to sleep when it tried to draw into this layer (or modify its clipping-rectangle definition) will not be put to sleep if it tries again.

UnlockLayerInfo

Syntax of Function Call

UnlockLayerInfo (layerInfo)
A0

Purpose of Function

This function unlocks the specified LayerInfo structure previously locked when the same task called the LockLayerInfo function. When UnlockLayerInfo returns, all other tasks can modify this LayerInfo structure.

Inputs to Function

LayerInfo   A pointer to a LayerInfo structure

Discussion

There are seven functions that work with the LayerInfo structure: DeleteLayer, Dispose-LayerInfo, FattenLayerInfo, LockLayerInfo, NewLayerInfo, ThinLayerInfo, and Un-lockLayerInfo. Read the other function discussions to learn more about working with the LayerInfo structure.

There should be an UnlockLayerInfo function call for every LockLayerInfo function call. Many Layers Library functions (for example, CreateBehindLayer, CreateUp-frontLayer, and DeleteLayer) call the LockLayerInfo function automatically. They also call the UnlockLayerInfo function just before they return. See the discussion of the New-LayerInfo function for the definition of the LayerInfo structure.

Anytime you wish to modify a Layer structure in ways not directly provided by the Layers Library functions, you should precede and follow your changes with calls to the LockLayer and LockLayerInfo and UnLockLayer and UnLockLayerInfo functions pairs.

UnlockLayers

Syntax of Function Call

UnlockLayers (layerInfo)
                         A0

Purpose of Function

This function first unlocks all layers associated with the specified LayerInfo structure. This allows other tasks to modify these layers' bitmap and clipping-rectangle definitions. The function then unlocks the LayerInfo structure itself.

Inputs to Function

layerInfo   A pointer to a LayerInfo structure

Discussion

The LockLayers and UnlockLayers functions allow you to manipulate all the layers associated with a specific LayerInfo structure simultaneously. You can call the LockLayers function in your current task to lock a group of related layers from change by any task other than the current task. Then, when you want to allow other tasks to change some or all of these layers, you can call the UnlockLayers function to unlock all related layers.

You should match every LockLayers function call in a task with an eventual Unlock-Layers function call in that same task definition. Then, when any other task gains control of the machine and tries to draw into or change the clipping-rectangle definitions of any of the layers associated with the specific LayerInfo structure, it will no longer be put to sleep.

UpfrontLayer

Syntax of Function Call

```
success = UpfrontLayer ( layerInfo, layer)
D0                      A0        A1
```

Purpose of Function

This function places the specified layer in front of all other layers. It does this by swapping bits in and out of the current display bitmap with other layers presently displayed. This function returns a Boolean value. If the function is successful, it returns TRUE; if the function is not successful, it returns FALSE.

Inputs to Function

layerInfo   A pointer to a LayerInfo structure

layer   A pointer to a Layer structure

Discussion

There are three functions that deal with the relative position of a layer in the layer stack on the display screen: BehindLayer, UpfrontLayer, and MoveLayerInFrontOf. These functions allow you to reorder your layers on the display screen of the Amiga. This capability is especially useful in a windowing environment such as Intuition and in an applications program that wants to mimic Intuition-style windows and screens. Each time you want to change the stacking order of your layers, you should call one of these three functions.

When a layer is brought to the front of the display, many parts of it will become newly exposed. If the layer is a smart-refresh or superbitmap layer, some drawing into the off-screen buffers may have occurred while those portions were not visible on the display screen. If the layer is a simple-refresh layer, however, the obscured parts will have been lost, which is why BeginUpdate and EndUpdate, which deal with the damage-list, must be used when obscured portions of simple-refresh layers are to be redrawn.

In general, the Layers Library functions split the drawing area for all types of layers into various clipping-rectangles. When your drawing task calls the various drawing functions, these functions draw only into the areas defined by the clipping-rectangles. Drawing outside of these rectangles is clipped at the rectangle boundaries (hence the term clipping-rectangle).

In particular, if you update a smart-refresh layer or a superbitmap layer, that layer may be partly obscured while the updating is taking place. Even so, when you call the drawing functions to redraw that layer, the Layers Library makes sure that both the exposed and obscured parts get updated if the drawing functions indicate drawing should occur in both parts. The on-screen update will be visible; the off-screen update will not be visible, though it does indeed occur.

Using clipping-rectangles, the Graphics Library drawing functions will be able to tell how the drawing area is split and where drawing updates should occur. The system handles this automatically once you define the type of layer you are drawing into. Note that the situation for simple-refresh layers is somewhat different. (See the discussion of the BeginUpdate function.)

If the layer in the UpfrontLayer function call is a simple-refresh layer, the UpfrontLayer function collects its clipping-rectangle damage-list and sets bits in the Layer structure's Flags parameter associated with this layer.

If the layer in the UpfrontLayer function call is a backdrop layer, the UpfrontLayer function can still put this layer in front of all other screen layers. To do this, however, you must first clear the LAYERBACKDROP bit in the Layer structure's Flags parameter with this program statement:

layer->Flags &= LAYERBACKDROP;

This is the program statement you should use to turn the backdrop layer flag on again:

layer->Flags |= LAYERBACKDROP;

The set of clipping-rectangles that makes up the current to-be-drawn areas of a layer is placed on a clipping-rectangle list. The clipping-rectangle list is represented and handled by the ClipRect structure.

The ClipRect Structure

Each Layer structure contains a pointer to a ClipRect structure. The ClipRect structure is used to manage the set of clipping-rectangles needed when a layer drawing update is initiated. The ClipRect structure is defined as follows:

```
struct ClipRect {
    struct ClipRect *Next;
    struct ClipRect *Prev;
    struct Layer *lobs;
    struct BitMap *BitMap;
    struct Rectangle bounds;
    struct ClipRect *_p1,*_p2;
    LONG reserved;
    LONG flags;
};
```

The Next parameter points to the next ClipRect structure, and the Prev parameter points to the previous ClipRect structure. These structures are part of a linked list that defines the areas where drawing updates should occur for a particular layer. The BitMap parameter points to the BitMap structure with which this ClipRect structure is associated. The bounds parameter is the name of a Rectangle substructure that defines the boundaries of the clipping-rectangle associated with this ClipRect structure. The remainder of the ClipRect structure parameters are for system use.

See the discussion of the CreateBehindLayer function for a description of the Layer structure. See the discussion of the NewLayerInfo function for a description of the LayerInfo structure.

WhichLayer

Syntax of Function Call

```
layer = WhichLayer (layerInfo, x, y)
D0                   A1       D0D1
```

Purpose of Function

This function finds the layer bitmap in which a particular x,y pixel point is located. The WhichLayer function looks through the layers consecutively, starting with the current topmost layer. This process continues until it either finds the point in a layer or runs out of layers. If it finds a layer with this point, it returns a pointer to that Layer structure. If it does not find a layer with this point, it returns a null value.

Inputs to Function

layerInfo	A pointer to a LayerInfo structure
x	The pixel x-coordinate of the point in the layer bitmap
y	The pixel y-coordinate of the point in the layer bitmap

Discussion

There are seven functions that allow you to manipulate individual layers in the group of layers handled by a specific LayerInfo structure: DeleteLayer, LockLayer, MoveLayer, ScrollLayer, SizeLayer, UnlockLayer, and WhichLayer. Read the other function discussions to learn more about working with individual layers.

If the screen viewing area has been separated into several layers, you may want to find out which layer is topmost at any particular screen pixel location. In other words, you may want to know which layer bitmap definition is producing the visible pixel displayed at this specific on-screen location.

Intuition does this very thing when keeping track of the mouse position. When you move the mouse into a specific area of the screen and click the Menu button, Intuition must locate the window in which the Menu button is being clicked. Intuition calls the WhichLayer function to get this information. WhichLayer then gives the Layer structure pointer to Intuition, and Intuition makes that window the active window.

There is one potential problem in using the WhichLayer function. In the time required to determine the layer to which a specific screen pixel belongs, one of the tasks in the system may be in the process of changing the layer bitmap definitions in the system. That is, if a task switch occurs during this time, some other task may call the UpfrontLayer, BehindLayer, CreateUpfrontLayer, DeleteLayer, MoveLayer, or SizeLayer function before control returns to the current task and the WhichLayer function returns its layer pointer. If this happens, the Layer structure pointer returned by WhichLayer may no longer be valid.

To prevent this, you should call the LockLayerInfo function before you call the WhichLayer function. This will prevent any other task from changing the layer arrangements before the WhichLayer function returns. As soon as WhichLayer returns, you will have the layer pointer in a temporary pointer variable. Then call the UnlockLayerInfo function to allow other tasks to continue operating on that layer bitmap.

The Intuition Functions

Introduction

Intuition is the Amiga user's interface. It is a library containing 60 built-in functions that allow you to design with ease applications programs that interact with the user through windows and screens on the colorful Amiga display screen. The Intuition functions are designed to make the manipulation of windows, screens, requesters, gadgets, menus, and so on as simple as possible.

Gadgets and requesters are the main method of communication your program has with the user. There are two types of gadgets: applications program gadgets and system gadgets. System gadgets are provided automatically in your windows and screens if you set appropriate flag bits in the Screen and Window structures. Note that you cannot use the Intuition functions to remove these system gadgets. There are four types of system gadgets:

■ The sizing gadget, which appears in the lower-right corner of a window or screen

■ The drag gadget, which appears anywhere on the screen or window title bars

■ The depth-arrange gadgets (bring-to-front and send-to-back), which appear in the upper-right corner of a window or screen

■ The close gadget, which appears in the upper-left corner of a window or screen

You can arrange your program so that with the exception of the close gadget; it never needs to know that the user selected a system gadget. Your program does not need to look for and process message signals coming from these gadgets. You can attach these system gadgets to your windows and screens and let Intuition do the work of responding to the user.

Requesters are screen prompts that act like menu information exchange boxes. They can be displayed in windows by either the system or your applications programs. You can also have requesters that the user can bring up on demand. Requesters require the user to satisfy the request before continuing with input to that window.

In addition to gadgets and requesters, you can design alerts. Alerts are error messages that appear automatically on the display screen when a critical condition is present. Alerts fall into two classes: system alerts and applications program alerts. An example of a system alert is an "out of memory" alert. You can design your applications program alerts to warn the user of any condition that is dangerous to the continued execution of your program. An alert appears in red and black with text and a blinking border.

Your programs can use two methods of window input/output. Program input is provided through the Console device and IDCMPs (Intuition direct communication message ports). Program output is through the Console device or directly to the Graphics Library functions. The Graphics Library functions allow your programs and tasks (one foreground task and many possible background tasks) to pass data and other information among themselves internally.

Intuition Screens and Windows

Screens and windows are both rectangular. When you first open a screen, it covers the entire Amiga horizontal display-screen surface. It need not cover the entire vertical screen surface. The size of a window when first opened depends on the settings in the Window structure. Like windows, screens can be depth-arranged using front and back depth-arrangement gadgets.

Each screen opened by your program can use any of the display modes offered by the Amiga. These include the low-resolution, high-resolution, noninterlaced, interlaced, single-playfield, dual-playfield, and hold-and-modify modes. The color combinations and restrictions that apply to these modes when using the Graphics Library functions also apply when using the Intuition functions.

Each program can open one or more of its own virtual terminals. A *virtual terminal* is simply a window in a screen; the user accesses each virtual terminal through a window. Each window has the entire machine and display system to itself. Program input and output takes place through windows. Your program can open as many windows as it needs to satisfy its input/output requirements.

Your program can ignore the user shaping and moving windows around the display screen because Intuition handles these types of display-management tasks automatically. As far as your applications program is concerned, the virtual terminal assigned to your window has control of the entire Amiga display screen. Outside of this virtual terminal is only a user with a keyboard and a mouse and perhaps other kinds of input devices.

One concept you should understand is the concept of the *containing display element*. A containing display element in Intuition is a specific piece of the display in which another piece of the display is contained and positioned. For example, a screen is a containing display element; within a screen is a window display element. A window is also a containing display element; within a window is a requester display element.

When an element is added to the display, it is placed within another element. This shows up both in the display itself and in the mechanics of dealing with the structures that define display elements. In particular, when an additional display element is added to an existing containing element, its position is most often referenced to the containing element's coordinate system, usually a coordinate system with the 0,0 point in the upper-left corner of that containing element.

The offset position usually shows up in the added display element's structure as the LeftEdge and TopEdge parameters. For example, the Screen, NewScreen, Window, NewWindow, Menu, MenuItem, Requester, Gadget, Border, and Image structures all include LeftEdge and TopEdge parameters as part of their structure definitions. Therefore, when you are about to add new Intuition display elements, always keep in mind the containing element and its reference point to position the added display element properly.

At the time of writing, the starting x-position for a screen is the left side of the display screen. That is, a screen must occupy the full width of the Amiga display screen. In addition, the final y-position point for a screen cannot be above the bottom of the Amiga display screen. Screens can be overlapped, but the bottom line of a screen cannot be above the bottom line of the display screen. In contrast, windows can be positioned and overlapped without any restrictions.

Screens can be moved vertically but not horizontally; in contrast, windows can move in all directions within a screen. Screens can also be moved in front of and behind other screens; so can windows.

Only one window can be active at any given time. This is the window that the current task is using for its input and output. Other windows can work on some task that doesn't require input from the user. Therefore, you can have a number of background tasks, each with its own priority, that operate on data already given to those tasks by the user. (See the discussion of the Exec SetTaskPri function for more on this.) However, the currently active window can be used to give data to the background tasks continuously through internal programming mechanisms operating between the one foreground task and many potential background tasks.

All windows are associated with (assigned to) screens. All windows associated with a particular screen inherit the display characteristics defined for that screen. This includes the display mode and the colors of that screen.

As the user moves the mouse, a selection pointer moves on the display screen. This pointer allows the user to make selections, change the active window, and otherwise manipulate the screens and windows. You can use the standard Intuition arrow pointer or design your own pointer. The SetPointer and ClearPointer functions are provided for this purpose. The user can move the pointer around the screen using either the mouse or the keyboard.

Screen Types

There are two types of screens in the Intuition system: standard screens and custom screens. Currently, the Workbench screen is the only standard screen. Every other Intuition display component (windows, gadgets, requesters, etc.) is defined in terms of the screen with which it is associated. In particular, all windows inherit the display characteristics (display modes, colors, etc.) of the screens in which those windows are opened. Therefore, if your program needs windows that have various display characteristics, you will have to open new screens and then open those windows in those new screens.

Standard screens differ from custom screens in three basic ways. First, standard screens (with the important exception of the Workbench screen) close and go away when all of their windows close and go away. Intuition's standard screens are the full height and width of the Amiga display screen. An applications program can display more than one window in a standard screen, and more than one applications program can open windows in the same standard screen (including the Workbench screen) at the same time.

Second, an Intuition standard screen—again with the exception of the Workbench screen (see the OpenWorkBench function)—is opened when one of its windows is opened with the OpenWindow function. This represents an indirect way to open a standard screen. Custom screens are opened differently; see the discussion of the OpenScreen function.

Third, you cannot change the display characteristics of any of the standard screens. The parameters that fix these characteristics have been predefined in the system's standard-screen structures. This allows all programs that use standard screens to present a uniform interface to the program user. Standard screen characteristics are defined and held constant by the internal routines of the Intuition system. Again, the only exception is the

Workbench screen, which the user can change with the Preferences program or the programmer can change by redefining the Preferences structure parameters.

The most important standard screen is the Workbench screen. It is a high-resolution, noninterlaced mode, 640-by-200-pixel display screen. Developers of text-oriented applications programs will find the Workbench screen the best screen to open windows into. The Workbench screen does not close automatically when you close all of its open windows; the other standard screens do close under this circumstance.

The Workbench screen is also memory-efficient. If you use the Workbench screen, you do not have to allocate memory for the bitmaps and structures that are required if you use another standard screen. However, note that the Workbench screen can be closed with the CloseWorkBench function. If you make this call, you will free up the memory assigned to the Workbench screen.

The Workbench program, which is automatically invoked when the Workbench screen is open, allows you to use and interact with the Amiga filing system. Your programs can therefore use icons and other graphic images to represent files. You then have access to the library of Workbench-related functions, which allow you to create and manipulate the Workbench applications program's objects and icons. The Workbench functions are discussed in Chapter 7.

You can create two basic types of custom screens. The first type is managed completely by the Intuition system without using any Graphics Library functions. The second type uses the Graphics Library functions to write directly into the screen's bitmap.

If you use this second type of custom screen, you are responsible for the detailed definition of its bitplanes, bitmap, and complete raster. You can also produce color animation, screen scrolling, patterned line drawing, patterned fills, and other detailed screen features. You can then combine such a custom screen with Intuition screens, windows, and other graphics entities. The interactions involved with these types of complex, nonstandard display definitions can lead to unexpected effects. Therefore, unless you are a very experienced programmer, you should probably stick with the standard and custom screens defined within the context of the Intuition functions.

When you design your custom screens, you can use Intuition's supplied features (text, gadgets, requesters, menu items, graphic images, etc.) or you can design features to suit your own purposes. Of course, you can combine some of the Intuition features with others of your own design to arrive at hybrid custom screens.

Your programs can place text into each of your screens and windows. To do this, you can create your own font or use the system default text font, which is Topaz. Topaz is a fixed-width font that comes in two sizes—Topaz-60 and Topaz-80. Topaz-60 is nine display screen lines tall and provides 64 characters per line of display in high-resolution mode and 32 characters in low-resolution mode. Topaz-80 is eight display screen lines tall and provides 80 characters per line of display in high-resolution mode and 40 characters in low-resolution mode.

Window Types

Intuition provides a number of unusual window types you may want to use in your programs. First, there is the borderless window. You set the BORDERLESS flag in the

NewWindow structure to get this type of window. (With all other types of windows, Intuition creates a thin border around the window.) Although a borderless window has no visible borders, it can have invisible borders. These invisible borders are determined by the location of various visible gadgets and text in the border areas of the window. However, if the window is designed with no border gadgets or text, there will be no visible identification of the boundary of the window; the window display will not be distinguishable from the background screen display. This is normally confusing, but you can put this type of window to good use.

In particular, if you make this window the full size of the display and declare it to be a backdrop window, you can draw into this backdrop window almost as freely as writing directly to the display memory of a custom screen. In addition, you will not run the risk of trashing menus or other windows in the display when you are drawing.

Second, there is the gimmezerozero window, which is specified by setting the GIMMEZEROZERO flag in the NewWindow structure. The gimmezerozero window actually consists of two windows: an inner window and an outer window. The outer window contains the window title, any window gadgets, and the window border, if any. The inner window contains all additional drawing information for this window. A separate bitmap is automatically assigned to the inner and outer windows when you create a gimmezerozero window. The main advantage of the gimmezerozero window is the freedom it gives you to draw into the inner window without worrying about drawing over the window title, window gadgets, or window borders.

Third, there is the backdrop window, which is specified by setting the BACKDROP flag in the NewWindow structure. A backdrop window always appears behind all other windows in a screen on the Intuition display. Its main advantage is that other windows can overlap it and be depth-arranged without ever going behind it.

The backdrop window differs from other windows in two ways:

1. The backdrop window is always behind all other windows in a specific screen. This includes any other backdrop windows that have been opened before this backdrop window was opened. You cannot depth-arrange your screen windows to put another type of window behind a backdrop window in the same screen.

2. You can attach only the close system gadget to a backdrop window.

The fourth type of window is a superbitmap window, which you specify by setting the SUPERBITMAP flag in the NewWindow structure. A superbitmap window has its own bitmap, which can be larger than the screen's window bitmap for this window—hence, the name superbitmap. The superbitmap contains all the bitplane pixel information needed to define the window display, both the visible and invisible parts. For this reason, the superbitmap provides all the information to refresh the window when part of the window is obscured by the user.

Screen and Window Titles

Each screen has two titles associated with it: the default title and the current title. The default title is contained in the NewScreen structure and is displayed when the screen first opens. The current title is associated with the window currently active in that screen. The characteristics (colors, etc.) of the current screen title depend on the preferences settings of the window currently open in that screen.

Each window in a screen (standard or custom) can have its own title, which appears in the window title bar, as well as its screen title, which appears in the screen title bar. When a window is active, it displays its own title in the screen title bar. The Intuition SetWindowTitles function allows you to specify, change, or delete either of these titles. The ShowTitle function also plays a role in window and screen title interactions.

Sprites in Intuition

In general, neither simple nor virtual sprites behave well in the Intuition system. The Graphics Library functions manage sprites independently of the Intuition display. This leads to a number of problems:

■ Sprites cannot be attached to any particular screen. Instead, they always appear in front of every Intuition screen.

■ When a screen is moved, the sprites do not automatically move with it. If you want the sprites to move, you must specifically call the Graphics Library animation MoveSprite or Animate functions.

■ Hardware sprites travel out of windows and screens.

Intuition System Structures

There are a number of structures defined and used internally by the Intuition software system. These structures sit in RAM at locations determined by the programmer. Some of these structures are static; they are initialized by your program task and remain in that state throughout the task's execution. The NewWindow and NewScreen structures are static structures. Others are dynamic; their contents change continuously as the user moves the mouse. The Window and Screen structures are examples of dynamic structures.

Most Intuition structures contain the following categories of structure information:

■ A set of substructure pointer parameters. An example of this is the FirstGadget parameter inside the NewWindow structure; this parameter points to the first gadget in a linked list of gadgets that can show in this window when it is displayed.

■ A set of location and size parameters. For example, the NewWindow, NewScreen, Window, and Screen structures all contain the LeftEdge, TopEdge, Width, and Height parameters. These parameters define the initial or current size of a specific display element.

■ A Flag parameter or parameters. The bits in this Flag parameter control various options associated with this structure and other structures to which it relates.

■ A set of display-element dimension-controlling parameters. Any display element that can be resized by the user has this type of parameter. The most obvious example is the Window structure, which has the parameters MinWidth, MinHeight, Max-Width, and MaxHeight. These parameters determine the allowable size variations of the dynamically changing window under user control.

■ A set of miscellaneous parameters required to fully define that display element. For example, the Window structure has the MouseX and MouseY parameter to indicate the current position of the mouse in the window.

The NewWindow Structure

The NewWindow structure contains all the parameters required to define a new window. This is how a NewWindow structure is defined:

```
struct New Window [
    SHORT LeftEdge, TopEdge;
    SHORT Width, Height;
    UBYTE DetailPen, BlockPen;
    ULONG IDCMPFlags;
    ULONG Flags;
    struct Gadget *First Gadget;
    struct Image *CheckMark;
    UBYTE *Title;
    struct Screen *Screen;
    struct BitMap *BitMap;
    SHORT MinWidth, MinHeight;
    SHORY MaxWidth, MaxHeight;
    USHORT Type;
};
```

Here is a list of the parameters in the NewWindow structure:

■ The LeftEdge parameter contains the initial x-position of the window.

■ The TopEdge parameter contains the initial y-position of the window.

■ The Width parameter contains the width of the window's raster bitmap.

■ The Height parameter contains the height of the window's raster bitmap.

■ The DetailPen parameter contains the color register number to use for window details such as gadgets or text in title bars.

■ The BlockPen parameter contains the color register number for block fills. This pen is used for the window's title bar.

■ The IDCMPFlags parameter contains a set of IDCMP flags. (See the discussion of the ModifyIDCMP function for a description of these flag bits.)

- The Flags parameter contains a number of bits for specifying window gadgets and other features of the new window.

- The FirstGadget parameter points to the first in a linked list of Gadget structures for gadgets to be placed in this window.

- The Checkmark parameter points to an Image structure for a custom check-mark image for menu displays.

- The Title parameter points to a null-terminated text string to be displayed in the window title bar when this window becomes active.

- The Screen parameter points to a Screen structure for custom screens. The window's bitmap is a subsection of this screen's bitmap.

- The BitMap parameter points to a BitMap structure for custom screens that have an associated superbitmap for refreshing purposes.

- The MinWidth, MinHeight, MaxWidth, and MaxHeight parameters contain a set of minimum and maximum values for sizing this window.

- The Type parameter contains the screen type for this window. This can be WORKBENCHSCREEN or CUSTOMSCREEN.

The Window Structure

The Window structure contains information about the changing condition of a window. You create the Window structure with a call to the OpenWindow function. The OpenWindow function requires a pointer to the NewWindow structure you previously defined in RAM. When OpenWindow returns, the Window structure will be initialized with the settings supplied in the NewWindow structure. Then, as the window is moved and acted on in other ways by the user, the Window structure keeps track of the changing state of the window. This includes the current size parameters of the window, the current number of requesters displayed in the window, and any other items that define the current state of the window.

This is how the Window structure is defined:

```
struct Window {
    struct Window *NextWindow;
    SHORT LeftEdge, TopEdge;
    SHORT Width, Height;
    SHORT MouseY, MouseX;
    SHORT MinWidth, MinHeight;
    SHORT MaxWidth, MaxHeight;
    ULONG Flags;
    struct Menu *MenuStrip;
    UBYTE *Title;
    struct Requester *FirstRequest;
    struct Requester *DMRequest;
```

```
        SHORT ReqCount;
        struct Screen *WScreen;
        struct RastPort *RPort;
        BYTE BorderLeft, BorderTop, BorderRight, BorderBottom;
        struct RastPort *BorderRPort;
        struct Gadget *FirstGadget;
        struct Window *Parent, *Descendent;
        USHORT *Pointer;
        BYTE PtrHeight;
        BYTE PtrWidth;
        BYTE XOffset, YOffset;
        ULONG IDCMPFlags;
        struct MsgPort *UserPort, *WindowPort;
        struct IntuiMessage *MessageKey;
        UBYTE DetailPen, BlockPen;
        struct Image *CheckMark;
        UBYTE *ScreenTitle;
        SHORT GZZMouseX;
        SHORT GZZMouseY;
        SHORT GZZWidth;
        SHORT GZZHeight;
        UBYTE *ExtData;
        BYTE *UserData;
};
```

The parameters in the Window structure are as follows:

- The NextWindow parameter is a pointer to a Window structure that represents the next window in a linked list of windows in a screen.

- The LeftEdge parameter contains the current x-coordinate of the left edge of the window represented by this Window structure. The system will change this parameter as the user moves and resizes the window.

- The TopEdge parameter contains the current y-coordinate of the top edge of the window represented by this Window structure. The system will change this parameter as the user moves and resizes the window.

- The Width parameter contains the current width (in number of pixels) of the window represented by this Window structure. The system will change this parameter as the user moves and resizes the window.

- The Height parameter contains the current height (in number of pixels) of the window represented by this Window structure. The system will change this parameter as the user moves and resizes the window.

- The MouseY and MouseX parameters contain the current y- and x-coordinates of the mouse pointer relative to the upper-left corner of the window represented by this Window structure. The system will change these parameters as the user moves the mouse inside the window.

■ The MinWidth and MinHeight parameters contain the minimum allowed width and height (in number of pixels) of the window represented by this Window structure.

■ The MaxWidth and MaxHeight parameters contain the maximum allowed width and height (in number of pixels) of the window represented by this Window structure.

■ The Flags parameter contains a set of flag parameter bits for the window represented by this Window structure. These include the WINDOWCLOSE, WINDOWDRAG, and WINDOWDEPTH flag bits. Other flag bits are detailed in the Intuition INCLUDE file.

■ The MenuStrip parameter is a pointer to a Menu structure, which represents the first menu in a linked list of menus associated with the window represented by this Window structure.

■ The Title parameter is a pointer to a null-terminated text string, which represents the title of the window that is represented by this Window structure. This is the title that will be displayed in the window title bar when this window is opened in its screen.

■ The FirstRequest parameter is a pointer to a Requester structure that represents the first requester in a linked list of requesters for the window represented by this Window structure.

■ The DMRequest parameter is a pointer to a Requester structure that represents a DMRequester for the window represented by this Window structure. See the ClearDMRequest and SetDMRequest functions.

■ The ReqCount parameter contains a count of the current number of active requesters blocking input to the window represented by this Window structure.

■ The WScreen parameter is a pointer to the Screen structure that represents the screen inside of which this window will appear when opened. If you opened the window in a custom screen, you already have a pointer to the Screen structure for the custom screen. However, if you opened the window in a standard screen (for example, the Workbench screen), this parameter provides the address of the Screen structure associated with that screen. See the GetScreen Data function.

■ The RPort parameter is a pointer to a RastPort structure that represents the drawing-control information for all drawing inside the window represented by this Window structure.

■ The BorderLeft, BorderTop, BorderRight, and BorderBottom parameters contain the pixel coordinates of the left, top, right, and bottom edges of the window border represented by this Window structure.

■ The BorderRPort parameter is a pointer to a RastPort structure that contains the drawing-control information required to draw the borders of the window represented by this Window structure.

■ The FirstGadget parameter is a pointer to a Gadget structure that represents the first gadget in a linked list of gadgets for the window represented by this Window structure.

■ The Parent parameter is a pointer to a Window structure that represents the window where the icon for this window appeared before it was opened. That window is the parent (in an AmigaDOS file tree) of this window.

■ The Descendent parameter is a pointer to a Window structure that represents a window whose icon appears in the window represented by this Window structure. That window is the descendent (in an AmigaDOS file tree) of this window.

■ The Pointer parameter is a pointer to sprite data for the mouse pointer sprite.

■ The PtrHeight and PtrWidth parameters contain the current height and width (in number of pixels) of the mouse pointer. These are used only for user-defined mouse pointers. For example, the system changes these when you change the pointer definition using the Preferences program.

■ The XOffset and YOffset parameters contain the current x- and y-offsets (in number of pixels from the top-left corner of the window) of the mouse pointer in the window represented by this Window structure.

■ The IDCMPFlags parameter contains a set of user-selected IDCMP flag parameters. These flag bits are defined under the ModifyIDCMP function discussion.

■ The UserPort parameter is a pointer to a MsgPort structure that represents the Intuition message port used to communicate with the task whose window is represented by this Window structure. Messages are passed back and forth between this message port and the message port pointed to by the WindowPort parameter.

■ The WindowPort parameter is a pointer to a MsgPort structure that represents the task reply port used to communicate with Intuition. That task is uniquely associated with the window defined by this Window structure.

■ The MessageKey parameter is a pointer to an IntuiMessage structure that is used to pass messages back and forth between the UserPort and the WindowPort message ports.

■ The DetailPen parameter contains the color register number of the Graphics Library drawing pen that will be used to render graphic details in the window represented by this Window structure.

■ The BlockPen parameter contains the color register number of the Graphics Library drawing pen that will be used to render block graphics in the window represented by this Window structure.

- The CheckMark parameter is a pointer to an Image structure that is used to define the image for the checkmark used in menus when menu items are selected.

- The ScreenTitle parameter is a pointer to a null-terminated text string that represents the screen title of the window represented by this Window structure. This is the title that will be displayed in the screen title bar when the window represented by this Window structure becomes the active window in the screen.

- The GZZMouseX and GZZMouseY parameters contain the mouse x- and y-coordinates (in number of pixels) relative to the origin of the inner window of a Gimmezerozero window.

- The GZZWidth and GZZHeight parameters contain the current width and height (in number of pixels) of the inner window of a Gimmezerozero window.

- The ExtData parameter is a pointer to the first of two user-defined data areas for the window represented by this Window structure.

- The UserData parameter is a pointer to the second of two user-defined data areas for the window represented by this Window structure.

The NewScreen Structure

The NewScreen structure is referenced in the Screen structure when you want to define a new screen in the system. As with the NewWindow structure, you define the NewScreen structure in RAM and provide a pointer to it when you call the OpenScreen function. The NewScreen structure defines all of the display characteristics for your new screen, including the size characteristics, the DetailPen, the BlockPen, and the gadgets attached to that screen.

The NewScreen structure is defined as follows:

```
struct NewScreen {
    SHORT LeftEdge, TopEdge;
    SHORT Width, Height;
    UBYTE DetailPen, BlockPen;
    USHORT ViewModes;
    USHORT Type;
    struct TextAttr *Font;
    UBYTE *DefaultTitle;
    struct Gadget *Gadgets;
    struct BitMap *CustomBitMap;
};
```

These are the parameters of the NewScreen structure:

- The LeftEdge parameter contains the pixel x-position of the left side of the screen when it is first opened.

- The TopEdge parameter contains the pixel y-position of the top of the screen when it is first opened.

- The Width parameter contains the pixel width of the screen. Use 320 for a low-resolution mode screen or 640 for a high-resolution mode screen.

- The Height parameter contains the pixel height of the screen. Use 200 for a non-interlaced mode screen or 400 for an interlaced mode screen.

- The Depth parameter contains the number of bitplanes in the screen bitmap. This can be a number from 1 to 5 for a single-playfield mode display or from 2 to 6 for a dual-playfield mode display.

- The DetailPen parameter contains the color register number to use for the screen details such as gadgets and text in the screen title bar.

- The BlockPen parameter contains the color register number for block fills such as the area filled in the screen title bar.

- The Type parameter indicates the type of screen. Set this to CUSTOMSCREEN.

- The Font parameter points to a TextAttr structure to be used for this screen. Set this to null if you want to use the Intuition default fonts (Topaz-60 and Topaz-80).

- The DefaultTitle parameter points to a null-terminated text string that you want displayed in the screen's title bar.

- The Gadgets parameter points to a Gadget structure for the first gadget in a linked list of gadgets to appear in that screen.

- The CustomBitMap parameter points to a BitMap structure used to define the display memory for this screen.

The Screen Structure

The Screen structure contains information about the changing condition of a custom screen. You create the Screen structure with a call to the OpenScreen function, which requires a pointer to the NewScreen structure you previously defined in RAM. When OpenScreen returns, the Screen structure will be initialized with the settings supplied in the NewScreen structure.

This is how a Screen structure is defined:

```
struct Screen {
    struct Screen *NextScreen;
    struct Window *FirstWindow;
    SHORT LeftEdge, TopEdge;
    SHORT Width, Height;
    SHORT MouseY, MouseX;
    USHORT Flags;
    UBYTE *Title;
    UBYTE *DefaultTitle;
    BYTE BarHeight, BarVBorder, BarHBorder;
    BYTE MenuVBorder, MenuHBorder;
```

```
        BYTE WBorTop, WBorLeft, WBorRight, WBorBottom;
        struct TextAttr *Font;
        struct ViewPort ViewPort;
        struct RastPort RastPort;
        struct BitMap BitMap;
        struct Layer_Info LayerInfo;
        struct Gadget *FirstGadget;
        UBYTE DetailPen, BlockPen;
        USHORT SaveColor0;
        struct Layer *BarLayer;
        UBYTE *ExtData;
        UBYTE *UserData;
    };
```

The parameters in the Screen structure are as follows:

- The NextScreen parameter is a pointer to a Screen structure, which represents the next custom screen in a linked list of custom screens.

- The FirstWindow parameter is a pointer to a Window structure, which represents the first window in the screen represented by this screen structure.

- The LeftEdge parameter contains the current pixel coordinate of the left edge of the screen (after movement or resizing) represented by this Screen structure. The system maintains this value and your program can look at this parameter to see where the user has currently positioned this screen.

- The TopEdge parameter contains the current pixel coordinate of the top edge of the screen represented by this Screen structure. The system maintains this value and your program can look at this parameter to see where the user has currently positioned this screen.

- The Width parameter contains the current width (in number of pixels) of the screen represented by this Screen structure. This parameter is not currently used by Intuition. However, for upward compatibility, always set this to 0.

- The Height parameter contains the current height (in number of pixels) of the screen represented by this Screen structure. This can be up to 200 for a non-interlaced mode display or up to 400 for an interlaced mode display.

- The MouseY and MouseX parameters contain the current y- and x-coordinates of the mouse pointer relative to the upper-left corner of the screen represented by this Screen structure. The system maintains this value and your program can look at these parameters to see where the user has currently positioned the mouse pointer.

- The Flags parameter contains a set of flag parameter bits, including WORK-BENCHSCREEN and CUSTOMSCREEN. Other bits are defined in the Intuition INCLUDE file.

- The Title parameter is a pointer to a null-terminated text string, which represents the title of the screen that is represented by this Screen structure. This is the title that will be displayed in the screen title bar when no window is currently active in this screen.

- The DefaultTitle parameter is a pointer to a null-terminated text string, which represents the default title of the screen represented by this Screen structure. This is the title that will be displayed in the screen title bar if no window in the screen has a screen title defined. This is also the screen title that is displayed when the screen first opens.

- The BarHeight parameter contains the height of the screen title bar for the screen represented by this Screen structure.

- The BarVBorder parameter contains the y-coordinate of the bottom of the screen title bar for the screen represented by this Screen structure.

- The BarHBorder parameter contains the x-coordinate of the right side of the screen title bar for the screen represented by this Screen structure.

- The MenuVBorder parameter contains the y-coordinate of the bottom of the menu bar for the menus associated with this Screen structure.

- The MenuHBorder parameter contains the x-coordinate of the right side of the menu bar for the menus associated with this Screen structure.

- The WBorTop parameter contains the y-coordinate of the top of the screen border for the screen represented by this Screen structure.

- The WBorLeft parameter contains the x-coordinate of the left of the screen border for the screen represented by this Screen structure.

- The WBorRight parameter contains the x-coordinate of the right of the screen border for the screen represented by this Screen structure.

- The WBorBottom parameter contains the y-coordinate of the bottom of the screen border for the screen represented by this Screen structure.

- The Font parameter is a pointer to a TextAttr structure, which represents the default font for all text displayed in the screen represented by this Screen structure.

- The ViewPort parameter contains the name of a Graphics Library ViewPort substructure, which contains the viewport definition of the screen represented by this Screen structure.

- The RastPort parameter contains the name of a Graphics Library RastPort substructure, which contains the drawing-control definitions of the screen represented by this Screen structure.

- The BitMap parameter contains the name of a Graphics Library BitMap substructure, which contains the pixel definitions of the screen represented by this Screen structure.

- The LayerInfo parameter contains the name of a Layers Library Layer substructure, which contains the layer definition of the screen represented by this Screen structure.

- The FirstGadget parameter is a pointer to a Gadget structure, which represents the first gadget in a linked list of gadgets for the screen represented by this Screen structure.

- The DetailPen parameter contains the color register number of the Graphics Library drawing pen that will be used to render graphic details (gadgets and text in the screen title bar) in the screen represented by this Screen structure.

- The BlockPen parameter contains the color register number of the Graphics Library drawing pen that will be used to render block graphics (for example, the screen title bar background area) in the screen represented by this Screen structure.

- The SaveColor0 parameter contains the color register number of the Graphics Library drawing pen that represents the background color for the screen represented by this Screen structure. The default value represents blue.

- The BarLayer parameter is a pointer to a Layer structure, which represents the layer used to define drawing information for the screen and menu title bars for the screen represented by this Screen structure.

- The ExtData parameter is a pointer to the first of two user-defined data areas for the screen represented by this Screen structure.

- The UserData parameter is a pointer to the second of two user-defined data areas for the screen represented by this Screen structure.

As the screen is moved and acted on in other ways by the user, the system changes parameters in the Screen structure to keep track of the changing state of the screen. This includes the current size parameters of that screen, the current mouse position in that screen, and any other items that define the current state of that screen. The Screen structure also includes the RastPort, ViewPort, BitMap, and LayerInfo substructures as part of its definition. These substructure definitions can be used by advanced programmers to examine and modify the details of an Intuition screen using the Graphics Library functions discussed in Chapter 2.

Other Structures

The Amiga Intuition functions work with several other structures:

BitMap	IntuiMessage	MenuItem	Remember
Border	IntuiText	Preferences	Requester
Gadget	Menu	PropInfo	StringInfo
Image			

If you want to know more about these structures, you should print and study the Intuition INCLUDE file. Their names suggest their use and purpose.

Programming under Intuition

Intuition is implemented as a library of C language functions. Applications programs can use these functions along with simple data structures to generate program displays and interact with the user.

Follow these basic steps to implement the Intuition software system in your programs:

1. Make sure you have the Intuition header (INCLUDE) files on a C language disk. These INCLUDE files contain all of the definitions of Intuition structures, data types, constants, and macros. Intuition contains six macros that deal with menu operations: MENUNUM, ITEMNUM, SUBNUM, SHIFTMENU, SHIFT-ITEM, and SHIFTSUB. As their names suggest, they deal with menus, menu items, and menu subitems. The only argument used in each is the menuNumber argument as defined in the ItemAddress function. Read the discussions of the individual macros.

2. Remember that Intuition is implemented as a library. For this reason, you must declare a pointer variable named IntuitionBase and call the Exec OpenLibrary function before you can use any of the Intuition functions.

3. Define each of your custom screens. Define a NewScreen structure and then call the OpenScreen function with a pointer to the NewScreen structure.

4. Define your windows. Define a NewWindow structure and then call the Open-Window function with a pointer to the NewWindow structure.

If you want to use assembly language, note that the 68000 registers are allocated in ascending order from register 0 to register 7 in each category (address registers and data registers). To find the correct association of register names with Intuition function arguments, look at the specific function and use the address registers for structure pointer arguments in the function call, starting with A0. In the same way, look at the specific function and use the data registers for data arguments in the function call, starting with D0. Note that the only exception to these rules occurs for the UnlockIBase functions as noted in that function discussion.

Assembly language programmers can use the Intuition assembly language INCLUDE file named Intuition.i to get the appropriate structures, etc. for their work.

Intuition Screens, Windows, and Menus: The User Interface

Figure 6.1 depicts the features of a typical Intuition display screen. Here you see a single screen with three windows. The main features of the screen are the screen close gadget, the screen title bar, the screen depth-arrangement gadgets, and the screen size gadget. It is important to understand that there may be other screens behind this screen. This is the foremost screen (with the highest video priority) at this time—possibly due to a previous depth-arrangement sequence.

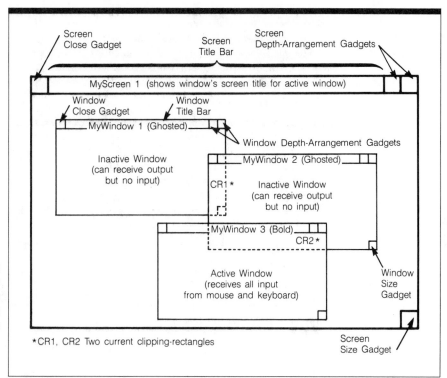

Figure 6.1:
Intuition Screen
with Windows
and System
Gadgets

If another screen has been defined, the screen depth-arrangement gadget can be used to send this screen behind the other screen. When this is done, that other screen will appear on the display screen; that newly displayed screen will then present its windows (if open) to the user.

The main features of each window in the screen are the window close gadget, the window depth-arrangement gadget, the window size gadget, and the window title bar.

Note that there is only one active window in the screen at any given time. This is pictured as Window 3 in Figure 6.1. This is the window that will receive input when the user moves the mouse over the menus or types from the keyboard. Each window can be resized using the size gadget of that window. The window does not need to be active to be resized. In the same way, each window can be moved or dragged around the screen without being the active window. However, a window will become active when these operations are completed.

In addition, a window is made active when the mouse Selection button is clicked anywhere inside that window. Note that the screen title of the active window appears in the screen title bar; when the active window is changed, the title in the screen title bar changes. The text in the title bar of the active window is always presented in bold type. The window title text of all inactive windows are always presented in dimmed (ghosted) text.

When the user presses the mouse Menu button the menus of the active window are displayed below the screen title bar. The user can then move the mouse pointer to the menu text and select menu items or subitems.

The selection of menu items and menu subitems is illustrated in Figure 6.2. In this figure a screen is displayed with a number of menus associated with the currently active window. The menu titles of each window menu appear in the screen title bar.

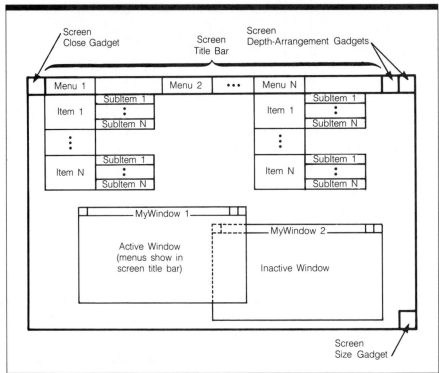

Figure 6.2:
Intuition Menus,
Menu Items,
and Menu
Subitems

Note that this figure actually shows the menu items and menu subitems for more than one menu displayed simultaneously on the display screen. This is just for illustration purposes and cannot be achieved on the Intuition display screen. In fact, if the user selects a specific menu with the mouse Menu button, the menu items for only that particular menu appear on the screen. If the user further selects a menu item with the mouse Menu button, all menu subitems for that menu item appear.

Structure Linkages in the Intuition System

The main characteristics of the Intuition software system are illustrated by the series of diagrams presented in Figures 6.3 through 6.7. These diagrams illustrate most of the structure linkage connections in the Intuition system. Learning how to deal with these linkages is the essence of Intuition programming using standard C language programming procedure.

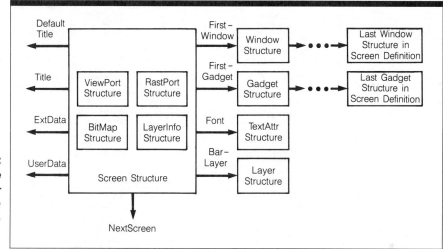

Figure 6.3:
Structure Linkages for Each Screen Structure

Keep in mind that not all of the structure parameters are represented in these figures; just the ones that deal with structure linkages and pointers. Consult the Intuition INCLUDE files to determine all the parameters required to define a structure. Also keep in mind that not all of these parameters are specified by the programmer; some are specified and maintained by the system.

The large rectangle in each of Figures 6.3–6.7 represents the structure being discussed. For example, in Figure 6.3, the Screen structure is being discussed. Each small rectangle inside the Screen structure rectangle represents a substructure. Arrows represent pointer parameters in the structure being discussed. Each small rectangle pointed to represents a specific instance of another structure type.

Screen Structure Linkages

Each Screen structure has zero or more window structures linked to it. These Window structures are represented by the upper row of small rectangles. The FirstWindow parameter points to the first of these window structures. In addition, each Screen structure has

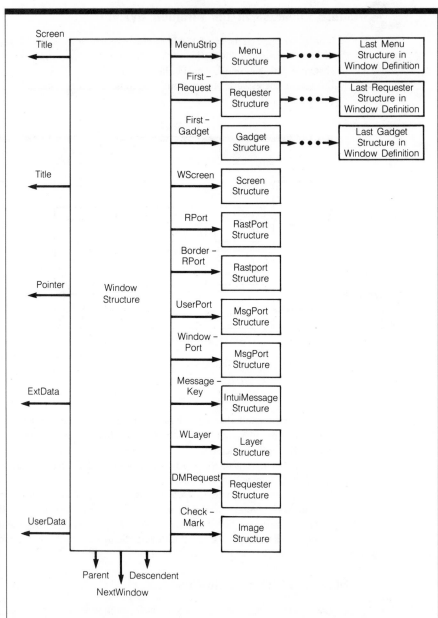

Figure 6.4:
*Structure
Linkages for
Each Window
Structure*

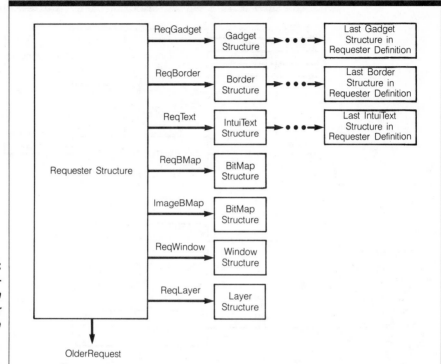

Figure 6.5:
Structure Linkages for Each Requester Structure

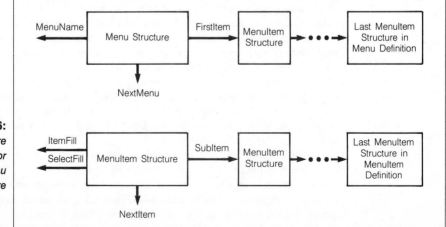

Figure 6.6:
Structure Linkages for Each Menu Structure

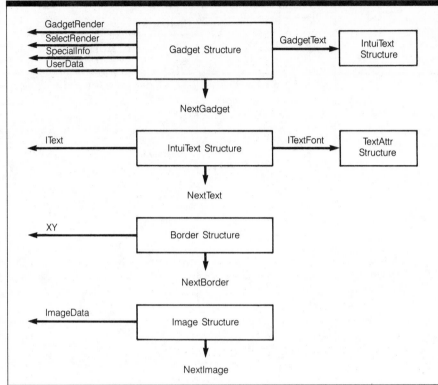

Figure 6.7:
Structure Linkages for the Gadget, IntuiText, Border, and Image Structures

zero or more Gadget structures linked to it. The FirstGadget parameter points to the first of these Gadget structures. These Window and Gadget structures in turn contain pointers to the next in a series of linked structures. Each of these structures is singly linked (versus doubly linked); each points to the next one in that specific sequence, but each does not point to the previous one in that sequence.

In addition, each Screen structure points to a TextAttr structure using the Font pointer parameter, a Layer structure using the BarLayer pointer parameter, a set of string data in memory pointed to by the DefaultTitle and Title parameters, and a set of user-defined screen data, pointed to by the BxtData and User Data parameters. (These last appear on the left side of the figure.)

Finally, each Screen structure possibly contains a pointer (NextScreen) to another Screen structure linked to this particular Screen structure.

Each Window structure is linked to its owning Screen structure (see the WScreen parameter in Figure 6.4). You should study Figure 6.3 until you understand how to define a screen and the windows in that screen. However, keep in mind that each screen usually starts with a definition of the NewScreen structure. Finally, always keep in mind that managing screens is nothing more than using these linkages together with the Intuition functions to manipulate your screens. Once created, all of these screens can be depth-arranged using either Intuition functions or user mouse commands.

Window Structure Linkages

Figure 6.4 shows a Window structure, represented by the large rectangle, together with a series of pointers to small rectangles that represent other structures specified in the Window structure. In addition, each Window structure contains pointers to a set of data in memory at locations named by the ScreenTitle, Title, Pointer, ExtData and UserData pointer parameters. These appear on the left side of the figure.

Notice that each Window structure possibly contains information to define a set of singly linked Menu, Requester, and Gadget structures. These linkages define three linked lists for this window. These lists define all the menus, requesters, and gadgets associated with this window. Nine other pointer parameters (WScreen to CheckMark) point to a series of other structures required to manage the window associated with this window structure.

In addition, each Window structure possibly contains a pointer (NextWindow) to another Window structure for a window in a particular screen. Finally, the Parent parameter points to the Window structure that was the parent (contained an icon for) this Window structure. The Descendent parameter points to a Window structure for a descendent window, a window whose icon appears in this window. Both of these parameters are maintained by the system.

If you study these linkages you will see how to define a linked list of Window structures. Once created, all of these windows will open in the screen pointed to by the WScreen parameter.

Requester Structure Linkages

Figure 6.5 shows a Requester structure, represented by the large rectangle, together with a series of pointers to small rectangles that represent other structures specified in the Requester structure. In addition, each Requester structure may point to another Requester structure with the OlderRequest pointer parameter.

Each Requester structure possibly contains a set of information to define a series of singly linked Gadget, Border, and IntuiText structures related to that Requester structure. The Gadget structures define the gadgets that are displayed when this requester is displayed in a window; the Border structures define all the border lines associated with this requester; the IntuiText structures define all the text associated with this requester.

If you study these linkages you will see how to define a linked list of Requester structures. Once created, all of these requesters will open in a particular window as designated by the ReqWindow parameter.

Menu and MenuItem Structure Linkages

Figure 6.6 describes how to design a window menu strip in Intuition. A menu strip consists of a number of menus, menu items, and menu subitems. First, the figure shows a Menu structure, represented by a large rectangle, together with two small rectangles that represent a linked list of MenuItem structures specified in the Menu structure. The First-Item parameter points to the first MenuItem structure in the linked list. In addition, each Menu structure contains a pointer (MenuName) to a null-terminated text string to define the name of the menu. Finally, each Menu structure possibly contains a pointer (Next-Menu) to another Menu structure for a menu in this window.

The second large rectangle in the figure represents a MenuItem structure, which may point to another MenuItem structure referenced by the pointer parameter NextItem. The SubItem pointer parameter points to the first in a linked list of MenuItem structures that define the menu subitems for this menu item.

If you study these linkages you will see how to define a linked list of Menu structures for a menu strip in an Intuition window.

Gadget, IntuiText, Border, and Image Structure Linkages

Figure 6.7 shows the linkages for the Gadget, IntuiText, Border, and Image structures. Note that these linkages are very simple compared to the other Intuition structures.

The first large rectangle in Figure 6.7 shows a Gadget structure. There are only two linkages in the Gadget structure. The first is defined by the GadgetText pointer parameter, which points to an IntuiText structure, which in turn points to a null-terminated text string defining the gadget text. Also, each Gadget structure possibly contains a pointer (NextGadget) to another Gadget structure for a gadget in a particular gadget list.

The next large rectangle in Figure 6.7 shows an IntuiText structure. There are only three linkages in the IntuiText structure. The first is defined by the ITextFont pointer parameter, which points to a TextAttr structure. The second is defined by the IText pointer parameter, which points to the null-terminated text string that defines the IntuiText structure text. Finally, each IntuiText structure possibly contains a pointer (NextText) to another IntuiText structure for a text definition in a particular text definition list.

The next large rectangle in Figure 6.7 represents a Border structure. There are only two linkages in the Border structure. The first is defined by the XY pointer parameter, which points to a set of line definitions (x,y values) to define a border. In addition, each Border structure may contain a pointer (NextBorder) to another Border structure for a border definition in a particular border list.

The last large rectangle in Figure 6.7 shows an Image structure containing the ImageData pointer parameter, which points to an image definition in memory, and possibly containing a pointer (NextImage) to another Image structure in this particular image list.

If you study these linkages you will see how to define a linked list of Gadget, IntuiText, Border, and Image structures. Once created, all of these structures can be used to define useful items in your screens, windows, and requesters.

ActivateGadget

Syntax of Function Call

success = ActivateGadget (gadget, window, requester)

Purpose of Function

This function activates a string gadget either directly in a window or in a requester in a window. This saves the user the additional step of activating the string gadget when he or she wants to enter text into that string gadget. If specified conditions are met, Activate-Gadget will return a TRUE value; otherwise a FALSE value is returned.

Inputs to Function

gadget   A pointer to a Gadget structure that represents the gadget you want to activate; the Gadget structure must represent a string gadget

window   A pointer to the Window structure for the window that contains the gadget

requester   A pointer to the Requester structure for the requester that contains the gadget; set this to null if the gadget is not in a requester

Discussion

ActivateGadget is one of the four 1.2 release functions that deal with gadgets and the gadget list in the Intuition software system.

The ActivateGadget function saves the user some work. When the user chooses a string gadget, he or she will not need to click the Menu button to activate the string gadget. Instead, the user can proceed to type text characters directly into the string gadget once it is displayed. This is an improvement over the earlier releases of the Amiga software.

Several conditions have to be met in order that the ActivateGadget function operate properly. These are as follows:

■ The specified gadget must be a string gadget.

- The window argument must point to the Window structure for the window that actually contains the gadget pointed to by the gadget argument. Any mismatch in these two parameters will cause a problem.

- If the gadget is in a requester, the window must contain the requester and a pointer to the requester must also be included in the function call. The requester argument will only be accepted if the associated Gadget structure has the REQGADGET flag parameter set.

- The window must be currently active. You can set the IDCMP ACTIVEWINDOW flag to make sure that your task receives a message to sense when a particular window is currently active. Then you can check the WINDOWACTIVE flag in the Window structure to verify that a window is currently active.

- No other gadgets can be currently in use; that is, the user cannot be playing with them at the time when ActivateGadget is called. This includes system gadgets such as those for window sizing, dragging, etc.

- If the gadget is in a requester, that requester must be currently active. You can use the IDCMP REQSET and REQCLEAR flags to receive an IDCMP message to sense when a requester is active. Then you can check the REQACTIVE flag in the Requester structure to verify that a requester is currently active.

ActivateWindow

Syntax of Function Call

ActivateWindow (window)

Purpose of Function

This function activates a window. It acts as a supplement to the ACTIVATE flag parameter in the Window structure. You should call this function synchronously with some action by the user. The window will not become active until the user has finished playing with gadgets or is finished sizing or dragging that window or other windows.

Inputs to Function

window   A pointer to the Window structure for the window you want to activate

Discussion

There are two 1.2 release functions that deal with windows in the Intuition software system: ActivateWindow and RefreshWindowFrame.

There are several ways to make a window active. First, you can set the ACTIVATE parameter in the Window structure to activate a window when it is first opened in a screen. Second, the user can activate a window by clicking the mouse Selection button anywhere in that window at any time the window is displayed. Third, you can activate a window using the ActivateWindow function.

Note that the window may not become active immediately. Instead, the action may be deferred until the user completes some ongoing action such as playing with the window gadgets or menus. Your program can test the WINDOWACTIVE flag in the Window structure to determine when the window actually becomes active. To do this, you must set the ACTIVEWINDOW flag in the IDCMP for that window.

AddGadget

Syntax of Function Call

gadgetPosition = AddGadget (pointer, gadget, position)

Purpose of Function

This function adds the specified gadget to the Intuition system gadget list for the designated window or screen. The gadget is placed into the gadget list for that window or screen. If the SCRGADGET flag is set, the pointer variable argument refers to a Screen structure. If this flag is not set, the pointer variable argument refers to a Window structure. AddGadget returns the gadget list position for that window or screen in the gadget-Position variable.

Inputs to Function

pointer   A pointer to the Window or Screen structure with which this gadget is associated

gadget   A pointer to the new Gadget structure

position   The integer position in the list for the new gadget; zero is the first position in the list

Discussion

There are six Intuition functions that manage gadgets: AddGadget, OnGadget, OffGadget, RefreshGadgets, RemoveGadget, and ModifyProp. There is more information on gadgets in the discussions of each of these functions.

Gadgets added to a screen or window are added into a linked list. The position argument in the AddGadget function call determines where in the linked list a specific gadget will be placed. If you set this position to 0, the gadget will be added at the head of the list; if you set it to 1, the gadget will be inserted after the first gadget but before the second. If you specify the position argument to be greater than the current number of gadgets in the list, the new gadget will be inserted at the end of the list; this is equivalent to appending the gadget to the gadget list. A safe way to ensure that a gadget is appended is to use a − 1 position argument.

The system itself manages a number of gadgets in each window and screen. These gadgets are placed at the front of the gadget list. This is a safety measure; if you position your own gadgets in a way that interferes with the graphic representation of the system gadgets, the system gadgets will appear on top of your gadgets and will be selected first by the user. This protects the system gadgets. If you start adding gadgets to the front of the list, you will interfere with this plan. If the image definitions of your gadgets never overlap the system gadgets, this problem will not occur.

AddGList

Syntax of Function Call

actual_position = AddGList (window, gadget, position, number_gadgets, requester)

Purpose of Function

This function adds a gadget list to the already existing gadget list of a window or requester. The new list then becomes a sublist inside the new bigger list. The new gadget sublist is linked into the original list at the ordinal list position specified by the position argument. AddGList returns the actual ordinal position of the newly added gadget sublist.

Inputs to Function

window   A pointer to a Window structure for the window that will contain the gadgets in the new gadget list

gadget	A pointer to the Gadget structure for the first gadget in the gadget sublist
position	The ordinal position where the first gadget in the gadget sublist should be inserted into the original list of gadgets; the original gadget list index starts at gadget position 0
number _gadget	The number of gadgets from the new gadget sublist to be added; if the entire new gadget sublist is to be added, use −1 for this parameter
requester	A pointer to the Requester structure for the requester that will display the gadgets in the new gadget sublist

Discussion

AddGList is one of the four 1.2 release functions that deal with gadgets and the gadget list in the Intuition software system.

Each window in the system can have a number of gadgets associated with it. At different stages of your program, you may find it useful to add some gadgets to the list of gadgets you associate with some of your windows or requesters in those windows. This is the purpose of the AddGList function. The system maintains information about gadgets and gadget lists using two structures new to the 1.2 release software. These are the GadgetInfo and GListEnv structures. You can study these structures by looking at the Intuitionbase.h INCLUDE file.

Note the following when you use this function:

■ The requester argument must point to a Requester structure for a requester that is actually associated with that particular window. Any mismatch here will cause AddGList to fail.

■ The REQGADGET flag parameter (the GadgetType parameter) must be set or cleared consistently for all gadgets in the gadget sublist; either they are all requester gadgets or they are not.

■ When AddGList returns, the NextGadget parameter in one Gadget structure (the one with sublist ordinal position value number_gadgets) will be changed to a null value. Thus, if you are adding three gadgets from a linked sublist of five gadgets, the link between the third and fourth gadgets in the sublist will be broken when AddGList returns; NextGadget will be null in the third Gadget structure. This is also true if you place all gadgets in the sublist into the original gadget list; the NextGadget parameter in the last Gadget structure in the sublist will be set to null when AddGList returns.

■ AddGList will add gadgets from the sublist to the original gadget list until the number of gadgets in number_gadgets are added or until the NextGadget parameter in one of the Gadget structures is null. This provides two ways to put part (and perhaps all) of the sublist into the original gadget list.

AllocRemember

Syntax of Function Call

memBlock = AllocRemember (rememberKey, size, flags)

Purpose of Function

This function allocates a block of memory to be used in your program. It not only allocates the stated memory block but also links it to other memory blocks associated with this specific Intuition program task. This linkage allows your program task to deallocate all assigned memory blocks at once at a later time. If the memory allocation is successful, AllocRemember returns the byte address of your requested memory block in the memBlock variable. A node to reference that block will also be linked into the list pointed to by your rememberKey pointer variable. If the allocation fails, AllocRemember returns a null and the list pointed to by rememberKey, if any, will not be changed.

Inputs to Function

rememberKey	The address of a pointer to a Remember structure; initialize this pointer to null before your first call to AllocRemember
size	The size in bytes of the memory block allocation
flags	The specification for the memory block allocation

Discussion

There are two Intuition functions that deal directly with memory allocation, AllocRemember and FreeRemember. The Intuition system automatically establishes a linked list of memory assignments, simplifying the job of memory maintenance.

The AllocRemember function calls the Exec AllocMem function. (Read Chapter 1 to see how the AllocMem function works.) AllocRemember also links this memory allocation into a master list of memory blocks (a Remember structure) assigned to this task.

You create an anchor to this Remember structure by creating a pointer variable to it (rememberKey). You initialize that variable to null before your first AllocRemember call. Whenever you call the AllocRemember function, it actually performs two allocations. The first allocation is for the memory block itself; the second allocation is for the Remember structure. The Remember structure is filled with data that describe the memory allocations in your program.

You can later call the Intuition FreeRemember function to deallocate in one call all the memory blocks allocated by all AllocRemember function calls in a specific task.

An example of this is as follows:

```
struct Remember *RememberKey
RememberKey = NULL
AllocRemember (&RememberKey, BUFSIZE, MEMF_CHIP)
FreeRemember (&RememberKey, TRUE)
```

AutoRequest

Syntax of Function Call

```
response = AutoRequest (window, bodyText, positiveText,
                         negativeText, positiveFlags,
                         negativeFlags, width, height)
```

Purpose of Function

This function places a requester on the display screen. It then waits for a response from the user (or the system) to satisfy that request. If the response is positive, AutoRequest returns TRUE; if the response is negative, AutoRequest returns FALSE. These values are returned in the Boolean response variable.

Inputs to Function

window	A pointer to a Window structure
bodyText	A pointer to an IntuiText structure
positiveText	A pointer to a second IntuiText structure
negativeText	A pointer to a third IntuiText structure
positiveFlags	Flag bits for the IDCMP
negativeFlags	Flag bits for the IDCMP
width	The width in pixels of the requester
height	The height in pixels of the requester

Discussion

There are seven Intuition functions that deal directly with requesters: AutoRequest, Build-SysRequest, ClearDMRequest, FreeSysRequest, InitRequester, Request, and SetDM-Request. These functions provide all the facilities you need to create and manipulate requesters (screen prompts) in windows and screens. There is more information on requesters in the discussions of each of these functions.

AutoRequest produces a very simple requester on the display screen that asks the user for a yes or no response. The positiveText argument is a pointer to an IntuiText structure containing a pointer to the text you want associated with the user's "Yes," "True," or "Retry" responses. The negativeText argument is a pointer to an IntuiText structure containing a pointer to the text you want associated with the user's "No," "False," or "Cancel" responses.

The text for positive responses is automatically placed in the lower-left corner of the requester; the text for negative responses is automatically placed in the lower-right corner of the requester. The IDCMP flag bits allow either positive or negative external events to satisfy the requester. For example, inserting a disk in a drive is a positive external event that can satisfy a requester.

When you call the AutoRequest function, Intuition will build the requester, display it, and wait for a response from the user. If the designated window can hold the requester, it is displayed in that window. If the designated window cannot hold the requester because of information already in that window, another window is opened to display the requester.

The AutoRequest function calls the BuildSysRequest function to provide a requester on the display screen. The arguments to the AutoRequest function call are passed automatically to the BuildSysRequest function. If the BuildSysRequest function returns a Window structure pointer, the Window structure will have its IDCMP message ports and flags initialized according to the AutoRequest function arguments; otherwise, BuildSysRequest returns a TRUE or FALSE value to the AutoRequest function.

BeginRefresh

Syntax of Function Call

BeginRefresh (window)

Purpose of Function

This function sets up a simple-refresh window for optimized refreshing. It sets Intuition internal states and then calls the BeginUpdate function in the Layers Library. This function does not return any values.

Inputs to Function

window   A pointer to a Window structure whose window needs refreshing

Discussion

There are twelve Intuition functions that work directly with windows: BeginRefresh, CloseWindow, EndRefresh, EndRequest, MoveWindow, OpenWindow, ReportMouse, SetWindowTitles, SizeWindow, WindowLimits, WindowToFront, and WindowToBack. There is more information on windows in the discussions of each of these functions.

The purpose of the BeginRefresh function is to ensure that window refreshing is done only to those portions of the simple-refresh window that need to be redrawn. The BeginRefresh function uses the clipping rectangles of the layer to determine which part of the window should be refreshed. It calls the BeginUpdate function in the Layers Library to exchange the appropriate DamageList and ClipRect structure pointers.

Intuition provides three different ways to refresh window displays. These are the simple-refresh, smart-refresh, and superbitmap-refresh methods. The concepts involved in these three different refreshing methods are closely tied to the layer and clipping-rectangle concepts, which are discussed in Chapters 2 and 5.

The window always shares part of the screen's bitmap. In fact, the bitmap information for the screen area where a window is displayed is the bitmap information for that window. However, as windows are moved, resized, and so forth, portions of the window are obscured. The three methods of screen refreshing differ in how they handle the bitmap information for these obscured areas. Obviously, the bitmap information for the obscured areas is not part of the screen bitmap. If it were, it would show on the screen. Therefore, the bitmap information for obscured areas is elsewhere in the system.

In the simple-refresh method, your program is responsible for redrawing the display of obscured parts of a window. When a window is partly obscured using simple refreshing, the obscured portion is discarded from the screen's bitmap and is not saved in an off-screen memory buffer. When this obscured area is to be newly exposed, your program must redraw that part of the screen. This means that the program must use the Graphics Library functions (AreaDraw, AreaMove, AreaEnd, etc.) to redraw those portions of the screen display. Note that this effectively places new bitmap information into the screen bitmap. If the user merely drags the window around, however (without obscuring part of it), Intuition will keep the display of that window up to date without the help of your program.

The simple-refresh method is slower than the smart-refresh and superbitmap-refresh methods, because simple-refresh operations require execution of drawing functions. However, because no off-screen buffers are saved, the simple-refresh method is more memory efficient; it uses only the screen's display memory for the window's display.

With the smart-refresh method, Intuition keeps all information about the obscured portions of the window in a group of off-screen RAM buffers. Then, if the user reveals parts of a window (or the entire window) that were previously obscured, Intuition automatically gets the bitmap information for those areas, transfers this information into the screen bitmap, and redraws the screen. The smart-refresh method uses the screen's display memory for the current window display as well as off-screen buffers for the obscured parts of the window display.

To set up a smart-refresh window, merely set the Flags parameter in the New-Window structure to SMART_REFRESH. This tells the system to refresh the window according to the smart-refresh method. The buffers used for off-screen portions of the display are allocated automatically by the system and can be scattered throughout memory. It is obvious that the smart-refresh method uses more display memory, but it redraws the window display faster than the simple-refresh method.

With the superbitmap-refresh method, a separate bitmap of the window is kept in a single off-screen buffer area. The term superbitmap comes from the size of the off-screen bitmap; a superbitmap is usually larger than the portion of the screen bitmap that holds the on-screen window. Your program never has to worry about redisplaying obscured portions of a superbitmap window. Once the window is designated as a superbitmap window, Intuition automatically refreshes that window using the information in the superbitmap RAM area.

These are the steps involved in setting up a superbitmap window:

1. Allocate RAM space for the superbitmap. You can use the Graphics Library Alloc-Raster function for this purpose. Note that this area of memory can be larger than the window subsection of the screen bitmap.

2. Create a BitMap structure. This BitMap structure will contain a pointer to a bitmap to be used as the superbitmap for this window. The Graphics Library function InitBitMap can be used to initialize the contents of the BitMap structure.

BuildSysRequest

Syntax of Function Call

window = BuildSysRequest (window, bodyText, positiveText,
negativeText, IDCMPFlags, width, height)

Purpose of Function

This function builds a requester in the window specified by the window argument. If all goes well, BuildSysRequest returns a pointer to the Window structure associated with this window.

Inputs to Function

window	A pointer to a Window structure
bodyText	A pointer to an IntuiText structure
positiveText	A pointer to a second IntuiText structure
negativeText	A pointer to a third IntuiText structure
IDCMPFlags	The IDCMP flag bits you want to use for the initialization of the IDCMP of the window containing the requester
width	The pixel width of the requester
height	The pixel height of the requester

Discussion

There are seven Intuition functions that work directly with requesters: AutoRequest, BuildSysRequest, ClearDMRequest, FreeSysRequest, InitRequester, Request, and SetDMRequest. There is more information on requesters in the discussions of each of these functions.

There are several steps required to use a requester properly in your program:

1. You must declare and allocate a Requester structure.

2. You must initialize the Requester structure with a call to the InitRequester function.

3. You must fill out the requester with specifications for the gadgets, text, borders, and imagery.

4. If you are using the IDCMP channel for requester input, you must decide whether to use the special functions provided by the IDCMP.

5. You must call either the Request or SetDMRequest functions to display the requester.

Follow these steps to create a Requester structure:

1. Initialize the Requester structure with a call to the InitRequester function; this will set most of the Requester structure variables to their default values—several will be set to null values. Fill in the unused values explicitly with structure parameter assignment statements in your program.

2. Set up a gadget list. Your requester can manage a linked list of gadgets. You should take care not to specify gadgets that extend beyond the requester rectangle boundaries. If you are using custom gadgets designed with your own bitmaps, you must

make sure that there is a well-defined correspondence between the gadget's selection boxes and the requester images you supply.

3. Supply a BitMap structure if this is a custom requester with its own bitmap.

If system conditions are such that the requester cannot be rendered in the window, Build-SysRequest will call the DisplayAlert function. The text for the requester will then be passed to the DisplayAlert function. What happens next depends on the user's actions. Specifically, the value (TRUE or FALSE) passed to the DisplayAlert function will be TRUE if the user pressed the Selection button on the mouse (the left button) and FALSE if the user pressed the Menu button (the right button).

If you are using the IDCMP (Intuition direct communications port) method of window I/O (see the ModifyIDCMP function), you can use some IDCMP flags to add refinements to your requesters. There are three IDCMP flags that are especially important:

■ REQVERIFY. When this flag is set to 1, you can use it to make sure that your program is ready to allow a requester to appear in a window. When your program receives a REQVERIFY message, the requester will not appear in the window until your program task replies to the message.

■ REQSET. If this flag is set to 1, your program will receive a message when the first requester opens in the window.

■ REQCLEAR. If this flag is set to 1, your program will receive a message when the last requester is cleared from the window.

You can set these flags either when you create a NewWindow structure or with a call to the ModifyIDCMP function.

ClearDMRequest

Syntax of Function Call

notinuse = ClearDMRequest (window)

Purpose of Function

This function clears the double-menu requester from a window. This is the special requester you attach to a double-click of the mouse Menu button. If the double-menu requester is not currently in use, ClearDMRequest zeroes the DMRequester pointer in the Window structure and returns TRUE for the notinuse Boolean variable. If the double-menu requester is currently in use, the DMRequester pointer in the Window structure is not changed and the ClearDMRequest function returns FALSE for the notinuse Boolean variable.

Inputs to Function

window   A pointer to the Window structure whose window is to be cleared of a double-menu requester

Discussion

There are seven Intuition functions that work directly with requesters: AutoRequest, BuildSysRequest, ClearDMRequest, FreeSysRequest, InitRequester, Request, and SetDMRequest. There is more information on requesters in the discussions of each of these functions.

A double-menu requester is displayed only when the user double-clicks the mouse Menu button; once this happens, all input to that window is blocked. Note that this same blocking behavior occurs when Intuition (or your program) brings up a requester without user intervention. In addition, a message stating that the requester now appears in the input window is placed into the window's input stream. If you want to stop the user from bringing up a double-menu requester in a particular window, you can unlink it from that window by using the ClearDMRequest function.

ClearMenuStrip

Syntax of Function Call

ClearMenuStrip (window)

Purpose of Function

This function clears a menu strip from a designated window. It does not return a value.

Inputs to Function

window   A pointer to a Window structure

Discussion

There are five Intuition functions that work directly with menus: ClearMenuStrip, Item-Address, OnMenu, OffMenu, and SetMenuStrip. These functions provide all the capability you need to create and manipulate menus and menu items in windows and screens. There is more information on menus in the discussions of each of these functions.

A menu strip is a linked list of Menu and MenuItem structures. This list is used to define all the text in a menu and its submenus. Eventually, you must remove every menu strip that you submit to Intuition. You can always clear the menu strip with a call to the ClearMenuStrip function. In addition, you can use the ClearMenuStrip function in another way: if you want to change the menu strip definition, call ClearMenuStrip, change the menu-related structures, and then call the SetMenuStrip function.

The flow of events for menu operations is as follows:

1. Call the OpenWindow function to open a window.

2. Call the SetMenuStrip and ClearMenuStrip functions in pairs to set and clear menu strips in the window you just opened.

3. Call the CloseWindow function to close that window.

Clearing the menu strip before closing the window avoids problems that can occur if the user is accessing a menu when the program closes the window.

ClearPointer

Syntax of Function Call

ClearPointer (window)

Purpose of Function

This function clears a task-specific definition of a mouse pointer image. The Intuition default pointer image is then displayed in that window every time the window becomes active. If the window is active when the ClearPointer function executes, the task-specific pointer image is changed immediately to the default Intuition arrow pointer image. Clear-Pointer does not return a value.

Inputs to Function

window   A pointer to a Window structure whose window is to be cleared of its pointer image definition

Discussion

There are two Intuition functions that work directly with pointer images, SetPointer and ClearPointer. These functions allow you to establish a window with its own pointer image and later clear that pointer image from that window. In this way, you can create your own pointer images and avoid using the arrow pointer image supplied as the default pointer image in the Intuition system.

The default Intuition pointer is always hardware sprite 0 and is designed with the light source coming from the top-right of the display screen. You should consider the same perspective when you are designing your own pointer; it will appear bright on its upper-right side. These are the color assignments used with the Intuition pointer sprite data:

color 16   Transparent (hardware color register 16)
color 17   Medium-intensity color (hardware color register 17)
color 18   Low-intensity color (hardware color register 18)
color 19   High-intensity color (hardware color register 19)

To be consistent with the Intuition default pointer, your customized pointer should be framed by either color 17 or color 19. You can set the colors of your customized pointer image by calling the Graphics Library function SetRGB4.

See the discussion of the SetPointer function for information on constructing and using a customized pointer in your programs.

CloseScreen

Syntax of Function Call

CloseScreen (screen)

Purpose of Function

This function closes an Intuition custom screen and deallocates all memory assigned to the screen. CloseScreen does not return a value.

Inputs to Function

screen   A pointer to a Screen structure whose screen should be closed

Discussion

There are seven Intuition functions that work directly with Intuition display screens: OpenScreen, CloseScreen, MoveScreen, MakeScreen, ShowTitle, ScreenToBack, and ScreenToFront.

The CloseScreen function not only closes the screen but also deallocates the memory assigned to the Screen structure. It also unlinks the Screen structure from the associated ViewPort structure. If the screen has open windows, CloseScreen still closes the screen. If this is the last screen closed, the Workbench screen will appear automatically on the display screen.

CloseWindow

Syntax of Function Call

CloseWindow (window)

Purpose of Function

This function closes an Intuition window, deallocating any memory assigned to that window. If the window appears in a system standard screen (with the exception of the Workbench screen) and is the last window to close in that screen, that screen is also closed by the CloseWindow function call. CloseWindow does not return a value.

Inputs to Function

window   A pointer to a Window structure whose window should be closed

Discussion

There are twelve Intuition functions that work directly with windows: BeginRefresh, CloseWindow, EndRefresh, EndRequest, MoveWindow, OpenWindow, ReportMouse, SetWindowTitles, SizeWindow, WindowLimits, WindowToFront, and WindowToBack. There is more information on windows in the discussions of each of these functions.

Before you call the CloseWindow function, your program must make sure that all messages in the window's IDCMP queue have been answered. If there are any messages in the message-port queue that have not been replied to before you close the window, they will be lost; their memory will be deallocated and they will disappear from the system. Therefore, always process all messages in the window's message queue before you close the window.

In the same way, if you have placed a menu strip in the window using the SetMenuStrip function, you should clear it before closing the window. You can use the ClearMenuStrip function for this purpose. The CloseWindow function does not check whether the menus of your window are currently being used before it executes. If menus are being used when you execute this function, the system will crash.

If the window is the last to close in a standard screen, the associated screen will also close when you close the window (with the exception of the Workbench standard screen). If the window is the last to close in a custom screen, however, the custom screen will not close when this window is closed. If you also want the custom screen to close, you must call the CloseScreen function after your call to the CloseWindow function.

CloseWorkBench

Syntax of Function Call

close = CloseWorkBench ()

Purpose of Function

This function attempts to close the Workbench screen and returns a Boolean (TRUE or FALSE) value in the close variable. First, it tests to see whether any applications program currently has open windows on the Workbench screen. If so, it returns a FALSE value and does not close the Workbench screen. If CloseWorkBench does not discover open applications program windows, it first cleans up any special buffers and then closes the Workbench screen and returns a TRUE value. This makes the Workbench screen disappear; however, the Workbench program will still monitor disk activity.

Inputs to Function

This function uses no arguments.

Discussion

There are four Intuition functions that allow you to deal directly with the standard Workbench screen display: OpenWorkBench, CloseWorkBench, WBenchToBack, and WBenchToFront. There is more information on manipulating the Workbench screen in the discussions of each of these functions.

At this time, the Workbench screen is the only standard screen in the Intuition system. Eventually, there may be other standard screens. The Workbench screen is the only screen besides your custom screens that you can explicitly close. Also, like custom screens, the Workbench screen does not close when you (or the user) close all of its open windows. The Workbench screen automatically reopens when all other screens are closed; your custom screens will not do this.

If your applications program needs more RAM, you can call CloseWorkBench to free the memory used by the Workbench screen. However, if you do this, you should call the OpenWorkBench function just before your program exits. In fact, you should make it a habit to call the OpenWorkBench function just before your program exits, regardless of events leading up to your program exit. This will ensure that the Workbench screen will always be presented when the user leaves your applications program, regardless of any adverse effects caused by that program.

CurrentTime

Syntax of Function Call

CurrentTime (&Seconds, &Micros)

Purpose of Function

This function gets the current time values for a task to examine and use; it places the current seconds and microseconds values into the memory locations indicated by the two function arguments.

Inputs to Function

&Seconds   A pointer to a longword variable (four bytes) that will receive the current seconds value

&Micros   A pointer to a longword variable (four bytes) that will receive the current microseconds value

Discussion

CurrentTime is the only Intuition function that deals directly with the system time variables. You use the CurrentTime function to get current values of the clock variables into your program. You can then use these values in any program that wants to time a sequence of events. Just call the CurrentTime function and place the current time values into the variable locations identified in the ULONG statement

ULONG Seconds, Micros

Then your program can reference the values at these locations.

Note that both time values are four bytes long. This allows the seconds value to range up to 2^{32} which is about 139 years. When the seconds value reaches this value, it returns to a zero value.

DisplayAlert

Syntax of Function Call

alert = DisplayAlert (alertNumber, string, height)

Purpose of Function

This function creates a specific alert display (error message) on the screen and returns a Boolean value (TRUE or FALSE) in the alert variable. If this is a DEADEND_ALERT,

FALSE is always returned. If this is a RECOVERY_ALERT, the return value will be TRUE if the user presses the mouse Selection button in response to the alert's message; if the user presses the mouse Menu button, the return value will be FALSE.

Inputs to Function

alertNumber	The number of the alert message; the ALERT_TYPE bits must be set to RECOVERY_ALERT or DEADEND_ALERT; the rest of this number is ignored
string	A pointer to an alert-message string
height	The total number of display lines required for the alert

Discussion

DisplayAlert is one of the Intuition functions that does not fall into any specific category. There are two types of Intuition alerts: system alerts and applications program alerts. System alerts are defined and managed entirely by Intuition; applications program alerts are managed by the DisplayAlert function. Both of these alerts display absolutely essential information; they should be reserved for situations where the user must take some immediate action to prevent a worse situation from developing. An impending system crash is one example of a critical situation; another example is an applications program fatal error.

The alert display (for both types) has a black background, a red border, and a 640-pixel horizontal resolution; it will be as tall as you specify in the height argument. The alert appears at the top of the display. If the rest of the display is still not affected, that part of the display is moved automatically down to accommodate the alert. If the problem that produced the alert is a fatal error, however, the system is about to go down. In this case, the alert immediately takes over the entire display.

There are two types of system and applications program alerts: RECOVERY_ ALERT and DEADEND_ALERT. The RECOVERY_ALERT flashes the alert's red border and displays the alert text. If the user presses the mouse Selection button in response to the alert's text, the DisplayAlert function returns a TRUE value. The DEADEND_ALERT displays the alert's text and returns FALSE immediately. The only way to recover from a DEADEND_ALERT is to reset the system.

The DisplayAlert string argument points to an alert-message string that is made up of one or more substrings. The first component of each substring is a 16-bit x-coordinate and an 8-bit y-coordinate. These define the screen location where you want the alert text to appear. The y-coordinate defines the y-position of the text base line. The second component is the text itself. This is a null-terminated text string. The last component is the continuation byte. If this byte is zero, the current substring is the last substring in the alert message. If this byte is nonzero, there is at least one more substring in the alert message.

Note that in many cases you should avoid using alerts—save them for extreme situations. Often, you can use requesters with warning messages instead. Requesters are less jarring to the user and can handle more types of user responses.

DisplayBeep

Syntax of Function Call

DisplayBeep (screen)

Purpose of Function

This function flashes the video display with the background color of the specified screen. If the screen argument is null, every screen in the system will flash. DisplayBeep does not return a value.

Inputs to Function

screen   A pointer to the Screen structure whose screen you want to flash; if this argument is a null, every screen in the current display will flash

Discussion

DisplayBeep is one of the Intuition functions that does not fall into any specific category. The Amiga machine has no internal bell or speaker. Therefore, system and applications program problems cannot be brought to the attention of the user through sound unless you have an external speaker hooked into the Amiga sound channels. This is the reason for the DisplayBeep function.

You should reserve the DisplayBeep function for situations that are not severe enough for alerts. For example, Intuition uses the DisplayBeep function when a user types a non-integer character into a gadget that accepts only integer input.

Note that you can flash all screens in the system. This includes all custom screens created by all tasks and programs currently residing in the system. The easiest way to do this is to use a null argument in the DisplayBeep function call. Then every screen in the display will be flashed. However, there is seldom a good reason to flash all Intuition screens.

DoubleClick

Syntax of Function Call

gooddoubleclick = DoubleClick (startSeconds, startMicros,
                                          currentSeconds, currentMicros)

Purpose of Function

This function compares the difference between the startSeconds and currentSeconds values and the difference between the startMicros and currentMicros values against the time values stored in the Preferences structure. These time values define the allowable time span for double-clicking. If the computed time differences are within the range set in the Preferences structure, DoubleClick returns a TRUE value in the gooddoubleclick Boolean variable. If the differences are greater than the values in the Preferences structure, DoubleClick returns a FALSE value.

Inputs to Function

startSeconds   The seconds value of the start of a double-click time period

startMicros   The microseconds value of the start of a double-click time period

currentSeconds The seconds value of the end of a double-click time period

currentMicros   The microseconds value of the end of a double-click time period

Discussion

DoubleClick is one of the Intuition functions that does not fall into any specific category. Your program must be able to decide whether two clicks of a mouse button are intended as a double-click or two separate clicks. This is the purpose of the DoubleClick function; it examines the actual double-click time period and compares it to the double-click criterion time values previously installed in the Preferences structure.

When the user presses the mouse Selection button, Intuition examines the state of the system and the position of the mouse pointer on the display screen. Intuition uses this information to decide whether the user is trying to select an object, an operation, or an option. There are some times when the user double-clicks the mouse Selection button.

Double-clicking an applications program icon to start execution of that program is one example of this.

The mouse Menu button is most often used for information transfer in menu operations. Pressing the Menu button usually displays the active window's menu title over the screen's title bar. Double-clicking the Menu button brings up the double-menu requester.

DrawBorder

Syntax of Function Call

DrawBorder (rastPort, border, leftOffset, topOffset)

Purpose of Function

This function draws a set of lines (borders) into the specified raster bitmap definition. Borders can be any sets of lines drawn at any angles on the display screen. The lines are defined by a set of x,y values pointed to by a Border structure. If part of a line's definition lies outside the bitmap limits, the line will be clipped at the edge of the bitmap. DrawBorder does not return a value.

Inputs to Function

rastPort	A pointer to a controlling RastPort structure
border	A pointer to a Border structure
leftOffset	The offset that will be added to the x-coordinate of each line before it is drawn
topOffset	The offset that will be added to the y-coordinate of each line before it is drawn

Discussion

The DrawBorder function allows you to add any number of lines to a containing display element (a window, a requester, or a gadget). The DrawBorder function works with the Border structure.

The Border Structure

The Border structure includes a number of parameters:

- The LeftEdge and TopEdge parameters contain the starting pixel positions of the line (border) with respect to the upper-left corner of the containing display element. These positions are measured according to the horizontal and vertical resolutions of the containing display element.

- The FrontPen, BackPen, and DrawMode parameters are used to define the color of the line. FrontPen is actually a color register value. BackPen is currently unused. DrawMode can be either JAM1 or XOR. The JAM1 drawing mode uses the FrontPen color to draw the line and makes no changes to the background of the containing display element. The XOR drawing mode draws the line as the binary complement of the pixel at the line pixel location. For example, if the line is being placed on top of a white background, it is drawn in black; no changes are made to the background of the containing display element.

- The NextBorder parameter points to another Border structure. With this pointer, you can link Border structures together. Each Border structure can define a set of lines.

- The XY parameter points to an array of x,y coordinate pairs. This array is associated with the current Border structure. Other linked Border structures might have additional XY arrays associated with them.

- The Count parameter contains the number of x,y coordinate pair values in the current XY array associated with this Border structure.

DrawImage

Syntax of Function Call

DrawImage (rastPort, image, leftOffset, topOffset)

Purpose of Function

This function draws the specified image into the raster bitmap. If the image definition lies outside the bitmap limits, the image will be clipped at the edge of the bitmap. DrawImage does not return a value.

Inputs to Function

rastPort	A pointer to a controlling RastPort structure
image	A pointer to the Image structure that defines each pixel of the image
leftOffset	The offset that will be added to the image's x-coordinate before it is drawn
topOffset	The offset that will be added to the image's y-coordinate before it is drawn

Discussion

The DrawImage function allows you to add a custom-designed image definition to a containing display element (a window, a requester, or a gadget). The DrawImage function allows you to construct images that are placed inside the containing display element. DrawImage works with the Image structure.

The Image Structure

The Image structure contains a number of parameters:

- The LeftEdge and TopEdge variables contain the starting pixel positions of the image with respect to the upper-left corner of the containing display element. These positions are measured according to the horizontal and vertical resolution of the containing display element.

- The Width and Height variables contain the pixel width and height of the image.

- The Depth variable contains the number of bitplanes required to define the image.

- The ImageData pointer points to the ImageData structure that defines each pixel of the image. The ImageData structure contains a number of two-byte words used to define the color of each pixel in the image definition. See the discussion of the SpriteImage structure (Chapter 3) for information on constructing an ImageData structure.

- The PlanePick parameter tells the system which bitplanes in the containing display element's bitmap will receive bits from the image pixel data bits. If the PlanePick parameter contains all 1 bits, every bitplane of the containing element's bitmap will receive bits from the image bitmap. If any bit in the PlanePick parameter is 0, the containing element's bitplane corresponding to that bit will not receive bits from the image bitmap.

■ The PlaneOnOff parameter tells the system what to do with the containing element's bitplanes where the image's bitplane data is not placed. This variable can turn off the display of pixel information already in specific containing-element bitplanes. For example, if you have a containing element with a two-bitplane bitmap and you set PlaneOnOff to 00, any bits in the containing element's bitplane will be set to 0 (effectively ignored) at the image's location in the containing element's bitmap.

The PlanePick and PlaneOnOff parameters require a bit of study to understand. See Chapter 3 for more about these two parameters.

EndRefresh

Syntax of Function Call

EndRefresh (window, complete)

Purpose of Function

This function ends the refreshing of a simple-fresh window started by a call to the BeginRefresh function. It completes the process by calling the EndUpdate function in the Layers Library to reverse the exchange made by BeginUpdate and allow the ClipRect structure to once again control the drawing process. This function does not return a value.

Inputs to Function

window   A pointer to a Window structure currently in an optimized refreshing mode

complete   A Boolean TRUE or FALSE value describing whether the window bitmap is completely refreshed

Discussion

There are twelve Intuition functions that work directly with windows: BeginRefresh, CloseWindow, EndRefresh, EndRequest, MoveWindow, OpenWindow, ReportMouse,

SetWindowTitles, SizeWindow, WindowLimits, WindowToFront, and WindowToBack. There is more information on windows in the discussions of each of these functions.

Calls to the BeginRefresh and EndRefresh functions should be made in pairs. The purpose of the BeginRefresh function is to start the optimized refreshing of your window; optimized refreshing means that only those parts of the window that are obscured will be redrawn. The purpose of the EndRefresh function is to stop the refreshing process for a window. A call to the EndRefresh function restores the state of the internal structures related to a window. When the EndRefresh function returns, the entire window, not just the obscured portions, will be drawn.

It is important to understand that several tasks or programs can deal with and draw into the same window in a given screen. Each of these tasks or programs share the responsibility for updating the window when it becomes obscured due to the user's window manipulations.

The complete argument in the EndRefresh function call allows you to indicate whether the current task's BeginRefresh call is the last BeginRefresh call to be made for this window. If you have additional tasks waiting to update this window, you should set this flag to FALSE. Then, when your tasks switch, the next task can also add its refreshing information to the window. When the last task involved in refreshing this window has completed, you can call the EndRefresh function in that task with a complete argument of TRUE. When the window is redisplayed, all obscured parts will be correctly refreshed.

EndRequest

Syntax of Function Call

EndRequest (requester, window)

Purpose of Function

This function ends the display of a requester in a window and resets the window. Only this requester is erased from the window; any other requesters remain in the window. EndRequest does not return a value.

Inputs to Function

requester   A pointer to the Requester structure whose requester is to be removed

> **window** A pointer to the Window structure in whose window the requester appears

Discussion

There are twelve Intuition functions that work directly with windows: BeginRefresh, CloseWindow, EndRefresh, EndRequest, MoveWindow, OpenWindow, ReportMouse, SetWindowTitles, SizeWindow, WindowLimits, WindowToFront, and WindowToBack. There is more information on windows in the discussions of each of these functions.

Requesters, like menus, are information-exchange boxes that can be displayed in windows by Intuition or by your applications programs. These information-exchange boxes are called requesters because they require the user to input specific information before the ongoing dialog between a program and the user can continue. You can place requesters anywhere in windows; bring one up whenever your program needs to elicit a response from the user.

Requesters are brought up in three ways: by the Intuition system, by the applications program, or by a user double-clicking the Menu button.

Even though a window with a requester displayed is blocked for further input until the requester is satisfied, it is not blocked for further output. Nothing prevents your task or program from writing to that window. However, if you try to output to a window when a requester is displayed, you run the risk of overwriting the requester display itself. This may render the requester useless.

The purpose of the EndRequest function is to remove the requester's display from the window with a program statement in your current task. Note that other requesters may still remain in the window; each one can be removed from the display with a call to the EndRequest function.

FreeRemember

Syntax of Function Call

FreeRemember (rememberKey, ReallyForget)

Purpose of Function

This function frees a set of RAM blocks allocated by the AllocRemember function. It can free either the Remember structure alone or both the Remember structure and the RAM buffers, depending on the value of the ReallyForget argument. The Remember structure provides a way to link all the memory blocks allocated in an Intuition program. Free-Remember does not return a value.

Inputs to Function

rememberKey The address of a pointer to a Remember structure

ReallyForget A Boolean TRUE or FALSE value describing whether you want to free only the Remember nodes (FALSE) or all of the memory (TRUE), both the nodes and the memory buffers pointed to by the nodes

Discussion

There are two Intuition functions that deal directly with memory allocation, Alloc-Remember and FreeRemember. The Intuition system automatically establishes a linked list of memory assignments, which makes memory maintenance much easier.

The FreeRemember function has two uses. First, if you are developing a task procedure involving quite a few memory allocations (an OpenWindow or OpenScreen procedure, for example), one of those memory allocations may fail due to lack of sufficient memory. In this case, you might want to abort the entire procedure and start again after you have freed additional memory blocks. Abandoning the current procedure involves freeing all the memory blocks you have already allocated. All you have to do is call the FreeRemember function; all the memory blocks in the linked list will then be deallocated and you can restart the procedure.

Secondly, when you exit from an Intuition program for the last time, you may want to free all the memory blocks used by that program. You can free all blocks originally allocated with the AllocRemember function with one call to the FreeRemember function.

FreeSysRequest

Syntax of Function Call

FreeSysRequest (window)

Purpose of Function

This function frees the memory that was allocated to a Requester structure by a call to the BuildSysRequest function.

Inputs to Function

window   The Window structure pointer variable returned by a previous call to the BuildSysRequest function

Discussion

There are seven Intuition functions that are used to manage requesters: AutoRequest, BuildSysRequest, ClearDMRequest, FreeSysRequest, InitRequester, Request, and SetDMRequest. There is more information on requesters in the discussions of each of these functions.

   If the BuildSysRequest function was successful, it returned a pointer to a Window structure. Your program could wait on the message port of that window to detect an event that satisfies the requester. If the BuildSysRequest function was not successful and did not return a pointer to a Window structure, you should not call the FreeSysRequest function.

GetDefPrefs

Syntax of Function Call

prefBuffer = GetDefPrefs (prefBuffer, size)

Purpose of Function

This function gets a copy of the default Intuition Preferences structure data and writes that data into a RAM buffer. By setting the size argument appropriately, the GetDefPrefs function allows you to make a partial copy of the default Preferences structure data. GetDefPrefs returns a pointer to the buffer; this is the same value supplied in the function call.

Inputs to Function

prefBuffer   A pointer to the memory buffer that will receive the copy of the default Preferences structure

size   The number of bytes in the prefBuffer; this is the number of bytes you want to copy from the system's Preferences structure

Discussion

There are two Intuition functions that work directly with the Preferences structure, Get-Prefs and GetDefPrefs. These functions allow you to get a copy of the default Intuition preferences settings (GetDefPrefs) and the current Intuition preferences settings (GetPrefs). You can then use this information in any way that is useful to your program. For example, the serial port baud rate is the third item in the Preferences structure. This parameter could be read and written by a communications program.

The default preferences are those supplied by Intuition when it first opens. You can take a full or partial copy of the Preferences structure. If you set the size parameter small enough, you will take a partial copy of the default preferences; you will get the most important Preferences structure data. This data is grouped near the top of the Preferences structure.

The Preferences Structure

The Preferences structure defines the display screen colors, the mouse-button response timing, and other system-wide parameters in the Amiga hardware system. Following is a summary of the parameters in the Preferences structure.

- The FontHeight parameter contains either of two values: nine scanning lines for Topaz-60 or eight scanning lines for Topaz-80.

- The PrinterPort parameter is set to PARALLEL_PRINTER or SERIAL_PRINTER to describe the type of printer attached to the printer port.

- The BaudRate parameter is the baud rate for the serial port.

- The KeyRptSpeed and KeyRptDelay parameters are Timeval substructures within the Preferences structure. Each Timeval structure contains two parameters—a seconds value and a microseconds value.

- The DoubleClick parameter contains the maximum time allowed between mouse clicks for a pair of mouse clicks to be considered a mouse double-click.

- The information to define the sprite data for the default Intuition mouse pointer.

- The XOffset and YOffset parameters are offsets from the upper-left corner of the default Intuition pointer image to the active spot (a spot near the tip) of the pointer image.

- Color17, Color18, and Color19 are color register definitions for the mouse pointer.

- The PointerTicks parameter contains the number of mouse-movement ticks required for the mouse pointer image to move one increment on the display screen.

- Color0, Color1, Color2, and Color3 are color register definitions for the Workbench screen default colors.

- The ViewXOffset and ViewYOffset parameters describe the view offset from the screen position where it was first displayed. These offsets keep track of the position of the screen on the monitor.

- The ViewInitX and ViewInitY parameters contain the initial x and y positions of the view.

- The EnableCLI parameter controls the display of the CLI icon when the CLI tool is available. The CLI (command line interface) is a tool for writing and debugging programs.

- The PrinterType parameter contains the definition of available printer types.

- The PrinterFileName [FILENAME_SIZE] buffer contains the default file name of the printer configuration file. FILENAME_SIZE is the number of bytes in the printer file name.

- The PrintPitch, PrintQuality, and PrintSpacing parameters contain various printing attributes.

- The PrintLeftMargin and PrintRightMargin parameters contain the character spacing of the print margins.

- The PrintImage, PrintAspect, and PrintShade parameters contain the printer page attributes.

- The PrintThreshold parameter describes the intensity threshold required to trigger printing of a pixel in simple monochrome printer displays.

- The PaperSize, PaperLength, and PaperType parameters contain the printer paper attributes.

GetPrefs

Syntax of Function Call

prefBuffer = GetPrefs (prefBuffer, size)

Purpose of Function

This function gets a copy of the current Intuition Preferences structure. It writes the data into a RAM buffer. By setting the size argument appropriately, GetPrefs allows you to make a partial copy of the current Preferences structure data. GetPrefs returns a pointer to the buffer; this is the same value supplied in the function call.

Inputs to Function

prefBuffer   A pointer to the memory buffer to receive your copy of the current Intuition preferences settings

size   The number of bytes in the prefBuffer; this is the number of bytes you want to copy from the current Preferences structure

Discussion

Two Intuition functions deal directly with the Preferences structure, GetPrefs and GetDef-Prefs. The user can change the preferences settings from the Workbench screen by choosing the Preferences icon; this starts execution of the Preferences program. If you want your program to know about any changes the user has made in the preferences settings, you can use GetPrefs to inquire about them. If you are using an IDCMP for program input, you can set the IDCMP flag NEWPREFS. Each time the user changes the preferences settings, your task or program will be notified automatically that a change has taken place. You can then call GetPrefs to place some or all of the Preferences structure data into a buffer of your choice for further examination.

Developers of printer drivers should always call the GetPrefs function before every print job, because the user may change printer parameters by running the Preferences program. The user can select paragraph size, right and left margin, continuous or single sheets, draft or letter quality, pitch, and line spacing. If the user chooses the Preferences display "Graphic Select" gadget, a requester appears from which the user can select shade (gray-scale printing), aspect (normal or sideways), positive or reverse image, and threshold for black and white printing. The last setting defines which colors are printed as black and which as white.

GetScreenData

Syntax of Function Call

success = GetScreenData (buffer, size, screen_type, screen)

Purpose of Function

This function copies all or part of the data in a Screen structure into a buffer specified by the buffer location argument. Your program can then examine and use the data in the Screen structure. If a standard screen (WBENCHSCREEN) is requested and that screen is not currently open, the GetScreenData function will open it. If GetScreenData is successful, it returns a TRUE value in the success variable; otherwise it returns a FALSE value.

Inputs to Function

buffer	A pointer to the RAM location that will contain all or part of the Screen structure data
size	This is the number of bytes in the buffer. You can specify less than the total number of bytes in the Screen structure.
screen_type	This is the screen type as specified in the Screen structure. This is either CUSTOMSCREEN or WBENCHSCREEN. If WBENCHSCREEN, the fourth argument (screen) is ignored.
screen	This is a pointer to a Screen structure for a custom screen. If the type argument is set to WBENCHSCREEN, this argument is ignored.

Discussion

GetScreenData is the only 1.2 release function that deals with screens in the Intuition software system. To get the data for the Workbench screen, use the following call:

**success = GetScreenData (buffer, sizeof (struct
Screen), WBENCHSCREEN, NULL)**

To get the data for a custom screen use the following call:

**success = GetScreenData (buffer, sizeof (struct
Screen), CUSTOMSCREEN, screen)**

Here, the fourth argument is a pointer to a Screen structure for a specific custom screen.

The first six items in the Screen structure are the NextScreen parameter, the FirstWindow parameter, and the LeftEdge, TopEdge, Width, and Height parameters. If you specify a buffer to contain these parameters, your program can then examine them as needed after the GetScreenData call. Otherwise, you can specify a full Screen structure buffer as described above.

The most common use for the GetScreenData function is to find the size, title bar height, and other parameters for the Workbench screen; the screen structure for the Workbench screen is defined by Intuition and this function allows you to access it.

InitRequester

Syntax of Function Call

InitRequester (requester)

Purpose of Function

This function initializes a Requester structure for general use. When the InitRequester function returns, you need fill in only those Requester structure values that fit your needs; all other values in the Requester structure are set to null. InitRequester does not return a value.

Inputs to Function

requester   A pointer to a Requester structure

Discussion

There are seven Intuition functions that are directly concerned with managing requesters: AutoRequest, BuildSysRequest, ClearDMRequest, FreeSysRequest, InitRequester, Request, and SetDMRequest. There is more information on requesters in the discussions of each of these functions.

A Requester structure can be initialized by using explicit structure-parameter assignment statements or by using the InitRequester function. In many cases Requester structure initialization is accomplished using a combination of these two methods. First, the InitRequester function is used to initialize most of the Requester structure parameters. This leaves most of the Requester structure parameters as null values. Then, explicit parameter assignment statements are used to define initial values for other values in the Requester structure definition.

The Requester Structure

Following is a brief summary of the parameters in the Requester structure:

- The OlderRequest variable is a link maintained by Intuition. It points to requesters that were rendered before this one in the same containing display element.

- The LeftEdge and TopEdge variables contain the requester's pixel offsets from the edges of the containing display element.

- The Width and Height variables contain the size of the requester rectangle.

- The RelLeft and RelTop variables contain the location of the requester with respect to the window pointer image. This is one method of positioning the requester in the window.

- The ReqGadget pointer points to the first in a linked list of gadgets that will appear in this requester's containing display element.

- The ReqBorder pointer points to a Border structure that defines the requester's borders.

- The ReqText pointer points to an IntuiText structure that defines the requester's text.

- The Flags pointer contains bits that are set by both Intuition and your applications programs. Your programs can set the POINTREL flag, which tells the system to draw the requester relative to the current window pointer image, and the PREDRAWN flag, which tells the system to use a custom bitmap image that will be used for the requester. Intuition sets the REQOFFWINDOW flag, which indicates when a requester is currently active and when some part of a requester's gadget was rendered outside of the requester's window; the REQACTIVE flag, which indicates when this requester is currently being used; and the SYSREQUEST flag, which Intuition sets when this is a system-generated requester.

- The BackFill parameter contains the pen for requester background drawing.

- The ReqCRect and ReqBMap parameters are used by Intuition to create the requester image for a custom bitmap requester.

- The ImageBMap pointer points to a custom bitmap for this requester.

IntuiTextLength

Syntax of Function Call

textwidth = IntuiTextLength (intuiText)

Purpose of Function

This function looks at the current font settings and computes the width in pixels of a text string stored in an IntuiText structure; it returns that width in the textwidth variable.

Inputs to Function

intuiText   A pointer to an IntuiText structure

Discussion

There are two Intuition functions that work directly with text in the system, IntuiTextLength and PrintIText. These functions deal specifically with the IntuiText structure. The IntuiText structure contains a representation of text in a null-terminated text string pointed to by the IText parameter. The IntuiTextLength and PrintIText functions allow you to return the length (actually the pixel width) of that text string and to print (actually draw into a bitmap) that text string according to controlling arguments in the PrintIText function. The IntuiTextLength function can be used, for example, when you want to find the length of a menu item text string.

The IntuiText Structure

Following is a summary of the contents of the IntuiText structure.

- The FrontPen parameter is the color used to draw the text characters themselves. The BackPen parameter is the color used to draw the background areas around and between the text characters; the BackPen color is used only when the JAM2 drawing mode is specified.

■ The DrawMode parameter is set to one of three drawing modes used for text in Intuition. See the discussion of the PrintIText function for an explanation of these drawing modes.

■ The LeftEdge parameter contains the starting pixel x-coordinate position of the text as an offset from the upper-left corner of the containing display element.

■ The TopEdge parameter contains the starting pixel y-coordinate position of the text as an offset from the upper-left corner of the containing display element.

■ The TextAttr pointer points to a structure containing a customized font description. You can set this to null if you want the default Intuition font (either Topaz-60 or Topaz-80).

■ The IText pointer points to a null-terminated text string.

■ The NextText pointer points to another instance of an IntuiText structure. This allows you to specify a linked list of text strings to display in a containing display element. Set this to null if this IntuiText structure is not part of a linked list or if this is the last structure in the linked list of IntuiText structures.

ItemAddress

Syntax of Function Call

menuItem = ItemAddress (menu, menuNumber)

Purpose of Function

This function returns a pointer to a MenuItem structure for the menu item specified by the menuNumber argument. You can use this function to get the address of a menu item from the menuNumber variable value sent to your task by Intuition after the user has made a menu selection.

Inputs to Function

menu   A pointer to the first Menu structure in a menu strip

menuNumber   A value that contains the packed data that selects the menu, the menu item, and the menu subitem

Discussion

There are five Intuition functions that manage menus directly: ClearMenuStrip, ItemAddress, OnMenu, OffMenu, and SetMenuStrip. There is more information on menus in the discussions of each of these functions.

The ItemAddress function requires that the arguments are well defined. If the menuNumber argument is a null value, the ItemAddress function returns a null value. If the menuNumber value is not null, it should include at least one valid menu item number and one valid menu subitem number.

For more information on menus, menu items, and menu subitems, see the discussion of the SetMenuStrip function.

ITEMNUM

Syntax of Macro Call

ITEMNUM (menuNumber)

Purpose of Macro

This macro extracts the ordinal menu item number from the menuNumber argument. This number starts at 0 and increases to 63. This macro is necessary to allow the IDCMP menu-selection message flag (MENUPICK) to be compared to the current menu item definitions to determine which menu item the user has selected.

Inputs to Macro

menuNumber   A 16-bit packed binary number that defines the menu number, the menu item number, and the menu subitem number

Discussion

There are six macros that deal with menus, menu items, and menu subitems: MENUNUM, ITEMNUM, SUBNUM, SHIFTMENU, SHIFTITEM, and SHIFT-SUB. You should read the discussions of each of these macros to see how menu-related items are handled by Intuition.

The ITEMNUM macro gets a value ranging from 0 to 63; the number indicates which specific menu is being referenced by the user. The menuNumber argument can be one of several possible classes of values:

■ A valid menu number defining a menu, a menu item, and possibly a menu subitem. Note that the menuNumber value must always define at least a menu and menu item. The system does not allow the user to select only a menu.

■ MENUNULL if no menu selection was made or if the user made a menu selection improperly. For example, if the user selected a menu but did not go on to select at least a menu item, the menuNumber will be MENUNULL.

To determine the menu item number, use the following program statement:

MyItemNumber = ITEMNUM (menuNumber)

Then MyItemNumber will be either a valid value (0 to 63) or the special value NOITEM if no menu item was selected. The values of MENUNULL and NOITEM are defined in the last part of the Intuition INCLUDE file, along with the precise definition of the MENUITEM macro.

LockIBase

Syntax of Function Call

lock_value = LockIBase (lock_number)

Purpose of Function

This function grabs an Intuition internal semaphore so that your program can examine the IntuitionBase structure safely. When LockIBase returns, the IntuitionBase structure will be locked from changes by Intuition or any other task in the system. LockIBase returns a ULONG value in the lock_value variable. This variable can then be used to free that specific lock later with the UnlockIBase function.

Inputs to Function

lock_number This is a long unsigned integer that represents one of the Intuition internal locks that you want to get. Normally, you will not know how to identify a specific Intuition internal lock number. Therefore, this argument should be zero for all foreseeable uses of the LockIBase function. Future enhancements may allow you to specify this argument explicitly.

Discussion

There are two 1.2 release functions that deal with locks in the Intuition software system: LockIBase and UnlockIBase.

The IntuitionBase structure contains all the parameters Intuition needs to maintain ongoing bookkeeping requirements in the Intuition software system. Normally, only Intuition can access the parameters in the IntuitionBase structure; when it does so, it locks the structure—using its internal semaphores—from access and changes by any other task in the system.

The LockIBase function allows your program to do the same thing that Intuition does; namely, to lock the IntuitionBase structure, thus preventing Intuition or any other task from changing its contents for a period of time. Your task then has complete control over the IntuitionBase structure. In this way, you can gain access to one of the Intuition-Base structure locks before Intuition changes any IntuitionBase structure parameters. For example, you can look at the ActiveWindow and FirstScreen parameters knowing that their values will not change while you are looking at them. You can also look at linked lists of windows and screens in this way under the protection of the lock.

It is important to note that calls to LockIBase and UnlockIBase must be paired. Also, your program should not use these locks for an extended period of time; Intuition will wait for your program to free the lock with a call to UnlockIBase before it can continue with input processing.

MakeScreen

Syntax of Function Call

MakeScreen (screen)

Purpose of Function

This function generates the Copper instruction list for an Intuition custom screen by calling the Graphics Library MakeVPort function.

Inputs to Function

screen   A pointer to a custom Screen structure

Discussion

There are seven Intuition functions that work directly with Intuition display screens: OpenScreen, CloseScreen, MakeScreen, MoveScreen, ShowTitle, ScreenToBack, and ScreenToFront. There is more information on display screens in the discussions of each of these functions.

Each Intuition custom screen is created by initializing a NewScreen structure and then calling the OpenScreen function to allocate the required memory and set up the Screen structure and all its substructures. Each Intuition Screen structure contains a ViewPort substructure. This makes each custom screen in the Intuition system a viewport as defined by the Graphics Library functions. For this reason, the internal system procedure required to display that screen is identical to the procedure used by the Graphics Library functions to display any other viewport. This procedure is accomplished by calling the Graphics Library MakeVPort function.

MakeVPort defines the Copper instruction list for a viewport and incorporates those Copper instructions into the full set of Copper instructions required for the complete display definition. When the MakeScreen function returns, call the RethinkDisplay function to incorporate the new viewport of your custom screen into the Intuition display.

ViewPort Structure Flags

Here is a summary of the flag bits in the ViewPort structure:

- HIRES. If this flag bit is 1, the viewport to which this screen belongs will be high-resolution mode.

- INTERLACE. If this flag bit is 1, the viewport to which this screen belongs will be interlaced mode.

- SPRITES. If this flag bit is 1, the viewport to which this screen belongs will have sprites.

- DUALPF. If this flag bit is 1, the viewport to which this screen belongs will have two playfields.

- HAM. If this flag bit is 1, the viewport to which this screen belongs will be hold-and-modify mode. This allows you to display up to 4,096 colors simultaneously.

MENUNUM

Syntax of Macro Call

MENUNUM (menuNumber)

Purpose of Macro

This macro extracts the ordinal menu number from the menuNumber argument. The ordinal menu number starts at 0 and increases to 31. This macro is necessary to allow the IDCMP menu-selection message flag (MENUPICK) to be compared to the current menu definitions to determine which menu the user has selected.

Inputs to Macro

menuNumber A 16-bit packed binary number that defines the menu number, the menu item number, and the menu subitem number

Discussion

There are six macros that deal with menus, menu items, and menu subitems: MENU-NUM, ITEMNUM, SUBNUM, SHIFTMENU, SHIFTITEM, and SHIFTSUB. You should read the discussions of each of these macros to see how menu-related items are handled by Intuition.

Intuition refers to menu, menu item, and menu subitem positions using two methods. The first method uses a 16-bit packed binary number (MenuNumber) to represent all three menu components as one of three subfields in the binary number. Bits 0 to 4 represent the menu number; bits 5 to 10 represent the menu item number; and bits 11 to 15 represent the menu subitem number. The ItemAddress function works with the MenuNumber variable, returning the address of a specific MenuItem structure, which represents a specific piece of a menu, menu item, or menu subitem.

The second method represents every part of the menu as an ordinal number indexing that menu component. The Intuition IDCMP message system requires the ordinal number representation to recognize the user's menu selections correctly when an IDCMP MENUPICK message is generated by a user menu selection.

The menu selection message IDCMP flag, MENUPICK, represents the specific menu choice as the ordinal position in each of the subfields of the packed binary number.

Therefore, to allow your program to determine the menu selected by the user, you will need to use these menu macros to extract the ordinal numbers corresponding to each of the subfields of the MenuNumber representation.

To determine the menu number, use the following program statement:

MyMenuNumber = MENUNUM (menuNumber)

The proper way to process a user menu selection is as follows:

```
while (menuNumber != MENUNULL){
    MenuItem = ItemAddress (menuStrip,menuNumber);
    /# process this item #/
    MenuNumber = MenuItem->NextSelect;
};
```

Here, NextSelect is one of the parameters of the MenuItem structure. If the user has made only one menu selection (not an extended menu selection), this parameter will be null. If the user has made more than one menu selection, this parameter will not be null.

ModifyIDCMP

Syntax of Function Call

ModifyIDCMP (window, IDCMPFlags)

Purpose of Function

This function modifies the state of a window's IDCMP settings to reflect the flag bits in the IDCMPFlags variable. If the IDCMPFlags argument is null, this function will close the IDCMP if it is currently open. If the IDCMPFlags argument is not null, this function will reset the flags in an IDCMP that is already open or open a new IDCMP in the window. ModifyIDCMP does not return a value.

Inputs to Function

window	A pointer to a Window structure
IDCMPFlags	The flag bits describing the desired state of the IDCMPs

Discussion

ModifyIDCMP is one of the Intuition functions that does not fall into any specific category. This function allows for one of four actions to be taken:

1. If there is no IDCMP assigned currently to the window and the IDCMPFlags variable is null, the window remains without any of these ports.

2. If there is no IDCMP assigned currently to the window and the IDCMPFlags variable is not null (some of the flags are set), the window is assigned a pair of these ports.

3. If the IDCMPs for the window are opened and the IDCMPFlags variable is null, the IDCMPs assigned to that window will be closed.

4. If the IDCMPs for the window are opened and the IDCMPFlags argument is not null, new flag bits will be set for that window. This allows your program to recognize and process a whole new set of events produced by the user.

You can handle input into each window in the Intuition system in two ways: you can assign either a Console device or an IDCMP (Intuition direct communications port) to the window. If you use an IDCMP, you can regulate the information that your Intuition applications program will recognize. This information falls into six categories: mouse messages, gadget messages, menu messages, requester messages, window messages, and miscellaneous messages.

Most of these messages are generated by user mouse and keyboard activity. Your program needs to know about some of this activity. Therefore, you set up an IDCMP channel to receive these messages. When you do this, the IDCMP is set up with an Exec user message port that belongs to your program. In addition, the window is assigned an Exec window message port. Read the discussion of the AddPort function in Chapter 1 for more information on the operation of these message ports.

The information that is recognized and flows back and forth between the user port and the window port is controlled by the flags set in the IDCMP definition. You can set these flags in the NewWindow structure and later modify them with the ModifyIDCMP function. Following is a brief summary of the IDCMP flags.

Mouse Message Flags

- MOUSEBUTTONS. If this flag bit is set, reports of Menu button up-and-down events are sent to your program after they are processed by Intuition. Any events that Intuition doesn't use and process will be passed along to your program.

- MOUSEMOVE. If this flag bit is set, reports of mouse movements are sent to your program.

- DELTAMOVE. If this flag bit is set, reports of mouse movements are sent as delta values rather than as absolute current mouse coordinates.

Gadget Message Flags

■ GADGETDOWN. If this flag bit is set, reports of gadget selection are sent to your program.

■ GADGETUP. If this flag bit is set, a report will be sent to your program when the user releases a gadget.

■ CLOSEWINDOW. If this flag bit is set, a report will be sent to your program when the user selects the window-close gadget.

Menu Message Flags

■ MENUPICK. If this flag bit is set, a report will be sent to your program when the user selects a menu.

■ MENUVERIFY. If this flag bit is set, all drawing operations in a window will be completed before the user is allowed to start menu operations.

Requester Message Flags

■ REQSET. If this flag bit is set, a report will be sent to your program when the first requester opens in a window.

■ REQCLEAR. If this flag bit is set, a report will be sent to your program when the last requester is cleared from your window.

■ REQVERIFY. If this flag bit is set, all drawing operations in a window will be completed before a requester is added to that window.

Window Message Flags

■ NEWSIZE. If this flag bit is set, Intuition sends your program a message when the user resizes a window.

■ REFRESHWINDOW. If this flag bit is set, a message is sent to your program whenever a window needs refreshing.

■ SIZEVERIFY. If this flag bit is set, all window drawing will be completed before the user can resize the window.

■ ACTIVEWINDOW. If this flag bit is set, your program will receive a message whenever a window becomes active.

■ INACTIVEWINDOW. If this flag bit is set, your program will receive a message whenever a window becomes inactive.

Miscellaneous Message Flags

■ RAWKEY. If this flag bit is set, raw (untranslated) keycodes from the keyboard are sent directly to your program.

- NEWPREFS. If this flag bit is set, a message will be sent to your program when the user changes the preferences settings.

- DISKINSERTED. If this flag bit is set, a message will be sent to your program when the user inserts a new disk into a disk drive.

- DISKREMOVED. If this flag bit is set, a message will be sent to your program when the user removes a disk from one of the disk drives.

ModifyProp

Syntax of Function Call

ModifyProp (gadget, pointer, requester, flags, horizPot, vertPot, horizBody, vertBody)

Purpose of Function

This function allows you to modify the current parameters of a proportional gadget as specified in its PropInfo structure. The Gadget structure for the proportional gadget contains a pointer to the PropInfo structure. The Gadget structure is recycled and the image of the gadget is redisplayed. If the SCRGADGET flag is set, the pointer variable argument refers to a Screen structure; if the SCRGADGET flag is not set, the pointer variable argument refers to a Window structure. The requester variable can point to a Requester structure. If the Gadget structure has the REQGADGET flag set, the gadget is part of requester and the pointer must necessarily point to a Window structure. If the gadget is not associated with a requester, the requester pointer argument may be null. ModifyProp does not return a value.

Inputs to Function

gadget	A pointer to a Gadget structure for a proportional gadget
pointer	A pointer to the containing element structure for this gadget; either a Window structure or a Screen structure
requester	A pointer to a Requester structure; this may be null if this gadget is not part of a requester

flags	A one-byte value to be stored in the Flags parameter of the PropInfo structure
horizPot	A one-byte value to be stored in the HorizPot parameter of the PropInfo structure
vertPot	A one-byte value to be stored in the VertPot parameter of the PropInfo structure
horizBody	A one-byte value to be stored in the HorizBody parameter of the PropInfo structure
vertBody	A one-byte value to be stored in the VertBody parameter of the PropInfo structure

Discussion

There are six Intuition functions that manage gadgets: AddGadget, OnGadget, OffGadget, RefreshGadgets, RemoveGadget, and ModifyProp. There is more information on gadgets in the discussions of each of these functions.

A proportional gadget allows or requires the user to specify some kind of proportional setting and to display proportional information. The color-control gadgets presented by the Preferences program are good examples of proportional gadgets. The proportional gadget can be designed in two ways: first, you can use the imagery furnished by Intuition. Second, you can design an image for a slider or knob for the user to choose a proportional setting.

A proportional gadget has several parts that work together to produce the complete gadget. These are the pot variables, the body variables, the knob, and the container. The word *pot* is short for potentiometer. There are two pot variables because proportional gadgets can be adjusted along both the horizontal and vertical axes. Typically, pot variables are initially set to 0 and then adjusted by the user with the proportional gadget. You can read the current user-adjusted values in the pot variables at any time once you have designed the proportional gadget for Intuition.

The horizBody and vertBody variables describe the increment by which the pot variables change in each direction. You can set the body variables to the same or different values. Then, when the user clicks in the proportional gadget container, the pot variables are adjusted by the amount set in the body variables.

The knob is the object actually manipulated by the user to change the pot variables by the increments specified in the body variables. With every click of the Menu button, the pot variable is increased or decreased by one increment value as set in the body variables.

The container is the area in which the knob can move. The container is actually the select box of the gadget. The size of the container can be relative to the size of the window, increasing in size when the user makes the window bigger and decreasing when the user makes the window smaller.

MoveScreen

Syntax of Function Call

MoveScreen (screen, dx, dy)

Purpose of Function

This function attempts to move the screen by increments specified in the dx and dy arguments. If these arguments are out of the currently allowed movement range for this screen, the screen will be moved as far as possible in the specified direction. MoveScreen does not return a value.

Inputs to Function

screen	A pointer to a Screen structure
dx	The distance to move the screen on the x-axis
dy	The distance to move the screen on the y-axis

Discussion

There are seven Intuition functions that allow you to work directly with Intuition custom display screens: OpenScreen, CloseScreen, MoveScreen, MakeScreen, ShowTitle, ScreenToBack, and ScreenToFront. There is more information on custom screens in the discussions of each of these functions.

The MoveScreen function will eventually allow you to move the screen in both the x and y directions. However, at the present time, there is a restriction on movement of screens: no x-movement is allowed. The dx argument is therefore not presently used.

Note that all Intuition screens, both standard and custom, are currently restricted to the full width of the Amiga display screen. In a future software update, these restrictions will most likely be changed to allow for screens that are narrower than the full display and screens that can be moved in the x as well as the y direction.

MoveWindow

Syntax of Function Call

MoveWindow (window, dx, dy)

Purpose of Function

This function attempts to move the window by certain increments in the x and y directions. The window will be moved the next time Intuition receives an input event. MoveWindow does not return a value.

Inputs to Function

window	A pointer to a Window structure
dx	A signed value defining how far to move the window on the x-axis
dy	A signed value defining how far to move the window on the y-axis

Discussion

There are twelve Intuition functions that work directly with windows: BeginRefresh, CloseWindow, EndRefresh, EndRequest, MoveWindow, OpenWindow, ReportMouse, SetWindowTitles, SizeWindow, WindowLimits, WindowToBack, and WindowToFront. There is more information on windows in the discussions of each of these functions.

When you call the MoveWindow function, the window is moved as soon as Intuition receives an input event. This happens at a minimum rate of ten times a second and a maximum rate of sixty times a second.

Note that the MoveWindow function does not check for errors. Therefore, if you specify dx and dy values that are outside of the window's screen pixel limits, some or all of the window will disappear from the screen.

OffGadget

Syntax of Function Call

OffGadget (gadget, pointer, requester)

Purpose of Function

This function disables the specified gadget in a window or screen. If the SCRGADGET flag is set, the pointer argument refers to a Screen structure; if the SCRGADGET flag is not set, the pointer argument refers to a Window structure. The requester variable points to a Requester structure. If the Gadget structure has the REQGADGET flag set, the gadget is part of a requester and the pointer must therefore point to a Window structure. If the gadget is not associated with a requester, the requester pointer argument can be null. OffGadget does not return a value.

Inputs to Function

gadget   A pointer to the Gadget structure you want to disable

pointer   A pointer to either a Screen or Window structure, determined by the SCRGADGET flag of the Gadget structure

requester   A pointer to a Requester structure; this can be null if it is not a requester gadget

Discussion

There are six functions that manage gadgets in the Amiga system: AddGadget, OnGadget, OffGadget, RefreshGadgets, RemoveGadget, and ModifyProp. There is more information on gadgets in the discussions of each of these functions.

When you execute the OffGadget function, the gadget image becomes ghosted, meaning that the normal gadget image is overlaid with a pattern of dots, making it less distinct on the display screen. This gadget can no longer be selected by the user. The Gadget structure contains a flag bit to indicate the state of a gadget. This is the GADGET-DISABLE flag bit. You initialize this flag bit to 1 if you want the gadget to appear ghosted when it is first presented on the display screen.

After you submit a gadget to Intuition, you can change its ghosted or nonghosted state with the OnGadget and OffGadget functions. If the gadget belongs to a requester, that requester must already be displayed for the OnGadget and OffGadget functions to have any effect.

OffMenu

Syntax of Function Call

OffMenu (window, menuNumber)

Purpose of Function

This function does one of three things: it disables a specified menu item, it disables a specified menu subitem, or it disables an entire menu. OffMenu does not return a value.

Inputs to Function

window   A pointer to a Window structure

menuNumber   A four-byte variable that defines the menu piece to be disabled

Discussion

There are five Intuition functions that work directly with menus: ClearMenuStrip, ItemAddress, OnMenu, OffMenu, and SetMenuStrip. There is more information on menus in the discussions of each of these functions.

The menuNumber argument used in the OnMenu and OffMenu functions is a 16-bit variable. Five bits are used for the menu number, six bits are used for the menu item number, and five bits are used for the menu subitem number. Bits 0 through 4 are used for the menu number; bits 5 through 10 are used for the menu items within the menu; bits 11 through 15 are used for the subitems within the menu items.

The three subfields in the menuNumber variable are binary numbers between 0 and 11111 (or between 0 and 111111 for menu items). Every piece of information is specified by its ordinal position in a list of items of the same level. For example, if you want to select menu 1, set the first field to 00001. If you want to select the third menu item, set the second subfield to 000011.

This means that for each level of menu item and subitem, up to 31 menu-related pieces can be specified. Therefore, there are 62 pieces that you can build under each menu. The value of each of the subfields with all bits set to 0 means that no selection of this particular menu item was made.

If the item number referenced in the menuNumber variable argument equals one of the actual item components in a Menu or MenuItem structure, that menu component will be disabled. To enable or disable a single item and all subitems attached to that menu item, set the menuNumber variable argument to the item component ordinal number. For example, to enable item 3 and all its subitems, set the menuNumber variable to 0000000001100000. If your menu item has a subitem list, set the subitem component of the menuNumber variable to NOSUB. To disable a single subitem, set the menu item and subitem parts of the menuNumber variable argument appropriately.

If the item component referenced by the menuNumber argument equals NOITEM, the entire menu, including all its items and subitems, will be disabled by your OffMenu function call.

The current definition of the NOSUB and NOITEM parameters can be found in the Intuition.h INCLUDE file.

OnGadget

Syntax of Function Call

OnGadget (gadget, pointer, requester)

Purpose of Function

This function enables a specified gadget in a window or screen. It displays the gadget image and allows the user to select the gadget. If the SCRGADGET flag is set, the pointer argument refers to a Screen structure; if the flag is not set, the pointer argument refers to a Window structure. OnGadget does not return a value.

Inputs to Function

gadget   A pointer to the Gadget structure that you want to enable

pointer   A pointer to either a Screen or Window structure

requester   A pointer to a Requester structure; this item can be null if this is not a requester gadget

Discussion

There are six Intuition functions that work with gadgets: AddGadget, OnGadget, OffGadget, RefreshGadgets, RemoveGadget, and ModifyProp. There is more information on gadgets in the discussions of each of these functions.

Use the following steps to add gadgets to your Intuition programs:

1. Create a Gadget structure for each gadget.

2. Create a linked list of Gadget structures for each display element that has a gadget or gadgets attached to it. These display elements can be screens, windows, or requesters.

3. Set the gadget pointer variable in your screen, window, or requester to point to the first gadget in the list.

A Gadget structure typically specifies the following items:

■ The gadget image and/or gadget border. Use null values if the gadget has no imagery or border graphics.

■ The select box of the gadget. This is the gadget area Intuition uses to detect if the user has selected the gadget.

■ The left and top offsets inside the gadget's containing display element. These are either absolute or relative to the current borders of the screen, window, or requester.

■ The gadget width and height with respect to the containing display element. These are either absolute or relative to the current borders of the screen, window, or requester.

■ The gadget type. A gadget is either Boolean (TRUE or FALSE settings), integer (integer settings), proportional (a range of values in the x and y directions), or string (a text value).

■ How you want Intuition to behave while the user is manipulating the gadget.

OnMenu

Syntax of Function Call

OnMenu (window, menuNumber)

Purpose of Function

This function enables the specified menu item or an entire menu. The specific choice is determined by the value of the menuNumber argument. If the base of the menu number matches the menu currently revealed, the menu strip is also redisplayed. OnMenu does not return a value.

Inputs to Function

window   A pointer to a Window structure

menuNumber A four-byte variable that defines the menu, menu items, and menu subitems to be enabled

Discussion

There are five Intuition functions that work directly with menus: ClearMenuStrip, Item-Address, OnMenu, OffMenu, and SetMenuStrip. There is more information on menus in the discussions of each of these functions.

Menu Structure Flags

There are two flags in the Menu structure that are worthy of note:

- The MENUENABLED flag bit indicates whether the menu is currently enabled. If this flag is set, the menu header and all items below it will be enabled. The user will then be able to select a menu item. If this flag is not set, all menu items will be disabled.

- The MIDRAWN flag bit indicates whether the menu items are currently displayed.

MenuItem Structure Flags

There are a number of flags in the MenuItem structure that are important to know about:

- The CHECKIT flag bit tells Intuition that this menu item is an attribute item; you want a check mark to appear next to that menu item when it is selected by the user.

- The CHECKED flag bit is set or reset when you initialize the MenuItem structure before submitting it to Intuition. If you want this menu item to be selected initially, set this flag bit; if you don't want this menu item to be selected initially, reset this flag bit. Intuition maintains this flag according to the checked or unchecked status of that menu item.

- The COMMSEQ flag bit, when set, indicates that this menu item has an equivalent command-key sequence associated with it.

- The ITEMENABLED flag bit indicates whether this menu item is currently enabled.

- The HIGHFLAGS flag bit indicates that highlighting will be used for this menu item when it is displayed. The next four flag bits indicate the specific type of highlighting.

- The HIGHCOMP bit, when set, complements all pixel bits contained within this menu item's select box.

- The HIGHBOX bit, when set, draws a box outside this item's select box.

- The HIGHIMAGE bit, when set, displays an alternate image as defined in the SelectFill image definition.

- The HIGHNONE bit, when set, disables any highlighting.

- The ISDRAWN flag bit is set by Intuition when the item's subitems are currently displayed to the user; Intuition clears this flag bit when the item's subitems are not displayed.

- The HIGHITEM flag is set by Intuition when the item is highlighted; Intuition clears this flag bit when the item is not highlighted.

OpenScreen

Syntax of Function Call

screen = OpenScreen (newScreen)

Purpose of Function

This function opens an Intuition custom screen. It allocates all the required memory and sets up the Screen structure and all related substructures. OpenScreen also links this screen into the full scheme of Intuition screens. OpenScreen returns a pointer to a Screen structure for the new screen.

Inputs to Function

newScreen   A pointer to a NewScreen structure

Discussion

There are seven Intuition functions that work directly with custom screens: OpenScreen, CloseScreen, MoveScreen, MakeScreen, ShowTitle, ScreenToBack, and ScreenToFront. There is more information on custom screens in the discussions of each of these functions.

The first step in creating a new custom screen is creating a NewScreen structure. For this reason, the NewScreen structure is very important. See the introduction to this chapter for a definition of the NewScreen structure.

Intuition Screens

Intuition screens fall into two general classifications: standard screens and custom screens. The Workbench screen is the only standard screen currently available in the Amiga Intuition system; however, other standard screens are planned. Standard screens will differ from custom screens in four ways:

1. Standard screens will always be the full width and height of the video display. At this time, custom screens are required to be the full width of the video display, but they are not required to be the full height.

2. Standard screens (with the exception of the Workbench screen) will close and go away if you or the user closes all of their windows.

3. Standard screens will open differently from custom screens, which use the OpenScreen function.

4. Standard screens (with the exception of the Workbench screen) will have set colors, a standard display mode, and other set parameters that you will not be able to change.

You can create two types of custom screens from within Intuition. The first type is managed entirely by Intuition. The second type is more difficult to create and manage, because you have to use the Graphics Library functions.

If you design an Intuition-managed custom screen, you can set many of the screen parameters, including the following:

■ You can set the height and vertical starting point of the screen when it first opens.

■ You can set the depth of the screen bitmap; this determines how many colors you will use for this screen.

■ You can choose the colors for drawing screen details, including screen gadgets and the screen title bar.

■ You can choose the type of screen display mode from four modes ranging from low-resolution, noninterlaced mode to high-resolution, interlaced mode.

■ You can choose between single-playfield mode, dual-playfield mode, and hold-and-modify mode.

■ You can design custom gadgets for the screen.

■ You can choose the RAM location for the beginning of the display memory.

These are the steps to use to create the second type of custom screen:

1. You must allocate memory for a NewScreen structure. Initialize a NewScreen structure with the screen characteristics you want for your custom screen.

2. You must call the OpenScreen function with a pointer to your NewScreen structure. The OpenScreen function returns a pointer to the Screen structure for your new screen.

3. You should deallocate the memory assigned to the NewScreen structure.

Before you initialize the contents of the NewScreen structure, you must decide on the type of custom screen you are about to design:

■ You must choose the screen height and the starting y-position for the screen.

■ You must decide the total number of colors you want to use in the screen. This includes the screen background color, the color of text characters, the colors used in screen gadgets, the colors for borders and other lines in the screen, and the colors for filling block areas such as the screen title bar.

■ You must choose the screen display mode. This can vary from a low-resolution, noninterlaced mode display to a high-resolution, interlaced mode display.

■ You must choose the screen text font. This text font is used for all windows that open in the screen.

■ You must choose the text characters to be displayed in the screen title bar.

■ You must design the custom gadgets to be used in the screen's display.

■ You must decide how the display memory will be handled. Either Intuition or your program can allocate and deallocate display memory.

OpenWindow

Syntax of Function Call

window = OpenWindow (newWindow)

Purpose of Function

This function opens an Intuition window with the parameters specified in the New-Window structure. It also places all the system gadgets in the window and allocates all the RAM needed to support the display of this window. OpenWindow returns a pointer to the Window structure for the new window.

Inputs to Function

newWindow   A pointer to a NewWindow structure

Discussion

There are twelve Intuition functions that manage windows: BeginRefresh, CloseWindow, EndRefresh, EndRequest, MoveWindow, OpenWindow, ReportMouse, SetWindowTitles, SizeWindow, WindowLimits, WindowToFront, and WindowToBack. There is more information on windows in the discussions of each of these functions.

Before you call the OpenWindow function, you must create and initialize a New-Window structure. Then, in your call to the OpenWindow function, you provide a pointer to the NewWindow structure associated with your new window. The NewWindow structure is a very important structure in the Intuition system. It is defined in the introduction to this chapter.

Once the NewWindow structure is properly initialized, you can call the Open-Window function with a pointer to the NewWindow structure. Once the window is opened, the OpenWindow function will return a pointer to the Window structure associated with your new window. At this point you can deallocate the memory previously allocated to the NewWindow structure.

NewWindow Structure Flags

The Flags variable in the NewWindow structure includes the following flag bits:

- WINDOWSIZING. If this flag bit is set, the user can resize the window using the mouse. Usually, the sizing gadget is in the lower-right corner of the window. However, if the SIZEBRIGHT flag bit is set, the sizing gadget will be placed in the right border area of the window; if the SIZEBBOTTOM flag bit is set, the sizing gadget will be placed in the bottom border area of the window.

- WINDOWDEPTH. If this bit is set, the user can use the mouse to depth-arrange the window.

- WINDOWCLOSE. If this bit is set, Intuition transmits a close-window message to your applications program when the user selects the close gadget. Your program must then call the CloseWindow function to close the window.

- WINDOWDRAG. If this bit is set, the entire title bar of the window becomes a drag gadget.

- GIMMEZEROZERO. If this bit is set, the window will be a gimmezerozero window.

- SIMPLE_REFRESH. If this bit is set, every time an obscured portion of the window is revealed, your program must specifically refresh the newly revealed area using the Graphics Library drawing functions.

- SMART_REFRESH. If this bit is set, the smart-refresh mode of window refreshing will be in effect for this window.

- SUPER_BITMAP. If this bit is set, this window will use the superbitmap refreshing mode.

- BACKDROP. If this bit is set, this window will be a backdrop window.

- REPORTMOUSE. If this bit is set, mouse movement within the window will be reported to your program.

- BORDERLESS. If this bit is set, the window will be created without borders.

- ACTIVATE. If this bit is set, this window will be active when it is opened.

- NOCAREREFRESH. If this bit is set, your program will not receive refresh messages when obscured portions of the window are revealed.

- ACTIVEWINDOW. If this bit is set, your program will receive a message when this window becomes active.

- INACTIVEWINDOW. If this bit is set, your program will receive a message when this window becomes inactive.

OpenWorkBench

Syntax of Function Call

open = OpenWorkBench ( )

Purpose of Function

This function opens the Workbench screen. If successful, it returns a TRUE value in the open Boolean variable; if unsuccessful, it returns a FALSE value.

Inputs to Function

This function uses no arguments.

Discussion

There are four Intuition functions that work directly with the standard Workbench screen display: OpenWorkBench, CloseWorkBench, WBenchToBack, and WBenchToFront. You use these functions to manipulate the Intuition Workbench screen.

Workbench is both a screen and an applications program (or tool). At this time, it is the only Intuition standard screen. It is a high-resolution, noninterlaced mode (640-by-200 pixels) display screen. The default colors are blue for the background, white and black for details, and orange for the cursor and mouse pointer.

The Workbench screen is used both for the CLI (command line interface) program and the Workbench program. You can also use the Workbench screen for windows in your applications programs. If the Workbench program is active, the Workbench screen displays both the Workbench program windows and your applications program windows. In this way, you do not have to create a custom screen to contain your program windows. Just set the screen type as WBENCHSCREEN in the NewWindow structure when you are about to define a new window for your program.

Text-oriented applications programs are especially efficient if all windows are opened in the Workbench screen. If the Workbench screen is the only screen in the system, the user will be able to work without the confusion of changing screens when changing windows. In addition, your applications program will not need to open any custom screens; this will obviously save on RAM space.

The OpenWorkBench function merely opens the Workbench screen. If there is not enough RAM, the OpenWorkBench function will fail. Also, if the Workbench program is available, all the windows of the Workbench program will automatically open on the Workbench screen. This includes the Preferences program window, which allows the user to change the color and other characteristics of the Workbench screen.

PrintIText

Syntax of Function Call

PrintIText (rastPort, intuiText, leftEdge, topEdge)

Purpose of Function

This function draws text according to the intuiText argument. If you try to draw text outside of the window's boundaries, your text will be clipped at the window's edge. PrintIText does not return a value.

Inputs to Function

rastPort	A pointer to a controlling RastPort structure
intuiText	A pointer to an IntuiText structure
leftEdge	The left offset of the text in the raster bitmap
topEdge	The top offset of the text in the raster bitmap

Discussion

There are two Intuition functions that deal directly with text in the Amiga system, IntuiTextLength and PrintIText. These functions deal specifically with the IntuiText structure. The IntuiText structure contains a text representation. The IText parameter in the IntuiText structure points to a null-terminated text string to be displayed. These two functions allow you to return the length (actually the pixel-width) of an IText string and to draw an IText string according to controlling arguments in the PrintIText function.

The IntuiText structure provides a simple way to display Intuition text strings on the Amiga display. The best example of this is an array of IText strings used to develop the menu displays in the Intuition system.

To define and display text, you need to decide the following:

- The colors you will use for your text

- The colors you will use for the background of your text

- The starting position in the containing display element for your text

- The font you will use, either the default font (Topaz-60 or Topaz-80) or your own special font

- Whether you want to create a linked list of IntuiText structures to hold multiple text strings

You can choose from three drawing modes to define the colors in your text. If you choose the JAM1 drawing mode, the text characters will be drawn in the FrontPen color; the background area around the characters will not be affected. JAM1 is also called over-strike mode.

If you choose the JAM2 drawing mode, the character image is drawn in the Front-Pen color; the background area around characters will be drawn in the BackPen color. Using this mode, you completely change the colors in and around the text characters.

If you choose the XOR (equivalent to COMPLEMENT) drawing mode, each pixel of the text characters is drawn in the binary complement color of the pixel at the destination location. For example, if the original color at a pixel position was all bits 1 values, the character text pixel at that position will be all bits 0 values. The FrontPen and Back-Pen settings in the IntuiText structure are ignored.

RefreshGadgets

Syntax of Function Call

RefreshGadgets (gadgets, pointer, requester)

Purpose of Function

This function refreshes all the gadgets in the gadget list starting with the specified gadget. If the SCRGADGET flag is set, the pointer variable refers to a Screen structure; if the SCRGADGET flag is not set, the pointer variable refers to a Window structure. RefreshGadgets does not return a value.

Inputs to Function

gadgets   A pointer to the first Gadget structure in a list of gadgets to be refreshed

pointer   A pointer to either a Screen or Window structure

requester   A pointer to a Requester structure; this will be null if this is not a requester gadget list

Discussion

There are six Intuition functions that work with gadgets: AddGadget, OnGadget, OffGadget, RefreshGadgets, RemoveGadget, and ModifyProp. There is more information on gadgets in the discussions of each of these functions.

There are two main reasons for using the RefreshGadgets function. First, if you have modified the imagery of some of the gadgets in your display, you will want to display the new imagery. Second, if some gadget operation you just performed has ruined the imagery of your gadget display, you will need to renew it.

When you refresh your gadgets, you may want to consider the three available highlighting methods:

1. You can highlight by complementary color. Here, you highlight by complementing all the colors in a gadget's select box. Complementing means that you use the binary-complement color register in setting the color for the gadget image. For example, if the pixel at a specific location in your gadget has the 001 bit combination, it will use the 001 color register to set the color at that location. However, if you choose complementary highlighting, the 110 color register will be used for that pixel.

2. You can highlight by drawing a box around the gadget's select box.

3. You can highlight by supplying an alternate image or border imagery. Then, when the gadget is selected, the alternate image or border is displayed in place of the nonhighlighted imagery.

RefreshGList

Syntax of Function Call

RefreshGList (gadget, window, requester, number_gadgets)

Purpose of Function

This function refreshes (redraws on the display screen) gadgets in a gadget list starting with a specified gadget. This is useful for refreshing gadgets in a window or requester. This function returns no value.

Inputs to Function

gadget   A pointer to the Gadget structure for the first gadget in the gadget list

window   A pointer to a Window structure for the window that will contain the gadgets in the gadget list

requester   This is a pointer to the Requester structure for the requester that will display the gadgets in the gadget list. In order to associate gadgets with requesters, the REQGADGET parameter must be set in the Gadget structure for the first gadget in the gadget list. Use null if the gadgets are not in a requester.

**number
_gadgets**   This is the maximum number of gadgets in the complete gadget list to be refreshed. If the entire gadget list is to be refreshed, use −1 for this parameter. However, if a null value is found in the NextGadget parameter of one of the Gadget structures, that gadget will be the last one to be refreshed.

Discussion

RefreshGList is one of the four 1.2 release functions that deal with gadgets and the gadget list in the Intuition software system. You should also read the discussion of the RefreshGadgets function, which is closely related to the RefreshGList function.

RefreshGList is useful when the redisplay of a series of gadgets in a window or requester is required for any reason. RefreshGList allows you to refresh all gadgets in a gadget list with one function call. In this sense RefreshGList is a superset of the RefreshGadgets function; it deals with all gadgets in a window or requester, not just the gadgets in a specific sublist.

RefreshWindowFrame

Syntax of Function Call

RefreshWindowFrame (window)

Purpose of Function

This function refreshes the border of a window, including the title bar region and all of the window's gadgets. You should make this call to update the display of your window borders. Typically, this function will be used to recover from unavoidable window border display corruption.

Inputs to Function

window   A pointer to a Window structure whose windowframe should be refreshed

Discussion

There are two 1.2 release functions that deal with windows in the Intuition software system: ActivateWindow and RefreshWindowFrame. The contents of a window border are specified by five parameters in the Window structure for that window. These are the BorderLeft, BorderRight, BorderTop, and BorderBottom parameters together with the BorderRPort parameter. The RefreshWindowFrame function uses these parameters to determine how to refresh the window when user action leads to corruption of the graphics display in the border area of that window.

RemakeDisplay

Syntax of Function Call

RemakeDisplay ( )

Purpose of Function

This function remakes the entire Intuition display. First, it calls the MakeScreen function for every screen in the system. Then it establishes the display relationships of the various screens and determines the correct Copper display lists to produce the current Intuition display frame. RemakeDisplay does not return a value.

Inputs to Function

This function uses no arguments.

Discussion

There are two Intuition functions that deal directly with the entire display, including all the screens and windows that define that display. These are the RemakeDisplay and RethinkDisplay functions.

The RemakeDisplay function allows you to redefine the display automatically for all combinations of windows, screens, viewports, and views you have previously defined. The MakeScreen function is called automatically for each screen when you call the Remake-Display function. For this reason, RemakeDisplay can be considered the grand manipulator of the Amiga Intuition display.

The Amiga display can be very complex. You can have a number of custom screens, and every one of your custom screens can have a number of windows. The windows currently open in a custom screen can belong to one program or several programs.

Each window in a screen can be a backdrop window, a superbitmap window, a borderless window, or a gimmezerozero window. In addition, you can have the Workbench screen open on the Amiga display.

Because of the extensive amount of information involved, the RemakeDisplay function can take several milliseconds to execute. During this time, all other tasks are locked out of the system. The system does this automatically by surrounding the RethinkDisplay function call statements (called indirectly by RemakeDisplay) with calls to the Forbid and Permit system routines.

All of this display complexity requires a fair amount of display memory. However, if you have an Amiga equipped with at least 512K of RAM, you can achieve most of these display combinations.

You can think of MakeScreen, RethinkDisplay, and RemakeDisplay as a hierarchy of functions. The MakeScreen function is at the bottom of the hierarchy; it deals with a single custom screen in a display. Next in line is the RethinkDisplay function; it deals with the entire Amiga display, with all its potential complexity. RethinkDisplay produces a completely new display of all your windows and screens. If you call MakeScreen for each of your custom screens, you can then call the RethinkDisplay function to redisplay each of them. Finally, there is the RemakeDisplay function, which does the job of the

MakeScreen and RethinkDisplay functions combined; it remakes all of your custom screens and then creates the new display that these screens bring about.

If you want to remake only one or two of your custom screens and you have several of them, it is more efficient to call the MakeScreen function for each of those screens and then call the RethinkDisplay function. RethinkDisplay takes your new screen definitions and combines them with the other unchanged screen definitions (including the Workbench screen) to produce the new display. If you have a fair number of screens, but only need to update one or two, this process will probably be faster than calling the RemakeDisplay function.

RemoveGadget

Syntax of Function Call

> **gadgetposition = RemoveGadget (pointer, gadget)**

Purpose of Function

This function removes a gadget from a window or screen. If the SCRGADGET flag is set, the pointer argument refers to a Screen structure; if the SCRGADGET flag is not set, the pointer argument refers to a Window structure. RemoveGadget returns the ordinal position number of the gadget in the gadget list in the gadgetposition variable. If the Gadget structure pointer points to a gadget that is not in the appropriate list, or if there are no gadgets in the list, a -1 is returned.

Inputs to Function

pointer	A pointer to either a Screen or Window structure
gadget	A pointer to the Gadget structure that you want to remove

Discussion

There are six Intuition functions that work with gadgets: AddGadget, OnGadget, OffGadget, RefreshGadgets, RemoveGadget, and ModifyProp. There is more information on gadgets in the discussions of each of these functions.

There is a very important distinction between disabling a gadget and removing a gadget. If you disable a gadget (using the OffGadget function), it remains on the system gadget list. The OnGadget function can then return that gadget to its normal display image. If you remove a gadget (using the RemoveGadget function), that gadget is taken off the system gadget list; you cannot use the OnGadget function to display it again. If you want to restore the display of that gadget, you must add it to the system with the AddGadget function. Note that you cannot use the RemoveGadget function to remove a system gadget.

RemoveGList

Syntax of Function Call

position = RemoveGList (window, gadget, number_gadgets)

Purpose of Function

This function removes a gadget sublist from the complete gadget list of a window or requester inside a window. The new gadget list for that window or requester is then shortened by the number of gadgets actually removed. The number_gadgets argument determines how many gadgets are removed from the original list. RemoveGList returns the ordinal position of the first gadget removed from the gadget list. If the specified gadget was not found in the gadget list, or if there are no gadgets in the gadget list, a −1 is returned.

Inputs to Function

window	A pointer to a Window structure for the window where gadgets will be removed
gadget	A pointer to the Gadget structure for the first gadget in the gadget sublist
number _gadgets	The number of gadgets from the gadget list to be removed; if the entire gadget list is to be removed, use −1 for this parameter

Discussion

RemoveGList is one of the four 1.2 release functions that deal with gadgets and the gadget list in the Intuition software system.

Gadgets in windows and requesters can be maintained in gadget lists (and sublists) as defined in the AddGList function discussion. RemoveGList allows you to remove a sublist of gadgets from a specific window or from a requester in a specific window. In this sense, the RemoveGList function is the inverse of the AddGList function.

The first Gadget structure determines if the specified gadget sublist belongs to a window or a requester in the window. If the REQGADGET flag is set in that first Gadget structure, then all gadgets in the sublist belong to a requester.

ReportMouse

Syntax of Function Call

ReportMouse (window, report)

Purpose of Function

This function tells Intuition whether to report mouse movement in a window when this window becomes active.

Inputs to Function

window   A pointer to a Window structure

report   A TRUE or FALSE value specifying whether to turn window mouse-movement reporting on or off

Discussion

There are twelve Intuition functions that manage windows in the Amiga system: BeginRefresh, CloseWindow, EndRefresh, EndRequest, MoveWindow, OpenWindow, ReportMouse, SetWindowTitles, SizeWindow, WindowLimits, WindowToFront, and WindowToBack. There is more information on windows in the discussions of each of these functions.

Both windows and window gadgets need to know about mouse movement. The ReportMouse function allows you to control the reporting of mouse movements in windows. In particular, each time the mouse pointer moves into an applications program or Intuition system gadget (the sizing gadget, drag gadget, close gadget, bring-to-front gadget, or send-to-back gadget) you will usually want Intuition to report mouse movement to your task or program. To be sure that this happens, call the ReportMouse function immediately after your OpenWindow function call. Then your program can take the appropriate action (for example, move the window) corresponding to that particular mouse movement.

If the specified window is active when the ReportMouse function is called with report set to TRUE, mouse-movement reports will start coming immediately. If the specified window is not active when ReportMouse executes, mouse movements will be reported once the window becomes active.

Both the NewWindow structure and the Gadget structure have flag bits for detection of mouse movements. The NewWindow structure has the REPORTMOUSE flag bit; the Gadget structure has the FOLLOWMOUSE flag bit. If the REPORTMOUSE flag bit is set, mouse movements will be reported when that window is open. The ReportMouse function can later override the window's setting. If the FOLLOWMOUSE flag bit is set, your program will receive mouse movement messages whenever the user moves the mouse pointer inside the gadget. The ReportMouse function does not override this setting.

If you call the ReportMouse function when a gadget is selected, reporting of mouse movements in the gadget will occur only while that gadget is selected. Once that gadget becomes unselected, the FOLLOWMOUSE flag bit in the Gadget structure is examined once again. If that flag bit is set, mouse movements inside the gadget will also be reported the next time the gadget is selected.

Calling ReportMouse when no gadget is selected will change the state of the window's REPORTMOUSE flag bit; however, it will have no effect on any gadget subsequently selected.

Request

Syntax of Function Call

reqopen = Request (requester, window)

Purpose of Function

This function activates a requester in a window. If the requester is opened successfully, the Request function returns TRUE in the reqopen Boolean variable; if the requester could not be opened, the Request function returns FALSE.

Inputs to Function

requester   A pointer to a Requester structure

window   A pointer to the Window structure that is to receive this requester

Discussion

There are seven Intuition functions that work directly with requesters: AutoRequest, BuildSysRequest, ClearDMRequest, FreeSysRequest, InitRequester, Request, and SetDMRequest. There is more information on requesters in the discussions of each of these functions.

AutoRequest, BuildSysRequest, InitRequest, and SetDMRequest merely prepare a requester for display; the Request function is the one that actually displays the requester in a window.

There are two ways the system can get pixel information for the display of a requester. The first method requires you to supply enough information for internal Intuition requester definitions to render the requester. The second method requires you to supply a custom bitmap requester image in RAM. How you fill in (initialize) the Requester structure depends on which method you use.

If you want Intuition to render the requester, you must supply a list of requester gadgets, a pen color for filling the requester background, and one or more IntuiText and Border structures to define the text and borders of the requester. If you want to define your own requester through a custom bitmap, you must define and supply the gadget imagery in bitmaps of your own design.

RethinkDisplay

Syntax of Function Call

RethinkDisplay ( )

Purpose of Function

This function works together with the MakeScreen function to produce a new Amiga display.

Inputs to Function

This function uses no arguments.

Discussion

There are two Intuition functions that work directly with the entire display, Remake-Display and RethinkDisplay. The entire display consists of all defined screens (standard and custom) and windows required to define that display. The RethinkDisplay function allows Intuition to redefine the Copper lists needed to drive the display hardware for this display frame definition, thereby combining all screens you have previously defined for that particular display frame.

In the Amiga multiscreen display system, you can have a number of custom screens as well as the Workbench screen in a specific display definition.

Each time you finish a drawing process that changes the pixel information in a custom screen bitmap, you want to include that information in your display. You can do this in two ways. First, you can change some of your custom screen definitions and call the RemakeDisplay function. The RemakeDisplay function will take your new custom screen definitions, all previous unchanged custom screen definitions, and the current Workbench screen definition and build a Copper instruction list to define the entire display that results from this information.

Alternatively, you can change some of your custom screens and call the MakeScreen function for each one. Then you can call the RethinkDisplay function to create the new display. If you have a fair number of screens but only need to update one or two of them, this process will probably be faster than calling the RemakeDisplay function.

Because of the extensive amount of information involved, the RethinkDisplay function can take a fair amount of time (several milliseconds) to execute. During this time, all other tasks are locked out of the system. The system does this automatically by surrounding the RethinkDisplay function call statements with calls to the Forbid and Permit system routines.

ScreenToBack

Syntax of Function Call

ScreenToBack (screen)

Purpose of Function

This function sends the specified custom screen to the back of the display.

Inputs to Function

screen   A pointer to a Screen structure

Discussion

There are seven Intuition functions that manage custom screens: OpenScreen, Close-Screen, MoveScreen, MakeScreen, ShowTitle, ScreenToBack, and ScreenToFront. There is more information on custom screens in the discussions of each of these functions.

When you have a multilayered Intuition display, the display order at any given time depends partly on the order in which screens and windows are opened and partly on the prior history of any depth-arrangement operations done in that display.

In any case, the current order of screens and windows will follow these rules:

1. If you have created backdrop windows in the deepest screen in the current display, the deepest part of that screen will consist of a backdrop window. The presence of backdrop windows in a screen depends on the setting of the BACKDROP flag in the NewWindow structure when you first create a window. Although you can have several layers of backdrop windows in a screen, there is usually no reason or advantage to having more than one. If you do have more than one backdrop window in a screen, the order of these backdrop windows will depend on the order in which you created (opened) them. The deepest backdrop window in a screen is the most recent one created for that screen.

2. Next, you can have a number of additional custom screens open in the display. The number is limited only by the amount of display memory at your disposal. Each of these custom screens can have a number of open windows, some of which can once again be backdrop windows. Each open window, regardless of its type, is a virtual terminal in the system. When that window is active, all I/O coming from the mouse, keyboard, or other I/O devices is directed through that window. All windows currently open in a custom screen can belong to one applications program. Alternatively, a number of applications programs can simultaneously open windows inside one custom screen.

3. Next, you can have any of the Intuition standard screens; at this time, only the Workbench screen is available. In each standard screen, you can open any number of windows, limited only by the amount of display memory available. Each of these windows can belong to one applications program, or several applications programs can share the Workbench screen to open and display their windows.

Note that the current order of screens and windows changes as the user (and your program) changes the depth-arrangement of screens and windows on the display. The order of screens and windows is controlled by the Layers Library functions. Read Chapter 5 to learn more about these ideas.

ScreenToFront

Syntax of Function Call

ScreenToFront (screen)

Purpose of Function

This function brings the specified custom screen to the front of the display.

Inputs to Function

screen   A pointer to a Screen structure

Discussion

There are seven Intuition functions that work directly with custom screens: OpenScreen, CloseScreen, MoveScreen, MakeScreen, ShowTitle, ScreenToBack and ScreenToFront. There is more information on custom screens in the discussions of each of these functions.

You can depth-arrange your custom screens with the ScreenToFront and ScreenToBack functions. This type of depth-arrangement is in addition to the depth-arrangement you use for windows inside custom and standard screens; these are two separate and distinct types of depth-arrangement mechanisms.

You can use the ScreenToFront and ScreenToBack functions whenever the user makes a menu choice that calls for a new screen display. At that time, you can send one screen to the back and bring another screen to the front of the display.

SetDMRequest

Syntax of Function Call

reqdisplay = SetDMRequest (window, dMRequester)

Purpose of Function

This function selects a specific double-menu requester for a window and causes it to be displayed in that window. The double-menu requester is the special requester that your program attaches to a double-click of the Menu button. SetDMRequest will have no effect if the double-menu requester is already active in the window. SetDMRequest returns TRUE in the reqdisplay Boolean variable if the double-menu requester was not already displayed in that window; otherwise it returns FALSE.

Inputs to Function

window   A pointer to a Window structure

dMRequester   A pointer to a Requester structure for a double-menu requester

Discussion

There are seven Intuition functions that work directly with requesters: AutoRequest, BuildSysRequest, ClearDMRequest, FreeSysRequest, InitRequester, Request, and SetDMRequest. There is more information on requesters in the discussions of each of these functions.

The double-menu requester, like other requesters, blocks input to the window in which it appears. Your graphics must be designed to allow the user to remove the requester from the window so that input can continue for that window. Therefore, all requesters (double-menu requesters and others alike) must have at least one gadget that will satisfy the request and allow window input to continue.

For each gadget that ends the user-requester interaction, your program should set the ENDGADGET flag in the Gadget structure flags variable. Each time one of the requester gadgets is selected, Intuition examines the ENDGADGET flag in the Gadget structure associated with that gadget. If the ENDGADGET flag is set to a value of 1, that requester is erased from the window and unlinked from the window's active-requester list.

SetMenuStrip

Syntax of Function Call

SetMenuStrip (window, menu)

Purpose of Function

This function attaches a specified menu strip to a window. It causes the specified menu strip to be displayed and accessible when the user presses the Menu button.

Inputs to Function

window	A pointer to a Window structure
menu	A pointer to the first Menu structure in a menu strip

Discussion

There are five Intuition functions that manage menus: ClearMenuStrip, ItemAddress, OnMenu, OffMenu, and SetMenuStrip. There is more information on menus in the discussions of each of these functions.

A menu strip contains all the information needed to define a set of interactive menus. Intuition menu strips have three components: menus, menu items, and menu subitems. There are two structures that deal with menus and their items: the Menu and MenuItem structures. The Menu structure contains data to define the basic unit of the menu strip. A menu strip consists of a linked list of Menu structures. Each Menu structure contains data to define the header or topic name for a list of menu items that can be selected by the user. The user never selects a menu alone, but rather a menu and at least one of its menu items.

This is the general procedure you should use to design your menu strip for windows:

1. Design the Menu structures and link them together into a menu strip.

2. Submit the menu strip to Intuition with the SetMenuStrip function; this attaches the menu strip to a window.

3. Arrange for your program to respond to Intuition's menu-selection messages (see the discussion of the ModifyIDCMP function).

For each Menu structure, you must decide the following:

- The menu names that will appear in the screen title bar
- The menu items that will appear when the user selects a menu item
- The position of each menu item in the menu item list
- The text or graphics input for each menu item
- The highlighting method used for each menu item when the user positions the mouse pointer over it
- Any equivalent command-key sequence to be associated with each menu item
- Whether any of your menu items will have subitems; for each subitem, you have to make the same decisions as you did for each menu item

The Menu Structure

The Menu structure contains the following information:

- Menu bar text that appears across the screen's title bar when the menu button is pressed
- The position for the menu bar text
- A pointer to the next Menu structure in a linked list of Menu structures that help define a menu strip
- A pointer to the first in a linked list of MenuItem structures that help define a menu strip

The MenuItem Structure

The MenuItem structure contains the following information:

- The position of the menu item with respect to the select box of its menu display
- A pointer to a text or graphics image
- An identification of the highlighting method to be used when the user selects the menu item
- An equivalent keyboard command sequence (if appropriate)
- A definition of the select box for the menu item; this is used to detect selection and also for some of the highlighting modes
- Other menu items that are mutually excluded by selecting this menu item
- A pointer to the first in a linked list of subitems

■ The menu number of the next selected menu item; when more than one menu item is selected, this field provides the link between these menu items

Each subitem of a menu item uses the same form of data structure as the menu item itself with a few differences: the subitem's location is relative to its menu item's select box, and the subitem's subitem link (to other nonexistent subitems) is ignored.

SetPointer

Syntax of Function Call

SetPointer (window, pointer, height, width, XOffset, YOffset)

Purpose of Function

This function gives a window its own customized display pointer. The customized pointer image is defined in a SpriteImage structure. When this window becomes active, that sprite pointer image will be displayed in the window. If the specified window is active when the SetPointer function is called, the new pointer is displayed immediately.

Inputs to Function

window	A pointer to a Window structure
pointer	A pointer to a SpriteImage structure
height	The height of the pointer-image sprite
width	The width of the pointer-image sprite
XOffset	The offset for your sprite from the current x-position of the default Intuition pointer
YOffset	The offset for your sprite from the current y-position of the default Intuition pointer

Discussion

There are two Intuition functions that work directly with mouse pointer images in windows, SetPointer and ClearPointer. These functions allow you to establish a window with its own pointer image and to clear that pointer image from that window. With these functions, you can create your own pointer images rather than use the arrow pointer image supplied as the default pointer image in the Intuition system. To define the pointer, you have to set up a SpriteImage structure which is Chapter 3.

Once you set up your custom pointer, you can change its colors at any time using the SetRGB4 function as described in Chapter 2. Note that the Intuition pointer is always sprite 0.

Use the following procedure to replace the Intuition pointer with a custom pointer of your own design. First, create a SpriteImage structure. This structure is made up of words of data needed to define the colors of each pixel in the sprite used for the custom pointer. The first two words and the last two words are all zeros. All the other words define the appearance of the pointer.

Then call the SetPointer function. If your window is currently active, the new pointer appears in the window immediately. The XOffset and YOffset variables used in the SetPointer function call are used to offset the upper-left corner of the custom pointer image from what Intuition regards as the current position of the Intuition default pointer. Intuition measures this offset from the center of the Intuition pointer (called the *hot spot*) at 7,7.

For example, if you specify XOffset and YOffset as 0,0, the top-left of your custom pointer will be placed at the center of the current Intuition pointer position. On the other hand, if you specify an XOffset of − 7, the custom pointer will be centered over the current Intuition pointer position. If you specify an XOffset value of − 15, the right edge of your custom pointer will be directly over the center of the Intuition pointer.

SetWindowTitles

Syntax of Function Call

SetWindowTitles (window, windowTitle, screenTitle)

Purpose of Function

This function sets the text of the window titles for both the window and the screen in which that window is displayed. If you set the windowTitle and screenTitle arguments to − 1, the current title remains unchanged; if you set these arguments to 0, there will be no titles in the specified window.

Inputs to Function

window	A pointer to a Window structure
windowTitle	A pointer to null-terminated text string
screenTitle	A pointer to null-terminated text string

Discussion

There are twelve Intuition functions that work directly with windows: BeginRefresh, CloseWindow, EndRefresh, EndRequest, MoveWindow, OpenWindow, ReportMouse, SetWindowTitles, SizeWindow, WindowLimits, WindowToFront, and WindowToBack. There is more information on windows in the discussions of each of these functions.

The window's title appears inside the window's title bar. The window's screen title appears in the screen title bar whenever this window is active.

When the SetWindowTitles function executes, the window title is changed immediately. The window does not have to be active for the window title to be changed. The window does have to be active, however, for the screen title to change.

Read the introduction to this chapter and the discussion of the ShowTitle function to learn more about window and screen titles.

SHIFTITEM

Syntax of Macro Call

SHIFTITEM (menuNumber)

Purpose of Macro

This macro first performs an And operation of the menuNumber value with a 0x3F hex value and then shifts the result five places to the left. This has the effect of shifting the present menu number to define a new value for the menu item number.

Inputs to Macro

menuNumber	A 16-bit packed binary number that defines the menu number, the menu item number, and the menu subitem number

Discussion

There are six macros that deal with menus, menu items, and menu subitems: MENUNUM, ITEMNUM, SUBNUM, SHIFTMENU, SHIFTITEM, and SHIFT-SUB. You should read the discussions of each of these macros to see how menu-related items are handled by Intuition.

The precise definition of the SHIFTITEM macro is included in the last part of the Intuition INCLUDE file under the Miscellaneous heading.

SHIFTMENU

Syntax of Macro Call

SHIFTMENU (menuNumber)

Purpose of Macro

This macro extracts the ordinal menu number—which starts at 0 and increases to 31—from the menuNumber argument. Its operation is identical to the MENUNUM macro. These two macros can be used interchangeably. SHIFTMENU is included only so that a menu counterpart exists for the SHIFTITEM and SHIFTSUB macros.

Inputs to Macro

menuNumber   A 16-bit packed binary number that defines the menu number, the menu item number, and the menu subitem number

Discussion

You should read the MENUNUM discussion to learn about the operation of the SHIFT-MENU macro. The precise definition of the SHIFTMENU macro is included in the last part of the Intuition INCLUDE file under the Miscellaneous heading.

SHIFTSUB

Syntax of Macro Call

SHIFTSUB (menuNumber)

Purpose of Macro

This macro first performs an And operation of the menuNumber value with a 0x1F hex value and then shifts the result 11 places to the left. This has the effect of shifting the present menu number to define a new value for the menu subitem number.

Inputs to Macro

menuNumber   A 16-bit packed binary number that defines the menu number, the menu item number, and the menu subitem number

Discussion

There are six macros that deal with menus, menu items, and menu subitems: MENUNUM, ITEMNUM, SUBNUM, SHIFTMENU, SHIFTITEM, and SHIFT-SUB. You should read the discussions of each of these macros to see how menu-related items are handled by Intuition. The precise definition of the SHIFTSUB macro is included in the last part of the Intuition INCLUDE file under the Miscellaneous heading.

ShowTitle

Syntax of Function Call

ShowTitle (screen, ShowIt)

Purpose of Function

This function either displays or hides the screen's default title when a backdrop window is open in that screen.

Inputs to Function

screen	A pointer to a Screen structure
ShowIt	A Boolean TRUE or FALSE value; the screen title bar text is displayed if TRUE and not displayed if FALSE

Discussion

There are seven Intuition functions that work directly with custom screens: OpenScreen, CloseScreen, MoveScreen, MakeScreen, ShowTitle, ScreenToBack, and ScreenToFront. There is more information on custom screens in the discussions of each of these functions.

The screen's title text is used for two reasons: to identify the screen, much like the identification on a file folder, and to designate which window is the active window in that screen.

Although the screen title is set when the NewScreen structure is initialized, it can change as new windows open in the screen. Each screen has two types of titles that can be displayed in the screen's title bar:

1. The default title is the title in the NewScreen structure; it is displayed when the screen first opens.

2. The current title is the title associated with the currently active window in this screen; it depends on the title settings in the Window structure associated with the active window.

Part of the specification of the NewScreen structure is the DefaultTitle parameter. This is a pointer to a null-terminated text string to be placed in the screen's title bar as the text of the screen's title. The NewScreen structure also contains a pointer to the default TextAttr structure, which contains a description of a font to be used in the screen's title bar text. You can either use this default Intuition font (Topaz-60 or Topaz-80) or provide your own TextAttr structure. A TextAttr structure is very simple; it merely contains the attributes of a text font. See Chapter 4 for information on the TextFont structure.

The screen's title bar can be behind or on top of any backdrop windows that are opened on that screen. When the ShowIt argument is TRUE, the screen title bar is shown in front of any backdrop windows.

The screen's title bar is always displayed in front of any backdrop windows when the screen is first opened. Other window types always appear in front of the screen's title bar, no matter how ShowTitle is set up.

SizeWindow

Syntax of Function Call

SizeWindow (window, dx, dy)

Purpose of Function

This function resizes a window by the values indicated in the dx,dy arguments. The window will be resized the next time Intuition receives an input event for that window.

Inputs to Function

window	A pointer to a Window structure
dx	A signed value describing how many pixels to resize the window on the x-axis
dy	A signed value describing how many pixels to resize the window on the y-axis

Discussion

There are twelve Intuition functions that work directly with windows: BeginRefresh, CloseWindow, EndRefresh, EndRequest, MoveWindow, OpenWindow, ReportMouse, SetWindowTitles, SizeWindow, WindowLimits, WindowToFront, and WindowToBack. There is more information on windows in the discussions of each of these functions.

When you call the SizeWindow function, the window is not resized until Intuition receives the next input event for that window, which occurs at a minimum rate of ten times a second and a maximum rate of sixty times a second. You can discover when your window was resized by setting the NEWSIZE flag of the IDCMP assigned to your window.

Note that the SizeWindow function does not check for errors. Therefore, if you specify dx and dy values that are outside of the window's screen-pixel limits, some or all of the window will disappear from the screen.

SUBNUM

Syntax of Macro Call

SUBNUM (menuNumber)

Purpose of Macro

This macro extracts the ordinal menu subitem number from the menuNumber argument. The ordinal subitem number starts at 0 and increases to 31. This macro is necessary to allow the IDCMP menu-selection message flag, MENUPICK, to be compared to the current menu subitem definitions to determine which menu subitem the user has selected.

Inputs to Macro

menuNumber   A 16-bit packed binary number that defines the menu number, the menu item number, and the menu subitem number

Discussion

There are six macros that deal with menus, menu items, and menu subitems: MENUNUM, ITEMNUM, SUBNUM, SHIFTMENU, SHIFTITEM, and SHIFT-SUB. You should read the discussions of each of these macros to see how menu-related items are handled by Intuition.

To determine the menu subitem number, use the following program statement:

MySubItemNumber = SUBNUM (menuNumber)

Then MySubItemNumber will be either a valid value (0 to 31) or the special value NOSUB if no menu item was selected. The values of MENUNULL and NOSUB are defined in the last part of the Intuition INCLUDE file, along with the precise definition of the SUBNUM macro.

UnlockIBase

Syntax of Function Call

UnlockIBase (lock_value)

Purpose of Function

This function releases one of the Intuition internal locks for your program to use. The lock must first be obtained with the LockIBase function. Note that the lock-value argument is passed in register A0 (rather than D0).

Inputs to Function

lock_value   A long unsigned integer that represents the Intuition internal lock you want to free; this is the same value originally returned by the LockIBase function call

Discussion

There are two 1.2 release functions that deal with locks in the Intuition software system: LockIBase and UnlockIBase. UnlockIBase is the inverse of LockIBase. These two functions must be called in pairs and reasonably close together in time. When UnlockIBase returns, Intuition can once again access and change the parameters in the IntuitionBase structure and continue with input processing.

ViewAddress

Syntax of Function Call

view = ViewAddress ()

Purpose of Function

This function returns a pointer to an Intuition View structure. If you want to use any of the Graphics Library drawing, display, text, or animation functions to render objects in an Intuition display, call the ViewAddress function to determine a pointer to the appropriate View structure to use.

Inputs to Function

This function uses no arguments.

Discussion

You can design all of your Intuition procedures without calling ViewAddress. However, if you want to use any of the Graphics Library functions to draw directly into the views of your Intuition displays, you will need the address of the Intuition View structure. This structure is a specific instance of a Graphics Library View structure; it is simply a linked list of all the ViewPort structures needed to define the Intuition display screen view.

For example, if you want to create an image in an Intuition display with the Area-Draw, AreaMove, and AreaEnd functions, you will need a pointer to the Intuition View structure.

When you use the Graphics Library functions to draw into an Intuition view and you allow the user to move and resize windows, the underlying screen bitmap information is destroyed. A blank background is displayed where the window was previously displayed. Obviously, this is an undesirable situation.

To avoid this problem, you should define all windows in that Intuition view to be unmovable and nonresizable. You can do this by setting the appropriate flags in the NewWindow structure when you first define each new window.

See the discussion of ViewPortAddress for a list of Intuition program instructions you can use to obtain a View structure pointer for an Intuition window or screen.

ViewPortAddress

Syntax of Function Call

viewPort = ViewPortAddress (window)

Purpose of Function

This function returns a pointer to the specified window's ViewPort structure. This is the ViewPort structure belonging to the screen in which this window is displayed. If you want to use any of the Graphics Library drawing, display, text, or animation functions to display objects in an Intuition viewport, you need to call ViewPortAddress for a pointer to the appropriate ViewPort structure.

Inputs to Function

window   A pointer to a Window structure

Discussion

ViewPortAddress works much like ViewAddress. The discussion under the ViewAddress function applies equally well to the ViewPortAddress function. You should read that discussion to understand how and when to use the ViewPortAddress function.

You can obtain a pointer to any RastPort, ViewPort, or View structure for a given Window structure with the following Intuition program instructions:

```
struct Window *myWindow;
struct RastPort *myRastPort;
struct ViewPort *myViewPort;
struct View *myView;

myWindow == OpenWindow ();
myRastPort == myWindow->RastPort;
myViewport == ViewPortAddress(myWindow);
myView == ViewAddress ();
```

Use these program instructions to obtain structure pointers for a given Screen structure:

```
struct Screen *myScreen;
struct RastPort *myRastPort;
struct ViewPort *myViewPort;
struct View *myView;

myScreen == OpenScreen ();
myRastPort == myScreen->RastPort;
myViewport == ViewPortAddress(myScreen);
myView == ViewAddress ();
```

WBenchToBack

Syntax of Function Call

wasopen = WBenchToBack ( )

Purpose of Function

This function places the Workbench screen behind all other screens on the display. This affects only the depth-arrangement of the Workbench screen with respect to other currently displayed screens; the Workbench screen is not moved up or down by the WBench-ToBack function. This function returns a TRUE value in the wasopen variable if the Workbench screen was open when the call was made; otherwise it returns FALSE.

Inputs to Function

This function uses no arguments.

Discussion

There are four Intuition functions that work directly with the Workbench screen display: OpenWorkBench, CloseWorkBench, WBenchToBack, and WBenchToFront.

When the WBenchToBack function sends the Workbench screen to the back of the display, most (if not all) of the windows currently open in the Workbench screen will not be visible or accessible to the user. Which windows are visible depends on the exact size and arrangement of all screens on the Amiga display. Any Workbench screen windows that are still visible can be made active by the user. Once active, they can process I/O in the usual way.

WBenchToFront

Syntax of Function Call

wasopen = WBenchToFront ( )

Purpose of Function

This function places the Workbench screen in front of all other screens on the display. This affects only the depth-arrangement of the Workbench screen with respect to other currently displayed screens; the Workbench screen is not moved up or down by the WBenchToBack function. This function returns a TRUE value in the wasopen variable if the Workbench screen was open when the call was made; other-wise it returns FALSE.

Inputs to Function

This function uses no arguments.

Discussion

There are four Intuition functions that work directly with the Workbench screen display: OpenWorkBench, CloseWorkBench, WBenchToBack, and WBenchToFront.

The Amiga display can consist of a number of screens arranged in layers (depth-arranged). To provide a common user interface for applications program windows, the Workbench screen should always be present. Some or all of its windows (including the Preferences program window) can be open or closed. You can also have a number of custom screens in the display. The WBenchToFront function brings the Workbench screen in front of all other screens. Once the Workbench screen is in front, the user can open, work in, and close all of its windows. If one or more of your applications programs have windows open in the Workbench screen, WBenchToFront gives the user access to those windows.

WindowLimits

Syntax of Function Call

limitsOK = WindowLimits (window, min_width,
min_height,max_width,max_height

Purpose of Function

This function redefines the minimum and maximum limits for the size of a window. You must call this function if you want to change the resizing limits for a window in its Window structure. If all function arguments are valid, the Window-Limits function returns

TRUE in the Boolean variable limitsOK; if any of the arguments are out of range, WindowLimits returns FALSE.

Inputs to Function

window	A pointer to a Window structure
min_width	The new minimum width for this window
min_height	The new minimum height for this window
max_width	The new maximum width for this window
max_height	The new maximum height for this window

Discussion

There are twelve Intuition functions that work directly with windows: BeginRefresh, CloseWindow, EndRefresh, EndRequest, MoveWindow, OpenWindow, ReportMouse, SetWindowTitles, SizeWindow, WindowLimits, WindowToFront, and WindowToBack. There is more information on windows in the discussions of each of these functions.

When you first create a window (using the NewWindow structure together with the OpenWindow function), the initial window size is set by the LeftEdge, TopEdge, Width, and Height parameters in the NewWindow structure. In addition, the MinWidth, MinHeight, MaxWidth, and MaxHeight parameters set the window-resizing limits. When OpenWindow returns, these values are also placed in the Window structure for that window.

The WindowLimits function allows you to change the values of the MinWidth, MinHeight, MaxWidth, and MaxHeight parameters in the Window structure. Then you can use the SizeWindow function to resize the window in one of your screens according to these new limits.

If you want to leave one of the window's size parameters unchanged, set the corresponding argument in the WindowLimits function call to 0. The previous setting (either the NewWindow setting or a previous WindowLimits function setting) will then remain in effect.

If any of the WindowLimits function arguments is out of range (minimums greater than the current window size, maximums less than the current size), that particular limit will be ignored, and those limits that are in range will still take effect. If the user is currently resizing the window, the new limits will not take effect until the user completes the resizing operation.

WindowToBack

Syntax of Function Call

WindowToBack (window)

Purpose of Function

This function sends a window to the back of the display. The specified window is placed behind all other windows in the same screen. WindowToBack does not return a value.

Inputs to Function

window   A pointer to a Window structure

Discussion

There are twelve Intuition functions that work directly with windows: BeginRefresh, CloseWindow, EndRefresh, EndRequest, MoveWindow, OpenWindow, ReportMouse, SetWindowTitles, SizeWindow, WindowLimits, WindowToFront, and WindowToBack. There is more information on windows in the discussions of each of these functions.

Each of several applications programs can have multiple windows open in one screen. Only one window can be active at a time. This is the window that receives user input from the keyboard and mouse while all other windows are inactive.

When the WindowToBack function returns, a specific window will be moved behind all other windows in the same screen. This function does not change the window's active state. If that window was active, it will remain active; if it was inactive, it will remain inactive. The user can always change the active window by moving the mouse pointer anywhere in the window and clicking the Menu button.

WindowToFront

Syntax of Function Call

WindowToFront (window)

Purpose of Function

This function places a window in front of all other windows in the currently displayed screen. The specified window becomes the active window. WindowToFront does not return a value.

Inputs to Function

window   A pointer to a Window structure

Discussion

There are twelve Intuition functions that work directly with windows: BeginRefresh, CloseWindow, EndRefresh, EndRequest, MoveWindow, OpenWindow, ReportMouse, SetWindowTitles, SizeWindow, WindowLimits, WindowToFront, and WindowToBack. There is more information on windows in the discussions of each of these functions.

You can depth-arrange your Intuition windows using the WindowToFront and WindowToBack functions. When you use these functions, it is important to remember that all depth-arranging takes place within a given screen, specifically the screen with which the window is associated. The screens themselves can form a series of display layers; within these screen layers are a series of window layers. The deepest window layer in a screen is always the most recent backdrop window opened. (Note, however, that it would be unusual to define more than one backdrop layer per screen.) This is followed by the other windows in that screen and then by the other screens in that display.

When the WindowToFront function executes, the window will be moved up front as soon as Intuition receives an input event, which occurs at a minimum rate of ten times per second and a maximum rate of sixty times per second.

The WindowToFront function changes the active window in a particular screen. The user can also change the active window for any window that has a set of depth-arrangement gadgets. If the programmer or the user changes the active window, the task or program associated with this window takes control of the machine.

The Workbench Functions

Introduction

This chapter defines and discusses the Icon Library functions. These functions allow you to design applications programs that display icons and open windows on the Amiga Workbench screen. The Intuition system presented in Chapter 6 provides the most obvious example of programs—the Preferences, System, Utility, and Demo programs, among others—that interface with the Workbench program to display information on the Workbench screen.

The Icon Library functions fall into seven categories:

- The general memory-management functions: AddFreeList and FreeFreeList, for adding memory blocks of specific sizes to specific free-memory lists and releasing all memory blocks in a specific free-memory list

- The Workbench object info file memory-management functions: AllocWBObject and FreeWBObject, for allocating and deallocating the memory assigned to a Workbench object info file

- The Workbench object info file disk-transfer functions: GetWBObject and PutWBObject, for reading and writing a Workbench object info file from disk into memory and from memory to disk

- The disk-object memory-management function, FreeDiskObject, for freeing the memory previously assigned to a disk object by the system when that disk object info file was loaded from disk into memory

- The disk object info file disk-transfer functions: GetDiskObject, GetIcon, PutDiskObject, and PutIcon, for reading and writing a disk object info file from disk into memory and from memory to disk

- The applications program (tool) name-management functions: FindToolType and MatchToolValue, for finding the value of a tool type string and checking a tool type substring for a particular value

- The file-renaming function, BumpRevision, for generating a new name for a file that is a direct copy of another file

The term Workbench refers to both a program (tool) and a display screen. The Workbench program resides in a file on the Workbench disk. You can copy this file onto a number of disks, each with a number of applications programs on them. In this way, you can use the facilities of the Workbench program to present a uniform interface (the Workbench screen) to a user. One example of this interface is the Intuition system. The Intuition Workbench screen, one of the standard screens of the Intuition system, is the screen where all of the Intuition applications program windows, icons, and so forth are displayed. The Intuition Library provides four functions that deal with the Workbench screen.

The Workbench program contains a set of routines that interact with applications programs to provide a uniform user interface for those programs. In particular, the Workbench program provides a uniform procedure for starting and executing a set of applications programs. It allows these applications programs to display icons and open windows on the Workbench screen. The applications program user can select the icons on the Workbench screen to do things that are useful to the execution of each specific applications program.

The Workbench program also allows users to interact with the Amiga disk operating system by using icons for disk directories, applications programs, and applications program files. The Icon Library functions, which interact with the Workbench program, provide facilities for manipulating the applications program's windows and icons. Among other things, the Workbench program provides for automatic execution of programs (the default tool mechanism) and automatic opening of applications program windows to direct input and output to specific windows. You can use all of these user-interface features to ease your applications programming efforts.

The WBObject structure, discussed under the AllocWBObject function, contains all the information that the Workbench program needs to deal with applications programs. The WBObject structure is a part of the Workbench object info file, which can be either in memory or on disk. The GetWBObject and PutWBObject functions work with the Workbench object info file, transferring it between disk and memory. The actual data in the Workbench object info file depend on the icon type of the disk objects you have created. Note that any graphic image can be used for any icon type in the info file. In fact, the graphic image need not be unique for each type of icon. However, it is strongly recommended that each type of icon have a unique graphic image associated with it.

In addition, the Workbench program works with a set of disk object info files. These files represent the icons associated with specific applications programs. Each of these files contains an icon image definition and other information needed for the disk object to interact with the Workbench program. Part of a disk object info file is a DiskObject structure, which contains information about the applications program represented by that disk object info file. Specifically, each DiskObject structure contains a Gadget structure to define the applications program icon and a pointer to a data structure to define the drawer window in which that icon should appear. (A drawer is a window that displays a set of icons for all of the files in a disk file directory.) The DiskObject structure is discussed under the FreeDiskObject function.

The Workbench object and disk object files are called info files for two reasons: first, they contain all the information required to display an icon associated with each of these object types and to relate that icon to windows and applications program software that should be brought into execution when the user selects the icon. Second, they appear in the directory of the disk with the characters .info appended to their file names.

The Workbench program allows the user to do the following things on the Workbench screen:

■ Select any icon for subsequent operations

■ Start an applications program

■ Open a drawer window

■ Make an applications program window

■ Open an applications program data file

You select an icon for subsequent operations by single-clicking the mouse Selection button; most icons can then be moved around on the Workbench screen.

You start an applications program by double-clicking the Selection button on either an applications program icon or an applications program file icon on the Workbench screen. The Workbench program senses the mouse message and sends a message to the applications program to start execution, open any applications program I/O windows, and so forth. The Workbench system provides for automatic activation of default applications programs through a set of parameters in the WBObject and DiskObject structures.

If the user selects a project icon, the default tool is the applications program that originally produced that project file. For example, if the user selects a word-processing file icon, the word-processing applications program (tool) will be activated automatically. If the user selects a drawing file icon, the drawing program will be activated automatically. Both the project file and the applications program that produced the file must be on the Workbench disk.

Drawers are opened by double-clicking the Selection button on a drawer icon on the Workbench screen. A drawer contains a number of displayed file icons and is equivalent to a file directory; it is represented by a DrawerData structure.

Each applications program provides different ways to open windows and data files. Usually, windows are made active when the user clicks the Selection button anywhere in that window. Applications program data files are usually opened by selecting the data file icon and making an open file menu selection or by double-clicking a project (applications program data file) icon. In the second case, the applications program window is made active at the same time.

Lists in the Workbench System

The Workbench system maintains and uses four lists: the MasterList, the SelectList, the ActiveDisks list, and the UtilityList. The MasterList is a list of all disk object info files currently in the system. The SelectList is a list of all icons currently selected; these are the highlighted icons on the Workbench display screen. The ActiveDisks list is a list of all disks that are currently logged into the system and therefore active. Usually, this will contain only one or two entries. A disk icon for each active disk will appear on the Workbench screen in the upper-right corner. The UtilityList is a list of all system utility programs currently in the system. The NotePad and Calculator programs are two examples of utility programs.

Each time you call the GetDiskObject, GetIcon, or GetWBObject functions, the MasterList is updated. Each time you select or unselect an icon on the Workbench screen, the SelectList is updated. Each time you log in a new disk, the ActiveDisk list is updated. And each time you bring a utility program in from disk, the UtilityList is updated.

Icons Used by the Workbench Program

The Workbench program recognizes and works with the following types of icons:

- WBDISK. This icon represents the root of the Workbench disk directory; it appears as a white, orange, and black icon in the upper-right corner of the display screen when the Workbench disk is inserted. It has the characters "Workbench" under it in white against the blue background of the Workbench screen.

- WBDRAWER. This icon represents a directory on the Workbench disk. If you double-click a drawer icon, it opens up into a drawer window. This window contains a separate icon for each of the system programs, applications programs, and utility programs on the Workbench disk.

- WBTOOL. This icon represents a directly executable disk object applications program; it is one of the icons in the drawer window that appears when the Workbench disk icon is double-clicked. The Intuition Preferences program icon is one example of this type of icon. If you double-click this icon, you start execution of the Preferences program.

- WBPROJECT. This icon represents an applications program data file. For example, if the Workbench disk has any word-processing files in its root directory, these will appear in the window that opens when the Workbench disk icon is double-clicked. Each of these word-processing files is represented by a project icon. You can double-click on an icon of this type to start execution of the applications program that produced this file. (The applications program file must be on the Workbench disk.)

- WBGARBAGE. This icon represents the trashcan drawer; it is a directory of all the files currently in the trashcan. If you double-click the WBGARBAGE icon, it will open into a drawer window containing a set of WBDRAWER, WBTOOL, and WBPROJECT icons that are currently contained in the trashcan. No icons will appear in the trashcan drawer unless the user selects them and drags them into the trashcan.

- WBKICK. This icon represents a non-DOS disk such as the Kickstart disk, which doesn't have the system tracks written on it.

The Gadget Structure of an Icon

The Workbench program works with the Intuition Gadget structure to define the graphics images used for icons. The Icon Editor (discussed in the Amiga manuals) is available for changing icon images. You can access the Icon Editor by opening the Workbench disk icon into its drawer window and double-clicking the System icon in that window. This will open a new window showing the Icon Editor icon image. Then you can double-click on that icon to start execution of the Icon Editor program.

Each icon with which the Workbench program deals has an Intuition Gadget structure associated with it. When the user selects the icon associated with that gadget, a message is sent to the Workbench program. In turn, when the user selects an applications program file icon directly, or a project file icon (which selects an applications program indirectly), the Workbench program sends a message to the applications program associated with that icon.

The Gadget structure used by the Workbench program always represents a TRUE/ FALSE gadget; the Workbench program sees the icon as either selected or not selected. However, the Workbench program does not use all of the items in the Intuition Gadget structure. Those that are not used should be set to zero. Here is a list of the Gadget structure parameters used by the Workbench program:

- The Width and Height parameters contain the width and height in pixels of the icon's active region. When the user presses the mouse Selection button in this region of the icon, the Workbench program interprets the action as a selection of the icon.

- The Flags parameter contains bits to set the gadget image. Currently, the gadget image flag must be GADGIMAGE. This ensures that the gadget is rendered as an image rather than a border. In addition, the Workbench program supports three highlighting modes, which define how the icon appears when it is selected: GADGHIMAGE, GADGBACKFILL, and GADGHCOMP. The GADGH-IMAGE mode uses an alternate image when the icon is selected. The GADGH-COMP mode complements the pixels of the icon image when it is selected. The GADGBACKFILL mode is similar to GADGHCOMP but ensures there is no orange ring around the selected image when it is selected. All other bits in this parameter should be set to zero.

- The Activation parameter should have only the RELVERIFY and GADGIMME-DIATE bits set. These settings allow the Workbench program to detect gadget selection, mouse movements within the gadget while it is selected, and release of the mouse button when the mouse pointer is over the gadget.

- The Type parameter contains the gadget type; it should be BOOLGADGET indicating a purely TRUE/FALSE gadget.

- The SelectRender parameter should be set only if the icon highlight mode is GADGHIMAGE.

Icon Library Structures

The Icon Library works with a number of structures. These structures are identified in the following paragraphs.

The WBObject structure is the main structure used by the Workbench program. It is part of the Workbench object info file and contains a set of four Node substructures to define all four lists in the system. It also contains a set of other information needed to control the Workbench object info file once it is brought into memory from disk. The WBObject structure is discussed in the AllocWBObject function.

The DiskObject structure is the main structure used by the Workbench program to deal with applications program icons on the Workbench screen. These icons allow the Workbench program to start and control execution of applications programs when a user selects a project or applications program icon. The DiskObject structure is a part of the disk object info file; it is discussed under the FreeDiskObject function.

The DrawerData structure manages the drawer window display for a disk object info file. It contains a NewWindow substructure and specifies the position of the drawer window on the Workbench screen. In addition, the DrawerData structure contains a number of Intuition Gadget, Image, and PropInfo substructures to define the imagery of the drawer window on the Workbench screen. The DrawerData structure also contains a pointer to a WBObject structure that associates a Workbench object info file with this DrawerData structure. The DrawerData structure is defined later in this introduction.

The FreeList structure manages the free memory available for disk objects once they are brought onto the Workbench screen. Each FreeList structure contains the number of free-memory blocks and an Exec MemList substructure. The FreeList structure is discussed under the AddFreeList function.

The WBStartup structure contains all the information required to start an applications program with a Workbench program. This includes a Message substructure and a MsgPort substructure, which allow messages to be passed back and forth between the Workbench program and an applications program. It also includes a pointer to an applications program window and a pointer to a WBArg structure, which contains the argument list passed by the Workbench program to an applications program. The WBStartup and WBArg structures are defined later in this introduction.

All of these structures are defined in the Workbench.h, Startup.h, and Icon.h INCLUDE files (for C language programmers) and in the Workbench.i, Startup.i, and Icon.i INCLUDE files (for assembly language programmers).

Workbench Operations

The Workbench system always follows a general sequence of steps, although its actual operations are based on the actions of the Workbench user and the design of various applications programs in the Workbench system.

When the Amiga is first started, the Workbench disk icon appears in the upper-right corner of the display screen. When the user double-clicks that icon to open the Workbench window, a set of icons appears for the System programs, the Demo programs, the Clock program, the Preferences program, the Trashcan program, and so on. Icons also appear for any applications programs on the Workbench disk, together with any project files.

The user can double-click any of the applications program icons or project icons to start any of the applications programs on the Workbench disk. When he does so, the gadget for that icon image sends a TRUE (selected) message to the Workbench program, and the Workbench program looks at the DiskObject structure associated with that icon and determines the type of applications program tool it represents. The Workbench program then sends a message to the applications program to load and start its execution. In turn, the applications program sends a reply message to the Workbench program to indicate that this was done.

If the clicked icon represents a project file, the Workbench program looks in the DiskObject structure to see which applications program is associated with that project icon. It then sends a message to the applications program to activate it. Once again, the applications program will send a reply message to the Workbench program. At this point, the applications program can run as intended.

The WBStartup Structure

The sequence of operations just described is managed by the WBStartup structure, which has the following form:

```
struct WBStartup {
    struct Message sm_Message;
    struct MsgPort *sm_Process;
    BPTR sm_Segment;
    LONG sm_NumArgs;
    char *sm_ToolWindow;
    struct WBArg *sm_ArgList;
};
```

Here is the meaning of each of the parameters in the WBStartup structure:

- The sm_Message parameter contains the name of a standard Exec Message substructure assigned to an applications program. This structure handles messages passed back and forth between the Workbench program and the applications program. The Workbench program has a message port to receive messages coming from the applications program.

- The sm_Process parameter is a pointer to a standard Exec MsgPort structure for the applications program's task. This message port acts as a reply port for messages coming back from the Workbench program.

- The sm_Segment parameter is a pointer to a process descriptor for the applications program code as loaded by the LoadSeg system routine. This provides the mechanism for a double-click event on an icon to reach and start execution of the task routines associated with a specific applications program.

- The sm_NumArgs parameter contains the number of arguments in the argument list passed to the applications program by the Workbench program.

- The sm_ToolWindow parameter is a pointer to a description of the window to open for the applications program. This is the same string as the DiskObject structure's do_ToolWindow parameter. It is passed here so that the applications program's setup code can open a window for that applications program immediately when it starts execution. If this parameter is null, no default window is opened.

■ The sm_ArgList parameter is a pointer to a WBArg structure that handles arguments passed by the Workbench program to the applications program.

The WBArg Structure

The WBArg Structure has the following form:

```
struct WBArg {
    BPTR wa_Lock;
    BYTE *wa_Name;
};
```

The wa_Lock parameter is a pointer to a directory lock descriptor. This parameter is either a directory lock or null if that applications program does not support directory locks. This parameter is used to prevent an applications program from accessing the files in a specific directory.

The wa_Name parameter is a pointer to the name of the applications program argument list. If the applications program is not a default tool or a drawer, this name will be the same as the string displayed under the applications program icon. A default tool will have the text of the wo_DefaultTool pointer in the WBObject structure; a drawer will have a null name passed.

The DrawerData Structure

Each time a new drawer window is opened on the Amiga display screen, the Workbench program uses a DrawerData structure to define the contents of the drawer. Each drawer window is a visual representation of some part of a disk directory. The DrawerData structure has the following form:

```
struct DrawerData {
    struct NewWindow dd_NewWindow;
    LONG dd_CurrentX;
    LONG dd_CurrentY;
    LONG dd_MinX;
    LONG dd_MinY;
    LONG dd_MaxX;
    LONG dd_MaxY;
    struct Gadget dd_HorizScroll;
    struct Gadget dd_VertScroll;
    struct Gadget dd_UpMove;
    struct Gadget dd_DownMove;
    struct Gadget dd_LeftMove;
    struct Gadget dd_RightMove;
    struct Image dd_HorizImage;
    struct Image dd_VertImage;
    struct PropInfo dd_HorizProp;
    struct PropInfo dd_VertProp;
```

```
    struct Window *dd_DrawerWin;
    struct WBObject *dd_Object;
    struct List dd_Children;
    LONG dd_Lock;
};
```

The meaning of the various parameters in the DrawerData structure is as follows:

■ The dd_NewWindow parameter contains the name of an Intuition NewWindow structure used to define the drawer window.

■ The dd_CurrentX and dd_CurrentY parameters contain the current x- and y-coordinates of the origin of the drawer window on the Workbench screen.

■ The dd_MinX, dd_MinY, dd_MaxX, and dd_MaxY parameters contain the minimum width, minimum height, maximum width, and maximum height for the drawer window.

■ The dd_HorizScroll and dd_VertScroll parameters contain the names of the Intuition Gadget substructures for the horizontal and vertical scroll bars in the drawer window.

■ The dd_UpMove, dd_DownMove, dd_LeftMove, and dd_RightMove parameters contain the names of the Intuition Gadget substructures for the up-move, down-move, left-move, and right-move gadgets in the drawer window.

■ The dd_HorizImage and dd_VertImage parameters contain the names of the Intuition Image substructures for the horizontal and vertical images in the drawer window.

■ The dd_HorizProp and dd_VertProp parameters contain the names of the Intuition PropInfo substructures for the horizontal and vertical proportional gadgets in the drawer window.

■ The dd_DrawerWin parameter is a pointer to an Intuition Window structure for the drawer window.

■ The dd_Object parameter is a pointer to a WBObject structure associated with the drawer window.

■ The dd_Children parameter contains the name of an Exec List structure which contains the names of file items in the drawer.

■ The dd_Lock parameter contains the directory lock indicator for the directory represented by this drawer.

AddFreeList

Syntax of Function Call

status = AddFreeList (freeList, memBlock, length)
D0   A0   A1   D1

Purpose of Function

This function adds the specified memory block to the specified free-memory list. If the AddFreeList function call fails, it returns a zero value in the status variable. You can then use the system IoErr routine to determine the cause of the error.

Inputs to Function

freeList	A pointer to a FreeList structure
memBlock	A pointer to the first byte of the memory block to be added to the free-memory list
length	The length in bytes of the memory block to be added to the free-memory list

Discussion

There are two functions in the Icon Library that manage general memory: AddFreeList and FreeFreeList. These functions add a memory block of a specific size to a specific free-memory list and release all the memory blocks in a specific free-memory list.

The Icon Library can maintain a number of free-memory lists. A specific FreeList structure is used to manage each of these lists. Each time an applications program finishes with a block of memory, you can add that memory block to one of these free-memory lists with the AddFreeList function. When AddFreeList returns, the list will be extended. If there is not enough memory to complete the call, a null value will be returned. Note that the AddFreeList function does not allocate the requested memory; it merely adds the block of already allocated memory to a specific free-memory list.

The FreeList Structure

The AddFreeList function works with the FreeList structure, which has the following form:

```
struct FreeList {
    WORD fl_NumFree;
    struct List fl_MemList;
};
```

The fl_NumFree parameter contains the number of eight-byte free-memory blocks available for allocation. The fl_MemList parameter contains the name of the List substructure that keeps track of memory in the Workbench system for this particular FreeList structure.

AllocWBObject

Syntax of Function Call

```
wBObject = AllocWBObject ()
D0
```

Purpose of Function

This function allocates all memory required for a Workbench object info file. In particular, it allocates memory for a WBObject structure and initializes its FreeList substructure. If successful, AllocWBObject returns a pointer to the WBObject structure. If the memory cannot be allocated, the function returns a null value.

Inputs to Function

There are no inputs to this function.

Discussion

There are two functions in the Icon Library that directly manage Workbench object memory: AllocWBObject and FreeWBObject. These functions are used to allocate and deallocate the memory assigned to a Workbench object. These functions are intended only for programmers who want to track internal changes in the Workbench program.

For example, if you wanted to examine the Gadget structure for the Workbench disk icon, you could use the AllocWBObject function to get a pointer to the Workbench info file. Then you could use the Gadget substructure within that structure to look at and modify the image data for that gadget. The Workbench disk icon appears in the upper-right corner of the display screen when the Workbench disk is inserted.

The WBObject Structure

The version 1.1 software release WBObject structure has the following form:

```
struct WBObject {
    struct Node wo_MasterNode;
    struct Node wo_Siblings;
    struct Node wo_SelectNode;
    struct Node wo_UtilityNode;
    struct WBObject *wo_Parent;
    #ifdef SMARTCOMPILER
    UBYTE wo_IconDisp:1;
    UBYTE wo_DrawerOpen:1;
    UBYTE wo_Selected:1;
    UBYTE wo_Background:1;
    #else;
    UBYTE wo_Flags;
    #endif
    UBYTE wo_Type;
    USHORT wo_UseCount;
    char *wo_Name;
    SHORT wo_NameXOffset;
    SHORT wo_NameYOffset;
    char *wo_DefaultTool;
    struct DrawerData *wo_DrawerData;
    struct Window *wo_IconWin;
    LONG wo_CurrentX;
    LONG wo_CurrentY;
    char **wo_ToolTypes;
    struct Gadget wo_Gadget;
    struct FreeList wo_FreeList;
    char *wo_ToolWindow;
    LONG wo_StackSize;
    LONG wo_Lock;
};
```

Here is the meaning of each of the parameters to the WBObject structure:

■ The wo_MasterNode parameter contains the name of a Node substructure used to construct a list where all current disk objects are kept.

- The wo_Siblings parameter contains the name of a Node substructure used to construct a list of all members in a drawer.

- The wo_SelectNode parameter contains the name of a Node substructure used to construct a list of all currently selected icons on the Workbench screen.

- The wo_UtilityNode parameter contains the name of a Node substructure used to construct a list of all currently selected Utility program icons.

- The wo_Parent parameter is a pointer to a parent WBObject structure in the linked list of WBObject structures.

- The wo_IconDisp, wo_DrawerOpen, wo_Selected, and wo_Background parameters contain Workbench object flag bits. Note that these parameters are each a bit in a packed-bit parameter. If wo_IconDisp (bit 0) is set, the Workbench object icon represented by this structure is currently displayed in a window. If wo_Drawer-Open (bit 1) is set, the Workbench object icon represented by this structure is currently in a drawer and the drawer window is open. If wo_Selected (bit 2) is set, the Workbench object icon represented by this structure is currently in a drawer and is selected. If wo_Background (bit 3) is set, the Workbench object icon represented by this structure is currently in a drawer and is in the background (not currently active). Only certain types of compiles (SMART) can recognize packed-bit parameters.

- The wo_Flags parameter contains the flag bits for this WBObject structure. These flag bits have the same meaning (and location) as the four bits in the packed-bit parameter above.

- The wo_Type parameter contains the type of the Workbench object. Workbench objects can be one of six types: WBDISK, WBDRAWER, WBTOOL, WB-PROJECT, WBGARBAGE, or WBKICK.

- The wo_UseCount parameter contains the number of references already made to this particular Workbench object.

- The wo_Name parameter is a pointer to a null-terminated text string representing this Workbench object's name. This is the name that appears under the Workbench object icon on the Workbench screen.

- The wo_NameXOffset and wo_NameYOffset parameters tell the system where to place the Workbench object icon name string on the Workbench screen.

- The wo_DefaultTool parameter is a pointer to the name of the default applications program that should execute when this Workbench object icon is selected by the user.

- The wo_DrawerData parameter is a pointer to a DrawerData structure to be used if this Workbench object icon represents a disk directory or a subdirectory on that disk. The DrawerData structure contains a NewWindow substructure to define a window for the icon to open into when it is selected by the user.

■ The wo_IconWin parameter is a pointer to the Window structure that defines a window where each Workbench object icon will be displayed.

■ The wo_CurrentX and wo_CurrentY parameters contain the current x- and y-coordinates of the Workbench object icon in the drawer window.

■ The wo_ToolTypes parameter is a pointer to a pointer (the two asterisks denote this double indirection) to a list of tool-type names for Workbench object tools.

■ The wo_Gadget parameter contains the name of a Gadget substructure to be used with this Workbench object structure.

■ The wo_FreeList parameter contains the name of the FreeList substructure that keeps track of the free memory associated with this Workbench object.

■ The wo_ToolWindow parameter is a pointer to a window-title string to be used in this tool's window.

■ The wo_StackSize parameter contains the size of the stack assigned to this particular Workbench object program.

■ The wo_Lock parameter is an applications program lock. If the icon for this applications program is currently in a backdrop window, this parameter will be set to lock that applications program from execution.

You should note that the five parameters starting with wo_IconDisp:1 and ending with wo_Flags are in a conditional define sequence. Study the Workbench.h INCLUDE file to see how this works.

BumpRevision

Syntax of Function Call

```
result = BumpRevision (newBuf, oldName)
D0                     A0      A1
```

Purpose of Function

This function takes an icon's file name and turns that name into "copy of name". When the user generates copies of copies, BumpRevision produces names for those copies accordingly. BumpRevision will truncate the new name to the maximum AmigaDOS name size of 30 characters. The character buffer that holds the new name must be at least 31 characters long (one character is assigned to the null that terminates the buffer). BumpRevision returns the actual size of the newly allocated name buffer in the result variable.

Inputs to Function

newBuf   A pointer to the buffer that will receive the character string of the new name

oldName   A pointer to the character string containing the original name

Discussion

BumpRevision generates a new name for a file that is a direct copy of another file. You can use the BumpRevision function to create a series of names for a series of files that are direct copies of a single file. The BumpRevision function only creates a new name for the file copy; it does not create a new copy.

This function is called indirectly any time a Workbench user uses a file copy command to copy a file and place an icon for that copy on the Workbench screen. BumpRevision generates the name that appears below the new file icon. For example, if you copy a file called Text, an icon will appear with the file name "copy of Text" below it. If you make a second copy from the first copy, its name will be "copy 2 of Text".

FindToolType

Syntax of Function Call

```
stringPointer = FindToolTypes (toolTypes,  typeName)
D0                             A0          A1
```

Purpose of Function

This function searches a ToolTypes array for a given typeName entry. It returns a pointer to the first character after the equal sign, which appears after the typeName character string. It returns a null value if no entry matching the typeName argument can be found in the ToolTypes array.

Inputs to Function

toolTypes   A pointer to a ToolTypes array in RAM

typeName   A pointer to a literal character string to search for in the ToolTypes array

Discussion

There are two functions in the Icon Library that deal with ToolTypes array strings: Find-ToolType and MatchToolValue. FindToolType allows you to determine a pointer to a specific ToolTypes array string entry; MatchToolValue allows you to check a ToolTypes array string entry for a specific character substring.

The purpose of these two functions is to allow one disk object icon to be related to a set of valid applications program tools. Then, when the user selects an icon, any one of this set of tools can start to execute. Which one actually executes is determined by other specified conditions.

To use the FindToolType function, you must first define a ToolTypes array in RAM. This array is simply a set of character string entries. Each entry contains information about a specific disk object info file and the applications programs that can use that file.

Each character string consists of two major character substrings separated by an equal sign. On the left side of the equal sign is the tool-type name parameter; on the right side of the equal sign is a list of string values associated with that tool-type name parameter. Each of the substrings on the right side of the equal sign is separated from the next by a vertical bar ($|$).

The general format for each character string entry in the ToolTypes array is

typename = substring1 [|substring2][|substring3]...[|substringN]

where typename is the tool type name and substring1 to substringN are specific character substrings to associate with that name. The substrings are usually names of applications programs or the names of the general category in which a file belongs. For example, a ToolTypes array entry for the source code of a BASIC program might be

FILETYPE = ABASIC.program |text

Any applications program that can work with either a text file (for example, a word-processing program) or a BASIC program will be able to use the disk object info file with this entry in its ToolTypes array. That is, when that icon is selected by the user, either a word-processing program or an ABASIC compiler or interpreter can be brought into execution.

If you specify the typeName argument in the FindToolType function call as the literal value FILETYPE, the function will return a pointer to the A character in the

ABASIC.program |text

string. This is a character string with two character substrings; ABASIC.program and text. You can use the MatchToolValue function to compare each of these specific substrings with the full string whose pointer was returned by the FindToolType function. If the MatchToolValue function indicates a match, your program will know that this file can be used with a specific applications program. It is important to remember that the FindToolType function returns a pointer to the tool string rather than the string itself. When MatchToolValue makes its comparison, it uses that pointer internally to check for a valid tool.

When you define the character string entries in the ToolTypes array in RAM, you are free to define them to suit your own special purposes. Your only restriction is that each ToolTypes array entry must contain information that tells the system which applications programs can use this disk object file, since this is the purpose of the array.

A ToolTypes array character string can be up to 32K bytes long. However, it is best if each character string is less than one line (about 60 characters) long. The characters for these strings can be chosen from the eight-bit ANSI (American National Standards Institute) character code. (This is the same as the seven-bit ASCII—American Standard Code for Information Exchange—code, with the eighth bit used for foreign language character extensions. You can see what these foreign characters look like if you type on the Amiga with the Alt key held down. For example, you can do this in the Notepad file.) The case (uppercase versus lowercase) of the characters in the character strings is significant; also, use only printable characters in these strings.

Once the entries of a ToolTypes array are all defined, place the ToolTypes array in RAM at a named location. Then provide a pointer to that location in the definition of the DiskObject structure. This is the do_ToolTypes pointer to the ToolTypes array. When you use the PutDiskObject function to place that disk object in a disk object info file, the ToolTypes array will also be written to disk. Later, when you use the GetDiskObject function to read that disk object info file back into RAM, the ToolTypes array will also be brought back into RAM.

FreeDiskObject

Syntax of Function Call

FreeDiskObject (diskObject)
A0

Purpose of Function

This function frees all memory associated with a disk object info file; it also frees the memory assigned to the DiskObject structure. Memory for the disk object info file was originally assigned by the system when the file was loaded into RAM by the GetDisk-Object function.

Inputs to Function

diskObject   A pointer to a DiskObject structure

Discussion

FreeDiskObject is the only function in the Icon Library that explicitly manages disk object info file memory. It frees the memory previously assigned to a disk object info file by the GetDiskObject function.

The FreeDiskObject function does its job by calling the FreeFreeList function. FreeDiskObject can be used only for DiskObject structures allocated by the GetDiskObject function; you cannot use FreeDiskObject for DiskObject structures allocated by the GetIcon function. The GetDiskObject function takes care of all the initialization required to set up the object's FreeList structure.

The DiskObject Structure

The FreeDiskObject function works with the DiskObject structure. The form of the DiskObject structure is as follows:

```
struct DiskObject {
    UWORD do_Magic;
    UWORD do_Version;
    struct Gadget do_Gadget;
    UBYTE do_Type;
    char *do_DefaultTool;
    char **do_ToolTypes;
    LONG do_CurrentX;
    LONG do_CurrentY;
    struct DrawerData *do_DrawerData;
    char *do_ToolWindow;
    LONG do_StackSize;
};
```

Here is the meaning of each of the parameters in the DiskObject structure:

■ The do_Magic parameter contains the literal constant WB_DISKMAGIC. The PutDiskObject function puts this value in the DiskObject structure when it places that structure on disk. This parameter identifies this file as a disk object info file. The GetDiskObject function will not load a file unless it has this value in the DiskObject structure within that file.

■ The do_Version parameter contains the version number of the icon file. Right now, its value is the literal constant WB_DISKVERSION. The PutDiskObject function sets this value when it places the DiskObject structure on disk.

■ The do_Gadget parameter contains the name of an Intuition Gadget structure used to hold the imagery for the disk object icon.

■ The do_Type parameter contains the icon type. It can be WBDRAWER, WBDISK, WBTOOL, WBPROJECT, WBGARBAGE, or WBKICK.

- The do_DefaultTool parameter points to the program name string for a default tool—an applications program that will start execution automatically when the user selects the icon associated with this DiskObject structure. Default tools are used for project and disk icons. A default tool is the applications program that starts execution when the user double-clicks the disk object icon.

- The do_ToolTypes parameter points to a pointer (double indirection) to an array of free-format strings defining applications programs that can work with the file information represented by this disk icon. The Workbench program does not enforce any rules on strings, but they are useful for tying disk object icons to specific applications programs. (See the discussions of the FindToolType and MatchToolValue functions.)

- The do_CurrentX and do_CurrentY parameters contain current x- and y-coordinates of an icon in the drawer window. Each drawer is a visual representation of a directory or subdirectory of files on a disk. Each icon in the drawer window has a position in the window's coordinate system. The user can scroll around in the window using the scroll gadgets on the drawer's window. If each of these parameters have the value NO_ICON_POSITION, the Workbench program picks a reasonable value for an icon to be newly placed in a drawer window. The icon will be placed in an unused portion of the drawer window. If there is no space in the drawer window, the icon will be placed just to the right of the visible region of the window.

- The do_DrawerData parameter points to a DrawerData structure. The WBDISK, WBDRAWER, and WBGARBAGE type icons can be opened as drawer windows. Part of the DrawerData structure is a NewWindow structure. The Workbench program uses this NewWindow structure to hold the window size and the current window position. The system uses these window parameters to ensure that a window will reopen in the same place as the user opens and closes windows on the Workbench screen. The CurrentX and CurrentY positions of the origin of the window are also stored in the NewWindow structure.

- The do_ToolWindow parameter points to a file that contains the definition of a window. This parameter is used only if this DiskObject structure represents an applications program (do_Type = WBTOOL). If this parameter is set, this window will be opened and made the standard input and output window of the applications program. By default, the Workbench program will start a program without an open window to receive I/O for that program.

- The do_StackSize parameter contains the size of the stack used for running the applications program tool. This parameter is used only if this DiskObject structure represents an applications program (do_Type = WBTOOL). If the size is null, the Workbench program will use a reasonable default stack size (usually 4K bytes).

FreeFreeList

Syntax of Function Call

FreeFreeList (freeList)
A0

Purpose of Function

This function deallocates all the memory in a series of structures tied together in the specified FreeList structure, as well as the memory assigned to the FreeList structure itself.

Inputs to Function

freeList   A pointer to a FreeList structure

Discussion

There are two functions in the Icon Library that manage general memory: AddFreeList and FreeFreeList. These functions are used to add memory blocks of specific sizes to specific free-memory lists and to release all memory blocks in a specific free-memory list.

A FreeList structure contains an Exec MemList structure as a substructure. The FreeList structure is used to place all free-memory blocks on a list maintained by the Workbench system. There is a FreeList substructure in the WBObject structure; that FreeList structure manages all the memory associated with that Workbench object. However, there is no FreeList structure associated with the DiskObject structure; memory associated with the DiskObject structure is managed by the system when the disk object info file is loaded. See the GetDiskObject function discussion. See the discussion of the AddFreeList function for a definition of the FreeList structure.

FreeWBObject

Syntax of Function Call

FreeWBObject (wBObject)
A0

Purpose of Function

This function frees all the memory previously allocated to the specified Workbench object info file; it also frees the memory assigned to the WBObject structure. FreeWBObject is implemented using the FreeFreeList function.

Inputs to Function

wBObject   A pointer to a WBObject structure

Discussion

There are two functions in the Icon Library that manage Workbench object info file memory: AllocWBObject and FreeWBObject. They are used to allocate and deallocate the memory assigned to a Workbench object info file.

The AllocWBObject function allocates all memory for a Workbench object info file. In particular, it allocates memory for the WBObject structure itself. In addition, it initializes the WBObject structure's FreeList substructure. The FreeWBObject call frees all memory previously allocated. Each WBObject structure has a FreeList substructure. FreeWBObject does its job by calling the FreeFreeList function to free the memory defined by that FreeList structure. See the AllocWBObject function for a definition of the WBObject structure.

GetDiskObject

Syntax of Function Call

```
diskObject = GetDiskObject (fileName)
D0                          A0
```

Purpose of Function

This function reads a disk object info file from disk into memory. Part of the info file is a DiskObject structure. If successful, GetDiskObject returns a pointer to that DiskObject structure in RAM. If the call fails, it returns a zero value. The reason for the failure can be obtained with the IoErr system routine.

Inputs to Function

fileName   A pointer to the file name of the disk object info file you want to load

Discussion

There are four functions in the Icon Library that deal with disk object info file transfer operations: GetDiskObject, PutDiskObject, GetIcon, and PutIcon. The GetDiskObject and GetIcon functions both read a disk object info file from disk into memory; the Put-DiskObject and PutIcon functions both write a disk object info file from memory to disk.

The GetDiskObject function is very similar to the GetIcon function. However, Get-DiskObject is easier to use because it requires only the name of the disk object info file. When GetDiskObject returns, a DiskObject structure is allocated automatically by the system. A FreeList structure associated with (but not part of) that DiskObject structure is also allocated. You can use the FreeDiskObject function later to deallocate the memory that was allocated with the GetDiskObject function.

The DiskObject structure is defined under the FreeDiskObject function. The FreeList structure is discussed under the AddFreeList function. Remember that the disk object info file will have a name parameter with .info automatically appended to it; the disk will be searched for a file of that name.

For example, if the disk object info file name was Mytext (a text project file produced by a word-processing program—do_Type = WBPROJECT), the GetDiskObject function would search the disk directory for a file named Mytext.info. This file would contain the DiskObject structure and other information about the disk object.

GetIcon

Syntax of Function Call

status = GetIcon (fileName, diskObject, freeList)
D0   A0   A1   A2

Purpose of Function

This function reads a disk object info file into memory. All memory required for the file's DiskObject structure is allocated automatically and stored in the specified FreeList structure. If the call fails, a zero value is returned. You can use the IoErr system routine to determine the cause of the error.

Inputs to Function

fileName	A pointer to the file name of the disk object info file you want to load
diskObject	A pointer to a DiskObject structure
freeList	A pointer to a FreeList structure

Discussion

There are four functions in the Icon Library that deal with disk object info file transfer operations: GetDiskObject, PutDiskObject, GetIcon, and PutIcon. The GetDiskObject and GetIcon functions read a disk object info file from disk into memory; the PutDiskObject and PutIcon functions write a disk object info file from memory to disk.

The only difference between the GetIcon function and the GetDiskObject function is that GetIcon allows you to specify the RAM location for the DiskObject and FreeList structures. The GetDiskObject function allows the system to determine these values for you. Therefore, the GetIcon function provides more control than the GetDiskObject function.

GetWBObject

Syntax of Function Call

```
wBObject = GetWBObject (fileName)
D0                      A0
```

Purpose of Function

This function reads a Workbench object info file from disk into memory. If successful, it returns a pointer to the WBObject structure in that Workbench object info file. If the call fails, the function returns a zero value. The system IoErr routine can be used to determine the cause of the error. This function is intended only for programmers who want to track internal changes in the Workbench program. See discussion of the AllocWBObject function for an example.

Inputs to Function

fileName   A pointer to the file name of the Workbench object info file you want to load

Discussion

There are two Icon Library functions that transfer Workbench object info files from memory to disk and from disk to memory: GetWBObject and PutWBObject. GetWBObject reads a Workbench object info file from disk into memory; PutWBObject writes a Workbench object info file from memory to disk.

Part of the Workbench object info file is a WBObject structure. The WBObject structure is discussed under the AllocWBObject function. Remember that the Workbench object info file has a name parameter with .info automatically appended to it; the disk will be searched for a file of that name.

MatchToolValue

Syntax of Function Call

stringfound = MatchToolValue (stringPointer, subString)
D0   A0   A1

Purpose of Function

This function searches a ToolTypes character string array for a specific substring. If the substring is found, the function returns a value of 1 in the result variable; if the substring is not found, it returns a 0 value.

Inputs to Function

stringPointer   A pointer to a ToolTypes string array returned by the FindToolType function

subString   A pointer to the substring you are searching for

Discussion

There are two functions in the Icon Library that work with ToolTypes array strings: FindToolType and MatchToolValue. FindToolType allows you to determine a pointer to a specific ToolTypes array string entry; MatchToolValue allows you to check a ToolTypes array string entry for a specific matching character tool substring.

Use the MatchToolValue function to compare a specific substring with one or more substrings whose pointer was returned by the FindToolType function. If the Match-ToolValue function indicates a substring match, the info file that contains a pointer to the ToolTypes array can be used with a specific applications program. Read the discussion of the FindToolTypes function.

MatchToolValue knows how to parse the syntax of a ToolTypes array string for a specific substring. In particular, it knows that the vertical bar (|) character separates a group of substrings in a ToolTypes array entry.

PutDiskObject

Syntax of Function Call

```
status = PutDiskObject (fileName, diskObject)
DO                      A0        A1
```

Purpose of Function

This function writes a disk object info file containing a DiskObject structure from memory to disk. It returns a value in the status variable. This variable is nonzero if the call succeeded. If the call fails, a zero status value is returned. You can find the reason for the failure by calling the system IoErr routine.

Inputs to Function

fileName   A pointer to the file name to be assigned to the disk object info file

diskObject   A pointer to a DiskObject structure to be included in that info file when placed on disk

Discussion

There are four functions in the Icon Library that deal with disk object info file transfer operations: GetDiskObject, PutDiskObject, GetIcon, and PutIcon. The GetDiskObject and GetIcon functions read a disk object info file from disk into memory; the PutDiskObject and PutIcon functions write a disk object info file from memory to disk. The filename parameter of the PutDiskObject call is used to fix the resulting disk file name.

The PutDiskObject and PutIcon functions are functionally identical. In fact, they are just two different names for the same function. (Note that this is not true of the GetDiskObject and GetIcon functions.) The PutIcon function was added to the system so that the GetIcon function would have a counterpart in the Icon Library.

PutIcon

Syntax of Function Call

```
status = PutIcon (fileName, diskObject)
D0               A0        A1
```

Purpose of Function

This function writes a disk object info file from memory to disk. It is functionally identical to the PutDiskObject function.

Inputs to Function

fileName	A pointer to the file name to be assigned to the disk object info file
diskObject	A pointer to the DiskObject structure to be included in that file when placed on disk

Discussion

There are four functions in the Icon Library that deal with disk object info file transfer operations: GetDiskObject, PutDiskObject, GetIcon, and PutIcon. The GetDiskObject and GetIcon functions both read a disk object info file from disk into memory; the PutDiskObject and PutIcon functions both write a disk object info file from memory to disk.

See the discussion of the PutDiskObject function to understand how the PutIcon function works.

PutWBObject

Syntax of Function Call

```
status = PutWBObject (fileName, wBObject)
D0                     A0       A1
```

Purpose of Function

This function writes a Workbench object info file from memory to disk. If the call fails, the function returns a zero value in the status variable. You can use the system IoErr routine to determine the cause of the error. This function is intended only for programmers who want to track internal changes in the Workbench program. Read the discussion of AllocWBObject for an example of this.

Inputs to Function

fileName   A pointer to the file name that will be assigned to the Workbench object info file containing the specified WBObject structure

wBObject   A pointer to the specified WBObject structure to be included in that file when placed on disk

Discussion

There are two Icon Library functions that transfer Workbench object info files from memory to disk and from disk to memory: GetWBObject and PutWBObject. GetWBObject reads a Workbench object info file from disk into memory; PutWBObject writes a Workbench object info file from memory to disk.

Part of the Workbench object info file is a WBObject structure. The WBObject structure is discussed under the AllocWBObject function. The filename parameter of the PutWBObject call is used to fix the resulting disk file name. Remember that the file name you specify will have .info appended to it automatically; the Workbench object info file will be written to disk with the full name.

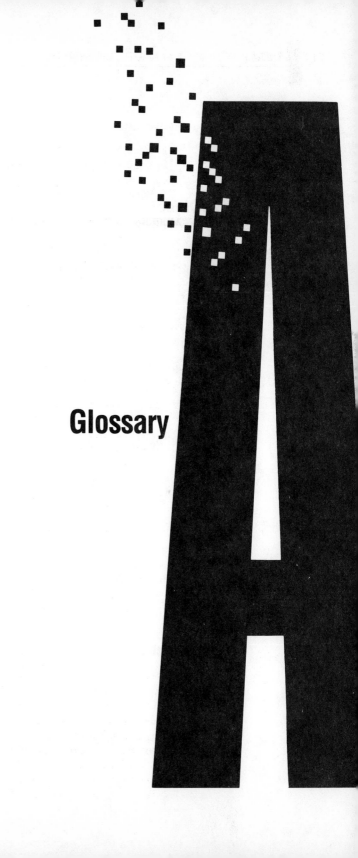

Glossary

Active window

In Intuition, the active window is the window currently receiving user input through the keyboard or mouse (or some other controller). All other windows are inactive. The user can change the active window by clicking the Selection button when the mouse pointer is positioned anywhere in an inactive window.

Allocate

To allocate memory is to set aside an area of memory for some use. You can use the Exec Library AllocMem, AllocEntry, and Allocate functions for this. In addition, most of the other libraries have their own memory allocation/deallocation functions. All structures and the individual bitplanes in a bitmap must be allocated contiguous memory blocks.

AmigaDOS

This is the portion of the operating system that controls the operation of the disk system. AmigaDOS commands include Copy, DiskCopy, and Delete. These commands represent the operating system at its highest level. The ROM-BIOS Exec functions are at the next level. The lowest level of control involves the direct control of the hardware. This is usually done with assembly language programs.

Animation component

This is the second highest level in the heirarchy of animation entities. Animation components are composed of bobs, and a group of animation components can define an animation object.

Animation entity

This can be a hardware sprite, a virtual sprite, a bob (Blitter object), an animation component, or an animation object. Only bobs can be combined into animation components and animation objects.

Animation object

This is the highest level in the animation entity hierarchy. Your animation efforts are directed at producing animation objects, which are then moved around the display screen to produce the animation effects you describe.

Backdrop window

This type of Intuition window stays anchored to the back of a screen. All other windows in that screen are placed in front of the backdrop window. In this sense, backdrop windows always have the lowest video priority of any Intuition window.

Bitmap

A bitmap is an area of memory composed of bitplanes. A bitmap can include up to six bitplanes. Each bitplane must be in a contiguous section of memory. However, the various bitplanes in a bitmap do not have to be next to each other in memory. The terms bitmap, raster, and raster bitmap are used interchangeably in this book.

BitMap structure

This structure contains information to define the bitmaps associated with views and viewports as well as Intuition screens and windows. Each BitMap specifies the size and depth of a specific bitmap.

Bitplane

This is a series of contiguous memory words, treated as if it were a rectangular drawing area definition. You can build up to six bitplanes in memory to define a bitmap.

Blanking interval

This is the period of time when the video beam is outside the visible display screen area. There is both a vertical and a horizontal blanking interval. The vertical blanking interval, when the video beam is first below, then above, the physical display screen, is used by the system routines and the Copper coprocessor to define the upcoming display frame.

BlitNode structure

This is a structure used by the system to queue Blitter requests coming from many different drawing tasks. In addition, the BlitNode structure provides a mechanism to call a user-defined Blitter routine when a particular Blitter request is executed. Blitter requests are placed in a FIFO queue. This scheme allows more than one task to use the Blitter by placing Blitter requests into the Blitter request queue.

Blitter

This is a special coprocessor inside the graphics animation chip that manipulates data information very quickly. The Blitter controls an Amiga DMA (direct memory access) channel and can transfer up to a million pixels from one area of memory to another in one second. Because of its speed, the Blitter DMA channel is used for data copying and line drawing. The Blitter is also used to manipulate the bobs (Blitter objects) used in graphics animation. The TrackDisk device uses the Blitter to encode and decode track data.

Bob

Bob is an acronym for Blitter object, which is an object drawn by the Blitter DMA channel. Each part of an animation component and therefore each part of an animation object is a bob. Each bob is defined by a Bob structure.

Chip memory

Chip memory consists of the first 512K bytes of memory. It is the only area of memory that the special-purpose Amiga chips (the graphics animation chip, the animation custom chip, the peripherals-sound custom chip, and others) can read information from and place information into. These chips sometimes compete with the 68000 CPU for the bus, thus slowing down CPU memory accessing. The other types of memory are fast memory and public memory.

Clip

To clip means to truncate a drawing operation to the area inside a specific section of a bitmap, defined by a single clipping-rectangle or a set of clipping-rectangles that have been combined to define a (clipping) region.

Collision

A collision is an overlap between graphics elements or between a graphics element and a playfield boundary. Collision detection is monitored by the system, which can detect collisions between any combination of bobs, virtual sprites, and playfield boundaries.

Color-descriptor words

These are pairs of words that define the pixel image for each line of a hardware or virtual sprite. Both types of sprites are 16 pixels wide and can be as many as 200 screen lines tall in noninterlaced mode operation.

Color indirection

Color indirection is the process of defining the color of a pixel on the display screen by a collection of data bits, each coming from a different bitplane in memory, rather than by a single data bit in memory. These data bits are combined into a binary number whose decimal equivalent forms an index into a colormap table. The colormap table uses that index to determine the hardware color register to use to define the color at that pixel location.

Color register

A color register holds the definition of one of 4,096 colors. There are 32 sixteen-bit color registers. The four most significant bits in each color register are not used. The 12 least significant bits define the intensity of the red, green, and blue colors currently assigned to that color register. Each of these colors is controlled by four bits in the color register; this allows 16 color intensities for each primary color.

Colortable array

A colortable array contains the set of colors available for a given section of the display screen. It maps the value of the bitplane bits to one of 32 hardware color registers. Each register represents one of 4,096 possible colors. In any given area of the screen, the color palette can vary; that is, the contents of the colortable array can be changed in midscreen to provide a different set of colors for screen areas lower in the display frame.

COMPLEMENT

COMPLEMENT is one of four drawing modes used by the graphics drawing functions. For each 1 bit in the bit pattern of the current foreground pen (FgPen), the corresponding bit in the target drawing area is complemented—its state is reversed (0 bits to 1 bits and vice versa). COMPLEMENT mode is most often used for drawing and then erasing lines.

Coordinate pair

This is a pair of numbers in the form x,y where x and y are offsets from the left side and top of a display element (bitmap, view, viewport, screen, window, etc.). Coordinate pairs are used in many of the Intuition and Graphics Library functions to place something into a bitmap or to add something to a graphics display element in Intuition.

Copper

The Copper is a special-purpose coprocessor in the animation custom chip whose instructions control display-related hardware in the system. Each part of a display frame is defined by a Copper instruction list. Copper instructions are placed in RAM and executed along with the 68000 instructions to produce screen displays. The operation of the Copper coprocessor is synchronized to the progress of the video beam as it produces each line of the video display.

Copper instruction list

A Copper instruction list is a set of MOVE and WAIT Copper instructions that allow the Copper to control the video beam as it defines each pixel in the display screen. The Copper instruction list is sorted by the system in increasing y,x order. This allows the Copper to change the colors and resolution of the display screen in midscreen.

Damage-list

A damage-list is a set of clipping-rectangles that define the obscured portion of a simple-refresh window. Each damage-list is defined by a DamageList structure. In Intuition, the system uses the DamageList structure to redraw obscured portions of simple-refresh windows produced when the user moves and resizes those windows.

Deallocate

To deallocate memory is to free memory for other uses that the system or applications program may require. Memory is freed by using the memory-management deallocation functions found in the Exec Library and other libraries.

Device

In hardware terms, devices include the disk drive, the keyboard, the gameport, and any other input or output devices. In software terms, a device is an interface specification involving a Device structure and a set of device routines. The Device structure is identical to a Library structure. In fact, the MakeLibrary function is used to construct both standard software libraries and device libraries.

Device commands

This is a command used to manipulate data coming to and from devices. These commands include Flush, Read, Write, Reset, Update, Clear, Start, and Stop.

Device message

This is a message passed to a device from a task currently running in the Amiga. The message is passed through the I/O Request Block structure associated with that device. Each device has an I/O Request Block structure that must be set up before that device can be used.

Display memory

Display memory consists of the areas of memory set aside to hold the bitplanes and bitmaps required to define the display frames of the Amiga video display. These areas of memory are assigned by the Graphics Library AllocRaster function. All bitplanes and bitmaps must be in the first 512K of RAM.

Display mode

The Amiga has several display modes that can be used in various combinations. The low-resolution mode uses 320 pixels of display information on each scan line; the high-resolution mode uses 640 pixels of information on each scan line. Non-interlaced mode has 200 scan lines in the vertical direction; interlaced mode has 400 scan lines in the vertical direction.

Display overscan

This is the portion of the display information (pixels on a display line) that is outside of the viewable display screen. Display overscan is used to avoid the edge distortion of the video display image that results from the curvature of the monitor's surface. Usually, one speaks of horizontal overscan, but there is also some overscan in the vertical direction.

DMA channel

A DMA (direct memory access) channel provides a quick way to move memory data around in the system without using the 68000 CPU. The Blitter is the best example of how a DMA channel is used to speed data movement between two memory blocks. The

Amiga provides up to 25 channels of DMA that your programs can use to improve their performance.

Double buffering

Double buffering is the use of two areas of memory for identical or similar bitmaps, Copper instruction lists, etc. This mechanism allows one area of memory to be updated while the other produces the display actually seen on the screen at that time. Although double buffering uses twice as much display memory, it allows for smooth, nonflickering operation of the Amiga video display.

Doubly linked list

A doubly linked list is a mechanism for grouping related structures. Each node in the list contains a pointer to the predecessor node and a pointer to the successor node. Because of this arrangement, nodes can be added and deleted without destroying the continuous nature of that list—the entire list remains properly linked.

Drawing mode

A drawing mode is a RastPort structure setting that defines how data will be added to a bitmap during a drawing operation. There are four drawing modes: JAM1, JAM2, INVERSVID, and COMPLEMENT.

Dual-playfield mode

This display mode allows you to manage two separate display memories, providing two separately controllable display playfields at the same time. The video priority of each playfield can be set to determine which playfield appears in front and which appears in back. If the front playfield has a transparent section, it allows a portion of the second playfield to show through that transparent area. Both playfields can be scrolled independently, thus producing a dynamic three-dimensional effect.

Exception

An exception is an unusual condition that occurs as a task is running; the task is interrupted and a special exception-code segment is entered to deal with the condition.

Fast memory

Fast memory is memory above the 512K-byte memory boundary. This includes all memory up to the eight-megabyte limit of the Amiga machine. This area of memory cannot be addressed by the Amiga special-purpose chips; only the 68000 CPU can use it. For this reason, there is no bus contention for this block of memory and CPU memory access is fast.

FIFO list

This is a doubly linked list where the first element in is the first element out. This is the type of queue used to hold device messages in the device ports of the Amiga. Contrast this type of list with the LIFO list, which defines a software or user applications program stack.

Free memory

Free memory is free for the system to allocate and use as required. All of this memory is kept in a free-memory pool that is managed by the system. Your programs as well as system routines can gain access to this pool of free memory, as required, to execute programs.

Gadget

A gadget is a multipurpose input device of the Intuition system. Most of the input to an applications program takes place through the gadgets in Intuition screens, windows, and requesters. Each Intuition gadget is defined by a Gadget structure.

Gel

This is an acronym for graphics element. There are two types of gels in the Amiga system: virtual sprites and bobs. All currently defined graphics elements are placed on a graphics-element list, which is used by the animation system to draw graphics elements in the proper order.

Gimmezerozero window

This is a special type of Intuition window that actually consists of two windows: an inner window and an outer window. The outer window contains the window title, the window gadgets, and the window border. The inner window contains any additional drawing information for this window.

Hardware interrupt

This is a 68000 CPU interrupt caused by some part of the Amiga hardware that needs the attention of the CPU. For example, the system responds to floppy-disk, hard-disk, audio-input-channel, and modem-input-channel interrupts. Each hardware device has an interrupt-server routine. These routines are located in memory and reached by jump vectors in the software libraries.

Hardware sprite

This is one of eight sprite DMA channels in the Amiga system. Each hardware sprite defines a 16-bit-wide, moveable object that can be as tall as the full display screen. Each hardware sprite is limited to three colors plus transparent. Each of these eight hardware sprites can be mapped into a virtual sprite to increase the number of moveable sprite objects on the display screen.

High-resolution mode

This is the display mode that produces 640 pixels of horizontal resolution on the display screen.

Hold-and-modify mode

This is the display mode that provides for extensive color selection. You can display up to 4,096 colors on the display screen simultaneously with this mode.

Icon

An icon is a graphic image on the Amiga display screen. Icons are used by the Workbench program to display a small image associated with a disk, an applications program, an applications program project file, a file directory, or the trashcan. A user can double-click on an icon to start an applications program.

IDCMP

This is an acronym for an Intuition direct communication message port. It is the primary communication path for user input through the currently active window in Intuition applications programs.

Initialize

This means to establish the initial data in a structure or data block in memory. Most of the software libraries contain a set of structure-intialization functions.

Input device

Input devices for the Amiga include the keyboard, the floppy-disk or hard-disk drives, the mouse, and any number of other devices connected to the Amiga expansion connector.

Input event

Each of the hardware devices attached to the Amiga (both internally and externally) generates input events. The hardware signals for these events are passed to the device's internal routines using its I/O Request Block structure.

Interrupt-handler routine

This type of Amiga interrupt routine is basically a subroutine that returns control to the system once it has executed, using a 68000 RTS (return from subroutine) instruction. Sometimes this routine is used to send a signal to a sleeping task to wake it up.

Interrupt-server routine

This is one of one or more interrupt routines that are linked together to form a chain. Each interrupt server in this chain has a priority assigned to it and its own Interrupt Server structure. The order of execution of these interrupt routines is determined by the priority in the Interrupt Server structure.

INVERSVID

INVERSVID is one of four drawing modes used by the graphics drawing functions. When INVERSVID is specified, all bits of the item to be drawn are reversed (0 bits to 1 bits and vice versa) before the item is transferred to the receiving bitmap. INVERSVID can be used with JAM2 to produce inverse-video text characters.

I/O Request Block structure

This is an Exec structure reserved to hold information needed to pass messages to and from devices. It is also known as the IORequest structure.

JAM1

JAM1 is one of four drawing modes used by the graphics drawing functions. If JAM1 mode is set, one color is "jammed" into the raster bitmap when a drawing operation is executed. The current color of the foreground pen (FgPen) is used to define colors whenever JAM1 is specified.

JAM2

JAM2 is one of four drawing modes used by the graphics drawing functions. If JAM2 mode is specified, two colors are "jammed" into the raster bitmap when a drawing operation is executed. The current colors of the foreground pen (FgPen) and background pen (BgPen) are used whenever JAM2 is specified.

Layer

A layer is a section of a bitmap that can be brought onto or taken off the visible display screen using a set of Layer library functions. Layers provide the screen and window quilting effects produced when many windows are displayed at one time on the Intuition display screen. Each Intuition window is usually associated with a Layer structure. A set of Layer structures is used to manage the display of Intuition windows.

Library

A library is a collection of jump instructions, a Library structure, and a data segment. System and user software are divided into modules called libraries. The routines reached by these libraries can be shared by many concurrent programs in the multitasking system. There are two types of libraries: resident and transient. A resident library remains in memory at all times; it is loaded upon startup. A transient library is brought into and out of RAM as required by the task that is currently executing. In addition to executable routines, libraries can also contain global data that can be used by all library functions and routines. Libraries can be opened and closed as necessary.

Library data segment

This is the part of a library definition that contains nothing but data. The data is usually used only by the library routines, but it can also be accessed by any task instructions that it.

Library structure

The Library structure allows named libraries to be linked together into a list of libraries maintained by the system. It also contains all the information needed to manage the library.

List structure

This is a doubly linked list that contains at least one Node structure for a head node and one Node structure for a tail node. Each Node structure in the List structure contains pointers to a predecessor Node structure and a successor Node structure.

Loading a view

To load a view is to render the information in a view's bitmap definition on the Amiga display screen. The Graphics Library LoadView function tells the system to use the bitmap definition of a display frame together with the Copper instructions for that display frame to tell the display hardware how to render that display frame.

Low-resolution mode

This is a display mode with 320 pixels of information across the width of the display screen.

Menu button

The Amiga Menu button is the right-hand button on the Amiga mouse. The Menu button is used to activate a menu, menu item, or menu subitem. Once these items are selected, they can be used to transfer information in a program or between programs.

Menu strip

An Intuition menu strip is a collection of structure definitions required to define complete menus, menu items, or menu subitems. The result of the menu strip structure definitions is a menu strip with a menu bar and its text, one or more menu items and their text, and possibly one or more menu subitems and their text. Intuition provides the mechanism to link all menu strip structures together.

Message port

This is a software mechanism managed by the Exec functions that allows intertask communication. Each message port is defined by a MsgPort structure. Each task and device in the system can send and receive messages through its assigned message ports. Many structures in the system have pointers to or include actual MsgPort substructures to allow message communication between that structure and another structure in the system.

Motion-control animation

This is one of two types of high-level Amiga animation. Motion-control animation uses a sequence of position, velocity, and acceleration values to define the motion of animation objects on the display screen. Sequenced-drawing animation is the second type of high-level animation.

Multitasking

Multitasking means running several tasks on the Amiga concurrently. Each task acts as a unique virtual terminal and appears to have complete control of the 68000 CPU and associated system hardware. You can define and add as many tasks to the system as the memory configuration will allow. Each task is associated with a Task Control Block and is assigned a priority in the system. Tasks communicate with each other using software induced signals sensed by their Task Control Block structures. Only one task runs at a time. Task switching is triggered by task priority settings, new tasks being added to the system, and interrupt events in the system. The Amiga's multitasking capability allows the programmer to change the definition of the display while the system continues to monitor the keyboard, disk drives, and so forth.

Noninterlaced mode

This is the video display mode that presents 200 scan lines on the display screen.

Output device

Output devices for the Amiga include the monitor, the floppy-disk drive, the hard-disk drive, and any number of devices connected to the Amiga expansion connector.

Pen color

This is the value of the color register setting assigned to a given drawing pen. The graphics system uses three drawing pens: the foreground drawing pen, denoted by FgPen (or FrontPen in Intuition); the background pen, denoted by BgPen (or BackPen in Intuition); and the area-outline pen, denoted by AOlPen. In addition, Intuition uses a DetailPen and a BlockPen.

Pixel

A pixel is the smallest item of display information on the screen. At maximum resolution, you can place 256,000 (1640 times 400) pixels on the screen. In hold-and-modify mode, each of these pixels can display one of 4,096 colors.

Playfield

A playfield is one of the two basic elements in Amiga graphics. It is the background for all other display elements. The playfield is the static part of the display and forms a surface on which sprites can move. Views and playfields are interchangeable terms. Intuition screen definitions are also equivalent to playfields.

Playfield animation

This is one of two types of low-level Amiga animation. In playfield animation you use the fast data-movement capabilities of the Blitter DMA channel to move individual bobs at high speeds around the display screen. The Blitter moves data fast enough to present the illusion of true animation. Virtual sprite animation is the second type of low-level animation.

Playfield scrolling

Playfield scrolling means moving playfield displays vertically or horizontally on the display screen.

Pointer

There are two meanings to this term: the Intuition pointer is used to select objects on the screen; the C language pointer is used to point to C language structures, arrays, strings, etc. in memory.

Predecessor node

This is the node in a list that precedes the current node.

Preferences

This is a program on the Intuition Workbench disk. The Preferences program allows the user to open a number of windows in which the preferences settings can be changed by using various gadgets. These windows and their gadgets define the Preferences display. The gadgets allow the user to set the colors, key repeat rate, and other aspects of Amiga operation. These settings can be used throughout a session or saved for the next time the user turns on the Amiga.

Primitive

This term refers to the collection of Amiga Library functions. This includes all functions in all libraries discussed in this book.

Public memory

This memory is shared by different tasks and devices in the system. A public memory block can be allocated anywhere in the entire memory space (up to eight megabytes) of the Amiga. In contrast, chip memory blocks are restricted to the first 512K and fast memory is above 512K.

Public structure

This is a structure having an associated Node substructure and placed on a list and named (using the ln_Name parameter in the Node substructure). Once the name is assigned, any and all tasks can reference that Node substructure by name using the FindName function. FindName will then return a pointer to that Node substructure. Furthermore, if the containing structure is a Task structure, the FindTask function can be used to obtain a pointer to that Task structure. If the containing structure is a MsgPort structure, the FindPort function can be used to obtain a pointer to that MsgPort structure. In these cases, both the Task and MsgPort structures can be made public structures if they are added to a list using the AddTask or AddPort function, respectively.

Queued I/O

This is a form of task-device I/O that uses an I/O Request structure and places the request represented by that structure in a device input request queue. I/O requests are then processed in FIFO order when they reach the top of the device queue (list) for that device.

Quick I/O

This is a form of device-task input/output that proceeds without hesitation. Quick I/O is used mostly for single-character I/O, when each character can be transferred with a single I/O request. Quick I/O provides a way of reducing the overhead associated with this type of I/O request.

Raster

This term refers to the RAM bitmap that defines a section of the display screen. The terms raster, raster bitmap, and bitmap are used interchangeably in this book. In this context, raster does not refer to the raster display of the monitor or television.

RastPort structure

This is the data structure that is used to control the addition of drawing areas to a bitmap. The RastPort structure is probably the most important structure in the entire graphics system. It contains drawing control information that defines how each portion of a display frame is drawn. The RastPort structure plays a big role in the static graphics functions, the graphics animation functions, and the graphics text functions.

Refresh

To refresh is to repaint the video display based on new information in the display memory of the Amiga.

Region

A region is a section of a bitmap to which a drawing operation is limited. Any drawing operations that attempt to draw outside the region will be clipped to the area inside the region. A region is built up from a set of clipping-rectangles.

Render

To draw is to define bit information in a bitmap; to render is to place that information on the display screen. Rendering occurs when the LoadView function is used to present the bitmap and Copper instruction lists to the Amiga display hardware.

Reply message

This is an intertask or task-device message. When a task or device receives a message, that message is placed in the message queue of one of its message ports. When the task or device retrieves the message from the queue, it takes the action required by that message. It then sends a reply message to the sending task or device, notifying it that the message has been processed.

Reply port

This is the message port through which a task or device sends a reply to another task or device.

Requester

A requester is an Intuition display element that requests the user to respond in some way in order to proceed with the next action in a program sequence.

Screen

This term has two meanings. First, it refers to the physical display screen of the Amiga. Second, it means an Intuition screen—either a standard screen or a custom screen. Intuition screens allow any number of applications programs to open and close windows on the display.

Selection button

The Amiga Selection button is the left-hand button on the Amiga mouse. The Selection button is used to select icons and to transfer information in the Intuition system. In Intuition, double-clicking the Selection button on an applications program icon automatically starts that program; double-clicking the Selection button on a project icon automatically starts the applications program that originally produced that project file.

Sequenced-drawing animation

This is one of two types of high-level Amiga animation. With sequenced-drawing animation, you supply a number of views of the animation object and spell out when and how these views are to be presented on the display screen. Compare this to motion-control animation.

Signal wait mask

This is a 32-bit mask parameter that specifies which signals a task can accept and process. This parameter is defined for each task in its Task Control Block structure.

Simple refresh

This is the method of refreshing screen and window displays in which obscured areas must be redrawn by the applications program when they are newly revealed. Compare this to smart refresh and superbitmap refresh.

Smart refresh

This is the method of window refreshing that uses a number of small off-screen bitmap buffers to refresh the display. These bitmap buffers correspond to the obscured areas of the display. The system automatically updates these off-screen buffers. Compare this to simple refresh and superbitmap refresh.

Software interrupt

This is a 68000 interrupt caused by the system or applications software, as opposed to the system hardware.

Sprite

A sprite is a generic term for an object that you create and move on the playfield display. Sprites are usually 16 pixels wide, but some of the 16 pixels can be transparent, thus producing a narrower sprite. Sprites can be as high as you specify, up to the entire height of the display screen. See also hardware sprite and virtual sprite.

Sprite mode

This is a display mode that allows you to have sprites in your Intuition windows.

Structure

This is a C or assembly language data definition used for libraries, devices, graphic display elements, etc. Each element of data in the structure is assigned the name of a structure parameter. The Amiga software system uses structures extensively. The definitions of all these structures are contained in the INCLUDE files.

Successor node

This is a node in a doubly linked list that follows the current node in the same list.

Superbitmap refresh

This is one of three methods of window refreshing. With superbitmap refresh, obscured areas of the display do not have to be redrawn; they are simply copied from a single off-screen bitmap (the superbitmap) area that is at least as large as and usually larger than the on-screen bitmap it is refreshing. Compare this with simple refresh and smart refresh.

Superbitmap window

In Intuition, this is a window type that uses its own separate bitmap (not the screen's bitmap) to develop the window display or refresh the window.

Supervisor stack

This is the stack in RAM reserved for information required by the 68000 CPU when it goes into supervisor mode.

System free-memory list

The system free-memory list keeps track of free memory blocks managed entirely by the system. In addition, each task can create a task-related free-memory list to keep track of free-memory blocks associated with a specific task.

Task

A task is a unique set of software instructions associated with its own Task Control Block structure. A task can be a simple subroutine, an interrupt-handler routine, an interrupt-server routine, or part of an applications program.

Task Control Block structure

This is the data structure that defines a task. It contains information to point to all structures needed to manage a task. It also contains a Node structure to define the task's priority. It appears as the Task structure in the INCLUDE files.

Task message

Tasks communicate with each other using messages passed through the message ports defined in their MsgPort structures. Each message can induce a signal when it arrives in a task's message port.

Task priority

This is a number between −128 and +127 used to assign a running priority to a task in the system. Task priority is determined by the priority parameter of the Node substructure inside the Task structure. The system uses this Node substructure to maintain a list of tasks and their execution priorities. Higher-priority tasks run first.

Task signal bit

Each task can send and receive messages through the message ports assigned to that task. Each message port induces a specific signal bit when a message arrives in that port. Signal bits allow a group of tasks to communicate with each other in the multitasking system. The Task Control Block structure of each task contains a 32-bit variable (tc_SigAlloc) that indicates which signals have been assigned to a task. Sixteen of these bits are reserved for system use; the other sixteen can be assigned to the various task-specific signals.

Task stack

Each task is assigned its own task stack, which is a specific instance of a 68000 user mode stack. The task stack is used to save and restore the contents of the 68000 CPU registers and to store local variables and subroutine return addresses.

Task switching

This is the process of switching the attention of the 68000 CPU from one task to another in the system. For example, task switching occurs whenever a task of higher priority than the current task is entered into the system or whenever a task is put to sleep due to an unavailable resource.

Text attribute

This is one of the several characteristics of a text font. Text attributes include the font width, height, and style. All of these attributes are contained in the TextAttr structure, which the system uses to search memory and disks for the appropriate font definition.

Trace mode

This is one of three modes for the Motorola 68000 CPU; the other two modes are user and supervisor. Trace mode is used to debug programs. In trace mode, a program exception is forced after each instruction is executed, thereby allowing a debugging program to monitor the execution of the program being tested.

Transparent

This is a special color-register definition that allows a background color to show through on the display screen. For example, you can simulate looking through a window (a real window) of a house from inside a room in the house. That window would be a transparent part of the screen with the highest video priority. The screen just behind the first screen would simulate the outdoor landscape. The first color register assigned to both hardware and virtual sprites always produces a transparent pixel where that color is assigned in those sprites.

UART

This is an acronym for universal asynchronous receiver/transmitter. It is a circuit and chip that controls the serial link to the peripheral devices.

User port

This is the message port created when you use the IDCMP method of Intuition applications program communication. Your program sends and receives mouse and keyboard messages to and from the user through this port. This user port is implemented as a specific instance of an Exec MsgPort structure. All input/output events coming from or going to the active window are sent through this port. Each window—whether active or inactive—has its own user port.

Vector

This term has two meanings. First, a vector is a 68000 jump instruction used to locate different pieces of software in the system. The system software library routines are placed at the locations specified by these vectors. This term is also used to refer to a line segment on the display screen.

Video display

This term refers to everything that appears on the screen or monitor. The video display is composed of some, but not necessarily all, of the following: playfields, screens, windows, bobs, and sprites. It is a multilayered display, each layer having its own video priority.

Video field

This is a series of 200 scan lines on the display screen. Each video field is produced in 1/60 of a second. In noninterlaced mode, one video field is equal to one display frame. In interlaced mode, two video fields comprise a display frame.

Video priority

Each display object has a video priority. This priority determines which objects (playfields, screens, windows, bobs, and sprites) are shown in the foreground and which are shown in the background on the Amiga display screen. Higher-priority objects appear in front of lower-priority objects. In addition, the Layers Library functions provide a mechanism to define a quilted display consisting of different pieces of screens and windows, each of which can overlap the other.

View

A view is the part of the Amiga display screen that is the full width of the screen but not necessarily the full height. Each view can consist of one or more viewports. Each view is defined by a View structure and has its own horizontal and vertical resolution. All viewports in a view are displayed with the resolution assigned to the view of which they are a part.

Viewport

A viewport is a rectangular piece of the Amiga display. Each viewport is usually the full width of the display screen but can be narrower. A viewport is a subrectangle within the larger view rectangle. Intuition windows are examples of viewports. There are one or more viewports in a view.

Virtual sprite

A virtual sprite is a sprite described by a VSprite structure. The term "virtual" is used because the sprite is not assigned to a piece of hardware. This allows any number of virtual sprites to use one of the eight Amiga hardware sprite DMA channels. The size and color restrictions defined for hardware sprites also apply to virtual sprites. Virtual sprites can be used in collision detection but cannot be used to define animation components or animation objects.

Virtual terminal

There are two meanings to this term. First, it is an Intuition window that accepts input from the user and displays output. Second, it is a task running in the Amiga system (not necessarily with a window) that has complete 68000 CPU attention. All other tasks in the system are unaware of this virtual terminal task. Each task in the system acts like a unique virtual terminal when it becomes active; it takes over the complete machine (memory, display, and disk drives).

Window

A window is a rectangular area that can be opened within an Intuition display screen. Each window can have a set of system and user-defined gadgets to control the operation of that window. Each Intuition display can consist of one or more screens; each screen can have one or more windows. Only one window can be active at a time; this is the window that is receiving user input.

Workbench

A program for manipulating file icon images on the display screen. Icons can represent whole disks, file directories, applications programs, devices, or applications program files. The Icon Library functions provide a uniform way to deal with these icons on the Workbench screen.

Workbench screen

This is the screen that opens when the Workbench program is loaded. By double-clicking the Workbench disk icon, you can reveal the icons included on the Workbench screen: the Clock, Preferences, Utilities, System, Empty, and Demos icons. You can also copy the Workbench program to another disk to allow you to design an application that uses the icon management functions for your set of applications programs and the directories and files with which they work.

Amiga Display Modes

There are four video display modes in addition to the single-playfield mode discussed in Chapter 2. These are dual-playfield mode, double-buffered mode, hold-and-modify mode, and extra-half-brite mode. These modes provide additional display options as described in this appendix.

Dual-Playfield Mode

The dual-playfield mode of display allows you to use two playfields in the design of your views. Don't confuse this mode with double-buffering mode, which is described in the next section. In dual-playfield mode, the two playfields are independent of each other; each can have a number of viewports that follow most of the rules of single-playfield mode displays. You can set the relative video priority of the playfields to make playfield 1 appear in front of playfield 2 or vice versa.

These are the programming steps to define a dual-playfield mode display:

1. Allocate two BitMap structures. Each BitMap structure will describe a separate raster bitmap in the dual-playfield mode display. Save the pointers returned by the memory allocation functions; these values will be used in the RasInfo and RastPort structures to point to each of the two BitMap structures alternately.

2. Use the AllocRaster function to allocate the memory required for two bitmaps. One of these bitmaps will be used to define the foreground playfield (playfield 1); the other will be used to define the background playfield (playfield 2). You can have up to three bitplanes per bitmap. Each bitmap can be a different width and height.

3. Allocate memory for two RasInfo structures. These two structures will be linked together by the Next RasInfo structure pointer in the first RasInfo structure. These RasInfo structures define the boundaries of each of the two playfields with respect to the two bitmaps.

4. Allocate memory for two RastPort structures. You will use these to draw into each of the two bitmaps.

5. Allocate memory for each ViewPort structure that you will have in your view. You need only one ViewPort structure for each viewport, because you will set the DUALPF Mode parameter in the ViewPort structure to indicate a dual-playfield mode display. Therefore, one ViewPort structure handles both playfields for each viewport.

6. Allocate memory for one View structure. One View structure will handle both playfields, because you will set the DUALPF Mode parameter in the View structure to indicate a dual-playfield mode display.

7. Use the InitBitMap function to initialize two BitMap structures. Use the pointers previously returned by the memory allocation functions to point to each BitMap structure.

8. Use the InitRastPort function to initialize each of the RastPort structures. Use the pointers previously returned by the memory allocation functions to point to these RastPort structures. Set the bitmap pointer in the first RastPort structure to point to the first BitMap structure; set the bitmap pointer in the second RastPort structure to point to the second BitMap structure.

9. Use a series of four structure parameter assignment statements to initialize a separate RasInfo structure for each of the two raster bitmaps. Playfield 1 is defined by the first RasInfo structure; playfield 2 is defined by the second RasInfo structure. Set the BitMap pointer in the first RasInfo structure to point to the first of the two BitMap structures you have created; set the BitMap pointer in the second RasInfo structure to point to the second BitMap structure. Also set the Next RasInfo structure pointer in the first RasInfo structure to point to the second RasInfo structure; this links these two structures.

10. Use the InitVPort function to initialize the ViewPort structures you allocated previously. Set the DUALPF parameter in the ViewPort structure to indicate a dual-playfield mode display. Also don't set the PFBA Mode parameter if you want playfield 1 to appear in front; set this parameter if you want playfield 2 to appear in front. Do this for each viewport in the view. Recall that each ViewPort structure has a pointer to a RasInfo structure. The RasInfo structure, in turn, has a pointer to a BitMap structure. Therefore, each ViewPort structure knows about both RasInfo structures and both BitMap structures. Set the RasInfo structure pointer in every ViewPort structure to point to the first RasInfo structure.

11. Use the InitView function to initialize the View structure you allocated previously. Set the DUALPF parameter in the View structure to indicate a dual-playfield mode display. Also don't set the PFBA Mode parameter if you want playfield 1 to appear in front; set this parameter if you want playfield 2 to appear in front.

12. Use the MakeVPort function to define the Copper instruction lists for each viewport. This will generate the intermediate Copper list for each viewport. It will also define the association of the various viewports to the view.

13. Call the MrgCop function to combine all Copper instructions required to define the view. This will merge all viewport intermediate Copper lists into the view hardware Copper list.

14. Call the LoadView function to load the view Copper instructions to produce the dual-playfield mode display.

Each playfield in a dual-playfield mode display is formed from one, two, or three bit-planes. The colors (up to seven plus the transparent setting) in each playfield are taken from different sets of color registers. Tables B.1 through B.3 define this more precisely.

Note that low-resolution mode can use up to three bitplanes in each playfield, while high-resolution mode can use up to two bitplanes in each playfield. Table B.3 shows which bitplanes are used to form the bit combinations. The bit from the highest-numbered bitplane has the highest significance when forming the binary number that determines the color reigster.

Bit Combination	Playfield 1	Playfield 2
000	Color register 0 (transparent)	Color register 8 (transparent)
001	Color register 1	Color register 9
010	Color register 2	Color register 10
011	Color register 3	Color register 11
100	Color register 4	Color register 12
101	Color register 5	Color register 13
110	Color register 6	Color register 14
111	Color register 7	Color register 15

Table B.1:
Color Register Assignments for Low-Resolution Dual-Playfield Mode

Bit Combination	Playfield 1	Playfield 2
00	Color register 0 (transparent)	Color register 8 (transparent)
01	Color register 1	Color register 9
10	Color register 2	Color register 10
11	Color register 3	Color register 11

Table B.2:
Color Register Assignments for High-Resolution Dual-Playfield Mode

Number of Bitplanes Used	Bitplane Numbers for Playfield 1	Bitplane Numbers for Playfield 2
1	1	None
2	1	2
3	3, 1	2
4	3, 1	4, 2
5	5, 3, 1	4, 2
6	5, 3, 1	6, 4, 2

Table B.3:
Assigning Bitplanes in Dual-Playfield Mode

A Dual-Playfield Mode Programming Template

The following listing shows the necessary program statements to define a dual-playfield mode display. You can use this program segment as a template for any of your dual-playfield mode programs.

This example illustrates three viewports in one view. XOffset1, XOffset2, YOffset1, and YOffset2 are the viewport raster offset values that you must choose based on the size of your raster bitmap and the origins of your viewports in that bitmap. You also specify the values of yourposition1, yourposition2, and yourposition3 to fix the positions of the three viewports in the view on the Amiga display screen. Each viewport is three bitplanes deep to allow eight colors to be simultaneously displayed in each viewport.

The DEFINES describe a low-resolution noninterlaced mode display. You will notice that there is only one view defined. Also notice that the PFBA parameter in the ViewPort and View structures is left undefined; the system places playfield 1 on top of playfield 2. If you want playfield 2 on top of playfield 1, set the PFBA parameter in all three View-Port structures and also in the View structure. Finally, notice that the structures are allocated statically; you can use the same programming pattern if you allocate your structures dynamically.

```
/* INCLUDES */

#include "exec/types.h"
#include "exec/memory.h"
#include "exec/exec.h"
#include "graphics/gfx.h"
#include "graphics/gfxbase.h"
#include "graphics/gfxmacros.h"
#include "graphics/view.h"
#include "graphics/copper.h"
#include "graphics/gels.h"
#include "graphics/regions.h"
#include "graphics/clip.h"
#include "graphics/text.h"
#include "hardware/blit.h"
#include "hardware/custom.h"
#include "hardware/dmabits.h"

/* DEFINES */

#define DEPTH 3
#define HEIGHT 200
#define WIDTH 320

/* structure declarations allocated statically */

struct BitMap BitMap1, BitMap2;
struct RasInfo RasInfo1, RasInfo2;
struct RastPort RastPort1, RastPort2;
```

```
struct ViewPort ViewPort1, ViewPort2, ViewPort3;
struct View MyView;

for(i = 0; i<DEPTH; i + +){
   BitMap1.Planes[i] = (PLANEPTR) AllocRaster(WIDTH, HEIGHT);
   BitMap2.Planes[i] = (PLANEPTR) AllocRaster(WIDTH, HEIGHT);
};

InitBitMap(&BitMap1, DEPTH, WIDTH, HEIGHT);
InitBitMap(&BitMap2, DEPTH, WIDTH, HEIGHT);

InitRastPort(&RastPort1); InitRastPort(&RastPort2);

RastPort1.BitMap = &BitMap1; RastPort2.BitMap = &BitMap2;

RasInfo1.BitMap = &BitMap1;
RasInfo1.RxOffset = XOffset1; RasInfo1.RyOffset = YOffset1;
RasInfo1.Next = &RasInfo2;

RasInfo2.BitMap = &BitMap2;
RasInfo2.RxOffset = XOffset2; RasInfo2.RyOffset = YOffset2;
RasInfo2.Next = NULL;

InitVPort(&ViewPort1); InitVPort(&ViewPort2); InitVPort(&ViewPort3);

ViewPort1.Modes = DUALPF;
ViewPort1.DWidth = WIDTH; ViewPort1.DHeight = HEIGHT;
ViewPort1.DxOffset = 0.0; ViewPort1.DyOffset = yourposition1;
ViewPort1.RasInfo = &RasInfo1;
ViewPort1.Next = &ViewPort2;

ViewPort2.Modes = DUALPF;
ViewPort2.DWidth = WIDTH; ViewPort2.DHeight = HEIGHT;
ViewPort2.DxOffset = 0.0; ViewPort2.DyOffset = yourposition2;
ViewPort2.RasInfo = &RasInfo1;
ViewPort2.Next = &ViewPort3;

ViewPort3.Modes = DUALPF;
ViewPort3.DWidth = WIDTH; ViewPort3.DHeight = HEIGHT;
ViewPort3.DxOffset = 0.0; ViewPort3.DyOffset = yourposition3;
ViewPort3.RasInfo = &RasInfo1;
ViewPort3.Next = NULL;

InitView(&MyView);
MyView.ViewPort = &ViewPort1; MyView.Modes = DUALPF;

MakeVPort(&MyView, &ViewPort1);
MakeVPort(&MyView, &ViewPort2);
MakeVPort(&MyView, &ViewPort3);
```

```
/* Now draw into bitmap 1 using the RastPort1 structure */

/* Now draw into bitmap 2 using the RastPort2 structure */

MrgCop(&MyView);
LoadView(&MyView);
```

Double-Buffered Mode

The term double-buffering means that you are using two identically sized sections of RAM (referred to as buffers) to hold two versions of raster bitmap information. Each bitmap is related to the other. In fact, most of the time they are mere copies of each other. This is what distinguishes double-buffered mode from dual-playfield mode.

Double-buffering allows your program to draw into one of these bitmaps while it displays the other. In this way, you can produce smoothly flowing graphic displays without any screen flicker. It is particularly useful when you want to produce smooth animation. This method supplements the procedure of drawing into a single raster bitmap after the video beam passes a certain point on the display screen. Read the discussion of the QBSBlit function to understand how this approach also enables you to avoid screen flicker.

When you are considering whether to use double-buffering, you should remember that all graphics information has to fit in the first 512K of memory. For example, if you have a 320-by-200-pixel raster with five bitplanes, each bitplane will require 8,000 bytes; a complete raster bitmap will require 40,000 bytes; and a double-buffered display will require 80,000 bytes. This is still not too demanding on memory. However, if you double the resolution in each direction (640,400), the double-buffered raster bitmap information will require 320,000 bytes of RAM. You can see that things are now getting tight.

The key to double-buffered graphics programming is the correct sequence of programming statements. You want to alternate the pointer to the bitmap currently being displayed so that your program displays one bitmap while it draws into the other; then you can reverse their roles.

Here is a summary of the programming steps required to define a double-buffered mode display:

1. Allocate two BitMap structures. Each BitMap structure will describe a separate raster in the double-buffered display. Save the pointers returned by the memory allocation functions. These pointers can then be used in the RasInfo structure (and the RastPort structure) to point to each of the two BitMap structures alternately.

2. Use the AllocRaster function to allocate the memory required for two separate bitmaps. You can have up to five bitplanes per bitmap. Each bitmap must be the same width and height.

3. Allocate memory for one RasInfo structure. You will use only one RasInfo structure, but you will keep changing the BitMap structure pointer in that RasInfo structure.

4. Allocate memory for one RastPort structure. You need only one RastPort structure because you can change the BitMap structure pointer in the RastPort structure to point to each of your two bitmaps alternately.

5. Allocate memory for each ViewPort structure that you will have in your view.

6. Allocate memory for one View structure. You need only one View structure because you will be displaying the information in one bitmap at a time.

7. Use the InitBitMap function to initialize two BitMap structures. Use the pointers previously returned by the memory allocation functions to point to each BitMap structure.

8. Use a series of four structure parameter assignment statements to initialize the RasInfo structure you allocated previously. Set the BitMap pointer in the RasInfo structure to point to the BitMap structure corresponding to the first bitmap you will draw into.

9. Use the InitRastPort function to initialize the RastPort structure you allocated previously. Set the BitMap pointer in the RastPort structure to point to the BitMap structure corresponding to the first bitmap you will draw into.

10. Use the InitVPort function to initialize the ViewPort structures you allocated previously. Recall that each ViewPort structure has a pointer to a RasInfo structure. The RasInfo structure, in turn, has a pointer to a BitMap structure. Therefore, by changing the pointer to the BitMap structure in the RasInfo structure, each ViewPort structure is always associated with the correct bitmap. Also initialize other parameters in each ViewPort structure.

11. Use the InitView function to initialize the View structure you allocated previously.

12. Use the Graphics Library drawing functions to draw into the first bitmap. The other bitmap is now sitting idle.

13. Call the MakeVPort function for each viewport in the view. This will generate the Copper instruction list for each of the viewports in the view based on the bitmap into which you have just drawn.

14. Call the MrgCop function. This will merge all the viewport Copper instruction lists together based on the first bitmap; it will tell the system to create the Copper list to define the display of the first bitmap. The system will create pointers for the View's LOFCprList (long-form Copper list) and SHFCprList (short-form Copper list) for the first of the two alternate displays. The system will also automatically allocate memory for these lists. The short-form Copper list is used only for interlaced mode displays, whereas the long-form Copper list is used for both interlaced

mode and noninterlaced mode displays. The pointers to these two Copper lists are initialized by the system in the View structure. As a result, the Copper instruction stream includes references to the first BitMap structure.

15. Save the current LOFCprList and SHFCprList pointers in backup variables. Then set the values of the LOFCprList and SHFCprList pointers in the View structure to zero.

16. Now you are ready to deal with the backup bitmap. Switch the BitMap structure pointers in the RasInfo and RastPort structures to point to the second BitMap structure. Now use the Graphics Library drawing functions to draw into the second bitmap.

17. Call the MakeVPort function for each viewport in the view. This will create the Copper instruction lists for the backup bitmap.

18. Call the MrgCop function. This will merge all the viewport Copper instruction lists together to define the display of the second bitmap. When you call the MrgCop function, the system automatically allocates another memory area to hold new lists of Copper instructions. Once again, pointers to these Copper instruction lists (the long-form Copper list and the short-form Copper list) will be built into the View structure.

The result of all this is two sets of display-frame Copper instruction streams co-existing in RAM. The path to one of these is saved in a pair of pointer variables; the path to the other has been newly created and is in the View structure. You can also save this set of pointers. Then you can substitute the set you want to display when you call the LoadView function. Recall that LoadView works with the View structure. By changing the Copper list pointers in the View structure, you can load each of the two different bitmaps for display.

In the meantime, your graphics task can be drawing into the bitmap that is not currently being displayed. Make sure you are using the correct BitMap structure pointer at each stage of your drawing definition in the RasInfo and RastPort structures. Remember that you will have to call FreeCopList for both sets of intermediate Copper lists when you are finished.

A Double-Buffered Mode Programming Template

The following listing shows the necessary program statements to define a double-buffered mode display. You can use this program segment as a template for any of your double-buffered mode programs.

This example illustrates three viewports in one view. XOffset and YOffset are the viewport raster offset values that you must choose based on the size of your raster bitmap and the origins of your viewports in that bitmap. You also specify the value of yourposition1, yourposition2, and yourposition3 to fix the position of the three viewports in the view on the Amiga display screen. Each viewport is five bitplanes deep to allow 32 colors to be simultaneously displayed in each viewport.

In addition, the DEFINES describe a low-resolution noninterlaced mode display. You will notice that there is only one view defined. Also notice that there is no special mode setting in the ViewPort or View structures to tell the system you are using double-buffering.

This example shows you how to do the following:

1. Handle the hardware CptList structure pointers in the View structure

2. Create one View structure

3. Save the CprList structure pointers in temporary variables

4. Create another View structure

5. Save the CprList structure pointers once again

You can then continue to alternate between the two bitmaps and their associated Copper lists using these two sets of pointers. Notice that the structures are allocated statically; you can use the same programming pattern if you allocate your structures dynamically.

```
/* INCLUDES */

#include "exec/types.h"
#include "exec/memory.h"
#include "exec/exec.h"
#include "graphics/gfx.h"
#include "graphics/gfxbase.h"
#include "graphics/gfxmacros.h"
#include "graphics/view.h"
#include "graphics/copper.h"
#include "graphics/gels.h"
#include "graphics/regions.h"
#include "graphics/clip.h"
#include "graphics/text.h"
#include "hardware/blit.h"
#include "hardware/custom.h"
#include "hardware/dmabits.h"

/* DEFINES */

#define DEPTH 5
#define HEIGHT 200
#define WIDTH 320

/* structure declarations allocated statically */

struct BitMap BitMap1, BitMap2;
struct RasInfo RasInfo;
```

```
struct RastPort RastPort;
struct ViewPort ViewPort1, ViewPort2, ViewPort3;
struct View MyView;

for(i = 0; i<DEPTH; i++){
   BitMap1.Planes[i] = (PLANEPTR) AllocRaster(WIDTH, HEIGHT);
   BitMap2.Planes[i] = (PLANEPTR) AllocRaster(WIDTH, HEIGHT);
};

InitBitMap(&BitMap1, DEPTH, WIDTH, HEIGHT);
InitBitMap(&BitMap2, DEPTH, WIDTH, HEIGHT);

RasInfo.BitMap = &BitMap1;
RasInfo.RxOffset = XOffset; RasInfo.RyOffset = YOffset;
RasInfo.Next = NULL;

InitRastPort(&RastPort);

RastPort.BitMap = &BitMap1;

InitVPort(&ViewPort1); InitVPort(&ViewPort2); InitVPort(&ViewPort3);

ViewPort1.DWidth = WIDTH; ViewPort1.DHeight = HEIGHT;
ViewPort1.DxOffset = 0.0; ViewPort1.DyOffset = yourposition1;
ViewPort1.RasInfo = &RasInfo;
ViewPort1.Next = &ViewPort2;

ViewPort2.DWidth = WIDTH; ViewPort2.DHeight = HEIGHT;
ViewPort2.DxOffset = 0.0; ViewPort2.DyOffset = yourposition2;
ViewPort2.RasInfo = &RasInfo;
ViewPort2.Next = &ViewPort3;

ViewPort3.DWidth = WIDTH; ViewPort3.DHeight = HEIGHT;
ViewPort3.RasInfo = &RasInfo;
ViewPort3.DxOffset = 0.0; ViewPort3.DyOffset = yourposition3;
ViewPort3.Next = NULL;

InitView(&MyView);
MyView.ViewPort = &ViewPort1;

/* Now draw into bitmap 1 */

MakeVPort(&MyView, &ViewPort1);
MakeVPort(&MyView, &ViewPort2);
MakeVPort(&MyView, &ViewPort3);

MrgCop(&MyView);

/* Now display bitmap 1 */

LoadView(&MyView);
```

```
/* Now prepare to draw into bitmap 2 */

BitMap1LOFCprList  =  MyView.LOFCprList;
BitMap1SHFCprList  =  MyView.SHFCprList;

MyView.LOFCprList  =  0.0;
MyView.SHFCprList  =  0.0;

RasInfo.BitMap  =  &BitMap2;
RastPort.BitMap  =  &BitMap2;

/* Now draw into bitmap 2 */

MakeVPort(&MyView,  &ViewPort1);
MakeVPort(&MyView,  &ViewPort2);
MakeVPort(&MyView,  &ViewPort3);

MrgCop(&MyView);

/* Now display bitmap 2 */

LoadView(&MyView);

/* Now prepare to draw into bitmap 1 again */

BitMap2LOFCprList  =  MyView.LOFCprList;
BitMap2SHFCprList  =  MyView.SHFCprList;

MyView.LOFCprList  =  BitMap1LOFCprList;
MyView.SHFCprList  =  BitMap1SHFCprList;

/* Continue drawing and switching CprList pointers in the View struc-
ture. */
```

Hold-and-Modify Mode

The main advantage that hold-and-modify mode offers over other display modes is the ability to display up to 4,096 colors on the screen simultaneously. Contrast this with the limitations of the other drawing modes, which allow 32 colors in a low-resolution, noninterlaced mode display and only 16 colors in a high-resolution, interlaced mode display.

To use hold-and-modify mode, follow these steps:

1. Use six bitplanes to define your raster bitmap. Bitplanes 1 to 4 are used to define one of 16 colors for a pixel at that raster location. Bitplanes 5 and 6 are used to tell the hardware system how to "hold" and modify those colors.

2. Initialize the ViewPort structure for each viewport in each view. Set the HAM flag in each ViewPort structure's Mode parameter.

When you draw into the raster bitmap from which each viewport originates, you have a choice of several different drawing methods. If you draw using color numbers 0 to 15 (based on bitplane 1–4), the pixel will be drawn in the color specified in that particular color register. Recall that you set the color number with the SetAPen and SetBPen functions and the SetOPen macro.

If you draw with a color value from 16 to 63 (based on bitplanes 1–6), the color actually drawn at that pixel location will depend on the color of the pixel immediately to the left of that pixel in the raster bitmap. The current pixel's color will be based on two of the three primary colors (RGB) of the previous pixel. The system will hold constant the intensity of two of these primary colors (color intensities can have 16 variations) and change the intensity of the current pixel's third primary color. To define how the third primary color should be treated, the display system hardware will use the current pixel's lower four bitplane bits. For example, you can hold the red and blue color intensities based on the previous pixel's values for these two primary colors. The green intensity will be based on the bits in bitplanes 1 through 4 at the raster location of the current pixel. In this case, you have held the red and blue constant and modified the green. This is how this display mode gets its name.

Bitplanes 5 and 6 are used to determine which of the primary colors are held from the previous pixel and which are modified. If the 6-5 bit combination for any pixel is 00, the normal color-selection method is used. In this case, the bit combination of bitplanes 1 through 4 are used to define the color at that pixel directly. The pixel to the left is not used to modify the colors of the current pixel. This option allows you to specify hold-and-modify mode for some pixels in your display and prevent it at others.

If the 6-5 bit combination for a given pixel is 01, the color of the pixel immediately to the left of this pixel is duplicated and then modified. In this case, the bit combination of bitplanes 1 through 4 are used to determine the blue color intensity at that pixel location. Thus, you hold red and green and modify blue. If the 6-5 bit combination for a given pixel is 10, you hold blue and green and modify red. If the 6-5 bit combination for a given pixel is 11, you hold blue and red and modify green. In all cases, the color intensity that is not duplicated (held) from the pixel to the left is modified according to the current pixel's color definition (described by the bits in bitplanes 1–4).

From this, you can see that you must make a decision about hold-and-modify mode early in the design of your graphics program. Then you can specify all bits in your six bitplanes to achieve the hold-and-modify mode behavior you want at each pixel location in your raster.

A Hold-and-Modify Mode Programming Template

The following listing shows the necessary program statements to define a hold-and-modify mode display. You can use this program segment as a template for any of your hold-and-modify programs.

This example illustrates three viewports in one view. XOffset and YOffset are the viewport raster offset values that you must choose based on the size of your raster bitmap and the origins of your viewports in that bitmap. You also specify the value of yourposition1, yourposition2, and yourposition3 to fix the positions of the three viewports in the view on the Amiga display screen. Each viewport is six bitplanes deep, which allows the simultaneous display of up to 4,096 colors.

The DEFINES describe a low-resolution noninterlaced mode display. Notice that there is only one view defined. Also notice that the HAM Mode parameter in the ViewPort and View structures is set. Now when you draw into the bitmap, the bits in the bitmap will be interpreted in hold-and-modify fashion to define the colors at each pixel location.

Finally, notice that the structures are allocated statically; you can use the same programming pattern if you allocate your structures dynamically.

```
/* INCLUDES */

#include "exec/types.h"
#include "exec/memory.h"
#include "exec/exec.h"
#include "graphics/gfx.h"
#include "graphics/gfxbase.h"
#include "graphics/gfxmacros.h"
#include "graphics/view.h"
#include "graphics/copper.h"
#include "graphics/gels.h"
#include "graphics/regions.h"
#include "graphics/clip.h"
#include "graphics/text.h"
#include "hardware/blit.h"
#include "hardware/custom.h"
#include "hardware/dmabits.h"

/* DEFINES */

#define DEPTH 6
#define HEIGHT 200
#define WIDTH 320

/* Structure declarations allocated statically */

struct BitMap BitMap;
struct RasInfo RasInfo;
```

```
struct RastPort RastPort;
struct ViewPort ViewPort1, ViewPort2, ViewPort3;
struct View MyView;

for(i = 0; i<DEPTH; i+ +){
   BitMap.Planes[i] = (PLANEPTR) AllocRaster(WIDTH, HEIGHT);
};

InitBitMap(&BitMap, DEPTH, WIDTH, HEIGHT);

InitRastPort(&RastPort);

RastPort.BitMap = &BitMap;

RasInfo.BitMap = &BitMap;
RasInfo.RxOffset = XOffset; RasInfo.RyOffset = YOffset;
RasInfo.Next = NULL;

InitVPort(&ViewPort1); InitVPort(&ViewPort2); InitVPort(&ViewPort3);

ViewPort1.Modes = HAM;
ViewPort1.DWidth = WIDTH; ViewPort1.DHeight = HEIGHT;
ViewPort1.DxOffset = 0.0; ViewPort1.DyOffset = yourposition1;
ViewPort1.RasInfo = &RasInfo;
ViewPort1.Next = &ViewPort2;

ViewPort2.Modes = HAM;
ViewPort2.DWidth = WIDTH; ViewPort2.DHeight = HEIGHT;
ViewPort2.DxOffset = 0.0; ViewPort2.DyOffset = yourposition2;
ViewPort2.RasInfo = &RasInfo;
ViewPort2.Next = &ViewPort3;

ViewPort3.Modes = HAM;
ViewPort3.DWidth = WIDTH; ViewPort3.DHeight = HEIGHT;
ViewPort3.DxOffset = 0.0; ViewPort3.DyOffset = yourposition3;
ViewPort3.RasInfo = &RasInfo;
ViewPort3.Next = NULL;

InitView(&MyView);
MyView.ViewPort = &ViewPort1; MyView.Modes = HAM;

MakeVPort(&MyView, &ViewPort1);
MakeVPort(&MyView, &ViewPort2);
MakeVPort(&MyView, &ViewPort3);
```

/* Now draw into the bitmap using the RastPort structure */

MrgCop(&MyView);
LoadView(&MyView);

Extra-Half-Brite Mode

Extra-half-brite mode allows you to define viewports which display an additional 32 colors that are half as bright as the colors defined by color registers 0–31. This allows you to define a sequence of display frames that start out at normal color intensity and gradually fade to the background display using the extra-half-brite mode as an intermediate step.

Extra-half-brite mode requires six bitplanes and a single-playfield mode display. You cannot use extra-half-brite with hold-and-modify mode. To use extra-half-brite mode, set the EXTRA_HALFBRITE mode parameter flag in the viewport structure. Then each pixel with a 1 bit in bitplane 6 will be displayed with the RGB colors half as bright as normal. The colors are defined by bitplanes 1–5.

The hold-and-modify mode listing can be easily modified to produce a template for an extra-half-brite mode example. Just change the HAM mode parameter in the ViewPort and View structures to EXTRA_HALFBRITE. Then the bitmap information in the six bitplanes of the bitmap will be interpreted in extra-half-brite fashion.

Index

Selections from The SYBEX Library

HOME COMPUTERS

Amiga Programmer's Handbook, Volume I (Second Edition)
Eugene P. Mortimore
624pp. Ref. 367-8

The complete reference for Amiga graphics programming. System commands and function calls are presented in detail, organized by funcitonal class: Exec, Graphics, Animation, Layers, Intuition and the Workbench. Includes AmigaDOS version 1.2.

Amiga Programmer's Handbook, Volume II
Eugene P. Mortimore
365pp. Ref. 384-8

In-depth discussion of Amiga device I/O programming—including programming with sound and speech—with complete details on the twelve Amiga devices and their associated commands and function calls. Inclues AmigaDOS version 1.2.

Programmer's Guide to the Amiga
Robert A. Peck
352pp. Ref. 310-4

A programmer's hands-on tour through the Amiga system—AmigaDOS, Exec, Graphics, Intuition, Devices, Sound, Animation, and more—packed with in-depth information and sample programs (in Amiga C) showing proper use of system routines.

DOS

The ABC's of DOS 4
Alan R. Miller
250pp. Ref. 583-2

This step-by-step introduction to using DOS 4 is written especially for beginners. Filled with simple examples, The ABC's of DOS 4 covers the basics of hardware, software, disks, the system editor EDLIN, DOS commands, and more.

ABC's of MS-DOS (Second Edition)
Alan R. Miller
233pp. Ref. 493-3

This handy guide to MS-DOS is all many PC users need to manage their computer files, organize floppy and hard disks, use EDLIN, and keep their computers organized. Additional information is given about utilities like Sidekick, and there is a DOS command and program summary. The second edition is fully updated for Version 3.3.

Mastering DOS (Second Edition)
Judd Robbins
700pp. Ref. 555-7

"The most useful DOS book." This seven-part, in-depth tutorial addresses the needs of users at all levels. Topics range from running applications, to managing files and directories, configuring the system, batch file programming, and techniques for system developers.

Amiga Programs and Other Support
AVAILABLE ON DISK

If you would like to have four C language programs illustrating some of the functions in this book, you can send for a disk containing the following information:

■ An Exec program illustrating two tasks with message ports and messages and signals passed back and forth between these tasks (approximately 300 lines of code)

■ A single-playfield graphics program automatically displaying a sequence of different screens (approximately 300 lines of code)

■ An animation program illustrating hardware sprites and single-playfield graphics in multiple automatic display screens (approximately 300 lines of code)

■ An Intuition program illustrating a custom screen, a text window, a graphics window, and a set of menus (approximately 350 lines of code)

All of these programs represent a convenient starting point for a useful Amiga program. We provide full explanations, source code, and executable programs.

In addition, the disk contains three discussions explaining how to optimize the AmigaDOS command system for efficient multitasking editing, compiling, and use of a RAM disk.

To obtain this Amiga disk, complete the order form and return it along with a check or money order for $11.95. Pennsylvania residents add sales tax.

Micro Systems Analysis, Inc.
P.O. Box 46
Bethel Park, PA 15102

_____
NAME

_____
ADDRESS

_____
CITY   STATE   ZIP

Enclosed is my check or money order. (Make check payable to Eugene P. Mortimore)

SYBEX is not affiliated with Micro Systems Analysis and assumes no responsibility for any defect in the disk or programs.